The Internal Auditing Handbook

The Internal Auditing Handbook

K. H. Spencer Pickett

(*assisted by Gerald Vinten*)

JOHN WILEY & SONS

Chichester • New York • Weinheim • Brisbane • Singapore • Toronto

Copyright © 1997 Spencer Pickett
Published by John Wiley & Sons Ltd,
  Baffins Lane, Chichester,
  West Sussex PO19 1UD, England

  National   01243 779777
  International (+44) 1243 779777
  e-mail (for orders and customer service enquiries):
  cs-books@wiley.co.uk
  Visit our Home Page on http://www.wiley.co.uk
            or http://www.wiley.com

Other Wiley Editorial Offices

John Wiley & Sons Inc., 605 Third Avenue,
New York, NY 10158-0012, USA

VCH Verlagsgesellschaft mbH, Pappelallee 3,
D-69469 Weinheim, Germany

Jacaranda Wiley Ltd, 33 Park Road, Milton,
Queensland 4064, Australia

John Wiley & Sons (Asia) Pte Ltd, 2 Clementi Loop #02-01,
Jin Xing Distripark, Singapore 129809

John Wiley & Sons (Canada) Ltd, 22 Worcester Road,
Rexdale, Ontario M9W 1L1, Canada

Library of Congress Cataloging-in-Publication Data
Pickett, Spencer.
    The internal auditing handbook / Spencer Pickett with Gerald
  Vinten.
      p.   cm.
    Includes bibliographical references and index.
    ISBN 0-471-96911-7
    1. Auditing, Internal.   I. Vinten, Gerald.   II. Title.
  HF5668.25.P53   1997
  657′.458–DC20   96–42896
                                                      CIP

British Library Cataloguing in Publication Data

A catalogue record for this book is available from the British Library

ISBN 0-471-96911-7

Typeset in 10/12pt Times from the author's CRC
Printed and bound in Great Britain by Bookcraft (Bath) Ltd
This book is printed on acid-free paper responsibly manufactured from sustainable forestation,
for which at least two tree are planted for each one used for paper production.

This book is dedicated with my deepest love to my wife, Jennifer

Contents

Foreword   xv

Acknowledgements   xvii

List of Abbreviations   xviii

List of supplements on disk   xx

Part One   The Theoretical Framework   **1**

1 Definition of Internal Audit   3
   1.1   Introduction   3
   1.2   The Auditing Practices Board (APB) Definition   3
   1.3   The Institute of Internal Auditors (IIA) Definition (1991)   4
   1.4   The New Definition of Internal Auditing   5
   1.5   Is there a Right Model?   6
   1.6   The Five Main Elements   9
   1.7   Implications of the Wide Scope   10
   1.8   The Managerial Control System   14
   1.9   Scope within Different Time Frames   15
   1.10 Resourcing the Agreed Scope   16

2 The Development of Internal Audit   17
   2.1   Introduction   17
   2.2   The Evolution of the Audit Function 17
   2.3   The Development of Internal Audit Services   18
   2.4   Moving Internal Audit out of Accountancy   22
   2.5   The Role of the Statement of Responsibility   25
   2.6   The 1947 Debate   26
   2.7   Current Topical Issues   28
   2.8   The Future for Internal Audit   32
   2.9   Conclusions   37

3 The Concept of Auditing Standards   38
   3.1   Professionalism   38
   3.2   The Role of Standards   41

	3.3	Institute of Internal Auditors' Standards	43
	3.4	Auditing Practices Board (APB) Standards	44
	3.5	Other Standards	45
	3.6	Can Standards be Universal?	47
	3.7	Can Standards Apply to Smaller Organisations?	49
	3.8	The National Health Service Experience	50
	3.9	Contribution of the Institute of Internal Auditors (IIA)	50
	3.10	Establishing Internal Audit	51
	3.11	Conclusions	52
4	Approaches to Internal Audit		53
	4.1	Different Approaches	53
	4.2	Investigations Versus Systems Auditing	55
	4.3	Conclusions	57
5	Independence		58
	5.1	Introduction	58
	5.2	The Meaning of Independence	58
	5.3	Factors Affecting Independence	60
	5.4	Courtemanche on Independence	63
	5.5	The Rittenberg Model	64
	5.6	A Working Model	64
	5.7	Chambers	66
	5.8	Managing the Director of Finance	67
	5.9	Reconciling the Consultancy Branch	69
	5.10	The External Audit Experience	71
	5.11	Defining the Fundamentals	72
	5.12	Conclusions	73
6	Behavioural Aspects of Auditing		75
	6.1	Introduction	75
	6.2	Human Behavioural Aspects	75
	6.3	The Churchill Studies	77
	6.4	CIPFA Survey	77
	6.5	HA Survey – Mints	78
	6.6	More Recent Research	79
	6.7	Audit Relationships	80
	6.8	Dealing with People	82
	6.9	Audit Roles	85
	6.10	Role Theory	87
	6.11	A Model of Audit Styles	88
	6.12	Understanding and Participating with Management	92
	6.13	The Expectation Gap	96
	6.14	Managing Negotiation Skills	98
	6.15	The Link into Marketing	100
	6.16	Managing the Delinquent Manager	101
	6.17	What of Independence?	102
	6.18	Conclusions	104

7   Audit Committees   105
     7.1   Introduction   105
     7.2   The Role of the Audit Committees   105
     7.3   The Audit Committee's Constitution   106
     7.4   Pros and Cons   106
     7.5   Utilising the Audit Committee   106
     7.6   The Internal Audit Perspective   110
     7.7   The IIA-UK Professional Briefing Note   114
     7.8   Conclusions   115

8   The Audit Charter   116
     8.1   Introduction   116
     8.2   The Role of the Audit Charter   116
     8.3   The 1986 Survey   117
     8.4   Key Issues   117
     8.5   Structure of the Charter   122
     8.6   The Audit Charter – An Example   122
     8.7   Conclusions   123

9   Code of Ethics   124
     9.1   Introduction   124
     9.2   Relevant Factors   124
     9.3   Underlying Models   127
     9.4   Whistleblowing   128
     9.5   The Moral Maze   129
     9.6   Applying a Three-Part Model   130

10   Standards on Audit Work   132
     10.1   Introduction   132
     10.2   IIA Standard 400   132
     10.3   The Auditing Practices Board (APB) Standards   132
     10.4   Applying a Suitable Model   133
     10.5   The Implications for Internal Audit   133
     10.6   Professional Proficiency   135
     10.7   Conclusions   136

11   External Audit and Others   138
     11.1   Introduction   138
     11.2   The Different Objectives   138
     11.3   Background to External Audit   138
     11.4   The Main Similarities   139
     11.5   The Main Differences   141
     11.6   The Auditing Practices Board (APB) Statement   145
     11.7   The Brink and Barratt Survey   146
     11.8   Other Review Agencies   148
     11.9   Conclusions   153

12   Fundamentals of Control   154
     12.1   The Concept of Control   154

12.2	Control Criteria	157
12.3	Controls in Practice	159
12.4	The Suitability of Controls	162
12.5	Managements' Role	165
12.6	Audit's Role	167
12.7	The IIA Briefing Note on Internal Control	168
12.8	Recent Developments	169
12.9	Managerial Control Mechanisms	170
12.10	The Managerial System Control Attributes	172
12.11	Conclusions	172

Part Two   Audit Techniques   **175**

13	The Planning Process	
13.1	Introduction	177
13.2	The Planning Process	177
13.3	Advantages of Planning	178
13.4	Disadvantages of Planning	181
13.5	Long-term Planning	182
13.6	The General Survey	184
13.7	Strategy Versus Resources	187
13.8	A Risk Profile	187
13.9	The Business Plan	189
13.10	The Annual Audit Plan	190
13.11	The Preliminary Survey	192
13.12	Assignment Planning	195
13.13	Conclusions	198

14	The Systems Approach	199
14.1	Systems Thinking	199
14.2	Systems Auditing	203
14.3	Ascertaining and Recording Systems	210
14.4	Evaluating Systems	217
14.5	Managerial Systems Components	225
14.6	Conclusions	227

15	The Concept of Risk	228
15.1	Introduction	228
15.2	Developing a High-level Risk Strategy	229
15.3	Risk Analysis	231
15.4	The Risk Matrix and Control Evaluation	233
15.5	Performance Indicators	234
15.6	A Risk Index	235
15.7	Conclusions	238

16	Testing and Working Papers	239
16.1	Background to Testing	239
16.2	The Four Types of Tests	241
16.3	Testing Considerations	242

16.4	Testing Techniques	244
16.5	Achieving Control Objectives	248
16.6	The Hundred Percent Interrogation Theory	250
16.7	The Meaning of Compliance	252
16.8	Issues in Testing	253
16.9	Evidence and Working Papers	254
16.10	Permanent Files	258
16.11	Current Files	259
16.12	Standardisation	261
16.13	Statistical Sampling	263
16.14	Advantages of Statistical Sampling	266
16.15	Applying Statistical Sampling to the Audit Process	268
16.16	Some Basic Rules for Applying Statistical Sampling	273
16.17	Conclusions	275
17	Interviewing	276
17.1	Introduction	276
17.2	Structuring Interviews	277
17.3	Behavioural Aspects of Interviewing	281
17.4	Types of Questions	285
17.5	Conduct During an Interview	287
17.6	Barriers to Good Interviews	289
17.7	Fraud Interviews	292
17.8	Standardised Procedures	293
17.9	Conclusions	295
18	Audit Reporting	296
18.1	Introduction	296
18.2	Types of Reports	296
18.3	Activity Reports	298
18.4	The Reporting Process	301
18.5	Defining the Client	305
18.6	Objectives of the Audit Report	306
18.7	Underlying Components of Action	309
18.8	The Review Process	316
18.9	The clearance Process	319
18.10	Formulating the Action Plan	319
18.11	Change Management	320
18.12	Logical Presentation	320
18.13	Oral Presentations	331
18.14	The Audit Manual	338
18.15	Conclusions	339
19	The Audit Manual	340
19.1	Introduction	340
19.2	The Role of the Audit Manual	340
19.3	Relevant Sources of Information	346
19.4	Main Issues	341

19.5   Building a Conceptual Model of the Audit Manual   346
19.6   Using Models   347
19.7   Selecting the Right Model   350
19.8   Overcoming the Creativity Problem   352
19.9   Structuring the Audit Manual   354
19.10 Implementing the Manual   355
19.11 Conclusions   356

Part Three   Management of Internal Audit   **357**

20   Audit Objectives and Strategies   361
     20.1   Setting Audit Objectives   361
     20.2   Defining Audit Strategy   362
     20.3   PESTL and SWOT Analysis   365
     20.4   Features of Audit Strategy   368
     20.5   Successful Strategic Implementation   371

21   Audit Structures   373
     21.1   Introduction   373
     21.2   Factors Influencing Structures   374
     21.3   Conclusions   381

22   Resourcing the Audit Unit   382
     22.1   Introduction   382
     22.2   Attributes of Auditors   384
     22.3   The Importance of Clear Personnel Policies   390
     22.4   Recruitment Selection   391
     22.5   The Career Development Profile   396
     22.6   Factors for Implementing an Auditor Appraisal Scheme 399
     22.7   Methods of Staff Appraisal   401
     22.8   Pros and Cons of Performance Appraisal   404
     22.9   Good Appraisal Schemes   406
     22.10 Dealing with Problem Staff   413
     22.11 Disciplinaries   415

23   Quality Assurance and Procedures   424
     23.1   CIA's Responsibilities   424
     23.2   Features of Quality Assurance   425
     23.3   IIA Standard 500   427
     23.4   Audit Procedures   429

24   Audit Information Systems   434
     24.1   The Effect on Audit Work   434
     24.2   The Development of Information Systems   436
     24.3   Resourcing IT   439
     24.4   The Hierarchical Structure   440
     24.5   End-user Computing   441
     24.6   The Workstation Concept   442
     24.7   An IT Strategy   443
     24.8   Managing IT Acquisitions   445
     24.9   The Need for Computer Standards   447

24.10 Time Monitoring Systems 449
24.11 Conclusions 452

25 Marketing Audit Services 453
25.1 Introduction 453
25.2 Should Internal Audit Adopt a Marketing Profile? 453
25.3 Different Approaches to Marketing 463
25.4 Conclusions 464

26 Training and Development 465
26.1 Introduction 465
26.2 Benefits of Training 466
26.3 The Common Body of Knowledge (CBOK) 468
26.4 Training Auditors 470
26.5 The Role of the Institute of Internal Auditors 474
26.6 Action Learning 475
26.7 Monitoring Training 476
26.8 The Link into Development 477
26.9 National Vocational Qualification (NVQ) 478
26.10 Building on Existing Knowledge 479
26.11 Conclusions 479

27 Managing Change 480
27.1 Introduction 480
27.2 The Need for Change 480
27.3 Implications of Change 482
27.4 Strategic Development 485
27.5 Change Problems 487
27.6 The Change Strategy 492
27.7 Implementing Change 493
27.8 Changing Culture 501
27.9 Stress and Change 504
27.10 The Impact on Managing Internal Audit 505

Part Four Specialist Auditing **507**

28 Managing Computer Audit 509
28.1 Introduction to Computer Audit 509
28.2 Approaches to Computer Auditing 511
28.3 Controlling Information Technology (IT) 513
28.4 Staffing and Planning Computer Audit 516
28.5 Dealing with the PC Environment 520
28.6 The Audit Role in Systems Development 520
28.7 Controlling Applications 526
28.8 Controlling the Computer Centre 531
28.9 Disaster Planning 534
28.10 Data Protection 538
28.11 Computer Assisted Audit Techniques (CAATs) 542
28.12 Acquiring Computer Facilities 545

29	Investigating Fraud	550
	29.1 Background to Fraud	550
	29.2 The Concept of Evidence	558
	29.3 Interviewing Techniques	564
	29.4 Surveillance	576
	29.5 Advance Disclosure of Evidence	578
	29.6 Investigating the Fraud	580
	29.7 Computer Abuse	588
	29.8 Cheques: Fraudulent Encashment	602
	29.9 Dealing with Public Sector Benefits Fraud	607
	29.10 Preventative Techniques	614
	29.11 Conclusions	623

References 624

Index 625

Foreword

Internal audit is enjoying a higher profile than ever before as it proves its worth in the marketplace. Internal audit is not only seen to be in partnership with managers but also with directors. This places internal audit at the centre of action and debate on corporate governance, and internal audit is increasingly tooled up to assist at the highest levels of strategic planning in addition to its more traditional involvement at operational level.

Internal audit has developed a professional dignity in its own right and its scope is so broad that it is closer to management accounting and the art and science of management itself than to financial accounting and the external audit with which it has often been associated. In such a comprehensive service to the organisation in which it resides, there is much to absorb. Indeed, so much so that extensive extra material is included in the accompanying computer disk. This includes copies of forms which have improved the orderly progressing of internal audit work, as well as self-help questions and answers that reinforce the essential messages of the handbook. There is no point in re-inventing the wheel when there is a collective wisdom and knowledge as to what works best and what seems to be best practice.

This handbook represents that body of knowledge and practice which has proved successful the world over. It is valuable to the junior auditor searching for initial ideas on a subject as well as to the more experienced auditor who cannot be expected to have explored every angle of the subject. For those undertaking professional examinations the handbook is a useful first read as well as a continuing aid to revision. (The documentation supplied on disk is similar to that on offer commercially at a considerably higher price.)

The present product started life years ago as a dissertation for an MSc degree in Internal Audit and Management for which I was privileged to act as supervisor. It was based on an exhaustive survey of current best practice. It then continued as a time-consuming and all-embracing labour of love, with a continuation latterly of the earlier collaboration. Nobody should under-estimate the time and effort that goes into such a venture, and the proof that the time was wisely invested will be in the value-in-use of the handbook and the foreseeable need for future updating editions.

The production of such a handbook and the activity to which it refers witnesses to the growing stature of internal audit and a sense of professionalism. The handbook is as impressive as anything produced for external audit, and considerably more readable. For those contemplating a rewarding career, the richness of activity portrayed in the handbook shows that internal audit has much to offer, either as a means of top executive training or as a career in its own right.

Professor Gerald Vinten
President,
Institute of Internal Auditors,
United Kingdom and Ireland, 1995–1996
Editor, *Managerial Auditing Journal*

Acknowledgements

A special thanks to Gerald Vinten, Eric Hall, Keith Wade, Graham Westwood, Mrs Joycelyne Milne, Mr & Mrs Livermore, Mr Harry Pickett, Master Jakab, Mohammed Khan, Audit Group 8F (Richard, Horace, Tony, Dipa, Suman & Vernon) and all those many friends and colleagues I have had the pleasure to have known and worked with over the years. For their patience, a thank you to my two children, Dexter and Laurel-Jade.

List of Abbreviations

AC	Audit Committee
ACCA	Chartered Association of Certified Accountants
APB	Auditing Practices Board
BA	Benefits Agency
BACS	Banks Automated Clearing System
BSI	British Standards Institute
BV	Book value
CA	Computer Audit
CAAT	Computer Assisted Audit Techniques
CBOK	Common Body of Knowledge
CCAB	Consultative Committee of Accountancy Bodies
CCT	Compulsory Competitive Tendering
CD	Compact Disk
CE	Chief Executive
CIA	Chief Internal Auditor
CIMA	Chartered Institute of Management Accountants
CIPFA	Chartered Institute of Public Finance and Accountancy
CPE	Continuing Professional Education
CPS	Crown Prosecution Service
CTB	Council Tax Benefits
DA	District Auditor
DB	Database
DF	Director of Finance
DP	Data Protection
DP ACT	Data Protection Act
D.S.S.	Department of Social Security
DSS	Decision Support System
EA	External Audit
EDP	Electronic Data Processing
EEC	European Economic Community
EIS	Executive Information System
EUC	End User Computing
FAST	Federation Against Software Theft
GIAM	Government Internal Audit Manual
HB	Housing Benefits

HRM	Human Resource Management
IA	Internal Audit
IC	Internal Control
ICA	Institute of Chartered Accountants
ICES	Internal Control Evaluation System
ICT	Internal Control Team
ICQ	Internal Control Questionnaires
ID	Identity
IDEA	Interactive Data Exchange
IIA	Institute of Internal Auditors
IIA.INC	Institute of Internal Auditors. United States of America
IIA.UK	Institute of Internal Auditors. United Kingdom
IT	Information Technology
ITSG	Information Technology Steering Group
JD	Job Description
JS	Job Specification
MBA	Master of Business Administration
MBO	Management By Objectives
MCS	Management Control System
MIS	Management Information Systems
MUS	Monetary Unit Sampling
NAO	National Audit Office
NED	Non-Executive Directors
NHS	National Health Service
PACE	Police and Criminal Evidence Act
PC	Personal Computer
PESTL	Political, Environmental, Social, Technical & Legal
PI	Performance Indicator
PR	Public Relations
PS	Preliminary Survey
PSR	Preliminary Survey Report
PTB	Poll Tax Benefits
QA	Quality Assurance
QiCA	Qualification in Computer Auditing
RAM	Random Access Memory
RCW	Record of Control Weakness
SBA	Systems Based Auditing
SD	Systems Development
SDLC	Systems Development Life Cycle
SLA	Service Level Agreement
SOR	Statement of Responsibilities
SWOT	Strengths, Weaknesses, Opportunities & Threats
TMS	Time Monitoring System
TOR	Terms of Reference
TQM	Total Quality Management
VFM	Value For Money
VDU	Visual Display Unit

Supplements on Disk

Supplement 1   Establishing a new audit function
Supplement 2   Dealing with managerial problems
Supplement 3   Delegating audit work
Supplement 4   Audit investigations
Supplement 5   Management controls
Supplement 6   Assignment questions
Supplement 7   Answers to assignment questions
Supplement 8   Specimen forms

PART ONE

THE THEORETICAL FRAMEWORK

INTRODUCTION TO PART ONE

The handbook starts with the theoretical framework of internal auditing. This sets a foundation on which approaches to audit work may be explained and developed in parts two, three and four. We deal with the definition of the internal audit role and some of the standards compiled over the years to promote professionalism. With the audit role fast developing, trends are isolated and considered in terms of how they may affect the future. We include an account of working relationships and the conflicts that have to be reconciled by the auditor in balancing a client based approach with the need to explore and report. This leads into a discussion on independence, as the prime factor in the behavioural models that are dealt with. Mention is made of the conceptual basis of controls, rather than the operational areas to be found in standard audit texts. There are chapters on the audit charter, audit committees, and the code of ethics. Part one establishes conceptual models that direct the way the audit role is perceived and discharged through professional standards. Many auditing textbooks include a brief account of the work of the internal auditor as a support to external audit work. The two roles are entirely different and this forms the reasoning behind part one, where internal auditing warrants discussion in its own right. The main differences between external and internal audit are detailed. Note that there is some repetition in the parts since each chapter is self-contained.

The key items in part one are:

- Definition of internal audit.
- The development of internal audit.
- The concept of auditing standards.
- Approaches to internal audit.
- Independence.
- Behavioural aspects of auditing.
- Audit committees.
- The audit charter.
- Code of ethics.
- Standards on audit work.
- External audit and other review agencies.
- Fundamentals of control (a list of managerial controls is set out in the accompanying diskette).

Part one is founded on the premise that the auditor must have a clear understanding of his/her role, responsibilities and professional standards before relevant auditing techniques found in part two can be applied. Once these techniques have been mastered we move into managerial aspects of auditing in part three, while part four describes practical aspects of performing specialist internal audit work. There are a number of assignments (along with suggested answers) in the accompanying diskettes that are case-study based. These may be attempted as a way of thinking through the issues involved.

CHAPTER ONE

DEFINITION OF INTERNAL AUDIT

1.1 Introduction

The starting place for internal audit theory is the definition of internal audit. A standard definition is made up of important issues that form the basic framework of internal audit principles. Each component may be considered in turn as an isolated topic although their role in coming together to form a defined function has to be carefully examined and fully appreciated before we can move further into the world of internal auditing. The divergence of interpretation of the audit role is explored in terms of the way we may in practice move away from the standard definition. Internal auditing is performed in a variety of ways each with its own approach and style. Accordingly it is important that a formal definition is devised and agreed since it will have a vital impact on the perceived role of the audit function. Management often asks auditors exactly what aspects of an operation they are responsible for and a variety of responses may be received. Some auditors feel that they should police the organisation while others are convinced they must check the accuracy of accounting records. Still others feel obliged to search out poor value for money or new and improved ways of using resources. Much depends on the audit charter and management expectations. One must have a model developed by the profession which represents the true scope of internal auditing. In this model, management is clearly responsible for controlling resources to ensure objectives are met, whilst the scope of audit work is based on reviewing key controls. When management asks an auditor what their responsibilities are, the answer must be precise.

1.2 The Auditing Practices Board (APB) Definition

The APB Auditing Guidelines - "Guidance for internal auditors" was published in October 1990. The definition of internal auditing is:

> *"Internal audit is an independent appraisal function established by management for the review of the internal control system as a service to the organisation. It objectively examines, evaluates and reports on the adequacy of internal control as a contribution to the proper, economic, efficient and effective use of resources."*

This definition tends to be adopted by CCAB accountants and includes the three Es (economy, efficiency and effectiveness). It was under revision in 1996 as a Practice Note with more convergence towards the IIA definition and emphasis on corporate governance.

1.3 The Institute of Internal Auditors (IIA) Definition (1991)

> *"Internal auditing is an independent appraisal function established within an organisation as a service to the organisation. It is a control that functions by examining and evaluating the adequacy and effectiveness of other controls."*

Although brief, it contains the basic principles on which internal audit is based. We analyse this definition in detail by examining each of the material concepts:

"Internal auditing": The service is based within the organisation and is distinct from the external audit role. Years ago the IIA considered changing the name of internal auditing to reflect the modern and increasingly professional approach. No alternative was forthcoming and the idea was dropped.

"Independent": The concept of independence is fundamental. Internal auditing cannot survive if it is not objective. All definitions of internal audit must feature an element of independence, although its extent, and how it is achieved, is a topic in its own right. The audit function must have sufficient status and be able to stand back from the operation under review for it to be of use. If this is not achieved, then this forms a fundamental flaw in the audit service and some internal audit functions may not be able to subscribe to the standards.

"Appraisal function": This part of the definition refers to the role of internal auditing in weighing up the various factors relevant to the area under review. This in turn would require an amount of professional expertise that provides the ability to appraise. As a function, internal audit has to perform a defined process and this conjures up the image of some form of standardised input/output system with a clear end-product.

"Established within an organisation": The fact that the internal audit function is located within the organisation makes it clear that it is wholly responsible to the organisation and not some external regulatory body. In general it therefore owes its allegiance solely to the organisation which lies over and above the concept of a loyalty to the public at large. Also some form of permanence is required to meet the criterion "established".

"As a service to the organisation": As a service, auditing has to form a client base and understand the needs of the organisation. Here the service role should lead to a defined benefit to the organisation rather than internal audit working for its own mysterious goals. Having said this, by serving the organisation it is possible to de-prioritise the needs of individual managers by reporting direct to corporate management, perhaps in the form of an audit committee. This then becomes the real audit client superseding specific officers of the organisation.

"Control": This brings into play the notion of audit as a master control floating above and advising on the various control systems. The idea that audit has a clear responsibility for advising on controls comes to the fore with its importance to management in developing control issues and bringing them to management's attention.

"That functions by examining": The task of examining brings out the detailed analytical functions that are seen during testing routines. The need for adequate evidence is also highlighted as this is derived from the examination routines.

"And evaluating": Evaluation involves applying creativity to a particular problem and lifts audit from the potential doldrums of continual testing procedures. Evaluation is

dependent on professional judgement and one can imagine a high level of expertise being required to reach this stage.

"The adequacy": Assessing adequacy presupposes an acceptable level that may be defined and applied. The audit role may be assurance as well as identifying problems for management. Management, with advice from audit, needs to establish operational standards and existing controls need to meet these.

"And effectiveness": Effectiveness is a bottom-line concept based on the notion that management is able to set objectives and control resources in such a way as to ensure that these goals are in fact achieved. The link between controls and objectives becomes clear, and audit must be able to understand the fundamental needs of management as it works to its goals. The complexities behind the concept of effectiveness are great, and by building this into the audit definition, the audit scope becomes potentially very wide.

"Of other controls": Restating the audit role as working on controls places this feature firmly in the audit mission. We can extend this idea and suggest that auditors are the experts in controls, and all matters that materially impact on control issues across the organisation need to form part of the audit plan. Concentrating on controls may mean moving away from the obsession with investigating delinquent transactions that forms the premise for many audit-testing programmes.

1.4 The New Definition of Internal Auditing

1991 saw a new definition in the IIA's updated standards and guidelines:

> *"Internal auditing is an independent appraisal function established within an organisation as a service to the organisation. The objective of internal auditing is to assist members of the organisation and on the board, in the effective discharge of their responsibilities. To this end it furnishes them with analysis, appraisals, recommendations, counsel, and information concerning the activities reviewed."*

Whilst the first sentence is the same, the next two add new features: "the provision of advice, and information that assists management in discharging their responsibilities". The development of these changes is dealt with later.

1994 changes

The 1994 definition of internal auditing from the IIA statement of responsibilities reads:

> *"Internal auditing is an independent appraisal function established within an organisation to examine and evaluate its activities as a service to the organisation. The objective of internal auditing is to assist members of the organisation, including those in management and on the board, in the effective discharge of their responsibilities. To this end internal audit furnishes them with analysis, appraisals, recommendations, counsel, and information concerning the activities reviewed. The objective includes promoting effective control at reasonable cost."*

The additional last sentence is taken from the 1988 definition of internal audit. This brings back into play the practicality and reasonableness that should attach to audit recommendations. All organisations now have to be cost conscious since most controls impact on resources.

1.5 Is there a Right Model?

Several well known authorities have used definitions outside of the IIA standards:

Lawrence Sawyer (1988)
"Internal auditing is a systematic, objective appraisal by internal auditors of the diverse operations and controls within an organisation to determine whether financial and operating information is accurate and reliable, risks to the enterprise are identified and minimised, external regulations and acceptable internal policies and procedures are followed, satisfactory standards are met, resources are used efficiently and economically, and the organisation's objectives are achieved; all for the purpose of assisting members of the organisation in the effective discharge of their responsibilities."

This definition includes most of the key areas although described in a unique fashion. Internal policies and procedures are only seen as important where they are acceptable which brings in the common-sense approach to auditing where practicalities are taken on board, in contrast to a less flexible stance. The important concept of risk is highlighted throughout. The final point is the emphasis on assisting members of the organisation in their responsibilities.

Allan J Sayle (1988)
"A management audit is an independent examination of objective evidence, performed by competent personnel, to determine whether or not the auditee:
- is assisting or is capable of assisting the company to achieve its policies and/or;
- is capable of, or is assisting the company to fulfil its contractual and legal obligations and;
- has integrated management systems to do so; and/or,
- is effectively implementing those systems.
- it is also the true and fair presentation of the results of such examination."

What appears an unusual view of auditing becomes increasingly relevant when one considers the importance of quality assurance systems, now a fundamental part of an organisation. It brings out clearly the key components of achieving objectives, having sound management systems and ensuring that they are being used. This moves closer to the systems based approach that is the foundation of audit work and allows one to develop a professional auditing methodology. We may also note the need for the audit to provide a true and fair representation of the work carried out. The definition relates to management auditing.

Government Internal Audit Manual (1988)
"Internal audit is an independent appraisal within a department which operates as a service to management by measuring and evaluating the effectiveness of internal control."

This straightforward definition brings out the basic role of internal audit. It is biased towards central government by including the term "department" and so applies to a specific branch of internal auditing. There is debate on whether there needs to be a separate definition for the public sector or whether it is simply part of the wider profession of auditing. A shortcoming with the definition is the lack of scope for consultancy work to provide advice and assistance to management.

Mautz (1984)

"Internal auditing which is ultimately responsible to the owners of the enterprise is a service to senior management and other enterprise interests that includes:

- monitoring management controls.
- anticipating, identifying and assessing risks to enterprise assets and activities.
- investigating actual and potential lapses of control and incidents of risk.
- making recommendations for improvement of control, the response to risk and the attainment of enterprise objectives."

Unlike the previous definition, this brings out the wider scope of the internal audit role, particularly on lapses in control. These lapses allow threats to value for money, fraud and breach of procedure, sub-optimal performance, and unreliable information systems. It differentiates between owners and senior management which implies an audit committee that represents the interests of the organisation. The main deficiency is not to acknowledge the importance of independence and information systems.

There are many similarities in the various published definitions of internal auditing. Most revolve around the view of internal audit as an independent service to the organisation reviewing systems of internal control. One futuristic model is quoted by Gerald Vinten (1990). This emphasises the need to direct audit resources at the future welfare of the organisation as opposed to being pre-occupied with past events in the form of recorded transactions and incidents that have already occurred:

> *"Internal auditing is the recurrent comprehensive investigation into apparently healthy organisations with the objective of achieving an insight into the state of the organisation and also its environment with the objective of achieving better control over its future operations."*

An audit department more concerned about future control issues than past events may have a dynamic impact on the organisation although it requires a new approach to discharging the audit role. An analysis of job advertisements reveals the wide variation in audit designations and duties. There is no one right model of internal audit and the final role adopted depends on the elements shown in figure 1.1.

FIGURE 1.1 FACTORS IMPACTING ON THE AUDIT ROLE

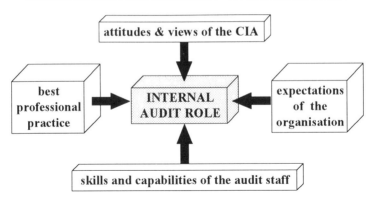

The relative influence of each of these will define the final model of internal audit that is applied in an organisation. The current trend is to move towards a consultancy-based approach that, as a result, is based on a very wide interpretation of the audit role. In this respect special projects may be included in the range of work which in reality could mean almost anything that urgently needs doing. Best professional practice is based on the auditor discharging the requirements of professional auditing standards. This represents an idealistic model but may be used as a suitable reference point. The fact that many auditors are essentially accountants first, underpins the need for formal auditing standards to maintain some form of balance. Organisational expectations become more significant in a market-led strategy where the client's needs are seen as paramount. Unfortunately we cannot simply do what managers want us to do, as this would mean the audit function being indistinguishable from management consultants. The type of staff involved in discharging the audit role acts as a barrier to the resultant activities in that we can only perform work that staff are capable of performing. This becomes less material where qualified auditors are employed, in contrast to using all who happen to end up in the audit unit. The Chief Internal Auditor (CIA) has the final say in role definition as the person most responsible for delivering the defined services. The background and experience of this person will have great impact. This in turn is influenced by the job description that is drawn up as a basis for appointing the CIA. An organisation establishing a new audit function is advised to use the services of an audit consultant to draw up terms of reference and recruit a suitable CIA. One interpretation of the audit role is:

> *"Internal audit is an established independent appraisal function that seeks to secure improvements in material systems of internal control within an organisation. The objective of internal audit is to provide guidance in this and related matters to the organisation so as to assist management in the discharge of its responsibilities for installing and maintaining controls that ensure organisational objectives are achieved. To this end it furnishes them with analyses, appraisals, recommendations, counsel, and information concerning the activities reviewed."*

1.6 The Five Main Elements

The scope of internal auditing is found in the Institute of Internal Auditors' professional standard 300 on reviewing the adequacy and effectiveness of key managerial controls in five areas:

- Management information systems.
- Compliance with laws, policies, procedures and regulations.
- Safeguarding assets and interests.
- The economy and efficiency with which resources are applied.
- The accomplishment of organisational goals and objectives.

The scope of internal audits encompasses the examination and evaluation of the adequacy and effectiveness of the organisation's systems of internal control and the quality of performance in carrying out assigned responsibilities:

310 Reliability and integrity of information. Internal auditors review the reliability and integrity of financial and operating information and the means used to identify, measure, classify and report such information.

320 Compliance with policies, plans, procedures, laws and regulations. Internal auditors should review the systems established to ensure compliance with those policies, plans, procedures, laws and regulations which could have a significant impact on operations and reports, and should determine whether the organisation is in compliance.

330 Safeguarding assets. Internal auditors should review the means of safeguarding and, as appropriate, verify the existence of such assets.

340 Economical and efficient use of resources. Internal auditors should appraise the economy and efficiency with which resources are employed.

350 Accomplishment of established objectives and goals for operations and programmes. Internal auditors should review operations or programmes to ascertain whether results are consistent with established objectives and goals and whether the operations are being carried out as planned.

Internal audit reviews the extent to which management has established sound systems of internal controls so that objectives are set and resources applied to these objectives in an efficient manner. This includes being protected from loss and abuse. Adequate information systems should be established to enable management to assess the extent to which objectives are being achieved via a series of suitable reports. Controls are required to ensure the achievement of value for money and it is these areas that internal audit is concerned with. Compliance, information systems, and safeguarding assets are all pre-requisites to good value for money. There is a fundamental link between quality assurance and VFM as it is the quality systems that underpin the achievement of VFM. This point is expanded in IIA standard 350, accomplishment of organisational objectives. If management includes efficiency and safeguarding assets as part of achieving objectives, then standard 350 becomes the single most important area that must be controlled.

It may then be possible to restate the control objectives to read that controls are required for the achievement of organisational objectives in an efficient manner, ensuring that:

- Information systems are adequate.
- Policies and procedures are complied with.
- Assets are protected.

Internal audit would be primarily concerned with those controls that promote effective managerial decisions for moving the organisation from point (a) to point (b). If this is the case we can reword our definition of internal audit:

> *"Internal audit is an independent appraisal function established within an organisation that seeks to review the extent to which management is able to achieve organisational objectives in an efficient manner. This entails an appraisal of key controls associated with management information and protection of assets through compliance with quality control systems, as a service to the organisation."*

1.7 Implications of the Wide Scope

The scope of internal auditing defined above is necessarily wide and this implies:

Expertise

Great expertise is required from auditors to enable them to provide advice on the wide range of key control objectives. Since we are charged with auditing anything and everything, we need some knowledge of almost all organisational activities. The ideal internal auditor may be the most experienced employee of the organisation in terms of an overall knowledge of the different areas, second only to the Chief Executive. Whilst this ideal is unrealistic it represents a major challenge for the auditor. Unfortunately traditional internal audit departments who are locked into a never-ending regime of checking the output from basic accounting systems will find it impossible to achieve the high standards that underpin this wide scope of audit work. Factors that assist the process of incorporating wide scope into the range of audit work performed include:

- Ensuring the audit plan covers all aspects of the organisation starting from top downwards. The plan is a statement of intent, that should then be delivered. The higher one aims, the more one is likely to achieve. It should be policy to tackle the most difficult and sensitive of work areas as well as the more basic audits. The plans, more than anything else, determine the direction of the audit function.
- Mobilising all available techniques and automated procedures and ensuring that auditors are well trained in management studies/practices and are able to assimilate them into everyday audit work. The duel concepts of being proficient in both auditing skills and management techniques allow one to meet the challenges arising from a wide view of audit work. In fact the better the appreciation of management techniques, the more efficient becomes the auditor's input into systems of management control. This equation is fundamental to an understanding of professional internal auditing.

- Ensuring the audit charter caters for the wide scope of audit work and that this is understood throughout all levels in the organisation. This requires a programme of ongoing publicity and marketing.

- Recruiting auditors from a variety of backgrounds in addition to those from a traditional accounting role. This enables service delivery promises to be kept by developing the wide skills base needed to resource the underlying work. This is easier said than done since one must buy in new skills and new experiences whilst getting these people to work as a team. Skills must be interfaced to form one complete whole, far removed from the narrow scope adopted by the single-minded accountant.

- Developing auditors to professional auditing standards via an appropriate internal audit qualification. Whatever the defined skills base, one must ensure that audit staff are above all, auditors. A short-cut to this is to release those who fail their auditing examinations. The other option of using ad-hoc consultants on a needs basis makes it even more difficult to solve the interface problem.

A useful test is to ensure that audit reports interest the Chief Executive as well as the Director of Finance. Resources directed at anything less than this, may be of little use to the organisation. Where the CE assumes a control orientation then the CIA must assume an educational role in promoting the right culture. This is easy if one considers that controls ensure organisational objectives are achieved. Once high standards have been established, this raises expectations which must be met. This can be achieved by implementing quality auditing systems:

FIGURE 1.2 ENSURING QUALITY AUDITS

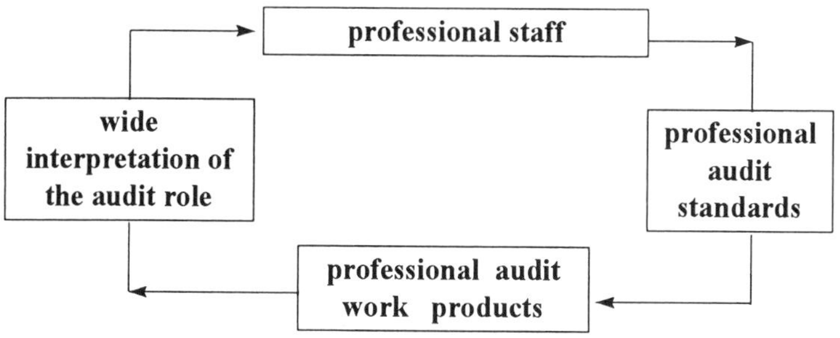

Safeguarding assets

It is necessary to establish who is responsible for investigating frauds since this is resource-intensive. Where internal audit is wholly responsible for investigating fraud, error and irregularities, this may become a drain on audit resources. Adopting a wide scope of work and having the necessary skills to operate at this level will be of little use where most of the available time is spent responding to management referrals on matters of regularity. High-level fraud investigations do require an associated level of skills and there is potential for major impact on the organisation. There is a defensive stance that may be assumed to preserve audit resources that will be effective in the short term. This is to plan a comprehensive programme of compliance checks and verification routines to protect organisational assets. It is then possible to calculate the minimum resources to fund such a programme and it is in this way that the audit budget may be preserved. The main drawback is the need to deploy armies of junior resources to carry out the basic checks of compliance work, which militates against working to high professional standards.

Balancing is required and it is the CIA's task. Management is, in the final analysis, responsible for safeguarding assets.

The compliance role

Controls over compliance may include an inspection routine and audit's role in this should be clearly defined. Do we provide a probity-based service on behalf of management and visit all relevant locations or merely provide an advisory function to management on promoting compliance? It is useful for internal audit to be supported by a range of control teams located close to each operation:

FIGURE 1.3 COMPLIANCE MECHANISMS

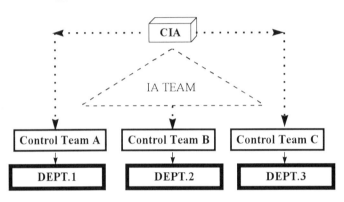

This will work where the CIA sets up the following systems:

The control teams report to the appropriate department's director but the CIA has a functional responsibility for their work. This responsibility means that the CIA will be concerned with the standards and performance of the teams and want to see them excel. We would expect to see the CIA or a suitable representative present on any selection panel that chooses senior internal control staff.

The control teams provide work programmes for each time-period (e.g. each quarter) which will have to be approved by the CIA. This can work on a number of levels; it may simply involve receiving work plans for approval or being actively involved in their formulation. The important point is that these plans are wholly interfaced with the current internal audit plans.

The control teams are required to furnish regular reports on progress against plan to the CIA (e.g. quarterly). The CIA may care to furnish the audit committee with this information. These reports constitute a major control over the teams in that they force them to formally account for their time as well as installing the discipline of weekly timesheet recording. Comparing planned against actuals is an accepted statistic that should highlight possible problems.

The CIA will provide the teams with suitable procedures based around the audit manual that will set the direction and methodology of their work. This may become a slimmed down version of the audit manual dealing with basic probity checks that would form the basis of the control team's work. Furthermore comprehensive audit programmes specially drafted for the control teams can be of great use, particularly where the team members are fairly new in their posts. This approach allows the CIA to review standards set via the audit manual.

The CIA will carry out regular quality reviews of these teams and require that any operational deficiencies are corrected. Compliance with procedures will also be assessed. These reviews consider the extent to which the teams meet their stated objectives. It also allows the CIA to judge whether reliance can be placed on their work and so reduce any internal audit coverage.

Where operational practices are adequate, the CIA will be able to issue internal audit warrants to the control teams that will allow them access to organisational records. Control teams will not ordinarily have access to most systems particularly those that are centralised or of a corporate nature. The power to issue or withhold audit warrants, that permit access across the organisation, consolidates the CIA's functional responsibility over the control teams. It gives credence to the review process where material problems with their performance may result in a suspension or complete withdrawal of the warrant. As with all important powers this must be exercised with care.

Information systems

The audit of management information systems (MIS) is crucial since this may involve reviewing MIS as part of operational audits, or these systems can be audited separately. MIS cannot be tackled without expertise. Auditing MIS may follow two main routes. We may review information systems as a concept in terms of looking at the way they are applied to enhancing the overall efficiency of operations. The assessment of MIS must be related to business objectives. The advantage is that one can concentrate expertise on the specific application that will almost certainly be computerised. Alternatively, it is possible to incorporate the assessment of MIS into all audits so that this becomes a fundamental feature of general audit work. This not only builds an appreciation of the importance of MIS by general auditors but also allows expertise to be acquired. It is easier to link MIS into operational objectives when this information is viewed in conjunction with the wider elements of the audit. Moreover, information systems cannot be ignored and this is wholly within the scope of audit work.

Value for money

The concept of economy, efficiency and effectiveness (or VFM) is another sensitive issue. Auditors can assist management's task in securing good arrangements for promoting VFM or alternatively undertake a continual search for waste and other poor VFM. These two different perspectives of the audit role will continue to arise in many different areas as it is based on the fundamental distinction between systems audits and investigations. A systems approach considers the managerial systems for promoting VFM and judges whether this is working. Investigatory work, on the other hand, furnishes management with suggestions as to alternative operational methods. In terms of defining the scope of audit work, the former approach is purist auditing work that falls within our definition. The investigatory stance is more akin to a consultancy approach that, whilst in line with the scope of work, falls closer to a management role. VFM is relevant to audit work whatever the adopted approach.

Management needs

A wide scope requires a good understanding of the operations being reviewed and it is necessary to include management's needs in the terms of reference by adopting a more participative style. Unlike the narrow approach that underpins traditional probity-auditing, this depends on getting inside management objectives. It is then impossible to operate as outsiders and work primarily from documentation and records. This will hinder the ability to achieve high level results. Close working arrangements with management are essential.

Specialists
The five elements of the key control objectives may require specialists in each of the defined areas and the level of expectation may place great demands on the audit service. One might imagine that the audit function will eventually be broken down into defined fields with experts specialising in different ones. This point is explored below in the section on resourcing the wide scope of audit work.

1.8 The Managerial Control System

The scope of internal auditing may be broken down into five components (IIA standard 300) and one can apply dedicated resources to specialising in each. The systems approach calls for management to formulate suitable arrangements for achieving each of these five main control objectives and once they are in place, management may be said to be in control. Likewise the managerial control system is based on the fundamental principles of management control over resources. This control loop must be in place to ensure control, and systems auditing will review the extent to which this is the case and whether they are operated and work in practice. The control system appears as:

FIGURE 1.4 THE MANAGERIAL CONTROL SYSTEM

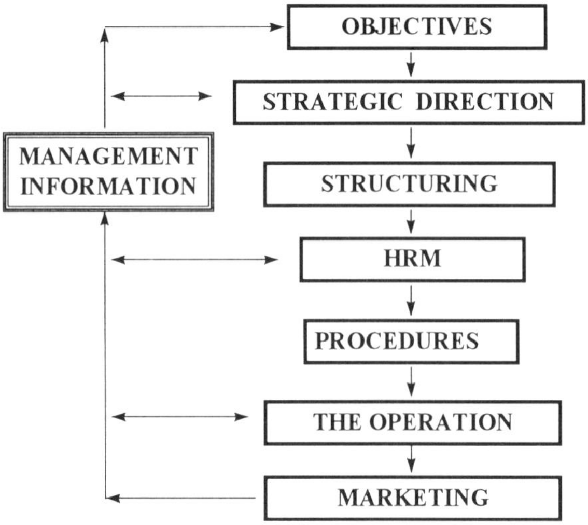

There are several fundamental managerial functions to be discharged before any operation can be said to be controlled. The five key control objectives may be achieved if the loop is in place to ensure that:
- Information is suitable for reviewing the success of strategy.
- Compliance with procedures occurs.
- Assets are protected via a well-controlled environment.
- Efficiency is secured.
- Operational objectives are formulated and may in turn be accomplished.

An audit involves reviewing each of these aspects or components of managerial controls. Each of the components is linked together to form a whole system of controls and they are dependent on each other. No matter how much effort management has placed in devising good operational procedures (i.e. the procedures component is strong), if poor staff are being recruited and no training provided (i.e. the staffing component is weak), then there will always be control problems. The auditor needs to recognise this relationship and incorporate it into the work carried out and areas addressed. This may be achieved only if the audit manual caters for a clear methodology geared into this wider view of control systems.

1.9 Scope within Different Time Frames

Scope has been described as the range of audit work that may be performed within the overall terms of reference for the audit function. This concept is affected by the time frame applied. There are several relevant points:

Charter

The major impact of the scope of audit work arises when the audit charter is being formulated, since this will set the whole direction of the audit function. A predetermined wide scope will necessarily require high profile, senior staff and an enhanced level of professionalism if it is to be achieved. These factors will have to be considered at conception stage, when the audit function is first set up.

Long-term plans

The next level at which the question of scope is relevant appears at the long-term planning stage where an audit strategy is being devised. Here the scope of work will determine how audit work will be interfaced with the organisation. Audit objectives and the way in which they fit into overall organisational needs will have to be defined in line with a comprehensive strategy for audit work. Since the scope of work partly sets out our responsibilities, there are obvious repercussions on the resultant strategy for discharging these responsibilities.

Medium-term plans

Scope next appears on the agenda during the medium-term planning stage. It is here that the audit field is fully defined, risk analysis applied and a formal audit plan produced for consultation. The scope of audit work will apply here as it may be used to isolate the audit field and determine how these work areas will be tackled.

Assignment planning

The final way in which scope is important is in terms of its impact on the assignment planning process. In practice we will not be able to tackle all parts of a planned audit since in one sense every audit is open-ended. It will be necessary to assess each of the key control issues and then decide, through a process of preliminary review, which will be prioritised for the audit in question. The use of scope makes this task easier and sets a clear frame for the necessary assessment.

1.10 Resourcing the Agreed Scope

There are resource implications of adopting a wide scope of audit work that will have to be catered for by audit management. This is because the act of assuming the stance whereby "everything of importance to controlling the organisation will be audited" brings with it the need to meet these enhanced expectations. One might promise much, but it is the delivery of associated results that will be monitored, not mere statements of intent. The following illustration sets out the process of resourcing the wide scope of audit and how this might be managed:

FIGURE 1.5 RESOURCING THE WIDE SCOPE OF AUDIT WORK

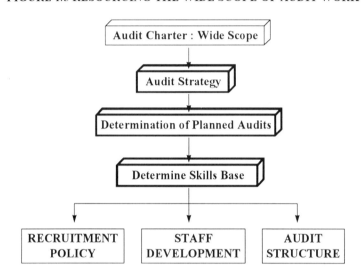

The idea is to ensure that the wide scope of audit work is taken into consideration when obtaining, developing and structuring audit staff. All relevant factors are accounted for when deciding how the agreed audit services will be delivered to management. While auditors are concerned about matters of compliance, information, fraud and VFM, one can use audit resources efficiently by advising management on steps they can take to promote good controls in these areas. As long as resources have been applied to achieving a defined goal, an operation may be audited by considering the following:

FIGURE 1.6 AUDIT COMPONENTS

OBJECTIVES → RESOURCES → ACHIEVEMENTS

Internal audit may adopt an open-ended stance which suggests that anything may be subject to audit. This includes policies, major issues, structures, communications, attitudes, and culture. The only caveat is the availability of skilled staff and reliable evidence to support such audits.

CHAPTER TWO

THE DEVELOPMENT OF INTERNAL AUDIT

2.1 Introduction

Internal audit is a developing profession. An individual employed in internal audit ten years ago would find an unrecognisable situation in terms of the audit role, services provided, and approach. For a full appreciation of internal auditing, it is necessary to trace these developments and extend trends into the future. Included is a section that outlines topical issues facing internal auditing.

2.2 The Evolution of the Audit Function

The internal audit function has moved through a number of stages in its development:

Extension of external audit

Internal audit developed as an extension of the external audit role in testing the reliability of accounting records that contribute to published financial statements. Internal audit reduced external audit work, based on a detailed programme of testing of accounting data. Where this model predominates, there can be little real development in the professionalism of the internal audit function. It would be possible to disband internal audit by simply increasing the level of testing in the external auditor's plans. Unfortunately there are still organisations whose main justification for resourcing an internal audit service is to reduce the external audit fee.

Internal check

The testing role progressed to cover non-financial areas, and this equates the function to a form of internal check. Vast numbers of transactions were double-checked to provide assurances that they were correct and properly authorised by laid-down procedures. The infamous audit stamp reigned supreme indicating that a document was deemed correct and above board. Internal control was seen as internal check and management was presented with audit reports listing the sometimes huge number of errors for their attention. The audit function usually consisted of a small team of auditors working under an assistant chief accountant. This encouraged management to neglect control systems on the grounds that errors would be picked up by auditors on the next visit. It locks the audit role tightly into the system of control making it difficult to secure real independence. If existence within an organisation depends on fulfilling a service need, then this need must be retained if one is to survive. The temptation is to allow failings in the systems of control so that each visit will result in a respectable number of audit findings. Wide-ranging recommendations for solving these control gaps (which cause these errors in the first place) will therefore not be made by the auditor. This destroys the foundation of objectivity on which independence is partly based.

Probity work

Probity work arrived next as an adaptation of checking accounting records where the auditors would arrive unannounced at satellite locations and offices, and perform a detailed series of tests according to a pre-conceived audit programme. Management was presented with a list of errors and queries that were uncovered by the auditors. The auditors either worked as a small team based in accountancy or had dual posts where they had special audit duties in addition to their general accounting role. Audit consisted mainly of checking, with the probity visits tending to centre on cash, stocks, purchases, petty cash, stamps, revenue contracts and other minor accounting functions. The main purpose behind these visits was linked into the view that the chief accountant needed to check on all remote sites to ensure that accounting procedures were complied with and that their books were correct. The audit was seen as inspection on behalf of management. This militates against good controls, as the auditor is expected to be the main avenue for securing information. Insecure management may then feel that their responsibility stops at issuing a batch of detailed procedures to local supervisors and nothing more. The auditors would then follow-up these procedures without questioning why they may not be working. The fundamental components of the control systems above local level will fall outside the scope of audit work that will be centred on low-level, detailed checking.

Non-financial systems

The shift in low-level checking arose when audit acquired a degree of separation from the accounting function with internal audit departments being purposely established. This allowed a level of audit management to develop which in turn raised the status of the audit function away from a complement of junior staff completing standardised audit programmes. The ability to define an audit's terms of reference stimulated the move towards greater professionalism, giving rise to the model of audit as a separate entity. Likewise, the ability to stand outside basic financial procedures allowed freedom to tackle high-level problems which is the main premise upon which audit professionalism is based. It is now possible to widen the scope of audit work and bring to bear a whole variety of disciplines including civil engineering, statistics, management, computing, and quality assurance.

Chief auditors

The final thrust towards a high profile, professional department was provided through employing chief internal auditors with high organisational status. They could meet with all levels of senior management and represent the audit function. This coincided with the removal of audit from the finance function retaining a functional link. The audit department as a separate high profile entity encourages career auditors able to develop within the function. This is as well as employing auditors able to use the experience as part of their managerial career development. The current position in many large organisations establishes a firm framework from which the audit function may continue to develop the professional status that is the mark of an accepted discipline. When assessing risk for the audit plan one asks what is crucial to the organisation before embarking on a series of planned audits that in the past may have had little relevance to top management. Professionalism is embodied in the ability to deal with important issues that have a major impact on success. The recent rise in the profile of internal auditing confirms potential for significant development.

Audit committees
Audit committees bring about the concept of the audit function reporting to the highest levels and this has a positive impact on perceived status. Securing the attention of the chief executive, managing director, non-executive directors and senior management provides an avenue for high level audit work able to tackle the most sensitive corporate issues. This is far removed from the early role of checking the stock and petty cash. Internal audit is now poised to enter all areas. In a wider sense, an entire nation's international policies and associated programmes may be audited in future.

2.3 The Development of Internal Audit Services
The developmental process outlined above highlights the way the function has progressed in assuming a higher profile and a greater degree of professionalism. The type of audit service has changed to reflect these new expectations. The development of services may likewise be traced:

Internal check procedures
Internal audit was seen as an integral component of the internal checking procedures designed to double-check accounting transactions. The idea was to re-check as many items as possible so as to provide this continuous audit. One might imagine an audit manager giving staff an instruction that "your job is to check all the book entries" on an ongoing basis.

Transaction based approach
The transactions approach came next, where a continuous programme of tests is used to isolate errors or frauds. This checking function would have become streamlined so that a detailed programme of tests may be built up over time to be applied at each audit visit. This systematic approach is readily controlled so that one might expect the auditor to complete hundreds of checks over a week long period during the course of completing this pre-determined audit programme.

Statistical sampling
Statistical sampling was later applied to reduce the level of testing along with a move away from examining all available documents or book entries. A scientific approach was used whereby the results from a sample could be extrapolated to the entire population in a defendable manner. The problem is that one is still adopting the external audit stance which seeks to give an accept or reject decision as the final product. Like the sophisticated computer interrogation now used in audit work, this is an example of how a new technique is limited by a refusal to move away from traditional audit objectives. The downfall of many a computer auditor has been failure to understand the full impact of the audit role. Computerised investigations now allow 100% checks. Much depends on whether we perceive this as a valid audit task or a managerial responsibility.

Probity based work
Probity based work next developed, again featuring the transaction approach where anything untoward was investigated. The probity approach is based on audit being the unseen force that sees and hears all that goes on in the organisation. Instead of double-checking accounting records and indicating those that should be corrected, the probity

approach allowed the Chief Accountant to check on financial propriety across the organisation. The auditor would represent the Director of Finance by visiting all major units and carrying out these audit test programmes.

Spot checks

It was then possible to reduce the level of probity visits by unannounced spot checks so that the audit deterrent (the possibility of being audited) would reduce the risk of irregularity. Larger organisations may have hundreds of decentralised locations that would have been visited each year by the auditor. This service depends on employing large teams of junior auditors who would undertake these regular visits. As management started to assume responsibility for their operations, the audit service turned increasingly to selective as opposed to periodic visits. Rather than a guaranteed visit each year, one sought compliance with procedure by threatening the possibility of a visit.

Risk analysis

The transaction/probity approach could be restricted by applying a form of risk analysis to the defined audit areas so that only high-risk ones would be visited. There are many well-known risk formulae that are designed to target audit resources to specific areas based around relevant factors. Each unit might then be ranked so that the high-risk ones would be visited first and/or using greater resources. Risk analysis used in conjunction with statistical sampling and automated interrogation gives the impression that internal auditing is carried out wholly scientifically. This is steeped in the dated version of internal auditing.

Systems based approach

Then came a move away from the regime of management by fear to a more consultancy based service. Systems based audits (SBA) are used to advise management on the types of controls they should be using. Testing is directed more at the controls than to highlight errors for their own sake. The problems found during audit visits will ultimately be linked to the way management controls their activities. This new-found responsibility moves managers away from relying on the programmed audit visit to solve all ills. Systems of control become the key words that management adopts when seeking efficiency and effectiveness, and it is here that the audit service may better be directed. The application of SBA was originally directed at accounting systems where internal control questionnaires devised by external auditors were adapted and used. Basic financial systems were covered by tailoring ready-made audit programmes that looked for a series of pre-determined controls. These were applied by internal auditors although it was in the shadow of external audit work.

Operational audit

Attention to operational areas outside the financial arena provided an opportunity to perform work not done by the external auditor. The concepts of economy, efficiency and effectiveness were built into models that evaluated the value for money implications of an area under review. Looking for savings based on greater efficiencies became a clear part of the audit role. Purpose built value for money teams were set up to seek out all identifiable savings. The worst-case scenario came true in many organisations where these teams had to be resourced from the savings they identified. It is one thing to recommend a whole series of savings but another to achieve them. As a result many teams were later disbanded. On the other hand, operational audit teams that encourage management to look for their own VFM savings had more success and this is now an established audit role.

Management audit

Management audit moves up a level to address control issues arising from managing an activity. It involves an appreciation of the finer points relating to the various managerial processes that move the organisation towards its objectives. This comes closer to the final goal of internal audit where it is deemed capable of reviewing all important areas within the organisation by adopting a wide interpretation of systems of control. The ability to understand and evaluate complicated systems of managerial and operational controls allows audit to assume wide scope. This is relevant where controls are seen in a wider context as all those measures necessary to ensure that objectives are achieved. The systems based approach offers great potential with the flexibility in applying this approach to a multitude of activities and developing a clear audit methodology at corporate, managerial and operational levels. This potted history of internal auditing may read:

FIGURE 2.1 DEVELOPMENT OF INTERNAL AUDIT

FINANCIAL AUDITS

OPERATIONAL AUDITS

MANAGEMENT AUDITS

CORPORATE AUDITS

SOCIAL AUDITS

This illustrates how the audit profile has moved up through various levels with the increasing sensitivity and importance of the areas reviewed. Gerald Vinten (1990) argues that social auditing is the highest plane that internal audit may reach and defines this as:

> *"A review to ensure that an organisation gives due regard to its wider social responsibilities to those both directly and indirectly affected by its decisions and that a balance is achieved between those aspects and the more traditional business or service-related objectives."*

This is no linear progression with many forces working to take the profession back to old models of the audit role with compliance and fraud work (financial propriety) the key services in demand.

2.4 Moving Internal Audit out of Accountancy

Many of the trends behind the development of internal audit point to the ultimate position where the audit function becomes a high profile autonomous department reporting at the highest level. This may depend on moving out audit functions based in accountancy.

Advantages

It is possible to establish internal audit as a separate profession so that one would employ internal auditors as opposed to accountants. This is a moot point in that there are those who feel that the auditor is above all an accountant. Not only is this view short-sighted but it is also steeped in the old version of the internal auditor as poor cousin of the external auditor. The true audit professional is called upon to review complicated and varied systems. The most complicated and sensitive ones may sometimes be financially based. A multi-disciplined approach provides the flexibility required to deal with operational areas. Many organisations require internal auditors to hold an accounting qualification or have accountancy experience. A move outside the finance function allows staff to be employed without an accounting background.

There are clear benefits in this move in terms of securing a firmer level of independence from the finance function. The traditional reporting line to the Director of Finance (DF) may have in the past created a potential barrier to audit objectivity. It may be said that there is little real audit independence where the CIA works for the Director of Finance. There are many models of internal auditing that see this function as a compliance role, representing the DF's interest in financial propriety. The auditor is able to comment on non-compliance so long as it does not extend to criticising the DF. The corporate view of financial management relies on the DF taking responsibility for establishing sound financial systems, that are then devolved across an organisation. The heart of any financial system will be based in the DF's department and this creates a problem for an auditor who may have found inadequacies in the way the DF has managed these systems. A defensive DF may ensure that the auditor does not produce material that forms a criticism of his/her financial services. This impairs the basic concept of independence where the auditor may be gagged, notwithstanding the presence of an audit committee.

One might therefore give greater attention to the managerial aspects of providing financial systems and move away from merely checking the resulting transactions. This is one sure way of extending the potential scope of internal audit to enable it to tackle the most high-level, sensitive areas. The audit terms of reference will move beyond fraud and accounting errors to take on board all important issues that impact on organisational controls. We are not only concerned with the matters affecting the DF but also that which is uppermost in the minds of the corporate management team headed by the Chief Executive. At this extreme, it becomes possible to audit the whole direction of the organisation in terms of its corporate strategy that is a far cry from checking the petty cash and stocks.

The relationship with external audit may become better defined where the differing objectives are clarified. The temptation for the Director of Finance to treat internal audit as an additional resource for external audit may decline. It may be possible to encourage external auditors to cover the main financial systems, with internal audit turning its attention more towards operational matters. If internal audit assumes a high profile and reviews the major activities, then the relationship between internal audit and external audit may be reversed. External audit may be seen to feed into the all-important internal audit process. This may be seen as a final achievement where internal auditors rely on external audit after having reviewed the quality of it.

The audit approach may move from an emphasis on financial audits to the exciting prospect of reviewing the management process itself. This change in emphasis is important; it is based on viewing the principal controls in any system of internal control as embodied in management itself. We would not consider the personalities of individual managers. We are more concerned with the formal managerial processes that have been established and how well they contribute to the efficient and effective application of resources to organisational objectives. This allows the scope of internal auditing to move to almost unlimited horizons. We may illustrate the depth of available management techniques by visiting any library that specialises in management to consider the thousands of textbooks that together comprise only part of the body of management knowledge.

The potential for establishing a powerful CIA may arise which might be compared to the previous position where the CIA merely acted as a go-between for the Director of Finance and the audit staff, giving them batches of projects that the DF wanted done. In an ideal world the CIA will have the ear of the Chief Executive (CE) who may turn to audit for advice on major organisational issues that impact on underlying control systems. This has a knock-on effect with the CIA assuming a senior grade commensurate with his/her role in the organisation. Likewise, audit managers and other staff will benefit. The internal audit department could end up with higher grades than the accountancy department.

Disadvantages
There is the possibility of isolation and lack of support where audit goes it alone. The weight of the Director of Finance (DF) may provide added force to difficult audit recommendations as will the DF's presence at senior management team meetings. This may be lost and a separate audit function may become either a tremendous success or a complete failure. In times of financial constraint, the "Centre" is the first place that budget cuts are made. This may affect the level of audit resources particularly if we are only aligned with the Chief Executive (CE). The power of the DF in assigning resources via the budget will be missed where we can no longer shelter under the umbrella of financial propriety in times of cut-backs. Whilst the CE may have many one-off uses for internal audit, it may be that the DF is the only Chief Officer who fully understands the real value of the audit function as a permanent fixture albeit in its narrow financial role. If audit is going through a bad patch, perhaps with staffing problems or poor client relationships, the CE may be tempted to restrict its role. Without direct and ongoing support from the DF well versed in the need for internal audit the scope of audit may be adversely affected. This may lead to eventual decline.

Career blocks may occur where internal audit cannot attract accountants as they might feel that they will not be able to return to mainline accountancy. In turn internal audit may well be comparatively lowly graded in comparison to accountancy and it may not be possible to achieve a degree of grade parity for an autonomous audit function. The separation of internal audit depends on a source of qualified auditors or a well-resourced training programme. There are traditional links between internal audit and accountancy that will be hard to ignore. An example is the accepted view that accountancy trainees should have a period in internal audit as part of their training programme. A full commitment to developing internal auditors that is supported by a formal training programme must be firmly in place before internal audit could separate from accountancy.

While accountancy is an established profession, internal audit may be seen as a developing quasi-profession. One could not rely on the high accountancy profile to secure the prestige necessary to promote the image of the audit function throughout the organisation. The risks are great and the move will only be successful where internal audit has strong management, efficient procedures and a high level of support throughout the organisation. Again this is a crucial decision that would have to be made as part of a long-term strategy that allows for each of these relevant factors, if the risks attached to any move are to be minimised.

The balance
We have to balance two considerations in deciding on any proposed move away from accountancy:
- The need to secure a level of independence from the finance function that is commensurate with the increasingly high profile of the internal audit function.
- And, the need to secure the full commitment of the Director of Finance to support the continuing presence of the internal auditing function.

Graphically this appears as:

FIGURE 2.2 MOVING AUDIT AWAY FROM ACCOUNTANCY

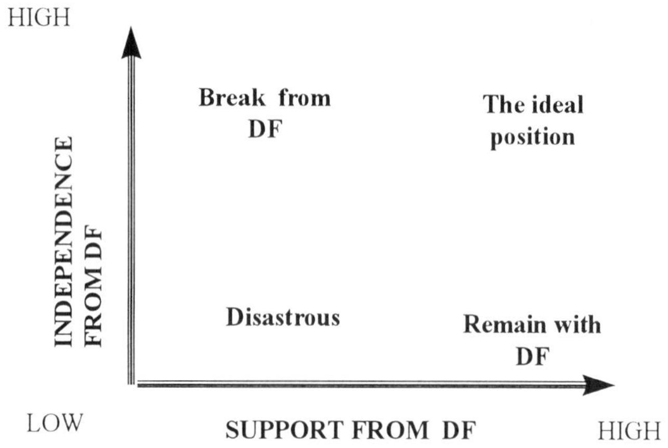

The ideal position is represented in the top right hand corner where both independence and support from the DF are secured. This may mean a formal link with the DF and powers to maintain financial propriety through adequate systems of internal control. It will also entail a direct reporting line to a forum such as an audit committee so that this element of independence is preserved. In short we would need to be close to, but at the same time, some distance from the DF.

2.5 The Role of the Statement of Responsibility

The Institute of Internal Auditors (IIA) has issued various statements of responsibilities (SOR), each new one providing a revision to the previous. It is possible to trace much of the development of internal audit through these SORs from 1947 to 1981:

1947: Original SOR setting out the first formal definition of internal audit. This saw the perceived role of internal audit as dealing primarily with accounting matters and is in line with the view that it arose as an extension of the external audit function.

1957: Internal audit dealt with both accounting and other operations. Although the accounting function was the principal concern, non-accounting matters were also within the audit remit.

1971: The breakthrough came in viewing the audit field as consisting simply of operations. Accounting operations have to compete with all others for audit attention with no automatic right to priority.

1976: This is the same as in 1971 but is made gender-neutral so as not to assume that all auditors are male.

1981: The major change in this SOR is the alteration of defining internal audit from a service to **management** to a service to the **organisation.** It directs the audit function to the highest levels of management. This impacts on independence in that the welfare of the organisation becomes paramount as opposed to the requirements of individual managers. The new role of internal audit means more attention to corporate areas with such a high profile audit function.

1991: Several important changes should be noted:
1. The statement gives the responsibilities of internal audit but no longer sets out the role. This then allows more flexibility in interpreting the concept of an internal auditing service.
2. The idea of internal audit as a control over controls is removed. This allows one to build on the consultancy role of internal audit in terms of performing work that does not necessarily comment on control systems.
3. The reference to assisting management and the board is removed, which lessens the extent to which the client has been defined so allowing us to report to an audit committee.
4. The audit objective including promoting effective control at reasonable cost is removed.
5. The section on independence is elevated to come before the section on responsibility and authority.
6. There is stronger emphasis on the CIA being responsible to a high status individual to promote independence.
7. The view that auditors should have an honest belief in their work product is taken out.
8. The point that auditors should not subordinate their judgement to that of others is included.
9. The point that internal audit is an integral part of the organisation is brought in.
10. The charter should now clarify the independence of internal audit.

11. Compliance with the standards is seen as essential.
12. We are now obliged to comply with the code of ethics.

This SOR provides for greater flexibility to include a wider range of audit and consultancy services. This is balanced by raising the profile of the all-important concept of independence that is so difficult to achieve fully in practice. Issues of compliance with standards and ethics are more actively addressed which must be accompanied by a firmer stance on member discipline that appears to be the trend with the IIA. Some of the more restrictive elements have been removed which again allows a wider view of the audit role. To summarise; the statement recognises that we may move further into consultancy but have to retain both professional standards and sufficient independence.

1994: The latest definition appeared in the IIA standards in 1994 and includes the concept of ensuring that recommendations are made having due regard to the costs of implementing them. We may go further and suggest that all recommendations should incorporate a consideration of balancing costs with benefits before they may be applied. Interestingly, a return to a previous view can represent development. Basic audit concepts need not be thrown away with time.

2.6 The 1947 Debate

When the original SOR was being devised in 1947 it involved debate as to the precise role and scope. Issues to be resolved before a clear model of audit could be constructed included:

Part of the system
Is internal audit part of the system of internal control in terms of consisting mainly of checking the output from each main system before certifying that it is acceptable? This was certainly true in a number of internal audit departments where for example, the "audit stamp" meant that large payments were vetted before release and the auditor had other duties such as controlling important stationery. Despite this, it was generally felt that this type of role was inappropriate and that internal audit should not be part of the routine systems-control procedures. We have certainly reached the point where audit cannot be locked into the systems of control to impair independence.

Reporting lines
Who should internal audit report to? Here internal audit was seen primarily as part of the accounting function. One of the drawbacks is the continuing view that internal audit is mainly responsible for checking the accuracy of financial data. This would be in addition to its duties as a supreme force checking on operational management and their staff. The ability to audit the accounting function would be severely restricted by this position. Internal audit being outside the accounting function continues to be a lively debate to this day. Most auditors accept that many internal audit functions, particularly those established by legislation, are based in the finance department and that this does not necessarily mean a sufficiently independent service cannot be provided. Audit committees have now become popular and this may be seen as the ultimate client for audit services.

Control over controls

Should internal audit be a control over internal controls? The response stresses the need for internal audit to be outside the system of internal control although in this case a clearer link is defined. This is that audit reviews and evaluates the systems of control while not being an integrated component within the actual control routines. The definition of internal audit as a control over controls is clearly open to debate. Does this mean that the controls can operate without this floating control over them? Alternatively, does this floating audit control simply apply to areas planned for audit review via an appraisal of the relative risks of each unit? The definition of internal audit in the 1991 SOR suggested the definition was dated, although this comes back in the 1994 definition.

External audit

Co-ordination with external audit is accepted and all internal audit standards include this. The change that is now apparent is that internal audit should be an equal partner as opposed to an extension of external audit, and this depends on establishing a professional base. Internal audit has more to offer an organisation where a wider scope of its activities has been agreed and documented in an audit charter. There is still imbalance in the internal/external audit relationship apparent in organisations where, by convention, the external auditor reviews the internal audit function. The type of relationship that is assumed will depend on the personal strengths of the CIA. It should be based on the extent to which internal audit has adopted professional auditing standards.

Management's role

Internal audit should not relieve management of responsibilities. Management designs, implements and maintains effective systems of internal controls while audit's role is to review these systems and advise on those high-priority risk areas where control weaknesses need to be redressed by management. A system approach would tend to be the most efficient way of achieving this. This is in contrast to a continual search for delinquent transactions that are generated by poor systems. This latter approach might imply that management need not secure good control since audit will catch all material errors. Unfortunately this important principle is less easy to achieve in practice due to the political pressures found in all organisations. The temptation to prop up management and make oneself indispensable is far too evident for poorly conceived audit services. Being around at all times to bale senior managers out where they have not bothered to install proper systems of control, may enhance the status of the audit function in the short term. By perpetuating this failure to secure good control the long-term objective of the audit role in terms of improving control will not be achieved and this will eventually be exposed.

Audit theory

The debate continues as to whether internal audit should be based on pure theory or what is actually going on in practice. Imposing excessively high standards may create problems by excluding a proportion of the audit departments that are unable to meet these demanding requirements. Flexibility and professional standards are concepts that have to be reconciled so that suitable ideals may be defined but at the same time are attainable in practice. One must be wary of taking this concept of flexibility to the extreme since this may suggest that anyone can do an audit and there are in reality no clear standards to be observed. Theory must have some bearing on reality and if it is too far removed, then it may need to be adjusted through clear reasoning based on sound research. What is unacceptable is for audit practitioners to be ignorant of the range of audit theory and adopt suspect practices based on this lack of knowledge. This is quite different from assessing the current theory and, based on local factors, deciding to adopt a different, less demanding approach. The need to master the agreed common body of knowledge is fundamental to the advancement of internal auditing as a profession. It would appear however that we will need to establish just which services are covered by the internal audit umbrella and whether we adopt an open-door or more restrictive policy. This is linked to the wider question of whether we accept that internal audit is becoming progressively fragmented as a discipline, or whether we seek to exclude linked functions such as operational review, quality reviewers, inspectorates, and systems security. One solution would be to create a licensed internal audit practitioner. This individual would have to be a qualified member of the internal audit profession as a prerequisite to practising. This would be particularly relevant where internal audit's presence is mandatory, since the requirement could be built into legislation/codes of practice.

2.7 Current Topical Issues

Contracting out internal audit

All internal auditing departments are under threat. In the private sector, where internal audit is generally not mandatory, the in-house unit may be deleted, downsized or replaced by an inspectorate, quality assurance or operational review service. This is equally so in financial services where the compliance role may not necessarily be carried out by internal audit. The public sector is in the front line, facing external competition like an army preparing for war. Outsourcing in central government and compulsory competitive tendering in local government provide an avenue for public sector internal auditing to be undertaken by firms of accountants. This cannot be said to be targeting internal audit since it represents overall governmental policy with universal application across many countries of varying political persuasion. All Chief Internal Auditors should have a number of key issues uppermost in their minds including:

- A formal strategy for meeting competition from internal and/or external sources.
- The audit budget and current charge-out rates for each auditor and how these figures compare to other departments.
- The pricing strategy will fall between the following ranges:

FIGURE 2.3 AUDIT PRICING STRATEGY

CHEAP & CHEERFUL		EXPENSIVE & SOPHISTICATED

- The pricing strategy cannot be completed until marketing research has been carried out that establishes exactly what the client wants. This marketing exercise should be completed or commissioned by the CIA and incorporated into the formal strategy.
- The level of resources should be assessed and compared to the current complement. One will have to consider the actual staff employed. Changes should be made over time

so staff can be retired, made redundant, recruited and developed until a best possible position is achieved.

- The whole concept of quality audit procedures and methodologies will need to be subject to constant review. We can take a short cut in explaining what this entails by simply stating that all material matters would be covered if the audit manual is reviewed and updated as a priority.

If the CIA is not concerned with the above matters then the future welfare of the internal auditing function is left to chance, like a rudderless ship. These matters should therefore represent the most pressing concerns for the CIA over and above the day-to-day workload.

Globalisation

The big picture of internal auditing must include that it is a discipline universally applicable throughout the world. There is no formal requirement that all CIAs be qualified apart from organisational job specifications. There is no worldwide concept of an internal auditor able to practice in any country. There is a move to spread professional auditing practise from the developed world to the less developed. The Institute of Internal Auditors is the only body established solely for the promotion of internal auditing. The IIA's professional standards are applied in each member country with slight changes in terminology, to accommodate local requirements. The growing trend towards globalisation brings with it searching questions as to the extent to which practice may be standardised to form universally acceptable methodologies. This brings the associated question of whether there is one real audit service or a range of services in line with client needs and local legislation.

Total quality management

The current interest in total quality management (TQM) is derived from a desire to secure excellence in service/product delivery. This allows a top downwards review of existing practices. Internal auditors are well versed in the principles and practice of management which is examined in IIA examinations. There are two main implications for internal audit of TQM:

As a service, we will have to consider the way that we might adopt the principles of TQM so that we can guarantee value for money from the investment in audit resources. On the question of quality, several internal audit departments have achieved accreditation under British Standards Institute 5750 by implementing suitable procedures to show that they have met the defined quality standards. At some time in the future it will be very difficult to justify why BSI 5750 (now ISO 9000) has not been secured. This may well indicate some failing or inefficiency in the audit service.

Internal audit will have to assess where it stands in the thrust towards quality standards. We may wish to add to our services and include a review of quality standards as part of the corporate systems of control. This may represent a major opportunity to enhance the status of the internal audit function which, if missed, may be captured by a potential competitor. If grasped it may alter the direction of audit and have impact if TQM initiatives become a major feature of organisational life.

The compliance role

There is debate on the role of internal audit in compliance with procedure. The technical view argues we moved away from detailed checking as the profession developed. One may now audit corporate systems of importance to the entire welfare of the organisation. There are organisations that make great play of compliance checks and have a need for a probity service that management knows and understands. Aspirations to professionalism may have to take second place to getting permanent business and guaranteeing one's future welfare. The picture is not as grey as might appear at first sight. There are many new compliance roles linked into major issues such as software piracy, quality assurance, financial regulations, contract tendering and computer security that raise the profile of internal audit. The secret is to perform these services as an add-on to the main systems role.

Independence

Much has been written on independence and it is no longer treated as an esoteric entity that is either held on to, or given up through greed or ignorance. A response to the threat of external competition from the big accountancy firms was that they could not be independent. This argument is insufficient. Independence is perceived more practically as the basic ability to do a good job. It is therefore possible to offer consultancy services in addition to traditional audits, recognising this new-found realism. How far this concept can be extended is a matter for informed judgement and debate.

The expectation gap

Audit services will have to be properly marketed which is essentially based on defining and meeting client needs. This feature poses no problem as long as clients know what to expect from their internal auditors. It does however become a concern when this is not the case, and there is a clear gap in what is expected and what is provided. Management may want internal auditors to:
1. Check on junior staff on a regular basis.
2. Investigate fraud and irregularity and present cases to the police and/or internal disciplinaries.
3. Draft procedures where these are lacking.
4. Draft information papers on items of new legislation or practice.
5. Investigate allegations concerning internal industrial disputes and advise on best resolution.
6. Take responsibility for data protection and check that the rules are complied with.

One cannot give up professional integrity but, at the same time, the above matters cannot be ignored. If new resources are brought in to cover these services, they may end up competing for the internal audit role. The secret is to maintain planned systems audits whilst also securing resources to cover what is part of the consultancy branch. If these additional services are important then management will have to be prepared to finance them. It is important not to sacrifice systems work by diverting audit resources to carrying out client-expectation services. This does not mean a participative approach to audit work cannot be adopted.

Legislation

This is an important component in the development of internal auditing:
• It may alter the audit role by providing additional work.
• It may bring into the frame, competitors for the current audit contract.
• It may on impact the status of internal auditing, e.g. any moves towards mandatory audit committees.

New legislation should be considered and the effects anticipated. The audit strategy and business plan should take on board these additional factors in a way that promotes the continuing success of the audit function. This means that the CIA must resource the continual search for new legislation that affects the organisation's control systems or impacts on the future of internal audit.

Corporate governance
The Cadbury report on Corporate Governance was published in the wake of various large-scale scandals in the 1990s such as Maxwell and BCCI. The report draws attention to the need for effective internal controls and the fact that responsibility for these rested with management. It sets out the role of Directors who are responsible for monitoring how well these controls operate. Internal audit is mentioned in the report and the establishment of an internal audit function is seen as good practice where they monitor these systems of control. Cadbury notes the ability of internal audit to investigate frauds and asks that the CIA has unrestricted access to the chair of the audit committee to ensure independence. There is no actual requirement to establish an internal audit function although the report admits that internal and external audit services are complementary. The code requires an audit committee for all listed companies serviced by at least three non-executive directors. There should be a statement on the effectiveness of systems of control that may well raise the profile of controls and internal audit. The three main recommendations of the 1995 Cadbury Committee are:
1. That the Boards of listed companies comply with a Code of Best Practice.
2. A statement of compliance with this Code should be included in their annual report and accounts. Reasons for any areas of non-compliance should be given.
3. That the companies' compliance is reviewed by external auditors before publication.

The Code covers nineteen main areas:
[1] The board should meet regularly, retain full and effective control over the company and monitor the executive management.
[2] There should be a clearly accepted division of responsibilities at the head of a company, which will ensure a balance of power and authority so that no one individual has unfettered powers of decision.
[3] The board should include non-executive directors of sufficient calibre and number for their views to carry significant weight.
[4] The board should have a formal schedule of matters specifically reserved to it for decision to ensure that the direction and control of the company are firmly in its hands.
[5] There should be an agreed procedure for directors, in the furtherance of their duties to take independent professional advice if necessary at the company's expense.
[6] All directors should have access to the advice and services of the company secretary, who is responsible to the board for ensuring that board procedures are followed and that applicable rules and regulations are complied with.
[7] Non-executive directors (NED) should bring an independent judgement to bear on issues of strategy, performance, resources, including key appointments and standards of conduct.
[8] The majority of NEDs should be independent of management and free from any business or other relationship which could materially interfere with the exercise of independent judgement, apart from their fees and shareholdings.

[9] NEDs should be appointed for specified terms and re-appointment should not be automatic.

[10] NEDs should be selected through a formal process and both this process and their appointment should be a matter for the board as a whole.

[11] Directors' service contracts should not exceed three years without shareholders' approval.

[12] There should be full disclosure of a director's total emoluments and those of the chairman and highest paid UK directors.

[13] Executive directors' pay should be subject to the recommendations of a remunerations committee made up wholly or mainly of NEDs.

[14] It is the board's duty to present a balanced and understandable assessment of the company's position.

[15] The board should ensure that an objective and professional relationship is maintained with the auditors.

[16] The board should establish an audit committee of at least three NEDs with written terms of reference which deal clearly with its authority and duties.

[17] The directors should explain their responsibility for preparing the accounts next to a statement by the auditors about their reporting responsibilities.

[18] The directors should report on the effectiveness of the company's system of internal control.

[19] The director should report that the business is a going concern, with supporting assumptions or qualifications as necessary.

Note that corporate governance is an ongoing issue that has not yet been resolved.

Control self assessment

The control self assessment has featured in Canadian business life for some time, in line with the growing recognition of the importance of internal controls. Control self assessment is not seen as replacing the internal audit role but more as a complement to scarce audit resources in large organisations. The IIA.UK issued professional briefing note seven in June 1995 to address this. It mentions advantages and disadvantages. It is important to see this development in conjunction with other audit type roles assumed by management, normally based around the drive for more quality systems. It recommends a role for internal audit in advising management about their self assessment and underlying training needs. It does not recommend acting as facilitators to the programme in that this will bring audit too far into management responsibilities. The move to make management responsible for their systems of internal control takes on a higher profile where this promotes the view that reviewing these controls is also part of this role.

2.8 The Future for Internal Audit

If we use the development of internal audit as a guide to the level of change that we might see in the world of audit then prospects for the future are excellent. There are many possibilities open to internal audit ranging from continuous progress in the established trends through to ventures into new areas. Internal audit future developments may be listed as:

Audit field

The level at which internal audit has targeted resources has the potential to progress from financial, operational, managerial, corporate, social, through to advising international communities on the audited effect of their high-level policy decisions. Imagine audit reports on sensitive areas that could influence national strategy with the emphasis on independent, objective reports based on firm evidence and testing procedures. There is increasing globalisation with the merging of development agencies combining to fund international projects to underdeveloped countries along with the trend towards international partnerships. All these programmes require sound controls where one might be managing large sums at any one time. The internal audit function attached to the World Bank seeks to assess controls over grants that are approved. The increasing use of audit consortia is another example of how the profession is able to offer services for a range of different organisations. There are now internal audit departments that have successfully tendered for audit contracts in other organisations and so have a spread of expertise.

Computer audit

Computer audit and the thrust into management information systems (MIS) and decision support systems now means that the audit role may be crucial to controlling the growth of end user systems and information technology (IT). The audit of MIS may include the managerial aspects of IT as well as the technical parts and the vast majority of auditors become primarily experts in MIS based controls. Information is the resource of the future as the most vital factors in organisational success, with all auditors becoming computer auditors. There are organisations who insist that a computer auditor is attached to all large computer development projects as a way of promoting good control. The press report continuing problems with new systems that have come on-line despite major flaws that impair their proper functioning. Audit departments may decide to build on their areas of responsibility by assuming control of systems security procedures as part of the consultancy role. There is no ignoring the growing use of automated systems in financial and operational areas.

Compliance legislation

The compliance factor is increasingly important and legislators in sensitive sectors such as financial services look to the internal auditor to advise the organisation. This appears to move internal audit backwards but really provides a distinct branch of audit in contrast to financial, MIS, operational and project review audits. This is particularly true in areas such as employee legislation, health and safety, data protection and environmental protection. The detailed audit programme may make a return but this time for more material corporate issues. This development is linked to fraud deterrents and it only takes a few major frauds for politicians to start calling for more auditors. It is also linked to increased regularity work in response to disaggregated budgets and decentralised controls. New information technology may result in growth in internal audit. However, such thinking may encourage a return to the old tick-and-check routines that gave internal audit a bad name in the past.

Specialisms

There is a call for auditors to provide specialist services be it in contracts, computers, engineering, exporting, or take-overs. These specialist fields may create specific categories of auditors with particular skills. Transfers between the specialities may become difficult with proponents demanding their own specialist internal auditing qualification. The IIA-UK offer a specialist qualification in computer auditing. There is the ever-present question of how much expertise the auditor requires before tackling a specific operational area. As organisations become increasingly complicated to survive in a high-tech environment, the auditor must respond. This makes demands on the auditor who may be called upon to tackle complicated legislation, detailed reengineering processes, huge capital contracts and newly automated operations. Options for meeting this potential skills shortage are:

1. Sub-contract parts of the audit to specialists.
2. Use consultants as advisors to the audit.
3. Second appropriate staff into the audit department for specialist projects.
4. Employ full-time specialists such as civil engineers, forensic scientists, fraud investigators, computer programmers and statisticians.
5. Extend audit training to cover these specialisms in outline terms as part of the professional studies or in one-off training courses.
6. Concentrate on the fundamental principles of control that may be applied to any specific area through lateral thinking and questioning insight. This will have to be linked to an extensive library of relevant material that the auditor would have access to as part of the audit. One may call in specialists for advice as a permanent solution to the skills problem.

The unlimited scope of internal audit whilst giving the potential for unrestricted development, demands a vast array of skills and expertise. This may represent the biggest challenge for the profession over the next decade.

Systems thinking

It is possible to imagine the systems based school of internal audit branching out to include managerial components in the overall systems of internal controls. This should promote comprehensive research into systems thinking by internal auditors. It is difficult to understand the lack of involvement from the auditing profession in general systems thinking, considering its relevance. We not only use a systems approach to breaking down the audit process into defined stages; we also seek to review controls that form systems of control in the area under review. Many auditors cannot visualise systems as extending outside basic accounting checking procedures and reject systems based auditing (SBA) for more complicated audits. By extending the SBA concept to cover all organisational activities greater progress will be possible. This does require us to be at the forefront of systems thinking as are engineers and social scientists. By building on this research and applying it to the internal audit arena much can be achieved now and in the future.

Effectiveness audit

The growing interest in effectiveness auditing may lead to audit resources being directed at this area. One can see the Chief Executive turning to internal audit for an effectiveness audit of the latest policy implemented. Audit might follow the systems out to the client or consumer, with an emphasis on the marketing systems. This might be the only way the organisation obtains an objective view regarding confidential corporate issues. Effectiveness impacts on marketing, PR, consumer behaviour, profits and the overall success of the organisation. Environmental issues come into play as one considers the net result of organisational activities. The ability to balance short-term gains with long-term issues such as the reputation of the organisation, is another feature of business life that has to be controlled. Where there is a control, there should be an associated audit review. Effectiveness auditing is extremely difficult in that it requires an assessment of complicated factors that compete for attention. Everyone in an organisation has a different perspective of what constitutes success. It is these inconsistent ranges of managerial decisions that make it hard to judge the resultant impact on the welfare of the organisation. Where one is able to audit this web of managerial processes, a clear and objective view may be secured that will help direct the flow of energies.

Consultancy
The consultancy aspect of internal audit may lead to an increase in project work moving outside of the strict audit role to a more detailed input into operational systems and advising on important executive decisions. One would have to balance this with the pure audit role although managerial pressure may demand this service. On the other side of the coin, where management has to rely on external consultants because internal audit turns these projects away, then the consultants may seize the opportunity to perform powerful work. They will then be best placed to bid for the internal audit role. There is nothing wrong with doing consultancy work as long as this is built into the audit charter and is distinguished from planned systems audits. It is important to balance the audit and consultancy roles so that sufficient independence is retained. This is a difficult but unavoidable aspect of business life that is possible only if the CIA has a firm grasp. Consultancy can be applied to control self assessment where audit encourages management to improve their control systems.

Public sector
Developments in the public sector in the form of social charters and a defined level of public services operating to formally adopted standards, cannot be ignored. The growth in implementing quality assurance principles may lead to a differing role of internal audit in performing comprehensive operational service reviews as part of the assurance that public services are operating to acceptable standards. To ignore this trend may open the door to an assortment of reviewing agencies that are able to gear into complicated quality issues, with the internal audit role then relegated to checking accounting data. The move towards creating business units has to be quickly grasped by the audit department. To retain credibility, internal audit must be at the forefront of all major developments by implementing quality assurance standards, performance measures, human resource programmes, and operational procedures. Internal audit may become the satellite for all important business initiatives that impact on service delivery and so move deeply into the research arena. Part of meeting the challenge from competition may mean an aggressive approach, taking business away from traditional areas so that we become responsible for matters such as corporate databases of reference information, quality standards, financial modelling, and research on control techniques. This is a far cry from the backwaters of yesteryear in which the audit department was located. The internal auditing standards issued by the Auditing Practices Board (APB) and the Institute of Internal Auditors are designed to be applied to all audit departments regardless of which industry their organisations operate within. They cover both the private and the public sectors and allow for any differences therein. A number of interesting points may be mentioned in respect of private versus public sector organisations:
• While the private sector has the crucial indicator of profitability to measure performance this cannot be readily applied to the public sector.

- Political sensitivity is an important concept in the public sector and in some instances may override the actual service delivery criterion.
- The accountancy profession is not as diversified as in the past with CIPFA members now working in the private sector and Chartered, Certified and Management accountants being found in the public sector.
- Privatisation and compulsory competitive tendering initiatives mean that separate business units are being established within the public sector and private firms are now providing public services.
- Accountability is central to the public sector and resources are applied to achieve this.
- The two fields are growing closer together and there is much transferability of staff.
- Statements of Standard Accounting Practices apply to both sectors.
- There is no specific legal requirement for internal audit in the private sector.
- Public sector internal auditing may be contracted out.
- External auditors are now moving into the VFM field.
- Compliance is now high profile in the private sector in building societies and financial services.

All indicators point to the growing convergence of the private and public sectors and auditors may find themselves securing experience in both fields during their career. There are trends that impact on these developments and the politicians may turn towards internal audit to tackle large-scale fraud where major business scandals call for action to stave off corruption. In the public sector, the growing recognition of quality assurance as a crucial function may put pressure on internal audit to provide this type of service. The presence or absence of legislation requiring an audit cover affects the type of service provided. Many parts of the public sector including most of central government, as with the private sector, do not have this provision. Contracting out the audit service also has major repercussions and many argue that this will turn audit into a quasi-consultancy type function.

Regularity
Fraud never goes away and always reappears on the agenda. New scandals highlight the difficulty in controlling corruption where it is entrenched in an organisation. The external auditor has been criticised for a failure to become fully involved and many look towards legislation to provide direction. Research on organisational ethics is one way to advance acceptable standards of conduct. It is the internal auditor who is called when the topic of fraud appears. On the basis of securing more business, we will have to resource the detection and investigation of frauds as part of the add-on services attached to the audit function. We may see the growth of inter-organisational forums that address common problems of fraud possibly funded through member organisations. There are already specialist firms that provide this type of service, operating primarily in the private sector. The police admit to problems in dealing with corporate and public sector fraud and the resources such investigations consume. Fraud is big business for both the fraudster and the investigator and so we should resource this service. There are those waiting to secure this work although as insiders, audit has an advantage.

2.9 Conclusions

One cannot understand one's existence unless one understands the past. This is true for internal audit and we have suffered our full share of poor reputations. Recent developments tend to be based on the concept of lifting the audit profile to deal with complicated specialist high profile areas/issues. This brings prestige but also the need to meet high expectations. It can only be achieved where the audit function is actively implementing a strategy with clear steps for enhancing professionalism. The ability to offer a wide range of services whilst still retaining a formal methodology steeped in professionalism, will be the feature of the new internal audit department. It will be necessary to market the audit service for those managers who still hold the old fashioned view of the profession as a ticking and checking function. Taking responsibility for parts of the control systems is another strong possibility hard to resist. So long as a two-tier system with basic low-level audits, and contrasting complicated reviews does not result in an imbalance, then this service differentiation will be one solution. The client may demand the basic fraud/probity work that falls within the expectation frame where managers wish gaps in control to be closed in a way that will not form a criticism of their role. This is in contrast to the systems approach that seeks to locate responsibility for control at management's doorstep. The CIA of the future will need the ability to balance these two major and sometimes conflicting considerations.

CHAPTER THREE

THE CONCEPT OF AUDITING STANDARDS

3.1 Professionalism

Before studying the standards attached to internal auditing we consider the main features of a professional discipline:

Training programme

A long specialised training programme that has to be undergone by the student before reaching practitioner status. This will typically last several years covering topics that are dedicated to (or have a direct link with) the particular discipline. Architects, doctors, lawyers and accountants spend many years engaged in study and development before securing the full qualification.

Common body of knowledge

A common body of knowledge (CBOK) attaches to the discipline and is to be mastered. This represents a minimum level of knowledge that is studied and understood. Some feel that the practitioner need not memorise an extensive range of facts as in practice one would have access to reference material. There is though a level of knowledge that should be at the instant recall of the practitioner. The extent to which various subjects are relevant to the discipline will have to be addressed when defining the content of the CBOK. The process of setting the CBOK will partly determine the boundaries of the profession and the areas considered important. The precise content may alter as the profession changes and adapts. For example, many professionals such as doctors and lawyers find it necessary to develop IT skills to use information systems that promote greater efficiency in service delivery.

Code of ethics

A code of ethics covering the required conduct expected from individual members of the profession. This is a fundamental requirement for all true professions in that it sets a moral framework within which individuals may practice. When one is acting as a professional, one in fact represents the entire profession. A suitable code of ethics will not only refer to the standards to which work will be performed. It will also set an overall code of conduct based around complete honesty and integrity as generalised concepts. This then sets the framework within which members are expected to conduct their affairs over and above mere compliance with the laws of the land. The invisible bond between the individual practitioner and the professional body allows a mutual trust that directs the respective activities of the two parties at all times.

Sanctions

The sanction of the community applies to ensure that members perform to the required standards to form a formal bond between the profession and society in general.

The hierarchical nature of professional standards might appear as:

FIGURE 3.1 BUSINESS ETHICS AND SOCIETY

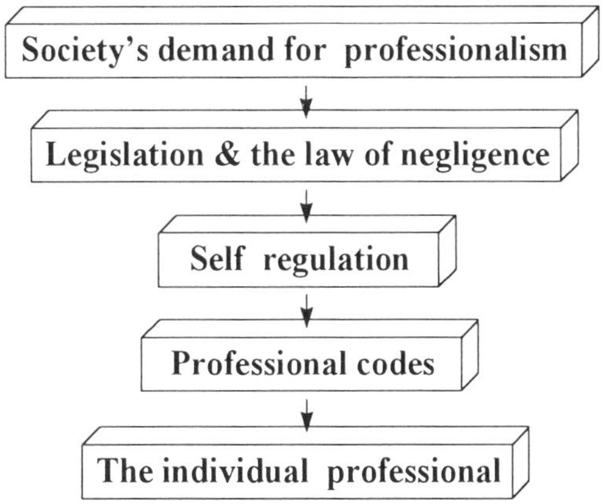

```
┌─────────────────────────────────────┐
│  Society's demand for professionalism │
└─────────────────────────────────────┘
                  ↓
┌─────────────────────────────────────┐
│   Legislation & the law of negligence │
└─────────────────────────────────────┘
                  ↓
        ┌─────────────────────┐
        │    Self regulation   │
        └─────────────────────┘
                  ↓
        ┌─────────────────────┐
        │  Professional codes  │
        └─────────────────────┘
                  ↓
      ┌─────────────────────────┐
      │ The individual professional │
      └─────────────────────────┘
```

If the profession is unable to regulate itself, then society will resort to legislation to ensure that these demands are achieved. This is due to the importance of the services in question, in terms of their impact on society. Non-professionals will tend not to attract this degree of attention from society.

Control over services
A professional person should be able to withdraw services where the situation is morally unacceptable. True professionals work to extremely high standards that cannot be compromised. If they were compromised, the individual should be in a position to withdraw from the situation. Such a level of professional freedom is vital to retain one's standing in the community. Unfortunately this requirement is difficult to achieve and many would-be disciplines fall down on this as a criterion.

Qualified practitioners
The practice should be limited to qualified practitioners who have mastered the common body of knowledge. Some form of licence would be issued. Licensed practitioners would be recognised by society as the only people allowed to carry out this type of work. This constitutes a formal barrier to the achievement of professional status as it is difficult to argue that a profession can be carried out by anyone without restriction. Many specialities will fail as a result of this principle. It is difficult to assess the extent to which formal qualifications are demanded as normal practice for a position in most organisations without carrying out research. As long as one person is practising without being a member of the profession in question then this criterion has not been met.

Morality
The concept of morals over pure profits means that the discipline moves to a higher level above simple employment. One should be practising through a desire to develop the profession and a wish to make a positive contribution. One would not expect a member to hold a second job (as opposed to voluntary work) that is in no way related to the main role. The professional would be asked to work within the formal moral framework and not seek profit-making as an overriding objective.

Technical difficulty

The services provided should be technically difficult and this is linked to the concept of a common body of knowledge. There should be some level of technical difficulty that has to be mastered through extensive training and several years practical experience. If anyone can do the required work there is no justification for deeming the area as meeting the requirements of professionalism.

Examinations

Formal examinations form part of the learning process in showing that the participant has acquired the various skills and techniques required. Although the extent to which examinations represent real-life situations that the practitioner will have to face is debatable, they remain an important component. The trend is towards course-work and desk-top training where the link between studies and practice is more readily achieved. Formal exams are still a useful method of testing what has been learnt over a defined syllabus. They impose pressure which may emulate business pressures. The process of formulating the examinations syllabus is useful for it forces one to define the scope of work and level of competence demanded.

Journals

The publication of a journal and literature dedicated to the subject is another hallmark of professional status. One would expect to see a relevant monthly journal that contains technical updates and useful articles along with features on social meetings. Another main sign of professionalism is research studies that examine subjects of interest to members. These studies should result in changes to the direction and focus of the profession in specific areas. Textbooks play an important role, with major works representing academic standards in terms of providing a comprehensive coverage of relevant subject matter. It is difficult to visualise a profession unable to display a major range of textbooks.

Professional body

A professional body represents the interests of its members and this is a pre-requisite for many of the matters outlined above. We may wish to see:
1. A formal corporate status such as a company limited by guarantee.
2. A headquarters.
3. A complement of full time staff.
4. A suitable logo.
5. Members' district societies.
6. Regular meetings and seminars/conferences.
7. Various committees to represent the interests of members.
8. Close contact with individual members.
9. Steps taken to commission research.

Compliance with rules

The professional body would have to enforce various sanctions against members who failed to comply with any of the requirements of membership. One would wish to see a formal process (say with an ethics committee) to receive, consider and decide on cases referred to the professional body concerning the conduct of their members. There should be formal representation, and an appeals process. The results of individual cases may be published in the journal, with or without names.

Service to society
A major feature of a profession is the overriding concept that its members are providing a service to society as opposed to individual clients. The ethos of the profession should be embodied in the view that it is there to fulfil an important role in society which is over and above the role it plays in servicing clients. Any conflict should be resolved by placing the duty of care to society first, which may serve to rule out many contenders who cannot show this. The Institute of Internal Auditors has a vital role to play in promoting this and some of them pose challenges to establishing internal auditing as a fully fledged profession. Each of the hallmarks of professionalism represents a challenge to be met over time as emergent professions develop and progress.

Internal audit's position
It is possible to estimate the degree of achievement within these hallmarks:

1. **A long specialised training programme** - We have specialist professional training although this is generally takes less time to complete than most other professions.
2. **A common body of knowledge** (CBOK) - This is in place.
3. **A code of ethics** - This is in place.
4. **The sanction of the community** - Auditors tend to be criticised where organisations collapse. Because we are not seen as an influential force these criticisms are generally limited and have a greater focus on external auditors.
5. **Ability to withdraw the services** - There are major problems with "whistle-blowing" which in the main is not encouraged.
6. **Practice limited to qualified practitioners** - Although there are many qualified accountants and auditors, the qualification is not mandatory in all organisations (even at CIA level).
7. **Morals over pure profits** - Once the internal auditor has reported the results fully there is little left to do. Most practitioners will protect their jobs by leaving senior management with the decision of how to respond to the findings. There is no moral obligation to go any further, at least without seeking legal advice, which may represent a major problem in corrupt organisations.
8. **Technically difficult** - This is more or less achieved although there are still many poorly trained audit staff doing low-level routine testing.
9. **Formal examinations** - This is in place.
10. **Journal and literature** - This is in place.
11. **A professional body** - This is in place.
12. **Enforce sanctions against members** - This is now falling into place.
13. **Members provide a service to society** - It appears that the internal audit service is established solely for the benefit of the organisation and not society at large.

Internal auditing is a developing or quasi-profession that still has some way to go. The questions to ask are, how much further should we go, and do we need to address any barriers that may hinder progress?

3.2 The Role of Standards
Internal auditing needs defined standards and this contributes to the development of professional audit services. A number of issues should be considered when assessing the role of standards:

IA as trustees

There is increasing recognition of the importance of internal controls and most larger organisations install a level of senior management to act as trustees for the owners. This involves maintaining an adequate system of internal control, and professional managers now study controls as part of their training programmes.

Expectations

As a result, the organisation and individual managers tend to be more prepared to accept the internal audit role. Where audit has moved more into a partnership with management, they will have to adopt sufficiently high standards to meet management expectations. A major factor relates to the overall quality of audit work and reports. The dilemma is that the greater the demands placed on audit by management, the greater the strain on resources which in turn creates pressures to get work completed quickly. Standards tend to take a back-seat unless the CIA takes a firm hand. Furthermore, audit cannot always do what management wishes. Political manoeuvring can turn the audit function into a device for distracting attention from the real cause of problems. Balancing this factor with the need to keep clients happy is no easy task.

External audit

With the growing status of internal audit, the external auditor may place greater reliance on internal audit work and they will want to see high auditing standards adhered to. Initial contact between the two audit functions should be based around reviewing each other's standards before any other interface. The level of competence of internal audit will in part be determined by the extent to which formal professional standards have been adopted.

CIA

The Chief Internal Auditor will need to apply a set of auditing standards both as guidance on the audit role and to measure the performance of the audit department. Audit standards start and stop at the CIA's door. Any consultant who wishes to solve the problems of a badly run organisation need only find out whether its directors and chief executive have established professional standards. If not then they are to blame; if there are standards then again they are to blame for not ensuring they work. This same principle applies to the CIA of an audit function.

Improved practice

Standards are required to improve the practice of internal audit. The need to promote a constant drive towards improving the audit product underpins the development of internal audit and this should be built around the adopted standards. There is clear and direct benefit derived from implementing formal auditing standards.

A common definition

Standards help define the role of internal audit by establishing a common definition that sets out the scope of audit work. This sets the frame for any dialogue between management, audit, and third parties. Each relies on professional standards to cover the activities of the audit function. So long as we are observing our standards it will be possible to challenge any criticisms that may be directed against us, perhaps for political reasons.

3.3 Institute of Internal Auditors' Standards

Internal auditing standards are based on the established principles of the profession and tend to be fairly consistent despite variation in style and the material covered. There is a variety of published material that represents internal auditing standards. The Institute of Internal Auditors' standards consist of five general standards in a series from 100 through to 500 within which twenty-five specific standards with accompanying guidance are set out. The main requirements may be summarised as follows:

100 INDEPENDENCE
Internal auditors should be independent of the activities they audit.

110 Organisational status - The organisational status of the internal auditing department should be sufficient to permit the accomplishment of its audit responsibilities.

120 Objectivity - Internal auditors should be objective in performing audits.

200 PROFESSIONAL PROFICIENCY
Internal audits should be performed with proficiency and due professional care.

210 Staffing - The internal auditing department should provide assurance that the technical proficiency and educational background of internal auditors are appropriate for the audits to be performed.

220 Knowledge, skills and disciplines - The internal auditing department should possess or obtain the knowledge, skills and disciplines needed to carry out its audit responsibilities.

230 Supervision - The internal auditing department should provide assurance that internal audits are properly supervised.

240 Compliance with standards of conduct - Internal auditors should comply with professional standards of conduct.

250 Knowledge, skills and disciplines - Internal auditors should possess the knowledge, skills and disciplines essential to the performance of internal audits.

260 Human relations and communications - Internal auditors should be skilled in dealing with people and in communicating effectively.

270 Continuing education - Internal auditors should maintain their technical competence through continuing education.

280 Due professional care - Internal auditors should exercise due professional care in performing internal audits.

300 SCOPE OF WORK
The scope of internal audits should encompass the examination and evaluation of the adequacy and effectiveness of the organisation's systems of internal control and the quality of performance in carrying out assigned responsibilities.

310 Reliability and integrity of information - Internal auditors should review the reliability and integrity of financial and operating information and the means used to identify, measure, classify and report such information.

320 Compliance with policies, plans, procedures, laws and regulations - Internal auditors should review the systems established to ensure compliance with those policies, plans, procedures, laws and regulations which could have a significant impact on operations and reports, and should determine whether the organisation is in compliance.

330 Safeguarding assets - Internal auditors should review the means of safeguarding and, as appropriate, verify the existence of such assets.

340 Economical and efficient use of resources - Internal auditors should appraise the economy and efficiency with which resources are employed.

350 Accomplishment of established objectives and goals for operations and programmes - Internal auditors should review operations or programmes to ascertain whether results are consistent with established objectives and goals and whether the operations are being carried out as planned.

400 PERFORMANCE OF AUDIT WORK

Audit work should include planning the audit, examining and evaluating information, communicating results, and following-up.

410 Planning the audit - Internal auditors should plan each audit.

420 Examining and evaluating information - Internal auditors should collect, analyse, interpret, and document information to support audit results. Information should be sufficient, competent, relevant and useful to provide a sound basis for audit findings and recommendations.

430 Communicating results - Internal auditors should report the results of their audit work. Audit findings should be based on the attributes of criteria, condition, cause and effect.

440 Following up - Internal auditors should follow up to ascertain that appropriate action is taken on audit findings.

500 MANAGEMENT OF INTERNAL AUDITING

The chief internal auditor should properly manage the internal auditing department.

510 Purpose, authority, and responsibility - The chief internal auditor should have a statement of purpose, authority, and responsibility for the internal auditing department.

520 Planning - The chief internal auditor should establish plans to carry out the responsibilities of the internal auditing department

530 Policies and procedures - The chief internal auditor should provide written policies and procedures to guide the audit staff.

540 Personnel management and development - The chief internal auditor should establish a programme for selecting and developing the staff of the internal auditing department.

550 External auditors - The chief internal auditor should ensure that internal and external audit efforts are properly co-ordinated.

560 Quality assurance - The chief internal auditor should establish and maintain a quality assurance programme to evaluate the operations of the internal auditing department. This includes complying with the professional standards and code of ethics, and a programme of supervision, internal reviews and external reviews.

3.4 Auditing Practices Board (APB) Standards

The APB standards are applicable to all members of the main accountancy bodies in the UK. This covers ACCA, ICAs, CIMA and CIPFA. These major UK accountancy bodies have combined to form a consultative committee called the CCAB. The CCAB have in turn established an Auditing Practices Board for its member bodies and from time to time they issue audit guidance. They issued an auditing guideline - "guidance for internal auditors" in January 1990 that in effect should be adopted by most UK accountants who work in the internal auditing arena. These replace the CIPFA statement on internal auditing that was in place before the APB guidelines were issued in January 1990. The guidelines cover eight main areas for effective internal auditing as follows:

1. INDEPENDENCE
The internal auditor should have the independence in terms of organisational status and personal objectivity that permits the proper performance of his duties.

2. STAFFING AND TRAINING
The internal audit unit should be appropriately staffed in terms of numbers, grades, qualifications and experience, having regard to its responsibilities and objectives. The internal auditor should be properly trained to fulfil all his responsibilities.

3. RELATIONSHIPS
The internal auditor should seek to foster constructive working relationships and mutual understanding with management, with external auditors, with any other review agencies and, where one exists, with the audit committee.

4. DUE CARE
The internal auditor should exercise due care in fulfilling his responsibilities.

5. PLANNING, CONTROLLING AND RECORDING
The internal auditor should adequately plan, control and record his work.

6. EVALUATION OF THE INTERNAL CONTROL SYSTEM
The internal auditor should identify and evaluate the organisation's internal control system as a basis for reporting upon its adequacy and effectiveness.

7. EVIDENCE
The internal auditor should obtain sufficient, relevant and reliable evidence on which to base reasonable conclusions and recommendations.

8. REPORTING AND FOLLOW-UP
The internal auditor should ensure that findings, conclusions and recommendations arising from each internal audit assignment are communicated promptly to the appropriate level of management and he should actively seek a response. He should ensure that arrangements are made to follow up audit recommendations to monitor what action has been taken on them.

3.5 Other Standards

Central government
Central government auditors will not necessarily be members of professional bodies and they subscribe to a Treasury publication called The Government Internal Auditing Manual (GIAM). GIAM in effect sets out a series of requirements that have the status of auditing standards. The GIAM standards are summarised as follows:
Scope - Internal audit should embrace the whole internal control system of a department including all its operations, resources, services and responsibilities for other bodies.

Independence - Internal audit must be sufficiently independent to perform its duties in a manner which will allow professional judgements and recommendations to be effective and impartial. Internal audit should be a separate entity.

Planning - Internal audit work should be planned at all levels in order to establish priorities, achieve objectives and ensure the efficient and effective use of audit resources.

Audit approach - Internal auditors should ensure that audit objectives and methods enable them to discharge their responsibilities to evaluate the internal control system. Internal auditors should obtain and record relevant, reliable and sufficient audit evidence to support audit findings and recommendations.

Controlling - Internal audit work should be controlled at all levels of operation to achieve objectives and ensure the economic and efficient use of audit resources.

Reporting - The findings and recommendations arising from each audit should be promptly reported to management and followed up to ascertain action arising therefrom.

Due professional care - In carrying out their duties internal auditors should exercise due professional care, that is with competence based on appropriate experience, training, ability, integrity and objectivity.

Relationships - Relationships with management, staff, external auditors and other review agencies should be centred on the need for mutual confidence, understanding of role and co-operation.

Staffing and training - Internal audit should be appropriately staffed in terms of numbers, grades and experience, having regard to its objectives and standards. Internal auditors must be properly trained to fulfil their responsibilities.

National Health Service

Internal auditors who work for the National Health Service (NHS) are covered by their own specific manual that again acts as a set of auditing standards. This was produced to help improve previously poor auditing standards in this Department. The minimum auditing standards are summarised as:

Overall consideration (planning) - Planning must include a formal consideration on an annual basis by the Treasurer and CIA of the structure, competence, training, specialisms and independence of the section and its staff.

Strategic audit plan - Planning must include the completion of a strategic audit plan, using an established field of operations and including a Resource Plan.

The systems based audit - The systems based approach should generally be adopted.

Monitoring and control - The internal audit section should be monitored and controlled both in day-to-day operations and while performing the audit work. This should include supervision during the planning, execution and closure of an audit, liaison with other auditors, job appraisal and counselling and reporting progress to management.

Computer audit planning - Work on computer systems must be planned as part of the Strategic Audit Plan. The needs of the specialist aspects of the audit of computer systems must be considered.

Value for money audit planning - VFM audits should be identified and integrated within the Strategic Audit Plan.

Planning - Cumulative audit knowledge and experience should be added to the system as ascertained to formulate the Audit Planning Memorandum.

Work programme - A work programme should be compiled based on the minimum level of testing.

Execution - Testing should be undertaken to conclude on each key control within the system and therefore each system objective.

Closure - Review of working papers should take place and evidence of the review and resolution of points raised should form part of the working papers. A report should be generated for each audit, discussed, and a reply received. A post-audit meeting can be held to act as a debrief on the audit assignment.

It appears strange that there are so many auditing standards and it is not always obvious as to which one should operate, particularly where auditors have different qualifications. As previously mentioned, the standards are generally consistent and since they each seek to improve auditing performance they should be supported. The position simply reflects the currently disjointed state of the internal auditing profession and a certain amount of professional jealousy where each body wishes to retain their own version of auditing standards.

3.6 Can Standards be Universal?

We have already established the fact that there are a variety of standards that cover internal auditing. Despite the real-life situation it is nevertheless interesting to discuss the concepts of universality of standards and whether there are barriers to having one set of internal audit standards applicable throughout the world. The IIA set is adopted by all members in the various countries they are established in. Writers such as Gerald Vinten (1990) have recognised the problems with international standards and some of the issues that relate to the question of universalism are now discussed:

Mandatory?
Should the standards be mandatory or just best practice and if mandatory, should we accept that not all countries could comply? This also brings in the issue of how one might enforce mandatory standards across international boundaries. It may be better to set standards as targets that should be aimed at, as opposed to enforceable regulations. The problem arises where there is non-compliance and it is not clear whether any action should or can be taken. The world of external audit is fast moving towards the view that substandard work lowers the auditing profession's reputation and that firms must be policed as part of a review and certification process. This presumably will eventually be the case for the internal auditor in time to come to reinforce our claim that many sectors of society rely on our work. The contrasting view will argue that we cannot afford to be too rigid in forcing working practices in audit units that are less able to meet professional standards.

Local factors
How far do local factors affect the profession particularly where local legislation affects that role of internal auditing by setting out some of their compliance based duties? Can one set of standards anticipate all such eventualities? It is clear that some aspects of legislation in many countries envisage internal audit as having a major role in regularity audits as a safeguard against fraud. Where different countries have specific legislation that impacts on the audit role then it becomes even more difficult to set standards to any degree of detail. Furthermore countries with large geographical areas with less developed communications systems may require their internal auditors to feedback basic information

on these outstations. This information gathering function may be far removed from the professional systems based approach that forms the basis of modern-day auditing.

Standardisation
To what extent should the standards require a standardised approach and how much flexibility should be built into discharging their requirements? Building on the above point, we would wish to create a balance between two competing positions.

FIGURE 3.2 INTERNATIONAL INTERNAL AUDITING STANDARDS

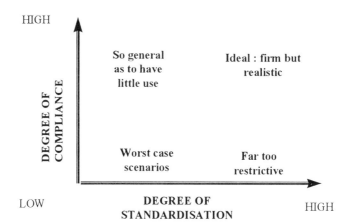

There are ways that we can move closer towards this ideal:
• We must recognise the practicalities of real-life auditing and formulate standards that provide statements of intent rather than comprehensive procedures.
• Translate the standards into suitable work practices and incorporate them into the audit manual.
• Make compliance with standards a major issue that is uppermost in the minds of all staff. To this end any barriers to compliance should be addressed immediately.

IIA Committee
Can the IIA's committee process take on board all the different interests across the world? This might involve a high degree of representation from each member country with strategically located Committee meetings rotated between continents. In practice there is a major problem getting sponsorship to pay the expense of attending meetings, particularly for poorer countries. So meetings that appear to offer an open invitation may in reality be restricted to a few of the bigger, more advanced countries. The only solution would be to hold a central fund and ensure that all member countries are able to attend and have an equal voice.

Translation
The language problems and translation costs can be prohibitive. In fact it is sometimes difficult to find appropriate translations for certain words to convey the technical content and spirit of the matter being addressed. As a result one dominant language (e.g. English) may reign supreme and so produce a slant towards the main language speakers.

Nationalism

Nationalism and political manoeuvring can make life difficult. It may become clear that a group of countries may possess most of the legislative powers with smaller countries more or less excluded from the main processes. Politics is almost unavoidable in any international forum and generally results in a disproportionate spread of power across members. This may be the single most important factor in securing a level of agreement in terms of the universal application of auditing standards. It is clear that there are barriers to universalism although the IIA have made some ground in breaking them down. It is also questionable as to whether full standardisation is a good thing bearing in mind the different models of the internal audit role that exists throughout the world. What is more defensible is the view that there should be some agreement on the basic principles of internal audit, which is a fundamental base from which to assist the development of internal audit as a profession.

3.7 Can Standards Apply to Smaller Organisations ?

Internal audit standards set out ideals that should be striven for and in the main are based on healthy, growing audit departments with a CIA and a complement of audit staff. Where the audit function consists of one officer and a desk, the question arises as to whether standards can be applied in this situation:

Lower status

Small audit departments may have a low status and therefore little of the necessary level of independence essential for the performance of good audit work. Most auditing standards require that they are separate entities headed by a senior officer (e.g. a CIA). As such small units located in an obscure part of the accountancy section may fall outside this requirement. It would be pointless to adopt standards that one knows cannot be achieved bearing in mind that any review of internal audit will comment on this non-compliance. Where internal audit is only recognised in terms of dual accountancy/audit posts, again problems with adopting IIA standards will ensue.

Type of work

Smaller audit departments may be established essentially to provide extra resources for the external auditor and in this way be far removed from the models that the standards are based on. The audit work carried out may therefore be centred on testing routines and bear little resemblance to the modern audit role. Again independence may be compromised to the detriment of audit performance. Any move towards higher level systems based auditing may be unattainable and standards that are based around the systems concept will be difficult to achieve. Where internal audit work programmes flow from external audit plans, standards that require the internal audit department to plan in its own name may be, in this scenario, unrealistic.

Level of expertise

There may be a lack of certain expertise in areas necessary for a rounded collection of knowledge, skills and disciplines that may be essential to discharging a high profile audit role. This may be true in areas such as computers, capital contracts, management accountancy and so on. Audit training and development standards may be too far advanced for less developed auditing practices. Smaller audit departments may be less well developed and at a major disadvantage than larger ones. In fact the audit role may be being discharged by one sole officer who struggles to make it work, far removed from the luxury of a structured, well-staffed internal audit department. Having said this, one may use internal auditing standards as professional targets that set the frame for the current audit function no matter how far this has developed to date. This is so long as this is not used to criticise the efforts. In the final analysis the idea is that all audit departments are covered by the relevant standards and should attempt to comply as far as possible. It may well be the case that small but efficient/professional audit departments may become so successful that they eventually receive the support necessary for expansion.

3.8 The National Health Service Experience

The role of internal auditing standards can be seen clearly in the way they were developed for the National Health Service (NHS) in the United Kingdom. As a case study, it is interesting to consider how problems with an audit service were tackled through implementing suitable standards. A brief history may be set out as follows:

1. A Comptroller and Auditor General report on the summarised accounts for 1979/80 noted various weaknesses in NHS internal audit including deficiencies in planning, reporting, computer coverage and low staffing numbers.
2. The Salmon Report of 1982 reviewed internal audit and made a number of major recommendations covering the role of audit and the approach to audit work. As well as staffing shortages, the low level of grades meant that professional standards were hard to attain.
3. As a result of these criticisms, an audit manual was issued in 1987 with a revised update version becoming mandatory from 1990.
4. The APB standards provided a framework but were not industry specific, i.e. tailored to the requirements of the NHS that were and still are going through major changes.
5. As well as setting qualitative standards the manual also helped determine principles of coverage, raised expectations and raised the profile of specialist skills such as computer audit.

The NHS manual is a direct response to external criticism that it met by setting formal standards to cover the direction and approach of the audit function. This point is made clear in the foreword to the standards. Although there has been some concern over the way staff have been developed to meet these new expectations, this is nonetheless a positive way of tackling the problem of poor performance. It is not enough simply to state that the IIA (or APB) standards will be adopted. One must go on to formulate detailed guidance that relates to the specific circumstances of each individual business sector.

3.9 Contribution of the Institute of Internal Auditors (IIA)

Main points relating to the contribution of the IIA are:

1. The IIA has developed a common body of knowledge that is examined before membership is acquired. In addition it publishes a set of standards, a code of ethics and a statement of responsibilities. Each of these is dealt with in detail in separate parts of the handbook.

2. The IIA has sanctions for dealing with breach of professional requirements and is now developing the mechanisms for enforcing them. Members have in the past been reprimanded for misconduct.

3. IIA members are not "approved practitioners" as there is no requirement for CIAs to be qualified members. It would appear that anyone can be an internal auditor and sign-off formal audit reports, although this will be subject to an individual organisation's employment policies. In fact there is a mistaken view that anyone can be an internal auditor without any training at all. This issue can be resolved at junior level but becomes more difficult where senior staff (with say contract or computing skills) are brought into internal audit with no intention of developing or understanding auditing skills. This reinforces the view that there is little or no use in employing unqualified people, or retaining those that are unable (or unwilling) to pass their auditing examinations.

4. The general spirit of the IIA standards stresses loyalty to the organisation and the professional concept of a duty to society takes second place. In a potential whistle-blowing situation there is no automatic requirement to protect the interests of society in general.

5. Internal auditors have not been sued for negligence and because of their position inside the organisation they are generally not exposed to this risk. This may alter as firms of accountants start to take on individual internal audit contracts where the internal audit function has been contracted out.

3.10 Establishing Internal Audit

Part three of the handbook covers managing internal audit and deals with the necessary managerial mechanisms that must be in place to ensure quality services are provided. (There is also supplementary material on establishing an internal audit function in the accompanying diskette.) Here we deal briefly with the question of establishing a new audit function and there are a number of related issues concerning standards that may be briefly considered before a new audit function is set up:

One would have to develop and publish a suitable audit charter that becomes the agreed terms of reference for the internal audit role. This should be signed by the organisation (i.e. the audit committee). This formal audit charter would set out the defined objectives, role and responsibilities of the internal audit function. As such it becomes fundamental to the start-up process.

It is necessary to engender support at the highest levels of the organisation as well as across management generally. Adopting and complying with professional auditing standards is the best way to approach this task and by publicising this, it can reinforce a positive image of the audit function. Securing quality standards is an additional device for promoting the image. Once in place, the task of maintaining this support should be paramount in the CIA's mind. A formal complaints procedure can assist this process.

A clear policy on independence should be linked to the dual planks of objectivity and organisational status. Once one's position in the organisation has been determined it will be very difficult to alter one's status, particularly upwards. An audit unit that is lowly placed in an organisation and which employs poorly paid unqualified staff will most probably be doomed to failure.

Access throughout the organisation has to be agreed and to a certain extent depends on the level of support that has been acquired. This policy should ensure unrestricted access in the performance of audit work. The audit charter should make this point crystal clear and ensure that it is publicised widely. Note however, undue reliance on formal access powers will indicate a problem with the audit ethic.

Reporting status will be defined and the various components that underlie the concept of independence need to be firmly established along with the involvement of any audit committee. Whilst audit reports will go to the relevant client's management, a final arbitrator in the form of the audit committee should be established to enhance independence.

A strategic plan will have to be formulated and implemented in line with the audit mission. This plan should then be supported by suitable resources operating at a professional level with the requisite level of expertise and numbers. It is better to have the resource profile led by strategy as this will ensure the right levels of staff are acquired. Remember strategy must be developed from a one-off review, analysis and reformulation, which likewise will effect the staffing equation. Many audit units employ a core staffing complement and add temporary staff as and when required. This allows flexibility and means that resources can alter in parallel with strategic analysis and review. On a less positive note, it is much easier to get rid of poor staff when they are on temporary contracts. Unfortunately this must be a major consideration of the CIA.

Professionalism is not just an academic concept but is also something that should be put into action as the audit function is managed and developed. To this end a formal set of audit standards should be adopted based around formal training and development programmes.

Above all, the audit function must offer and then deliver a professional audit service in line with clear standards and no amount of publicity can replace this fundamental truth. Marketing should be used to help define the type of services that should be provided, so long as the audit committee is deemed the ultimate client.

Lastly a formal audit manual should be compiled and implemented, which will reflect the underlying requirements of the professional standards whilst incorporating and codifying all the matters that have been listed above.

3.11 Conclusions

Standards play a crucial role in internal auditing and support the concept of auditing as a professionally based discipline. This complements the drive to full professional status that internal audit is now embarking on although we still have some way to go. It is however clear that published statements are of little use unless they have been fully implemented and subject to continual review. The audit manual is the right mechanism for this process and it is through this that formal standards may be set and adopted. There are stringent tests that are applied to assessing whether a discipline has attained professional status and these revolve around the concept of providing a service to society in general. As the internal audit role develops it passes many of these tests although there is still some way to go. While internal audit may be referred to as a profession in its own right it may be seen more as a quasi-profession that is developing towards its full potential. The IIA and APB versions of internal auditing standards are different in structure but are generally not inconsistent. All internal auditors should ensure that they have copies of these standards and that they are able to comply with their main requirements.

CHAPTER FOUR

APPROACHES TO INTERNAL AUDIT

4.1 Different Approaches

Introduction

Internal auditing may be performed in many different ways and there are a variety of models that may be applied to discharging the audit role. The organisation will define its audit needs and this will help to establish which types of audit services are provided. The CIA is then charged with providing this service to professional auditing standards. This chapter explores some of these different approaches and the way that they relate to the role of internal auditing, whilst this theme is expanded in part four.

Audit variety

The development of internal auditing, as a profession, is based on the premise that the practice of internal audit is a defined discipline subject to professional standards. At the same time it is clear that there is a great deal of variety in the way the audit role is discharged. This results from different approaches and in some cases, a different interpretation of the underlying principles. Some of the more common ways that the audit role is expressed may be found in the descriptions of vacant audit post designations that are advertised, such as:

- Management audit.
- Operational audit.
- Systems audit.
- Corporate audit.
- Probity audit.
- Compliance audit.
- Contract audit.
- Computer audit.
- Social audit.
- VFM audit.
- Fraud investigations.
- Performance review.
- Quality audit.

This wide variety in the use of audit based terms does not necessarily mean that there is no clear discipline of internal auditing. It is not merely common-sense work that any untrained person may perform. What is evident is the way that the audit role is discharged will vary according to the agreed terms of reference (or audit charter). Variety creates a richness and degree of flexibility in the type of audit work that is undertaken. In many cases an audit department will contain different types of auditors who collectively discharge the audit function. Internal auditing is about evaluating controls and this should be a central theme in most audit work.

Audit approaches
There are many ways that the different approaches may be categorised:

☐ **Vouching**. This approach is centred on comparing one transaction with another to confirm their accuracy. These would normally be obtained independently and the cross-checking would isolate whether the item being examined is accurate, consistent, correct, complete and reliable. The principal objective would be to uncover errors and possibly identify who is responsible. It is associated with the technique of ticking documents and records and formulating a list of errors and query items to be corrected by the responsible management. One might picture a line manager saying to staff :

> *"make sure this entry is correct or the auditors will pick it up next time they come around."*

The auditor is generally associated with carrying out detailed checking of transactions that have been processed in some cases many months ago. In addition the auditor would tend to follow a detailed audit programme of tests that require little understanding of the managerial systems of control.

☐ **Verification**. This approach is used mainly by the external auditor to test the assets and interests that are stated in the balance sheet. This may include examining evidence of the cost, authorisation, value, existence, beneficial ownership and the way the item is presented in the accounts. The internal auditor may also make use of this technique particularly where assets (say in remote locations) have to be audited.

☐ **Problem-solving**. In some organisations the internal auditors are called upon to provide reports to management on particular managerial problems. This is due to the great flexibility in the way audit skills may be applied to specific problems and the level of objectivity that is associated with audit. An example may be deciding how best to close sub-stores and merge them with a central store. The principle behind this approach is that a function that is solving major managerial problems will always be supported by the organisation. The approach will also be based on defined terms of reference and an examination of the relevant factors and underlying causes of problems before corresponding solutions may be devised.

☐ **Response to management's needs**. One audit philosophy is based on total marketing of audit services by simply responding to the wide range of managerial requests for assistance that may be referred to the audit department. The argument is that audit will become indispensable to the organisation and achieve a reputation of getting things sorted out. While this includes rational problem-solving exercises it will also cover trouble-shooting, fraud investigations, taking out corrupt directors, analysis of the accounts of potential take-over bid companies and a whole host of associated activities. The main drawback with this approach is that much of the resultant work bears little resemblance to the systems reviews that audit should be undertaking. In addition the audit role will eventually assume a pure consultancy base and professional standards may be jeopardised where management set tight terms of reference for each project. The conceptual difficulty arises where the auditor is unable to appreciate that the value of the response-work to management is not being questioned. We are more concerned with proper role definition between management and the auditor and the long-term implications.

☐ **Fraud investigations**. The audit role in fraud investigations may be emphasised in an attempt to satisfy management's needs. Management feels particularly vulnerable when a fraud is alleged and tends to want to refer the entire matter to internal audit. Where audit takes on cases wholesale including any subsequent appearance as witnesses at court and presenting internal disciplinaries against the employee in question, a great strain on audit resources will occur. As well as the effect on planned work, there is a danger in not allowing management to acquire expertise in this area. This encourages them not to ensure that systems of control are effective in preventing most frauds and irregularities. Generally frauds arise where systems are unsound or are not being properly operated and the audit role is more effectively used when it is geared towards systems reviews.

☐ **Probity reviews**. Management is charged with establishing systems of internal control that include mechanisms for ensuring that these systems are correctly applied. This may well involve inspection based visits to remote establishments/offices and a certain amount of checks on compliance. If internal audit assumes this role then a formal programme of audit visits to all material establishments will consume audit resources. In fact there is a direct link between this approach and vouching where the auditor will tend to perform extensive vouching exercises when performing the necessary compliance checks. Probity audits revolve around checking the integrity of transactions and operational activities and tend not to involve systems evaluation.

☐ **Systems auditing**. This is seen by some as the principal way in which the audit role should be discharged as it necessarily involves evaluating systems of control. The idea is that systems are studied to assess whether they are sufficiently controlled so that managerial objectives may be achieved. Before a view can be taken it is necessary to test the operation of controls and the extent to which weaknesses impact on the end-product. These tests may well include vouching, verification and an assortment of checks and confirmatory routines. The point being that vouching here is used as a technique to assist the control evaluation, as opposed to the results being an end in themselves. In this way the emphasis is not on performing an endless series of tests but more on reviewing the system and its principal objectives.

4.2 Investigations Versus Systems Auditing

A more straightforward way of analysing audit approaches is to distinguish between investigations and systems work. Firstly one would argue that audit is about evaluating systems of control and then follow-on by viewing all control-related problems as matters that should be investigated. While it is management's role to investigate these areas (that may be referred to as delinquent transactions), internal audit may be asked to assist in this process as a contribution to the welfare of the organisation. So investigations may be undertaken as part of audit's consultancy role as long as management's primary responsibility has been clearly defined. In this way it is possible to view most of the audit activities that fall outside the defined systems role as audit investigations. These investigations may range through fraud, breach of procedure, poor VFM, rationalisation exercises, compliance checks, operational performance and so on. The important point is they do not cover control systems. Some would argue that they tend to occur due to weaknesses in controls. For example, poor value for money may arise where management has not set clear operational targets or has failed to monitor their resources.

Allocating audit resources

The conceptual differences between systems work and investigations may be used to assign audit resources via the audit plan. Systems reviews are necessary to discharge the audit role and may be planned via an agreed risk assessment process, subject to changing circumstances and any required rescheduling of planned audits. These audits will be agreed with management and investigations may be built into the plans as a recognition of audit's desire to assist management in solving its more immediate problems. Much investigatory work cannot be foreseen and planned for, which means a contingency allowance may be used to resource these tasks. In practice investigations generally call for a transactions based as opposed to systems based approach since transactions testing is the main feature of most investigatory work. Again it is important to stress the difference between these two types of work in that systems is formal audit work while investigations constitute additional assistance to management.

Levels of auditing

Before moving away from systems auditing as an approach, it should be pointed out that systems work is not merely limited to financial or informational systems which tend to be computerised. It involves a much wider concept. Systems in this context covers all managerial processes that ensure objectives are achieved. The managerial control system has been dealt with in chapter one and it should be clear that systems auditing will review these control features. As such, systems auditing views controls as a system in themselves while at the same time the audit work will also form a system in itself.

Force-field analysis

There are many different ways that internal auditing may be approached and some are investigatory/transactions based while others move towards a systems approach. There is an argument that the most efficient use of audit resources occurs where one concentrates on reviewing systems as opposed to the examination of individual systems' transactions. Management may tend to use internal audit for one-off problem-solving exercises particularly where there is a potential embarrassment factor if the matter is left unresolved. On the other hand where systems reviews are not carried out then breakdown and sub-optimal functioning may occur. This leads to delinquent transactions. It is possible to use force-field analysis to weigh up the factors that together define the actual audit approach that is applied in any organisation.

These forces may be set out as follows:

FIGURE 4.1 FACTORS IMPACTING ON THE AUDIT APPROACH

Each of these factors will apply pressure in defining the way that the audit role is discharged and some of the influences may appear as follows:

TABLE 4.1 FACTORS: MAIN REQUIREMENTS

BODY	REQUIREMENTS
The CIA	Systems reviews and satisfying audit clients.
Audit Committee	Systems reviews and major corporate issues resolved.
Line management	Management problems solved.
Professional practice	Corporate, managerial and operational systems reviews (+ consulting?).

4.3 Conclusions

There is a choice in the way internal auditing is carried out and although the professional standards do set conceptual guidelines, they do not promote a particular methodology. The final approach will result from a combination of factors that affect the audit role and resultant work carried out. The premise upon which the handbook is based considers systems auditing as the correct interpretation of the purist internal audit role, with all other matters falling under the generic term, investigations.

CHAPTER FIVE

INDEPENDENCE

5.1 Introduction

All definitions of internal audit contain the word "independence" and this is an important component of the audit role. It is both a concept and a process. One could assume that since internal audit is located within the organisation it cannot be independent. The counter argument suggests that internal audit has to be totally independent, or it has little use. The real position falls somewhere between. There are degrees and a quality of independence that has to be earned to ensure that audit is sufficiently distanced from the particular operation being reviewed.

5.2 The Meaning of Independence

Independence means that management can place full reliance on audit findings and recommendations. Positive images are conjured up by this concept of independence:

Objectivity

Behind this word is a whole multitude of issues that together form a complex maze. The main problem is that the whole basis of objectivity stems from a human condition of correctness and fair play. Any models that involve a consideration of the human condition have to deal with many psychological matters, and at times irrational behaviour. Although objectivity is located in the mind, it is heavily influenced by the procedures and practices adopted.

Impartiality

Objectivity may be seen as not being influenced by improper motives whilst impartiality is not taking sides. The question of impartiality is important because there is a view that internal audit, like all other units, will work in a politically advantageous way. This may result in audit taking the side of the most powerful party in any work that impacts on the political balances within an organisation. If this is allowed to occur unchecked then the audit evidence that supports any audit report may be secured with a view to assisting one side only. An absence of impartiality will undermine the audit process. If audit plans are changed, reports withdrawn and audits aborted because this suits certain parties in the organisation, this reputation will stay with the audit function and give it a poor image.

Unbiased views

When an audit report states that "the audit view is..." this should provide a comment on the state of internal controls. Where used to provide an advantage for the audit function, credibility is risked. The other aspect of audit bias is where certain officers/sections have been earmarked as "poor, uncooperative or suspect..." We go into an audit looking for any material that supports our original contentions. If taken to the extreme, the audit function will become a hit squad, conjuring up cases against people it does not like. It is difficult to build professional audit standards using this model.

Valid opinion

Readers of audit reports require the auditors to complete work to professional standards with the audit opinion properly derived from this work. This opinion must make sense having reference to all relevant factors. The audit role is not to please nominated parties or simply maintain the status quo; it is to present audit work in a professional and objective manner. The temptation to keep certain individuals happy may well result in a distorted audit opinion which in turn will make the underlying audit work unreliable. Managers will issue hundreds of reports during the course of their careers, each taking a stance that is derived from their position within the organisation. Internal audit on the other hand depends wholly on a reputation for reviewing an area, or performing an investigation, and producing an opinion that is valid. This is not to suggest that this opinion will be supported by all levels of management, but it should be accepted as a fair representation of the facts.

No spying for management

Professional objectivity means that audit does not fall into the trap of acting as spies for management, particularly where managers feel that their staff are not performing. Most general problems with staff can be related to a failure by management to install effective controls and this is a point that the auditor will return to time and time again. The latest definition of internal audit suggests that audit serves the organisation as a whole rather than targeting specific officers. This means that the welfare of the organisation is paramount as the audit role rises above the in-fighting that goes on in both private and public sector bodies. There is an issue surrounding the provision of audit consultancy services that makes this a complicated area which is dealt with later.

No "no-go" areas

There are senior managers who adopt a particularly aggressive stance to managing their areas of responsibility. All outsiders are treated with great suspicion. In fact there is a correlation between professional incompetence and this threatening posture, i.e. the less able the manager the more aggressive he/she becomes. If this results in certain areas being deemed out-of-bounds to internal audit then this means that audit's independence is impaired and they will have a lesser role. If audit can be kept away from certain areas then this restricts the audit field, and if this trend is allowed to continue it could set a damaging precedent. The net result may be that the audit field becomes relegated to defined parts of the organisation only. This is playing at auditing far removed from the demands of any professionally based audit practice.

Sensitive areas audited

To achieve its full status internal audit must be able to audit sensitive areas. Unlike the no-go areas, this potential barrier arises where the necessary skills and techniques are not available to the audit unit thus making it impossible to cover high-level areas. Where the audit scope is set within basic accounting systems for low-level checking, little important work can be undertaken and audit independence will not have been secured.

Senior management audited

There is a view that over 80% of system-controls are located within the management processes that underpin the operations. Where audit fails to incorporate this factor into the scope of audit work, a great deal will be missed. The problem is that managers may not wish to be audited, particularly where this exposes gaps in their responsibility to establish sound controls. The CIA will have a quiet life where he/she works only at a detailed operational level and ignores the whole management process. Again this restricts the audit role and so adversely impacts on the auditor's independence.

No backing-off
We do not expect auditors to back down without a valid reason when confronted by an assertive manager. This is not to say that auditors march unchecked across the organisation, unaware of any disruption they might be causing to front-line operations. It does however mean that they will pursue audit objectives to the full in a diplomatic and professional manner. If this is not the case then audit will be vulnerable to criticism from all sides. Audit reports would then reflect what managers allowed the auditor to do rather than the work required to discharge the terms of reference for the audit. In this instance audit can claim very little real independence.

The above provides a foundation for the audit practice at the heart of the audit role. This distinguishes it from management consultancy and other review agencies who provide professional review services but only to the terms of reference set by management. These factors must be in place for the audit function to have any real impact on the organisation. If managers are able to pick and choose which audit reports to believe, then this represents a major flaw in the audit service. It will eventually lead to its downfall, as well as a failure to meet professional internal auditing standards.

5.3 Factors Affecting Independence
Since independence is achieved in degrees, there are many factors that impact on the acquired level of independence:

Where internal audit is too closely involved in the design of systems, it becomes difficult to stand back at a later stage and audit the same system. People feel their work is correct and of a high standard. There are few who are able, at a later stage, to criticise their own efforts however objective they may claim to be. Systems designers take on some of the ownership of these systems which necessarily rules them out as independent systems assessors. All systems designed by audit will have to be taken out of the audit field thus restricting the scope of audit coverage. The vexed issue of audit involvement in computerised systems development is dealt with under computer auditing.

The internal audit role in systems development may mean that audit becomes responsible for the new system. The definition of professional audit services hinges on an agreed model where management is responsible for their systems and systems controls. Excessive involvement in systems design will interfere with this concept and locate responsibility with the auditor who will have to make recommendations to him/herself whenever reviewing a particular system. Any form of independence in this instance would be a non-starter.

Where internal audit is over-familiar with the client one may view its work as potentially biased by the relationship. There is a view that auditors should seek to remain outside the normal free associations between managers and officers who will strike up informal relationships. Two points addressed later are the audit role in providing consultancy services; and the need to avoid a perception (as well as the reality) that audit has close ties with defined managers such as to impair objectivity. An extreme example would be where an auditor has an intimate friendship with a manager although the relationship problem would apply wherever audit has provided assistance to particular managers.

Conflicts of interest can arise where the auditor cannot stand back from the system. This can happen where the auditor has developed a close social relationship with the manager of the operation under review. The ability to employ good inter-personal skills is a clear advantage to the performance of audit work. Where however this entails forming close friendships, one risks many subsequent disadvantages that outweigh the original benefits. A carefully formulated and implemented code of conduct is essential in dealing with this complicated subject.

The practicalities of the situation may make it difficult to preserve independence. Where there is no computer auditor available, it is difficult to provide an effective input into this area. One aspect of independence is based on a wide scope of audit coverage across the organisation. Where this is impracticable the audit impact will suffer accordingly. As such the CIA is charged with formulating a clear strategy to counter all problems that impair the ability to provide an efficient audit service.

Where internal audit reports to the Finance Director, a careful approach has to be negotiated to secure the degree of independence that promotes good audit work. This point is dealt with later.

Rotation of auditors between assignments gives a fresh eye to periodic audits and avoids the auditor becoming too involved with the system under review. It is not necessarily the relationship with the operational staff in question that is the issue. It is linked more to the level of boredom and sameness that creeps in where the same audit area is tackled again and again by the same person. This is not to say that one cannot assign specific parts of the audit field to specific auditors so that a degree of expertise can be acquired.

Gifts provided by the client can create obvious problems and firm audit policies must be provided for this matter. The position is not always wholly clear since free drinks, lunches and other minor perks may be part of the culture, with constant refusal causing embarrassment to both sides. There is always a balance to be struck between the following two extremes:

FIGURE 5.1 RECEIVING GIFTS

A cup of tea and biscuits  **All expenses paid holiday**

The real issue here is not so much the value of any perks received as part of working for an organisation. It is related more to an outsider's perception if the internal auditor is seen to be accepting favoured hospitality from the client.

Where auditors have recently come from a particular operation, it is advisable that they are not involved in auditing this area for a period of time during which they might be assimilated into internal audit. Where an auditor is due to leave internal audit and assume a line role in a particular operation, again they should not be party to audit work in the same area.

In terms of working relationships, there is in fact a dilemma felt by some less experienced auditors. Here they wish to perform an objective audit but also want to impress the client with a friendly and congenial approach. Striking up a positive working relationship is always encouraged but this should not be at the expense of professionalism in an attempt to simply please the client. Breaking these cosy relationships is generally recommended so that both sides may maintain a sense of proportion in performing their respective roles. Again clear policies on this matter are required.

The policy of talking to management and incorporating their needs into the project terms of reference creates a positive process but may be manipulated to lessen the level of independence. One would accommodate management's views but only to an extent, so as not to alter the original terms beyond recognition. We can extend this argument to cover those audit departments that have assumed an almost pure consultancy role responding fully to client requests rather than undertaking planned audit work. The difference between consultancy and audit must be fully recognised by the CIA when designing the type of audit services on offer.

When discussing factors that affect independence we must move from the position of deciding if we do or do not have independence. The true position is that an idealistic stance cannot be held onto at all costs. The practicalities of each individual case will mean that it merely has to be sufficient to support good audit work. What is important is that the many barriers to acceptable levels of independence should be recognised and addressed via the adopted audit philosophy.

The three component model
Mautz and Sharif (1961) tackle external audit independence through three fundamental components:
1. **Programming independence** - Here the auditor is free to define how the selected areas will be audited and what procedures will be applied.
2. **Reporting independence** - The right to report the full facts is seen as an important aspect of independence.
3. **Examining independence** - External auditors should have freedom to examine all areas that affect the financial accounts.

We have touched on the problems where internal audit is too immersed in the organisation's operations and cannot stand back and audit them. The acid test is:

> *"if internal audit were to be removed, the organisation would not come to a halt"*

This is excellent theory but does create secondary problems where the organisation does not fully understand the audit role thus making the audit function vulnerable. If this is the case, audit will be subject to a strong temptation to adopt a consultancy role and become part of the day-to-day controls so that its absence would be noticed immediately. Fearn's (1985) research into audit independence suggests that one should distinguish between the fact of objectivity that auditors are satisfied that they have, and the appearance to outsiders. It is important that internal audit is seen to be independent. Fearn felt that there was insufficient guidance on gifts and over-familiarity with the client. While most accepted that internal audit was independent from line managers, these same managers tended to view the auditors as intimately linked to senior management and in fact could not be independent from them. Operational management may adopt a more severe view of the internal auditor and consider them to be management spies who are not prepared to criticise senior management failings. Independence must not only be earned but must also be carefully managed.

5.4 Courtemanche on Independence

Courtemanche (1986) includes a chapter on independence in his book - *The New Internal Auditing*. He feels that the auditor's style and approach to work affect the degree and quality of independence that is secured. Where the auditor loses support from management, the status, scope and profile of the audit function will decline. Courtemanche discusses four styles of auditing that are akin to adopted audit philosophies:

The outsider
The auditor represents an outside interest with a regulatory role in the organisation. There is no recognition of the goals of the organisation and the approach becomes self-limiting with management restricting audit to those limited areas where it can be useful.

The manager by proxy
The audit role is as an agent for senior management and a special status is therefore acquired. After a while resentment builds up among auditees and pressure is applied to senior management. The tendency is then to restrict the audit role to where they can do least harm to morale.

The autonomist
This is the worst situation where the auditor is self-answerable and not to management or an outside regulatory agency. The auditor possesses a special wisdom and attempts to impose on the organisation regardless of suitability. The ideals may be engineered to meet managers' requirements for a while but will eventually break down when it becomes clear that auditors report to no one but themselves. This illusion of independence is quickly lost when management withdraws its support.

The absolutist
The auditor distorts the admirable qualities of honesty and integrity to "tell it like it is". The auditor then proceeds to spread trouble and discord throughout the organisation, rejecting all compromise until management's support wears down. The auditor has no professional base or leadership qualities, just a nagging insistence of rightness and the audit role will be restricted by management.

Courtemanche concludes that audit is not simply independent from management but that their independence is in fact dependent on management's support. He sees independence as based on a constructive auditor style while managing the follwing components:
* Access.
* Freedom to report.
* Responsiveness (by management) to audit findings.
* Diligence in performing work.
* Objectivity and professionalism.

5.5 The Rittenberg Model

An important model of audit independence that incorporates all the main ingredients was devised by Rittenberg (1977). The model is divided into two main sections: the organisation and the individual. Factors relating to the individual auditor are subdivided into economic and mental:

Organisation
This deals with the position of audit within the organisation and covers all relevant factors including reporting levels, top management support, audit committees and the audit charter.

Economic
These factors relate to the management of the audit department and include policies on designing systems, staffing the audit function, ethics, time restrictions on work and supervisory review.

Mental state
Factors in this category should ensure that the auditor does not subordinate his/her judgement as required by the standards. The important areas are personal attributes, objectivity, competence and professionalism in providing audit services.

Independence is a complicated issue with many features that must be both considered and properly managed. The two main features may be subdivided into various subsidiary categories giving a much wider view of independence.

5.6 A Working Model

Based on research it is possible to formulate a working model for assessing the level of independence. A number of components are considered and one works out the desirable, feasible and actual points on a continuum and then estimates how far one is from what is feasible. This model has been used by Keith Wade (1990) who sees the main factors as:

Position within the organisation
The higher one is located within an organisation, the greater the ability to offer an independent audit service. The status of each auditor is affected by the seniority of the CIA and where this is not on a high enough level one will only be able to pay lip service to the concept of independence. Furthermore it is extremely difficult for an auditor to liaise with senior management where he/she is of a much lower grade. The imbalance may impair one's ability to defend the audit view if required.

Reporting line
The people who are ultimately concerned with the auditor's conclusions concerning the state of controls in specific operations and generally throughout the organisation will impact on the level of independence achieved. The ability to resort to the most senior level of the organisation when required gives the audit function power which promotes audit objectivity. This access to the formal power structure need not ever be used in practice so long as it is clearly available if needed.

Scope of work

An ability to address control concerns at the highest level in the organisation is a major hallmark of audit independence. This must not only be built into the audit charter but must also be put into practice. A narrow definition of internal audit steeped in basic accounting systems is totally inadequate. The applied audit model must be based around professional definitions that view controls as all measures designed to assist the organisation in achieving its objectives. When complemented by a top-downwards approach to control, this allows one to audit the corporate process itself.

Level of audit resources

With all the best will in the world it will not be possible to achieve an independent audit coverage if the necessary resources are not in place. The right numbers and grades of auditors must be established before one can discharge a professional audit role. The requisite numbers will depend on the audit strategy, formal audit plans and the adopted approach to work. High-level professional audit work can only be carried out by high-level professional auditors.

Freedom from line operations

This is very important. Most audit units have now moved away from direct line functions such as certifying contractors' interim and final accounts before payment. However, a new trend has arisen where audit departments seek to discharge management's responsibilities for designing suitable systems and guarding against frauds. This results from mixing consultancy based work with audit work so that the lines of responsibility become blurred. Management no longer needs to think about the adequacy of their control systems as this role has been passed over to audit. These systems have no real owners and so drift into disrepair. The consultancy debate is outlined later.

Objectivity

The CIA should continuously seek out ways to improve the level of objectivity throughout audit and some of the relevant matters have been mentioned earlier. A great deal of this hinges on installing suitable policies and procedures. The aim being to remove any potential barriers to the auditor's ability to perform fair and unbiased work.

Competence

This is achieved through training and development programmes supported by performance appraisal schemes. Sound human resource management practices are the only means of ensuring that competent staff are employed and retained.

Planning work areas

An audit department with no formal audit plans can never be said to be independent. Not only are professional audit standards being flouted but it also means that audit responds to the pressures of the day, normally on a "he who shouts loudest" basis. This turns the audit resource into a political football that is used and abused on the excuse of providing a client response based audit service. A CIA who allows this disastrous condition to arise will be open to criticism.

Professionalism

This is based on employing qualified staff and ensuring they operate to professional standards. The principle of using unqualified staff who are able to operate on a similar level is inconsistent since there is then no reason why they should not have secured the full qualification. Since they are not members, they have no real allegiance to the methodologies that underpin professional audit services. Non-professionals will be employed where salary levels are relatively poor which means that the status of audit will likewise suffer as will the ensuing level of independence. Managing a tight audit budget and possibly competing against external suppliers of audit services may mean that audit staff should not be too expensive. Automated audit techniques will help as will a policy of employing junior staff for detailed checking. As long as supervisory auditors are qualified one will be able to work to quality standards.

5.7 Chambers

Andrew Chambers was reported in the IIA.UK's Journal, *Internal Auditing*, (December 1992) as saying:

- All those affected by audit work rely on audit independence of sufficient quality being in place.
- There is no such thing as complete independence as it is seen as falling on some point of a continuum. This positioning of internal audit on a point on the independence continuum should be such as to enable it to provide the service called for.
- The professional body, the units providing the service and the individual auditor each have an essential part to play in ensuring that auditors have adequate knowledge and understanding (to underpin independence).

The units providing the audit service

Here one would examine the CIA's reporting line that should ideally not be the Director of Finance. This will affect the scope of the audit service giving it a focus on accounting matters unless there is also a reporting line to an Audit Committee. The seniority of audit staff is also an important factor. The role in systems design and rotation of audit staff are seen as additional relevant factors.

The individual auditor

The audit staff should be carefully selected to ensure integrity and the right balance of authoritative behaviour. Adequate technical and professional development can act as safeguards against a personal loss of independence.

The professional bodies

These provide external authority and support and can act as a buttress against threats to independence.

Eleven factors that contribute to the auditor's independence:
1. Integrity.
2. High degree of understanding of the business in general.
3. Technical grasp of the audit subject.
4. Good professional auditing skills.
5. Resistance to accepting inadequate explanations.
6. Tact with firmness.

7. Avoidance of excessive explanations.
8. Avoidance of inappropriate social relationships.
9. Commitment to auditing.
10. Language skills as appropriate.
11. Understanding of the operating culture.

5.8 Managing the Director of Finance

There are many internal audit units that are located within the Director of Finance's (DF) department. Politicians when considering legislation on accountability, view the internal audit role as primarily concerned with promoting financial accountability on behalf of the chief financial officer. This is a fundamental misunderstanding of the true audit role as it fails to recognise that we cover systems at a corporate, managerial and operational level that includes the financial implications therein. It is nonetheless impossible to ignore forces (i.e. legislation) directed at expanding the audit role and profile. We will however have to address two basic questions when reporting to the DF:

•   Can we be truly independent in auditing the financial systems?
•   If we were in dispute with the DF on an audit-related issue how would this be resolved?

These two questions are directly related in that we can only be independent if we cannot be overruled by the DF in audit matters. There is an interesting equation that impacts on this consideration:

FIGURE 5.2 AUDIT AND THE DIRECTOR OF FINANCE

```
         The DF's contract in place

       Based on sound performance

     DF responsible for financial systems

   DF performance = sound financial systems

 Factors placing contract in doubt will not be well received
```

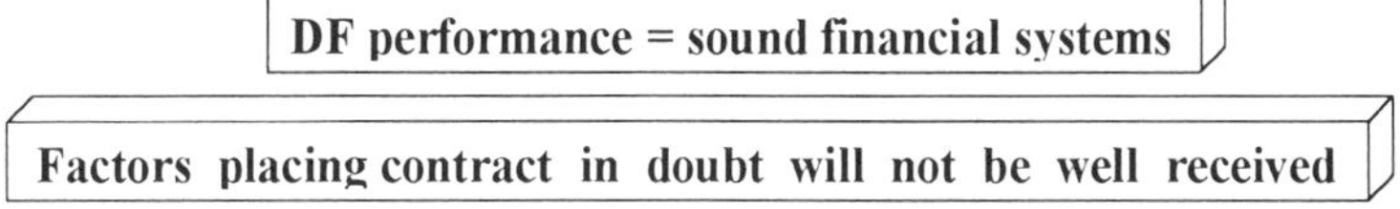

The secondary question then is: will internal audit reviews that might criticise financial systems adversely affect the personal welfare (i.e. the contract) of the DF? And as such will these criticisms be allowed to surface? The answer is that a competent and professional DF will wish to ensure that his/her systems are sound. Any material that suggests otherwise will be urgently received so that the required improvements can be quickly made. By the same token, a poor DF will wish to suppress any audit findings that embarrass him/her in a politically astute fashion. If the organisation is forced to choose between the DF and CIA, it will almost always support the former. This is because the DF will be a key member of the corporate management team with the power to affect the way resources are allocated across the organisation (i.e. political power). History recalls great battles between the DF and CIA, many resulting in the resignation of the loser (insert

"CIA"). There is no final solution to this problem although the following points concern the way that such a situation may be managed:

The audit plan should be compiled through a process of risk appraisal and consultation across the organisation. This will ensure that audit tackles high risk important areas through a process of selection that cannot readily be interfered with. If we are not protected by formal plans then there is a temptation to allow ourselves to be used as political footballs with an endless stream of special projects that are referred to audit from the DF and senior management.

Do not allow the DF to interfere with this plan either by removing parts or by including so many additional ad-hoc projects that it becomes impossible to resource planned work. Keep consultancy work and planned system reviews apart. Where the DF refers pet projects to the CIA for urgent action, this creates a potentially disastrous position. A cynic might argue that this enables a DF who feels threatened by external review to keep the CIA otherwise occupied through a constant supply of fabricated special projects. If each DF referral is resourced from a separate budget then the audit plan remains intact. The market for temporary audit staff should enable this policy to be applied. The CIA should ensure there is a specific code for recharging additional costs for DF initiated projects.

Encourage the DF to designate a manager responsible for each main area of financial services so that the DF is able to rise above the day-to-day running of these services. Where the CIA is immersed in the DF's management team then adopt a policy of keeping the designated audit manager free from this responsibility and so avoid clouding his/her judgement. The CIA may have a conflict between serving audit and supporting his/her line manager, the DF. In recognition of this, the audit manager may be given a degree of professional freedom to help counter this possible influence.

Encourage the DF to employ systems accountants who can manage the arrangements for development, control and quality standards over all main financial systems. In this way the auditor will not assume hands-on responsibility for controls and enforcing compliance. Make sure that financial systems control teams are also subject to audit review as with all other resources.

Above all, ensure that audit also reports to an audit committee on all issues that impact on systems control. This forms the ultimate safety valve where important matters are reported in full to an audit committee in line with the growing trend towards more corporate governance. Balancing the needs of the audit committee with that of an insecure DF line manager is in practice an impossible task. At some point in time a decision may have to be made based around declaring allegiance to one side. Remember these problems are less likely to arise with a professionally competent DF who has acquired good management skills.

Ensure that there is formal access to the Chief Executive and regular meetings are held. This acts as an additional reference point where required although note that in most cases, in any conflict, the Chief Executive will side with the DF and not the CIA.

If the organisation has employed an incompetent DF then the CIA might seek to distance him/herself from this person and maintain a formal relationship whereby all meetings and resultant decisions are documented. This is an unfortunate position and the CIA may seek to get the line management relationship terminated if this becomes untenable.

It is important that quarterly and annual audit reports that detail the current state of systems of control are published and presented to the audit committee. Full and fair reporting is one way of retaining one's professional status. Since systems auditing is about reviewing controls and not about naming names there is no reason why audit reports should be fully disclosed to the audit committee.

Being in the pocket of the DF is an unfortunate situation that the CIA may experience as a result of the political forces of the day and the assumed reporting line. Where this arises one's only real option for retaining professional integrity may be to resign on principle.

5.9 Reconciling the Consultancy Branch

The internal auditing arena is now facing a real threat to independence where it is being asked to reconcile two forces that are at times in conflict.

FIGURE 5.3 CONSULTANCY VERSUS SYSTEMS WORK

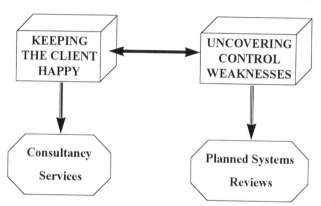

The client might wish to have internal audit perform a series of consultancy projects generated by ad-hoc problems that they as managers may experience. The professional auditing standards seek to promote audits that involve reviews of control systems as a service to the entire organisation as a wider concept. The conflict arises where the problems referred to audit by management result from inadequacies in controls. The act of propping up management reinforces the view that management need not concern itself about controls and that if there are control faults, audit will solve the ensuing problems. Here independence falls by the wayside and a response based audit service is resourced to the detriment of organisational controls. We will argue that the following holds true:

> *Unqualified staff employed in an audit unit that is located in the finance department to provide a response based service to managers will be unable to meet the requirements of professional auditing standards (including the requirements for independence).*

There are a number of ways to reconcile the competing forces present where consultancy and audit services conflict:

The audit charter should make clear that consultancy services are provided in addition to main-line audit services. Formal definitions will be required along with an explanation that makes clear the differences between these two types of services. Audit services would be based around planned systems reviews whilst consultancy consists of any other services that the client may require.

These additional consultancy services should not mean that the audit plan is not completed. Consultancy services should be separately resourced so as not to detract resources away from the audit plan. The approved audit plan is in fact a contract with the organisation and each project should be delivered in discharging the audit role. Consultancy services on the other hand consist of contracts with individual managers scattered throughout the organisation.

Where management referrals highlight the presence of control weaknesses in particular areas, the in-built flexibility of audit plans should allow these plans to be adjusted as a result of changing control priorities and risks. As such management problems are not simply ignored and if these relate to poor controls then audit plans should be adjusted so that high risk audits are featured. In this situation management's control concerns are not deemed to be consultancy work, but simply mean a change in planned audit priorities. It is only when management's problems do not relate to improving control that they fall under the category of additional client based services.

One way of emphasising the distinction between audit and consultancy services is to ensure that they are provided by different audit groups. This solves many problems relating to role definition and client contact. The difficulty is where the work becomes so far differentiated that they cannot really work together in teams. The other problem is that separate funding sources may mean that one side progresses more than the other. We have to mention the real possibility of professional jealousy where one type of work, say fraud investigations (i.e. consultancy), is deemed more attractive than the other. These issues will have to be resolved by the CIA by careful consideration and insight.

Where there is a conflict between consultancy and audit services, then audit services should reign supreme. This requirement should be formally stated in all agreements for the provision of consultancy services. As an example, say a consultancy project into poor performance finds a massive breach of important control arrangements, this may mean the operation will appear in the audit plans as a newly defined high risk area. We will have to provide consultancies with this in mind on a "take it or leave it!" basis. Anything less than this is unacceptable and interferes with audit independence.

Additional resources should be secured for major consultancy projects since, if they are deemed important, management will presumably be prepared to pay for them. A useful technique is to employ temporary staff to resource consultancy work and charge them directly to the client's budget. It is important that the project is costed at the outset so that these additional consultancy charges are agreed with the client. The work will obviously be led and directed by the in-house lead auditor.

The CIA should also make clear that any breach of procedure uncovered in the project will be reported to the appropriate officers. Internal irregularity discovered during the audit must be dealt with as issues of probity and not "glossed over" as is possible with management consultants who have no particular allegiance to the organisation. Again where management fails to accept this concept then they presumably will not wish to employ consultancy work from the internal audit function.

5.10 The External Audit Experience

At first sight the simple response when addressing the issue of audit independence in external audit in contrast to internal audit is to suggest that, as outsiders, external audit must be independent. Since internal auditors are insiders their level of independence may be seen as minimal. This response is too simple and does not cater for the factors that underpin the external auditor's search for independence. The two functions have different objectives. To balance this consideration of independence we consider points relating to the external auditor's independence:

Audit independence is a cornerstone of the external audit tradition and is enshrined in the legislation covering the provision of company audits. Unfortunately public scandals that question the reliability of the audit process place great strain on the auditing profession and do lead to much criticism. As a result there has been some debate over the reality of audit independence and whether this can be improved by any suitable measures, that will continue to rage for many years to come. Some impact on the internal audit role although many of these issues are confined to the external audit role in verifying financial statements.

There is a view that audit partners can develop extremely friendly relationships with company directors and this may affect the reliability of an ensuing audit. Rotation of partners may solve this problem and in the USA, companies registered with the Securities and Exchange Commission are required to change the partner in charge of the audit every seven years.

There is a major expectation gap concerning the perceived role of external audit in uncovering and investigating frauds. It is possible to explore this feature by examining the vast array of case-law relating to the laws of negligence where the auditor has failed to discover fraud that has later affected the welfare of the company in question. The topic of whistleblowing also has a bearing on independence. Auditors of financial services companies (banks, building societies and insurance companies) are often required to report suspicions of fraud to regulators. This allows the auditor access to an external agency although it does place an additional burden in defining a clearer role in respect of fraud. The idea is to enhance the level of independence through this additional facility, which may be built into auditing standards.

Independence is further impaired by the perceptions that some auditors will sign off an audit under pressure to retain the contract. This can arise where fees from any one client represent a large source of income although the view is that they should not exceed 15% of the total fee income. Some have floated the idea of a separate appointments sub-committee to ease the threat of a termination of the audit contract. A worst-case scenario exists where an auditor fails to report that a company is not a going concern for fear of placing the outstanding audit fee at risk where an adverse audit report would result in the banks calling in all loans.

The provision of consultancy services by large firms of auditors can be viewed as a potential conflict of interests. The situation where huge consultancy fees overshadow the relatively small audit fee may mean that audit issues are de-prioritised over keeping the client happy. Tasks such as the preparation of annual accounts, selection of new computer systems and tax advice may mean that the external auditor moves into purist consultancy. This is not always reconciled with their statutory responsibility to provide an external audit. The realities of managing this multi-million pound business may be far removed from the textbook principles of the external audit role and there is clearly the risk of impairing independence.

The audit fee may be determined at the outset of the audit as opposed to an open-ended hourly charge. Even where one charges on actual work done, there must be a base figure within which the final account will fall as agreed between the shareholders and external audit. Where this audit budget is overshot, there are major implications that impact on the degree of independence that is secured. A reduction in the work carried out will almost certainly involve less detailed testing of figures set out in the final accounts i.e. less verification work. There is then the temptation to expend all efforts in completing the audit rather than looking out for problems that may affect the final audit opinion. In this scenario independence will suffer although much of this can be avoided if work is carefully planned and controlled. Again the difficulty in reconciling theoretical principles with the realities of the business world means that the final solution will fall somewhere between the ideal position and a mere pretence at independence.

Independence has different meanings for external and internal audit as a result of their different objectives. There are however several lessons for internal audit that are derived from the external audit experience and this is the real value from studying this aspect of independence. Firstly, there is nothing inherent in being an external body that makes it easier to achieve greater objectivity. Secondly, many of the potential barriers to independence apply equally where the internal audit service has been contracted out to a firm of auditors.

5.11 Defining the Fundamentals

Much of the material set out above provides a framework within which independence may be defined. This is a wide concept with many associated factors. Independence cannot be seen as an absolute state, but more as a series of targets that together improve the overall effectiveness of the audit service. An alternative model that may be put forward is based on the following key factors:

1. The ultimate recipient of audit services must have the power to make executive decisions at the highest level of the organisation. The CIA must have unrestricted access to this forum as and when required and this should be formally established in the audit charter.
2. The audit strategy must be derived from a process that assesses high risk areas unimpeded, using a top-downwards approach that includes a level of consultation with clients. As such the most sensitive high level areas that impact on control systems should feature in a resultant audit plan. This plan must be supported by the officer/s noted in point 1 above.
3. The CIA must prepare up-to-date procedures that together form a defined audit methodology covering the way audits are managed and conducted. The underlying policies and procedures should be defined in a formal document (the audit manual).
4. The audit staff should be employed to discharge the audit plan and they should be professionally qualified and/or undergoing an individually tailored, ongoing training/development programme. Audit staff should be required to meet defined targets that together ensure the completion of audit plans within both time budgets and in line with professional standards and codes of ethics.
5. Work set out in audit plans should be carried out to the relevant standards (i.e. per the audit manual) and fully completed. The results of such work should be fully reported

without regard to any factors that do not form part of the formal audit findings and they should be followed up within a reasonable time period.

6. Management must be required to react to audit findings by implementing them or accounting for the implications of not doing so. This matter must be set out in officer job descriptions and the organisation's disciplinary code of practice.

7. Internal audit must be subject to a continuing process of review on a functional level and individual audit level, and any material problems must be reported and dealt with in the forum noted in the first point 1 noted above.

8. The CIA must have competent information systems that allow him/her to judge whether the requirements outlined above have been satisfied.

The above may be illustrated:

FIGURE 5.4 ASSESSING AUDIT INDEPENDENCE

5.12 Conclusions

We have seen that independence is a complicated concept that is affected by the audit approach. Its importance is shown in the way it has been given a higher profile in revisions to the Institute of Internal Auditors' Statement of Responsibilities published in 1991 and 1994. There are no absolutes and independence cannot be worn as a halo so as to allow the auditor to float above the realities of everyday events in the organisation. It cannot be guarded at all costs and one only needs sufficient independence to enable professional audit work to be carried out and acted on by management. The auditor must balance the right to plan areas of work with the need to involve management in this process. Providing a response based audit service with no formal audit plans will secure support from management but at the same time will diminish independence severely. The auditor cannot be a slave to independence, but at the same time a lack of it will undermine the entire audit role. As part of this process of balancing the various relevant factors, the need to adopt professional audit standards and well-thought-out policies and procedure becomes a fundamental prerequisite. We have developed four levels at which the issue of independence can be addressed by the CIA that cover the adopted structures, staffing, strategy and systems. For each of these four fundamental components there are four underlying sub-components making a total of sixteen separate factors. We can suggest that the degree to which these factors are in place equates to the degree of independence that has been secured.

CHAPTER SIX

BEHAVIOURAL ASPECTS OF AUDITING

6.1 Introduction

Most audit text books make reference to the impact that internal audit has not only on systems but also on people, and stress the importance of understanding human behaviour. This is sometimes extended by the view that auditors face various complicated issues because of their special position in the organisation. This chapter tackles some of these issues by adopting the stance that merely being genuine is not enough. One has to seriously consider one's position and the impact of the applied audit policies on the behavioural aspects of this role, to uncover any actual or potential barriers to good performance.

6.2 Human Behavioural Aspects

This covers a wide area and touches on topics such as industrial psychology, communication skills and group theory. The following should be noted:

IIA standard 260

IIA standard 260 states that auditors should be skilled in dealing with people and as such this aspect is seen as a valid audit skill. Unfortunately this skill does not always form part of the auditors' professional training and development programme. In fact a poor recruitment policy may result in bringing in auditors who see little value in developing good inter-personal skills. The old-fashioned detailed checker had little time to discuss the real-life issues that fall outside the scope of the audit programme. Nowadays auditors are required to do more than operate on a detailed technical level; they are expected to be able to converse openly with senior management.

Mautz and Sharif

Mautz and Sharif (1961) feel that internal control is essentially about people, which again highlights the need to frame audit work with this concept in mind. A large part of the control system depends on a close interface with the people who are involved in the system. An ability to understand documentation and system manuals comes a poor second to the need to appreciate how managers, supervisors and staff interact with the system so as to promote an acceptable degree of control. In contrast, if these people are simply ignored, it is doubtful whether one would be able to assess the relevant controls and form a sensible opinion.

The one minute manager

Research into the "one minute manager" shows that formal long-winded audit reports have little impact on busy managers. They want to know in short simple words "what the problem is, and what they should therefore do about it". While the auditor may present with pride a fifty page report containing ten separate appendices, it is doubtful whether this will be fully read by anyone, no matter how well written. Understanding the managers' needs and how the audit role may fit into this will help circumvent the frustrating process of producing audit reports that have little or no real use to managers (and the organisation). Later we will tackle the vexing issue of the "delinquent manager".

Audit intrusion

However well-meaning the auditor is, his/her intrusion into a manager's work area may well contribute to an increase in the overall level of managerial stress. The well-meaning opening phrase, "can I help you?", that the auditor may use to introduce his/her audit may be met with a cold silence with unspoken undertones of ("yes, by going away and letting me get on with my job!"). If we were management consultants we might then withdraw from the audit, but since this is not the case there is no simple answer.

Relevance

An audit approach that is obsessed with listing minor errors that occurred months ago, while at the same time ignoring issues affecting the whole future of the operation being reviewed, will have very little relevance to management. Auditors trapped in this obsession with basic detail are doomed to become obsolete with the passing of time, while professional auditors offer unlimited horizons. The old attributes of reliability and total accuracy (to the nth degree) are being replaced by newer ones of creativity and genuine enthusiasm linked into a commitment to organisational goals.

Management controls

Internal auditors who fail to recognise that the most fundamental control is the management process itself will necessarily perform sub-standard work. The ability to step into the management process is a major achievement. This is one reason that material relating to management techniques is included in part three of the handbook.

Management needs

Internal auditors who fail to appreciate management's needs will be unable to formulate sensible recommendations and as a result will leave themselves open to competition from other review agencies. Unfortunately the success criteria that management is working within may not be wholly clear when the audit is first started. Firm inter-personal skills are required to establish just what management is trying to achieve which, bearing in mind the importance of this factor, will have a major impact on the resultant audit. Again, these skills are over and above the basic audit techniques that most auditors will study as part of their training programme.

As a response to the above issues, auditors have the difficult task of balancing the need to understand management with the equally important need to fulfil their professional obligation not to subordinate their judgement on audit matters to that of others (IIA standard 120). Nothing short of a truly professional approach, having due regard to the available research into behavioural aspects, will enable internal audit to achieve the desired results.

6.3 The Churchill Studies

This limited research carried out many years ago by Neil Churchill (1965) was based on a pilot study of seven firms looking at auditees' attitudes towards internal audit. Attitudes towards internal audit were found to be:

TABLE 6.1 CHURCHILL - ATTITUDES TOWARDS INTERNAL AUDIT

ATTITUDE	%
NEGATIVE	26%
NEUTRAL	48%
POSITIVE	24%
MIXED	2%

When asked who internal auditors were most like the replies were broken down into the following:

TABLE 6.2 WHOM AUDIT MOST RESEMBLES

RESEMBLES	%
TEACHER	11%
POLICEMAN	58%
ATTORNEY	23%
MIXED	8%

The results have to be treated with caution since they are based on limited research. There are also vague areas such as the idea of an attorney, who could be a defendant's best friend or alternatively could be perceived as prosecuting a helpless individual. The work made it clear however, that feelings of suspicion, resentment and distrust of the internal auditor were felt by auditees.

6.4 CIPFA Survey

The Chartered Institute of Public Finance and Accountancy (CIPFA) held a seminar in 1973 on behavioural aspects of auditing. This addressed three basic questions:
1. What should be the scope of internal audit in local government?
2. Is there a conflict between the inspection and advisory aspects of the internal audit role?
3. Is there a need for training in inter-personal skills?

Research was then commissioned into this topic in four main stages:
Stage 1 Review of available research on behavioural aspects.
Stage 2 Interviews with auditors and auditees in a large local authority.
Stage 3 A questionnaire was then constructed for wide circulation to local authorities.
Stage 4 The results of this questionnaire were then analysed.

There was much congruence between the auditors and auditees on a wide range of issues. There was also some disagreement concerning the auditors' behaviour so that while auditors saw their behaviour as advisory, the auditee generally saw them as inspectors. Herein lies the role conflict where the auditor is convinced that he/she is here to help and finds it difficult to understand the auditees' sometimes negative response. The main implications of this research are:

1. The auditor needs to develop better communications skills and establish good working relations with the client.
2. Dealing with more complicated systems requires greater professionalism and expertise from the auditor.
3. The approach to work should be reviewed including the level of surprise visits, responsibility for fraud, systems based audits and testing routines.
4. Auditors need training in inter-personal skills.
5. An advisory role is more effective as opposed to blunt criticism.
6. Role-conflict can make an auditors' job more difficult and the participative approach should be considered, bearing in mind that internal control is all about people.

6.5 IIA Survey - Mints

In 1972 the IIA.Inc commissioned Frederick Mints to look into the auditee/auditor relationship and see what could be done about causes of unsatisfactory relationships. The approach was to:

1. Analyse background material.
2. Look into available research.
3. Interview audit managers.
4. Carry out laboratory experiments where puzzles were solved in two environments, one with a positive team based observer and the other with a critical formal observer giving the same advice. The observers were meant to represent the two different audit styles of advisor and inspector.
5. Carry out field study experiments applying the different styles using working conditions.

Mints highlighted views of internal audit behaviour. The police officer role saw good working relations as useful but not essential since, as long as the auditor was polite, this was enough. The consultancy approach was geared more to getting inside the managerial perspective based on positive working relationships. The main findings were:

1. Most audit managers felt that auditee relationships could be improved.
2. The participative style secured more favourable comments than the traditional style.
3. Audit managers' choice of style was:

TABLE 6.3 MINTS - CHOICE OF AUDIT STYLES

TRADITIONAL STYLE (A))	MIXED STYLE (B)		PARTICIPATIVE STYLE (C)
A	B	B/C	C
8%	53%	11%	28%

Mints set out a number of ways that auditor/auditee relations might be improved:

1. Better understanding and communications by the auditor.
2. Use a mutual problem-solving, rather than blame assignment approach in line with participative team building.
3. Educate auditees in the usefulness of audits.
4. Obtain management's view of the problem.

6.6 More Recent Research

Wood and Wilson

Research in the 1990s by Wood and Wilson into behavioural aspects has, amongst other matters, identified a whole range of views from management concerning their opinion of the audit function. A long list of positive terms was invoked by management when discussing the auditors such as:

> *"helper, advisor, friend, expert..."*

While others were not so complimentary, using terms along the lines of:

> *"inspector, police, informer, checker, gestapo..."*

It would appear that feelings run strongly at both extremes and the auditor should bear in mind the various possibilities and where he/she might stand in the organisation.

CIPFA 1991 research

This research considered the clients' view of internal audit and concluded that whilst managers saw a growing need for internal audit, its image needs enhancing. External audit on the other hand was perceived as appearing more professional. The researchers proposed a number of ways that this could be tackled:

- Assess the current position.
- Promote the service.
- Look for areas to expand into.
- Distance yourself as much as possible from any one department, e.g. finance.
- Build good relationships with clients.
- Maintain technical competence through adequate training.

IIA-UK 1992 Research

This survey was designed to assess how internal auditing as a profession was perceived in the market place. The last time the IIA carried out such a survey in 1986 this revealed that internal audit was under-utilised. The latest review was carried out against the background of many positive developments. These included the debate on corporate governance and an all-round demand for better accountability in the light of major scandals that was a feature of the 1980s and 1990s. Because the research was looking for untapped potential, the private sector was targeted as having greater scope for reversing the current trend in under-utilising internal audit. Based on an article (IIA Journal: March 1992), a summary of the responses to standardised questions was:

1. What is the role of internal audit? A variety of answers was received; consistent themes being control, accounting and computer audit along with some mention of independence.

2. What is the definition of internal audit? The definitions used in the private sector vary greatly with a great variety of job descriptions and the need for flexibility emphasised. The public sector was more consistent, sticking to official IIA terminology when defining the audit service.

3. Is it a professional career or a stepping stone? 50% of private sector respondents regarded audit as more of a stepping stone than a career while 70% from the public sector felt it was a career in its own right. Many saw audit as a good way of getting to know how an organisation works.

4. Attitudes towards the IIA.UK- 50% of private sector respondents were members of the IIA while this stood at 65% in the public sector. Many felt that the IIA was mainly a training and examining organisation rather than a source of current information.

5. Opinion on IIA Standards and Code of Ethics - The standards and code of ethics were well received.

6. Services expected from the IIA - Standards, communications and meetings were all placed high on the agenda.

7. Awareness of IIA and QiCA qualification - 62% felt that these qualifications compare unfavourably with that of the Chartered Accountants. Respondents felt that the IIA exams were not of the same intellectual status.

8. The image of internal auditing - Most felt that the profession has a poor image in the commercial world. "Policeman", "dull", "boring" and "dusty" were recurrent descriptions. Although there are individual auditors who are challenging this view, there is no collective move despite the great potential for internal audit to develop.

The IIA.UK are taking pro-active steps to improve the image of internal auditing and raise its profile.

6.7 Audit Relationships

Internal audit cannot be done in the audit office with no contact with management and operatives. The audit objective is based on providing sound advice to management on their systems of internal control. Here, the auditor requires a good understanding of the client's systems as a necessary prerequisite to effective audit work. It has been argued that internal control is people and if the people factor is missed then little useful work will ensue. The truly effective auditor is one who is able to extract all the required information from whatever source in an efficient manner. This requires talking to people, asking questions and securing assistance throughout the audit process and human relation skills may here be skilfully applied. Later on we deal with the concept of role conflict and how it may be managed and controlled so that the audit impact is maximised. This section in contrast deals with the wider issue of communicating and dealing with people generally.

Internal audit liaison
Contacts the auditor may experience include:
- Audit management.
- Corporate managers.
- Operational managers.

- Operatives.
- Delegates at various audit conferences and seminars.
- Government officials.
- Officials and lawyers at Courts of Law.
- Finance and computer specialists.
- External auditors.
- Staff from other internal review agencies.
- Members of the public.
- The organisation's clients.
- The local police and the fraud squad.
- Auditors from other organisations.

Each of these groups may require a different mode of communication and the auditor has to be flexible in meeting their expectations and at the same time satisfying the audit objective.

Transaction analysis
Here relationships are formed with staff who may be of a junior or senior grade or be part of one's peer group. The relationships consist of transactions between:

FIGURE 6.1 LEVELS OF RELATIONSHIPS

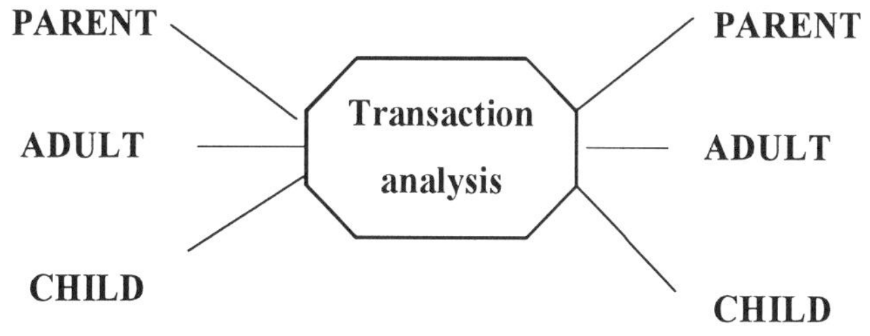

The most efficient working model is where the "adult" communicates with the "adult".

Emotional states (role playing)
Different people treat work in different ways and a major flaw in the human relations school of management theory is where employees do not see the work experience as a central life interest. It is possible to classify the emotional state of the employee under:

☐ **Withdrawal**. Where the employee feels unable to relate to work goals and so refuses to be committed to them. This can occur where the person feels frustrated by having their own views repressed by management. The result is that they minimise positive communications and become withdrawn.

☐ **Ritualistic**. Here the member of staff engages in an assortment of rituals that serve to confirm their position within the organisation. It may be that they are referred to by their surname or have a larger desk or office because of their grade or length of service. This is symbolised by having "the keys to the executive bathroom". The model of company car offered will tend to be related to seniority.

☐ **Pastimes**. This person sees work as an interesting pastime and may spend much time gossiping, securing favours and generally enjoying the social side of work. An auditor operating in this mode will typically work on never-ending fraud investigations following the audit nose and tracking down the perpetrators in a style reminiscent of that used in detective stories. Low productivity, long lunches and an extensive network of work friends and contacts are normally a feature of this approach.

☐ **Games**. Where the work culture is geared into excessive competition then a games culture may become the norm. This views one's success as dependent on another colleague's failure. Employees spend time catching each other out, gaining the upper hand and generally getting into favour with the power figures within the organisation. Many major decisions are made with the aim of scoring goals against colleagues. One's own goals may at times coincide with organisational objectives but they may also serve to sub-optimise performance. Over-reliance on one main performance indicator, e.g. ratio of recoverable to non-recoverable audit hours worked, may lead to managers distorting results and so playing games.

☐ **Work activity**. This emotional state may best serve the organisation in that it occurs where the individual is geared into work goals and has a clear well-defined purpose that he/she relates to. They are not easily side-tracked from these goals and the social aspects of working for an organisation assume second place to getting the job done in an efficient manner.

6.8 Dealing with People

There are certain obstacles that the internal auditor may come across when carrying out audit work, many of which relate to the behavioural aspects of work:

Traditional tick and check

Many auditors are seen as checkers who spend their time ticking thousands of documents and records. In this way management may treat the auditor as someone who has an extremely limited role that requires little skill and professionalism. At the extreme, managers may view audit staff with disdain and greet their presence with what can only be termed ridicule. This position can account for the strained atmosphere that many an auditor has faced when meeting with client managers at the outset of an audit. The perception that operational management is very busy doing important work while the auditor is simply checking some of the basic accounting data that relates to the area, can create a great imbalance. This sets the auditor at a disadvantage from day one of the audit. Where the auditor is only concerned with detailed testing programmes then this view is actually reinforced (see Figure 6.2).

FIGURE 6.2 THE IMPLICATIONS OF TRADITIONAL TICK AND CHECK

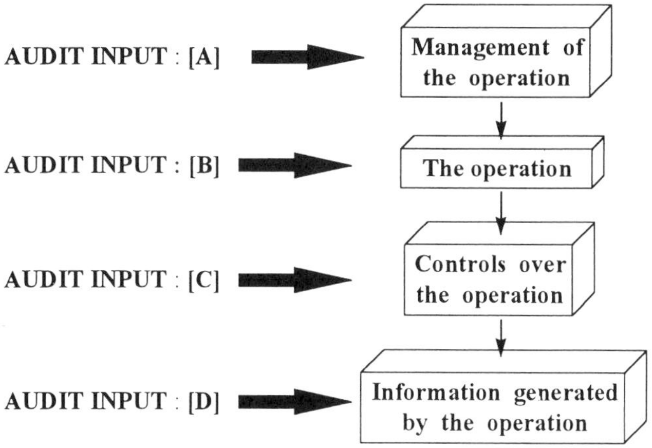

AUDIT INPUT : [A] ➡ Management of the operation

AUDIT INPUT : [B] ➡ The operation

AUDIT INPUT : [C] ➡ Controls over the operation

AUDIT INPUT : [D] ➡ Information generated by the operation

The auditor may aim to work at level [C] i.e. deal with controls over the operation and ensure that these are adequate and adhered to. Work geared towards the operation itself [B] will take the auditor to a higher level since an understanding of the operational processes provides the foundation for a better audit. The management techniques [A] applied by senior officers act as the ultimate control in any system. Work at this level will pay great dividends. [D] represents the lowest level of audit work and if this approach is adopted, then in contrast, it will reinforce the low esteem in which the auditor is held by management. Ticking and checking cannot justify the auditor's claim to professionalism.

The audit snoop

Line management and the various operatives may resent the audit as being mainly based on management's wishes to spy on them using audit staff for this unsavoury task. It is management's job to establish suitable controls over the areas that they are responsible for. This includes installing information systems that provide feedback on the way staff are performing so that corrective action may be taken whenever necessary. It is not acceptable for managers to simply ignore this responsibility and rely on the annual internal audit to obtain information on what their staff are doing. This is an incorrect interpretation of both management and audit's roles. The result is an arrangement whereby auditors are rightly seen as spies. Falling into this trap damages the audit reputation which if continued may become irretrievable. Where internal audit has not adopted this ill-conceived stance, then reliance may be given to staff at all levels in the area under review that audit are not acting as moles. The response in this case is to explain that audit reviews controls, not people; where people act as a control it is their role and not their behaviour that is being considered. This technique cannot be applied where we do in fact act as undercover agents for management.

Role of audit

There are audits that are undertaken and completed with a final report issued some time after the event that have little meaning to the operatives affected by the work. Many see internal audit as part of the internal control that is centred on extensive testing routines. Where the auditor cannot explain the precise audit objectives it may be seen more as a punishment than a constructive exercise to assist management. This creates a mystique surrounding the audit role that may be fostered by an uncommunicative internal auditor.

Interviewing

An audit interview may be a highly pressurised event for a more junior member of staff and if the auditor fails to recognise this, many barriers to communications may arise. The attitude of the auditor may be a crucial factor in determining whether the interview is successful or not. Audit objectives must be met but at the same time if the client's expectations are not satisfied (say in terms of clear explanations of the audit process) then the interviewee will be dissatisfied.

Audit committee

The relationship with the audit committee is a factor in the success of the audit function. The committee constitutes a principal audit client although the real support for audit comes from middle management who run the systems on a day-to-day basis. Bearing this in mind, the CIA will need to apply all his/her communications skills in forming a professional platform for the audit role.

Poor cousin of external audit

Where the internal auditors merely support the external audit function, the relationship may leave little scope for professional development. Any prospective CIA should establish the precise position before accepting a new appointment and ensure that the organisation is prepared to accept their interpretation of the auditors' terms of reference and scope of work.

Fear and hostility

Auditors who feel that hostile management has something to hide will perpetuate a cycle where they probe, management resists, they probe harder and so on. Fear and hostility may result from managers being unsure of the audit role and how it should be geared into their objectives and needs and it is here that the auditor may in fact have caused the poor relationships.

Advisor/inspector conflict

Problems will ensue where auditors are convinced that they are advisors whereas they are seen by management as only checkers. This results from a mismatch between words and deeds, where assurances are given to staff whilst at the same time searching for any errors that may be spotted no matter how unimportant. The resulting audit report will not be influential if this reflects an obsession with error-seeking.

Image problems

Internal audit departments can have a poor reputation. This will affect the type of contact that is had with other members of the organisation since one has to earn rather than demand respect. This can only be overcome if we adopt and apply professional standards and then seek to publicise this new-found image. There is some misunderstanding of the audit role and a need to improve overall image. Barriers to effective communications and problems when dealing with members of the organisation may result. An attempt was made some years ago to change the name of internal audit to reflect the growing professional base that is now developing although a suitable alternative was not forthcoming.

6.9 Audit Roles

We have noted the different groups that the auditor may be in contact with. Here we set out the different roles that the auditor may have to assume.

Staff training

Audit management should conduct in-house audit training courses and all audit staff should attend suitable courses in line with their individual developmental programmes. This type of relationship between tutor and students should be centred on the exchange of technical knowledge and the overall development of the internal audit function.

Public relations

Any client communication with a specific remit to develop the public relations aspect of internal auditing should be carefully managed. One trap is to groom an audit manager to do all the presentations and high-level meetings and ignore the rest of the audit staff who have to do the work that the public relations manager is promising the client. The public relations role should be assumed by all auditors as any contact with a member of the department will have a bearing on the audit image. This is an important concept that can change the audit style into a client based approach based on excellent communications skills. This leaves little room for the traditional auditor who greets all-comers with a cynical expression and a healthy mistrust of everyone inside and outside the organisation.

Marketing

Marketing is an extension of public relations where sufficient information is collected to form the basis of a marketing strategy. The auditor identifies client audit needs and whether these are being fully met by existing arrangements. This requires an open approach since clients will only give views on the audit service if they feel there would be no recriminations. One would search for concerns that the client may have and not assume problems are caused by the auditee.

Meeting management

Auditors may be at a disadvantage where they are asked to interview senior officers who have a comparatively high position within the organisation. There are times where the "parent-child" model may be assumed by management and the auditor will not be given all the information required to complete the audit. Audit policies should ensure that senior members of the audit department are available to handle certain types of meetings particularly at the start and close of the audit. Opening and wash up meetings are very important as the first one sets the scene for the coming audit while the wash up (or closing meeting) sets the tone of the draft audit report that will follow.

Crisis management

Senior members of the organisation may apply pressure on the auditors to respond to a constant stream of one-off matters that, although creating problems for individual managers, have little bearing on high-risk control issues facing the organisation. Audit management must weigh up the need to respond to management with the need to fulfil the audit plan agreed with the audit committee. The individual field auditor should be given formal guidance on this matter. It also impacts on the individual auditor as the original terms of reference for the work may be altered beyond all recognition as a response to management's concerns. The crucial ability to juggle the concepts of independence and client needs can only be acquired over time.

Staff appraisal
Audit management should appraise their staff and be appraised. Good appraisal schemes raise the level of motivation while poor schemes tend to de-motivate. All available skills in dealing with people will be called upon to administer successful staff appraisal schemes and in some organisations this is one of the biggest bones of contention.

Motivating staff
Management is charged with motivating staff and controls can be used to contribute to this function. The auditor must understand how controls affect operatives' lives and formulate their recommendations in line with this information. A control may be designed to promote efficiencies but if staff resent a recommended control, perhaps say a new signing-in form that tracks the movements of a particular document, then inefficiencies may actually result. It is necessary to go beyond the normal understanding of controls by appreciating staff motives and the way they affect efficiency levels and performance.

Obstructive management
There are times where management is being deliberately obstructive. The auditor will always hold the audit right of access although this should only be used where it is essential to do so. Audit management and the CIA should be brought into play where unreasonable barriers are placed in position by a manager. A formal meeting and referral to the managers' manager may at times be necessary as long as the CIA is satisfied that the auditor is not at fault. It is the case that impoverished managers may view the audit as a threatening instance of external scrutiny that will expose their incompetence. Incompetence means controls are ignored and must be reported by the auditor.

Strategic planning
This calls for agreement by management and the audit committee on the risk criterion used to assess which areas will be subject to audit attention. It determines the audit resources required and a formal strategy will result. It will require high-level liaison throughout the corporate components of the organisation and will probably be done by the CIA. The skills called for to discharge this role are based on a clear appreciation of the corporate direction of the organisation and how audit fits into this process. The most important thing to note is that this cannot be done from within an ivory tower; but must involve regular contact with the key decision makers.

Annual reporting
The annual audit report provides a forum for communicating audit performance and major control issues. This time the auditor (i.e. the CIA) will assume the role of the manager of an operation being reviewed (by the Audit Committee) via the annual report. In this way the CIA not only reports on the organisation but also reports on his/her operations and performance.

Audit review

Audit managers will review the work of their staff and here a constructive role should be assumed as well as the need to identify any poor performance by the auditor. It brings into play pure management skills of judging staff's work, correcting problems, discussing changes and encouraging high standards. This is not an easy task.

Technical aspects of audit work

The auditor may assume a technical expert role when addressing complicated areas such as computerised applications, production works, capital contracts and compliance with legislation. The key here is not to pretend or promise to deliver more than is possible. If the auditor remembers that auditors are mainly experts in control then they may communicate on an equal level with technical staff throughout the organisation. This is a major task, particularly when convincing junior auditors that they are not competing with the experts, i.e. operational staff.

An example will illustrate this:

> *A systems accountant had previous experience of the company's payroll systems. He was promoted and moved to internal audit as a senior auditor. The first task was to assist a more senior auditor who was reporting on the payroll system. He found this straightforward with years of experience of this system. After this audit he was asked to review a complicated investments system and made several complaints to the audit manager, suggesting that he could not be proficient in this work area. Despite many talks with the audit manager, he failed to understand the basic audit concept of mastering controls and not operations. After several months, he was transferred out of internal audit.*

The way the audit role is discharged and the way inter-organisational relationships are dealt with will in part be determined by the type of organisation and the culture that predominates. We would hope that a team-building approach reigns supreme where discussion, commitment and excellence are the applied buzzwords. Audit will then assume a similar brief. If this is not so and a management-by-fear policy is in place, then we will spend less time explaining the need for good controls and more time exposing management failings.

6.10 Role Theory

One interesting way of analysing the behavioural aspects of internal audit is found in role theory. Here the images projected to the person that we are dealing with are derived from three main factors:

FIGURE 6.3 DEALING WITH PEOPLE

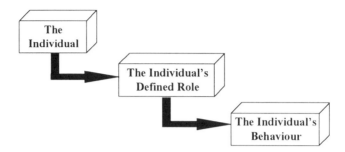

The internal audit role affects behaviour at work and the audit style adopted is important. The auditor's behaviour will be interpreted within the context of the auditor's perceived role. The client may see this role as one of a detailed checker who will make sure all incorrectly processed transactions are isolated through the "audit". This will then affect the entire interface between the client and the auditor. It will be hard to resist the temptation to assume this role and so meet the client's expectation. This poses no major problem for management consultants although it creates difficulties for the internal auditor as we shall see later on. Where there is a divergence between the two sides' understanding of these roles, then there will be some conflict and this will either be resolved through discussion or it will interfere with the ensuing communications.

6.11 A Model of Audit Styles

Participation involves forming a partnership with management where audit provides professional advice to assist managers in their search for better systems of internal control. This contrasts with the traditional audit approach that concentrates on uncovering errors and breach of procedure. The extreme version of participation occurs where the auditor and auditee carry out the review together as the audit progresses, and issue joint reports with the contents and recommendations agreed together. There are some related areas that should be considered:

☐ **Mintz (1972) research**. We have discussed how different styles of auditing affected the auditee and concluded that the participative style had a more positive impact than the traditional approach. Where managers are responsible for their systems of control, the audit role will become one of assisting them in discharging the requirements of these responsibilities. One might visualise the auditor providing oral presentations on matters such as formalising procedures, controls (such as authorisation, division of duties, documentation etc.), and the use of information in promoting control. This builds on the theory that argues that managers perform well when encouraged by audit (in terms of control issues), and that part of audit's role is to encourage and support management.

☐ **Likert management styles**. This is taken from management theory and develops styles of management that are used in different circumstances. Participative auditing builds on the approach that involves management by bringing them into the objectives of the actual audit itself. A mode of working that involves explanation, discussion and persuasion can be used when managers are open and enlightened. Using this approach, one might argue that different styles are required where a manager is openly adversarial to the auditors. In the extreme one may appear to be manipulative where various changes in style are applied in response to managers' reactions, as opposed to adopting a consistent manner. It is perhaps better to set basic professional standards in the way relationships are established and maintained, and then keep to these standards.

☐ **Agree objectives with client**. When the objectives are agreed with the client this may engender a feeling of commitment from management. It is important that the terms of reference and scope reflect what has been agreed and that changes will be made if necessary. This process can be extended by not formulating the terms until management have aired their views on the basis that it is their audit that is being performed. Getting full support from the outset can help cement relationships even where a manager has no wish to add to the terms being proposed by audit. The process of discussing the objectives of the audit can be used as a means of explaining the audit role without giving a lecture.

☐ **Seek advice from the client**. The participative style means that the auditor need not solve all control questions but tries to get management to contribute in this process. In fact one may set out identified problems in front of the client and then work together on a suitable solution. For example where the auditor feels that too much authority is vested in one person with little or no segregation, this point may be posed as a management problem. The auditor may seek ideas from management on ways that this problem may be overcome. It is not seen as an audit problem but a key managerial control issue that may be resolved in a number of ways.

☐ **Discuss the findings**. This is a fundamental part of the participative approach where the matters contained in the working papers are put in front of operational managers for initial reaction. This is far removed from the auditor who jealously saves up findings for the final report. Again with the participative approach, the idea is to share recommendations so that they are not reported as "audit's" or "management's" as such, but as a joint endeavour. The audit presence promotes better control by generally encouraging and educating in the importance and application of good controls. The findings become part of this process, not in terms of things done wrong by managers, but more to reveal the extent to which action needs to be taken. Findings are not seen as a battle ground to be dealt with at a confrontational meeting between the auditor and client. They almost become conversation pieces where the implications and solutions are debated in a brainstorming mode.

☐ **Shared views**. The whole report should reflect the shared views of the client and auditor as they together agree the contents of the report. This stage cannot be reached where there has been no communication between auditor and client during the course of the audit work. Sharing must occur throughout the fieldwork if it is to have real meaning. Joint working entails a change whereby the auditor actively seeks the views of the auditee in a joint problem-solving mode. Here the audit role may simply be to pose the problem and discuss ideas that line management may have in seeking improvement and/or solutions. The auditor will probe these ideas and decide whether an identified control deficiency has been resolved. Where this happens one may argue that the report then reflects this sharing of ideas and the actual wording applied in the draft will be readily agreed if it is derived from this process. Communication becomes the key to this type of arrangement:

> *An auditor was in the middle of an audit of an important general income system. On reviewing the findings that had been secured so far he began to deliberate on a specific problem concerning the way the computer was being used to account for this income. He decided to call the general income manager and discussed his concern that there was no one reviewing the daily logs generated by the computer. The general income manager agreed that this was a problem and admitted that he had never considered this issue before. On visiting the manager later the same day the auditor discussed the matter and asked that it be considered so that any suggested solutions could be reviewed when the audit was nearing completion. The manager was happy to provide this input and subsequently redefined the role of the systems administrator to reflect a greater control orientation.*

☐ **Interim reports**. Regular progress reports and draft findings are a feature of the participative approach as the audit is built up over time. The old fashioned routine where the draft report appears almost "out of the blue" turns the audit into a mystical process that the typical manager finds difficult to understand. Reports that are produced many weeks after the audit fieldwork has been completed will tend to be perceived as the auditor's report as opposed to a document that is primarily for the use of the client. When interim reports are developed as the audit progresses, they act as a device to keep the client up-to-date. In line with the fast changing pace of managing a business most managers would expect a weekly update on any work that affects their area of concern and it is not unreasonable for this policy to apply to the auditor. Notwithstanding the strategic planning process that will require a consideration of future influences, managers are mainly concerned with what is in front of their face on a day-to-day basis. The participative approach depends on close contact with the client. This is aided by keeping the audit in front of the managers on a daily/weekly basis. The format of interim reports may be regular meetings with management based around a formal report that sets the findings to date and outstanding work. Participation comes to the fore where the auditor works with management and does not feel the need to be isolated during his/her work before producing the report. The scenario where management knows exactly what has been completed each week is a fundamental component of the sharing process where secrets are revealed to each side via interim reports.

☐ **Errors are symptoms of weak controls**. The whole thrust of this approach is one of partnership and joint problem-solving with management. To this end, errors are not assigned to a defined individual (or postholder) since this will promote blame assignment. Instead, errors are seen as symptoms of weak controls and are presented to aid the search for effective solutions. Although we would seek to consider the cause and effect relationship that underpins systems weaknesses, the main preoccupation is with finding remedies to enhance control. An example of this position follows:

> *During a meeting between the auditor and management to discuss a draft audit report issued several days ago, there was debate over the findings. Management was worried about the way these were expressed and felt that they formed a criticism of their performance. The audit manager explained it was the recommendations that were more important to discuss and that adverse findings simply provided a clear impetus to seek improvements to controls. A more positive mode was assumed as the emphasis turned to the various changes recommended.*

☐ **Constructive appraisals**. The formal definition of internal audit contains the concepts of an appraisal activity whilst the participative approach requires that this be constructive. In this way blanket criticism is not seen to have a major role in the audit world. The principle of constructive criticism requires a sophisticated level of understanding the needs and problems faced by managers as they seek to achieve organisational objectives. It is a move away from a simplistic view of whether they have or have not installed a control mechanism but seeks to appreciate why there may be room for improved controls. The standard audit comment that "management has failed to establish formally documented procedures" is almost a throwaway audit finding. What would make more sense to management are constructive comments in the vein of "since the procedures manual was produced in 19xx there have been many changes that mean that the manual is now out-of-date. The lack of resources to maintain the manual is cause for some concern and this may be addressed by measures xyz…" The key is to support management as far as possible by taking a reasonable view of their efforts and any constraints that they might face.

☐ **Teamwork approach**. The essence of the participative approach is the idea that audit and management function as a team working together as one. This is far removed from the traditional audit approach that stresses the task of checking on management. This is not really consultancy since we are providing advice wherever possible and also bringing management into the process of seeking solutions to control problems. Teamwork involves people working together to an agreed goal, in this case based around the audit findings.

The participative approach brings audit closer to a consultancy role where management needs are foremost. Many audit departments have moved along this route and the explanatory models suggest that a continuum may be designed where one may move further along the direction of participation. It must however be noted that the more participation that is promoted, the greater the strain in maintaining a satisfactory level of independence. As such there will be limits on how far one might go. It is possible to use an established model of audit styles ranging from a traditional through to a participative style.

There is a continuum for each of the components of this established model as follows:

TABLE 6.4 TRADITIONAL VERSUS PARTICIPATIVE STYLES

FACTOR	TRADITIONAL STYLE	PARTICIPATIVE STYLE
ROLE	Policeman	Advisor
AUTHORITY	Formal	Informal
SOURCE OF AUTHORITY	Office	Personal attributes
SANCTION	Coercion	Suggestion

These are two extremes which might on the one hand mean that an audit function is imposed on management to police the organisation. Alternatively, the audit service may be more like a partnership with audit providing professional advice in line with management's needs. Clearly modern internal auditing is moving towards the partnership role with management as it does not report to itself, or work towards its own mysterious goals.

6.12 Understanding and Participating with Management

Where an auditor understands management and the management process it is easier to work in a partnership mode. It is possible to note some interesting areas:

Accounting staff
Accounting staff are more used to working with formal controls and auditors, whereas operational staff may feel that the audit process is more of an intrusion. We are suggesting that internal audit will move far outside the limited world of financial systems and tackle any and everything that is important to the organisation. While this sounds simple in theory, it does create many knock-on implications in terms of the effect this might have. Non-financial staff and managers may well find this uncomfortable, particularly where their only experience of an audit presence outside the finance department is where a fraud or breach of procedure is being investigated. This issue will need to be confronted and bridges built before any effective work may be carried out.

Basic planning
Basic planning is a fundamental part of control and crisis management tends to be much more difficult to control in a systematic fashion. Before ascertaining what management do in terms of achieving their business objectives, it is well to go one step back and ask what they plan to do. The planning task provides a framework against which the actual results may be measured and it is here that the role of planning as a major control comes to the fore. Managers who are consistently deep in crisis tend to make great demands on audit services as problems mount up. The provision of these consultancy-type projects makes it more difficult to subsequently review the systems particularly where there are major

weaknesses. In this scenario, trying to meet management's needs does not sit well with the task of reviewing the management process.

Budgetary control

Budgetary control is an important management control which also has human behavioural implications. This is because success tends to raise performance while failure has a tendency to breed further failures. Again the "people angle" of any control must be fully appreciated since it is little use recommending tighter budgets if this in fact de-motivates staff and so impairs performance. As with all controls, it has to be implemented in a reasonable fashion having due regard to all the relevant factors, some quantifiable and others not so readily apparent.

Management style

An auditor may find that management is applying a participative style where staff are treated as mature adults who want to perform. Alternatively, the style may be more akin to an authoritative approach involving management by fear. As well as affecting the overall performance this factor will also impact on the type of control systems in place in terms of fitting the defined culture. It is important that this factor is catered for during the audit process since it cannot simply be ignored. This can be difficult as culture is less tangible a product since it attaches to a whole body of people as opposed to one individual. It is still a significant component of the overall system of control and must be seen as such by the auditor.

Advantages of participation

The auditor should recognise the culture that exists in the area being audited and ensure that audit recommendations are framed in a way that fits into management's needs. Participative auditing means working with management rather than auditing them. This is in line with the view that controls belong to management and they should be encouraged to maintain and improve them. There is great scope in participative auditing and it has several positive features that can be summarised:

1. It involves management in the auditing process as part of the team rather than using audit as a management spy. It is essential that the initial terms of reference and approach are discussed with management at the outset as this will set the tone for the resultant audit.

2. It is not merely a question of being nice to the client as it has a more dynamic element that involves some flexibility on both sides. Artificial pleasantries are a far cry from working closely with a client in a problem-solving fashion.

3. It can be more interesting in that it is not geared into error discovery and the audit findings are placed into perspective according to a clear prioritisation process. The aim is not to report what was done wrong but more to report ways that management may better control their scarce resources.

4. It can be more demanding where many complicated issues have to be built into the work and the auditor will have to decide how far to alter draft reports to reflect management's views. The great audit preserve, the audit report, is no longer sacred and bearing in mind that a report is simply a device for securing improvement, this should not pose a major problem.

5. The results are discussed and agreed as the audit proceeds with regular interim reports and management may actually assist in developing proposed solutions. It is possible to

present a record of control weakness to management at a wash-up meeting and work with them in completing the remainder, i.e. the necessary recommendations. This then becomes a true partnership with all sides having a major input.

6. Managers are able to share their problems. It is also advisable to review the reports with lower levels of management. Working with the operational manager who is most in touch with the areas in question can be most rewarding. This is the person who will have to build on the recommendations that result from the audit. The participative style is designed to help develop the positive working relationships that would underpin such an approach.

7. It can engender more commitment all round. Discussing the audit as it progresses brings all parties into the debate and if carefully managed, can make everyone look forward to the resultant report.

8. The auditor is able to address major issues. It is only by becoming involved in management's control problems that one is able to deal with high level concerns. This process will bring a realism into the audit that allows the auditor access to the real problems, i.e. the important issues which in turn will raise the entire profile of the audit process.

9. It promotes good co-operation between audit and management that can be used to build a client base across the organisation. This in turn will engender a degree of support for the audit function that may be called on in times when central/support services are under financial constraints. The process of outsourcing (i.e. contracting out audit and other professional white collar services) may also be confronted knowing that there is a committed level of support within the organisation.

Disadvantages of participation

There are drawbacks particularly where the extent of participation with management is taken to the extreme:

1. There is a long consultation process in discussing and agreeing each stage of the audit. This slows down the fieldwork and means that managers must be taken along each part of the audit and if they are absent, one might not be sure whether to push ahead or wait. An auditor is never happier than when sifting through a set of files at leisure, that has been left by the line manager while he is away on holiday. With the participative style this should not be the case as most of the time should ideally be spent with the manager as problems are discussed and resolved.

2. It may not be cost-efficient particularly where audits have narrow terms of reference say to check that a budget has been properly administered. To avoid confusion one should have fully discussed terms of reference. This however is not the final answer as the audit process must have some in-built flexibility that allows the client to have additional concerns tackled so long as they fit with the audit in hand. Reference must be made to the audit manager if extra work is being taken on.

3. One cannot force participation onto management and they may resist becoming involved through lack of interest in the audit product or previous bad experiences with internal auditors. This is an unfortunate fact of life as not all staff will be converted to the audit view.

4. There may be some trade union resistance where auditors are seen to be siding with management. If we make a clear commitment to listen to all sides of an operation, this may mean unions asking to be in on the audit as it may affect their members' working

conditions. Whilst this is not wholly unreasonable, it may act as a restriction on the auditor as he/she tries to be fair to all sides.

5. There must be limits placed on participation or audit will assume a pure consultancy role with little or no independence. It is not possible simply to do what managers want audit to do. There has to be some regard to the best interests of the organisation in terms of assessing the adequacy of the systems of control and the implications of significant control weaknesses. Remember internal audit works for the organisation and not only individual managers. The audit committee concept is based on lifting the audit reporting line above management to the body that represents the entire organisation.

6. Some argue that internal audit thrives on an amount of tension between management and it is this that drives the auditor on. Others are very concerned with giving up too much independence and find it convenient to maintain a more traditional approach. Whatever the adopted formula it is important that the significant issues are understood, discussed and a view then taken on what might be the most appropriate model of audit services.

Self audit

This epitomises the participative approach by suggesting that management should perform its own audits. The standard model that argues that managers are responsible for installing and maintaining systems of internal control is extended. Management is asked to undertake a comprehensive review of their controls to assess adequacy and extent of compliance. They are said to be auditing their systems, with advice and support from their auditors.

The two models are:

FIGURE 6.4 STANDARD CONTROL SYSTEMS CYCLE

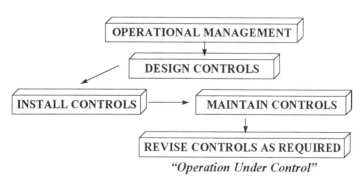

"Operation Under Control"

FIGURE 6.5. THE SELF AUDIT CONTROL SYSTEM MODEL

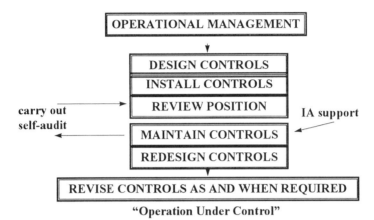

"Operation Under Control"

Control self assessment

The IIA.UK's professional briefing note number seven (1995) provides guidance on the growing trend towards assisting management in their responsibilities for sound systems of internal control:

> *"A control self assessment programme is a process which allows individual line managers and staff to participate in reviewing existing controls for adequacy (both now and in the predicted future) and recommending, agreeing and implementing improvements (modification, addition or elimination) to existing controls."*

The professional briefing note covers details of the control self assessment programme, its benefits and the internal audit role. One key point is that management should manage the programme and drive it forward. Internal audit on the other hand should advise and report on its design and operation. Internal audit is likely to be involved during the early stage, because of the nature of the programme. The final point made is that:

> *"It is a supplement to, not an alternative to, an independent appraisal activity such as internal audit."*

6.13 The Expectation Gap

External auditors are increasingly concerned about the expectation gap and this has received much press comment. For the external auditor there is little relief from the pressure to resolve this problem. This creates a perception that they should have a greater role in locating frauds and helping to sort out companies that are going wrong, despite the apparent healthy state of their financial statements. Internal auditors have a different problem in that we are able to adapt our role depending on what the organisation requires. This could involve a flexible interpretation of professional standards but so long as we retain some audit work, many additional services may also be provided. It is the extent of these additional services and whether they interfere with an ability to provide an internal audit of the organisation that is crucial. Client expectations of internal audit services typically consist of:

1. A check on remote establishments to ensure that they are complying with procedures.
2. The investigation of frauds where they have been detected within the organisation.
3. Investigations into employees who cause concern to management in terms of breaching procedure.
4. A continuous programme of checks over the output from various financial systems to assess whether these are correct.
5. On-the-spot advice as to whether proposed management decisions are acceptable in terms of compliance with procedure and best practice.
6. Ad-hoc investigations requested by members of the corporate management team.
7. Additional resources for computer system development projects.

The above creates a major problem for internal audit in that on the one hand, we have to market audit services and as such define what the client wants. On the other hand, we have to retain the right to provide a professional audit service which means essentially advising on systems of internal control as a result of an agreed programme of audits. If we fail to respond to management expectations then this will put us at risk in the long term while if we carry out the above work, this turns us into management consultants. The rules to be applied to managing this situation may be set out as:

1. Isolate two ranges of clients. The audit committee who will be the client for audit work (systems auditing), and managers who can receive additional consultancy services.
2. Make sure the audit committee understands the concept of planned systems audits and that a basic block of resources must be reserved for this task.
3. Provide consultancy as additional services that are clearly distinguished from audit work. Ensure that management understands that they are responsible for compliance, information systems, fraud investigations and achieving value for money.
4. Publicise the audit role through suitable brochures, presentations and correspondence.
5. Encourage managers to take a long-term view in promoting sound controls and so avoid the many problems that are derived from poor arrangements. This is a long process but is assisted by oral presentations in control that audit may provide to management.

If there is a situation where audit and consultancy services conflict in any respect, then ensure that the audit role reigns supreme. This is highly likely if the following (broken) cycle is observed:

FIGURE 6.6 THE CONTROL BREAKDOWN CYCLE

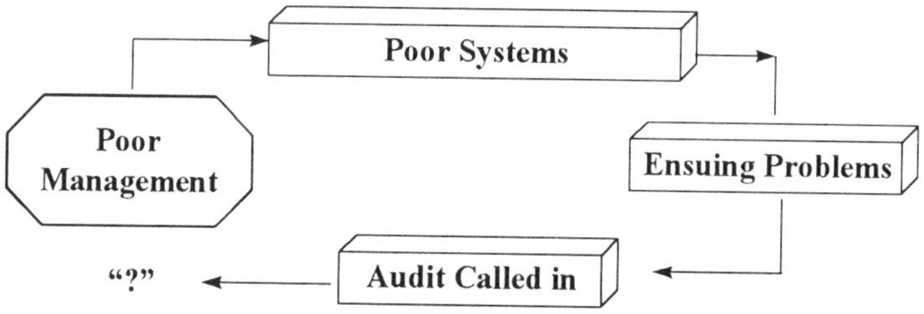

The correct answer to the above scenario is that audit should seek to close the gap in controls that is caused by management's failure to establish sound controls. Chasing the results of control weaknesses (i.e. frauds, errors, poor performance etc.) is in fact a poor use of audit resources. The worst scenario is where management purposely direct audit at fire-chasing so that the auditor has no time to locate the source of the problems (i.e. management themselves). We may restate that reconciling these two issues is no easy task and involves:

- Keeping consultancy and audit services separate so that investigatory work done as a response to management's direct requests does not interfere with the ability to deliver planned systems reviews.
- Making it clear at the outset that information from consultancy can and will be used in later systems work if there is a relationship.
- Making it clear at the outset that any breach of procedure identified during a consultancy project will be followed up and reported on separately.
- Where management has failed to install adequate controls and this is established via a consultancy project, this feature will also form part of the findings.

6.14 Managing Negotiation Skills

As part of the behavioural aspects of auditing it is as well to mention negotiations skills. In the 1989 research paper produced by the IIA.Inc "Persuasions and Negotiation Skills for Internal Auditors", Jim King considers that there are three main stages to the negotiation process:

1. **Conflict** - Where one side feels that the discussion is unbalanced.
2. **Goals** - Where the sides have different positions.
3. **Solutions** - Where a search for some compromise is made.

The idea is to view the process of getting audit work done, findings accepted and recommendations agreed, as one of constant negotiation. Superimposed on this is the great potential for role conflict that is inherent in the audit role. We return once again to the need for effective inter-personal skills. Points relating to negotiations and the auditor may be touched upon:

Time

Busy managers find it difficult to assign time (and their staff's time) to deal with the auditor. Arrangements will have to be agreed to suit all sides and it is here that negotiation skills will come to the fore. The approach will have to be that audit will minimise interference with the work staff are performing and limit the time they spend away from their work. It is not good practice to abandon the audit since the current trend is for systems to be constantly under development and change. Audit must work within this environment and time and time again the auditor will start a meeting by being told that the manager only has a short time available, only to be discussing key issues several hours later. When a manager indicates that there are problems allocating time for the audit, what he/she really means is that there is little point spending resources in areas that have little or no return. Employing professional auditors who are asked to work to formal standards is one way of avoiding this. All managers encourage developments that help them achieve their goals and if audit have assumed this reputation then it will not be difficult to get co-operation from managers and their staff.

Terms of reference

The opening terms of reference for the audit are always a difficult matter as each side feels the other out. There is always an element of suspicion from the client which itself is located in the whole issue of change management. The auditor must recognise the two main worries of the client:

- That the auditor may wish to recommend changes that will adversely affect the manager's position.
- That the auditor may in fact be investigating him, the operating manager.

Audit approach

The audit approach and general attitude will have an impact on the resulting negotiations. It is generally accepted that negotiation is about compromise and securing benefits for all sides in contrast to a win-lose stance. There are auditors who feel that they work for a supreme force and must not back down to anyone. This is one reason why audit suffers a poor image as enforcers, although it is entirely the CIA's fault if audit staff are behaving in this fashion.

Bottom line

One view of internal audit sees it as a function that seeks to leave the operation in a better position than it was before the audit. This does not mean that every detailed recommendation must be immediately implemented by management. It is based more on the view that management should be consulted and where essential, they will take on board recommendations although open to negotiation. It requires the auditor to negotiate recommendations and differentiate between those that are essential, important and merely useful. Using this approach, a little may be given up for the sake of progress in other areas.

Negotiation skills

Negotiation skills can be managed by applying the following rules:

1. Provide proper training in negotiation skills either in-house or via external programmes that help develop a suitable skills base in this topic. In this way we would hope to spread this expertise across the section rather than rely on one or two auditors who are able to represent the service on difficult issues. Where it is accepted policy that all audit staff have a base level of such skills there is more scope to move towards a professional service.

2. Include negotiation skills as one of the personal skills that are assessed via the performance appraisal scheme and built into the auditor's job description. Here we would seek to test the extent to which staff have acquired and are using this approach to their work. This recognises the requirement that audit staff possess a rounded level of skills which include not only technical competence but also an ability to work with management whilst still retaining the audit perspective. Negotiation is a matter of balance and not simply agreeing with the client. Good communication skills and a determination to pursue control issues must be tempered with a clear view of the audit objective.

3. Include a section on negotiation skills in the audit manual that sets standards on this matter. It will start by stating that the auditor should not subordinate his/her judgement to that of another. It will go on to state that the auditor will maintain high standards of conduct even where there is disagreement with management over a particular view. There will be material on for example, giving up minor points, redrafting points in

reports on management's requests, dealing with difficult people, referring matters to audit management, and the all-important "wash-up" meeting where audit findings are discussed before the draft report is issued.

4. Ensure that the audit review process includes a consideration of how well the auditor had negotiated throughout the course of the audit. So for example where the review process finds that files were not made available to the auditor, the audit manager must find out what action was taken, as a result. Where audit findings have been suppressed at the behest of management, this factor must also be subject to close review and consideration.

5. Encourage auditors to use their initiative and make clear decisions when dealing with management. The fully fledged auditor will have mastered many skills and the ability to make decisions without reference to audit managers is a great asset to the audit service. Negotiation cannot occur without decisions being made as the proceedings progress. This then requires a level of maturity that enables sound judgement to be applied within the context of the discussions at hand. Management appreciates being able to discuss findings with people who can provide instant feedback. It has been said by many that one must allow mistakes if any real progress is to be made in developing staff and this applies equally to auditors.

6.15 The Link into Marketing

Marketing involves defining and then meeting client needs. Is this the case for audit services? To answer this question we need to consider the following process:

FIGURE 6.7 MARKETING AUDIT SERVICES

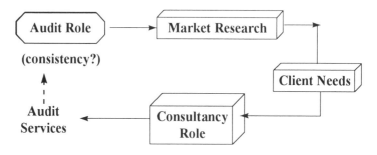

This model would be perfect for most business units that exist primarily to meet a client's need. There is a nagging question mark near the top left hand box that asks whether the type of services required by management is entirely consistent with the audit role. If not then we either:

1. Fail to meet clients' needs or,
2. We must alter the audit role.

Each of these solutions goes on to provide further problems for the audit service that may eventually impair its efficiency and effectiveness.

One response to solving this problem is:

FIGURE 6.8 MARKETING CONSULTANCY SERVICES

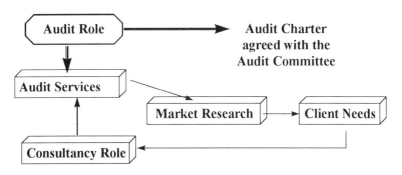

The refinement to the original model means that we are now able to provide a consultancy based service which can consist of any tasks/projects the client requires. This is in addition to our main line audit role that necessarily requires us to:

1. Define the audit field.
2. Assess the relative risk of each "audit unit".
3. Draft a plan aimed at these high risk areas.
4. Seek approval from the audit committee.
5. Resource and implement this plan of audits that involves assessing the adequacy and effectiveness of systems of control in each material audit unit.
6. Report the results to management and the audit committee.

6.16 Managing the Delinquent Manager

Much has been said about the need to feed the audit process into management needs and this is the only way for effective audit. This is because the business objectives are the paramount factors that drive the system and the subsequent systems' controls. Two other issues are: what to do about delinquent managers, and what to do in a corrupt organisation. Delinquent managers may be defined as senior officers who are working to objectives that are inconsistent with organisational objectives. As they achieve their objectives, the welfare of the organisation is impaired. There is little scope to discuss participative auditing and linking into managerial objectives. The difficulty comes in clearly identifying such people and either missing them or at the other extreme, assuming all managers fall into this category. If it is clear that a manager is acting in this way, the auditor must assume a reporting line with a more senior officer who is removed from this problem. The delinquent manager will seek to hinder the audit and get it aborted as a challenge to his/her position in the organisation. The question of manager's needs does not arise as the auditor must rise above the operation and politics that will certainly confront him/her. The auditor will be alerted and should carry out more detailed work into problem areas and report them to the most appropriate level of management. Where an entire organisation is essentially corrupt, a whole new set of problems will arise (see chapter 29). Returning to the lesser problem of the one-off delinquent manager, the following may be noted:

1. This problem must be discussed with the audit manager and an agreed departure from the participative approach will be required. The CIA should be kept informed.
2. The delinquent manager may operate a system of control that does not actually promote control so as to get around performance measures. This may typically include:
   - A lack of formal procedures.
   - An in-crowd of co-conspirators.
   - Not being available to the auditor.
   - No clear accountability.
   - Regular breaches of the corporate control systems such as the organisation's revenue budgetary setting process or ordering procedures etc.
   - A failure to respond to previous audit reports.

It may be possible to take disciplinary action against the officer in question particularly where breach of procedure has occurred. This factor should be discussed with senior management.

6.17 What of Independence?

We have highlighted the need to seek management support and apply high level inter-personal skills. These skills do not come easily and there are auditors who stubbornly stick to the old fashioned regime of viewing all employees as the enemy whose activities must be exposed (audited). This type of auditor will exhibit the following characteristics:

1. Almost non-existent communication with the auditee at operational level. The auditor appears almost as a spy, drifting into the relevant section, asking a series of blunt questions and then double-checking everything that he/she has been told. The auditor will restrict contact with operational staff unless absolutely necessary. It is almost as if the audit view will be tainted by anything that is disclosed by operational staff outside of formal interviews with the auditor.
2. Slightly more respect for senior management. This type of auditor quickly takes sides where senior management reflects the view that all their problems are caused by their staff. The audit becomes more of a check on the workers than anything else. There is no consideration of the principle that management is wholly responsible for the areas and staff under their control.
3. A view that all employees are guilty until proven innocent. Here one will look for non-compliance as the norm, based on the fact that most staff are not interested in their work at all. Taken to the extreme this results in a burning desire to identify wrongdoing whenever an audit is being conducted on the basis that this is the real audit role.
4. An intense resistance to discussing audit findings before they appear in a draft report for consultation. This auditor reports and runs. The report comes as a complete surprise to management as the findings have never been discussed or revealed. Communication is carried out through formal memoranda between auditor and client where points are raised and responded to.

This person achieved a basic distance from managers and operational staff that allowed him/her to act almost as an external review agency. The material on independence makes it clear that performing low level audits with no appreciation of business objectives militates against effective levels of independence in its wider sense. The question that arises relates to the difficult task of working amongst and with management, whilst still retaining some objectivity. There must be a limit on the extent to which we may co-operate with management since this impacts on the degree of objectivity. The more professional the manager, the less of a problem this poses as trained managers recognise the importance of sound systems of control and their responsibilities therein. Less able staff may not accept this principle particularly where systems are weak and performance therefore suffers. We have already described the way in which consultancy work may be resourced and kept away from main-line audit work. We have illustrated how the audit committee may be used for support. Pointers to secure an adequate level of independence while still promoting a participative approach are:

1. The audit charter agreed with the audit committee should be based on best professional practice including the provision for audit independence. The CIA should ensure that this is not interfered with so as to be unrecognisable and that the ensuing audit work follows the standards as defined via the charter. Working relations with management will be described as all-important but put within the context of delivering an effective audit service to the organisation.

2. The audit planning process should start with a clear risk assessment model (risk criteria) which should be agreed with the audit committee. The rest of the process of isolating the material for the audit plan should flow automatically from this. Once the planning mechanism has been agreed then the remainder of the process of formulating the content of audit work should fall entirely into the hands of the CIA. No one should be able to interfere with these plans. One will still have due regard for requests made by managers. The risk index should incorporate managers' requests as a relevant factor that determines the level of risk. In this way we would argue that the audit plan is sacrosanct since it is developed from an agreed process for isolating high-risk high-priority areas.

3. When discussing the terms of reference for the audit with the line manager, the key control objectives should form the basis for this discussion (MIS, compliance, safeguarding assets and VFM). Managerial problems should fit into one of these categories or they will have to form the basis of a separate consultancy project.

4. The regular discussions that should occur throughout the audit process should be based around the progress made to date. It should be made clear to the client that he/she should not seek to alter the original terms of reference beyond recognition by loading the project with one-off management problems that arise from time to time. Again additional consultancy work may be commissioned.

5. While the draft audit report should go only to the line manager for detailed consideration, the final cleared report may if necessary also be copied to members of the audit committee. This will act as an additional safety valve if there is any attempted blockage by management.

6. The audit manager should be readily available to address concerns the auditor may experience during the course of the audit. Although a participative approach involves working closely with management, any matters that impinge upon the auditor's independence should be dealt with quickly by the CIA. This control driven by the CIA should be firmly in place at all times.

6.18 Conclusions

The behavioural aspects of internal auditing have been widely researched and it is clear that audit management needs to decide on which policies and procedures to promote based on the available options. Being nice is not enough and the audit department needs to identify management's control needs, explain how it can assist in solving control weaknesses and take management with it through the whole audit process. This must be done so that positive working relationships are established and maintained while at the same time preserving professional independence necessary to carry out good audit work. This is no easy task and requires commitment, training and practice. The auditor must recognise the importance and potential problems that one may encounter when dealing with people. The success of the individual audits and the whole audit role may depend on how this is managed. The organisation and the auditor's own style will affect relationships and a team approach is helpful but can lead to becoming akin to a management consultancy service. The auditor must manage these relationships very carefully and apply professional skills and diplomacy in all circumstances. Auditors have great powers and may be misunderstood, although this will be partly the fault of the CIA if they operate under a cloud of mystery.

CHAPTER SEVEN

AUDIT COMMITTEES

7.1 Introduction
The topic of audit committees has an interesting background:

CIPFA
The Chartered Institute of Public Finance and Accountancy (CIPFA) has issued a statement on audit committees and concludes that they are very useful in the public sector. It suggests that local authorities do not require them, since they have their own version by reporting to the Finance (or Policy and Resources) Committee. In contrast their use is encouraged by central government.

The Treadway Committee
In the USA it is felt that audit committees help deter fraud and they are mandatory for companies quoted on the New York Stock Exchange. Treadway said that "The mere existence of an audit committee is not enough. The audit committee must be vigilant, informed, diligent and probing."

The Canadian experience
They are mandatory in Canada where a study carried out in 1993 concluded that "an audit committee can make a major contribution towards improving the quality of financial reports".

The IIA
The Institute of Internal Auditors (IIA) issued a position statement on audit committees and recommends them for quoted companies. They feel that the audit committee should be encouraged in government and the voluntary sector.

UK listed companies
The Cadbury report on corporate governance (1993) sets out a non-mandatory code of practice that requires an audit committee for all companies listed on the London Stock Exchange. Cadbury argues that the committee should be made up of at least three non-executive directors as a subcommittee of the main board.

7.2 The Role of the Audit Committees
The usual role of the audit committees may be summarised as follows:
- To consider the finances and expenditure of the organisation.
- To review the audit process, both external and internal and receive reports that impact on the welfare of the organisation.
- To consider the annual accounts and the external audit report that attaches to these accounts.

- To consider the adequacy of systems of internal controls. The current move to require directors to report on their systems of internal control means that this is starting to assume a higher profile.
- Involvement in the appointment of the external and internal auditors.

Audit committees are popular in the USA and although they tend to be concerned mainly with external audit, the more mature ones also turn their attention to internal audit. The IIA feels that their role in respect of the internal audit function should be to:
- Help co-ordinate external and internal audit efforts.
- Evaluate internal audit annually and consider the annual audit plans and reports.
- Approve the internal audit charter.
- Meet privately with the CIA.

7.3 The Audit Committee's Constitution

In the private sector the idea is that non-executive directors sit on audit committees with the remit to:
1. Improve the Board's decision-making role.
2. Expand the Board's horizon for strategies.
3. Monitor executive performance.
4. Look into sensitive financial matters.

The role of the audit committee's Chair is important and this should not be undertaken by the chairperson of the Board of Directors. However research suggests that the Board's Chairperson still has a great deal of influence, albeit informal, over the audit committee.

7.4 Pros and Cons

There are arguments for and against the audit committee. Advantages are that it:
1. Helps directors fulfil their role.
2. Improves communication.
3. Promotes objectivity.
4. Gives a high status to audit matters.
5. Strengthens the role of non-executive directors.

Arguments against are that:
1. It may split the Board of Directors.
2. It may encroach on management.
3. There is a shortage of non-executive directors and relevant expertise.
4. That it is time consuming.
5. Tends to be least effective in those sensitive areas where it is most needed.

7.5 Utilising the Audit Committee

Most view the audit committee from an external audit perspective and as such it has a principal role in enhancing financial reporting. Important control systems are perceived to be those that relate to the final accounts and financial management systems. There is danger that any internal audit function will also be seen in this same context and the wide role will not be fully appreciated. There are many ways that the audit committee can be used to increase the profile of internal audit as long as the relationship with the audit committee is properly managed. There are several points that may help the CIA in managing the audit committee:

The audit committee must be properly constituted. The key members must hold positions that act as a control over the powerful senior officers of any organisation. For the private sector this will be non-executive directors and for the public sector this will involve a political balance. In fact it can be argued that the opposition members will be more concerned with accountability than members of the party in power. So for example a local authority audit committee should ideally be chaired by the leader of the opposition party, and not the leader of the group in power.

The audit committee must have clear terms of reference and ensure that matters it deals with fall entirely within the scope of its role. There is always danger that the committee may feel it should be involved in the running of the organisation. This may mean it perceives its role as an executive decision-making body. The main concept of the committee is that of a higher level control over the people who administer the affairs of the organisation and it is here that a blurring of responsibilities may occur. In the public sector the committee may be used to further political goals and aspirations. Members may seek to prove that certain policies are wrong or that certain political positions can be criticised. This creates a new dimension to the audit role where it becomes a political football to be used and abused by all sides. The key safeguard against this is the terms of reference of the committee and the way it interfaces with the organisation. Whilst the Chief Executive cannot constrain the committee, there must nonetheless be a process by which its power can be contained within its official role without this resulting in a gagging situation. It should be a disciplinary offence for members of the committee to leak confidential papers that have been laid before it.

The CIA should agree clear terms of reference for involvement with the audit committee. This should build in unrestricted access to the committee and include regular private meetings with the Chair of the committee as well as a presence at each meeting. One firm rule is that the CIA will only submit reports that have been consulted on with the auditee and are available as final reports. This is not to say that audit necessarily agrees with any response from the auditee. It also means that where there has been no response despite sufficient time being made available to receive one, the report becomes by default, final. The audit committee should also be made fully aware of which audit reports they view are confidential and which ones have been given wider circulation.

The audit committee should act as an additional link into the organisation's power structure so that the CIA need not depend wholly on his/her official line manager (e.g. the Director of Finance). As such the members of the audit committees should be able to overrule the Director of Finance, where absolutely necessary, in matters of control, fraud and accountability.

The audit committee should have a clear understanding of the internal audit role and the different objectives that it has from the external auditor. A formal audit charter should be agreed with the audit committee and any changes to this document should also be subject to formal approval. No member of the committee should be allowed to convene business without first having been given relevant documents (such as the audit charter and annual reports). They should also have to attend a special briefing to explain the audit role and how this interfaces with management responsibilities.

The CIA should publish regular reports (on say a quarterly and annual basis) and these reports should provide an indication on the control state of health of the organisation's corporate, operational, computerised and financial systems. It may include executive summaries of all reports finalised since the last meeting with any action plans agreed with management. There needs to be a special item on the agenda that covers follow up audits which sets out the extent to which management has responded to agreed recommendations. Any clear barriers to improving controls should then be tackled urgently.

The audit committee should have an overseeing role in the recruitment and review of the CIA's contract and the audit budget. This is an important concept since if the CIA's job and funding are under constant threat from senior officers in the organisation then this can create a great pressure to please. Where the audit committee are involved in these types of decisions there is more scope for open scrutiny. In one sense the audit committee can become the CIA's employer in what will be a special arrangement in recognition of the fact that some independence must attach to this key officer. Some argue that "he who pays the piper calls the tune" and there is a high percentage of workers whose main preoccupation is to please their line manager. This is a sound practice for most although the auditor is probably the only person who has trouble applying this philosophy and still reporting in an open and sincere manner. As such the audit committee comes to the rescue by being an embodiment of the organisation which provides a second opinion where the auditor's work is being interfered with.

Abuse from the audit committee

One must be aware of the potential for abuse by the audit committee that takes different forms:

☐ **Political in-fighting**. Political pressures may also take place on a local level where staff vie for position within an organisation and so use audit to further their goals. The problem arises where these senior managers' goals do not coincide with organisational objectives and this leads to a dilemma for the auditor. To align oneself with competing interests creates an impossible task as meeting one level of expectations will probably impair one's ability to satisfy another committee member's view. Where these are mutually exclusive, say in support for one of two directors competing for the managing director position, then the auditor falls into a lose-lose position. Where the audit committee is ethically corrupt, there is little scope for the committee concept to be a positive development. It may be as well for an incoming CIA to establish the nature of the audit committee before signing any contract of employment with the organisation.

☐ **Special investigations**. One danger lies in the temptation for the committee to commission a series of special investigations into matters in which they have a personal interest. It is unfortunately the case that the vast majority of non-auditors have a complete misunderstanding of the internal audit role. Most feel that audit in some way investigates the actions of individuals employed by the organisation. They feel that systems auditing is simply a ploy to get into the relevant work area so that these undercover investigations can be completed. Sadly there are many auditors who, in practice, share this distorted view. Where the committee is able to throw up a constant stream of investigations into mysterious matters of breach of procedure or inaccurate reports in an area that they happen to know about, they make it impossible for the CIA to provide a professional audit service. This situation presents a trap that an unwary CIA may fall into. The need to provide a formal presentation on the real role of internal audit and the important emphasis on systems of control under management's responsibility cannot be over-stressed. Most commentators argue that the committee should be able to commission reviews by the CIA into areas they are concerned about. In this case the audit committee must have a budget that can be used to fund these projects without diverting the audit plans.

☐ **Restricted information**. Most members of the audit committee soon realise that they have direct access to information and reports that may have a great impact on the organisation. Time and time again major scandal and even the downfalls of large organisations have been traced back to a root cause in terms of poor systems of control. Being party to reports that discuss and comment on major controls can be a source of great power. Where internal audit gets involved in investigations into officer conduct, this provides a source of sensitive information that can implicate many employees. One has to consider very carefully who has access to this information via their role on the committee which is why they are normally non-executive directors (in the private sector). In the public sector there must be a proper balance of political allegiance for the committee to work. Take an example:

> *In one large local authority the audit committee was chaired by the Chief Executive and included a representative from one political party in the form of leader and deputy leader. The CIA and his line manager (the director of finance) sat on the committee. The CIA's only contact was quarterly formal presentations to this forum.*

There are several clear problems with this arrangement:
1. It is chaired by the chief executive who is ultimately responsible for the organisation. In principle this is wrong, as this person cannot independently consider the success of overall control arrangements since he/she is the key person who is responsible for these controls.
2. Since only one political party is represented on the committee there is a great temptation to instil bias into the proceedings, particularly where the committee is able to request that internal audit undertakes various special investigations carried out by the CIA.
3. There are no provisions for private meetings with committee. This means that any representations by the CIA are made in the presence of the chief executive and director of finance. As such, there is no scope to highlight any issues that may have a potential to embarrass these two top officers. The principles that underpin the functioning of the audit committee include the view that no officer is above the jurisdiction of the auditor. It recognises there are times where the conduct of senior managers has to be subject to review or investigation. The presence of the director of finance reinforces the typical line manager role that he/she has in terms of the internal audit function.

This scenario gives great potential for the internal audit function to be abused and used as political fodder, either by the politician or the chief officers. In either case the CIA is again in a lose-lose situation.

7.6 The Internal Audit Perspective

The audit committee has an overseeing role in terms of accountability and financial propriety. It must take an organisation-wide view of all matters that impair the proper running of the business. External auditors, consultants and internal reports will all be of interest to the committee and all relevant factors will be taken on board in the members' deliberations. We however are concerned primarily with the committee's interface with internal audit. In this respect there are a number of matters that should be considered:

□ **The relationship with internal audit.** We would seek to establish a positive relationship between the audit committee and internal audit. It is pointless establishing a committee that simply initiates an endless list of projects that the CIA must resource to further the aims of the various members. It is also unwise to report to a committee that is only concerned with performance indicators attaching to the audit function and reducing the audit budget wherever possible. The committee must have due respect for audit and seek to further the recommendations that are provided by the CIA. The committee should also support the CIA by removing any particular barriers that impair the successful completion of important audits. This factor must be carefully managed by the CIA and could have an important bearing on the future of the audit service if this is not the case.

□ **The need to balance the review role with client support.** The committee provides the special role of being the "ultimate client" for audit services. This means that planned audit work cannot readily be challenged by managers who dislike the external scrutiny that comes with an audit. Whilst all other support services must have due regard to the needs of their clients, internal audit may claim this as only one factor in that managers are clients only in as much as they promote good controls. Where this is not the case, the committee becomes the client and audit has someone to report the results of audit work to. The committee must endeavour to promote the client based view of audit that meets managers' needs and will make formal enquiries under quality assurance procedures. The committee must recognise the need to challenge impoverished managers who are interfering with the smooth running of the audit process. This is a fine balancing act and can only be performed successfully by committee members who have a clear understanding of the concepts involved.

□ **Reconciling the director of finance's needs.** We must return to the position where the director of finance is the formal line manager of the CIA, whilst at the same time audit furnishes regular reports to the committee. There will be times where the interests of the director of finance are not best served by reporting all findings to an external forum such as the audit committee. This may be the case where follow-up audits highlight a failure to act on audit recommendations resulting in actual losses or problems for the organisation. If it is necessary to assign responsibility, and this is seen as part of the audit role, then there may be a dilemma for the CIA. The CIA may arrive at the juncture where he/she has to ask "To report or not to report, that is the question..." The solution is made easier where the committee contains mature people who are able to discuss complicated issues without making emotive judgements impaired by personal motives. Likewise the CIA is charged with reporting the facts in a fair and open fashion and this high standard is expected at all times, regardless of the implications.

☐ **Using the committee as an ultimate control mechanism**. Audit is about getting managers to act wherever necessary in seeking improvements to systems of control. The CIA provides recommendations that are designed to assist this process and this is normally quite straightforward. However as a fail-safe mechanism, the committee may take up control issues that have not been properly dealt with via the normal report to management process. The committee may be seen as the ultimate control that swings into action where all else fails. The committee must understand this important role and be prepared to take a firm line where the CIA calls for special action to promote the welfare of the organisation. The hierarchical relationship in terms of reporting lines is:

FIGURE 7.1 RELATIVE REPORTING LINES

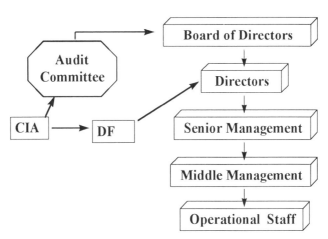

Here the CIA has an additional reporting line through to the committee which in turn advises the board of directors on the state of control across the organisation. This may be used as a superior reporting line rather than the CIA's official line manager (in many cases the director of finance).

The need for a clear focus
In times of public scrutiny and growing corporate governance, the concept of accountability has become a major issue in the business world. Various public scandals have cast doubt on the integrity of organisations' ability to control their activities in both the private and public sectors. Most large organisations feel the need to address this concern by taking pro-active steps in a highly publicised manner. An "it could never happen to us" strategy is generally deemed to be unacceptable. There are a variety of responses to this development, one of which is to establish an audit committee. In one sense this becomes a high-level control that supersedes all other efforts by management to promote better systems of internal controls and greater accountability. In terms of the impact on any in-house internal audit function that inputs into the audit committee, this is highly commendable. Unfortunately it is not the existence of the audit committee that is important, it is the role, responsibilities and activities that determine the value and impact of this corporate control mechanism. Its efficiency is by no means guaranteed and this is hindered by the absence of ready made experienced officials who are available to sit on the committee. Furthermore there is a great learning curve for newly established audit committees before they can mature and become fully functional. One setback appears

where there is a failure to set clear objectives at the outset which may mean the committee fails to gain any direction even with greater experience over time. In terms of the support provided to the internal audit function, there are several roles that should not fall within the remit of the audit committee:

[1] It should not provide a follow up service for internal audit reports. This role is properly located with the CIA.

[2] It should not provide an additional consultancy service for the chief executive. As such special projects (for internal audit) requested by the CE should not be presented to the audit committee for approval.

[3] It should not seek to reinforce line reporting structures whereby the CIA reports to the director of finance who in turn reports to the CE. To this end the audit committee should not require the DF or CE to review internal audit or carry out restructuring exercises. These tasks should be under the direction of the CIA and reported direct to the audit committee.

[4] Building on the above mentioned point, it is pointless asking that the DF or CE present audit reports to committee. This must be done by the CIA. Moreover, these reports should not be cleared (or rewritten by) the DF or CE but must go to committee directly.

[5] The audit committee is not meant to review the contents of individual audit reports. It needs only ensure that there are adequate mechanisms to allow such reports to be addressed by management through a suitable action plan. It is only failings in the adopted mechanisms that should be of concern to the audit committee. This is not to say that the audit committee need never consider audit reports and executive summaries (which should be made available as requested). It is more to the point that committee members should be concerned with an overview on the state of controls along with the adequacy of internal audit, and not individual one-off recommendations.

We have described some of the roles that should not be assumed by the audit committee. Based on these considerations, it is possible to set out one version of a more suitable role, again in terms of internal audit's areas of responsibility (i.e. systems of internal control and any failures therein). Suitable audit committee objectives may include:

[1] Ensuring that there is an adequate and effective audit function and that it operates to professional auditing standards.

[2] Ensure that there are suitable mechanisms that allow internal audit recommendations to be fully addressed by management in an appropriate manner.

[3] Ensuring that the organisation has established adequate systems of internal controls and that these are being operated efficiently. This should be particularly related to computerised and financial systems, corporate human resource management systems and all operational systems that impact on high-level business objectives.

[4] Ensuring that all material problems that impact on (or result from) internal control considerations are fully investigated and addressed.

[5] Ensuring that the organisation has established suitable corporate policies and procedures to prevent fraud or irregularity, to investigate any actual or alleged frauds, and to ensure that effective solutions are implemented.

[6] Ensuring that matters connected with any failure to comply with organisational policies and procedures, legislation and/or appropriate legislation are fully reported to the audit committee.

In addressing the above mentioned objectives we would expect the audit committee to receive the following reports on a regular basis (perhaps quarterly):

[1] A list of completed audits. One page executive summaries and management action plans should be included and the full reports available for inspection on request by members of the audit committee.

[2] Activity report from internal audit on work carried out over the relevant period (e.g. quarter), highlighting any major control concerns, with an emphasis on follow-up audits that disclose continuing problems.

[3] Schedule of frauds, irregularities and breaches of procedure identified in the period along with a report on implications.

[4] Statistical information relating to the performance of internal audit giving for example:
- Reports issued.
- The percentage of recoverable time charged.
- Aborted audits.
- Outstanding audits that have missed completion dates.
- Audits that have overrun budgets.
- Extent to which annual audit plan has been achieved.
- Details of staff leaving, joining, passing exams.

[5] Quality assurance report on the results of random checks, internal reviews and any external reviews of internal audit.

[6] Special papers, covering for example budget reduction exercises, special audits and important developments. Major fraud investigations and compliance issues should also be discussed.

Once a suitable agenda has been set, based on the above items the audit committee may then direct itself to key issues in line with the following:

IS THE ORGANISATION WELL CONTROLLED?

ARE INTERNAL AUDIT REVIEWS EFFICIENT AND EFFECTIVE?

IS MANAGEMENT ACTING ON AUDIT RECOMMENDATIONS?

This is in contrast to a poorly conceived audit committee that is immersed in detailed observations on specific audit reports.

Independence and the audit committee

There is one point that should be revisited regarding the reporting line between the CIA and the director of finance in the context of audit committees. It is the danger inherent in allowing the DF to present audits to the committee and take the lead whilst the CIA is required to respond only where the DF requires it. The ability of the DF to take the initiative with the audit committee and reinforce the reporting line over the CIA may neutralise the potential impact of the committee in overseeing the organisation's systems of internal control. This can be a difficult point in that it creates an inherent dilemma for the CIA, where the DF is negligent or incompetent (or a mixture of both) who may be tempted to cover for the DF.

An example may illustrate:

> *A newly convened audit committee asked that each audit report was*
> *accompanied by a response from management in the form of an*
> *action plan. The CIA proceeded to seek this action plan from his*
> *manager, the DF, who in the main had ignored the audit reports on*
> *financial systems despite these reports highlighting major control*
> *concerns. The audit manager who had overseen the preparation of*
> *the reports realised that the DF had failed to implement important*
> *audit recommendations. Since the audits under review by the audit*
> *committee were fairly recent there had been no follow-ups. The*
> *audit committee met and heard a presentation by the DF on the*
> *action taken in response to the audit reports that was more or less*
> *fabricated. The audit committee were satisfied by the DF's*
> *presentation which was supported by the CIA (in that this officer*
> *was present and made no comment). On his return to the office the*
> *next day the audit manager wrote a confidential memorandum to*
> *the CIA and expressed deep concern over the misrepresentations*
> *made by the DF and how this prevented the audit committee from*
> *addressing outstanding and material control weaknesses in*
> *financial systems. Nothing resulted from this memo and the audit*
> *manager eventually resigned.*

The audit committee must be able to address the real issues if it is to have any use at all. One further setback is where the members have little understanding of systems, controls, financial procedures, fraud, corporate governance and other issues relating to officer accountability. It is as well to provide regular presentations to the committee on each of these topics and so ensure that they are able to understand the audit issues and audit reports.

7.7 The IIA.UK Professional Briefing Note

This fourth professional briefing note was issued in 1994 and covers audit committees in both the private and public sectors. The use of committees has always been supported by the IIA who suggest that their role is to report to the board on:

- The financial reporting process.
- The audit thereof.
- The internal control of the business.
- The review thereof.

The briefing note calls for the committee to be formally established by the board and have an independent role outside of operational responsibilities assumed by other committees such as the finance committee. There is a move to ensure that members of the committee are independent and as such consist of non-executive directors. The finance director and chairperson are not seen as appropriate members although the CIA, director of finance and external auditor should attend meetings. One or more of these officers may be asked to leave the room when confidential matters are discussed. The committee will report to the board on recommendations concerning control regimes although it has no executive power to implement these changes. In terms of the relationship with the CIA, the briefing note suggests that the CIA report to the committee on:

1. Significant defects in control.
2. The degree of co-ordination with external audit.
3. Whether the systems of internal control are adequate.
4. Whether there is an appropriate level of internal audit coverage.

The briefing paper goes on to list many practical pitfalls of audit committees that can arise where there is insufficient consideration and planning. Whilst there is a great deal of useful information in this paper there are nonetheless several issues that have not really been addressed including:

1. The material that is relevant to a public sector environment, particularly the politically volatile experiences that exist in many local authorities.
2. There needs to be more guidance on ways that the chief executive or managing director can be controlled such that they do not have an unreasonable influence on audit committee members.
3. The advisory role of the audit committee means that control concerns may not necessarily be translated into executive decisions. Much depends on the board's perception of the importance of recommendations that originate from the committee.

7.8 Conclusions

The audit committee can be very useful but it must be carefully set up to be effective. The way it is administered and maintained can represent a reflection of the balance of power within the organisation with internal audit becoming a pawn within this process. Where internal audit reports to the Director of Finance, regular contact with a high profile audit committee may overcome any barriers to sufficient independence from the finance function. Again great care must be exercised to ensure that this is not designed to unfairly undermine the integrity of the Director of Finance. The main advantage is that the CIA is able to secure regular, formal contact with the highest levels of the organisation. It also ensures that senior management has a clear input into a continuing debate on the organisation's systems of internal control. The CIA should ensure that the audit committee works and that this forum is able to resolve any barriers to effective performance of the audit function.

CHAPTER EIGHT

THE AUDIT CHARTER

8.1 Introduction

The audit charter has a key role for the internal audit function in setting out exactly the audit terms of reference. This may be used in a positive fashion to underpin the marketing task that is discharged by audit management. It can also be used to defend audit services in the event of a dispute or an awkward auditee. The charter formally documents the raison d'être of the audit function. It is important that all audit departments both develop and maintain a suitable charter. The Institute of Internal Auditors has issued a statement of responsibilities that covers the role of internal auditing and this document may be used to form the basis of such a charter.

8.2 The Role of the Audit Charter

The audit charter constitutes a formal document that should be developed by the CIA and agreed by the highest level of the organisation. If an audit committee exists then it should be agreed in this forum although the final document should be signed and dated by the Chief Executive Officer. The audit charter establishes audit's position within the organisation and will address principal issues:

The nature of internal auditing
This should cover the general concept of auditing and the fact that it comprises the ultimate sanction over systems of internal control by providing that they are subject to formal review.

The audit objectives
The precise definition of internal audit should be set out. This will be in formal words and include references to the objectives of internal audit. There should be a clear link into organisational objectives and the way that the internal audit role contributes to these. If the audit role allows for a level of consultancy based services then this should be specifically provided for. It may be possible to use the formal definition of internal audit applied by a professional auditing body such as the Institute of Internal Auditors or Chartered Institute of Public Finance and Accountancy.

The scope of audit work
The main areas that internal audit covers should be a feature of the audit charter. This may be in line with the key control objectives that are found in the IIA standard 300 covering:
- Information systems.
- Matters of compliance.
- Safeguarding assets.
- Value for money generally.

Audit's responsibilities

It is important that the role of internal audit is clearly set out and that this is distinguished from management's responsibilities. For each of the components of the scope of audit (see above) the expectation of audit's role should be defined. This will include the audit role in respect of coverage of fraud, compliance matters and value for money. In the main one would expect management to be wholly responsible for addressing these matters while audit would review the controls that ensure these objectives are achieved. It is possible to provide further detail by outlining internal audit's duty to prepare plans and undertake the required work to professional auditing standards.

Audit's authority

The audit charter will have to refer to the rights of internal audit and the fact that they are confirmed through the charter itself. This will include unimpaired access to all information, explanations, records, buildings and so on that are required to complete audit work. It may be possible to insert a crucial clause that provides that this access be available without undue delay (perhaps within 24 hours). This is because the time factor can be controversial with some of the more difficult audits.

Outline of independence

No charter would be complete without a clear reference to the concept of independence. This must be perceived as a high profile, prioritised factor that underpins all audit work. While it is necessary in practice to strike a realistic balance, the intention to secure a high level of audit independence will be specifically documented in the charter.

8.3 The 1986 Survey

Tom Fanning's survey of audit charters carried out in 1986 included the following findings:

TABLE 8.1 ATTRIBUTES OF AUDIT CHARTERS

ATTRIBUTE	% of charters
Signed by management	26
Mentions adherence to standards	17
Mentions adherence to code of ethics	7
Contains a statement on fraud	7
Mentions co-ordination with external audit	65
Dated	26
Two pages or less	52

It would appear at this point in time, that not all of the principles behind good audit charters were being applied. However we would hope that much progress has been made since then.

8.4 Key Issues

There are several important points relating to the use of audit charters including:

The charter should be simple and short, preferably contained within a single sheet of paper. One might imagine the charter forming a colour "glossy" document that may appear at audit's reception. As such we may seek to prepare a summary document on one page for presentation purposes, whilst the actual charter itself may run across several pages. Accordingly the charter must be a short statement of roles and responsibilities and not a comprehensive description of audit policies and practices that would be very boring to the typical manager. We may go on to suggest that it should convey a basic message and in so doing be perceived as a mission statement that auditors can rally around. The fast pace of the business world does not cater for documents that run to many pages as these will not be read. In fact the fastest growing management skill is the ability to sum up a situation using the minimum number of words and this is now becoming a universally accepted principle.

The concept of audit independence should be highlighted. The charter must encapsulate the principle of independence as a key feature of the internal audit service. This must jump out at the reader and set out clearly the need to achieve this distance and authority to enable the CIA to discharge the audit role properly. Independence must not appear as a second thought or a minor matter that is expressed simply by saying "audit should be independent". What is required is a brief explanation of the importance of having sufficient independence and a hint at how it has been built into the audit service. Furthermore there must be a mention of fall-back mechanisms where there is any threat to the auditor's objectivity or the ability to get recommendations implemented.

If senior management in the organisation does not support the charter then considerable problems will ensue. The process of developing a formal charter will bring this point to a head. The document will call for a clear position for audit in the organisation and the ability to access all work areas. It will also make mention of the importance of recommendations and officers' responsibilities therein. These features may make audit potentially the most powerful section in the organisation and bringing these demands to the chief executive will highlight this factor. The organisation will get the type of service that it requires. This will vary from a low-level checking function through to a high profile professional service that tackles the most difficult of assignments. The charter represents a statement by the organisation that sets the terms of reference and scope of internal audit. This is something that the CIA cannot produce in private but must be a public document signed by the highest level of the organisation and widely publicised. It cannot be rubber stamped or simply signed and filed away. It must represent a living policy that is referred to time and time again by both audit and management.

The reporting process should be briefly described. This should indicate whom audit reports to, both in terms of the results of individual audits and for activity reports (e.g. quarterly and annual reports). It is here that the role of the audit committee may be mentioned as there is a clear link between the charter and the committee that raises the status of internal audit. The audit manual will obviously contain much detail on the reporting process from inception through to formalised final reports. This will include clearance procedures and the various management meetings that underpin the negotiation process. It is inappropriate to go into great detail in the charter although it is possible to issue a separate document to managers that sets out how audit reports are prepared and agreed. This will also explain the role of the audit committee that receives summarised versions of either all or perhaps just the more important audit reports. This is a useful device since there is a view that the audit committee may be somehow spying on managers via the audit process. As such it is as well to explain the role and objectives of the committee forum. One would go on to detail why audit also reports to a higher overseeing body in line with accepted best practice for organisational accountability. Whatever the final formula, the charter should contain a formal but brief statement on reporting that can be expanded on elsewhere.

Some reference to the auditors' code of ethics should be included in the charter. Whilst the charter may be seen as the authoritative service contract between the organisation and internal audit, the code of ethics provides the moral contract that underpins all professional work. Sophisticated concepts such as the requirement for auditors to seek to develop the audit service with the organisation are dealt with through the ethical code, along with many other similar issues. The act of establishing this link between the charter and the code of ethics gives proper organisational recognition to the matters dealt with in the code. As such there is an additional requirement for the auditor to comply with the code, not only to satisfy professional affiliations but also to adhere to corporate policy.

The requirement that internal audit assume no line responsibilities in the organisation should be noted. This is important, since there is much misunderstanding of the real role of internal audit. In the main misguided managers feel that audit checks the output from their systems as the main audit role, which makes them part and parcel of these systems. Audit meanwhile will restate professional auditing standards and argue that, if managers do not assume responsibility for ensuring that systems are controlled, then this defeats the key principles of control. No amount of theoretical argument will solve this problem where the rules are not set within the charter. Most managers would state that audit must surely perform in the way the organisation requires it to perform, and it is here that the charter becomes an important reference point in such a debate. Again so long as this specific point is contained in the charter, then the CIA's position is protected. Where this is not the case, there is more scope for misunderstanding.

The position regarding responsibilities for detecting, investigating and resolving frauds should be clearly established. We have mentioned several times before that the topic of fraud investigations can be a very sensitive matter. In the final analysis internal audit will most probably be the people to investigate such problems and the CIA should see this as extra work for his/her staff. Having said this, it is nonetheless important that the principle of ownership of responsibility is sound. In this way we would seek to make reference to management's duty to prevent, detect and investigate frauds and irregularities. Once set up in the charter, this statement confirms the corporate view that audit only assists managers in solving these types of problems and does not assume wholesale responsibility over and above the advisory role.

A note regarding the need for full co-operation with the organisation's external auditor may also be included. This simply links the two functions and recognises the need to interact from time to time. It also provides authority to copy what may be confidential reports to the external auditor and not have this act defined as whistleblowing. This can be useful where the CIA tackles a particularly sensitive problem and feels the need to get support from the external auditor. In the worst cases it may be that the organisation does not support the line of enquiries that the CIA is pursuing although there are matters that need to be subject to scrutiny and review. The ability to get the external auditor involved in debates that impact on the financial statements can provide an additional layer of comfort for the CIA where there is pressure to abandon or amend the project. Notwithstanding this it is good practice to develop a formal relationship with external audit in the normal course of developing and implementing audit plans.

The charter should be a statement of basic principles and not a procedures manual. As such it should be possible to keep it short and to the point. A useful point is to make reference to the audit manual as a way of drawing out the detailed management and operational standards that would direct the audit function. This may be used to give formal status to the audit manual since so long as auditors comply with the requirements of this document, then they can be said to be operating within their agreed terms of reference. If the audit manual is compiled to meet professional auditing standards then this means that the CIA can adhere to quality standards while at the same time conforming to a document that has been formally recognised by the organisation via the audit charter. It is for the CIA to ensure that the audit manual is drafted in a way that promotes an efficient and effective audit service and the audit committee should not interfere with this principle.

The charter should be formally approved at the highest level of the organisation. This sets the tone for all other documents prepared by the internal audit service and creates the authority to perform. The array of documents and policies established for audit should ideally flow from the audit charter in due recognition of this fact. The CIA would seek to prepare three types of documents that help direct and bind the audit service. These will operate as part of the audit manual process, the code of ethics and items that are formally released across the organisation. The first two, audit manual and code of ethics, are standards that are set for professional and quality purposes. The third item, publications, expands on the statements contained within the audit charter. To capture this model we may set out a suitable diagram showing the types of matters that may appear in each category, as an extension of the high-level audit charter:

FIGURE 8.1 STANDARDS THAT FLOW FROM THE CHARTER

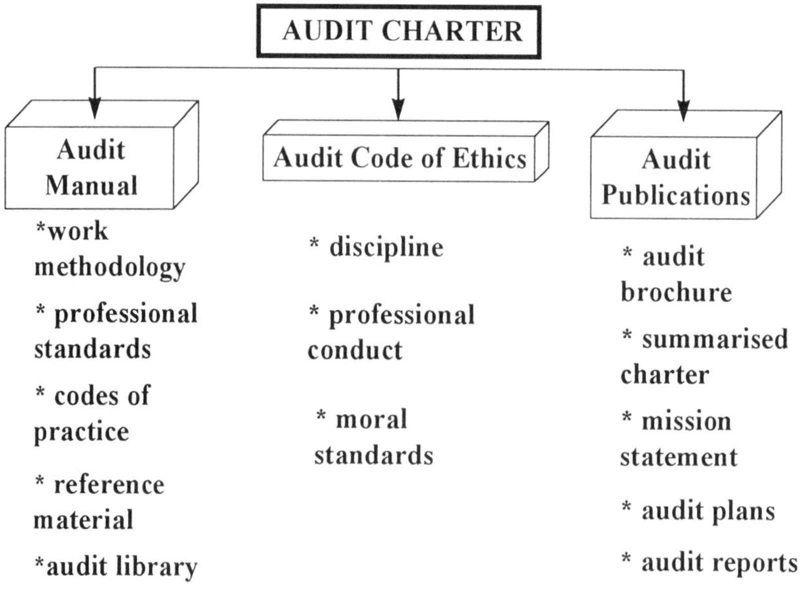

The key point that is derived from the above is that a poorly thought-out charter (or for that matter, where there is no formal charter in existence) has a knock-on effect on other standards that are really dependent on the formal authority to discharge an audit service.

Where the three main types of documents do not attach to any formal authority they may become mere pieces of paper that can be blown away by a stiff breeze. This is in contrast to the correct position where each document may be defended at all levels in the organisation if they are at all challenged.

As noted unrestricted access should be agreed within the charter and this should occur at all levels throughout the organisation. It is best to stay away from a financial bias and view the organisation as a collection of major management systems. Ideally one might consider adopting a management audit approach that will be able to take on board all areas of the organisation. The main point is that this wide scope of audit work should be referred to in the charter so that access is deemed to cover any and everything that may impact on the audit role. This is over and above the basic accounting systems that have been seen by management as the traditional province of audit. If the auditor arrives at a meeting to discuss the way corporate policy is controlled there should be no resistance from senior managers who perceive this to fall outside the agreed scope of audit work. A simple reference to the charter should enable the CIA to respond to this point, although one would have expected that marketing devices (such as the audit brochure) should have already addressed these types of issues.

The charter should not require frequent changes as any such alterations will have to go through the same approval process. As such it should contain statements of general principles that will tend to remain intact over the years. Having said this, it should be updated as and when required. One must remember that internal audit is a developing profession and we would expect changes as the style and emphasis of audit work develops over time. The charter then as a living document that reflects best auditing practice, should not be allowed to fall out-of-date. In one sense it is as well to bring the document before the eyes of corporate management as these people will change with resignations and new arrivals. Again to allow the charter to become a document that was agreed many years ago by people who have since left the organisation is extremely unwise. Following this line, one may argue that the charter should be revised say annually although this must not become a process of re-justifying the existence of the audit process each year. The original charter sets up the audit concept whilst the annual review simply allows for any adjustment to detail that may have become necessary. It is the adjustments that are approved not the entire charter.

The scope of audit work may include non-audit consultancy work as a direct response to meeting management's needs. It is important to differentiate between audit work and consultancy, which is an additional service. The charter will clearly set out the formal role of internal audit based around the systems work that is performed to discharge the audit role. At the same time authority to perform investigations under the consultancy role should also be agreed and referred to in the charter. The audit manual will obviously explain these two concepts in great detail which in turn will be summarised in glossy brochures released to management. What is needed in the charter is a simple reference to this matter.

Whatever the expectations implied by the charter, the CIA should ensure that the audit function can meet them. This final point is crucial since great power can readily be agreed but the exercise of this power then has to meet enhanced expectations. Not only does the charter contain a statement of rights but it will also require audit to discharge certain responsibilities against the background of the appropriate professional standards. The audit committee will support and promote audit but will also consider the extent to which they have achieved acceptable standards of work. This acts as a control over the audit function. We can go on to argue that the charter, in turn, also acts as a form of control in setting expectations of the organisation that must be seen as a key driving force for the CIA's work.

8.5 Structure of the Charter

It is possible to outline a suitable structure for the charter bearing in mind the different models that will be applied by different types of organisations:

FIGURE 8.2 STRUCTURE OF THE AUDIT CHARTER

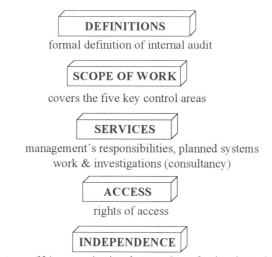

DEFINITIONS
formal definition of internal audit

SCOPE OF WORK
covers the five key control areas

SERVICES
management's responsibilities, planned systems work & investigations (consultancy)

ACCESS
rights of access

INDEPENDENCE
cornerstone of IA : organisational status & professional standards

8.6 The Audit Charter - An Example

Each individual charter will vary depending on the needs of the organisation, views of the CIA and type of services offered. We have produced a charter for a fictional company, Keystone Ltd:

KEYSTONE AUDIT SERVICES - AUDIT CHARTER

This audit charter sets out the role, authority and responsibilities of the internal audit function and has been formally adopted by Keystone Ltd on 1st January 19xx.

1. Role
Internal audit is an independent appraisal function established by an organisation as a service to the organisation. Audit is concerned with the adequacy and effectiveness of systems of internal control and whether they are managed, maintained, complied with and function effectively. To this end audit will evaluate controls that promote :

- efficient management information.
- compliance with procedures.
- protection of organisational assets and interests.
- and value for money.

2. Responsibilities
Internal audit is required to publish an annual audit plan to the audit committee and perform the systems audits that are contained within this plan, to the standards set out in the audit manual. The overall results of audit work will be reported quarterly to the audit committee (who in turn report to the Board of Directors). In addition, and subject to the availability of resources audit will seek to respond to management's requests for investigations into matters of fraud, probity and compliance that are management's responsibility. Furthermore, internal audit shall have no responsibilities over the operations that it audits over and above the furnishing of recommendations to management.

3. Reports
All audit reports will be cleared with the relevant management and once agreed will be copied to the audit committee and external audit. Management is expected to implement all agreed audit recommendations within a reasonable timeframe and each audit will be followed up to assess the extent to which this has happened.

4. Access
Internal audit has access to all officers, buildings, information, explanations and documentation required to discharge the audit role. Any interference with this right of access will be investigated and if found to be unreasonable, will be deemed a breach of organisational procedure and dealt with accordingly.

5. Independence
Internal audit is required to provide an objective audit service in line with professional auditing standards (as embodied within the audit manual) and the auditor's code of ethics. To this end it is essential that sufficient independence attaches to this work for it to have any impact on Keystone Ltd. This is dependent on sufficient organisational status and the ability to work to professional standards and the audit committee will undertake an ongoing review of the impact of these two factors.

CHIEF EXECUTIVE   CHAIR OF AUDIT COMMITTEE
DATE   DATE

8.7 Conclusions

The audit charter may be seen as the mission statement of internal audit and a clear definition may be documented to form the basis of later explanations that auditors may apply when describing their role to management. It may also come to the CIA's aid in the event of a dispute with management which is why it should be formulated by the CIA and agreed with the utmost care and consideration.

CHAPTER NINE

CODE OF ETHICS

9.1 Introduction

The auditing profession is charged with providing a high standard of audit services to each employing organisation and the audit charter forms a contract with the organisation in this respect. An extension of this concept is the view that audit professionals are also charged with performing their work with the highest of moral standards that one would expect from people in this position. Moreover the code of ethics (or code of conduct) forms a contract to cover the auditor's moral obligations. The organisation may therefore rely on this code for guiding the conduct of members of the audit department.

9.2 Relevant Factors

Dittenhoffer and Klem (1983) researched auditors' responses to a wide range of hypothetical situations. These were designed to reflect various issues of morality that one might face at work. Based on the results of this research, the Institute of Internal Auditors developed a code of ethics covering the auditor's behaviour that includes the following requirements

[1] **Members shall exercise honesty, objectivity and diligence in the performance of their duties and responsibilities**. This first item in the code in one sense summarises the basic requirements of good ethics. Here honesty is seen as essential and this sets the tone for the rest of the code. Objectivity is part of the process of achieving independence and again is a fundamental component of auditing. Diligence is less exciting an ideal but is as equally important as the rest in that it needs a dogged determination to achieve clear goals by basic hard work. This lifts audit from the spiritual level to a work based function that requires a degree of dedication. Moreover if one is truthful, fair and hardworking then there is little else that can be asked of an employee. The main problem here is that it is difficult to measure these concepts as they tend to be embodied within one's personality. It would take a degree of legal reasoning to establish if someone has breached any of these pointers, and it is not something that can be readily measured on a day to day basis. One may spot a severe case of a dishonest auditor but it is less easy to measure degrees of say honesty on the basis that one auditor is more honest than another. Nonetheless these are important components and do have a clear meaning to the everyday person in the street.

[2] **Members shall exhibit loyalty in all matters pertaining to the affairs of their organisation or to whomever they may be rendering a service. However, members shall not knowingly be a party to any illegal or improper activity**. This part of the code seeks to reconcile two potentially conflicting principles. There is above all an affiliation to the employer which for all practical purposes makes good sense. On the other hand there is a caveat whereby the auditor cannot become involved in illegal matters. This is somewhat incomplete in that the auditor will generally not be involved (i.e. party to) improper acts but will be aware of them as part of the audit office. To sit back and not

comment on possible probity problems or to be refused access to sensitive areas where probity has not been achieved, can be explained as part of this process of being loyal to the organisation. Admittedly it is rare for an entire organisation to be corrupt although, as the B.C.C.I. case shows, it is not impossible. What is more likely is for top managers not to care what their staff do so long as certain goals (e.g. defined profit margins) are being achieved. The difficulty arises where the two parts of this element of the code of ethics are mutually exclusive. Here the auditor's resignation would appear to be most appropriate although this is not always possible particularly where the economy is in recession.

[3] **Members shall not knowingly engage in acts or activities which are discreditable to the profession of internal auditing or to their organisation**. This provision brings in the external environment and one interpretation is that members convicted of criminal offences, the nature of which reflects badly on the auditing profession may find themselves excluded from membership. One would expect some consistency in the application of this rule, and some form of mechanism whereby relevant criminal convictions are brought before the IIA for deliberation and decision with all members being treated similarly. The key point is that the code then enters into the private life of the practising auditor and attaches to his/her behaviour even outside the work environment.

[4] **Members shall refrain from entering into any activity which may be in conflict with the interests of their organisation or which would prejudice their ability to carry out objectively their duties and responsibilities**. Here one would consider the auditor's activities that may be acceptable were he/she not employed by the organisation as an auditor. As an example visualise an auditor who engages in a business relationship with a main client for audit services that impairs his/her ability to carry out good audit work. The first part of this item is in itself quite interesting; the rule may be seen as part of a wider requirement to promote the interests of the organisation and is an extension of item [2] above. It imposes on the auditor a high level of commitment to the organisation that may not attach to other employees. As such it does make the IIA code somewhat demanding which cannot be a bad thing for the profession.

[5] **Members shall not accept anything of value from an employee, client, customer, supplier or business associate of their organisation which would impair or be presumed to impair their professional judgement**. The main implications of this factor are that gifts and bribes are more or less banned. A useful addition is the concept of presumption that gifts impair judgement. In practice there is no defence against such an accusation. One need only prove that an outsider would assume a relationship between receiving gifts and giving an audit opinion, rather than show an actual cause and effect. The only real problem is related to materiality since value may be defined as anything of any worth. Alternatively it may be seen as a real-life concept that sees value as something that is great enough to influence behaviour. The final point to note is the notorious difficulty in discovering a bribe that has been well organised. Notwithstanding this, if auditors abide by this part of the code of ethics then all uncertainty is removed.

[6] **Members shall undertake only those services which they can reasonably expect to complete with professional competence**. There is a clear link between this rule and the laws of negligence in that staff are required to turn down work that they cannot perform or at least to seek assistance. We might however expect some role for audit management as

they are responsible for setting work and ensuring that it is done to professional standards. One would not expect an individual member of internal audit to question an assignment that has been given to them by an audit manager. This may not go down too well. Likewise it would be embarrassing for a junior auditor to point out that this requirement of the code of ethics may be infringed. It is probably better to build the competence factor into the audit manual and force audit staff to bring to their manager's attention any reasons why an assignment cannot be properly completed. At the same time the CIA should be required to examine this factor whenever work is assigned and then undertaken. It becomes an organisational issue rather than a matter for individual auditors. This makes it more appropriate for it to be dealt with via the auditing standards as opposed to (or as well as) the code of ethics.

[7] **Members shall adopt suitable means to comply with the standards for the professional practice of internal auditing**. This may be seen as the most far-reaching part of the code as it brings into play the entire package of professional auditing standards.

What it may have gone on to say is:

> *The IIA will seek to review compliance with this and the other provisions of the code and will bring disciplinary action against any member who fails to comply with it.*

The rest of the code of ethics could then go on to define standards of personal conduct, with the assurance that professional standards, as the cornerstone of audit practice, are being achieved.

[8] **Members shall be prudent in the use of information acquired in the course of their duties. They shall not use confidential information for any personal gain nor in any manner which would be contrary to law or detrimental to the welfare of their organisation**. Herein lies the main reason why "whistleblowing" is now a fundamental issue to many internal auditors. The complete ban from disclosing information that has not been authorised for use by third parties can be read into this part of the code. One might argue that the welfare of the organisation relates only to legal objectives that may be pursued by those who run and direct the business. However, there is a problem where the entire organisation is corrupt. Here the auditor may well consider that the code of ethics acts as a restriction in alerting the authorities and getting "the organisation" into trouble. We can go on to suggest that the only acceptable reason why a CIA may wish to suppress the findings of a member of audit staff, would be that it is against the interests of the organisation. Again the code of ethics binds the auditor to confidentiality and makes it difficult to take any action that falls outside what is allowed by line management. The basic principle of keeping information private is sound. We can go further and propose that the auditor is duty bound to refrain from engaging in gossip, rumour and social discussion where matters that have come to his/her attention as a result of an audit are disclosed even where there is no actual gain. The code could be firmer and state that:

> *information obtained during the course of audit work should only be used in pursuing the objectives of the audit and should not be disclosed to unauthorised persons.*

[9] **Members, when reporting on the results of their work, shall reveal all material facts known to them which, if not revealed, could either distort reports of operations under review or conceal unlawful practices**. This rule provides a significant source of protection for the rights of the auditor and may be seen as the true ethical standard that lifts audit work to a higher plane. It can be summed up in the age-old adage "report and be damned", which makes internal audit quite different from other management services who are bound by their client. If we were to operate without this provision, there would be very little of the ethical considerations that make the audit task at times somewhat difficult. As it stands the auditor cannot simply pursue the task of satisfying management. The findings become the paramount factor in the audit report and these must be fully reported although where this rule conflicts with item [8] above then there is a problem. The requirement to report may result in a dilemma when all those officers surrounding the auditor either do not wish this report to be made, or intend to take no notice of it. In one sense the auditor is only required to report and cannot force managers to act since publishing the report discharges the main audit obligation.

[10] **Members shall continually strive for improvement in the proficiency, effectiveness and quality of their service**. The true professional has an affiliation with the service that is being delivered as a conceptual issue over and above the day-to-day work that is carried out. This internalised desire to seek improvements distinguishes the proficient auditor from the clerical record checker as a higher plane is sought. It must revolve around a strategic plan that sets direction and standards for the audit service which should be the key responsibility of the CIA.

[11] **Members, in the practice of their profession, shall be ever mindful of their obligation to maintain the high standards of competence, morality and dignity promulgated by the Institute. Members shall abide by the Articles and uphold the objectives of the Institute**. This catch-all category simply reinforces the point that the onus is on the auditor to comply with the requirements of the code of ethics and goals of the IIA.

Each internal audit department is advised to establish a suitable code based on the above but tailored to meet its specific requirements and organisational policies. Adherence to this code should be contained in the auditors' job description and the code should be fully set out in the audit manual.

9.3 Underlying Models

Gerald Vinten (1990) has developed three models of morality:

☐ **The regulatory model**. This approach sees the question of morals as being based on instructions from the appropriate authorities. As such one is told what to do and rewarded for following instruction. Regulation is also based on the threat of punishment where the rules are breached.

☐ **The aspirational model**. This model appeals to the higher levels of humanity with the concept of morals seen as something that glows from within. The feeling that people are born with a sense of morality pervades this model although there are problems where the aspirations are not being met.

☐ **The educational model.** This is the most appropriate model where morality is seen as a set of concepts that may be learned. The professional approach is linked into the demanding training and development programme that is followed by members of the internal auditing profession. This model has a great deal of scope and allows for the different views that people have on the topic of moral behaviour.

The above models can be used to build suitable frameworks for personal conduct. Even so, we return to the vexing question facing internal auditing where there would appear to be no duty owed to society at large outside of the requirement for loyalty to the employer.

9.4 Whistleblowing

This is where the internal auditor releases confidential information to an outside authority knowing that the senior management in the organisation would have forbidden it. This might occur where the auditor has uncovered a breach of regulation or legislation and finds that management wishes to suppress it. An example would be falsification of testing data by a cosmetics company to satisfy the regulatory authorities before releasing a new product onto the market. The auditor then decides to disclose the details to the appropriate authorities on the basis that it is a professional duty to society. Where this occurs the auditor tends to suffer. Dismissal, unemployment and a tarnished reputation are likely to follow. Unfortunately, there is little protection that is available to support the auditor. There is conflict between auditors' duty to society and professional loyalty and confidentiality to the employer. The IIA have issued a proclamation that suggests that a number of tests should be applied to any one potential whistleblowing situation:
1. Is the audit department complying with IIA standards?
2. Does the CIA have direct access to an audit committee where the facts have been fully reported?

If these two requirements are met, then there is generally no need to report outside the organisation. If they are not, then the problem is compounded and legal advice should be sought. The clear allegiance to the employer is seen in the IIA statements. The IIA Briefing Note Five (1994) deals with the "vexed issue of whistleblowing" by focusing on the professional issues involved. The IIA have developed a definition of whistleblowing:

> *"The unauthorised disclosure by internal auditors of audit results, findings, opinions, or information acquired in the course of performing their duties and relating to questionable practices."*

One key point that is made by the briefing note is that the existence of an audit committee falls in line with best professional practice. This committee is most effective where it agrees the appointment and removal of the CIA. This factor in conjunction with adequate reporting lines promotes the ability to achieve the IIA's professional auditing standards. The briefing note suggests that the CIA has a duty to report audit findings and if these are not sufficiently addressed then reports should be sent to higher levels within the organisation. The lack of a properly constituted audit committee would make it difficult to apply this principle. Disclosure to external parties should either be authorised by the organisation or fall under a legal obligation to do so (e.g. under a court order). The role of internal audit as an advisory function with no executive responsibility for correcting systems faults, is reinforced. The correction of wrongdoings is seen as falling outside the jurisdiction of the auditor since once problems have been reported, it is up to management (e.g. the board of directors) to take appropriate action. The more junior auditor who feels that audit management has not adequately addressed a finding is also bound by the rules on official reporting lines. Where audit seeks to report these matters to external interested parties, this is seen as destroying the relationship between management and their internal auditors. The briefing note goes on to summarise the position where auditors are able to use authorised reporting lines. Once exhausted, there is no further remit to report elsewhere even if the auditor has since resigned. The realities of whistleblowing are hinted at when the briefing note argues that:

> *"An auditor should weigh these considerations with great care. He or she should be aware that whistleblowers who "go public" have found it extremely difficult to enter similar employment elsewhere."*

The IIA.Inc details an additional provision in the position statement on whistleblowing (1988) whereby outside counsel should be obtained where the situation, after reporting internally, remains unsatisfactory.

9.5 The Moral Maze

The auditor can be faced with a moral maze. Ethical standards may be impaired by the realities of being a practising internal auditor. Official pronouncements deal with explicit problems where the organisation or certain managers have breached formal legislation or regulation. This poses the question of whether the auditor can bring the breach to the attention of external authorities which, in the main, appears not to be the case. The correct reporting mechanism, involving an independent audit committee and professional standards, is seen as a key necessity to underpin this adherence to formal lines of communication authorised by the organisation. However the defined position is in part dependent on the overall stance assumed by the government of the day. Whist the IIA code of ethics caters for most situations by imposing the highest standards on the auditor's conduct, there are various problems that on a day-to-day basis can be of concern to the auditor. Many of these revolve around the pre-reporting process where audit reports are redrafted as they embark on the journey to become final audit reports. This is illustrated in Figure 9.1. At each of the stages in the figure it is possible that an audit finding will be altered. This is not a problem where:

- The auditor has worked to professional standards.
- The client has not attempted to interfere with the fair reporting of findings.
- The CIA has a secure position within the organisation and is a member of the IIA (i.e. subscribes to the IIA code of ethics).
- Alternatively, the CIA should be a member of another relevant professional body.
- Management has a professional approach to controlling their operations.

- Audit reports are not used as ammunition for political in-fighting within the organisation.

FIGURE 9.1 PRE-REPORTING CLEARANCE PROCESS

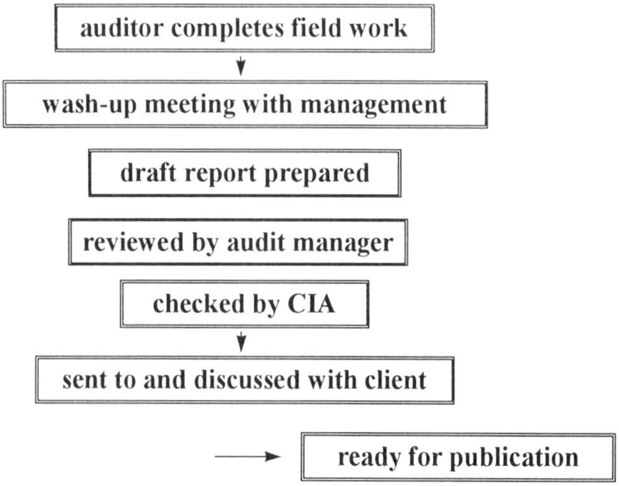

```
         ┌──────────────────────────────────┐
         │   auditor completes field work   │
         └──────────────────────────────────┘
                          │
                          ▼
       ┌──────────────────────────────────────┐
       │   wash-up meeting with management     │
       └──────────────────────────────────────┘

          ┌──────────────────────────────────┐
          │       draft report prepared       │
          └──────────────────────────────────┘

          ┌──────────────────────────────────┐
          │     reviewed by audit manager     │
          └──────────────────────────────────┘

            ┌──────────────────────────────┐
            │         checked by CIA        │
            └──────────────────────────────┘
                          │
                          ▼
        ┌──────────────────────────────────────┐
        │   sent to and discussed with client   │
        └──────────────────────────────────────┘


                  ──────▶  ┌─────────────────────────┐
                           │   ready for publication  │
                           └─────────────────────────┘
```

Any cracks in the matters that have been listed may lead to the suppression of audit findings at the request of management, through the application of severe pressures on the CIA. This is a more usual position experienced by some auditors where their reports have been "sanitised" so as not to upset anyone in a position of power. The CIA here adopts an unwritten policy of bowing to pressures and once established, this destroys the entire fabric of the audit function. Where the CIA reports to the director of finance and where this officer "vets" audit reports, we are entering a position where not only independence but also audit's ethical standards may reach unacceptably low levels. Much of the audit review process involves toning down reports so that they can be published without upsetting anyone. The junior auditor generally has a fixed idea of the control problems and wishes to expose these in no uncertain terms. As the report is considered the hard edges are removed and it becomes a routine document that contains no direct criticisms but concentrates on recommended improvements. In most cases this is acceptable. However, where managers have failed to effect proper control despite numerous audit reports and warnings, then we may move closer to the typical CIA "cover up" that some audit staff experience during their career. The tone of the auditor's ethical standards is set in favour of keeping one's job over aspiring to put morality first. One might argue that this policy sets a boundary that will stop internal audit from moving from a quasi-profession to a full blown discipline. It is not what the auditor says that should be a matter for ethical debate, but it is what by convention, is left unsaid that poses the biggest threat to the audit image in the eyes of the public.

9.6 Applying a Three-Part Model

It is possible to adopt a model of ethical considerations that helps direct the conduct of the auditor:

FIGURE 9.2 A MODEL OF ETHICAL CONSIDERATIONS

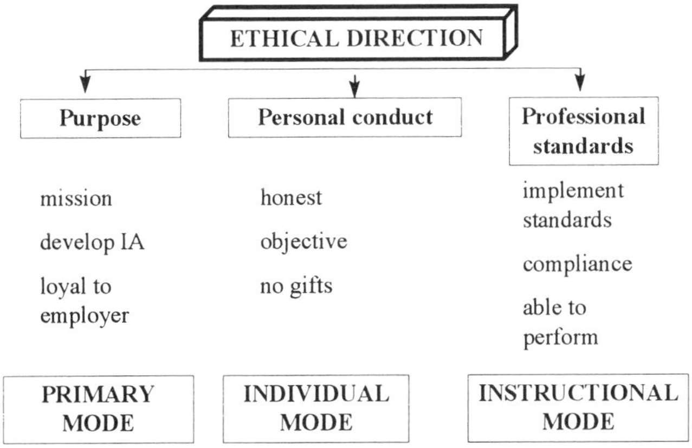

```
                          ┌─────────────────────┐
                          │ ETHICAL DIRECTION   │
                          └─────────────────────┘
            │                        │                       │
            ▼                        ▼                       ▼
    ┌───────────────┐     ┌────────────────────┐    ┌─────────────────┐
    │    Purpose    │     │  Personal conduct  │    │   Professional  │
    └───────────────┘     └────────────────────┘    │    standards    │
                                                     └─────────────────┘

       mission               honest                  implement
                                                      standards
       develop IA            objective
                                                      compliance
       loyal to              no gifts
       employer                                       able to
                                                      perform

    ┌───────────────┐     ┌────────────────────┐    ┌─────────────────┐
    │    PRIMARY    │     │    INDIVIDUAL      │    │  INSTRUCTIONAL  │
    │     MODE      │     │      MODE          │    │      MODE       │
    └───────────────┘     └────────────────────┘    └─────────────────┘
```

Some explanations follow:

1. The **purpose** forms the goals of the auditor as a form of spiritual guide that sets an overall direction of the audit effort. It is considered a primary code in that it provides this fundamental standard that determines the mission of the auditor, the need to develop the profession and an essential loyalty to the employer.

2. The **personal conduct** attaches to the daily activities of the individual auditor in its requirement for basic honesty and objectivity. This calls for high standards over the way one operates one's private and working life which for example makes it hard for a convicted criminal to perform an audit role.

3. **Professional standards** are linked more to the instructional component of the auditor's development. Here we are concerned with the way auditing standards are used and complied with by qualified persons.

We can now build on this model and look for key additional components of the ethical framework that would promote three basic matters:

- Honest and sincere auditors who have an honest desire to objectively conduct good audit work and prepare fully their findings.
- An audit function that is able to report all findings in a full and open manner notwithstanding the pressures to "play the organisational game".
- An organisation whose corporate body expects the highest ethical standards from all employees and top management, and supports any audit report that impacts on this issue.

The code of ethics is in fact a series of codes each of which depends on the individual auditor, the audit unit and the entire organisation. If there are gaps in any of these three parts, then a sub-optimal position arises. The code of ethics creates a special bond between the auditor and the employer. The internal auditor's position is easily abused and there are not many officers who will question the auditor's behaviour particularly where it appears that audit reports to some unseen higher authority. The code counters this problem and should be applied in an educational mode where auditors are encouraged to adopt the code as part of the training and development process.

131

CHAPTER TEN

STANDARDS ON AUDIT WORK

10.1 Introduction

Institute of Internal Auditors' (IIA) standard 400 covers performance of audit work and the criteria covering the way audit work should be carried out, while Auditing Practices Board standards paragraphs 45 to 78 deal with similar areas. Both standards address the requirement for professional proficiency in terms of the type of auditor employed and the need for due professional care. Most of the issues mentioned here are dealt with in more detail elsewhere in the handbook, and this chapter is a brief summary only.

10.2 IIA Standard 400

The main components of standard 400 are as follows:

- **Internal auditors should plan each audit (410):** Here the auditor is charged with meeting basic standards of planning. This is designed to ensure that the audit objectives are clear and properly controlled.
- **Internal auditors should collect, analyse, interpret and document information to support audit results (420):** This aspect of the standard requires the auditor to go about the audit in a systematic fashion relying on a clear process of securing good evidence before formulating findings.
- **Information should be sufficient, competent, relevant and useful to provide a sound basis for audit findings and recommendations (420.01.02):** Standards of evidence establish criteria that information must meet. The extent to which they meet each of the components is left to the professional judgement of the auditor.
- **Internal auditors should report the results of their audit work (430):** This appears at first sight fairly basic but there are auditors who carry out audit tasks and fail to prepare formal reports. This is particularly true for investigative audit services where "audit looks into certain matters" without producing a formal audit report.
- **Internal auditors should follow up audit work to ascertain that appropriate action is taken on reported audit findings (440):** This means that the auditor cannot simply report and then ignore the outcome. It does depend on a sound system for receiving a formal response from management and programming follow-up routines.

10.3 The Auditing Practices Board (APB) Standards

There is no corresponding standard for performance of audit work in the Auditing Practices Board standards. However there are areas that are covered in the APB standards that deal with issues relating to the main concerns that can be noted as follows:

- **Planning, control and recording (Paras 45 to 58):** The auditor should adequately plan, control and record his work.

- **Evaluation of internal control (Paras 59 to 62):** The internal auditor should identify and evaluate the organisation's internal control system as a basis for reporting on its adequacy and effectiveness.
- **Evidence (Paras 63 to 69):** The internal auditor should obtain sufficient, relevant and reliable evidence on which to base conclusions and recommendations.
- **Reporting and follow-up (Paras 70 to 78):** The internal auditor should ensure that findings, conclusions and recommendations arising from each internal audit assignment are communicated promptly to the appropriate level of management and he should actively seek a response. He should ensure that arrangements are made to follow up recommendations to monitor what action has been taken.

10.4 Applying a Suitable Model

As a short cut to isolating the principles upon which the operational elements of an audit are based, we may seek to devise a model:

FIGURE 10.1 MODEL OF BASELINE STANDARDS

ASSIGNMENT PLANNING (terms of reference)

ANALYSIS OF INFORMATION (evidence for terms of ref.)

FORMULATION OF FINDINGS   (interpretation)

COMMUNICATION OF FINDINGS (reporting)

FOLLOW-UP (assignment of risk)

Each individual audit has to meet a set of baseline standards if it is to be of acceptable quality, and as such the components outlined above will have to be firmly in place. If this is not the case then there is a strong argument to conclude that the audit has not been performed properly. We can go on to state that, where this is the norm for most audits then the audit function itself can in no way be proficient. In this instance, the CIA, if a member of a professional auditing body, should be disciplined by the professional body. This simple formula should be firmly in place or there is little hope for developing the practice of internal auditing. In this sense it may be the case that all chief auditors need to be members of an appropriate professional auditing body.

10.5 The Implications for Internal Audit

The standards pertaining to the performance of audits do have implications for the auditor, and there must be some consideration of a number of issues as follows:

Audit planning
Audit management must ensure that all audits are carefully planned before resources are spent on them. This will involve an assessment of the relative risk of each component of

the system of control and this information discussed with management before formal terms of reference are set. Furthermore plans help establish a process whereby the progress of the audit can be monitored as each task is completed and reviewed. This standard places an emphasis of proper audit work that has been derived from a considered process of setting objectives and assigning resources in contrast to a hit-or-miss affair that relies on the "audit nose". It is so tempting to sit back and wait for work on the basis that an assortment of special investigations is what management really wants from internal audit. It is so much more difficult to formulate a plan of work that by default sets targets that have then to be met by audit management. Planning can work on a macro level where long-term work programmes are agreed in contrast to planning applied to individual audits. Even where the audit is conjured up by say the audit committee, each job must be carefully administered via a formal scheme of work (i.e. a plan).

Analysis of information

Each part of the terms of reference should be subject to a process whereby the available evidence is analysed in the most appropriate fashion. This may involve the application of particular techniques such as statistical sampling or computer interrogation. Much of the work will require the use of audit testing programmes. The net result is that an approach that involves talking to managers and then reporting these discussions is not acceptable audit practice. Audit standards require information to be secured and dissected in a way that provides clear audit findings, whilst the auditor must furnish this information as a key feature of the audit process.

Formulation of findings

It will be necessary to seek to interpret the material that has been accumulated in the fact-finding/analysis stage mentioned above. This all-important process requires the auditor to make sense of all the work carried out so far, which in turn depends on clear standards set by audit management. The basis of the resultant audit report should be secured through this stage of the audit and here we would look for a level of insight and deliberation. The skills involved in isolating the influence of one factor on another, in a methodical way demand the highest level of creative perception as a consequence of this audit standard.

Communication of results

The reporting stage must also be determined by audit management and appropriate standards defined and implemented. This should cover all types of audits, be they systems work or ad-hoc investigations as a basic requirement. What at first sight sounds quite straightforward can be demanding for auditors who have not adopted the discipline of formally reporting their work. As a standard this rule does distinguish the well managed from the more chaotic audit functions. A new chief executive or director of finance need only ask to see the reports issued by internal audit over the last year to get a good idea whether it is worth retaining this resource.

Follow-up

An audit has not been performed unless it has been followed up. This will be based on a process of locating control risk with management where they may either improve controls to guard against risk, or accept and be responsible for allowing these risks to continue unabated. The follow-up routine brings into play an important concept that suggests a great responsibility over and above a duty to report. Following up involves detailed enquiries by the auditor concerning the extent to which the original report has been acted on and it is here that the audit role becomes more comprehensive. This standard implies a duty not only to suggest action by operational management but also a duty to actively seek, demand and get action on agreed recommendations, or at least make sufficient attempts.

We have shown that there are mechanisms that must be in place to satisfy the auditing standards that cover the performance of audit work. One acid test is to ask whether the procedures covering this issue would stand up in a court of law that wished to consider whether an audit had been performed to acceptable standards. Although this point is more relevant to firms of external auditors, it should nonetheless be noted by internal auditors as more public sector internal audit functions are being contracted out.

10.6 Professional Proficiency

This part of the IIA standard (200) deals with the basic principles that need to be satisfied before the audit department can be said to operate in a proficient manner. The term has important connotations for auditors since where they act proficiently, they properly discharge their professional responsibilities. Where this is not the case then a sub-standard audit service will result with obvious problems. The standard requires that internal audits should be performed with professional proficiency and due professional care. The main components of standard 200 are:

- **Staffing (210):** The internal auditing department should provide assurance that the technical proficiency and educational background of internal auditors are appropriate for the audits to be performed.
- **Knowledge, skills and disciplines (220):** The internal auditing department should possess or should obtain the knowledge, skills, and disciplines needed to carry out its audit responsibilities.
- **Supervision (230):** The internal auditing department should provide assurance that internal audits are properly supervised.
- **Compliance with standards (240):** Internal auditors should comply with professional standards of conduct.
- **Knowledge, skills and disciplines (250):** Internal auditors should possess the knowledge, skills, and disciplines essential to the performance of internal audits.
- **Human relations and communications (260):** Internal auditors should be skilled in dealing with people and in communicating effectively.
- **Continuing education (270):** Internal auditors should maintain their technical competence through continuing education.
- **Due professional care (280):** Internal auditors should exercise due professional care in performing internal audits.

The first three items refer to the audit department while the remainder refer to the individual auditors.

APB Standards
On professional proficiency, the APB model contains requirements similar to the IIA version:

- **Staffing and training:** The internal audit unit should be appropriately staffed in terms of numbers, grades, qualifications and experience, having regard to its responsibilities and objectives. The internal auditor should be properly trained to fulfil all his responsibilities (Paras 15 to 26).
- **Relationships:** The internal auditor should seek to foster constructive working relationships and mutual understanding with management, external auditors, with any other review agencies and, where one exists, with the audit committee (Paras 27 to 37).
- **Due professional care:** The internal auditor should exercise due professional care in fulfilling his responsibilities (Paras 38 to 44).

Professional standards emphasise a disciplined approach to the auditor's duties and work that is derived from best practice. To reinforce this view, CIPFA has started the move to require compliance with the APB standard on internal auditing by issuing a document to this effect late in 1994.

10.7 Conclusions

The IIA and APB standards bring together sound policies for performing audit work and although they appear at first sight fairly straightforward, they do demand good procedures. In addition the various requirements call for a professional approach to auditing where the work is planned, based on good evidence, reported and followed up. An audit department that does not establish suitable procedures to take on board all these matters cannot discharge the requirements of these standards. In addition the audit department must be staffed with personnel who between them have all the skills required to discharge the audit role. These skills are varied and cover a range of disciplines based on the whole body of audit knowledge that is studied during professional auditing examinations. If the CIA does not ensure that these skills are employed or readily available then professional auditing standards cannot be met. There may be a case for having internal audit functions that are able to meet performance standards, formally designated as "certificated internal auditors". This is in contrast to other audit functions that have no such allegiance or are unable to meet the required standards. Nothing short of this will raise auditing standards to a level where they have any real purpose. We can also take the view that the current search for quality assurance "Kitemarks" may become a thing of the past. The audit function will simply rely on statements to the effect that they are in compliance with professional standards as the chief marketing tool. Again taking a futuristic view of this position we may move towards the following quality control mechanism applied to professional internal audit units as a means of accrediting the audit service:

FIGURE 10.2 MONITORING PERFORMANCE STANDARDS

This is a simple concept which in reality requires some re-thinking by the internal auditor in terms of seeking a full professional affiliation, along with a degree of additional resources where professional bodies seek to perform this new role.

CHAPTER ELEVEN

EXTERNAL AUDIT AND OTHERS

11.1 Introduction

There is much guidance written about the relationship between the internal and external auditors and at times an amount of confusion. Certainly the client may find it difficult to appreciate the differences and many internal auditors have spent time explaining the two roles. This chapter attempts to show that there are basic differences that are important to understand, since the two functions are in practice completely different.

11.2 The Different Objectives

The starting place is to clearly set out the different objectives of the two disciplines:

The external auditor

The external auditor seeks to test the underlying transactions that form the basis of the financial statements. In this way they may form an opinion on whether or not these statements show a true and fair view. Reliance may be placed on those systems that produce the accounts so that less testing will be necessary where the system is found to be sound. The systems are however perceived as a short-cut to examining all the financial transactions for the period in question.

The internal auditor

The internal auditor, on the other hand, seeks to advise management on whether its major operations have sound systems of internal controls. To this end the auditor will test the resultant transactions to confirm the evaluation and determine the implications of any systems weaknesses. These systems are primarily designed to ensure the future welfare of the organisation rather than accounting for its activities.

It should be clear from the above that the external auditor uses systems as a short-cut to verifying the figures in the accounts. In contrast the internal auditor is primarily concerned with all systems of control that enable organisational objectives to be met. Note that in the public sector, the National Audit Office (NAO) and the Audit Commission (AC), as well as their role in final accounts, also examine operational matters and value for money issues. In addition, firms of auditors may be asked to undertake various consultancy projects in addition to their external audit role.

11.3 Background to External Audit

There are features of the private sector external auditor's role that may be noted to help understand the relationship between the two disciplines:

- External auditors are generally members of CCAB professional accountancy bodies and are employed under the Companies legislation to audit the accounts of registered companies.
- They are appointed annually at the annual general meeting by their clients, the shareholders.
- Their remuneration is fixed at general meeting.
- They have a right to attend general meetings to discuss any audit-related matters.
- They have a right of access to all books, information and explanations pertaining to the financial statements.
- In a limited company they can be removed by ordinary resolution with special notice.
- They cannot be officers, corporations or partners or employees of officers.
- In the event of their resignation they have to provide a statement of circumstances to the new incoming auditor that will document any specific problems with the audit cover.
- Where there is a problem with the accounts the auditor will fashion a suitable report to reflect the nature of the problem.

They can report that:

TABLE 11.1 EXTERNAL AUDIT REPORT FORMAT

	EFFECT ON THE ACCOUNTS	
AUDITOR'S VIEW	**MATERIAL**	**FUNDAMENTAL**
UNCERTAINTY	"subject to"	"disclaimer"
DISAGREEMENT	"except for"	"adverse"

In this way the external auditor will form an opinion on the accounts based on the adopted position. Note that the public sector will also be subject to external audits.

11.4 The Main Similarities

The main similarities are as follows:

Both the external and internal auditor carry out testing routines and this may involve examining and analysing many transactions. Where these revolve around financial systems then they may appear to be very similar, particularly for the operational staff who have to supply the required information to assist the audit in hand. There are many auditors who have tried to explain the different roles of the two functions to a confused manager who has seen both teams perform what appears to be exactly the same work. As testament to this, one will recall the many times where a client has handed a document to the internal auditor, who after much confusion, is able to work out that the document actually belongs to the external audit team. This confusion is enhanced where the size of the audit means that the external audit team is located within the organisation. Having said this, there are many ways that audit testing programmes applied to financial systems appear to be very similar and this does bring the two audit functions closer together in terms of working methodologies.

Both are concerned that the organisation complies with the laid down procedures and policies since good systems are generally based on this principle. The external auditor will be worried if procedures were very poor and/or there was a basic ignorance of the importance of adhering to them. Obviously the external auditor will be involved in matters that impinge on the financial statements although they may comment on the overall arrangements for setting standards and direction. Internal audit will tend to take this concept further in an attempt to promote suitable controls. The auditor's work is dependent on people doing things in the way that is laid down by the organisation and they will not take this factor for granted without applying appropriate compliance tests. Herein lies a basic similarity in terms of approaches to the all-important question of compliance.

Both tend to be deeply involved in information systems since this is a major element of managerial control as well as being fundamental to the financial reporting process. New computerised developments that impact on the figures presented in the final accounts must incorporate basic controls to ensure the integrity of the database and ensuing reports. Computer audit is a term applied to both external and internal audit as a follow-up to this principle. A good computer auditor may work in both types of audit roles throughout his/her career, as the skills applied to this type of work are wholly transferable. Take as an example computer interrogation routines that seek to identify correct functionality or say duplicate accounts; these may be applied to financial information systems by both external and internal audit although from different perspectives. The external auditor will seek to assess whether the information supplied by the computer that forms the basis of figures for the accounts is correct. The internal auditor will be concerned that the computer generates correct reports that enable management to achieve their objectives efficiently. Obviously the internal auditor will consider all major systems that impact on organisational objectives as opposed to just the accounting based ones. This makes for a concentration of resources on corporate managerial controls such as the systems development life cycle applied to new and developing computerised systems.

Both are based in a professional discipline and operate to professional standards. The external auditor's work is in the main covered by the APB auditing standards, that cater for matters such as starting an engagement, planning work and carrying out the required tasks. In the United Kingdom, the internal auditor makes reference to either the IIA standards or the APB equivalent. There is one key difference in the form of an added impetus to subscribe properly to auditing standards that applies to the external auditor. This is the ever-present threat of legal action that may be taken by a client or a third party who has relied on the financial statements and suffered a loss as a result. The ability to prove that one has operated to professional standards is almost a prerequisite to a successful defence against any claims of professional negligence. The internal auditor has two main forces that encourage compliance with professional standards. These appear in the form of the CIA's stance on this issue and the quality assurance procedures that should call for a review of compliance either done in-house or through external resources. The key point however is the view that both internal and external audit should seek to adhere to formal auditing standards that should form the foundation of their work. This would be translated perhaps as an in-house audit manual supported by suitable training and development programmes.

Both seek active co-operation between the two functions. IIA standard 550 covers this point whilst the external auditor has a remit, through APB guidelines, to place some reliance on the internal auditor's work wherever possible. This co-operation should operate on an equal footing and is partly designed to avoid embarrassing situations where both teams turn up at the same location at the same time.

Both are intimately tied up with the organisation's systems of internal control. Controls and the way they are interfaced with the organisation's operational arrangements should be seen as an important concern, that is fundamental to the audit role. Considerations relating to authorisation, segregation of duties, good documentation, audit trails, sound information systems, and supervision all fall under the remit of control systems that are key to the success of the business in hand. There is one external audit view that proposes the use of extended interrogation software to perform 100% testing of financial systems and so move away from the need to place any great reliance on controls. This however is based on the narrow definition of controls used by external audit based around the output from accounting systems being more or less correct. We can contrast this with the wider internal audit view on controls that considers them to be mechanisms that promote the achievement of organisational objectives. The importance of sound controls has been given greater recognition recently by the external audit world with the general acceptance of this issue as part of the annual reports issued by the directors. To this end we would expect the internal and external auditor to move closer together in relation to controls over financial systems. In practice we may speculate whether internal audit should have a key role in control evaluation where relevant statements do appear in the annual report and accounts. The APB guidelines on placing reliance on internal audit may need to be reviewed to reflect this concept.

Both are concerned with the occurrence and effect of errors and misstatement that affect the final accounts. This is a key concern of the external auditor where it has an impact on the audit report that is issued after reviewing the items set out in the final accounts. In this situation the internal auditors would be interested in the systems weaknesses that have led to the resultant errors in contrast to the external auditor's interest in the effect of incorrectly stated figures. Where there is close co-operation between the two functions, we may expect a great deal of close working to identify and resolve such problems.

Both produce formal audit reports on their activities. The external auditor has tended to report on an exception basis where comments relate specifically to the type of audit opinion that is provided. More recently audit standards require more information in audit reports that provide a more rounded view of work done and responsibilities. The problem for the external auditor is that the more that is said in a report the more the writer can be held to account. The internal audit report can be differentiated by its resemblance to the more conventional type of report with a formal structure, i.e. a beginning, middle and end. This can become a detailed document for larger audits although one would expect an executive summary to provide a brief statement of opinion, making it closer to the model used by the external auditor. Notwithstanding the differences in the report formats we can conclude that both sets of auditors have to assume the discipline of formally reporting their findings and carrying out their work with this obligation in mind.

11.5 The Main Differences

There are however many key differences and these are matters of basic principle that should be fully recognised:

The external auditor is an external contractor and not an employee of the organisation as is the internal auditor. Note however, that there is an increasing number of contracted out internal audit functions where the internal audit service is provided by an external body. In fact this external body is likely to be the same type of organisation (e.g. firm of accountants) as those that supply the external audit services. Having said this there is a third model that is being increasingly applied that involves a small in-house internal audit team supplemented by an outsourced contract that covers more routine audits. As such we are still dealing with internal auditors who are normally employees of the company. There is one further qualification to this where audit consortia are involved, as is popular in the UK's National Health Service; this is akin to an externally provided internal audit service.

The external auditor seeks to provide an opinion on whether the accounts show a true and fair view. Whereas internal audit forms an opinion on the adequacy and effectiveness of systems of internal control, many of which fall outside the main accounting systems. It is important to get this concept clearly in mind and an illustration may assist:

FIGURE 11.1 AUDITING CONTROLS VERSUS ACCOUNTS

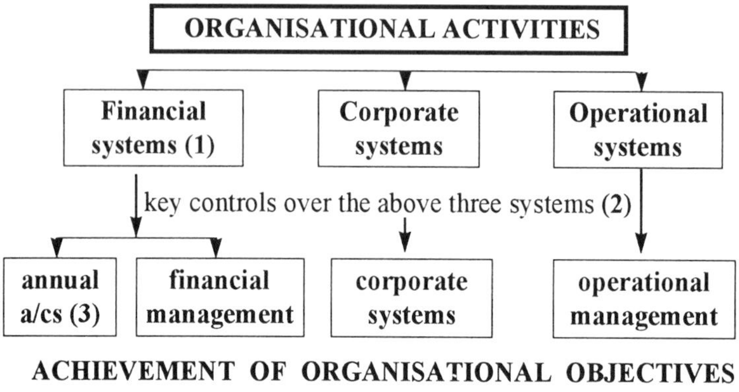

```
                    ┌─────────────────────────────────────┐
                    │     ORGANISATIONAL ACTIVITIES        │
                    └─────────────────────────────────────┘
                         │              │              │
                         ▼              ▼              ▼
              ┌──────────────┐ ┌──────────────┐ ┌──────────────┐
              │  Financial   │ │  Corporate   │ │ Operational  │
              │ systems (1)  │ │   systems    │ │   systems    │
              └──────────────┘ └──────────────┘ └──────────────┘
                    │  key controls over the above three systems (2) │
              ┌─────┴─────┐          │                      │
              ▼     ▼     ▼          ▼                      ▼
          ┌────────┬─────────────┐ ┌──────────────┐ ┌──────────────┐
          │ annual │ financial   │ │  corporate   │ │ operational  │
          │ a/cs(3)│ management  │ │   systems    │ │ management   │
          └────────┴─────────────┘ └──────────────┘ └──────────────┘
```

ACHIEVEMENT OF ORGANISATIONAL OBJECTIVES

The three key elements of this model are:
1. Financial systems may be considered by the external auditor as a short-cut to verifying all the figures in the accounts to complete the audit process. The internal auditor will also cover these systems as part of the audit plan.
2. Overall control arrangements are the main preoccupation of the internal auditor who is concerned with all those controls fundamental to the achievement of organisational objectives.
3. The final accounts are the main preoccupation of the external auditor who is concerned that the data presented in the accounts present a true and fair view of the financial affairs of the organisation.

It should be clear that the external audit role is really much removed from the considerations of the internal auditor both in terms of objectives and scope of work. The fact that there is some overlap in respect of controls over the accounting arrangements must be set within the context of these major differences.

External audit is a legal requirement for limited companies and most public bodies, while internal audit is not essential for private companies and is only legally required in parts of the public sector. Much of the external auditor's work is prescribed in outline by law. To an extent even working practices are affected by case law dealing with claims of professional negligence against the auditor. Rights, responsibilities and the role of external audit are found in legislation that contains clear definitions that are well understood by the business community. The world of the internal auditor, on the other hand is shrouded in mystery and generally not appreciated by management. The different methodologies applied by various internal audit functions and the fact that they need not necessarily be aligned to a professional body, also make it hard to develop one universal model of auditing that can be held up as an agreed standard. We may go on to suggest that the external auditor is more accepted by society than the internal audit counterpart as a result of the position we have just described. Unfortunately there are many internal auditors who can only get the attention of the business community by making mention of the importance of fraud investigations as a way of defining their role in society so as to avoid complicated discussions on other more significant aspects of their work. External auditors, on the other hand, have no need to enter the realms of conceptualisation to explain their main role in society.

Internal audit may be charged with investigating frauds, and although the external auditors will want to see them resolved, they are mainly concerned with those that materially affect the final accounts. Whilst there is a growing recognition of the external audit role in fraud investigations, the truth is that tackling fraud is not only hard work but also very resource intensive. Referring matters to internal audit is one good way of managing this issue if it comes about. Accordingly internal audit tend to claim this area as its own. In the public sector where probity is seen as a key issue, there is generally a need to investigate all occurrences and/or allegations of fraud even where they go back some time. In the private sector this type of work will tend to be at the behest of the board of directors. In some cases the fraud aspects of organisational affairs will fall under specially designated security officers.

Internal auditors cover all the organisation's operations whereas external auditors work primarily with those financial systems that have a bearing on the final accounts. This point should not be underestimated since if external audit spends a great deal of time on financial systems it may result in the internal audit function dealing primarily with managerial/operational areas. If this is the case the internal auditor may well commit only a small level of resources to the financial arena. Although this type of arrangement does depend on a close co-operation of the two audit functions, it also creates a clear differentiation in the two work areas that will tend to move them further apart in the long term. It also moves away from the alternative model where internal audit work is used primarily to allow a reduction in the level of external audit cover in designated areas. Reverting to the previous example, an exaggeration of the separation of systems into financial and others, in line with the different roles of external and internal audit, may allow the latter function to assume a fuller identity in its own right.

Internal audit may be charged with developing value for money initiatives that provide savings and/or increased efficiencies within the organisation. Interestingly, this may also apply to the external auditor under the consultancy head (although the level of consultancy provided by the external auditor is restricted so as not to provide a conflict of interests). It also applies to some external auditors in the public sector (e.g. Audit Commission and National Audit Office). Generally speaking though, internal audit will be concerned with operational efficiency whilst the external audit function has no remit to delve into these areas of organisational activities.

The internal auditor reviews systems of internal control in contrast to the external auditor who considers whether the state of controls will allow a reduced amount of testing. As such, external audit work is directed at the transactions that occurred within a past period in contrast to the future impact of good systems. As an example, the internal auditor may be concerned with the efficiency and effectiveness of the organisation's marketing systems whereas there is no clear role for external audit in this area.

Internal audit works for and on behalf of the organisation whereas the external auditor is technically employed by and works for a third party, the shareholders. This is an important difference in that the client base has a great deal of influence on the audit role and reporting arrangements. The external auditor is clearly reporting on the organisation's management as a fundamental part of their role. It is top management (i.e. the directors) who prepare and approve the accounts, and society views the external audit function as a direct check over the figures on the basis that it is not well to rely on the unchecked accounts as they stand. The internal auditor does not have this distinct philosophy for protection as it is management who decides to employ an internal auditor, not to check on them, but to seek improvements to systems. The point though is, having identified weaknesses, the internal auditor has no third party to go to if there is a lack of effective action to remedy these weaknesses. The internal auditor reports to the people in front of him/her, not some unseen force that periodically convenes as a group of shareholders watching over the organisation with interest and supreme authority. The ideal standard calls for an audit committee to fulfil this role although the directors and chief executive do tend to have a great influence on this forum and so diminish its capacity as an ultimate control over the organisation. This difference in reporting lines in turn creates a contrasting type of independence in that the external auditor is independent from the organisation whilst internal audit is independent from the operations being reviewed. There are pressures on the external auditor particularly for owner-run registered companies that can impair the level of audit independence. There are also time pressures that can lead to junior staff doing limited work in poorly managed firms of auditors although the drive for quality assurance procedures does diminish the frequency of this type of scenario. There are those that argue against any recognised degree of independence attaching to the internal audit function compared to external audit. Note that a separate chapter on this topic should provide a more rounded insight.

The internal audit cover is continuous throughout the year but the external audit tends to be a year-end process even though some testing may be carried out during the year. Having said this, some larger organisations have a permanent external audit presence who provide year-round coverage of account verification and substantiation. For smaller companies one might imagine the external auditor arriving at the finance department after the accounts have been closed and producing a suitable report after the requisite period of audit work. This is very different from the full time internal auditor who is consumed by the organisational culture as the years pass by, and colleagues across all departments become close personal friends. We may be tempted to argue that the internal auditor is as such "playing at auditing" as the years grow closer to retirement, if this did not expose a complete misunderstanding of the internal audit role.

It is possible to outline the key differences in table format over various relevant heads:

TABLE 11.2 INTERNAL VERSUS EXTERNAL AUDIT

FACTOR	INTERNAL AUDIT	EXTERNAL AUDIT
OBJECTIVES	sound controls	accounts = true & fair view
SCOPE OF WORK	over all systems: VFM, fraud, MIS & compliance	accounts, Profit & Loss a/c balance sheet, annual report & financial systems
INDEPENDENCE	from operations by professionalism and status	from company via statutory rights & APB codes
STRUCTURE	varies: CIA, managers, seniors & assistants	partners, managers, seniors & trainees
STAFF	competent persons e.g.: engineers, IT experts, accountants, quantity surveyors and so on	qualified and part qualified accountants
METHODOLOGY	systems based audits and investigations	vouching & verification
REPORTS	comprehensive structured reports to management & the audit committee	brief standardised reports to shareholders
STANDARDS	IIA and/or APB	various APB requirements
LEGISLATION	generally not mandatory apart from parts of public sector	companies legislation & various public sector statutes
SIZE	only larger organisations	all registered companies & public sector (small companies may have exemptions)

11.6 The Auditing Practices Board (APB) Statement

Because internal audit reviews systems and carries out testing routines it may produce much work that the external auditor might find useful. Reliance on internal audit's work reduces the external audit workload and may lead to lower fees. The Auditing Practices Board (APB) has provided guidance on this matter that includes the following:

External audit needs to assess the adequacy of internal audit before relying on its work and so reducing its own. Accordingly it will need to consider the following:

1. The internal audit work should be properly recorded.
2. The internal audit work should be properly controlled.
3. Internal audit should be adequately independent.
4. The scope of the internal audit work should be sufficiently wide.
5. Internal audit should have sufficient resources.
6. Internal audit should be competent.
7. It should carry out its work with due professional care.

Only where internal audit meets the above criteria may the external auditor restrict the amount of work based on the internal audit cover. In fact in a number of local authorities the district auditor (DA) has asked internal audit to undertake testing programmes of various central government claims before the DA signs the claim off. The budget for external audit services is reduced accordingly. On the one hand, this shows a level of confidence in internal audit that should be taken as a compliment. The downside though, is the creeping view that internal audit is there to simply back up the all-important external auditor, which harks back to the old model of the two audit functions. One solution is to support the external auditor by using specially brought-in internal audit resources for this purpose, whilst still maintaining the audit plan intact. It is quite easy to buy in short-term temporary auditors via a suitable recruitment agency that specialises in this type of resource. To simply divert internal audit resources for the external auditor can create an imbalance in the relationship between the two parties that can set a precedent for the future.

11.7 The Brink and Barratt Survey

Brink and Barratt (1980) carried out research on the relationship between internal and external audit with the following major findings:

- Internal audit is primarily concerned with internal controls, and assisting the external auditors in their work is seen as a secondary matter.
- External audit primarily gave assurances on the accounts with only a secondary concern with internal controls.
- Internal audit spent around half of its time on financial audits.
- Most internal auditors reported to officers and not the board of directors.
- Considerable co-operation is possible where working papers are exchanged.
- The audit committee is the right forum for planning co-operation.

We can now discuss some of the ways that may be used to foster greater co-operation that includes:

[1] **A common audit methodology**. A close co-operation can result from adopting a common approach to audit work. This may for example revolve around a systems based approach where one would seek to ascertain, evaluate, test and then report the relevant findings. In practice the policy would work better if it were based around developing clear but different methodologies that are understood by both audit functions. This recognises the differences in objectives, scope and approach to work that will attach to each type of audit, and deals with the difficulty in achieving a universal approach. So long as working methodologies are defined and publicised, then a basic appreciation should result which in turn would underpin any drive towards harmonisation.

[2] **Joint training programmes**. Again fully integrated training programmes, as an ideal, are not possible due to the different nature of the two audit functions. A policy of joint training can nonetheless be applied so long as this is limited to general audit techniques. These include flowcharting, statistical sampling, database interrogation, transactions testing, interviewing skills, control evaluation and so on. Time and resource may be rationalised where this approach is adopted. The disadvantage is the many limitations that must be placed on this approach since many of the techniques dealt with would have to be

discussed as conceptual matters, with no link into audit objectives (that do not really reconcile).

[3] **Joint planning of audit work**. This is the single most useful policy in terms of co-ordinating internal and external audit. Harmonisation of the planning task is fundamental in this respect.

There are several levels to which audit planning may be interfaced as follows:

FIGURE 11.2 INTERFACED AUDIT PLANNING

STAGE ONE
copies of plans exchanged when complete

STAGE TWO
a joint meeting where plans are discussed
and harmonised - issued separately

STAGE THREE
regular meetings where fully integrated
plans are issued as one composite document

The stages move from one through to three to reflect an increasingly greater degree of interface between internal and external audit. At the extreme it can result in one planning document being prepared for the organisation. This is more relevant in the public sector where external audit tends to assume a role in securing value for money. Stage one consists of a common courtesy where plans are exchanged, which in fact involves two sub-levels where draft plans are given (that can as a result be altered). This is in contrast to the less integrated stance where finalised plans only are provided.

[4] **Direct assistance with each other's projects**. A swap of resources creates further co-operation as the available audit skills base is added to as and when required. This can allow as an example an external computer auditor to run interrogation software to support the internal auditor's review of a large financial system. Internal audit may in turn complete a suitable testing programme that enables external audit to substantially reduce work in the area in question. Note that some of these issues have been mentioned earlier.

[5] **Exchanging reports**. This is a simple method of keeping each side informed although it is more relevant within a public sector environment. Unfortunately what at first appears straightforward may involve an amount of political manoeuvring where each side applies special rules for confidential reports or reports that have not reached final report status. A more explicit statement of co-operation occurs where pre-report stage material, such as the agreed terms of reference for the ensuing audit, is also exchanged.

The new external audit approach
An APB paper called "The Audit Agenda" was sent out for consultation where comments had to be submitted by April 1995. It has three major elements:

- It recognises that the audit requirements of listed and owner-managed companies are different.
- It advocates that an extended audit should apply to listed companies and major public companies. Here compliance with the Cadbury code of corporate governance becomes a major concern.
- It places a new emphasis on fraud detection where the auditor would be required to report on the appropriateness and adequacy of systems intended to minimise the risk of fraud.

These proposals highlight the developing format of the external audit role that is moving closer to the internal auditor's concerns with the way the company's affairs are managed and controlled. The Cadburys' code that advocates reports by directors and auditors on the systems on internal control also brings into the frame the concept of management's responsibilities for the overall control arrangements. Again we can see that the growing proximity of internal and external audit pursuits is evident, which calls for more urgency in developing the policies for good co-operation. This also calls for a better distinction of the two functions so that common interests are dealt with in an appropriate fashion and do not lead to a confusion of roles and responsibilities.

11.8 Other Review Agencies

There are other review agencies that have certain similarities with internal audit. In fact there are times when planned audits are cancelled where the operation in question has recently been subject to a review. Some of these review agencies may be listed:

Management consultants
These may be external or based in-house and may tackle a variety of projects that are required by management. In fact the current policy tends to be to disband in-house teams and call upon external consultants wherever necessary. Moreover, persons employed as corporate "policy analysts" may actually perform a quasi-consultancy role. In the case of management consultants, management sets the applied terms of reference that then restrict the consultant's work to specific concerns. Whilst there is a body called the Institute of Management Consultants, due to the wide variety of projects the types of skills differ and may in practice be pooled for a multi-disciplinary approach. Consultants may solve specific problems and unlike internal auditors may devise whole systems and go on to install them, depending on the terms of engagements. There are some internal audit departments that also offer a consultancy based service since there is a great deal of skills transferability. Furthermore, some audit departments argue that any non-systems based work carried out by internal audit is in fact "consultancy work" in nature. The relevant points to note when comparing consultancy and internal audit are:

Consultants have no claim to independence over and above the view that they perform their work to professional standards and report all noteworthy matters. The fact that the terms of reference are set entirely by management means that this is a client based service to managers rather than an independent view for the welfare of the corporate entity. A consultant may be asked to provide a report to management and then be removed from any further involvement in the ensuing decisions that may be taken based on this work. This stance cannot be accepted by the auditor who is charged with securing a response from management and then carrying out a follow-up review after an appropriate time.

Internal auditors can learn from the focus that consultants have for applying their skills to solving managerial problems. A good audit report will seek to address and resolve control disorders found during the course of the audit and the published report should be set with this emphasis in mind. The CIA should be concerned where management has called in a consultant to solve problems impacting on service delivery shortly after an audit has been completed in the particular area. The question should be posed as to the value of the audit if key problems have not been considered by the internal auditor bearing in mind that control means being able to deliver one's goals. The consultant should not necessarily operate on a higher plane than the auditor. Where this is the case, then it may be necessary to restructure the audit strategy to take on board major issues that have meaning to managers. Whatever the format, it is just as well to read any recent consultant's report that impacts on an operation that is soon to be subject to audit cover.

It is possible to form a link into the world of management consultants where internal audit reports that require the application of major change programmes may call for consultants to be used to support the change process. Conversely, the other main concern that the auditor has with consultants is where audit urges caution from managers who rely too heavily on these consultants. Where this occurs, one must beware relying on persons who have no ongoing responsibility for the area in question once they have completed the project and leave the organisation. This is particularly relevant for computer systems that are under development as management has to live with the system once it goes live.

Internal control teams
These teams will tend to report to the appropriate director and their work depends on the objectives that they assumed when being established. Management controls and directs work and they tend to carry out a great deal of testing either on larger systems or via a programme of visits to establishment. The main difference is their lack of independence although they may have some link into internal audit via training programmes, plans, secondments and so on. One model of internal audit is based on a core audit department with internal control teams (ICTs) located within each main Directorate that have a functional reporting line to the CIA. Furthermore to cement such an arrangement, the CIA may submit plans and progress reports on behalf of the ICTs to the audit committee as well as carrying out regular reviews of their work. There are four main types of internal control teams as follows:

- **Computer coverage:** these teams are based around the computer runs and are responsible for ensuring that all input is properly processed and reconciled to the resulting outputs.
- **Low-level fraud investigations:** these teams carry out basic investigations into matters of irregularity that impact on their particular area.
- **Probity programmes:** some internal control teams carry out basic checks on remote establishments where compliance with procedure is reviewed along with related matters of accountability.
- **Testing programmes:** there are control teams that concentrate on completing detailed test programmes that seek to ascertain the correctness of specific books and records.

The internal auditor should establish a formal relationship with all ICTs so that their work may be taken on board when planning and performing internal audit work. In one sense, time spent reviewing the efficiency of ICTs is time well spent, particularly where any transaction testing constitutes a key control over the operation in question. The CIA can argue the case for a functional responsibility over these teams and seek to have this built into the job descriptions of both him/herself and the ICT officers. Where this is the case and ICTs are deemed to be low level "satellite auditors", then the CIA should have a role in setting the terms of reference for the teams, recruiting staff, and recommending suitable procedures and standards that may be applied to controlling their work. One useful control is to have the CIA issue "audit warrants" to ICTs that allow them limited access to various corporate systems outside their operational area. This will enable them to carry out their work, so long as they are able to meet minimum standards set by the CIA. These standards and the extent to which they are being achieved will then be subject to ongoing review by (or on behalf of) the CIA. Furthermore it is possible to establish joint training programmes where ICT staff can attend and become involved in audit-type developments. Where internal audit has assumed a probity role in line with the adopted audit charter and approach, then the issue of ICTs assumes another dimension. Here one may seek to restrict the ICT role as it may constitute a challenge to the internal audit resource and form a type of devolution of the audit service down to each department. There is a strong case for ensuring the internal audit function consists of senior staff so as to contrast this with any ICT that will tend to employ more junior personnel. As such the CIA will need to monitor the spread of ICTs to ensure that they do not duplicate internal audit work.

Work study
Time and motion staff may be used to discharge the organisation's policies regarding work flows, bonus schemes, job evaluation and so on. Their work may affect procedures and lead to systems changes that audit should be made aware of. The teams that in the past have performed this work have tended to be disbanded particularly where support services have been susceptible to budget reductions. In many cases these duties, say in job evaluation, have been passed on to personnel departments. Nonetheless, it may be good policy for internal audit to be made aware of developments within the organisation that impact on structuring, officer duties and staffing generally. These may then be assimilated into the operational profiles that underpin the audit plans.

Inspectorate functions
These are growing in the public sector with the growing emphasis on contracted out services and quality/compliance inspection of services provided. Management is becoming increasingly aware of its responsibilities to have knowledge of what is going on throughout the organisation and the inspectorate function can provide the necessary assurances. There is a link into the quality assurance function and this may be a growth area. Internal audit should keep up-to-date with this initiative since much compliance based work may be being undertaken throughout the organisation. Any function that falls under the generic term "inspectorate" may become involved in work that impacts on the internal auditor. Furthermore, there should be suitable communications mechanisms in place to enable a proper exchange of information. Regular meetings, exchanging reports and generally developing a good working relationship would all be considered best practice in interfacing the work of internal audit and inspectorate teams. Having said this, the internal

auditor has the additional responsibility of auditing such teams as part of the ongoing cover applied to all significant areas of the organisation.

Project teams

These are one-off initiatives and can lead to changes within the organisation and as well as consuming resources, they may include control issues in their remit. Points to note regarding project teams are:

The most common type of project team is that relating to systems development. In most cases existing computer applications are replaced by new and improved versions that because of their magnitude constitute developments in their own right. The audit concern here is dealt with in more detail in the chapter covering computer auditing. At this stage we may merely note the controls over the new application and the way the project itself has been managed and controlled. This is as well as the overall changes that may occur within the organisation as a result of the new development. To this end it is as well to have in place a formal policy whereby all project teams involving new (or enhanced) computer systems have to involve internal audit in terms of consulting them on security issues, project planning techniques applied and control issues affecting the new system. In addition where there is a requirement for internal audit to perform a post-implementation review of all such developments, there is likely to be greater compliance with corporate standards covering this type of activity.

Other ad-hoc project teams may be established to address major issues that are of concern to top management. A good example is a devolution of centralised services to business units that requires a great deal of planning and consideration before it can be completed. A formal project team may be set up to effect the necessary changes in respect of this devolution. In this type of scenario again, internal audit would seek to be kept informed as to the changes that arise as a result of the matters dealt with by the project team. Papers that detail the proposed changes and implications thereof should be copied to internal audit for comments before implementation. In this way control issues would hopefully be isolated and dealt with before major changes occur.

Internal audit may be asked to join a project team as part of their overall duty to promote the welfare of the organisation. In this eventuality, the CIA will need to submit formal terms of reference for such a role and ensure that there is no conflict of interests with this and the performance of audit work.

Systems controllers/managers

A review team (or in many cases review person) may be in post to fulfil the role of systems controller for the larger more significant computer systems. The internal auditor will seek to establish links with these persons who have a vested interest in maintaining good controls over the application in question. This person may be a key contact for any audit carried out that is associated with the system under review. As such, audit may wish to review the role and responsibilities of the systems controller, verify that these duties are being carried out and use information relating to journals and control reports, during the course of the audit. The additional question that the auditor will pose is "who controls the systems controller?". To this end audit may consider further reports that detail the interface the systems controller has with the computer system. This is as well as assessing the facilities (such as on-line access to the database) that this person has at his/her disposal. A useful starting place when dealing with the issue of systems controllers at a corporate level is to review the job descriptions prepared for this work with a view to assessing the level of control that is promoted via this resource. Whatever the approach, it is certainly advisable to keep this organisational role under review as a key control over automated functions.

Systems analysts

These officers will tend to spend time documenting major systems and advising on new developments as well as helping to maintain existing computerised systems. This process could well assist the audit role in providing good information, records and flowcharts albeit in the format used by IT personnel as opposed to auditors. Systems analysis may be the source of many changes to systems as part of an ongoing review and development and this will impact on the auditor's work. Again as with other review functions that we have already mentioned, internal audit should establish links so that a suitable exchange of information is available. It is surprising how brief conversations with systems analysts can highlight many issues that affect the balance of controls as systems are improved. Generally, the systems analysts' role is not properly balanced where they are taking too much responsibility for a development, or business managers are not addressing the key IT issues in their development plans, or the corporate interfaces with other systems have not been fully thought out. This can occur where the terms of reference for the required developments exclude key representatives from other areas where what will be feeder and/or link systems are in place. The internal auditor will be concerned that the systems analysts are not being asked to make changes that do not fit with corporate IT standards (e.g. on the acquisition of hardware). This is one reason why it is good practice to keep abreast of work being performed at this level.

Compliance officers

Where legislation sets up strict rules then a compliance function generally follows. An example is the computer misuse legislation that makes it an offence to attempt unauthorised access to computer systems. This development may enable audit to free itself of many cumbersome compliance duties where it is covered by another resource. One problem is that the compliance officer may actually be based within the audit department where there are no obvious alternatives provided by the existing organisation chart. Instead of viewing this role as part of the audit field that will be covered in the audit plan, the various compliance officers and security staff may actually report to the organisation's CIA. Whilst politically this may mean an increased power base for the CIA, it does water down the audit role and involve one in executive decisions as an integral part of operational procedures. There are obvious benefits and problems with this approach. Adopting the compliance role will have to be carefully managed by the CIA and it is best to keep this function separate from the systems audit service that should be the main preoccupation of internal audit. Data protection may be mentioned here, where an administrative and compliance role is required to discharge the organisation's responsibilities under the Data Protection Act 1984. Again it is possible to assimilate this role into the internal audit service (if the CIA wishes to assume a growth strategy). Also, there is a tentative link between this and overall computer systems security from a compliance viewpoint.

Quality assurance

This growth area has resulted in new teams appearing in many different sections of some organisations under the generic term "quality assurance" (QA). They generally review the underlying procedures that ensure a quality service is provided. This is a change in emphasis, based on prevention whilst moving away from the old-fashioned teams of checkers who identified post-production problems. Accreditation under quality standards may be sought for the area in question although the current view is that the formal arrangements for this status do have a resource implication in terms of time and costs. Whatever the final format, this trend cannot be ignored by internal audit since much work appears to have an audit flavour, even to the extent of using traditional audit terminology. Quality assurance initiatives and associated teams should be subject to internal audit cover as with all organisational resources. Notwithstanding this, we must ensure that we have all material that is in the possession of the QA teams as a way of maintaining an equilibrium with this service. Obviously the best approach is to share information and audit need have nothing to fear since QA has no established professional base that can compare to internal auditing. It tends to come and go in conjunction with the changing views of corporate management. We must though, be watchful of any move to consume audit work into the QA role without the full agreement of the CIA.

11.9 Conclusions

When considering the relationship between internal and external audit we must mention issues such as professionalism, the audit image, training, marketing and good relations with external audit and others. This is because good relationships do not mean standing in external audit's shadow and being used by it as it pleases. It means an equal relationship with professional respect from both sides, which has to be earned before it can be demanded. Relationships with other review agencies should likewise be clearly established since there may be some scope for co-ordination. Internal audit should seek to ensure that it assumes a higher status in the organisation than these other review teams, which should also be subject to internal audit cover in the normal course of planned audit work. In terms of other review agencies, the internal audit role within the organisation should be firmly established and contrasted with other available services. In addition an element of competition may lead to the services becoming blurred. This is where a formal audit charter helps define and publicise the audit mission so long as this is supported by a base of professional audit staff. There is also a link into the audit approach and if there are no client based marketing plans, audit's future may become somewhat insecure. Whilst communication links should be established with all appropriate review agencies, we must always reserve our right to "audit" them as is the case with all relevant parts of the organisation.

CHAPTER TWELVE

FUNDAMENTALS OF CONTROL

12.1 The Concept of Control

Introduction

Control may be seen as one of the single most important topics that the auditor needs to master. The main justification for the internal auditing function revolves around the need to review systems of internal control with all other audit activities being to an extent, subsidiary to this task. Understanding the concept of control and how controls may be applied in practice is an important skill that takes many years to fully acquire. This chapter considers the traditional aspects of the concept of control and goes on to explore an alternative model based on viewing **control** and **management** as synonymous terms.

The IIA definition

It should be noted that we are using a very wide definition of control which brings us far outside the various control mechanisms that are found in basic accounting systems. The IIA definition reads:

> *"All means devised to promote, govern and check upon various activities for the purpose of seeing that enterprise objectives are met."*

An outline of internal control is found in the IIA standard 300.

Control as an issue

Following on from the definition used above, there are a number of issues that underlie the concept of controls:

Controls are all means devised to promote the achievement of agreed objectives. This is an extremely broad interpretation of the control concept that in theory brings into play everything that management does in pursuing their objectives. We will return to this issue later.

All controls have a corresponding cost and the idea is that the ensuing benefits should be worth the required outlay. Costs may be defined to include actual additional expenditure as in the case of a security officer employed to enhance controls over the safety of portable, moveable equipment held in offices. On the other hand costs may simply relate to the increased efforts applied by management in seeking compliance with for example a new document signing procedure that makes it easier to find out who was involved in a certain transaction. The types of controls that spring to mind during a typical systems audit must be set within the cost context if the ensuing recommendations are to have any real use. Moreover we must remember that these additional costs are borne by management and not the auditor.

Controls belong to those who operate them and should not be viewed in isolation. In this respect management is responsible for the controls and the success of its operations will be linked to the degree to which controls work. There is a view that there are certain "audit requirements" that have to be acted on when considering controls over operations. This term is in reality a fallacy since it implies that certain control criteria are not under management's responsibility but are in some way under the purview of internal audit. So for example audit may state that managers must install a mechanism that enables them to know the whereabouts of portable PCs at all times. To suggest that this is an audit requirement rather than a management procedure is to relieve management of this responsibility, and so distort the control orientation. The temptation to issue "audit instructions" should be resisted as it will bring this inconsistency into play.

Internal control is all about people since controls work well only if they are geared to the user's needs in terms of practicality and usefulness. What appears sound on paper may be very difficult to put into practice. One may recall the newly appointed auditor who asks the cashier to record all cheques posted out each day, only to be told that it would take a certain type of individual to be able to log thousands of items daily. Again a detailed user manual that explains how a computerised system may be operated is of little use where the staff using the system have no real IT competence. Likewise controls that involve an officer monitoring staff by observing their every movement may be very difficult to apply in practice. Where an auditor comes across staff who are not at all motivated then he/she may find a level of non-compliance that may be difficult to explain. The "people factor" must be properly recognised. This comes to the fore when a change programme is being developed, and new systems and procedures are installed within a short time-frame. The principle may be taken to the extreme where we might argue that if the right people are employed, then they will seek to develop their own controls as part of their every day responsibilities. Unfortunately the converse would be true where inadequate staff are taken on.

Over-control is as bad as under-control in that it results in an impression that someone, somewhere is monitoring activity whereas this may not be the case in reality. Burdensome controls reduce the efficiency of operations and create an atmosphere of extreme bureaucracy where everything has to be signed for in triplicate. We have all read novels where the fictional police detective makes all the important arrests by refusing to "do things by the book". The other danger with over-control stems from a view that someone else will provide the necessary checks and balances. This appears where accounts fail to reconcile but because so many parties become involved in the balancing process, differences are left in suspense on the basis that they will be corrected somewhere along the line. Where front-line managers do not take responsibility for controlling their areas of work, but rely on a whole army of control teams we again have a recipe for disaster. An example follows:

> *An auditor in a large organisation came across a finance officer who spent all his time checking in detail, mileage claims submitted by front line staff. He expressed concerns about the accuracy of a number of regular claims by certain officers and showed a few examples to the auditor. The auditor suggested that the manager who had approved the claims should be held accountable. It turned out that this manager did have some worries about the claims but felt that this would be picked up in finance and so signed them off. The extra control exercised by finance was actually stifling the main control, i.e. managerial review.*

Entropy is the tendency to decay and all control systems will under-achieve where they are not reviewed and updated regularly. This is a quite straightforward concept that simply means that controls fall out-of-date as systems change and adapt to the latest environmental forces. Control routines fall into disuse over time whilst new developments call for a change in control orientation. Most organisations have devolved their support functions to business unit level where what used to be corporate controls now fall under the remit of local business managers. The traditional control disciplines over say hiring and firing staff are no longer relevant in this new climate where local management has much devolved powers. If the control orientation (say better corporate standards) does not alter to reflect these types of developments then problems can ensue. Returning to the micro level, we can suggest that every time a form falls into disuse this represents a symptom of entropy at work. This is why it is as well to plan audits over say a two to three year cycle, so that we can judge whether developments have led to an impairment in controls. There is an argument for getting management to consult with internal audit on all material proposals for restructuring and new systems installations, so that these issues may be considered. An alternative would be to educate management in the various control techniques as part of an ongoing development programme. Here we would expect all feasibility studies to contain a section covering "control implications" that addresses any shift in balance of control as a mandatory consideration. The only other option is for audit to plan a cycle of work that ensures all key systems are reviewed say annually.

The organisational culture affects the type of control features that are in place that may be bureaucratic or flexible in nature. There is no one right answer since each activity will have its own control policies. This principle can be seen in a stark example whereby two different personnel sections were visited to cover an audit of recruitment practices with the following result:

> *The first section consisted of seven staff squeezed into a small area with files and boxes scattered throughout the four offices. Personnel officers ran around making tea and discussing cases while making regular searches for misplaced files. The other section held six timesheeted personnel staff who sat in tidy offices that generated a feel of efficient working practices. Control in the first scenario centred around regular meetings and close contact between the personnel manager and staff. The other section in contrast, operated controls based on formal reports of activities via timesheeted hours, with very little open communication. Different types of controls work for different environments and this fact must be acknowledged by the auditor if there is to be any value derived from the audit work.*

The managerial control system has been described earlier as a fundamental system that should be in place for all operational areas. Deficiencies in any of the individual aspects will adversely affect the whole process of achieving the defined objectives. We will return to this key point later.

One way of viewing the control system is to consider that each operation must be accompanied by a corresponding control system that is superimposed on the operation itself. In this way control should not be an alien concept that impinges on the activity being performed. Systems objectives should be dependent on the underlying control objectives with each working in harmony to ensure that activities are undertaken in a controlled fashion. We can argue that assets can be acquired so long as they are used for authorised purposes, reports prepared so long as they are accurate and useful, and operations managed so long as this is done in an efficient fashion. In this way control follows the activity. The only way to make managers responsible for control is to incorporate the key concerns within their objectives. So an objective to achieve something must also incorporate a requirement to do so having due regard to matters of regularity, efficiency, compliance with procedure and overall control.

Building on the above point, the five main control objectives (see IIA standards pp 43-4) should always be kept in mind when considering and evaluating a system. In this way management would have to ensure that in pursuing their goals, there is due regard to:

- The adequacy of information systems.
- Compliance with laws and procedures.
- Protection of assets.
- Overall value for money (i.e. economy, efficiency and effectiveness).

The growing recognition of chaos management brings with it a need to control what appears at first sight a situation out of control. This may be the single biggest challenge now facing internal audit. A bottom-line control given to a business unit may simply be encompassed in a defined gross profit margin and nothing else. Controls that do not impact on this figure may be deemed to have no relevance at all. This may result in a chaotic search for profits that has no regard for the traditional controls of authorisation, good documentation, supervision, reconciliation and so on. It may even be accepted that a line manager may abuse company resources so long as this profit target is met. The concept of control will be much different in this type of environment and this must be recognised. Many of the moves towards good corporate governance are based on the growing recognition that there must be some standards of conduct outside the bottom-line profit margin. The question of whether there is a right way of doing things is fundamental to any discussion of controls. One answer is to suggest that since controls are means by which objectives are achieved, then they must link directly into these goals to be of any use. If these goals are single-issue based then so will be the types of controls that support them.

12.2 Control Criteria

Good control mechanisms should exhibit certain defined attributes:

They should be clearly defined and understood by all users. Where a procedure is not fully appreciated by staff there will definitely be problems associated with compliance. They should be simple to operate and make sense. So for example, where two activities are segregated the ensuing work should flow in a sensible way and not constitute a basic duplication of effort. They should be realistic and not too cumbersome. An office environment that relies heavily on telephone contact will stagnate if staff are asked to record in detail each phone call made and received. Rules on documentation should, in this case, take on board the level of activity that is recorded and apply only to limited instances where there is a real need to write something down. They should be regularly reviewed and amended particularly where the operation has changed. We have touched upon the control aspects of systems amendment and it is important that managers recognise this when making decisions regarding the way they organise their resources.

They should be geared to the riskier aspects of the operation. This is a key factor since there is little point devising a whole series of procedures that do not relate to matters that should be of concern to management. In fact it is most frustrating to spend time controlling areas that do not feed directly into organisational goals. Note that we will be developing an alternative model of "controls" that builds on this view that they must be interfaced with the process of pursuing objectives. They should be consistent in the way they are designed and applied. For example, if performance appraisal is applied to one set of staff, it makes sense to extend this to all employees where performance is a major concern. Again devolved financial management and decentralised personnel management should all relate back to corporate standards that act as a high-level control over what can and cannot be done. As such controls should not really be dependent on the individual managers but should be part of general quality standards. Furthermore, matters of fairness and equity should be a clear part of the control process across the organisation.

Mechanisms should be established to monitor the extent to which control is being applied in practice. Control is a process that starts with setting standards and ends with reviewing the extent to which this has been successful. Checks over the way people are using procedures are an integral part of the control process that cannot be separated from the act of installing the control features in the first place. Non-compliance is a major concern for the auditor who will seek to test this factor before accepting that suitable controls are in place. This view however may be challenged where we deem the review of compliance as management's role, underpinning the control process rather than relying on separate checks by the auditor. As we have already hinted, a wider interpretation of the control concept can be used to cater for the need to integrate controls into the entire management process.

Their use should be agreed by management and the staff who operate them. This factor should be used by the auditors to ensure they get managers to "own" recommendations that impact on the systems of internal control. Suggesting that the devices that strengthen control in some way belong to the auditors creates a degree of distance between management and the control process. Managers must accept or reject a control process and this decision must be left up to them. Following this point, it is not for the managers to stand guard over their staff and ensure they do things properly. In the final analysis we return again to the principle that control is people, and that these people are located at all levels in the organisation. With this in mind, it is essential that the control process is driven not only by managers but also by the staff themselves. We can monitor this principle by examining management textbooks and training courses, which should include material on systems of internal control.

Types of control

Principal controls may be categorised in a number of different ways. One way is to view them as being classified as follows:

- Administrative.
- Informational.
- Managerial.
- Procedural.
- Physical.

Another way is to break them down into:

1. **Preventive** - to ensure that systems work in the first place. These may include employing competent staff, high moral standards, segregation of duties and generally establishing a good control environment.

2. **Detective** - These controls are designed to pick up transaction errors that have not been prevented. They cover controls such as supervisory review, internal checks, variance reporting, spot checks and reconciliations.

3. **Corrective** - The final category of controls ensures that where problems are identified they are properly dealt with. These include management action, correction and follow-up procedures.

12.3 Controls in Practice

Some of the more traditional control mechanisms that may be applied in practice include:

☐ **Authorisation**. The act of authorising something brings with it the process of granting permission on behalf of the organisation. This is normally associated with a signature from the authorising officer that records this decision. For this control to be of any use it must involve the following attributes:

FIGURE 12.1 THE EXERCISE OF AUTHORITY

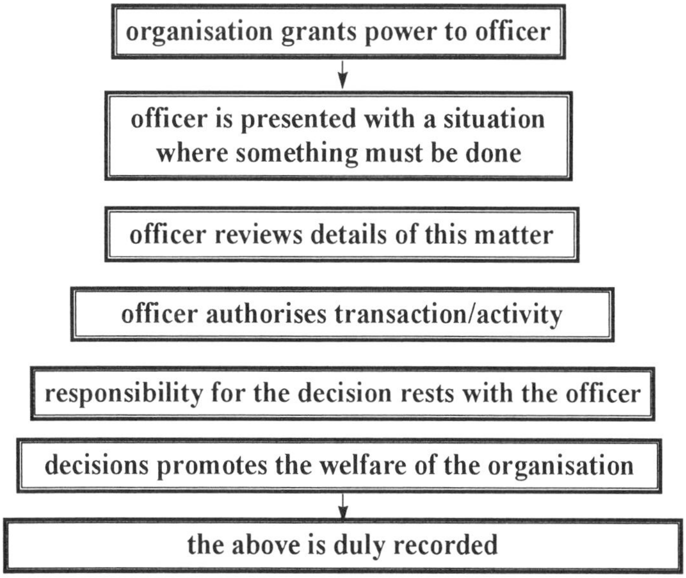

organisation grants power to officer
officer is presented with a situation where something must be done
officer reviews details of this matter
officer authorises transaction/activity
responsibility for the decision rests with the officer
decisions promotes the welfare of the organisation
the above is duly recorded

Each of the above components must be fully satisfied for this control process to be relied on. Where for example the detail presented to the officer is false or misleading, or not properly considered, the decision may be flawed. Likewise, if the officer can disclaim responsibility for the decision then again the process breaks down.

☐ **Physical access restrictions**. This should be applied to information through (say passwords), people (e.g. screens) and assets (e.g. locks). It is based on two principles. The first is the need to know/have policy that provides information or assets only where this is necessary for the performance of one's work. The second is based on the view that there is little point in leaving cash on a desk and so testing the resolve of people to resist temptation. Access restrictions only work where there is careful consideration given to the control of keys/passwords.

☐ **Supervision**. This control tends to have a dual nature whereby staff are observed first hand by their line managers, while at the same time these supervisors are available to help and assist their subordinates. Supervision will not really work unless these two features are firmly in place. When reviewing the success of supervision it is not enough to simply have line managers located with their staff but we must also consider what is achieved through the relationship. Where a supervisor ignores blatant breaches of procedure (say abuse of the telephones) then this in fact impairs control.

☐ **Compliance checks**. We have already discussed compliance as a fundamental component of the control systems and the way it is part of the process of doing things properly. Here we consider compliance in the context of special steps taken to check on whether authorised procedures are being applied as prescribed. This is a support control that seeks independent confirmation that staff are performing in the way that was originally intended. Control teams with a remit to carry out regular compliance checks are one way of doing this. Remember that compliance checks cannot be part of a quality assurance programme unless there is an in-built way of tracing identified problems back to their underlying cause and so correcting them. Straightforward compliance checks simply provide a device for making sure procedures are used.

☐ **Procedures manuals**. As a high level control, the organisation should set corporate standards that cover at least the following areas:
- Financial regulations covering income, expenditure, cash, banking, general accounting, contracts and related matters.
- Staff handbook covering recruitment, training and development, performance, discipline and so on.
- Purchasing code of practice on goods and services acquired by the organisation.
- Code of personal conduct with guidance on gifts and hospitality.
- Computer standards on the use of computer hardware and software.

Where there is a limited internal audit cover, it may be best to channel audit resources into reviewing the adequacy and effectiveness of the above mentioned procedures as the most efficient use of audit time. Corporate procedures should be related to lower-level operational procedures that set direction on matters that fall within the remit of front-line officers. These more detailed procedures also constitute important control devices so long as they are complied with.

☐ **Output inspection**. Another key control that should be firmly in place is related to a process whereby output is examined by line management. This may involve reviewing reconciliations, working papers, reports, physical products, achievements (e.g. a new contract agreed with the client) and so on. The point being that some form of check is made on that which staff produce. The output should be measured against a defined standard in line with the following process.

FIGURE 12.2 OUTPUT INSPECTION PROCESS

This process is linked to the principle of delegation whereby staff are able to act on behalf of management, but the resultant product is still the responsibility of the same managers, who have to sign-off the work done. As such a typical auditor's question that can be applied in almost any situation may appear as "how do you satisfy yourself that the work has been performed to the requisite standard?".

☐ **Recruitment practices.** We have indicated that most controls are based around what people do and the people factor cannot be ignored. The successful operation of basic controls presupposes that the staff involved are competent, motivated, honest, and alert so that they are both able and willing to perform. Whilst much of this is dependent on good management practices based around communication and team building, the foundation is derived from using the right people in the first place. This in turn is wholly dependent on sound recruitment practices. There are many auditors who will recognise the embarrassing situation where they have completed an audit and found many problems that essentially relate back to elementary staff incompetence. It is difficult to report this matter other than as a training need. It is becoming increasingly clear that impoverished organisations, particularly in the public sector, have suffered because of inadequate recruitment procedures that lead to staff being taken on, who are not equipped to perform in any respect.

☐ **Segregation of duties.** This control brings into play more than one officer during any one transaction that can lead to an actual gain or benefit. The idea is to stop one person from undertaking a transaction from start to finish. There are obvious examples such as a payments system where the preparation, authorisation, processing, and dispatch of the cheque should each be done by different people. The idea is not only to act as a check on each other's work but also to help prevent fraud. Internal check is a related procedure whereby the work of one person is checked by another again so as to minimise fraud and error. As such, reliance is not placed solely on the work of one person in recognition of the human frailty that allows mistakes to occur. An example of a basic check is where staff timesheets are cross-cast by an administrative officer before being input to a time recording system. Any errors on completing this document will hopefully be thereby isolated. Segregation of duties and internal check are becoming less prevalent as we move to flatter organisations where business units have devolved responsibility for systems such as payments, income collection and payroll. The new control culture seeks rejection routines, automated audit trails and exception reports to reveal whether there has been any fraud or abuse.

☐ **Sequential numbering of documents**. Valuable documents such as orders, cheque requisitions and cheques themselves have an in-built control in terms of the sequential numbers. All controlled stationery should meet this criterion. The ability to check and report on these sequences creates a useful control technique where missing, duplicated or inconsistent items may be readily isolated. Transactions sequencing can be applied to many situations where we wish to monitor what is going through a system and/or what documents are being used. It is good practice to review all documents in use and decide whether there would be any benefits in having them uniquely identifiable. Any processing systems would have to be set to record and report on this item for such a procedure to be of any use.

☐ **Reconciliations**. The act of balancing one system to another does in itself engender control. As a principle this should be applied to all systems that have an association in terms of data from one relating to data from another. Control reports based on the reconciliations can direct management to areas where there might be problems or error. Of course basic reconciliations also arise in accounting procedures where accounts are balanced before they are closed off and posted to the final accounts. Again, the auditor may ask for any system "what should this balance to and does this happen in practice?". As an example a creditors system may allow the inputter to write-off a payment that has been fraudulently encashed after the cheque has been intercepted in the post, so that a fresh cheque may be raised. A separate database of fraudulently encashed cheques may also be maintained. The creditors system may then report all items coded to "write off: fraudulent encashment", and this report should be reconciled to the fraudulent cheques database as a key control over this procedure.

The list may go on and on indefinitely since it is clear that control is about everything that management does in getting the right results. This concept will be developed later as we seek to construct a model that takes on board a wider interpretation of the control concept.

12.4 The Suitability of Controls

In terms of assessing the suitability of systems of internal control, there are some danger signs that should be looked for that might lower the efficiency of the control environment as follows:

☐ **Ability of senior management to override accepted control**. Many quite acceptable procedures constitute good control over staff activities so long as they are being applied. Furthermore compliance checks may help isolate staff who do not use prescribed procedures and action taken to remedy this. Informal groups with decision-making powers are also able to form a pressure group that may be able to overrule control routines. Formal control procedures that are written up and applied by all staff lead to good control. However, where there are matters that fall outside the norm, vague contingency arrangements may be in place that are in practice unwritten and in part, simply made up. Where this happens controls may break down and it may be very difficult to discover who made what decisions. The problem arises where managers are able to suspend controls at will, so as to expedite a required activity. An example follows:

> *A director ruled that reception staff must check all ID cards for staff arriving at the building even where they are known. This happened for a few weeks and suddenly stopped. Reception explained, when asked why the practice had ceased, that the same director when asked to produce his ID became most annoyed and refused. Since then it was felt that the extra checks should be abandoned.*

The difficulty arises where staff feel unable to challenge senior managers who are by-passing a standard control. Where controls can be suspended for emergencies this must be agreed and written into the procedure, and ideally subject to special checks when the emergency is over.

☐ **Lack of staff and vacant posts**. Control relating to authorisation, internal check, segregation and supervision can suffer where there are insufficient staff to enact the agreed procedure. For example a procedure for enveloping cheques that requires two people being present is very hard to apply where there simply are not enough staff. There needs to be a level of flexibility in designing controls so that unusual circumstances, where staff are not available, may be catered for. To compensate for this, it is essential that a management trail is present that allows one to ascertain who initiated a transaction for later review and consideration. Moreover, management must assume responsibility for failing to fill vacant posts or not arranging suitable cover such that controls are impaired. They cannot simply ignore this issue or blame it on budget restrictions.

☐ **Poor control culture**. The types of controls that we have mentioned above depend on managers and staff doing things properly. It normally takes longer and it is more cumbersome to perform these control arrangements and this in turn takes a level of all-round discipline. The aggregation of these views on discipline from all levels in the organisation constitutes what we may call the "control environment" or alternatively the "control culture".

An example:

> *A new employee was being shown around the office and came across a book marked "temps signing-in book". He was surprised to find it empty despite the fact that there were several temporary staff present who had been working for many months. On making enquiries he was told that the temps did not bother to sign-in and no one insisted that they did.*

☐ **Staff collusion**. Many controls depend on two or more officers' involvement as a form of a check over each other's activities. The idea is that whilst one person could be corrupt, this would be a rare occurrence which is catered for by not allowing an individual sole authority over one routine. This unfortunately does not take on board research that suggests many people are only as honest as controls require them to be. As such where dishonest staff conspire to defeat controls they can do a great deal of damage. When reviewing transactions the fact that there are two signatures attached to a document does not mean that it is necessarily correct and proper. In one sense, this is the auditor's nightmare, as there are some systems that can be wholly by-passed through collusion.

☐ **Reliance on a single performance indicator**. We have agreed that controls are in place to ensure that management is able to achieve its objectives. Where these objectives are centred on performance indicators then we would expect the associated controls to recognise this factor. The problem arises where management is given one basic indicator to work to, which is regularly reported. The temptation to base one's activities around one key factor can lead to many distortions that do not necessarily promote organisational objectives. A bottom-line ratio can have unforeseen side-effects that make many controls redundant as they do not contribute to the requisite figure. An example:

> *An internal audit section had one main performance indicator, the percentage of recoverable to nonrecoverable hours which was reported to the audit committee quarterly. The committee were not interested in the achievements from the recoverable hours (i.e. reports issued) and this led to staff dumping their time to recoverable jobs. There was very little attention paid to controlling time charged to active jobs.*

☐ **Reliance on memory**. There are some controls that are dependent on knowledge held only in the minds of employees. This may relate to identity and/or signature of authorising officers, procedures used for dealing with various activities, levels of delegated authority, key contacts, roles of respective officers and so on. Whilst on the one hand this gives well-deserved responsibility to long-serving employees, and as a result places them in a special position, it can also have many disadvantages. One is a lack of clarity as to precisely what actions the organisation has authorised. In addition inconsistency and misunderstanding can arise where there is undue reliance placed on the discretion of the person in question. It is surprising how many systems are based on this factor that, through custom and practice, develops over time. Control is not impossible within this model but there are many dangers that can result in an overall lowering of control standards. This point can be probed by the auditor who might continue to enquire "what happens when this person is away...? How can you be sure that this is the correct procedure...? and so on..." We can place reliance on memory next to the fact that long-serving and trusted employees can be involved in fraud, irregularity and basic mistakes. We move to a position where a more formalised arrangement may be required. Unfortunately, there is a socio-psychological influence that can come into play, where staff have learnt that it is better to operate on an informal footing in contrast to adopting formal written procedures. This is because, from experience, one may become almost indispensable where no one actually knows how to perform the tasks that attach to the job in question. Compiling formal documents and checklists can eventually lead to redundancy/removal for the person involved. It is therefore unfortunate that the best interests of staff do not necessarily coincide with the best interests of the organisation. Many an auditor has returned to a work area each year only to find that the procedures, checklists and standard documentation that he/she had previously recommended have not yet been drafted. What should be the motivation for this may be stifled by a motive that is driven by a stronger force. We return again to the question of reliance on memory and suggest that staff who seem to be muddling their way through the day in what appears to be a chaotic fashion may have actually engineered this position for their own reasons.

□ **Retrospective transaction recording**. There are many managers who feel that documentation that records and/or authorises a transaction is a matter of pure bureaucracy, that interferes with the day-to-day running of their work area. There are times when orders are placed over the phone with the associated paperwork compiled many weeks later. There are records that are written up as and when there is time available, in many cases the relevant detail is based mainly on memory.

□ **Uncontrolled delegation of tasks**. The idea of controls is linked into various management principles that include accountability and responsibility. Having someone in charge of an operation and responsible for the end-result is the best way of ensuring that there is a driving force that directs resources towards the defined goals of the organisation. This principle is fundamental to the business world as experience shows that consensus rule through various committees blurs the decision-making process and leads to excessive bureaucracy. Responsibility does not mean that tasks cannot be delegated to various levels under a manager's command and again this is generally good practice. The danger lies in excessive delegation that has not been controlled in any sense. In this scenario control suffers as staff assume responsibility for activities that should rightly be under the charge of more senior officers. It is not possible to assign tasks and walk away without checking on progress or caring about what happens. "Scapegoating" is now a serious political issue where middle management is frequently prone to disciplinary action if a problem can be traced back to an action (or failure to act). The question of exactly who is responsible for an activity where there are problems can be key to the process of instigating such disciplinary action. Delegation can in this respect be a useful management tool, or a weapon to be readily abused.

12.5 Management's Role

Management's role concerning systems of internal control is as follows:

□ **Determine the need for controls**. Managers must be able to isolate a situation where there is a need for specific internal controls and respond appropriately. For example when designing a new computer system, they must consider controls over both the development process and the resulting system at an early stage as part of their overall responsibility to promote the welfare of the organisation. The determination of need precedes the design stage as there is little point in resourcing a control routine that is not really required. Another good example of this principle is where a previously in-house service is contracted out to an external provider. Here the contract specification along with suitable contract management procedures constitute key controls over the contract where it is monitored and compliance checked. Management must consider the need for additional controls over and above the contract compliance issue. This may include a review of the database for say a debtors system where accounts that are left out may simply be ignored and so not collected. Checks over the completeness of this database may be required to protect the organisation where there would be no other way of knowing whether the database was being properly maintained. The decision on whether to install extra controls is obviously relevant here and this must be placed at the foot of management.

☐ **Design suitable controls**. Once the need for controls has been defined, management must then establish suitable means to install them. This is not a simple process that relies solely on doing what was done in the past. It involves much more including a formal process of assessing relative risks and seeking to guard against the types of problems that might arise, if controls are not firmly in place. We have already outlined the criteria that should be considered when devising controls and this and much more should be taken on board in the design process. Managers know their staff, work environment and type of culture they operate within better than anyone else, which makes them well placed for this task. Consultants, auditors, project teams and other sources of advice may be employed in the search for improved control, but notwithstanding this, responsibility still lies with the managers themselves.

☐ **Implement these controls**. Managers are then duty-bound to ensure that the control processes are carefully implemented. This entails at a minimum the provision of suitable guidance on how they should be used, ideally in written format and a mechanism by which staff can be coached in the application of the underlying actions. We may care to move back a step and suggest that managers have to think about the basic skills necessary to effect these controls and whether they are employing the right calibre of staff in this respect. Remember it is the responsibility of management to deem that defined posts attract certain minimum qualifications and experience. If these are not asked for, then there is no point then blaming staff for poor performance. It is generally the managers' fault that their subordinates are not able to discharge the requirements of their post. Training and development are the other techniques that seek to support basic performance standards. This must be fully applied in the pursuit of success in line with the control arrangements that underpin this search.

☐ **Check that they are being applied correctly**. Management and not internal audit is responsible for ensuring that control mechanisms are not being by-passed but are fully applied as they were originally intended. One cannot wait for the auditors for information on how controls are working as this defeats this important principle. We have already explained that the control process includes a review of compliance as an integral component. We have also described the control culture where management seeks to set control as a highly regarded discipline that deserves the respect of all staff and not an unnecessary set of rules that impair performance. All these things lead to an environment where control is fostered and publicised, again leading to the chance of greater compliance. It therefore becomes more and more difficult for managers to shrug their shoulders and declare that poor control is caused by junior staff and not them. Once we have arrived at this acceptance we have great scope for a well controlled organisation (substitute "well managed" for "well controlled").

☐ **Maintain and update the controls**. This feature is also important in that securing control is a continuous task that should be at the forefront of management concerns. The need to define control implications must be revisited as we reinforce the view that management must acknowledge this issue in a vigorous way. This includes the need to discard outdated control wherever necessary so as to avoid the unmanageable situation where controls are perceived as patchy, with some being applied while others have fallen into disuse. So as to avoid excessive debate on the question of updating control, we can merely suggest that up-to-date procedures can be a life or death issue as one newspaper headline reads:

> **"Hundreds killed by doctors relying on outdated manuals".**
> **(Sunday Times - 5 February 1995)**

☐ **Inclusion of the above noted matters within any appraisal scheme that seeks to judge management's performance**. We would expect management to consider the application of controls a part of management skills and training. Furthermore if this were built firmly into employee performance appraisal mechanisms then managers would be in the enviable position whereby they receive suggestions from their staff on how to better effect good control over the resources under their command.

12.6 Audit's Role

The auditors' role regarding systems of internal control is distinguished from management's in that it covers:

- Assessing those areas that are most at risk in terms of the key control objectives that we have already mentioned several times (i.e. MIS, compliance, safeguarding assets and VFM).
- Defining and undertaking a programme for reviewing these high profile systems that attract the most risk.
- Reviewing each of these systems by examining and evaluating their associated systems of internal control to determine the extent to which the five key control objectives are being met.
- Advising management whether or not controls are operating adequately and effectively so as to promote the achievement of the systems/control objectives.
- Recommending any necessary improvements to strengthen controls where appropriate, whilst making clear the risks involved for failing to effect these recommended changes.
- Following up audit work so as to discover whether management has actioned agreed audit recommendations.

The growing trend to self-auditing imposes a level of responsibility on internal audit for educating management on the need for good controls and risks that arise where this factor is not duly appreciated. Brochures, presentations, skills workshops, and close consultation with managers may be considered internal audit roles in this search for getting management committed to a clear control orientation. These initiatives however must be done in such a way as to reinforce and not dilute the extensive responsibilities of management for controlling resources.

The control system
One convenient way of discharging the audit role in evaluating controls is to consider the extent to which a control loop has been established and applied. The control system has been dealt with in chapter one. It is possible to examine the way in which each of these fundamental aspects of control are dealt with by management. Control is seen as inherent in effectively providing for these managerial components and it is this concept that audit will evaluate. The actual operation will incorporate the unique control mechanisms that are suited to the function that the system is designed to perform. This point is developed later on in this chapter.

12.7 The IIA Briefing note on internal control

The IIA.UK issued guidance (briefing note 6) on this topic in 1994 that contained much needed material in the wake of the Cadbury report that made mention of internal control as a defined concept. Whilst the briefing note covers 50 pages of relevant material, there are several extracts that can be quoted that impact on our discussions on this matter:

Effective internal control cannot solve all corporate problems, but defective internal controls may lead to serious corporate problems. Internal control is part of, but not the whole of the management process, and effective internal controls are not a remedy for poor decisions, ineffective management, or unpredictable external events. Good management and effective internal controls can help to ensure that an organisation is in a position to deal quickly and positively with adverse circumstances and can help to limit the worst effects (p.7). The primary purpose of an internal control system is to enable directors to drive their companies forward with confidence, at an appropriate speed and direction, in both good and bad times; the secondary, but no less important, purpose is to safeguard resources and ensure the adequacy of records and systems of accountability (p.8). Directors and top management can significantly enhance the likelihood of objectives and goals being attained if they adequately control, i.e., plan, organise and direct, the effective use of resources (p.9). The management process of every company includes an internal control system. If the internal control system is ineffective the management process will also be ineffective (p.10). Internal control is part of the management process. It is the action taken by management to plan, organise and direct the performance of sufficient actions to provide reasonable assurance that the following objectives will be achieved:

* Accomplishment of established objectives and goals for operations and programmes.
* The economical and efficient use of resources.
* The safeguarding of resources.
* The reliability and integrity of information.
* Compliance with policies, plans, procedures, laws and regulations (p.13).

For example, an effective control system will ensure that management received sufficient information to enable them to take action which will help them to achieve corporate objectives etc. However, if management chooses to ignore the information, or does not recognise the implications of the information, the organisation may suffer adverse consequences (p.14). Effective internal control is achieved through people. To make internal control effective requires directors, managers and others, to design, maintain, adhere to, and monitor the system of control (p.14). The effectiveness of the control systems can only be guessed at unless there is an effective monitoring system. However no monitoring system can give management absolute assurance of the effectiveness of, and adherence to the corporate controls (p.15). All corporate decisions lead to planning, organising, and directing actions. Each action needs to be:

- Planned to indicate the demands on company resources and the targets and goals.
- Executed within corporate/legal restraints.
- Recorded in accordance with corporate procedures.
- Reviewed against the targets or goals.

The review (of internal control) should concentrate on eliminating complacency, ignorance, inefficiency and waste, which will inhibit corporate performance. The review should also pay attention to the need to eliminate any unnecessary bureaucracy in the management process while ensuring that the essential controls exist and contribute to effective performance (p.17). As failures of quoted companies are invariably due to failures of internal controls it would seem reasonable to expect boards to regularly review the process adopted by them to achieve their objectives and goals (p.18). The effective management framework for management control covers:

- Philosophy and operating style.
- Plans, risks, goals and objectives.
- Human resources.
- Policies and procedures.
- Information systems.
- Monitoring and correction (p.20).

The briefing note goes on to make reference to the US Committee of Sponsoring Organisations of the Treadway Commission 1992 report (COSO) as providing important guidance on internal control. This report defines internal control as follows:

> **"Internal control is a process, effected by an entity's board of directors, management and other personnel, designed to provide reasonable assurance regarding the achievement of objectives in the following categories;**
> - **Effectiveness and efficiency of operations.**
> - **Reliability of financial reporting.**
> - **Compliance with applicable laws and regulations."**

COSO among other matters also states that the internal control system is intertwined with an entity's operating activities and exists for fundamental business reasons. Internal controls are most effective when they are built into the entity's infrastructure and are part of the essence of the enterprise. They should be "Built in" rather than "built on".

12.8 Recent Developments

The new business environment creates a growing emphasis on internal controls and the fact that there can be dire consequences where they break down, or are not there in the first place. The Cadbury report has been dealt with elsewhere and there is a view that corporate governance is equally relevant to the public sector as well as private enterprise. Paul Rutteman has chaired a working party that seeks to address the issues relating to internal controls and its impact on the business environment, within this regulatory context. We have also made note of that new development, control self assessment, elsewhere in the handbook. The accountancy/audit profession has responded to these demands by seeking guidance on directors' new responsibilities and reporting duties. There is also pressure to define the roles of both external audit and internal audit in this respect. Meanwhile during 1995, the IIA.UK introduced a new examination paper on "control" as part of their revised professional study programme. From what we have seen so far, for the late 1990s and going onto the year 2000, there will be many questions that need to be addressed including:

- How do we define (and re-define) controls and systems of internal control?
- How can directors discharge what may be seen as an open-ended responsibility for conceptual systems?
- How should external audit report on this responsibility?
- How can we control top managers who not only set up their own controls but may also be able to override them wherever they wish to?
- How do we contain risk in a business (such as trading in derivatives) that positively thrives on the risk factor?
- How can we promote a scandal-free business environment, when we have already argued that "control is people and people are control"?
- And lastly, and most importantly, can internal audit utilise this new development to assume a key role in controlling all important companies, authorities and government agencies?

12.9 Managerial Control Mechanisms

The concept of managerial controls

Auditing is based on comparing the "what should be" to the "what is in practice". Suitable control models must be devised as a basis for this comparison and herein lies the need to have an army of suggested controls that may be used to this end. On one level control can mean many things relating to the act of being in charge. These have synonyms including "command, conduct, direct, dominate, govern, have charge of, lead, manage, manipulate, oversee, pilot, reign over, rule, steer, superintend, and supervise." On the other hand it can denote a process of holding back with synonyms such as "bridle, check, constrain, contain, curb, hold back, limit, master, rein in, repress, restrain and subdue." This brings out the dual nature of the forces of control in that it involves both doing the right things as well as stopping the wrong things from occurring, so as to seek an acceptable equilibrium. Faced with this dilemma the starting place is to restate the official definition of a control which is the means by which management ensures that its objectives will be achieved. The first point that may be gleaned from this definition is that this means all the arrangements that management relies on, are potential controls, making this an extremely wide concept. If this line is pursued then we may have to suggest that all activities are controls and we need therefore to cover all possible management action. This is obviously an unacceptable stance to defend as well as being impossible to carry out in practice. Accordingly we will break down our references to systems of control in a number of ways that will then be used to structure this section of the material on control. One argument is to suggest that controls can be addressed and documented on a number of levels:

☐ **The managerial system control attributes**. Auditing that is performed at a corporate or managerial level will look for controls over the management process. The systems school of management may be used as a basis for defining the fundamental management processes that must be present. Each management process should exhibit certain features and we refer to these as "control attributes" that can be applied to the audit of any business unit.

☐ **Information systems controls**. The growing importance of management information systems (MIS) makes this a topic in its own right. While MIS is one of the fundamental managerial control processes it may also be viewed as a whole system in its own right. It is poor practice to audit an MIS without reference to operational aspects related to business objectives. Nevertheless, having a whole range of computer controls will assist the evaluation stage of an audit. This is why we would expect comprehensive notes on computer audit and related controls to be held in the audit library.

☐ **Subject-related trigger points**. Controls are in part viewed as fundamental concepts that may be applied in any situation. At the same time each operational area has its own special features, and these affect the way that underlying control systems are applied. Available control mechanisms have been described in many textbooks and papers relating to internal audit and external audit, and these are therefore not reproduced here. However the various relevant textbooks and ICQs should also be held in the audit library.

The above comprises a whole package of control attributes/mechanisms that should be used by the auditor in performing the control evaluation stage of a systems audit. Most operational areas may in this way, be reviewed by the auditor.

Applying the systems approach
Before launching into managerial control attributes, we must restate the way that controls relate to the systems auditing that we carry out. In this respect several relevant points may be listed:
- Controls must be incorporated into the various schedules that are used in the evaluation stage of systems auditing.
- It is not possible to throw controls at a client out of context. Controls must be related to business objectives or they will have no relevance whatsoever.
- Control weaknesses must be tested wherein the effects of weak control systems are established.
- Controls must be viewed as a system and many suggested mechanisms may be absent but are compensated for by strong controls at an earlier or later stage in the systems' process.

From our discussion so far, it should be clear that there is no such thing as an audit control. There are only management controls and in this context we should restate that management should establish business objectives and for each business objective there will be underlying control objectives to ensure that, the information is adequate, compliance occurs, assets are protected, value for money is promoted. Sufficient control mechanisms should be designed, installed and reviewed to ensure that these control objectives are achieved. These controls should form a system to cover control at a corporate, managerial and operational level.

12.10 The Managerial System Control Attributes

The managerial control system represents the fundamental processes that must be in place to control any operation. The systems school of thought uses General Systems Thinking to help define these processes and the way that they link together to form a complete system. When reviewing what may be viewed as a business unit (i.e. a defined set of resources under a manager working to achieve a defined objective) then we may consider the adequacy and effectiveness of the macro-based managerial control system. This is done by considering whether the various attributes (as set out below) are present. Potential weaknesses may be identified where any of these attributes are lacking. The areas that form the managerial control system (MSC) may be listed as follows:

- Objectives; a clear statement of goals.
- Strategic analysis; an efficient way of achieving the goals.
- Structuring; the way resources will be deployed.
- Human resource management; a process of acquiring the required resources.
- Quality standards; the standards that will be applied to the operation in terms of quality and quantity.
- Procedures; the way work will be undertaken.
- Operational activities; the activities themselves.
- Marketing; the way that clients' needs are defined and met.
- Management information; the information that is required to manage and control the activities.

A series of managerial control attributes are set out in supplement five in the accompanying diskette.

12.11 Conclusions

We can note that internal auditors are known by many names including computer audit, contract audit, compliance audit, fraud investigators, probity inspectors and so on. There is a view that the auditor should know more about the system under review than management and as such may tell them how best to perform their managerial duties. This is false since it is managers who must understand their areas of responsibility and audit's role is not to second-guess them. Above all the auditor is an expert in control armed with a comprehensive knowledge of control concepts. The available mechanisms and how they might be applied in practice are the main prerequisites for a professional internal auditor. Meanwhile the auditor should use the attributes that attach to each component of the managerial control system (MCS), whenever the audit evaluation covers a defined service. This is particularly relevant for auditing an operation, section, department or what may be considered akin to a business unit. An activity cannot be assessed outside of the context of the macro system of controls that form the basis of the MCS. A top-downwards approach (according to the MCS) will always be more effective than a review of isolated low-level transactions. In summary the two approaches that we have described in this section of the handbook are derived from two different views of controls:

FIGURE 12.3 TRADITIONAL CONTROL MODEL

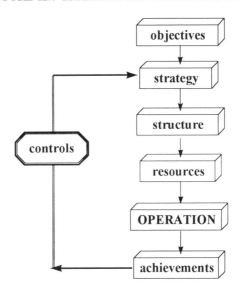

Here control is seen to shadow the management process as an additional system superimposed over and above this process to ensure that activities are carried out properly and objectives achieved.

FIGURE 12.4 MANAGEMENT CONTROL SYSTEM (AMENDED)

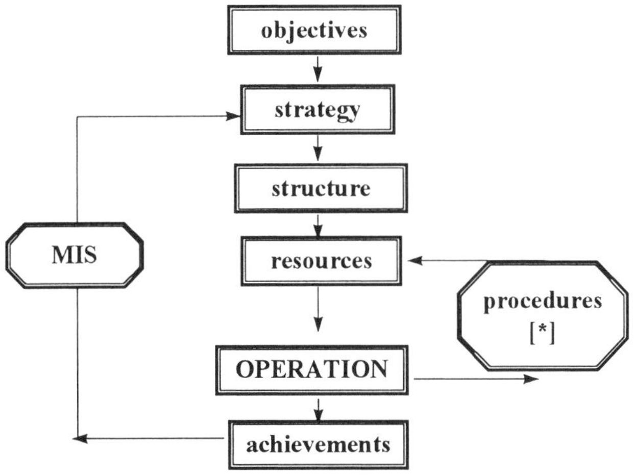

The alternative model simply argues that the management process constitutes the absolute control process which is impossible to separate from managers' main activities. This in turn calls for a quasi-management consultancy audit role, as we seek to tackle complicated management systems. We can surmise that at least 80% of control is exercised via the management processes whilst the remainder falls in line with the more traditional type of controls that are based around the actual operation (incorporated within operational procedures [*] above).

PART TWO

AUDIT TECHNIQUES

Introduction to Part Two

We have adopted a wide definition of "techniques" to include a range of auditing procedures that will feature in most audits. Emphasis is on systems based auditing, hence the material on systems thinking and its application. Most of the other techniques revolve around the process of achieving a systems audit. Part two deals with basic audit techniques such as:

- The planning process.
- The systems approach.
- The concept of risk.
- Testing.
- Interviewing.
- Audit reporting.
- The audit manual.

A number of specimen pro-forma documents that are on the accompanying diskette are referred to in part two. Note that computer audit and fraud investigations are in part four. Various auditing techniques are described and discussed although they have to be practised hands-on, to be mastered to any extent. There is some repetition in part two (as with the other parts) since each chapter is self-contained. Part one provides the theoretical foundation; part three covers the way an audit function is managed and controlled. Part four goes on to describe specific approaches to audit work. There are a number of assignments (along with suggested answers) in the accompanying diskettes that are case-study based. These may be attempted as a way of thinking through the issues involved.

CHAPTER THIRTEEN

THE PLANNING PROCESS

13.1 Introduction

Planning is fundamental to successful auditing and should involve the client in defining areas for review and risk assessment. Long-term planning allocates scarce audit resources to the huge audit field and it is impossible to audit everything. Auditors must be seen to be doing important work. The worst-case scenario is where they are unable to perform sensitive high-level investigations on management's behalf while at the same time appearing to be involved in routine low-level checking in insignificant parts of the organisation. A professional audit service tends to rely more on senior officers tackling serious control issues.

13.2 The Planning Process

Overall planning allows the audit to be part of a carefully thought-out system. This ensures that all planned work is of high priority and that audit resources are used in the best possible way. The main steps in the overall planning process are:

FIGURE 13.1 THE PLANNING PROCESS

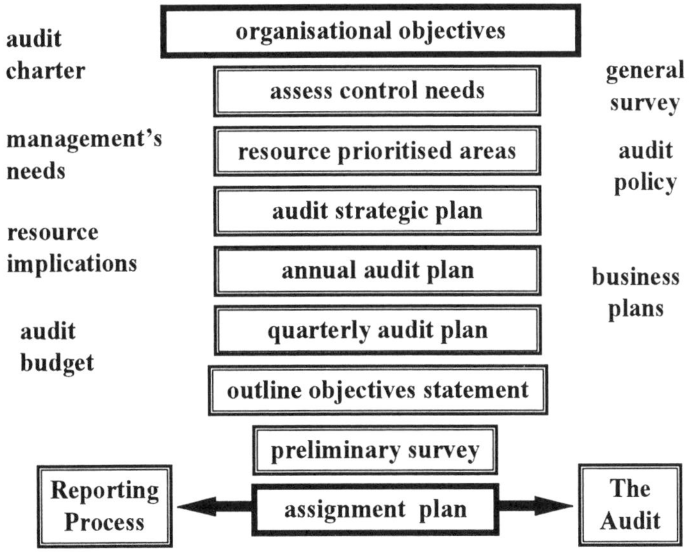

audit charter	**organisational objectives**	general survey
	assess control needs	
management's needs	**resource prioritised areas**	audit policy
	audit strategic plan	
resource implications	**annual audit plan**	business plans
audit budget	**quarterly audit plan**	
	outline objectives statement	
	preliminary survey	
Reporting Process ←	**assignment plan**	→ **The Audit**

Some explanations follow:

- **Organisational objectives**. The starting place for audit planning must be in the objectives of the organisation. If these objectives are based on devolution of corporate services to business units, then the audit mission must also be so derived. Management must clarify goals and aspirations before plans can be formulated and this feedback can be achieved by active liaison and communication.

- **Assess control needs**. The relative risks of each audit area must be identified.
- **Resource prioritised areas**. Suitable resources for these areas must be provided.
- **Audit strategic plan**. A plan to reconcile workload with existing resources should be developed. This should take on board the various constraints and opportunities that are influential now and in the future. The strategic plan takes us from where we are to where we wish to be over a defined time-frame, having due regard for the audit budget.
- **Annual audit plan**. A formal audit plan for the year ahead is expected by most audit committees.
- **Quarterly audit plan**. A quarterly plan can be derived from the annual plan. Most organisations experience constant change making the quarter a suitable time-slot for supportive work programmes.
- **Outline objectives statement**. Audit management can make a one line statement of expectations from an audit from work done so far in the planning process.
- **Preliminary survey**. Background research requires thought on key areas to be covered in an audit. This ranges from a quick look at previous files and a conversation with an operational manager to formal processes of many days of background work involving a full assessment of local control risks.
- **Assignment plan**. We can now draft an assignment plan with formal terms of reference, including budgets, due dates and an audit programme.
- **The audit**. Progress should be monitored with all matters in the terms of reference considered.
- **The reporting process**. Planning feeds naturally into reporting so long as we have made proper reference to our plans throughout the course of the audit.

Audit plans will then flow naturally from the organisation's strategic direction whilst the underlying process should be flexible and, as strategies alter, planned reviews be reassessed. The flow of planning components should be kept in mind as we consider each aspect of audit planning. The importance of linking plans to objectives can be illustrated:

> *A new chief executive joined a large organisation and announced far reaching changes. With several directors dismissed, a different approach to service delivery was evidenced. The audit committee requested a new audit plan in line with a drive to introduce formal risk assessment. The CIA argued it was pointless developing a risk assessment profile until the chief executive had determined the organisation's new direction. He argued that audit plans must attach to organisational strategy to be of any use.*

13.3 Advantages of Planning

Planning is not straightforward. There are advantages and drawbacks of preparing and working to formal audit plans. The main advantages are:

It promotes a professional image rather than being ad-hoc. Much of the control exercised by the CIA relies upon establishing a framework within which the audit service may be resourced and delivered. This depends on planning. Waiting for projects to arrive is akin to the management consultant's response based approach. There is no way a failure to establish plans can be defended.

It motivates staff by giving direction. Plans assign resources to problems and attach projects to people. Staff are aware of future projects as work is scheduled and publicised. This promotes a sense of direction as staff can focus on future workload.

Audit work may be carefully timed and programmed to suit staffing needs. Monthly and quarterly plans reconcile individual circumstances to the defined workload. Absences, development plans and other factors may be taken on board when formulating work programmes that cover available resources. Unforeseen conditions may interfere with plans, but this can be catered for where management assumes a flexible attitude towards planning. Audit management may record planned absences and events such as professional examinations and develop a resource availability profile for the coming months. A realistic profile of audit work may then be compiled.

Resources may be directed systematically. Procedures for assigning staff to jobs consider factors such as personal development and skill level. This is a managed rather than disjointed approach.

Management problems may be identified and incorporated into plans. Planning entails communication as profiles are developed of each key area within the organisation. This engenders close links with managers as their operations are discussed as part of the accumulation of background information. It is better to meet with managers on their proposed strategies than discuss past decisions. The key difference between internal and external audit results from the timeframe within which each operates. External audit (which some managers confuse with internal audit) considers past accounts. Internal auditors are concerned about the future and whether controls are keeping pace with expected changes. Planning enables this exchange of views with managers at a level they understand best: their future intentions.

Change is catered for and future developments put into audit plans. Concurrent auditing assesses what is happening now, while planned audits seek to incorporate projections that have been made. The entire reporting process revolves around assessment of future developments and how they impact on the organisation. Planning requires audit managers to raise themselves above day-to-day matters and consider the direction of developments that may have a control implication.

Assumptions and audit objectives are clearly documented. Where audit is asked to respond to daily pressures, there is little time to deliberate about the right and wrong application of audit time. There is scope for setting a basic framework for the audit role. Planning allows one to make decisions about the mission that should be pursued, as clear choices arise as to what should be included within audit plans and what may be left out as more a line management role. This is hard to achieve where most work is carried out at the urgent request of management.

Administrative arrangements include travel and annual leave. Timetables, hotels, team working, conferences and other mundane matters are better dealt with in a programme of future work.

Bids may be made for the audit budget where skills and number shortfalls are identified. Audit resources can only be properly defined in relation to needed and planned work. There may be a need to secure specialist skills to support the type of work. The required audit cover may not only be used to obtain additional resources. It may also support a formal audit strategy regarding the type of audit services that is required. We move into the dimension of strategic appraisals and sophisticated change programmes, which are dealt with in the chapters on managing internal audit. Major benefit accrues from formal planing where we are able to judge whether the existing staff complement will be able to support the projected workload. To retain existing staff levels may be the result of such an exercise, against the current environment where every support service budget is under strain.

Work areas are prioritised by considering all the activities in the audit field before applying suitable risk criteria. Risk assessment means that key areas within the organisation are identified and exposed to audit cover so that audit is seen to perform only what is most important. Without the planning process, risk assessment is isolated, and audits are undertaken as and when an issue appears. They may be important to the manager who refers the matter to audit, but in terms of the overall welfare of the organisation, the response based approach cannot address the longer term.

The only sure way that audit work can be controlled is to consider progress regarding a defined plan. It is one thing to report on achievements made by the audit function but this has no meaning unless it is set against the targets that naturally arise from formal plans. Internal auditors are not facing business realities if they refuse to formulate plans, and in so doing prepare a statement of intention that binds them to the organisation. Planning promotes professional freedom from simply responding to each crisis. The control aspects of planning are dealt with below.

Plans have a dual use in not only showing the areas that will be audited but also those operations that will not be covered in the near future. This is a useful side effect as there are times when internal audit may face some criticism where systems break down that have not been subject to audit cover. Plans will make it quite clear where a particular area has not been isolated through the risk assessment process.

It will be possible to co-ordinate plans better and create interface between different parts of the audit service. Where audit is arranged into teams or groups they should integrate activities to avoid a disjointed audit unit where each team is unaware of the other's workload. The planning process harmonises audit teams as each work area is considered and placed within an overall planning document. Planning is essential for establishing good liaison with the external auditor. It provides a convenient framework for exchanging plans and ensuring consistency. Audit plans avoid duplication of effort. Efficiency increases as information is provided to control teams, consultants, and other review services. Many parts of the organisation are interested in audit plans, ranging from the director of finance through to the chief executive.

Assignment plans help supervisors decide whether all the planned tasks have been adequately completed. Even where long-term plans are not prepared, there would be some effort made in at least formulating assignment plans. The problems that arise where there is a lack of audit plans are compounded by a failure to set formal assignment plans for the audit in question.

Access problems may be foreseen and dealt with in good time. Internal audit units that work to management requests for assistance without setting plans may be able to meet the expectations of those making the referrals; although other equally deserving areas may be left unattended. The constant stream of referrals to internal audit may be designed to detract audit from its real role in reviewing key systems. Planning brings out any potential resistance to audit access where high-level sensitive systems are placed into the plans. The potential resistance can be gauged and dealt with.

Planning enables the CIA to direct scarce audit resources at real issues as opposed to an assortment of sundry minor investigations better performed by management. Proper planning ensures best use of audit resources and gives assurances that due consideration has been given to the entire audit field. This is before each part is appraised and then placed (or not placed) into audit plans. This assurance is impossible to deliver where ad-hoc responsive work is carried out. What appear to be major issues to certain managers may in the long run be a waste of resources to the detriment of other key areas.

13.4 Disadvantages of Planning

Formal long-term planning is seen as almost mandatory for the auditor. It would be unfair to ignore some of the forces that stop the preparation of these plans. Various disadvantages may occur:

Planning can be tedious both in terms of aggregating information and preparing the plans. To start the entire planning process from scratch means preparing a systems listing with a definition of the entire audit field. Risk analysis is then applied to this field so that plans may be based on the high-risk topics. Such information must be "captured" from sources within the organisation, and this is time consuming. There is no substitute for assigning audit time to this planning task even though it lowers recoverable hours charged and detracts from front-line audit work. There has to be a firm decision based on a commitment to planning. This is in contrast to the temptation to put off this task as a non-urgent matter that can be tackled when there is enough time.

It may stifle the famous "audit nose" that needs to move around freely from place to place unhindered by the need to perform planned work. There are auditors who feel that they must be free to roam randomly around the organisation using intuition to target problem areas. The perception is that, if these problems could be foreseen then planning is valid, but less able to cope with problems only spotted by the eagle-eyed auditor. The key setback with problem hunting is the natural tendency to respond to political pressures from powerful quarters. The usual end result is that the auditor is used as a political football on issues to suit certain senior managers, with little or no independence. Another danger with the audit nose is being subject to the whims and fancies of the auditor.

Plans may become inflexible and not reflect the realities of current control problems. The "it gets quickly out of date" argument is used to counter having formal audit plans. This is valid if dusty plans are filed in desks with little relevance to the fast moving pace of a typical business. The argument is strongest in audit units that employ traditional planning techniques with five year outline plans and detailed annual programmes that seek to plan each day. It is less persuasive where the plans are realistic and derived from a flexible model that changes periodically as the organisation adapts and adjusts to influencing factors.

Staff shortages may upset the best-laid plans with expectations not met. If plans are based on actual staff in post, this may admit that there is no need to recruit additional staff. If plans are based on the full complement then they may not be achieved. If we expect a high level of absences through sick-leave or training leave, this may give out inappropriate messages whilst tighter plans will not be achieved. The best solution is to set long-term plans in outline whilst seeking to plan closely only at the short-term level.

Formal plans may mean that audit is unable to respond to managers' requests for assistance and therefore lead to a poor image. It can be frustrating for a line manager to watch an auditor going about the task of performing a systems audit of a large financial system, while apparently ignoring real problems that impair the efficient running of a different operation. The planning process tends not to support a response orientation that may be what management wants. Diverting audit resources from planned work at the request of management is one way of meeting the client expectation. Freed from the shackles of formal plans, the auditor may court senior managers and simply work on the topic of the day, so, as problems arise, they are solved. Management consultants adopt this model but there is difficulty reconciling it with the professional audit approach. So long as high risk projects are isolated in the plan, there is little justification for dropping these important corporate items, to set to work on a one-off managerial concern that could be dealt with by the manager.

Plans may lead to documented promises that cannot be delivered and lower audit credibility. Continual reporting of unplanned excesses and shelved projects may de-motivate audit staff. This is the subconscious barrier to planning as no manager likes to set unachievable targets. It is less a disadvantage than a poor excuse.

If the organisation does not generally plan then audit may fall out-of-step with management. We must recognise the culture and tone of an organisation. Organisations develop the culture that suits their objectives so as to employ appropriate people and systems. Where this does not promote formal planning say in favour of a project-by-project approach, then this also sets the frame for the auditor's work. Audit may need to fit with the organisation and if this discourages planning then there is a necessary impact on audit services. Internal audit would tend to be in breach of auditing standards if long-term planning was ignored and it is difficult to see how organisations can function in an unplanned environment. If there is no recognition of planning, the CIA may have to resign.

Auditing standards
The Institute of Internal Auditors' standard 500 on managing internal audit covers audit planning:
520.03 - Audit should ensure that the goals of the operation are capable of being accomplished within specific plans and budgets.
520.14 - Audit work schedules should be prepared.
520.05 - Staffing plans and financial budgets should be prepared.
520.06 - Activity reports should be submitted periodically by internal audit.
Assignment planning is dealt with in standard 400.

The APB standards cover planning in para 45 which reads: "Internal audit work should be planned, controlled and recorded in order to determine priorities, establish and achieve objectives, and ensure the effective and efficient use of audit resources." This sets the framework for audit planning and best practice by requiring that formal plans are devised and publicised.

13.5 Long-term Planning

Factors for long-term planning
There are numerous ways of assessing the audit field and many factors to be considered:
Available audit resources will impact on the type of work that may be undertaken. This is in terms of numbers, grades, expertise, qualifications and special skills of auditors.

It may be part of the human resource strategy to develop or bring in the required skills as dictated by the planned work. This is a longer-term strategy.

The sensitivity of the area to the organisation. The organisation's policies and strategy need to be understood and built into the planning process. A risk index that cannot account for sensitivity or potential embarrassment will not mean much to senior management.

Build in contingency allowances for audit hours that may fall outside the planning process to cope with requests from management for special audits. This may be based on experience. Anything over and above this should be dealt with by employing extra temporary resources for such special requests.

Managers' problems should be considered when formulating plans. If these are ignored, they will turn elsewhere. We have discussed the disadvantages of the response based approach where plans are not formulated but resources simply sent to support management requests. The needs and desires of management should never be ignored as it is possible to build them firmly into the planning mechanism. It is difficult to reconcile the needs of individual managers who may expect different things from the audit service. These must be catered for.

Financial materiality increases risk and much information is readily available from budgets and other financial data. Large operations consume resources and this impacts on plans.

Other reviews may influence audit plans. Reports issued by in-house or external consultants, project teams and other review agencies should be considered. They may indicate an area has received recent and excessive scrutiny with an audit better scheduled for later. Alternatively a review may hint at major control problems that call for urgent audit attention that could then be secured via re-prioritisation of the audit plan. A third position is reached where the review is invalid, politically motivated and should be ignored when formulating plans. Useful background information may be obtained from other review reports that are not unduly out-of-date.

Risk assessment is based on all factors that impact on the audit field with priority ratings assigned. It is more concerned with all relevant matters that should affect audit plans rather than being a single component of the planning process. Risk is explored in outline below and in a later chapter.

Deleted audit posts and vacancies have to be allowed for in long-term plans and it is unwise to be too ambitious where staff are not available. New audit posts may allow opportunities in new areas. Since planning reconciles workload to resources, the number of people available is a determining factor. The new model of staffing the audit function relies heavily on temporary staff to fill short-term gaps in coverage.

New legislation may require additional audit resources. Changes in rules derived from internal policies or external regulation, perhaps set for the industry in question, must be considered. This is relevant in the public sector where outsourcing of support and front line services is growing along with the business unit concept applied to in-house services. Audit plans must cope with a "what if..." model that seeks to cater for different outcomes where services may be provided through different mechanisms over time. Where an in-house service faces external competition internal audit may tighten the existing service to assist preparation for competition, or review controls around the database so that it is reliable as a basis for a formal contract specification. It can be handed intact to the external contractor. It may be based on continuing audit cover or setting a new approach around contract management. It cannot be based on ignoring trends. Legislation can involve a new emphasis on environmental concerns, or compliance with regulation (e.g. EU directives), or changes in staffing, or reductions in the budgetary provisions for parts of the public and private sectors. Many types of laws and regulations affect how organisations control and manage resources.

Research and change impact on the organisation. The auditor should be able to talk management language if audit resources are to be geared into the real issues. Trade magazines and developments based around increasing automation, new specialisms, growth or entrenchment strategies all alter the way goods and services are provided. To feed audit resources into organisational plans is the only sure way of supporting corporate resources.

The results of previous audit cover help assess proposed coverage either by directing resources to new areas or by demanding further examination in activities that continue to pose problems. Audit's past experiences will give much insight into types of control concerns. Auditors should enter all concerns in their working papers. This ensures that the results of past audit work are incorporated into future plans. A useful technique is to set up an "outstanding matters" document that captures all issues not resolved during the audit. It is also possible to feed general information received during an audit into the permanent files so that these feed into the risk assessment procedures.

New systems impact on audit plans particularly in high profile sensitive areas. The growing trend to de-centralised decision support systems may be strategically sound but the systems implications require much attention and may lead to greater risks. Audit resources must follow these changes. New computer systems change the balance of control in the relevant operational area as new working practices adjust to meet the changing conditions. The unknown presents a control issue as it may or may not be well controlled.

Take-overs and mergers cannot always be planned and even where the organisation publishes a growth strategy it tends to keep the operational details secret. The acquisition of a large enterprise can double the audit field overnight and the organisation may find it has two separate audit departments to be integrated. Such large-scale change will mean re-formulating the audit plan and now the flexibility factor comes into play. Take-overs cannot be predicted unless a clear expansion strategy has been adopted where even here, there is always uncertainty.

Previous frauds may mean the areas will assume a high profile in the future. Frauds result from a breakdown in control at some level, corporate, managerial, operational or informational. There is not always time to deal with the long-term systems implications during a fraud investigation. Wider control issues related to, for example, a lack of clear procedures can be referred to the long-term planning mechanism to be dealt with when resources are available as prioritised.

The complexity of the area is important for it may require more sophisticated controls such as may operate within an autonomous research and development unit. Those more difficult areas should not be left without audit cover. Work scheduling should employ required short-term specialist resources to undertake audits in all important parts of the organisation. The concept of operational complexity needs to be built into the audit planning mechanism via risk assessment factors.

13.6 The General Survey

Securing planning information depends on an efficient mechanism to be able to assimilate facts, data and general information into our planning framework. This relies on sophisticated information systems that feed vital material directly into the internal audit database. The CIA can be pivotal in setting up such a complex arrangement. The "general survey" accumulates material relevant to the audit field and assesses impact on predetermined risk criteria. In meetings with senior and line management the auditor is familiarised with the operation and its key managers. This fact-finding exercise enables data to be obtained and set into audit plans. The features of a general survey are the following:

Meeting with managers is an opportunity not only to get to know them but also introduces the audit role to clients and gains an appreciation of their concerns. Some of the mystique of audit may be removed. Marketing should be an active feature of client contact and so long as the auditor is competent and presentable, this should create a positive atmosphere. This is a by-product that complements the process of securing relevant material as part of a two-way exchange of information. Information straight from the source saves much time in contrast to straining through reports and decision sheets prepared months ago. Information received from managers is up-to-date and there is accompanying interpretation and informal remarks that put strategies into perspective.

It provides material to establish the real issues facing the organisation. The general survey provides useful high-level information that says more than the base operational data and detailed budgets from the audit filing system. Real issues provide real problems which need real controls. Where audit is able to isolate these concerns then plans become more dynamic and defensible.

A useful side-effect of the survey is that link officers may be established in each department/division and provide a vital communication device between the audit field and management. Regular exchange of information assists planning by making it more efficient and responsive. Communication needs to be two-way. The link officers will provide information to audit but will want advice and assistance on new problems with control implications. Providing on-line support to managers diverts resources from planned work. However, there is still a need to resource this type of service in addition to planned audits. We will be expanding this point later.

This close contact enables the auditor to follow matters that have been reported previously and get updates on progress in making required improvements to controls. Where a development is inconsistent with a previous audit recommendation, say relating to a live running date for a new computer system, then audit can take up this issue before it is too late. Keeping abreast can enable a form of concurrent audit where a breach of procedure may be spotted before it occurs as the proposed activities are reported in operational plans or committee/board reports.

The main objective of the general survey is to provide input to the risk assessment process so that suitable plans may be drafted. What is important to audit should also be for management, if these plans are to be used to interface audit with the organisation. The survey tackles high-risk issues through the constant search for information. As we link with managers the concept of risk will be the cause of much debate and discussion. Once established the risk criterion may be used to great effect as we sell the idea of risk throughout the organisation. Since it is agreed with the audit committee, the criteria can only be amended by formal change procedures.

There is the opportunity to listen to managers, on the basis that "listening" is a dynamic technique based around interactive communications. The feedback system can be used to supplement the formal complaints system since it can be used to identify problems with individual auditors or clarify matters complained about. Each of these feedback routines depends on communication systems that fall outside the formal audit reporting process.

The part of the general survey process that involves meeting with management is aided through questionnaires and checklists which shorten the interview process. Providing managers with extensive lists to complete will frustrate the process of communications links. The auditor who sits back and reads from the list of questions is doomed. A checklist is used to focus on predefined concerns and as an aide-mémoire during an interview. The auditor should prepare such a document and use this for discussions with senior management as part of the general survey which should cover matters such as materiality, sensitivity, the state of controls and managerial requirements.

Auditors should be given specific areas in the organisation that they will have responsibility for and then be charged with securing information on them. We will not only be concerned with internal information systems and reports but also with information that comes from external sources such as press releases and journals. Keeping this information current should be an important staff performance target reported on regularly. Attendance at seminars, meetings, reviews of new legislation, and publications are all part of the general survey procedure. This seeks to keep audit up to date with all matters that impact on the assessment of relative risk to controls throughout the organisation. This is no simple matter and the drive from the CIA and audit management should be such that it is deemed an important procedure. Audit management may not be aware of items that have been missed by an auditor under this arrangement so the motivation and interest must be maintained if files are not to fall into disuse. Rotation of assigned areas stimulates and maintains interest as do regular briefing sessions from staff. A key control is to ensure that material gathered is read and interpreted by the auditor before it is entered into the permanent files. It is possible to use a front sheet that forces the auditor to indicate the implications for audit plans of new information or developments. Changes in the risk factor should be automatically entered into the risk profile and so change audit plans at the regular review dates say, monthly or quarterly. Responsibility for these changes must be placed on staff as a control. Form 045 can be applied (see accompanying diskette).

A filing system can hold the database of information and so smooth the survey data. This records information relating specifically to the adopted risk criteria by providing a suitable document for each key factor. This focuses the survey by turning it from a general information gathering process to a structured method for ensuring key points are addressed. After the completion of each audit assignment we would remove documents with lasting influence from the current file and place them into the relevant permanent file. A firm picture is built up that "profiles" each audit area.

The survey brings management into the planning process and ensures that audit plans are based on the best up-to-date information. It requires skill and a professional approach so as not to become manipulated by management. It is discussion-led rather than a mathematically generated list of audits. Systematic risk analysis may be linked into the survey and this is considered later in the chapter.

Whilst the survey is based around meetings with management and reviewing information supplied to internal audit, there must be an element of independence in the way this information is procured and used. We cannot simply rely on material supplied by managers as this can give a distorted view. A level of objectivity should be built into the survey process for it to work as a suitable planning tool. The baseline for planning audit assignments must not be influenced by political in-fighting.

13.7 Strategy Versus Resources

There are two main models of the long-term planning process where each takes a different starting position to arrive at the list of planned audits. The first starts with the control needs of the organisation and resources this gap through the application of sufficient audit resources. The second starts with available resources and then assigns them to the defined audit field in the most efficient way. This difference of approach may be displayed as:

FIGURE 13.2 STRATEGY VERSUS RESOURCE LED PLANNING

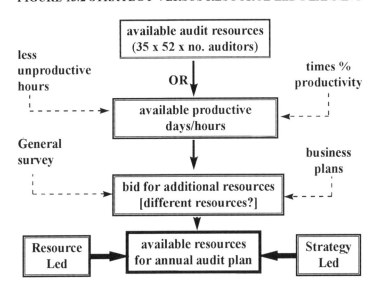

Explanations follow:

A limited version of strategic led planning occurs where we plan for a full complement of staff by assigning work to posts not filled. An expanded version appears where the required resource level is wholly dependent on the required extent and nature of audit coverage. This assumes full support from the host organisation where a new budget will be found to resource the planned audits. In a recession this is hard to defend although there is increasing use of temporary staff that can fill short-term gaps. The model more often applied is based on planning for the current resources that are available. More often than not there is ongoing pressure to restrict the current staff budget in an annual streamlining process, where it is very difficult to argue that extra resources are required. It is only the newly set up internal audit units that may be able to negotiate an expansion. In a competitive environment it is not always advisable to seek to increase the staff levels (i.e. budgets) as this may make the audit service more vulnerable as it becomes increasingly expensive.

13.8 A Risk Profile

Risk is dealt with later in the handbook. This section merely outlines one useful risk criterion for evaluating operations/systems before determining their place in the audit plans.

The four main factors that may be used in a basic model have earlier been defined:
1. **Materiality**
2. **Impact on success criteria (sensitivity)**
3. **Control concerns**
4. **Management's concerns**

Each system is appraised on how they score on these four features. They can be marked from say 1 - 10 so that the final score falls between 4 and 40 with the subsequent ranking being in line with the score. The background information for this assessment may be gathered from the general survey.
Each of the four factors is made up of several relevant points:

1. **Materiality**
   - Revenue expenditure.
   - Capital expenditure.
   - Income generated.
   - Level of output.
   - Amount of capital invested.
   - Space occupied.
   - Number of managers and other staff.

2. **Sensitivity**
   - Political sensitivity.
   - Type of service provided.
   - Number of sub-systems, inter-linked systems and dependent systems.
   - Importance of objectives.
   - Extent of managerial reliance.
   - Overall affect on the organisation's welfare.

3. **Control concerns**
   - Past breakdowns in control.
   - Previous frauds.
   - High levels of reported errors.
   - Inherent risks in the operation, e.g. funds transfers involved.
   - Reported evidence of control weaknesses.
   - Recent changes, e.g. new systems.
   - Managerial problems, e.g. long-term vacancies and poor recruitment procedures.
   - Generally lax controls with evidence of non-compliance.
   - Lack of reviews in the past.
   - Previous reviews (and audits) that show continuing control problems.

4. **Management concerns**
   - Direct requests for assistance.
   - Any potential for embarrassment.
   - Specific problem areas.
   - Lack of success that management may have had with previous reviews.

If this information is readily available, it will be possible to build up a risk profile on each major operation. The score in the risk profile will determine the place assumed by the operation in audit plans. Returning to the index factors, each individual operation will be assessed:

TABLE 13.1 RISK INDEX

RISK FACTOR	Score 1 - 10
MATERIALITY	
IMPACT ON SUCCESS CRITERIA (SENSITIVITY)	
MANAGEMENT'S CONCERNS	
CONTROL CONCERNS	
TOTAL SCORE	**4 - 40**

Forms 044 and 044A to 044D (see diskette) can be used to record the results of this type of risk assessment. Listing all "operations" is extremely important as it forces audit management to define fully what areas audit is responsible for covering. There are clear advantages in performing this task:

A suitable filing system is designed to reflect the way the audit field has been isolated. It requires audit management to apply their audit methodology through the way audits are defined. This will involve a combination of computer audits, contract audit, financial systems, operational areas, and corporate arrangements.

It provides a database of audits that can be added to as new developments occur throughout the organisation. This is the starting place for the audit mission to set out exactly what the organisation looks like in terms of its audit profile. This audit profile should be a mirror image of the organisation that moves in parallel with changes that arise over the months/years.

Audits that are performed can always be set within the context of audits that appear in the audit field. The terms of reference for an audit can be developed with the full knowledge of other distinct areas that are treated separately in terms of audit planning. For example, an audit of IT acquisition standards may bring in the question of overall purchasing arrangements for both IT and purchases generally. Where purchasing is listed as a separate audit, auditors are able to see clearly where their work stops and where a different audit takes over.

The listing will confirm that there is much work that needs doing and only a relatively small amount of resources to do it.

13.9 The Business Plan

In addition to planning the audit areas that will be included for future cover, the CIA must consider how the services will be provided. This requires a development plan that covers the strategic direction of the internal audit function. The issues addressed via the business plan include:

The current audit charter and whether it properly reflects the present situation. The role and objectives of the audit function are encompassed within the audit mission that sets the tone for the ensuing work that is performed. As a start, a regular review of this role and how it interfaces with the drive and direction of the organisation will help isolate any imbalance. It is notoriously difficult to bring together the hopes and aspirations of individual auditors when they each have a different perception of the audit role. A clear charter assists this process of bringing together competing views.

The current status of the audit function and whether this is sufficiently high to discharge the audit mission. A mission statement says what audit should do, the status provides a basis from which this happens. A business plan will include a consideration of this factor and any barriers that impair audit's ability to address the highest levels of the organisation.

Whether the existing audit approach is appropriate particularly in providing a client based audit service. The business plan should address the type of work that is performed and how this is perceived by clients. Marketing and client feedback should come into play as the continuing search for improving the service is undertaken. A good appreciation of audit's image may be obtained from reviewing material derived from a formal complaints procedure established with clients.

Auditors' career development and human resource management programmes should provide the level of skills required to discharge audit plans. This will be kept under constant review in line with formal training and programmes linked into performance appraisal. Recognition should be given to the overall levels of staff morale and whether personnel policies promote an effective audit service

The adequacy of the audit manual should have a firm place in the business plan. Most improvements and developments to the audit service require amendment to the audit manual. They revolve around developing new or improved procedures for how resources are employed and used.

A strengths, weaknesses, opportunities, threats (SWOT) and political, economic, social technological, legal (PESTL) analysis will isolate problem areas incorporating those factors that will affect the audit service in the future. The aim is that weaknesses should be rectified and opportunities maximised. The business plan would cover the way audit is staffed, marketed and the operational procedures that are applied, with any necessary adjustments being reflected in a revised audit manual. Facing up to external competition may be a feature of the business plan and one would need to review the efficiency and effectiveness of the audit function and the hourly charge-out rates. The CIA would be advised to produce an audit brochure that publicises available audit services.

13.10 The Annual Audit Plan

Audit will be required to publish an annual audit plan formally approved by the audit committee. This lists planned audits for the year and includes a reconciliation of audit resources to required audit cover. The annual plan may be resource led and based on available audit staff. Alternatively it may be strategy led and include a bid for additional staff/expertise to fulfil the proposed workload. The annual plan is important as it represents the justification for resourcing the internal audit service. Moreover, listed audits must be material to top management's search for commercial success.

Auditors will have around 214 days a year available although it is better to form long-term plans on a week-by-week basis. The annual audit plan will set out which parts of the listed systems will be subject to audit cover over the next twelve months without assigning resources to each audit. It is probably enough to simply list against each planned audit whether it is large, medium or small. As a start these categories may be set as an estimated figure, e.g. six weeks (large), four weeks (medium) and two weeks (small).

Some of the features of the annual audit plan are as follows:

It contains key audit areas for the next twelve months and explains why they were selected through a suitable preamble. This opening discussion should be a scaled-down version of the audit strategy with comments on the main problems facing the organisation now and in the immediate future.

Following from the above, the annual plan needs to be interfaced with the annual report. The report will talk about the state of control in general across the organisation, whereas the plan will explain how these concerns will be dealt with by internal audit.

The plan itself should be circulated to Directors for their consideration and comment before being finalised. It will explain the process of risk assessment and agreed risk criteria. The plan cannot be challenged although the basis of risk assessment may be commented on by management who may argue that it does not reflect actual risk because of new or changed information. Management cannot insist on a change to the risk assessment parameter as this can only be enforced by the audit committee, although they can certainly express reservations with the planning process. Once top management has seen the plan it will be presented to the audit committee to be formally adopted. Changes to the plan should likewise be confirmed at audit committee.

The annual plan should be well publicised both to the organisation and to individual auditors.

The quarterly audit plan
The quarterly audit plan provides an opportunity to take the planning process to greater detail where the various projects may be scheduled over a 13 week period. The quarterly period has much more meaning to both managers and auditors as a timeframe despite the fast pace of business life. Quarterly plans are no longer short-term matters as it becomes increasingly more difficult to predict what factors may influence the organisation as new developments arise. The annual plan sets a background to the quarterly plan. Three months is often an appropriate period within which to set priorities and assign work.

Within this planning framework it is possible to:
1. Build in the planned absences of individual auditors so that a good idea of the available resources for the period in question can be obtained. The quarterly period is ideal for this, in that we will have some knowledge of staff movements and training, annual leave, and sick leave.
2. Plan audit cover weekly as the basis of a work programme for each individual auditor.
3. Enter projected start and completion dates for each audit that can be in detail (e.g. the exact date) or more realistically the week within which the planned start and finish will fall. It is possible to set this level of detail with a manageable timeframe.

4. Allocate projects to auditors. This sets the right resources to the right projects in line with relevant factors. It includes skills, experience, special interests, and career development.

5. Re-prioritise projects on the annual plan. As quarterly plans are set, audits are reassigned on the annual plan as detailed changes are made. The link between the annual and quarterly planning mechanisms must be maintained as each is adjusted in line with changing circumstances.

The annual plan, quarterly plan and monthly work schedules can be documented using Forms 047, 048 and 049 (see diskette).

13.11 The Preliminary Survey

The annual audit plan lists those high-risk areas that are targeted for audit cover during the next twelve months. The quarterly audit plan provides more detail by setting out those audits that will be performed by specified auditors in the following three months. Before the full audit is started and resources committed, an assignment plan will direct and control these resources. Before we are in a position to formulate assignment plans, we need background information on the targeted operation. Preliminary work will be required, the extent of which will vary according to the size of the audit. This section sets out the principles behind the preliminary survey although the approach and level of detail will vary depending on the policies of each individual audit department.

Relevant factors

The preliminary survey seeks to accumulate relevant information regarding the operation under review so that a defined direction of the ensuing audit (if it goes ahead) may be agreed. There are several features of a preliminary survey:

The internal audit files will be the first point of call and any previous audit cover will be considered. All assignment audit files should contain a paper entitled "outstanding matters" that will set out concerns that were not addressed via the audit at hand. The files tell only part of the story as will the resultant audit report, and it is best to talk to the auditor who last performed work in the relevant area.

It is advisable to carry out background research into the area subject to the survey. This might include national research, committee papers, recent changes and planned computerised systems. Much of this information should really have been obtained via the general survey. It is always advisable to get some basic facts before meeting with management so as to create a good impression.

We can now meet with the key manager and tour the operational area. An overview of the real issues facing the manager in question can be obtained. A feel for the audit can be gathered from impressions gained from touring the work area, where the initial impression can be used to help direct the auditor towards particular problems. A checklist of matters to be covered in such an opening meeting should be drafted to form the basis of the discussions, covering items such as:

1. **Key control objectives;**
   - The reliability and integrity of information.
   - Compliance with laws, policies and procedures.
   - Safeguarding assets.
   - Economy and efficiency.

- Effectiveness.

2. Key managerial processes

- Operational objectives.
- Strategy.
- Structure.
- Human resource management.
- Information systems.
- Direction and supervision.

Operational procedures

Recent work carried out by other review agencies should be obtained and considered although watch out for bias where the work was commissioned for a particular reason. Reports contain natural bias set by the terms of reference. For example a staffing review commissioned by a union is more likely to recommend pay rises. The preliminary survey involves assessing local risk factors that affect audit objectives. No audit can cover all the relevant areas within a specific operation and the assignment plan states what will be done and what is not covered. It is the process of assessing local risk that allows the auditor to key into the target elements of the operational area. This is done at preliminary survey before the audit objectives and scope of the review can be drafted and agreed. The auditor must isolate the system for review and distinguish it from parent systems, sub-systems, parallel systems and link systems. Systems theory states that a system is defined in line with the perceptions of the reviewer. The system selected by the auditor has to be defined before it can be audited and the preliminary survey comes to the rescue. Systems boundaries can only be determined after the necessary information has been accumulated and digested. This must happen before the assignment planning stage so that a clear plan may be documented and shown to management. The aim of the preliminary survey will be to agree the objectives and scope and timing of the audit with management. What needs to be done, how and when it will be done, will be derived from the survey as a prerequisite to the proper preparation for the full audit. It will be necessary to note areas that will not be considered as outside the terms of reference. This is important because management often feel that an audit will reveal all that is wrong with a system. A clear definition of what was not included in the audit will help to avoid this. The preliminary survey provides an exclusion clause that is conveyed to management. The impact on audit work might be an issue either by re-directing resources or adjusting the scope of another audit that would be affected by the planned work. A major benefit of the preliminary survey is an understanding of the nature of the audit. This highlights the type of audit skills required, including special skills relating to automation and/or technically complicated matters such as contract law. Audit standards require audit management to ensure they can perform audits to professional standards. It is the responsibility of managers to use their resources properly and if it is clear that an audit is too difficult for the available resources then the project should be aborted. It is a useful policy to get senior auditors or audit managers to perform the preliminary survey and then assign the full audit to more junior staff. The survey is perhaps the most difficult part of the audit process since once the terms of reference have been set and a programme of work agreed the remainder can be fairly straightforward. It means that the audit manager has a full knowledge of the audit and can supervise and review the work as it progresses. The preliminary survey should result in a programme of work that has been identified as a result of the background work. This may be in the form of a detailed audit programme or simply a list of key tasks depending on the type of audit, the approach to work and the policies of the audit unit.

The audit programme
As well as isolating the system for review and determining the direction of the audit, the preliminary survey may result in an audit programme for use during the audit. This term should be carefully considered since an audit programme tends to be associated with a series of pre-defined testing routines. This does not promote the systems based approach since the direction of the testing procedures depends on the outcome of the control evaluation. The programme may be seen more as an audit guide and may include:

1. Defining the various tasks that need to be performed. Here a list of key tasks should be compiled for the lead auditor that sets the direction of the audit process that will now be carried out. This is not only a useful planning tool that can be used to monitor progress on the audit, but also provides firm guidance for the auditor on work that must be completed.

2. Defining the extent of work in a particular part of the operation. For smaller audits with a probity approach it is possible to list the various testing routines. Defining testing programmes makes the audit controllable. It is based around the required tests and in basic audits this may give the number of items that should be selected and how they are tested. Audit management can exercise firm control. This would not be appropriate for a systems based approach since it is controls that are tested after they have been assessed and testing is not carried out for its own sake.

The key differences between the systems and compliance/probity approaches to audit work are:

FIGURE 13.3 SYSTEMS BASED APPROACH VERSUS PROBITY

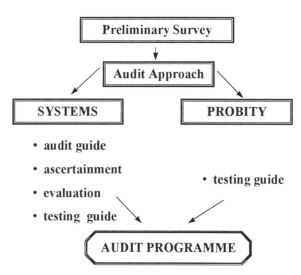

This is an important distinction. Compliance and probity audits emphasise transactions testing, and the audit programme is formulated at the preliminary survey stage. For systems audit this detailed testing programme can only be defined after the system has been documented and assessed. The programme of work that is set for a systems audit can be described as an audit guide that determines the work required to complete the audit and this may be drafted at preliminary stage. The programme will include target dates and perhaps a progress checklist for stages of the audit. Not only is it used as a monitoring tool but as each task is carried out, the date completed and reviewed should be entered on the schedule. This provides a comprehensive record of work. The audit techniques may be identified and this may affect the auditors assigned. Statistical sampling, flowcharting, interviewing, computer assisted audit techniques, product inspection, third party circularisation and other techniques may be planned where clearly required. Resourcing these techniques can be dealt with at the pre-planning stage. If the requisite skills are not available, audit management must secure them or suspend/abort the audit. The audit programme should be formally signed off by the audit manager to constitute an approved work plan for the field auditor/s. Attaching the programme to the associated terms of reference and budget for the work provides a management tool for controlling the audit. The audit programme sets direction for the testing stage. Be careful not to suppress the auditor's initiative or responsibility for the work. There must be direction but at the same time freedom to explore key issues and form an opinion on the state of controls. For systems audits, the test programme appears after most of the crucial evaluation work has been completed. For compliance audits it is essential that the auditor uses the programme as a means to an end and not an end in itself. This means tailoring the programme to fit the audit whilst retaining responsibility for the end results.

The preliminary survey report
It is advisable to present a formal preliminary survey report (PSR) once the work has been completed. This report goes to the audit manager, along with a brief description of the system to be used to prepare the assignment plan. The PSR of two or three pages will cover the following:
1. An outline of the system under review including systems objectives and boundaries.
2. The work undertaken in the preliminary survey.
3. An initial opinion on the risk areas based on the key control objectives covering compliance, information systems, safeguarding assets and value for money.
4. Recommendations for the proposed assignment in terms of the nature and extent of audit cover now required.
5. An appendix with outline systems notes and a draft audit guide/programme for the full audit.

The preliminary survey stage can be planned and recorded on Forms 050 to 058 (see diskette).

13.12 Assignment Planning

Introduction
Each audit must be carefully planned as this is the only way to control it. Assignment planning takes all available information and allows the objectives, scope, direction and approach to be defined. The preliminary survey will have been conducted before plans can be formulated and will provide much information for formulating the assignment plan. The preliminary survey report will set out the proposed objectives of the full audit stage. Factors to be addressed in the assignment plan are:

The terms of reference for the audit by audit management and disclosed to the client management. They guide audit work and feature in the resultant report with an audit opinion on each component.

The scope of work including areas for coverage and parts of the system not to be dealt with at this time. This may be referred to in a memorandum to client management publicising the pending audit.

Target dates for start and completion and key stages. For larger audits, break the task down into defined stages. Section the audit into manageable parts that may be reported on separately. This enables the auditor to maintain a focus on the objective at hand, and report before going on to deal with the next part. For example a corporate system, that has been devolved down to departments like personnel, budgeting, or expenditure processing, may be broken down into sections relating to each department. A separate report will be drafted for each department along with a composite report covering the corporate arrangements. Auditors can be drafted in to deal with each department if a suitable programme of work has been prepared and explained since the work programme requires extensive testing and interrogation of the corporate database. Once compiled, it can be completed by a variety of resources including temporary audit staff.

Special instructions covering particular problems seen by the auditor and matters that management has brought to the attention of the auditor in discussion. This may include any follow-up action taken on an audit report issued previously that impacts on the audit.

A full definition of the system under review including the points where it starts and finishes and interfaces with other related systems. This avoids unnecessary confusion over the duration of the audit with a clear focus on exactly what the system is. It allows the auditor to think through the associated systems and their impact on the audit (Form 059 - see diskette).

Identification of risk areas and critical points of the audit that may require special attention and/or resources. This may refer to the timing of the audit, say in relation to restructuring, a new computer system, a recruitment campaign or a new staff performance scheme.

Definition of the reporting and review arrangements including a list of the officers who will receive draft reports. Where the audit is geographically remote, the review arrangements must be determined so that this process does not hold up the progress of the audit report.

Establish a confirmed audit programme (or guide) for each part of the audit and the testing regimes (for compliance reviews). The audit techniques that should be applied may also be defined along with a list of standardised documents (having reference to the audit manual) in use in the audit unit.

The assignment plan will outline any travel and hotel arrangements along with subsistence allowances. This should recognise the need to save time and ensure efficient use of resources.

Identify the auditors assigned to the project and their roles. The assignment planning task must identify which auditors are assigned. The audit manager or lead auditor should perform the preliminary survey so that a good insight into the audit is obtained by those directing the work. Once done, the audit proper should be assigned. A trend is for a move away from teamwork with a single auditor being given an audit to streamline resources. It fits with the development profile of auditors who, apart from trainees, should be given responsibility for whole projects.

Assigning time budgets to audits

We must define an audit budget in terms of time allowed. Time is the key factor on any audit. Setting a time budget acts as a principle control over the assignment as the single most important concern of audit management. A viable audit is achieved within budget to professional audit standards and as a full discharge of its objectives. Budgeted hours must be realistic and achievable. An alternative approach is more basic and simply states (for example):

LARGE AUDIT:	6 WEEKS
MEDIUM-SIZED AUDIT:	4 WEEKS
SMALL AUDIT:	2 WEEKS

The extent of work done in such time frames depends on the skill and expertise of the individual auditor. A performance appraisal scheme rewards those who deliver quality reports within the time constraints. There are two different views. One seeks to perform the audit terms of reference to the full no matter how long this takes, even if budgeted hours are extended. This normally involves extensive testing and an inability to defer parts of the audit to a later stage. The other view is that audit management sets a defined number of hours according to the level of risk attached. When this budget expires the auditor must transfer to another work area, so recognising the risks of not dealing with the next planned audit. Extensions are not encouraged as the auditor has to perform as much work as possible during the budget hours and then move on to the next job. The adopted policy must be explained and detailed in the audit manual since work done on one audit detracts from work that might be done elsewhere. One solution is to disallow budget extensions unless there is good reason such as to avoid the psychological dilemma of "auditor attachment". This occurs where the auditor becomes so engrossed in an operation that they see themselves as an expert who has a duty to solve all problems after mastering the system. Client managers assimilate the auditor into an executive role by constantly seeking advice on operational decisions. The auditor becomes too closely associated with the operation, asking for more and more time to spend on the audit. The correct position is to provide budgeted hours for the audit and then remove the auditor from the work once this has expired. The working file will show what work is outstanding that may be deferred to the next audit. Auditor attachment can lead to audit saturation where there has been too much exposure.

The assignment planning process

The audit manager should provide all guidance in the assignment plan before the full audit commences. Objectives in the assignment plan should be achieved and the review should ensure this. The review will also check hours charged and quality of work to judge the value of work performed.

Planning documentation

There are many versions of documents that assist audit planning. They provide standards and checklists for the work and areas that should be covered in the plan. Basic examples are found on Forms 059 to 071(on diskette). They show each task and indicate:

1. The audit objective.
2. Who does what.
3. For how long.
4. Any particular guidance.
5. The review arrangement.

This control will not work unless there is an in-built monitoring system of continual supervision and review of progress. The audit manager should provide all necessary direction via the assignment planning process. The details above are the minimum information that should be contained in audit plans before the full audit is approved by audit management.

13.13 Conclusions

Planning is an important process to be resourced and carried out by internal audit. There are pros and cons. Most disadvantages may be overcome by careful plans that have in-built flexibility and contingency allowances. Long-term planning is a crucial tool for applying audit resources. If properly used it may mean that individual audits can be undertaken with the sound knowledge that they are geared into a long-term strategy and make sense. Resources spent in this activity should lead to a more professional audit service. Assignment plans enable each audit project to be controlled. The preliminary survey bridges the gap between the quarterly plan and the assignment plan. For smaller projects this may consist of a review of previous audit work and a discussion with the line manager. For larger projects this may be more extensive. Audit resources should not be scheduled and committed without background work being carried out. It would be wise for each audit department to formulate suitable policies on the use of preliminary surveys. Audit work should be designed to ensure that a defined audit product is delivered. If audit management provides no direction on what they require, then there is little hope that the field auditor will meet expectations. The assignment plan directs and controls the audit, and the objectives set by the plan become goals auditors have to meet. This is an effective way of controlling the audit work as long as deviations may be quickly spotted and rectified. The auditor's training in evaluating controls and the expertise that is acquired means there is no excuse for allowing audits to drift aimlessly. Audit management is charged with developing suitable planning mechanisms and standardised documents to ensure that the critical areas are considered and documented guidance provided.

CHAPTER FOURTEEN

THE SYSTEMS APPROACH

14.1 Systems Thinking

The systems approach to internal auditing has provided an extremely powerful technique for conducting audit reviews and has led to a change in auditing concepts. This requires an audit policy that stresses the importance of establishing good systems so that problems, errors and abuse may be avoided in the first place. Management is charged with devising and maintaining these systems with advice from internal audit. The move is away from error spotting with more emphasis on getting the system right. Systems auditing is based on systems theory and wider systems concepts.

Features of systems

Systems thinking is based on viewing operations and events as processes with the following flows:

FIGURE 14.1 A BASIC SYSTEM

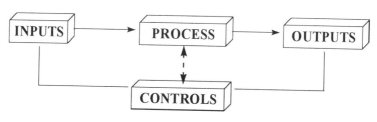

Defining a system:

> *"A set of objects together with relationships between these objects and their attributes connected or related to each other in such a manner as to form an entirety or whole."*

There are a number of concepts that underpin systems theory and these may be listed:

☐ **Connected components**. Each part of the system has some relationship to the other parts, so that together they comprise the system at hand. A link in a chain is connected by the two links that attach it to the chain as well as being connected to the other links by their relative position in the chain. Each link has a different proximity to the others but they still have some kind of relationship.

☐ **Affected by being in a system**. The components must be affected by being in the system in that there is some reason for it to be defined in this way. Going back to the chain, the links must be part of the process of forming a whole with the other links for there to be a system in existence. A spare link that is not attached is not affected by the activities of the chain and so falls outside the system.

☐ **Assembly of components does something**. This brings into play the important concept of systems objectives which means that the system must have some purpose that justifies its existence. A bicycle chain drives the wheels whilst a gold chain worn around the neck will exist mainly for ornamentation.

☐ **Assembly identified as being of special interest**. This is the most difficult part of the systems concepts in that there must be an underlying reason why something has been defined as a system. A system depends on what is being defined rather than being an absolute concept. If we view a bicycle chain as a system consisting of links, this may be because we wish to examine its properties so that its strength may be improved. We can alternatively define the system as comprising the chain and the pedals if we wish to consider the way energy is transferred from the pedals to the wheels via the chain. This may be to seek to improve the efficiency of this energy transfer. The system is deemed to be a system because we wish it to be so, which brings in the idea of it having a special interest.

The universal principles behind systems thinking can be applied in a wide variety of situations and there are several key features:

An open system is linked to the environment and should respond to changes in relevant external factors so as to optimise the systems process. A closed system by contrast is fixed and does not react to external pressures. So a central heating system may remain on for fixed time periods controlled by a timer and once set remains in this mode of operation. Where there are thermostat controls, the system is able to respond to changes in the temperature and so provide a more interactive service. Controls are part of this process of adjusting the system to ensure it is always able to deliver its defined objectives.

A system is a set of interrelated components and the idea of synergy comes into play. This suggests that the sum of the whole is greater than the sum of each individual component, which is expressed as:

$$\boxed{2 + 2 = 5}$$

Synergy may be seen in the example of a series of parts that go to make a motor cycle. When stripped down each part is a non-functioning component. When put together to form a motor cycle it becomes a transportation system with far greater potential in terms of ability and horizons.

Systems thinking is based on the idea of seeing a process as a whole, made up of related parts. This holistic view enables one to understand complicated operations by rising above each specific aspect and considering the whole. A major advantage of systems thinking is this potential for working at the highest levels by viewing an operation as a complete service. The auditor who is able to distinguish between low-level detail and material issues is the auditor of tomorrow. Viewing a system as a sub-system that feeds into a "big picture" is a skill that the auditor should acquire.

Key components are important parts that are crucial to the success of the process. Attention directed towards these will be of more value than the less material parts. The ability to isolate the key issues facing a managerial system has a fundamental impact on internal audit as our work moves towards higher levels in the organisation. For example, there are many control weaknesses that are derived from problems with the human resource management systems. As the auditor progresses in the work this factor may allow resources to be directed at this area as the most efficient use of audit time. The way the HRM systems interface with line operations can be captured by applying the systems view of the organisation as both strong and weak links are isolated.

Another theory derived from systems theory is that there are compensating influences. These can make up for weaknesses elsewhere in the system or simply provide an additional control. For example, a corporate financial system that is supposed to underpin budgetary control may be poor and only report actual spend after a delay of several months. Management may maintain its own record of spending to get up-to-date information of budget variances. The budgetary control system must be seen to include this compensating control if it is to be fully appreciated.

As well as the key components there are sensitive areas in any system. The dependency chain means that the whole process may be at risk where parts of the link are weak or break down. It is only by understanding the whole system that one is able to determine the effect of changes in any one area on other linked areas. This may be the single biggest benefit to accrue from adopting a systems approach in contrast to viewing individual operations and activities as discreet items.

We turn to the issue of link and parent/child systems which interface with the activities that we are considering. Returning to our example of a motor cycle, the associated systems may be illustrated as:

FIGURE 14.2 MOTOR CYCLE TRANSPORT SYSTEM

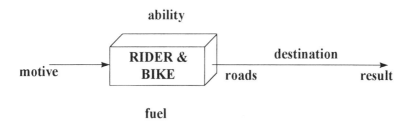

The rider and bike may be seen as the primary system that then feeds into link systems such as roads, fuel, and objectives. There is an infinite number of systems combinations that may be applied depending on one's perceptions. An audit terms of reference must state clearly where the system under review stops and starts.

We need to establish the conceptual cut-off point. The motorbike example can be extended to include maintenance, manufacture, cleaning, road maps, driving licence, and value for money.

General systems thinking

Brief mention of systems theory and an overview of this methodology appear below:

FIGURE 14.3 GENERAL SYSTEMS THINKING

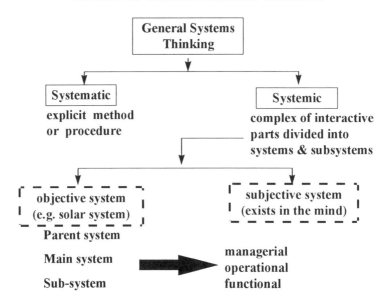

Explanations follow:
1. **Systematic**. The process of using a clear methodology is applied in systems based auditing by using a defined methodology for planning, progressing the audit, and then issuing the audit report.
2. **Systemic**. This use of systems theory is applied to the way the audit field is viewed as a series of systems and link systems.
3. **Subjective system**. Here the use of a set system's boundary to define the system under review is something that auditors should apply to provide an agreed picture of what will be subject to audit.
4. **Parent system, main systems and sub-systems**. The appreciation of systems relationships in a hierarchical manner, and as part of the associated system gives an insight into the way activities feed into each other.
5. **Managerial, operational and functional**. The translation of systems to organisational levels and types gives a start to deciding how to break down the organisation for audit purposes.

Entropy
This may be seen as a disorder, disorganisation, lack of patterning or randomness of organisation of systems. A closed system tends to increase in entropy over time in that it will move towards greater disorder and randomness. Entropy provides a justification for the audit role as systems break down and controls deteriorate over time unless they are reviewed and made to keep pace with change. The trend to removing a tier of management to achieve budget reductions may have a major impact on systems controlled through supervisory reviews by line and middle management. The balance of control changes with restructuring. If not, the imbalance becomes part of the overall entropy where a

deterioration in controls impairs the successful functioning of the system. This is why some audit units plan a cycle of reviews every few years.

14.2 Systems Auditing

We can use the principles of systems thinking to conduct systems audits. We are primarily concerned about the arrangements for effecting the five key control objectives that fall within the scope of internal auditing (see IIA standard 300):

• Suitable and accurate management information.
• Compliance with procedures, laws and regulations.
• Safeguarding assets.
• Securing economies and efficiencies.
• Accomplishing objectives.

We are concerned with reviewing and then advising management on their systems of internal controls that discharge these five objectives. So an activity should be undertaken with due regard for compliance with laws and procedures and this feature should be built into the system. Systems in control will subscribe to these key control features, in contrast to those that are not.

The transactions approach

Systems are designed to process transactions and internal audit is concerned with controls that ensure the systems objectives are met. Where this does not happen the system produces delinquent transactions that breach one or more of the five key control areas. An audit approach that ignores the systems but seeks to identify delinquent transactions may be seen as a transactions-based audit. Probity visits, fraud investigations, compliance testing programmes, spot checks, and VFM efficiency reviews may be based on the transactions approach. Any audit work that does not include evaluating and testing controls cannot be systems auditing. Systems auditing relies on some testing although this naturally flows from the review of controls.

FIGURE 14.4 SYSTEMS VERSUS TRANSACTIONS APPROACH

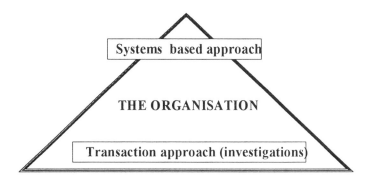

For example: An audit team used to follow vehicles to see whether they were being used on official business. This displays adherence to a transactions based approach, since a systems approach would seek to consider the controls that should be in place to ensure that vehicles are used only for business purposes. We might wish to observe several vehicles during the course of the audit but this would be to check the way these controls are operating and not as an audit in its own right. A systems audit of a payments system will seek to isolate and review controls over the process of preparing invoices and paying suppliers. A transactions approach examines a sample of payments to see if they are correct and proper without commenting on the underlying controls. The main principle is that systems auditing starts from the top (controls established by management), in contrast to the transaction approach which starts at the bottom (the end results of transactions processing).

Stages of systems based auditing (SBA)

System thinking is used twice in SBA. Firstly, we break down operations as systems, components of a system, sub-systems, parallel systems and parent systems. An overview may be adopted and links between operations may be identified and understood. Secondly, SBA is in fact a system in itself with defined stages and clear links between each step. The stages of a system based audit are:

FIGURE 14.5 THE SYSTEMS BASED AUDITING PROCESS

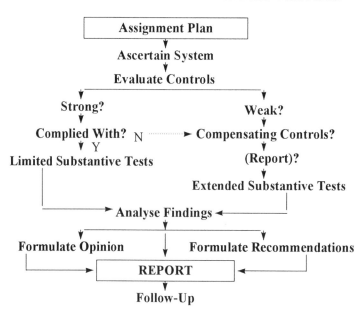

System auditing cannot be carried out without following the above steps.

Stage considerations

For each stage of the systems audit there are a number of matters to be considered:

☐ **Define clear objectives for the stage**. What we are aiming to achieve should be clearly stated at each stage so that the actual output can be measured against this.

☐ **Plan the work and approach to be adopted**. Planning is a continuous process that occurs before the audit and throughout the various above mentioned stages. It is possible to set a separate time budget for the stage and then seek to monitor hours charged before finalisation of the audit. It is also possible to carry out a review of work as the stage is completed to provide an ongoing supervision of the project by audit management.

☐ **Define any testing strategy**. Testing is applied at ascertainment (walk through), compliance (after evaluation) and substantive testing (after evaluation and compliance tests). The detailed work programme may be drafted and agreed as the appropriate stage is arrived at.

☐ **Define the techniques that will be used**. Audit techniques such as interviewing, flowcharting, database interrogation, negotiating and statistical sampling should be agreed again at the relevant stage of the audit. This will assist timing the work and enable additional skill needs to be identified.

☐ **Brief staff working on the project**. With a team approach it is useful to break down each stage so that a briefing can be held to discuss problem areas, progress and other matters. Not only will this act as a feedback device but it will also promote team working where ideas are exchanged.

☐ **Ensure that the work is formally documented**. Standardised documentation ensures all key points are covered and that the work is fully recorded. The stage end is a convenient time to consider whether the documentation meets quality standards (according to the audit manual) and contains all the necessary detail. The opportunity to obtain missing material is more readily available during and not after the audit. There is an obvious link between this and the audit manager review procedure.

☐ **Look for any control implications**. It is good practice to report as the audit progresses to save time and ensure that the report is fresh and dynamic. The auditor has the opportunity to assess the impact on the work done so far on the report and the testing strategy that will have to be developed at some stage. Control implications can enter the report so long as the repercussions have been tested. Since evaluation of controls occurs throughout the audit, the whole package of views on the state of key controls is developed as work progresses. This is a major part of the auditor's work.

☐ **Agree the direction of work for the next stage**. The link between stages comes naturally from the systems approach to auditing as one moves smoothly from one to another. The direction of the next stage must be considered by the auditor not only from a planning point of view, but also from the wider perspective of whether work should be expended, curtailed or adjusted. This is the point to discuss matters with the audit manager and also advise that the stage in question is complete.

Key systems issues
In a systems audit the auditor will comment on specific determinations of the state of controls that have been reviewed:

FIGURE 14.6 KEY SYSTEMS AUDIT ISSUES

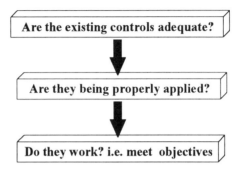

The detailed testing routines and comprehensive discussions with management all contribute. An obsession with the mechanisms of performing the audit and close examination of files and data should not detract from this point. The auditor must at the end of the day be prepared to comment on the systems of internal control.

The management control system
There is misunderstanding of systems based audits and some see this as applying only to basic accounting or computerised systems. Operational auditing is the term applied to non-financial audits and this is seen as being outside systems based audits. Operational auditors are then viewed as searching for "good ideas" to apply to the area they are auditing that improve efficient production methods. Some take this idea further and consider that auditors need to be experts in the area under review and may end up trying to convince line managers that the auditors actually know best. This conflicts with the basic principle of internal auditing, which is to assist managers with their systems and not to second guess. Auditors need only to be experts at systems auditing and controls and should not do management's job. It is possible to use systems thinking in its widest sense and consider that any operation being reviewed consists of systems of corporate policies, managerial activities and the actual operations. These systems are reinforced by support systems like IT, finance, and personnel. The managerial control system caters for all these systems through a comprehensive cycle of activities that encompass the concept of controlling resources. Control arises from developing, implementing and maintaining a suitable control system described in chapter one. This then becomes the system under review and touches upon all crucial control issues including the management of the activity. Systems auditing can be applied in its widest sense and its scope is in practice unlimited. The key control objectives may be superimposed on this control loop and this system has to be properly in place before management's objectives can be achieved. The managerial control system is a device that appears in various forms throughout the handbook.

Benefits of systems based auditing (SBA)
Keith Wade (1990) has argued that SBA has a number of benefits:
1. It is positive and forward-looking and considers the future strengths of control systems as opposed to isolating and reporting a series of past errors.
2. It promotes participation by involving the client in explaining the system and its objectives.

3. It promotes professionalism as opposed to churning out auditors who are experts in basic extensive testing routines.
4. It covers everything by being based on the system in operation.
5. It is constructive in seeking to improve systems.
6. It is preventive and views errors in terms of preventing them in the future rather than listing them for management to re-process.
7. It can be geared into career development as an experienced systems auditor is able to tackle very complicated operations.
8. It promotes respect by requiring the auditor to understand the systems and the client's needs.
9. It develops auditors as experts in control rather than checkers of management.
10. There is unlimited potential to extend systems auditing into all organisational activities.
11. Auditors generally find it more interesting with the emphasis away from testing transactions.
12. It can act as a vital aid to management with long lasting effects in strengthening controls.
13. It can be a very efficient use of audit resources since it looks for causes of problems and not just the consequential errors.
14. Since it is not error oriented it is not therefore seen as negative by management.
15. It is systematic and key areas may be identified and isolated for further attention.
16. It has a wide scope and application and may be used to audit almost anything.

Limitations of the transactions approach

We favour the systems approach since the main limitations of the transactions based approach are:
1. It tends to be directed at merely assigning blame without addressing the wider implications.
2. Errors may occur randomly and testing routines may not put the results into a fair perspective.
3. It is not systematic and may miss out more important issues facing the operation.
4. It can blur the management role and be seen as a chance to "catch them out". Management may be lax in preventing certain types of errors since these will be picked up by the auditors.
5. The audit deterrent principle that underpins some testing routines is negative since it is based on the theory that staff will perform badly unless under threat of being exposed.
6. It promotes an immature obsession with testing and checking.
7. It may engender little professionalism and become very boring, with repetitive rounds of visits to perform pre-designed audit programmes.
8. It may result in role conflict with the auditors insisting that their work assists management whereas they are seen primarily as checkers.
9. It ignores real managerial issues and underlying causes by a fixation with historic evidence that could be many months (or even years) old so as to isolate errors.
10. It is negative and backwards looking.

Implications of transaction auditing

Where internal audit emphasises testing programmes and probity visits, fraud investigations, compliance inspections, VFM reviews and contract compliance, this is indicative of the transaction auditing approach. The implication is that audit success criteria fall around errors that can be found as opposed to controls that may be improved. This "error industry" must have weak systems to survive and prosper in total conflict with the systems based approach. A whole army of checkers can be employed to search and report problems using junior staff with a "let's catch them" attitude that sets a tone of threat and intimidation. This approach leads to poorly controlled systems that defeat the professional audit objective which is to review and ensure management has installed adequate controls over organisational resources. The following diagram shows how controls when ignored tend to break down which reinforces the need to test for errors:

FIGURE 14.7 TRANSACTIONS APPROACH BOTTOM LINE - POOR SYSTEMS

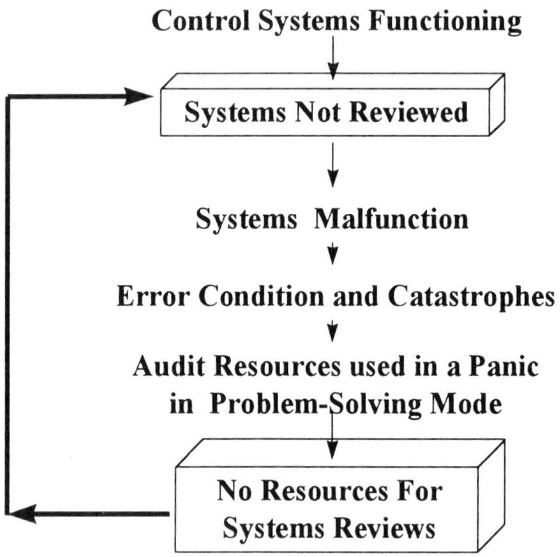

Transactions versus systems auditing
The systems based approach views the organisation as a series of control systems that cover corporate, managerial, operational and support service activities. The transactions approach views the organisation as a series of processes that can lead to errors and problems if the output is not examined by routine testing programmes that consider propriety and compliance with procedure. The systems approach will seek to install a suitable control environment within which managers plan, organise, monitor, and apply the resources under their direction so as to promote the achievement of organisational objectives. It is the controls that are emphasised and this has a major impact on the perceived internal audit role. Control weaknesses should be identified and the managerial control system seen to be firmly in place. Part of the control systems would require management to seek to monitor compliance with control standards and this then frees internal audit to concentrate on the controls themselves. Error conditions are traced back to their original cause in terms of weak, inadequate or vague controls. There is a move towards compliance auditing as more in line with management's expectations of the audit role and as a way of protecting the audit budget in times of financial pressure. This is based on a lack of appreciation of the importance of control standards at the highest levels of the organisation. The dilemma lies when top management feels threatened by the audit

presence in control systems since the audit reports are based on the premise that the same managers are responsible for these controls. Probity and compliance are seen more as matters that impinge on junior staff, and reports that comment on problems in these areas are always well received by top management. Internal organisational forces can work against the systems auditing model. This is a challenge that must be met. The other pressure that impacts on the systems ethos is that interrogation facilities can deal with entire databases that can be tested on a 100% basis. There are auditors who view this as the future of internal auditing. This is dealt with in the chapter sixteen on testing.

Service Based Systems Auditing (SBSA)
An enlightened approach to tackling internal audits is to view the organisation as a collection of services that are provided internally or externally. This is based on a number of principles:
1. The organisation is viewed as a series of business units where local management is deemed responsible for delivering the defined level and quality of service.
2. The management control system should be in place so as to transfer resources into services in line with a stated objective.
3. The various functional support functions including financial, operational, informational, and other corporate standards fall under this review if they impact on business objectives.

This approach is epitomised in a local authority where one need only obtain a directory of services such as libraries, child care, schools, refuse collection, highways repairs, housing, sports centres and hundreds of unique services. Each service then becomes an audit unit and subject to audit cover. This is obviously a subjective view of the organisation but addresses clearly the problem of defining systems in a precise fashion in line with a high-level approach to service based systems auditing.

FIGURE 14.8 SERVICE BASED SYSTEMS AUDITING

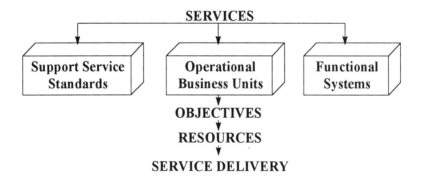

The above approach can be applied as follows:
1. List all services (business units).
2. List support services.
3. Apply risk appraisal to these services.
4. Set out audit plans.
5. Audit each service by applying the managerial control system.
6. Perform special investigations into problem areas using resources set aside for consultancy work.

14.3 Ascertaining and Recording Systems

Introduction
Systems based auditing relies on evaluating the whole system of internal controls that ensure operational objectives will be achieved. This task can only be performed where the systems that are being considered are properly understood which in turn relies on the auditor's ability to document the system efficiently. There are several alternative methods, each with its own advantages. Some of the more popular ones are mentioned here.

Alternative methods
The main options that the auditor has for documenting the system are:
1. Narrative notes.
2. Block diagrams.
3. Flowcharts.
4. Internal control questionnaire (ICQ).

There are different types of flowcharts which may be shown as follows:

FIGURE 14.9 TYPES OF FLOWCHARTS

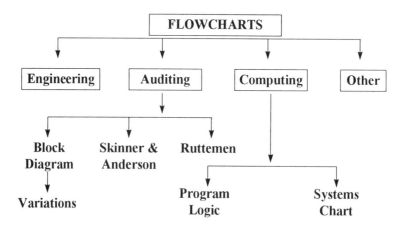

Despite clear differences between types of flowchart, there are basic principles:

FIGURE 14.10 BASIC FLOWCHARTING RULES

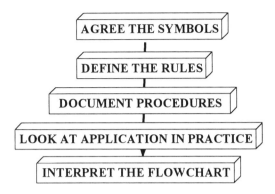

Securing the required information

Before the auditor can "capture" the system, information must be secured through fact finding:

The auditor interviews the line manager and operatives to elicit a picture of operations. Line managers will have an overview of what goes on in their areas of responsibility and this is the starting place for the full audit. It is only when the operatives are seen that a truer picture is obtained as answers highlight non-compliance and/or poor controls. The auditor decides how far to follow the system if it links into other systems. This is clear from the defined scope of the audit in the assignment plan. New information that extends the systems boundaries is brought back to the audit manager for further consideration. When the system is being written up, gaps in acquired information may require further investigation. Armed with predefined checklists the auditor should direct interviews to cover all important areas. Capturing the flow of documentation and information should be key concerns. The auditor should try to document the system and consider whether it equates to the "official system". Different versions of the same system may result from misunderstanding by operational staff and this should be seen as a finding in its own right. Walk through testing means that the auditor will point to examples as the system is explained by the auditee to help illustrate underlying processes. The information gathering process may bring out weaknesses which might be discovered by the auditor or expressed by the interviewee. This aids the auditor in evaluation, and it is not necessary to keep ascertainment and evaluation separate. It is dangerous for the auditor to jump to conclusions and start recommending action at the ascertainment stage no matter how impressive this might appear during initial interviews.

Narrative

Systems are set out by straightforward narrative where the main parts of the system are noted in point format. The processes are described from start to finish to convey the required information on which to base an evaluation. The bulk of these systems notes may be taken direct from the interview with the operations manager. For simple systems that do not involve much document flows, this may be sufficient. For more complicated systems it may be necessary to go on to draft a block diagram and/or a detailed flowchart.

Narrative provides a useful short-cut to systems documentation and as long as it conveys the right information clearly, it is a valid technique. It should be possible to cross reference relevant documents to the narrative and then attach them to the notes for future use. Structured narrative notes divide the operation into sections or people alongside brief notes on each activity to form a diagrammatic representation of events. This might appear as:

TABLE 14.1 STRUCTURED SYSTEMS NARRATIVE NOTES

SYSTEM STAGE	DEPT A	DEPT B	DEPT C
1	notes xxx	notes xxx	notes xxx
2	notes xxx	notes xxx	notes xxx
3	notes xxx	notes xxx	notes xxx
4	notes xxx	notes xxx	notes xxx
etc.			

This captures the system simply on a single document without needing detailed symbols and keys.

Block diagrams

Block diagrams fall in between detailed flowcharts and narrative. They consist of a series of boxes each representing an operation or control. It provides a simple diagrammatic representation:

FIGURE 14.11 A BLOCK DIAGRAM

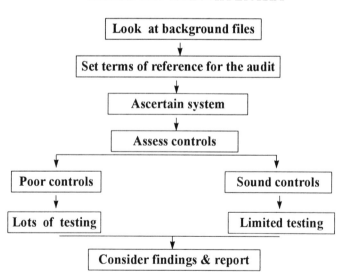

One may show the flow of information and the organisational arrangements. The main advantage is that this technique is quick and simple, and sample diagrams can be incorporated within the audit report to aid understanding by outlining the system. For high-level work that does not require a detailed analysis of documentation this can be an efficient way of recording the system. This contrasts with flowcharting where there is an obsession with the detailed movement of documents.

The rules of flowcharting

Flowcharts are detailed representations of documents and information that record most parts of a defined operation. The rules that are applied to audit charts are:

1. Provide clear headings and dates so that the system dealt with is clearly identified. Do not make them unnecessarily complicated as this consumes time and may not aid the audit process.
2. Look for exception routines and note these so that a complete picture is provided.
3. Test the flowchart against the client's understanding of the system.
4. Distinguish between operations/processes and controls so that the flowchart can feed directly into the control evaluation procedures.
5. Number the events in sequential order as they may be referred to in other audit working papers.
6. Keep the narrative brief to avoid making the schedule appear cramped.
7. Show destination of all documents by not leaving loose ends.
8. Distinguish between information and documentation flow.
9. Use a convention of moving through the system - top to bottom and from left to right.
10. Apply standardised symbols and keys that are fully agreed and detailed in the audit manual.

Rutteman

The Ruttemen convention is popular and tends to be used by ICA/ACCA trained auditors:

1. It has fewer symbols than the Skinner and Anderson system.
2. It has fewer operations.
3. There is less narrative in the margin.
4. Everything has to be concluded.

Some of the standard symbols used are listed in figure 14.2:

FIGURE 14.12 STANDARD FLOWCHART SYMBOLS

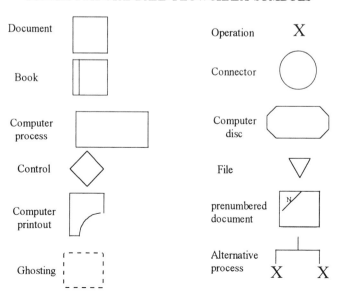

Documents that have been processed will normally be found in temporary or permanent files. Temporary files are those awaiting further instructions or information to complete the transaction:

TABLE 14.2 FILES

	Permanent	Temporary
Alphabetic	A	TA
Numerical	N	TN
Date order	D	TD

As a final outcome of all transactions we should find that they are:
1. Permanently filed.
2. Have left the system.
3. Destroyed.

Ghosting is applied when multi-part documents are used and the separate parts may be subjected to different sequences of operations so that a restatement of each part may be the simplest way to depict these operations. Sequences of operations representing a subroutine may be shown on a separate chart and ghosting can be used to restate the initial document in the chart. As a brief example of this flowcharting convention refer to this narrative:
1. Weekly requisitions received by Buyer from main office.
2. Three part order prepared by Buyer.
3. Documents sent to Accounts where they check the requisitions with the orders.
4. Requisitions are filed in date order.
5. Orders are entered into purchase ledger.

FIGURE 14.13 ORDERING SYSTEM - FLOWCHART

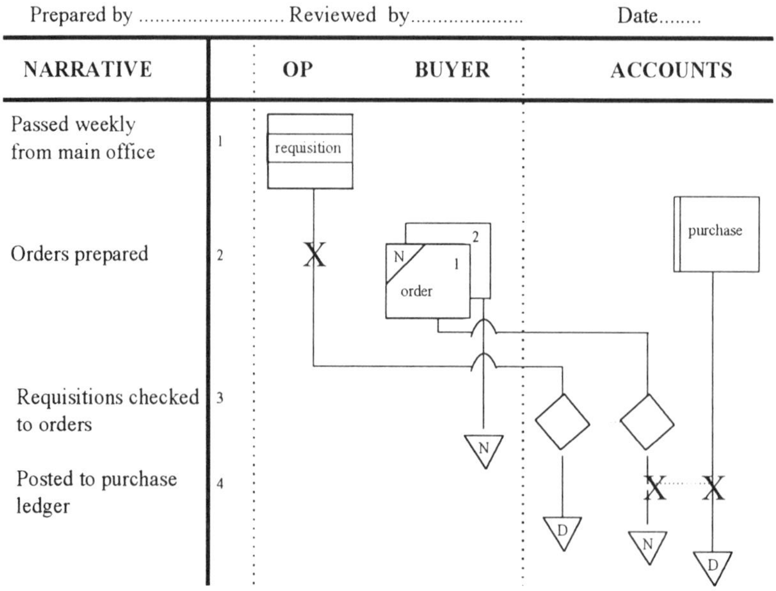

Prepared by .... Reviewed by..................... Date........

NARRATIVE	OP	BUYER	ACCOUNTS
Passed weekly from main office	1	requisition	
Orders prepared	2	X N / 1 order [2]	purchase
Requisitions checked to orders	3	N	
Posted to purchase ledger	4	D N	X ...... X D

Pros and cons of flowcharting

Main advantages:

- Highlights weak controls particularly relating to a lack of segregation of duties and authorisation.
- Indicates possible duplication of work where tasks are repeated.
- Permanent record of the system.
- Shows instances of formal authorisation.
- A logical and systematic procedure that can be learnt and applied by all auditors.
- Ensures the complete system is ascertained. Narrative notes may not follow all documents from initiation to conclusion and only by formally charting their flow may gaps be spotted.
- Used to highlight instances of internal check.
- Allows a birds-eye view of the system.

Disadvantages:

- Training in the techniques required for competent use.
- Time consuming as detailed operations are documented.
- Can be badly drawn and hardly understood by anyone.
- Tends not to be descriptive and suit complicated systems with lots of document flows.
- May be subject to constant change and require updating as systems change.
- Can show excessive detail and become very complicated.
- Becomes an end in itself instead of a tool to be sensibly applied as part of the overall audit process.
- Inappropriate for corporate and managerial systems with high-level controls to be explained rather than charted.

Using the flowchart

Flowcharts may be used in the following ways:

1. Weak areas or waste of resources may be isolated so that audit attention may be directed towards these parts of the system, or problems can simply be referred to in the report.
2. One can draw a second flowchart to show proposed improvements. The relevant stages may be highlighted in "before" and "after" charts that form the basis of discussions with management.
3. One may use the internal control questionnaire (ICQ) in conjunction with flowcharts, expanding on areas where there may be systems weaknesses. ICQs are also a form of systems ascertainment in that they relay the control features of the area under review.
4. Walk through tests may be used to take a small sample of transactions through the system so that the integrity of the documentation may be determined.
5. Automated flowcharting packages may be used.

Balancing the level of details required

There must be balance in the use of ascertainment techniques so that efficiency is maintained and there is perspective involved in applying flowcharting. For the best ascertainment options consider:

- **Narrative** - A simple descriptive overview gleaned directly from the interviews. It should be used wherever possible unless the level of documentation becomes too detailed to deal with in note form.

- **Block diagrams** -Illustrate the main stages of a system and the relationships between components. With the growing use of graphical presentation software, there is scope for attractive diagrams that can be imported into the audit report for ease of reading. Main systems stages have to be summarised for block diagrams to be of any use although the advantage is simplicity in design and ease of use.
- **Detailed flowchart** - These should be used sparingly and only where absolutely necessary. Because of time constraints and the move away from basic operational detail, they have limited use. Where a sensitive system, such as pre-signed cheque ordering, use and dispatch, must be carefully accounted for, monitored and controlled at all stages, detailed flowcharts will probably be required.

Standards on the above including appropriate conventions should be comprehensively dealt with in the audit manual. It is pointless to seek to flowchart in detail all organisational systems as this would be a momentous task. They would need constant change with little or no benefit to the audit service.

Other ascertainment techniques

It is possible to apply many different techniques to the task of ascertaining a system. The traditional methods chart the flow of information and documents. In operational auditing we tend to be more interested in the profile of a particular operational area that uses resources to produce a defined service (or product). We can use ascertainment to link directly into the evaluation stage and so concentrate on controls. In seeking to ascertain operational systems we may apply several approaches in conjunction with relevant parts of the specimen documents (found in the accompanying diskette):

1. For more complicated systems that interface with other systems we isolate the target area through the use of Form 068 where link systems are also noted.
2. For functional systems such as a creditors system, we describe the role of each section (or department) and isolate key controls accordingly. Form 073 can be used for this.
3. It is possible to view an operation as a discrete area that has inputs and operational processes which then result in a defined output. These may be "captured" through the use of Form 074 (for resources) or Form 075 (for the flow of information and documents).
4. Systems ascertainment should be carried out recognising that controls will generally prevent, detect and/or correct errors and problems. For each key process we record these types of controls and Form 076 can be used.
5. Managerial controls are located in the management control systems. For each key component, we may complete Form 077 to record the state of the relevant component (i.e. objectives, staffing arrangements, use of procedures).
6. The final example relates to recording the type of information system in place in the area under review and Form 078 can be used.

The choice of ascertainment technique depends on the type of audit and approach adopted. There is a wide variety of available methodologies and this adds to, rather than dilutes, the auditor's skills base. The audit manual is the right vehicle for setting such standards.

14.4 Evaluating Systems

Introduction

Evaluation may be seen as the most important stage in any audit review since this provides an opportunity for auditors to apply professional creativity to the fullest. The audit opinion and recommendations should flow from the systems weaknesses identified during the systems evaluation. Audit testing routines are carried out to confirm the original evaluation in terms of the application of controls and the effects of control weaknesses. If the evaluation is flawed then all the remaining audit work will suffer. Audit recommendations will provide sub-standard solutions to control problems.

Defining the system

The preliminary survey establishes which system is being audited. The statement on scope of audit work in the assignment plan will document what is being reviewed and it is this system that will be subject to evaluation. We then have to turn to the model of the system that is being evaluated. The system may be conceived as one of several models:

☐ **The prescribed system**. This perceived version of the system is laid down in procedure notes and official documents. The original systems intentions may be set out in old committee papers and formal reviews commissioned by management. The official description of the system will follow this formally agreed format. The auditor has to be concerned with this system since it may be the one that is officially approved by the organisation and if it has altered, then fresh approval may have to be sought. For example where the organisation has agreed a central purchasing function then any variation to this model, where managers place their own orders, should be formally authorised. If not, we may be in breach of procedure.

☐ **The alleged system**. This follows the procedures that are described by the management and staff operating the system. It allows for any changes to the official system that have been made by operatives over the years. Although the steps that constitute the operational system have been conveyed by line managers, they may in practice be carried out differently. When the auditor first starts the audit, management will tend to give the "Rolls Royce" version of the system in that all work is well managed, supervised and controlled. For example the manager of payroll may arrange work into three teams and argue that it is well managed and controlled. After a few days work the auditor may find that each team works to their own standards and as a result the overall payroll operations are fraught with inconsistency and error.

☐ **The planned system**. The system that management wishes to install may be called the planned system. The auditor may be asked not to review the existing operations but concentrate on management's proposal since it is this that will form the future system. On one level it is good to feed into development plans as a way of directing attention at major managerial concerns. The problem with this approach is the uncertainty of futuristic proposals that may simply exist as management ideas. Actual problems that relate to the existing arrangements cannot simply be ignored. For example a sundry debtors' function that had a poor collection record should be subject to an internal audit. There is no point in managers seeking to abort the planned audit on the basis that they are seeking to resolve the problems. The auditor notes the planned changes but will examine the scope of the problems and whether adequate controls have been or are being installed.

☐ **The emergency/contingency system**. Although the system may be clearly set out and applied on most occasions, there is also an emergency system that the auditor may wish to consider. This is based on the need to "get things done" in an emergency and may result in many overrides of official procedure. An example is where the organisation is making redundancies. Any audit review of controls where the operation is fully staffed and working normally, may be irrelevant where everything is subject to major change. Short cuts may be taken for expediency and these arrangements cannot be ignored. Emergency routes should form part of the system as exception routines and be included within the scope of the audit review. Exceptions create major vulnerabilities in systems as otherwise sound controls may be bypassed, normally by senior management.

☐ **The ideal system**. Published research on systems control and value for money studies, by their nature, use generalisations on how defined operations may be improved. The temptation to set out ideals on systems control may be seen as part of the drive to establishing an "ideal system". This can also occur where the package of controls is fine in theory but, becomes too cumbersome and complicated in practice. The auditor's recommendations will appear to be out of touch with operational reality if based on ideals that do not attach to actual working practices. This problem arises where the auditor insists on making snap judgements about devising new controls.

☐ **The auditor's preferred system**. The auditor's understanding of the systems processes and control weaknesses may convince him/her that certain improvements are required. These may be seen as the auditor's version of the ideal system. It is not the auditor who will be charged with operating these recommended controls so it must be supported by findings which identify the need for further improvements. Findings are generally obtained through the application of compliance and substantive tests. Marketing and negotiation may be required to "sell" the audit recommendations.

☐ **Staff's preferred system**. Supervisory staff and front line employees may have a vision of the type of controls that should be incorporated. The system preferred by management tends to be what the auditor finds during the review, unless management is not aware of non-compliance or the full implications of control weaknesses. Staff will tend to implant additional checks and records to assist them in their day-to-day work, many of which act as compensating controls. The issue of non-compliance may be related more to conscientious employees devising new routines rather than purposely bypassing formal controls. The auditor must try with caution to capture the real system.

☐ **The workable system**. This is the system that works in practice and retains all the required control features. It may fall somewhere between the ideal system, management's system, audit's preferences and the procedures applied by staff themselves.

☐ **The best system**. The question arises as to what is the best system. There would seem to be several interpretations. The "best" system is able to deliver management's objectives, which brings into play exactly how this criterion should be applied. The starting place is to isolate the success criteria that managers use to guide them in managing resources. We would expect these to coincide with the organisation's view of success. Where the internal auditor finds that management has failed to establish performance indicators this is a control weakness. If these indicators would have been reported to a Corporate Management Team forum, they may show what management believes they would show i.e. a poor result that is indefensible. Audit insistence that performance should be measured may fall upon deaf ears since the organisation's needs do not coincide with management's own interests. All systems have interested parties who depend on the services to different extents for different reasons. All systems have in-built constraints that limit the level of service delivered. We must still discover the systems objectives and ensure that the underlying controls promote the achievement of these. Once these have been isolated, the systems may be reviewed. To answer our original question we might argue that taking a pro-organisation stance, the best system will be that which delivers management's objectives and promotes the welfare of the organisation. Evaluation will be based on the system that is actually in operation although reference will be had to development plans and official procedures. Successful evaluation requires that the right techniques are applied in the right way, based on a good understanding of the system. The auditor's understanding of the system should include:

1. **Understanding the needs of the parties who rely on the system**. This not only includes front-line staff and middle managers but all those involved in systems that interface. These may sometimes conflict where one user (say line managers) requires readily available financial information while another (say the accountant) demands a high accuracy rather than speed.

2. **Understanding the adopted success criteria** and what the system is about in terms of the competing factors of quality, timeliness, quantity and value of the systems product.

3. **Understanding systems constraints** and the relationship between the cost and benefits of control.

Evaluation techniques

The system being reviewed is the system being applied in practice in line with management's operational objectives. The evaluation applied should be based on those controls required to ensure systems objectives are achieved with no great loss or inefficiency. Evaluation techniques include:

1. **Flowcharts**. These help identify systems blockages, duplication of effort and segregation of duties along with controls that depend on documentation flows and the way work is organised.

2. **Transactions testing**. By testing transactions one might pick up systems malfunctions that cause error conditions identified by the tests. Where we are able to manipulate large amounts of data, the ability to carry out a limited range of tests quickly arises. This cannot be seen as a systematic evaluation since it does not rely on a full understanding of the operation under review, but leaves matters to chance as samples are selected and examined.

3. **Directed representations**. One cannot deny the usefulness of information provided by persons who have knowledge of the system. If management states that there are defined systems weaknesses at the outset of an audit, one would be ill advised to ignore this source of information. Complaints from users, operatives, middle management and third parties can provide a short-cut to the evaluation process. One would look for bias in these comments as they could not be taken without some degree of substantiating evidence.

4. **Internal control questionnaires (ICQ)**. Dealt with below.
5. **Internal control evaluation system (ICES)**. Dealt with below.

We must make one point clear in the form of a formal statement on evaluations that reads:

FIGURE 14.14 EVALUATION

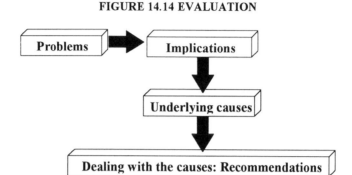

At some stage we apply this framework against what we find in practice. This is why the evaluation stage is where the auditor's creative abilities come to the fore.

Internal control questionnaires (ICQ)

Internal control questionnaires (ICQ) are widely used to assist the control evaluation process and there are many standard packages. They consist of a series of questions applied to a particular operation and designed so that a "no" answer indicates a potential control weakness. One might ask:

> *"Is the task of receipting income separated from the recording of this income?"*

The idea being that a "no" answer may mean that official duties are insufficiently segregated. The potential weaknesses are then further explored and compensatory controls looked for before testing routines are applied. ICQs have a number of specific advantages and disadvantages:

Advantages

1. Provides a permanent record of the evaluation stage. As the schedules are completed they automatically record the response to each key point examined as a ready made working paper.
2. A disciplined, systematic approach to evaluation not depending on the whims and fancies of the assigned auditor.
3. Helps audit supervisors as the standard of evaluation is set beforehand through compilation of the ICQ. The expectation that field auditors will ensure full coverage of the defined areas via this process provides a useful management tool for controlling the audit.
4. Provides direction to the auditor by setting out clearly the areas that are to be addressed. In this way the auditor can approach an audit armed with the necessary

tools i.e. the ICQ checklists. There is no need to rethink the control mechanisms that form part of the evaluation process as they are set out in the ICQ. The "what should be" model is then available to be used to assess the adequacy of existing practices. Some might argue that the ICQ provides indispensable guidance.

5. It is simple to use as the questions are directed at control objectives that should be present in the operation under review.

6. The technique can be used by inexperienced auditors who should find it simple to adapt their work to provide responses to the listed questions.

7. It de-personalises the audit by setting tried, trusted, and objective criteria for the controls in operation. The auditor can defend a charge of being too obsessed with control by referring to the ICQ standards adopted by the internal audit function and not devised in a hit or miss fashion.

8. ICQs promote a systems based approach. They emphasise controls as the main source of audit attention, rather than the testing programmes that may be the main basis for the audit. Controls are deemed by the ICQ to accomplish objectives that support the main thrust of the systems approach.

9. Provides good structure and form to the audit by defining beforehand the way systems will be assessed. Planning is easier as time can be assigned to completing the requirements of the ICQ and the work has a natural start and finish in line with the control standards used.

10. It results in comprehensive cover of an area by dealing with all foreseeable points. It is impossible for an auditor to be aware of all control features within an ICQ, particularly the more comprehensive ones. Having the checklist to hand enables one to take on board many factors.

Disadvantages

1. They can lead to a stereotyped approach where each year the auditor seeks to examine a series of predetermined factors that is wholly predictable. It may engender a bureaucratic approach where detailed enquiries are repeated time and time again with little or no real inspiration from the auditor.

2. It can become mechanical as the task of completing the never-ending checklist becomes so laborious that the auditor develops a secret desire to leave the profession.

3. They may be followed blindly by an auditor whose preoccupation is to complete schedules without really understanding why. It is one thing to provide comprehensive direction on audit coverage, but to simply employ form fillers is unacceptable. Where strict time limitations are placed on completing the schedules, there may be little time to think through the actual implications.

4. Detailed ICQs may stifle initiative. The inexperienced auditor may find the detailed guidance useful whereas the more skilled may feel frustration with this mechanical process. The wish to divert resources to new issues that may have been discussed with client management may be impaired by the fixation with the ICQ as documentation that needs to be completed. The professional auditor needs freedom to follow high-level issues to their conclusion as a way of targeting key risks.

5. Management may feel it is a cumbersome time consuming technique. Where the auditor is completing a checklist, that ranges from important matters to immaterial detail on insignificant parts of the system, it may appear amateurish. There will be some parts of the ICQ to be based on questions to line management and it may be tedious to seek the required responses. Some of the questions may elicit inappropriate

answers and some may display poor understanding by the auditor of the systems. Most of these disadvantages arise from a misuse of the ICQ procedure which, at its worst, ends up with the auditor sending a list of 101 questions to management.

There are a several ways that the ICQ technique may be applied more efficiently and effectively:

- Tailor the standardised ICQ to the specific circumstances based on understanding of the system under review. Make each question relevant. Using automated schedules makes this task much easier where the auditor can amend the document on computer disk.
- Gear the questions into control objectives as a way of interfacing them with the system. Once the key control objective has been agreed then the questions can be directed to the control issues.

Parts of the ICQ that relate to a stores system may appear as:

TABLE 14.3 CONTROL RELATED ICQ

QUESTION	YES	NO	TEST NO.
ORDERING SYSTEM			
CONTROL OBJECTIVE : To ensure that stores are authorised, delivered, correct, safeguarded and available.			
Q.1 Is person certifying the order independent of the storekeeper?			
Q.2 Are orders placed only with approved suppliers?			
Q.3 Does the order make reference to a purchasing contract?			
Q.4 Are stock level reports issued regularly for re-ordering purposes?			

Do not give them to the manager to complete but use them for fact-finding discussion. The ICQ should be completed by using all available sources of information from interviews, observation, initial testing, documents, manuals, representations, and past audit files. It is compiled as the audit progresses taking on board a wide range of information.

Internal control evaluation system (ICES)

The internal control evaluation system (ICES) is partly a conceptual model linked directly into the systems based approach and partly a mechanism for setting out the evaluation process in matrix format. Unlike ICQs it involves setting out the components of good evaluation in a schedule (or matrix) format so that a systematic series of steps can be undertaken before testing, conclusions and recommendation are made. The main headings may appear at the top of the schedule as:

- Systems objectives.
- Control objectives.

- Risk areas.
- Available control mechanisms.
- Existing control mechanisms.
- Initial evaluation.
- Testing strategy required.
- Test results.
- Conclusions.
- Recommendations.

The entire audit process is established in a formal systematic fashion although this technique tends to be used by more experienced auditors with a full understanding of the system. An example of this approach applied to an audit of a local authority small business grant approval system follows:

TABLE 14.4 BUSINESS ADVICE SERVICE CONTROL EVALUATION

CONTROL OBJECTIVE	DESIRABLE CONTROLS	EXISTING CONTROLS	INITIAL ASSESSMENT	TEST REF.
Awareness of grant	wide publicity	word of mouth only	inadequate	1.A
eligibility	information package	brief leaflet	not comprehensive	1.B
meet criteria	formal assessment	subjective selection	open to abuse	2
pay the correct person	ID & collection	posted out	can go astray	3
monitor effect etc.............	database follow-up	not done	VFM not assured	4

There are advantages to this approach:

1. It treats controls as part of the process of achieving objectives therefore it starts with what management is trying to achieve (i.e. the systems objectives). The entire audit process is seen to flow from this start point.
2. The auditor does not possess a pat answer to controls as suggested by the ICQ approach. It is a question of working out what control objectives are relevant (having regard to the systems objectives) and then seeking to determine what control mechanisms should be in place. This technique is more difficult to master as it requires a commitment to systems auditing. Instead of being armed with a list of questions, the auditor is armed with a database of control mechanisms.
3. The ICES requires the auditor to analyse the system and break it down into logical components as it flows from input, process through to the final output in chronological order.
4. The ICES deals with control risk and exposures as an extension of the evaluation procedure. This requires a considered understanding of the activities under review. A good appreciation of risk enables the auditor to direct control mechanisms at the right parts of the system.

5. The ICES flows naturally into the testing routines as after compliance has been reviewed, the poorer parts of the system are then subject to substantive testing.
6. The ICES forms a record of control weakness to be placed in front of management and discussed before the draft audit report is prepared. We are able to provide a full audit process encapsulated within the ICES schedules. This contains details of objectives, how existing controls compare with desirable ones, the test results obtained, final opinion and recommended improvements derived from resolving weak controls that were confirmed by tests applied.

Evaluation as a continuous process

This section has commented on some of the techniques that auditors use when evaluating systems. Although formal evaluation is a clear component of the audit process, it is also a function that can occur continuously throughout the audit. The final audit opinion will be derived from many factors and information that the auditor uncovers during the audit:

As flowcharts and systems notes are formulated they indicate systems weaknesses in problem areas. These should be separately noted for future reference when developing a testing programme. It is possible to get an initial impression when say touring the location and this adds to the auditor's understanding. If an auditor finds files and documents scattered, these initial impressions may be tested by checking the whereabouts of a selected sample.

Matters connected with the economy, efficiency and effectiveness of the operation may arise at any time during the audit. They may suggest that management has not taken reasonable steps to ensure they are providing value for money. These are all findings relating to the overall state of controls that may appear in the audit report.

Systems control objectives will have to be carefully defined in line with management views since this will have a fundamental bearing on the controls that are assessed. Where management has failed to set clear objectives there is little hope that they will have any success in discharging their responsibilities. If there are objectives but they fall out of line with organisational policies then this is a finding in its own right. We can go on to suggest that "auditing through business objectives" brings the auditor closer to the high-level issues than any other audit procedure. The success criteria that management apply will guide the auditor in deciding whether the controls are working.

The objectives of the system and management perception on what is being achieved have to be fully appreciated before controls can be reviewed. This requires the auditor to have a good understanding of the system under review and means management has to be fully involved in the auditor's work.

An understanding of the available control mechanisms again will assist the evaluation process. Imagine an auditor who has been given a computer notebook that contains the full text of the audit manual. In addition a comprehensive library of control mechanisms would also sit on the hard disk. Having been given terms of reference for the audit and a budgeted hours for the job, we would expect that the library of control mechanisms (used in conjunction with the audit manual) would guide the auditor in the most important task of control evaluation.

The level of existing controls should be assessed as a package that together forms a system of internal control which in turn has to be checked for compliance. The act of obtaining information on the proper functioning of these controls must occur throughout the audit and not just during control evaluation. We would hope that formal control evaluation would provide an opportunity to bring the findings together so that an actual opinion on controls may be provided. One way of summarising these findings is to relate control weaknesses to the five key control objectives.

Fraud is usually an indicator of poor control and where this has occurred in the past, the evaluation should be carried out with a view to preventing similar control breaches that might facilitate fraudulent activity. As such, matters relating to past frauds should be brought into play when considering the adequacy of the entire system of internal controls.

Compensating controls may be used by operatives where formal controls are inadequate or are not used in practice. They may be organic in nature and if formally adopted, may be more effective than official procedures. Key controls are fundamental control mechanisms that have to be in place as opposed to less material optional control features. An example of a key control is regular feedback for managers on operational performance.

The whole control environment including the operational culture, will have an impact on the way control mechanisms are defined and adopted. If the auditor ignores this then the evaluation will be sub-standard. The managerial control system ensures that fundamental control features involving objectives, resources and constant adjustment of strategy are pre-requisites for good controls. The macro evaluation concentrates on the managerial in contrast to the operational aspects of the system of internal control. An ICQ approach is better able to deal with this aspect of control whilst the ICES copes with detailed operational systems broken down into clear stages.

During control evaluation the auditor's judgement is perhaps the single most important factor and this will be based on experience and training. The whole process of reviewing the system will arise throughout the audit and the formal evaluation techniques may be used to confirm the auditor's initial opinion. Control findings have to be tested. Firstly they must be checked to see if controls are being applied as intended. Secondly the effects of weaknesses must be established and quantified:

FIGURE 14.15 EVALUATION CONFIRMATION CYCLE

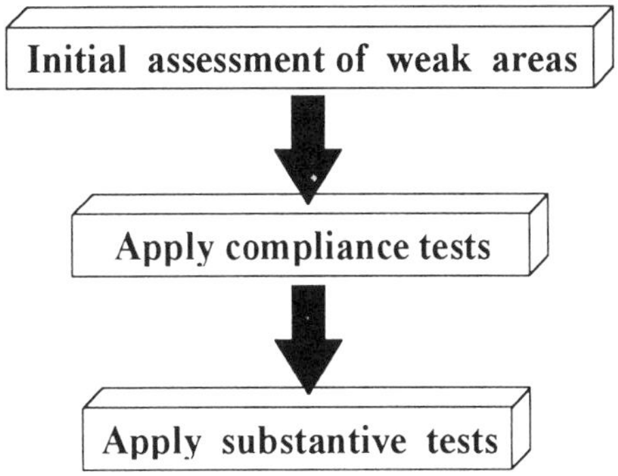

14.5 Managerial Systems Components

The control evaluation process may operate on a number of levels in line with the way an operation is organised and discharged. All operations involve the following components:

FIGURE 14.16 OPERATIONS

Another way of viewing an operation is by considering the fundamental questions to be addressed:

FIGURE 14.17 OPERATIONAL QUESTIONS

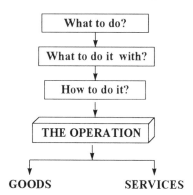

One way that managerial control may be tackled is to establish a managerial control system which itself constitutes a system of internal control. This is based on the premise that if any aspects of the managerial control components are missing then the resulting operation will be sub-optimised and objectives will not be attained. Bearing in mind that controls are all devices established by management to promote the achievement of organisational objectives then clearly managerial weaknesses are in fact control weaknesses. The managerial control system is explained in chapter one.

Control evaluation may include the managerial as well as the operational aspects of the system under review and one may assess managerial areas by:

• Reviewing managerial control attributes, i.e. the managerial arrangements inherent in the managerial control system. Some of these attributes are summarised in the section on internal controls (part 1) through an ICQ based approach.

• Reviewing operational control mechanisms, i.e. specific controls located in the operation related to the input, process and output functions through an ICES based approach.

So control attributes can be assessed by considering whether they meet a defined criterion and link into each other. The actual operation performed may be assessed by considering control mechanisms required to discharge the particular operational objectives which vary from system to system.

Evaluation by objectives
It is important to define business objectives and one view of control evaluation is that it should be linked firmly into these objectives. Objectives may flow as follows:

FIGURE 14.18 EVALUATION BY OBJECTIVES

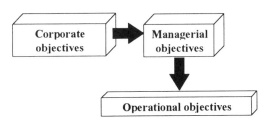

Systems objectives should be identified for each stage of an operation and corresponding control mechanisms then defined for ensuring these objectives are met. Some argue that the control system floats above the operational system and ensures that while systems goals are met, say an item of equipment is ordered, it is done with due regard for:

• Complying with purchasing procedures.

• Providing sufficient information on the transaction.

• Protecting the assets that are acquired.

• Economy and efficiency in the purchasing function.

• Operational effectiveness in that goals are set and achieved.

In this way the resourced activities are carried out in a controlled fashion and it is these control objectives that will be achieved in line with the defined systems objectives.

14.6 Conclusions

Systems based auditing permits the auditor to get involved in reviewing managerial arrangements. Audit resources may be very efficiently used by directing them at promoting better systems as opposed to checking everything that moves. The transactions approach is a bottom-up activity that involves the auditor in an endless stream of transactions and documents with little impact on the development of the organisation. Systems auditing can overcome these problems as long as control systems are understood to cover all activities in the organisation. No operation can be controlled without a suitable managerial control system in place and the auditors fail in their duties if they are not able to understand and apply this. Evaluation is the raison d'être for internal audit and is a very important stage of an audit. It will occur throughout the audit and many factors will contribute to the auditor's final opinion and recommendations. Evaluation may operate on a number of levels. It may be directed towards managerial parts of the system of internal control in recognition of the fact that control systems are formed by a link between each part of the managerial feedback loop. Several evaluation techniques are available with most applying auditing by objectives where management's operational objectives become the starting place with all controls being related back to the system under review. Evaluation must involve the consideration of what should be with what is in practice, and control models can be used as long as they are derived from the central systems objectives. Testing routines are a feature of most audits and they should be undertaken solely to secure more insight into the state of control. Testing that does not relate to controls has little use in systems based auditing that places the audit emphasis on the control evaluation function. It would be advisable for audit departments to build up a data-base of control mechanisms to be applied in systems evaluation.

CHAPTER FIFTEEN

THE CONCEPT OF RISK

15.1 Introduction

The concept of risk is fundamental to the audit role since it may conflict with the concept of control. Controls are designed to ensure that objectives are achieved; risk may prevent this. Overall risk should be reduced by adequate controls and the greater the degree of risk, the greater the need for good controls. Audit has a clear remit to expose and help minimise the level of risk facing the organisation. The study of risk pays good dividends for the auditor.

Types of risk

Risk has a number of related terms including:

> *chance, danger, gamble, hazard, jeopardy, peril, speculation, uncertainty.*

Risk appears to have negative connotations implying loss or misfortune. It is generally dealt with as an overall concept and different organisations may define it differently. Types of risk may be categorised as:

☐ **Operational risk.** This is inherent in the operation itself. Examples are a decentralised payroll system with department based remote terminals that allow salaries to be paid to staff; business units allowing discretion at local level; a grant or benefits operation that pays out funds where claimants meet defined criteria; purchasing functions where staff engage in major contracts with suppliers.

☐ **Control risk.** Operations inherently risky are generally well controlled. There is control risk if controls do not work well or are not complied with. The organisation believes it is in control but may not be. Entropy means that controls degenerate over time and systems that are not reviewed will assume control risk which is a principal justification for resourcing an internal audit function.

☐ **Residual risk.** The scope for error or systems faults remaining after controls are established by management. This is the degree of risk acceptable to the organisation in view of the cost of control. There is always risk in any operation and the audit role is to ensure that management appreciate the quantified implications of this residual risk. It is then for management to decide if the existing level of control is acceptable. Residual risk is quantified through testing routines.

☐ **Audit risk.** Systems may not be reviewed by internal audit, recommendations may be ignored or the audit may not be carried out properly with risk areas missed.

To illustrate the relationship between the above risk factors, visualise the underlying causes of a major systems failure that affected the whole organisation:

- The operation was inherently risky.
- Controls were not adhered to.
- The level of residual risk was therefore high.
- This operation was not included among internal audit's planned reviews and has therefore never been audited in the past.

There is a high chance that the organisation is jeopardised because of unacceptably high levels of risk. The internal audit presence is designed to counter audit risk and control risk and leave only an acceptable level of residual risk:

FIGURE 15.1 AUDIT AND RISK

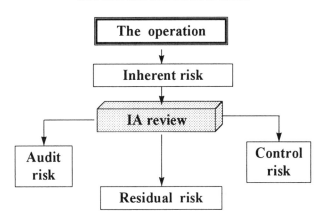

Risk appraisal allows the internal auditor to direct audit resources towards operations of importance that have high levels of control risk. Once identified, the parts of the operation that should be prioritised are gleaned from risk appraisal at the micro level.

15.2 Developing a High-level Risk Strategy

It is possible to develop a risk strategy that takes on board the nature of risk and the damaging affect it can have. This cannot be done by internal audit alone but must be based on a commitment from top management with advice and support from audit. The strategy may appear as follows:

TABLE 15.1 THE RISK STRATEGY

TYPE OF RISK	RESPONSE
INHERENT RISK	Stop doing it, e.g. a branch in a volatile country
CONTROL RISK	Review controls, watch out for entropy
RESIDUAL RISK	Examine impact, does this risk impact on achieving objectives?
AUDIT RISK	Use risk analysis, apply SBA not a transaction based audit

There is a form of "management risk" derived from the culture of the organisation when it fails to take a proactive approach to organisational problems. This is more difficult and relies on a change to a risk management culture. Such organisations are easy to spot through one basic question.

> *When claiming against an insurance policy does the organisation*
> *also review its risk management procedures?*

If there is no formal risk management policy then we can expect a poor appreciation of risk as a corporate issue, and the internal auditor's work becomes more difficult.

Risk factors
Control risk may be seen as the opposite side of the key control objectives:
- The risk that the organisation is not complying with laws and procedure.
- The risk that information is inadequate.
- The risk that assets are not safeguarded.
- The risk that value for money is not being achieved.

There are many reasons why these control objectives are not achieved. Features of risk are:
1. Risk is only important where the result would be material to the achievement of operational objectives. Larger more resource intensive operations should attract more attention. There is a view that operations largely dependent on staff as the main resource are not important, since there is only a limited amount of work to be done on staffing budgets. This ignores the main audit objective to review service delivery and it is the *products* that are audited and not the basic payroll figures.
2. The level of internal controls should correspond to the level of the risks. Management must direct controls towards risk areas. A new computer system that changes the balance of controls and allows staff direct on-line access to large databases, some with updating facilities, must be controlled. We would expect management to resource an IT security function.
3. The level of managerial awareness of risk bears on how controls are viewed. This affects the control environment and organisational culture. It is one thing to place responsibility for risk management with managers, but this has no real use if they are not supported in countering negative forces. The internal audit role may move to support and encouragement as we seek to heighten awareness of controls and threats to controls. An ideal scenario is where internal audit makes presentations to middle and top management on the topic of risk and its limitation.
4. Available audit expertise determines the type of work carried out. High-level sensitive operations cannot be audited by inexperienced junior staff. Audit risk is based on a lack of audit cover at the right level so that risk is not properly placed on management's agenda. Training and development programmes in line with an audit strategy to tackle high-risk areas, should help minimise audit risk.
5. The materiality of risk is determined by the probability of occurrence so that an operation may be vulnerable with a low probability of a major problem, or a high probability of less material problems. This moves us away from corporate systems to view all systems as important. Operations that are not necessarily material in the level of resources consumed may become major problems because of the lack of direct

attention, based on the view that they are only subsidiary systems. This is why risk appraisal considers all factors to arrive at a list of target audits.

6. It is necessary to ascertain management's future intentions since high-risk areas may be targeted for additional controls. Risk is dynamic and changes over time with new developments. It is futuristic as it indicates what might happen in any set of circumstances. Any review of risk criteria should take into account existing and potential factors so that predictions and audit plans can be made.

7. Risk assessment involves many subjective factors and it can never be strictly mathematical. It always has a "best guess" factor.

8. When assessing risk the auditor must recognise management's concerns and if these are not met the audit will not be successful. It is advisable to agree any risk index with management before it is used to perform audit work. It is as well to have the audit committee confirm the methodology before the resultant planning process, based on the agreed risk model, is undertaken.

9. Previous problems including past frauds provide ready-made indicators of risk. To retain audit credibility, any risk formula should be designed to pick these up.

10. Risk analysis is used to apply audit resources either to target areas or to concentrate on particular parts of an operation. Resources are defined in terms of numbers of auditors, grades, experience, special skills, amount of time, scope of work and timing of the audit.

11. Formal risk analysis is well suited where a probity based audit approach is used and each audit unit has similar features, or at least features that can be measured through one defined mechanism. A cycle of visits may be scheduled according to an agreed risk criterion based on targeting the locations that come out high on the risk ranking.

12. For a systems approach risk analysis must be based on specific attributes since the final system may be defined in a variety of ways, and this in practice will be more difficult to apply.

13. When considering risk one must pose the question "whose risk is being assessed?"

Many parties have a role in requiring operational risk to be controlled but it is line management who is primarily charged with running a successful operation and delivering the defined level of product/services.

15.3 Risk Analysis

There are many factors that contribute to the overall assessment of risk. It is advisable to establish a risk profile for each operational area as a prelude to formulating long-term audit plans. Risk indexes can become very complicated but most are based on this basic model:

FIGURE 15.2 RISK INDEX

$$\text{Risk Index} = \frac{\text{significance/materiality}}{\text{quality of internal control}} + \text{special factors}$$

More sensitive areas (in terms of size and impact on the organisation) produce a larger figure to reflect inherent risk. This is scaled down if the area is controlled. The better the control the smaller the final figure. Special factors allow scope to incorporate additional features in the calculation. Factors in the index may be subjectively derived but the model ensures consistency in that operations will be treated alike and so be comparable. A model of risk based audit cover is:

FIGURE 15.3 RISK BASED AUDIT COVER

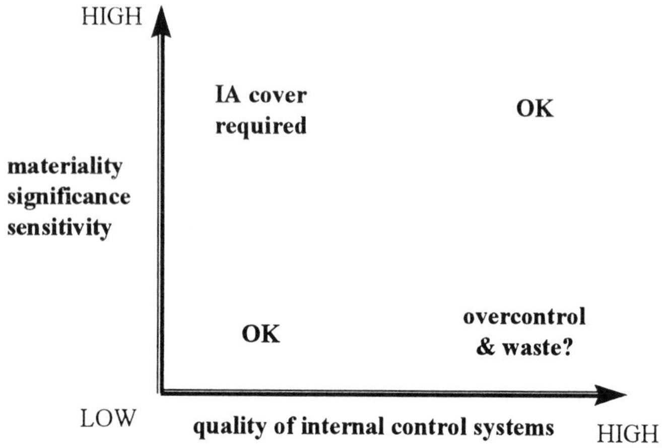

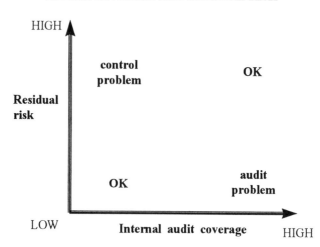

This suggests we need to target the important operations that potentially have poor systems of control, although it does depend on good compliance with controls, not always known to the auditor.

FIGURE 15.4 AUDIT AND RESIDUAL RISK

HIGH ↑

    control   **OK**
    problem

Residual
risk

     OK   **audit**
            problem

LOW   **Internal audit coverage** HIGH

This model suggests we need to target areas where there is still much exposure to risk after controls have done their best to remedy this. Where there has been insufficient audit cover in the past, this causes little problem unless there is high residual risk. Conversely, where audit resources are wasted by use on low residual risk areas, then an audit risk arises where the same resources are not being applied to the right operations. Putting these concepts together we view the overall risk position:

FIGURE 15.5 THE RISK HIERARCHY

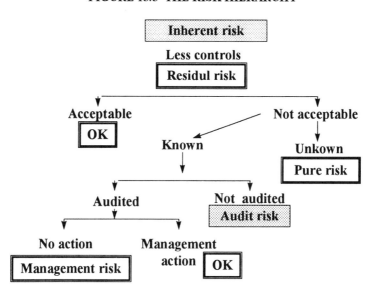

This brings in several additional risk concepts. One is that of "pure risk" where there is a completely unknown level of exposure that has not been guarded against. The other is of "management risk" which is failure on its part to take action despite warnings from internal audit. The combination of these risk components shows control weaknesses despite audit cover.

15.4 The Risk Matrix and Control Evaluation

A matrix approach to risk analysis may be used to build up a picture of those areas that audit should direct attention at. This may be used in long-term planning and during control evaluation, and the latter can be illustrated below:

FIGURE 15.6 THE RISK MATRIX

	possible exposure (risks)				
SYSTEM STAGES	compliance	MIS	assets	efficient	effective
1					
2					
3					
4					
5					
6					

By establishing possible risks that may attach to specific stages in the operation more attention may be then directed at the high-risk parts and weak controls identified. This may be performed at preliminary survey stage with the resulting risk assessment appearing in the assignment plan.

15.5. Performance Indicators

Performance indicators are a form of risk analysis that direct management towards areas requiring attention and most at risk. Performance indicators should:

☐ **Promote good control** by encouraging management to look for causes of problems and not become obsessed by the problem itself. An indicator is a signpost that points out a direction but without giving much more information. Further exploration is required to examine the risk implications.

☐ **Be reliable**. If PIs can be ignored because they are sometimes flawed then they can readily become obsolete. It is not only that they should be accurate but more that they should be derived from a consistent baseline so that different elements or time periods can be compared.

☐ **They should be available in good time**. PIs assist managers in directing their attention to risk areas and so make decisions according to the findings. These same decisions drive the organisation from point [a] to point [b] in line with a defined strategy. The time factor is important as decisions must be made quickly so as to influence the desired object.

☐ **They should be convenient**. The costs of collecting the underlying data should not exceed the value derived from their use. This is probably the single biggest drawback.

☐ **Consistent with objectives**. Achievements that impact positively on PIs accomplish organisational objectives. Management activities should make sense to achieve goals and be linked to the PI system. An audit PI based on the number of audit reports issued each quarter may mean that large audits that deal with major control issues are not tackled, as they take longer and decrease the total number of reports. In the long term this PI may lower the impact audit has on key operations. It is important that PIs flow from a whole package of indicators considered together. There may be abuse of the PI system, particularly where pay bonuses result. Where management rallies around one key PI, this may create imbalance with inappropriate use of resources or even mis-reporting. PIs must be both complicated and simple: simple to prepare but complex to give a rounded picture.

There is an abundance of suitable measures and their use will vary depending on the type of operation that is being controlled. Common ones are:

OUTPUT/COST OF OUTPUT   = EFFICIENCY MEASURE
COST OF OUTPUT/OUTPUT   = UNIT COST
INPUT/PLANNED INPUT   = ECONOMY
OUTPUT/PLANNED OUTPUT = EFFECTIVENESS

The movement in these indicators over time provides a useful measure of performance and helps management target their resources more efficiently. They also instil accountability where top management can keep a global eye on what is going on.

15.6 A Risk Index

One risk index allows the auditor to weigh up various audit units against each other so that long-term plans may be formulated according to their respective riskiness:

A = Volume of transactions
B = Systems characteristics (e.g. number of staff)
C = Scope and effect of system (importance)
D = Quality of internal control

It is then possible to weigh each component with a factor of say 1, 1.5 or 2. Each system is assigned a rating for each component of say between 1 and 5. The risk index then becomes:

$$(A \times 1.5) + B + C + (D \times 2)$$

Volume is given a weighting of 1.5 and the quality of IC a 2. When each system is rated one can rank them in order of sensitivity by listing the highest scoring systems first. The audit plans then reflect the level of risk in each unit with the most risky being tackled first and perhaps with more audit resources. One problem is whether this technique can be used with a systems based approach. This arises because systems run across operations and are not departmentally based, as is the detail required for the risk index. It deals with an audit unit as say one section or a remote location (an old people's home, a local bank or a retail outlet). This is tackled later.

The Civil Service model
The Civil Service three factor risk index is in the Government Internal Audit Manual (1996):
- Volume of transactions.
- Complexity of system.
- Sensitivity of systems.

The index is applied as follows:

TABLE 15.2 THE RISK STRATEGY

Factor	Point rating	Weighting Factors
A. Volume of transactions	1 - 5	2
B. Complexity of the system	1 - 5	3
C. Sensitivity of systems	1 - 5	4

The risk index can be summarised:

$$(A \times 2) + (B \times 3) + (C \times 4) = the\ index$$

Applying risk in internal auditing
Risk has been mentioned in formulating audit plans and evaluating controls. Risk has a wide application within the internal auditor's work and may cover:
- **Long-term planning**. Risk assessment has a main role in long-term planning by providing a formal basis upon which to assign audit resources across a wide audit field.
- **Preliminary survey**. The background work provides an initial assessment of high-risk areas in the planned audit.
- **Assignment planning**. The key parts of the operation under review will be determined through a process of appraising relative risk of each element of the system. The assignment plan directs the course of the entire audit in terms of the areas for consideration and the time available.
- **System ascertainment**. We only document important parts of the system, with reference to risk levels. We direct time to the key controls.
- **Systems evaluation**. The evaluation process must be within time budgets. Risk assessment will assist the review of parts of the system more susceptible to risk.
- **Testing controls**. Testing can take up considerable audit time with detailed examination of transactions. The concept of risk ensures tests are directed at important elements of the system.
- **Formulating audit opinions**. Providing an opinion and formulating and agreeing audit recommendations must have regard to what is important and what does not comprise a material exposure for management. Audit recommendations only make sense if they discuss salient points that impact on business objectives.
- **Agreeing a management action plan**. The task of negotiating action after the audit field work has been completed is an opportunity to install the principles behind risk profiling. Pointers to be given up, as opposed to retained, can be decided beforehand.

- **Following up audit recommendations**. The timing, staff levels and overall importance of follow-ups should be gauged having regard to a prioritisation process linked into risk appraisal.

Risk assessment is a continuous process that operates throughout the entire audit process.

A working model for long-term planning

The systems based approach can be reconciled to the use of risk analysis. Systems comprise control components required in any operation. Where the operation consists of objectives, resources and a resultant product, this becomes the "audit unit". Once an audit unit is defined a risk index can be applied, and risk factors assessed and quantified producing a ranked list of operations. The efficiency of many risk indexes is reduced by the detail required for the index factors. Some are so detailed that it would be necessary to perform most of the audit before the index could be applied. It is advisable to use the simplest possible risk index that does justice to the situation:

  Materiality
  Sensitivity
  Adequacy of controls
  Requests by management

Each operation is then assessed in terms of the above four factors and the highest scoring prioritised for audit attention. Further sophistication is given by adding different weighting factors to the risk components.

Installing the index

Key points about devising a suitable index for systems based audits (not investigations) are:

- Publish the risk criterion along with explanation.
- Get management to understand by providing formal presentations if required. Circulate a document that sets out the reasoning behind risk assessment and the way it is used to assist audit planning as well as performing work.
- Apply the agreed formula and set aside suitable audit resources for this all-important task.
- Carry out a comprehensive and regular review of the index and revise it when required.

Resource problems

Risk analysis is an ongoing long-term process. It depends on extensive information on operational areas over time. It is important to make a start and write a crude model with rule-of-thumb measures and then build on it. A formal identification of the audit field as a systems listing is a prerequisite to the risk assessment process. There is a link into the audit filing system as information is assimilated into the files and then into the risk index. This transition should be smooth and is assisted by suitable documentation that can be used to capture data as it is published or obtained. There is no short-cut to the time consuming task of collecting the database and feeding the information into the risk index. Once established it is simple to update, maintain and develop.

15.7 Conclusions

Risk is central to audit and allows auditors to decide how time should be applied to a vast audit field. Simple risk indexes, understood and agreed by the client provide a consistent way of assigning risk. This not only helps ensure the efficient use of audit resources but can be used to defend how audits are selected and undertaken. By viewing risk as impacting all aspects of an audit, the work may be carried out to the highest standard with important areas given greater attention.

CHAPTER SIXTEEN

TESTING AND WORKING PAPERS

16.1 Background to Testing

Testing is the act of securing suitable evidence to support an audit. It confirms the auditor's initial opinion on the state of internal controls. It is a step in control evaluation, although many auditors test for the sole purpose of highlighting errors or non-adherence with laid down procedure. It depends on the audit objective. We have included two related topics of evidence and statistical sampling since they are both linked to securing suitable evidence to support the audit report.

The testing process
IIA standard 420 states that the auditor should collect, analyse, interpret and document information to support audit results and this is done primarily through testing. Likewise APB standards require that the internal auditor should obtain sufficient, relevant and reliable evidence on which to base reasonable conclusions and recommendations (Paras 63 to 69). The testing process may be illustrated:

FIGURE 16.1 THE TESTING PROCESS

Define the test objective

Perform the test

Interpret the results

Determine the impact on audit objectives

Determine the next steps

Brief explanations follow:

□ **Define the test objective**. There must be clear reason for performing the test. In systems auditing this relates to the adequacy or effectiveness of controls. If we are concerned that there is no proper system for ensuring orders are properly authorised, then we may examine a sample of orders to see if they comply with the purchasing code of practice. The test objective is to judge the extent of problems.

□ **Define the testing strategy**. How test objectives are achieved is determined by the testing strategy. This lists the tests required and groups them to aid their efficient execution. If we need to examine application forms for a sample of employees as part of an audit of personnel procedures, we need to decide how this will best be achieved, the use of statistical sampling and how data will be extracted.

☐ **Formulate an audit programme**. The testing strategy can be defined in more detail and form an audit programme of work. This programme becomes a schedule containing space for the samples to be listed and the tests performed and documented. It provides a ready made guide to the completion of the testing strategies. The programme may appear in matrix format with space on the left for a list of payments made to sub-contractors that are selected at random. The rest of the schedule will be broken down into columns for each part of the tests. This could cover checks over order, contract number, payments, certificates, invoices, select list of suppliers, budget provision, and tax exemption. This checks whether procedures over the employment and payment of sub-contractors work.

☐ **Perform the test**. The detailed work of performing the tests is the main part of the testing process. The key point is that there is a tendency for the process to be lost in the vast amount of work that may be required during the test performance stage.

☐ **Schedule the evidence**. The results of testing should be summarised and fed into the report (via the record of control weakness) and be cross referenced in the working papers. Test results give an overview of results, and provide detailed schedules that may be sent to management for action. They may be referred to in the audit report as examples of actual problems. Where we have examined hundreds of payroll payments and found several categories of errors (say the wrong pay rates applied) we may mention the amount of over/under payments in each department in the report. The working papers should assist by allowing summaries to be compiled without extra effort. Interesting examples may be highlighted and the design of schedules should enable these items to be readily extracted.

☐ **Interpret the results**. The meaning of what is found feeds into the testing strategy. If we examine a series of committee reports for indications of misleading information being provided, we must have set criteria against which to measure findings. We must consider whether what was found is accurate and have access to a suitable model to make this judgement. If we check authorisations for new accounts on a computer system, the checks will only make sense if we have a list of authorising officers.

☐ **Determine the impact on audit objectives**. The link back to the original objectives should be firmly in place so that we take the mass of data and decide what it means for the audit. Auditors should give an opinion on areas covered. This will be based on the state of controls and whether this led to defined problems being identified through testing. This part of the testing puts the detailed work into perspective by providing an outcome. This cannot be to list errors found by internal audit, since this would be for management to do. The goal is to support an audit view of controls resulting in a recommendation.

☐ **Determine the next step**. Taking into account all that has been found, the direction of the audit should be agreed particularly if there is a need to change plans. One outcome may be to extend the testing routines into greater detail or other areas, or ask management to look into particular problems. We may find matters that were totally unexpected and there must be opportunity to review the audit and current position before going headlong into the next stage of the project.

16.2 The Four Types of Tests

The four types of tests are:

☐ **Walk through**. This involves taking a small sample of items that are traced through the system to ensure that the auditor understands the system. It occurs during the ascertainment stage of the audit and may lead into further tests later. The client may be asked to refer to named documents representative of the transaction cycle that will be cross referenced to the interview record to assist this process of "capturing" the system.

☐ **Compliance**. This determines whether key controls are adhered to. It uncovers non-compliance or unclear procedures. If key controls are not being applied, and this is not compensated for by the system, they become reclassified as weak controls.

☐ **Substantive**. These determine whether control objectives are being achieved. Weak controls imply objectives will not be achieved and substantive tests are designed to confirm this initial audit view. Substantive tests may isolate error, poor information, direct loss or a poor value for money.

☐ **Dual purpose**. This is not a test but a recognition of the practicalities of testing controls where one may wish to combine compliance and substantive testing. An example is to examine an invoice that is certified for payment (compliance test) and is valid (substantive test). It would be impractical to select this invoice twice for two different tests to be separately applied.

The important tests are deemed to be compliance or substantive as these are the two main techniques used to support audit work. The relationship between the four tests is shown below.

FIGURE 16.2 THE VARIOUS TEST PATTERNS

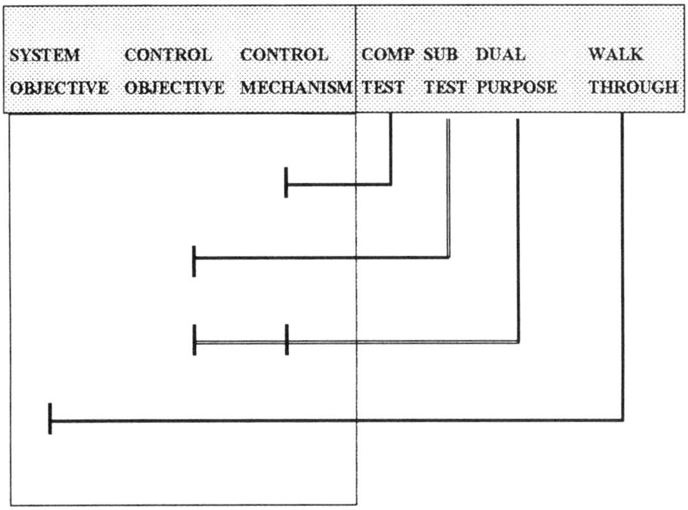

We summarise our discussion:
- Walk through tests seek to determine how the system's objectives are achieved.
- Compliance tests seek to determine whether control mechanisms are being applied.
- Substantive tests seek to determine whether control objectives are being achieved.
- Dual purpose tests check for both compliance and control weaknesses.

Comparing compliance and substantive tests
There are key differences between the two main types of test. We restate the systems based approach to auditing and how these tests fit into the audit process:

FIGURE 16.3 COMPLIANCE AND SUBSTANTIVE TESTS

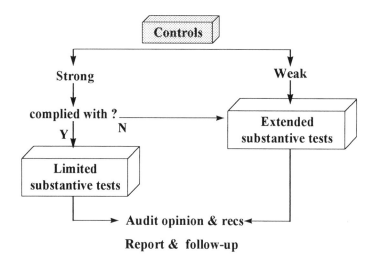

We look first for compliance with key controls then review results. Substantive tests are then directed towards all known weak areas including those where key controls are not being observed revealed through compliance testing. Forms 083 to 089 set a clear direction for testing and recording results (see diskette).

16.3 Testing Considerations

The decision on what to test and the extent of testing will be based on factors revolving around evaluation of the systems of internal control. These include:

☐ **The relative control risks**. The type of risks that arise where a system of control is inadequate or compliance is essential. The parts of the operation that are risky should be targeted for more testing than less sensitive parts. Where a payments system requires an additional signature for items over £1m this procedure becomes important and must be adhered to because of the large sums involved.

☐ **Management needs**. Where management has concerns about aspects of the system this should feed into the testing strategy. If in a large debtors system, senior management is concerned that staff may be suspending reminders where there is a query on the account without first investigating the matter, this may be explored by internal audit. We would want to see sensible controls installed over the process of stopping routine reminders as a long-term solution, but to establish the extent of this problem, some audit testing may be carried out beforehand.

□ **Previous audit cover**. The types of findings that were obtained in previous audits can assist planning tests in the latest review. This information may indicate areas of concern and areas where no real problems were found in the past. Testing can be used to support a follow-up of a previous audit. We can establish whether data is being entered onto systems in a disciplined fashion or haphazardly as identified in the previous audit.

□ **The auditor's own experiences**. The auditor may have come across systems in the past where there were certain parts that presented a difficulty. This may relate to the difficulty in retrieving past years' data where it had been archived.

□ **The level of managerial support for the audit**. One key factor in setting testing levels is related to the position assumed by management in respect of the audit. Where top management is aware of control concerns and is openly seeking advice from internal audit, there is little point in proving in detail that these problems exist. Test results will set the context of any required action by highlighting how bad the true position is, from the sample examined. Where no one needs convincing, the emphasis will be located with the recommendations and not the evidence from testing. The auditor must convince him/herself by performing some tests but there is little use in doing detailed work when all sides agree on the main control issues.

□ **The availability of evidence**. Testing starts from a hypothetical view of control problems and efforts to substantiate initial findings can look good on paper but be difficult to apply in practice. Where evidence is hard to obtain and analyse, this must be catered for when developing testing plans. All tests take time and no audit unit has the luxury of an open budget for "exploring issues". Time spent on testing is in the main fixed and where information or documents are hard to find, parts of test plans will have to be tailored to this. If the auditor is unable to comment because of such problems then the report will indicate this. Where evidence is withheld we enter the remit of fraud investigations.

□ **The audit objectives**. Much testing work depends on what one is trying to achieve in line with the stated audit objective. If we need independent third party verification to discharge the audit objective, say in confirming bank balances, then tests will reflect this.

□ **The level of materiality of the item reviewed**. As well as dealing with high-risk matters we are also concerned that we take on board materiality. When reviewing a purchasing system there is little point checking small value items that really have no significance to the entire operation as this detracts resources from the more important areas. An audit of a multi-million pound cashiering operation will have little concern for a £50 petty cash float administered by the system.

□ **The time available for the tests**. The more time available, the more transactions can be tested. There is a bottom-line position that states that time spent on one audit equals time not spent on another. We cannot go on extending tests because there are problems in one area. Testing always takes longer than planned and there must be a cut-off that indicates enough material to go to print.

☐ **The assessment of internal control.** This has to be included as the correct answer to the issue of extent and direction of testing. Testing is required to support an opinion on controls; for example - whether they work, are sound, stop error, stop fraud, promote efficiencies and assist in the proper management of resources. Testing will only be relevant when attached to a clear view of controls.

Analytical review
Analytical review is a technique that tends to be applied by external auditors and there is an APB statement on this. This involves looking at two or more sets of comparable information, say two years' balance sheets, and extracting new data that can be used to direct audit attention towards areas of particular interest. One would be looking for:
- Changes in key ratios.
- Absolute changes in key figures.
- General trends.
- Movement in the level of purchases and creditors.
- Movement in the cash and bank account balances.
- Movement in sales and debtors.

The main question that is posed is:

> *"are these trends consistent with one another and the overall performance of the organisation?"*

This directs the auditors' attention towards areas for investigation although because of the emphasis in comparing financial data the technique is mainly used by external auditors.

16.4 Testing Techniques

There are many ways that one can gather the necessary evidence to support the testing objective. The number and types of techniques are limited only by the imagination of the auditor:

☐ **Re-performance.** Re-checking a calculation or procedure can give evidence as to its reliability. This enables the auditor to comment directly on the accuracy by which transactions are processed although it does depend on the auditor being able to perform the necessary task. As an example we might wish to re-calculate the amount of money paid to staff who are made compulsorily redundant to ensure that controls, such as supervisory review over payments, are working properly.

☐ **Observation.** This is a useful method of information gathering since it is obtained first hand by the auditor. There are drawbacks in that what is presented to the auditor may be stage-managed although this may be a somewhat cynical view. For example, during one audit staff were observed exchanging passwords where they were already keyed into a terminal under their own password and wanted to use another terminal, which was a clear breach of procedure. Structured observation may be used to check controls that have a physical presence such as security and for example this may be used to check how cashiers carry out their end-of-day cash balancing operations.

☐ **Corroboration**. Having facts from one area confirmed by reference to another party is a good way of verifying the accuracy of these facts. The more independent the third party the more reliable the results. This technique should be used with care as it should not be an obvious act of re-checking what has been said elsewhere and is best used to follow the natural flow of a system. For example, a payment can be written-off by an officer who has placed a stop on the cheque, by writing a memo to a financial controller. Meanwhile, the financial controller should be asked to confirm this, as he/she is visited as part of the audit.

☐ **Analytical review**. Referred to above.

☐ **Inspection**. Inspection is a formal way of observing physical attributes against a set criterion. It implies the use of an amount of expertise to discharge this exercise that the auditor may or not possess. One might imagine the auditor wishing to inspect building work done by subcontractors that has been certified and paid for by the organisation. Again the auditor will not necessarily be able to carry out this inspection but may commission a consultant to make the required checks and provide a status report. In this case controls over the work certification process can be reviewed through this process of examining previous building jobs. Inspection can also be used to check the existence of assets that have been acquired by the organisation.

☐ **Reconciliation**. The process of balancing one set of figures back to another is based mainly on the principle of double entry bookkeeping that ensures the accounts balance at all times. The reconciliation may be something that is done by management as part of its normal work and this may be reviewed by the auditor using re-performance where necessary. It is also possible for the auditor to perform a new reconciliation to provide evidence of the adequacy of controls. For example the auditor may seek to balance payroll to personnel systems to establish how well these two systems interface. Any discrepancies may indicate a breakdown of communications between the two functions that could lead to real or potential loss to the organisation. The wider role of systems reconciliations can be used for fraud detection projects and this is dealt with in the chapter on fraud investigations.

☐ **Expert opinion**. This is less a technique and more a source of assistance linked to another technique. There are many times when the auditor has a problem in terms of securing relevant evidence pertinent to the audit at hand but being unable to perform the underlying work. For example a stores audit may disclose losses on fuel that management argues is due to the natural process of evaporation. The extent of these losses, having reference to this factor, may be reviewed for consistency by an expert who would examine the facilities and provide an opinion on the validity of the stated argument. The auditor in turn may then be able to comment on the state of controls over safeguarding fuel from unauthorised removal, where there are clear losses that cannot be fully explained through evaporation.

☐ **Interviews**. More often than not the best way to find something out is simply to ask and much useful information can be obtained through the interview forum. This facility is extremely convenient although the reliability of representations can vary, depending on the circumstances. Where persons provide information this must be verified as far as possible by asking for the document, report, policy, memorandum, minutes and so on that should support what is being said. There are some pointers that are simple to examine, where for example we wish to discover whether managers are using the organisation's financial regulations. If they are asked whether they possess a copy and cannot find one, then we can argue that they do not make reference to this document in their everyday work. If some of them have never heard of the regulation then we may comment adversely on the adequacy with which this procedure has been implemented in the organisation.

☐ **Review of published reports/research**. Another source of supportive evidence is to be found in reports that impact on the area under review. These can range from internal reports, say on staffing levels, externally commissioned reviews of for example, the potential for new IT, or national reports that contain relevant base data on, say, productivity levels. They may provide information that may be referred to in the audit report covering for instance the average cost per employee of payroll services. Alternatively, the existence of a report may simply be used as evidence that management had access to specific advice, that may or may not have been acted on. Any matters raised by the external auditors may also be of use when seeking material to support the internal audit opinion. Obviously reports must be used with care, since the auditor cannot verify the contents of most reports unless prepared from official sources (e.g. Government statistics).

☐ **Independent confirmation**. An obvious source of evidence is to get someone to independently agree defined facts. Where opinion is involved this becomes more difficult as subjective matters can be interpreted in different ways. Direct facts relating to dates, times, figures, agreements and so on can be readily double checked. The usual example of this technique is debtors' circularisation where moneys due to the organisation are confirmed by writing direct to the debtor in question. This is a useful device for the external auditor during asset verification. Independent verification may involve checking a representation made by the independent third party. So a stocktaker's certificate may be checked for authenticity by contacting the firm that has issued the document. The rule that the best evidence comes from people who have no vested interest in providing incorrect information is applied. However, this is not a way of viewing all others as somehow untrustworthy, but simply part of the drive to seek the best evidence wherever possible.

☐ **Receiving the service as a client**. Most operations that produce goods or services recognise the key concept of client care that means there must be a net value from what is being delivered. If we were going to audit McDonald's Restaurants, the first thing to do would be to purchase a meal from the outlet. Taking this further it is possible to visit or phone the audit field and experience the service as a client to obtain a feel for the way controls over this service are operating. If for example a line manager has said that all clients receive a complaints form so that feedback is obtained where the service user has experienced a problem, we can find out if this is the case. This technique may be used in conjunction with observation so that an overall impression can be gleaned. We would not be able to refer directly to evidence from this source but it may be used to concentrate attention in the direction of service delivery, if this suggests a breakdown in controls. The approach is not always possible to use but where it can be, it gives an important "feel" for the operation.

☐ **Mathematical models**. The auditor may construct a model that may be used to gauge particular features of an operation. This is generally not easy as there is a set-up cost involved and the question of credibility when it is used to support an audit report. However where we have a large audit where it is possible to apply conceptual models, this is a consideration. The example that students will see in most textbooks relates to setting reorder levels in a stores environment. Here the auditor may use a suitable model to test whether controls over stock reordering result in acceptable reorder quantities and frequencies. Other factors such as slow moving stock and stock-outs will also come into play to support or not support the findings from such a mathematical model.

☐ **Questionnaires**. Formal surveys can be used to assist the audit process. This is a useful device in an audit of an operation that has equivalents either within the organisation or in other comparable ones. Because an organisation does things differently from other bodies does not mean that this is wrong or right. Telephone surveys can be used to save time so long as full records are made and important matters separately verified in writing. We can elicit data on staffing levels, decentralised operations, use of new IT and other matters from asking questions from other services. We can compute averages and trends to be used to assess the existing position. These devices are best used for more comprehensive reviews that examine controls over value for money.

☐ **Comparison**. Vouching comes under this heading in that we can seek to check one item against another one which has an associated factor. There is little that can be said about comparison over and above the basic checking of two or more facts (usually documents). One point to note is that the auditor should maintain accurate records of these comparisons as they may be challenged at a later date. Furthermore where there is a discrepancy we would have to discover which item is wrong before such matters can be reported. We should also bring the actual error to the attention of management if it is material in terms of the need to make corrections.

☐ **User satisfaction surveys**. Obtaining direct feedback from persons who use the service/product delivered by the operation under review can provide an insight into the success or otherwise of the operation. These mainly test controls over the marketing function attached to the operation. In addition, they can provide a commentary on the quality assurance (QA) procedures that have been installed (these QA procedures would be deemed a key control). Such surveys can reveal much more than hours of conversations with management, as they should give a completely unbiased view of the service being audited.

We have already suggested that there is an open-ended list of testing techniques although, whatever techniques are applied it is important to record all results carefully. Clearly, testing is not just limited to basic financial systems but can be applied in any environment. For some of the more sensitive ones such as the client satisfaction survey, the auditor should make it clear to management that the exercise is being undertaken. Copies of the pro forma documentation that is being used for the purpose should also be provided.

Whatever the approach we must beware appearing to be spies, performing some type of undercover work, as this will probably impair the audit image.

16.5 Achieving Control Objectives

Tests check that control objectives are being achieved. This helps confirm the auditor's view of those controls that need improving and helps quantify the extent of the problem. Control objectives ensure that the systems objectives are achieved with regard to:

- The information systems.
- The extent of compliance.
- Safeguarding assets.
- Value for money.

When applying test results to determine if control objectives are achieved the auditor should consider:

☐ **The success criteria management is applying**. There is often a conflict between factors the auditor would look for when judging the success of a system. These range from timeliness, accuracy, presentation, client feedback, to performance targets. Not all these will be achieved at the same time. More important is the view of management success. Tests that highlight whether business objectives are being met must bear in mind the different interpretations of objectives. There is little point reporting that 2% of timesheets are not reviewed when management feels it so immaterial as not to be worthy of attention. The auditor should ask the important question whether the control objectives promote management systems objectives. An example may help:

> *An auditor reviewed the database for a pension administration scheme and found the details on employees' personal circumstances out of date. This was pursued with management who did not appear overly concerned. The auditor was not aware that the system was designed to hold historical data to be updated when an employee retired or left. Management's success criterion was based on getting the correct data quickly once it was clear that an employee was due to leave. It was not based on having a well-maintained database at all times.*

☐ **Any systems constraints**. There are always constraints over how a system operates. This may relate to resource levels, the availability of information, unforeseeable circumstances, and computer down-time. These lead to lack of clarity in the basic formula that reads "resources given direction allow one to achieve objectives". The formula becomes more akin to "resources given direction, notwithstanding problems, allow one to seek to achieve objectives". Test results that do not cater for the realities of business life will not be taken seriously by management.

☐ **The extent of achievement**. The auditor should recognise there is no such thing as 100% perfection in any business system. All systems have some imperfection that results in "error conditions" discovered through audit testing. These errors may not have a significant effect on the performance of the operation and can be tolerated by management. An obsession with these minor infringements can lead to a frustrating audit report that is immersed in the "findings" without any understanding of the real issues that confront management. Reports that put this into perspective will be better received. There are many managers who receive audit reports that emphasise the results of audit testing, by asking what the implications are. The "points sheet" approach adopted by some auditors can be misguided as the frantic search for errors makes it difficult to distinguish between important and irrelevant mistakes. Findings that have been exaggerated or appear to be insignificant may nonetheless be discussed in terms of the sample that was considered. The key question is to ask whether the sample used is representative of the whole position.

☐ **The need to secure good evidence for an audit opinion.** Testing provides direct material that can underwrite the audit report and conclusions that are contained therein. This is the proper relationship where detailed research backs up the action the auditor believes should be taken in seeking to develop better control systems. The imbalance lies where evidence from testing is secured and presented for its own sake, in the guise of a detailed report on audit findings. One technique that promotes a wider view of the role of testing is to stand back from the specific test results and ask how the various problems relate to underlying causes. This can be used to identify the cause, effect and solution relationship. This enables one to adopt a broader view of the system and how it can be improved. Instead of designing an audit report to read findings and recommendations, we would take findings, draw general conclusions, then provide suitable recommendations based on the wider picture:

FIGURE 16.4 PUTTING TESTING INTO PERSPECTIVE

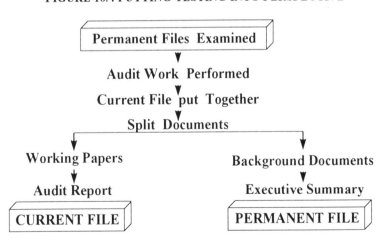

The idea is to gather the test findings into control issues in a compartmentalised manner, so that we may form a view not on the testing itself, but more on the underlying control implications. A lack of clear operational standards may lead to inconsistent work that promotes errors and oversights by staff. Rather than discuss how each error may be corrected, we may deal with the root problem.

16.6 The Hundred Percent Interrogation Theory

We deal with an important development that has growing support and is changing the direction of internal audit. This is the "100% test result" where the auditor uses automated techniques to examine all relevant data on a database. Designated fields are downloaded onto disk and the data manipulated using a package such as I.D.E.A. The audit role becomes testing, testing and more testing in a search for errors, inconsistencies, non-compliance, duplicates, unauthorised items, missing data, incorrect input, and suspect transactions. The view is that the audit occurs during this testing. This replaces the systems approach where controls are ascertained and evaluated with testing being seen as a minor stage. The fact that large databases are readily accessible makes this a real proposal with most of the audit work being done at a remote PC terminal as data is interrogated. In this environment we would expect an audit textbook to consist almost entirely of material on testing. This is in contrast to the approach adopted where this topic warrants one chapter only. The flaws in the "100% test result" approach can be noted in a series of relevant questions:

☐ **What about the control implications?** Testing may isolate specific errors and problems that are being targeted. The findings enable us to comment on the errors that are found but it is more difficult to relate these errors to a failing in control mechanisms. An example follows;

> *An audit of a contributory pension scheme found that data on employees was being exchanged through comments shouted across the office between the payroll and pension contributions section, located next to each other. A key control of a formal document representing information flows between the two sections was missing. This control weakness was identified through control evaluation. Tests applied to the audit included an attempt to reconcile the two databases (payroll and pensions administration. to identify any discrepancies). These tests could be directed at fields affected by the control weakness i.e. those that contain data that is exchanged, and we might then comment on the lack of formal section interface regardless of the test results. If the reconciliations were applied blindfolded, without the control evaluation stage, we would end up with a list of errors but no indication of how this happened. We may even find that there are no errors, which does not mean that we cannot report the weakness.*

☐ **What about managerial arrangements?** A large proportion of control is located in the managerial processes that should be in place before we can be said to be in control. These controls are set within the task of setting objectives and directing resources to meet these goals. One strategic goal may be to provide an automated interface between payroll and pension contributions. A list of discrepancies between the two systems is only of use if put within the context of managerial strategies for addressing the issue. The key difference between managerial deficiencies that result in problems, and problems discovered out of context, is that the former enables one to comment on real managerial issues. The interpretation of test results that are derived from extensive interrogation techniques is very difficult if these tests have not been directed at control issues. The relationship between managerial arrangements and detailed reports from database interrogations can only be established from a top downwards approach. The information system and data that are contained there, is only one minor part of the operation and only supports the services that are being delivered. Auditors immersed in the analysis of this data will have little time for the real performance issues. The 100% interrogation approach stems from the external audit view that seeks to verify the accuracy and fairness of financial information. An obsession with this approach stops the internal auditor from rising above the external audit perspective to assume the expanded role of an independent management systems control consultant.

□ **What is management's role?** Audit interrogations of the vast bulk of computerised data are designed to isolate matters of audit interest. If this interest is to support findings concerning how management has organised systems of control then we can argue that this is the audit role. If this interest is in discovering errors or inconsistencies in the data that is processed we will have to suggest that this is part of management's responsibilities. Any attempt to remove the role of ensuring the integrity of the database from them, will dilute managers' power and motivation. Any attempt to show managers how poor their data are, again is something that should be performed by managers themselves. At the extreme we can suggest that the auditor is being selfish by not passing over interrogation software to management and allowing it to carry out "cleansing" procedures.

□ **What about following up problems?** One problem when the auditor prints out a series of "suspect items" is that of follow-up. We come across the enigma of working out how to uncover the meaning of hundreds of delinquent transactions when each has a different reason for being incorrect. The 100% interrogation approach may be best used before an audit is carried out to help decide which areas should be subject to audit cover.

The 100% interrogations do have an important role in audit. The chapter on computer audit will argue that the auditor should have a suite of downloaded databases for each main computer system. This data should be examined through special audit tests looking for possible fraud and error. These limited "reviews" have a role in the audit plans and can be used to uncover much material that can be reported to management, or form the basis for further audit work. This cannot replace the all consuming systems based audits that should be the bulk of audit work. Within the context of systems auditing, 100% interrogations provide a powerful tool for discovering the condition of the data and commenting on the state of controls. This is less significant for systems that are not primarily there to process transactions, but have a service delivery profile. It is still important that all underlying information processes are correct and proper. Testing can prove this point so long as it is put into perspective. Returning to the audit of pensions, we can test the database to establish whether our concerns about information system controls are really operating. Our audit is not a series of interrogations of information systems but a considered opinion on the adequacy and effectiveness of managerial systems of control.

16.7 The Meaning of Compliance

Compliance testing seeks to establish the degree to which control mechanisms are being applied as prescribed and the results should highlight non-compliance in pursuit of the defined test objective. This simple concept hides a number of interesting questions:

☐ **What is the definition of compliance?** The starting place for a compliance check is the precise definition of what one is seeking to conform to. When considering whether a control is in use, we must decide the model of control adopted. Where management believes a key control is being applied, say use of unique and individual passwords, this should be subject to a further check before we can say it is an effective control. Passwords along with user IDs allow management to restrict access and know which people have interfaced with the system. Where these passwords are swapped at will, the control fails and we must have knowledge of this before we can determine the detailed test programme. Compliance testing then comes into the frame to decide whether parts of the operation should be subject to substantive tests as a prerequisite to forming an opinion.

☐ **Why do people not comply?** Compliance testing programmes will determine whether something is being done. The results will be used to help the auditor decide whether controls are adequate, by highlighting the improper use of what should be accepted procedure. What it cannot say is why certain operations that constitute controls are not being adopted. The auditor is charged with placing the results into context by understanding the reasons why matters are not as they should be. Where procedures are not being followed we may take a step back and suggest that the same procedures should be assessed for adequacy before we tackle the subject of adherence. Where they do not make sense or are out of date, there is little progress in stating that there is breach of procedure. We need to provide management with insight into what is going on. One question is whether it is necessary to comply at all and this is covered below on compensating controls.

☐ **Can controls be compensated for?** There are times where controls fall out-of-date or become inappropriate as the system adapts to its environment. Front-line controls fall out of place and back up controls appear as staff seek to ensure the operations work. We find staff deal with problems by establishing another level of control to fill in for any perceived gaps. A system for car mileage claims may state that managers should certify claims before they are paid as a key control. Where this task is not taken seriously then we may find payroll staff querying the claims where they are obviously inconsistent. This check by payroll acts as a compensatory control that may not appear in the official procedure in line with the principle that people generally want good controls. Systems of internal control operate together and where one part is weak (i.e. not adhered to) then another part may well take over. Auditors may need to look for these compensating controls. They will need to decide whether to recommend that management adopts them as official procedures, on the basis that they reflect the shifts in control balance that occur over time. Most compensating controls depend on a good control culture that means an organic view of procedures is adopted to a better effect. We cannot always take extra procedures as being the most efficient method, as they may not be based on an overview of the entire operation and interfaces. The auditor must test compliance with official controls and apply the same tests to compensatory ones.

16.8 Issues in Testing

The fraud investigation perspective

The increasingly high profile that internal audit has assumed in fraud investigations has been to meet the requirements of the "expectation gap" that calls for these types of services. We all appreciate that management is responsible for the prevention, detection and investigation of fraud and irregularity although we also know that this role is shared with (if not given to) the auditor. The link between the auditor and a profile in fraud investigations apart from the control implication, is the way testing can be applied to this type of work. This enables the auditor to research problems in a way that managers are unable to, in the search for the offender. Managers when confronted with a fraud, tend to want to confront the alleged offender and "have it out", while the auditor will tend to stand back and develop a series of test programmes to secure evidence concerning the fraud. Herein lies the main difference where auditors possess techniques that enable them to probe, examine and review material relevant to the case in question. We have mentioned various methods for securing relevant information and these are likewise applied to fraud investigations albeit with a different objective in mind. The key difference between a systems audit and a fraud investigation is the emphasis on purist testing routines that are applied to the latter work.

Substantive testing and the "expert" dilemma

The concept of substantive testing must be dealt with carefully. During substantive testing we establish whether a business objective is being achieved. This requires a considered judgement on whether something produces the right result. Questions such as "is this right? does it make sense? is it correct? is it proper? does it work?" all substantiate the true position. The application of substantive tests to traditional financial systems is easier since the control objective will be concerned with the value, timing and presentation of figures reported by the system, which may be measured. Where we tackle managerial and operational areas we turn to qualitative considerations that are more difficult to measure. These may relate to the impact of services on clients and value for money that require the auditor to substantiate whether controls produce the desired effect. Expanding the concept of effectiveness brings with it even more demands as this is difficult to quantify. The conflict between the need to directly substantiate something and provide a considered judgement can lead to problems for the auditor. This is where a substantive test depends on an interpretation of the results of the applied test procedure. These complications add to the spice of the audit task.

Do we need to mistrust everyone and everything?

Testing applies the principle of asking what, where, when, and why, which is ingrained into the auditor as part of training and experience. We commend the auditor who probes, and we recognise the need to examine in detail transactions from all systems. These skills are applied with great determination since we must test as much as possible and complete the test programme. The premise of this derives from mistrust of people and documents. We seek evidence from as independent a source as possible in line with the audit objective. There are implications of a position where we do not trust anything until confirmed. The way this potentially confrontational position is managed takes care and practice. Meeting with management the auditor requests many documents referred to in discussions. When managers say they wrote to staff on data protection, we ask to see the memorandum. When managers argue they sign all orders before dispatch, we examine a batch of them. The auditor verifies representations although comments may be reported accurately: "management has indicated that..." or "we were informed that...". We should ask for confirmation in a way that does not imply mistrust but falls under standard auditing procedures. The best approach is to explain to management this procedure to de-personalise it.

16.9 Evidence and Working Papers

Introduction
Audit testing results in much material that should support the reported audit opinion and associated recommendations. The test results along with other material gathered throughout the audit process will constitute audit evidence and this will be held in suitable audit working papers. Standards of working papers and documentary evidence are a topic that all auditors come across in the course of their work and generally there is a view that good standards are a prerequisite to good control. Note that the external auditor may be sued where their work may have been performed negligently and their working papers may be used in any defence to this charge. Here we look at some of the requirements for internal auditors' working papers and filing systems.

Information attributes
The information the auditor uses for the audit opinion should be:

☐ **Sufficient** - This is in line with materiality, level of risk and the level of auditors' knowledge of the operation. Sufficient means enough, which depends on circumstances. It should be enough to satisfy the auditor's judgement or persuade management to make any changes advocated by audit. It could mean enough to ensure there is a wide spread of material or an acceptable sample. Evidence is adequate when it meets the desired purpose. The audit opinion may range from "it is clear that...", "it would appear that...", "there are indications that...",and "there is the possibility that...". In the current environment of cost constraint, the amount of evidence secured should be the minimum to form an opinion in that it takes more resources to obtain relevant proof that conclusions are sound.

☐ **Relevant** - This ensures that evidence is directed to the control objectives. Relevance brings into play the legal concept of admissibility, that requires material to relate specifically to the issues at hand. It is wrong to refer to matters that do not impact on the arguments that appear in the audit report, as a way of blurring the issues at hand. The auditor must use professional judgement in deciding what is important. Test results that refer to low-level detail cannot be used to comment on material considerations that have a far reaching effect on management's ability to achieve. Relevance means that the evidence is associated to the key concerns and that it is material to them.

☐ **Reliable** - The information should be accurate, without bias and if possible produced by a third party or obtained directly by the auditor. The term "reliable" stimulates images of the evidence being "dependable, honest, sound, and true". This may in turn be applied to the audit report that is based on this evidence, as in one sense and in contrast, unreliable evidence creates an opposite impact by lowering the credibility of the auditor's work. The rules on obtaining audit evidence require it to be done in a way that minimises bias. The reliability factor must be applied by the auditor to satisfy him/herself and must also satisfy the perceptions of the report reader. Independence and accuracy are the main components of the reliability index that need to be fully addressed by the auditor, in the search for good evidence.

☐ **Practical** - One would weigh up the evidence required, the cost and time taken to obtain it and sensitivity. Some matters cannot be discovered through audit since it would take too much research. There are many examples of this that range from getting a definitive verdict on the state of the MIS database, through to obtaining a view on whether staff are well motivated. Not all matters may be studied and documented by the auditor since the general equation suggests that the greater the value of evidence the more resources will be applied to securing it. There is a constraint that means there is a strict limit on the time that can be applied.

Types of evidence
Material to support audit findings from testing would include:
1. Documents.
2. Re-performance by audit.
3. Analysis of figures.
4. Reconciliations.
5. Third party confirmation.
6. Reports.
7. Vouching checks.
8. Verification.
9. Testimonials.
10. Physical material e.g. photographs.
11. Interview records.

Working papers
Test results will be contained in working papers held in audit files. Working papers should:

☐ **Set out the objectives of the work**. All documentation is prepared or secured for a reason and this reason should be defined at the outset. The reason the work was carried out that resulted in the relevant working paper should be stated in a way that sets a firm context for the interpretation of the information contained therein. This will help indicate the extent to which the document being relied on by the auditor is pursuing the overall audit objectives.

☐ **Clarity.** The working papers should be laid out clearly to promote their use during report writing and review of work. Papers should be set out in a neat and orderly fashion that is logical and simple. This is aided where documents contain a list of abbreviations used and definitions of any common terminology and keys. One well-known test is that if one found a sheet of paper from any working paper file, it should be immediately identifiable.

☐ **Indexed**. The first enclosure of any file should always consist of an index to the papers. This should indicate where documents can be found and what each one contains. It is better to start the index sequence from the back of the file so that newer documents can be added.

☐ **Support the audit decisions/opinion**. Working papers are secured primarily to ensure that audit findings can be justified. Cross referencing should be applied whereby the report held on file contains references (in the margin) that relate to specific enclosures held in the working paper file. Figures, examples, quotations and charts should be able to be traced back straight to the file. This is particularly relevant where the report is contentious. Working papers are used at pre-report drafting stage where findings are being discussed with management.

☐ **The use of pro formas**. One way to promote the use of audit standards in working papers is to use standardised documents. These act as checklists, forcing the auditor to cover specified areas during the course of completing the required document and also form an aide-mémoire in guiding the auditor. The documents may be used as pure evidence where material is extracted from source records and then input onto the form. Alternatively they may be used to summarise the material from records and analysis that is attached to the pro forma. One further advantage is that they appear tidier as an alternative to reams of rough hand written notes. Automated working papers come a step closer where we are used to working with standardised documentation.

☐ **Cross referenced**. Working papers form a whole in that together they tell the story of the audit in terms of work carried out and resultant findings. In an audit each stage leads naturally into the next. Findings from one piece of research will impact on work done on other areas as the flow and direction of the audit changes with new findings. These links and associations should be reflected in the working papers by a suitable system for cross referencing. The file should be capable of being read in parts and if the files were to be reconsidered months (or even years) after the audit is completed.

☐ **Economically used**. Working papers contain evidence and material relating to the audit. The papers should not be prepared for their own sake but must relate to specific audit objectives. If we flowchart a system, this should be left out where due to circumstances, it is not required. Filling files with superfluous material will blur the real issues and lead to inefficient use of audit time.

☐ **Headed up**. All documents should contain headers with the name of the audit, date, relevant officers and other details. Any document prepared by the internal audit unit should be able to be identified by the headings.

☐ **Clearly show any impact on the audit report**. Some documents have a profound impact on the audit report while others provide background. The status of working papers should be clear in that items that feature in the report should be indicated. A scan of the working papers should give an idea of what points will appear. One way of providing this standard is to highlight (by a coloured pen) sections that will enter into the report to create this distinction. A brief review of the working paper file will isolate the key material without having to re-read all the contents of the file.

☐ **Signed by the auditor and the reviewer**. It is practice to place at the bottom of each document, boxes for "prepared by" and "reviewed by" along with spaces for the dates. This underpins an audit standard that dictates that all evidence indicates the preparer. It encourages the audit manager or senior auditor to record they have reviewed the document in line with quality assurance standards.

☐ **Show the work carried out**. Documents support the audit opinion and contain matters that may be referred to in the audit report. Whilst this gives a bottom-line use for the working papers it is equally important that the underlying work completed be fully identified. This sets a context for the conclusions that may be important at a later date. Factors relating to the way source evidence was examined and recorded should be documented as a formal account of the procedures. If missing there is a temptation to leave out controversial material not derived from fully understood procedures.

☐ **Show the source of information/data**. The origins of information in working papers should be clearly defined. Where the data was obtained from filing systems or computerised databases, the date and circumstances must be recorded, since the same data may be altered at a later date. Where an officer has made a representation that falls within the working papers, the source should be noted, particularly where it relates to specific figures.

☐ **Indicate which matters are outstanding**. A working paper will say what has been done and the results of this work. For the record it should make clear what work has not been undertaken as this may arise as an issue. Where parts of the system have not been addressed this should be made clear, particularly where a different level of work would have been required. Where samples have not been fully tested because of various practical difficulties this point should appear on the working paper to explain why certain items have no results listed against them. Examples may cover many different areas although the basic principle is simple in that qualifying information is just as important as positive findings in terms of providing an acceptable foundation for the report.

☐ **Show any impact on the next audit**. The working paper indicates what has been left for later consideration. The nature of audit work means that not all matters are addressed in any one operation and two audits can be carried out in the same area dealing with different aspects. It is helpful if files show where future resources may be concentrated in terms of covering gaps left from an earlier audit. This should "jump out" from the working files to feed directly into the next audit of the area.

☐ **Complete**. There is nothing more frustrating than reviewing a file that suggests that certain items have been missed for no apparent reason. Files should be complete, in that all they purport to cover is dealt with. For standardised documents this is particularly relevant since where a predetermined item is not deemed necessary it must be noted as "not applicable" with suitable explanation.

☐ **Consistent**. Working papers should be wholly consistent. This is important where the audit has been done over a long time period and/or involves several auditors, each dealing with a different part. If a figure or fact is quoted in one document, this should be the same as in another or differences explained. This rule also applies to statements and representation made during the audit and recorded in the working paper files. Where this does not occur and there are inconsistent facts then the normal option will be to exclude all reference, because of uncertainty and thus lowering impact of the report. Any audit manager's review of the working papers must seek to identify inconsistencies between the working papers and the draft audit report.

☐ **Include summaries wherever possible**. It is one thing to obtain and file vast volumes of reports, printouts, and documentation in that they impact on the audit. What is more important is to digest, analyse, and then summarise the material components of this information so as to avoid re-reading bulky material. So a consultant's report on an operation should be read by the auditor and then key points extracted and summarised. The consultant's report should not lie in the file without comment. Likewise extensive test results should not appear in spreadsheets without bottom-line conclusion that can go straight into the audit report. Detailed figures are meaningless if no conclusions can be drawn.

IIA standards 230, 420 and 520.04 provide further guidance on audit working papers. APB standards (Paragraph 58) cover this topic.

16.10 Permanent Files

These files contain standing information of a permanent nature such as:

1. **Organisation charts**. This shows names, designations and position of staff. It will fall out-of-date but indicates structure. Management may provide updates.

2. **System notes**. Notes and flowcharts from previous audits that document the movement of information and documentation should be held on file so that a good picture of the operations is secured in the permanent files. Again these will tend to fall out-of-date as changes arise.

3. **Research items and relevant publications**. Publications that relate to the operation will help provide an overview of current developments and keep the auditor in touch with the changing factors that impact on the particular work area. Bulky material may be held in the audit library and simply referred to in the permanent file.

4. **Summaries of frauds**. It is good practice to link fraud and irregularity to the systems work as a way of seeking improvements in controls that allow problems to arise in the first place. A reference to frauds that impact on the operation will assist.

5. **Management reports**. Reports prepared by consultants and management themselves should also be obtained and held on file or appropriately cross referenced. This is a good way of keeping in touch with matters that are of concern to management without performing an actual audit.

6. **Committee papers**. Reports that are submitted to committee (or the board) for approval usually involve new acquisitions or restructuring exercises. Relating these to the permanent files adds important knowledge concerning proposed and approved changes that may have a control implication.

7. **Budgets and other financial data**. Financial reports can be used to assess materiality. They can be further analysed to obtain a view of changes in spending patterns of interest to the auditor in planning future work. Permanent files have two main uses in that they help in setting long-term audit plans (via risk appraisal) and also provide background information.

8. **Previous audit reports**. The executive summary of previous audit reports should be held on file as each report should ideally run only to a few key pages. This is in addition to references to the full audit report that should be filed elsewhere.

9. **List of premises and addresses**. Useful information such as brief maps and transportation arrangements for each site can be of great aid to the auditor. We would also require a list of contact names and phone numbers. This will involve employees who have in the past been assigned to assist the auditor and recognises the protocol that is sometimes applied by management where they nominate specific link officers for the audit.

We would wish to retain in our permanent files, information of continuing relevance to the area in question so long as it is material to the audit objective. Armed with this we would want to derive a profile of each main operational area for planning purposes and as a way of developing a database of relevant information concerning key parts of the audit field. It would probably be advisable to assign specific parts of the audit field to auditors for continual updating and amendment. In addition close liaison with management should ensure that all relevant material is entered into the filing system. The updating process should also require the auditor to assess the impact of new information as it is placed on file. This may act as a funnel mechanism where all relevant information ends up in the correct place within the filing system.

16.11 Current Files

These files record the results of the audit assignment. They contain items such as:

1. **The objectives statement**. The first document that we might come across may be a statement of audit objectives that sets the tone for the resultant audit.

2. **The preliminary survey**. In the section on audit planning we have agreed that assignment planning starts with a preliminary survey where key risk areas are identified for proposed cover. The work done in this respect should be fully recorded on the current file.

3. **The scope of the audit**. Having completed the preliminary survey we may now define the scope of work in a formal document. This will be in two forms. One will be a file document that is agreed by the audit manager. The other will be a memorandum to the auditee advising on the scope of work that will be carried out in discharge of the audit objective. Both documents should be held on the current file.

4. **The assignment plan**. The work undertaken to prepare the assignment plan should be properly recorded on the current file. This will be used to set a frame against which the actual results can be measured and as such constitutes a major control over the audit process. The planning schedules will be updated as details of actual audit hours worked are made available. The documentation should also include an administrative schedule that sets out clearly who is responsible for what parts of the audit.

5. **The results of any background research carried out**. Interviews with staff and management should be fully recorded and held on file. These are important for later use as we may have to quote from representations made by management. Also a review of the working paper file will make it clear whether management has agreed that there are certain weaknesses and we may have made notes on the response to resolving them that can be reported on. It is best to hold interview notes in plastic pockets so that any documents referred to during the interview, can be placed next to the interview notes

themselves. It may be that something said by an officer conflicts with other views from auditees and it is as well to know which material was provided by which person.

6. **Systems notes and flowcharts.** These are obviously important file documents. The interesting point for these papers is that they will probably need to be copied and held also on the permanent file since they will have a continuing relevance to the audit unit in question.

7. **Any audit programme used.** Programmes come in two forms. Some list the tasks that need to be completed to perform the audit, while others contain space to record the results of the work carried out. Whatever the format, they are essential material for the current file as they feed directly into the audit reporting process. It is good practice to highlight those matters that will be used as examples of the implications of poor control, when the report is prepared. The format of the schedules should be carefully considered. It is one thing to list errors and concerns and quite another to have them ordered in such as way as to allow summary figures to be reported. So for example where we wish to report on the percentage of items exhibiting a particular type of problem the working papers should accommodate this requirement by allowing composite figures to be readily extracted.

8. **The system evaluation.** Much of the audit opinion is inferred from the evaluation of controls in terms of defining weaknesses that are then reported on. Some systems audits pay little attention to the evaluation stage and the working papers reflect this approach by not containing a great detail of control assessment. Notwithstanding this, the formal evaluation documentation, be it by ICQ or control evaluation schedules, should be held in the current file as a record of this process.

9. **The testing strategy.** Test programmes indicate what will be done as well as by default defining what will not be covered. Formal documentation on the current file is required as part of the working paper standards applied to current files. It is one thing to list the great lengths the auditor has gone to in performing testing and the detailed results that will probably be recorded. However the process of deciding what to test and how is sometimes lost amongst the vast amount of material that testing tends to produce. This factor can be very important at a later stage where for example a fraud occurs shortly after an audit has been completed having disclosed no material concerns. The way samples were selected and dealt with can be an important point where there is some dispute over the audit work. Again this initial strategy should be clearly set in the current file so that conclusions concerning this stage of the audit can be readily extracted.

10. **The test results.** We now arrive at the actual testing stage and this will normally produce material that will be referred to throughout the audit. The need to have this evidence recorded in a clear and accurate manner cannot be overemphasised.

11. **Record of control weaknesses.** This document should set out the control objectives, initial assessment of control mechanisms, the test results, the opinion, and recommendations. It will form the basis of the closure meeting with line management as the key points are discussed in some detail. We should end up with an initial management response that can also be entered onto the record of control weakness. Many of the matters set out in the record will enter directly into the draft report, and herein lies another reason why the document should be carefully drafted and held on the current file.

12. **The audit report.** A version of the audit report that contains direct references to the underlying working papers should also be held on the current file. We should make

sure that this is the same version as the final issued report, as we would expect several drafts to be prepared and revised during the course of a typical audit.

13. **Audit review notes**. The current file should contain a formal audit review record that should indicate what checks were made by the audit manager in question and that the audit meets quality standards. The main problem is where the review is not formally documented in the file. A further problem is where the audit manager has reviewed a draft report that ends up with many comments written on the report pages. The draft may then be destroyed as new versions are prepared and review points then lost. As such it is important that the audit manager details the review points (say concerning the draft report) and that this is held permanently on file, even if the draft report is destroyed. To expand this point it may also be advisable to record significant meetings between audit management and the lead auditor where the audit is discussed.

Linking permanent and current files

There is an obvious link between the permanent and current files as much of the material of continuing importance collected during the audit will end up in the permanent filing system.

FIGURE 16.5 PERMANENT/CURRENT FILES LINKAGES

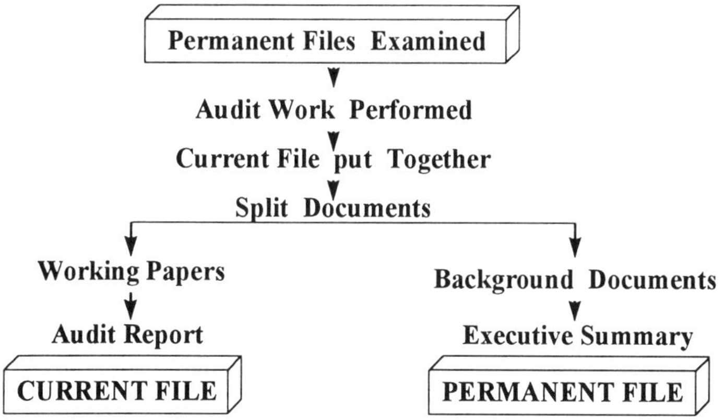

16.12 Standardisation

One way to formalise the above process is to define standardised working papers aimed at getting to the audit opinion with supporting evidence. These standardised documents will form the current file while the background material will either be held as a bundle of general papers or if relevant will enter into the permanent filing system. This approach forms the basis for an automated filing system where standardised forms are maintained on disk. Standardised documentation enables auditors to follow a systematic audit methodology and can contribute to overall audit efficiency. This point is explored later in the chapter on the audit manual. These are certain types of documents that might be standardised including for example:

• Preliminary survey report.
• Assignment plans.

- Flowcharts.
- Interview records.
- Internal control evaluation forms.
- Compliance and substantive test strategies.
- Record of control weakness.
- Issue analysis.
- Constraint analysis.
- Objectives statement.

We can seek to develop an entire suite of standardised documents and this is a feature of the specimen template documents on the diskette.

Filing systems
The adopted filing system should reflect the way information is stored and the different categories of files that will be compiled over the years. One might maintain the following files:
- The general survey work (permanent files).
- File updating exercises.
- Annual reports.
- Quarterly reports.
- Final assignment reports.
- Annual plans.
- Quarterly plans.
- Audit management files including personal files.
- Correspondence files.
- Fraud allegations forms.
- Assignment working paper folders - standardised forms.
- Assignment working paper folders - background notes.

It may be possible to adopt colour coding for files, for example:
1. **Orange** - General files on audit management (e.g. staffing issues), long-term plans and activity reports. General background information on the organisation, its strategies and general developments
2. **Blue** - Other permanent files, on the various systems in the audit field, broken down into defined audit units in line with the adopted audit approach.
3. **Buff** - Current audit files with standardised forms and background information on the audit.
4. **Lever arch** - Containing all general correspondence received and dealt with by internal audit that may be cross referenced in detail to the main filing system.
5. **Lever arch** - Containing all published audit reports with a further copy held in the current audit file. Each report can be given a reference number that can be used to readily trace the document.
6. **Time monitoring systems** - This file will detail the time recording systems along with timesheets and various standardised documents used by internal audit. Moreover job codes may be cross referenced to the numbering used in the filing system.

Each filing system will be unique and depend on the way the internal audit unit is organised. Bearing this in mind there is one interpretation of a filing standard that is set out below:

FIGURE 16.6 FORMAT FOR A FILING SYSTEM

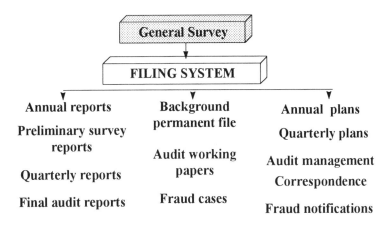

The above set-up should account for most types of files and information required to manage an internal audit function although files should be held on computer disk wherever possible.

Automation
Traditional material on audit working papers deals with the attributes and standards applied to paper files. This is important since standards need to be applied regardless of the media used. Automation strategies impact on the way working papers are maintained. Most information will be on disk or accessible from corporate systems as required. Document imaging means that source documents that contain signatures and original data can be stored on disk, without manual back-up files. A half way house is where manual files are held alongside automated files. A progressive automation programme involves destruction of paper files with information retrieval via permanent interface with computer databases. We retrieve information either on the file assigned to the audit unit or via a library system where all the material relevant to the audit unit is referenced. There is no working paper that cannot be stored on disk. We may also establish report generators that retrieve the data on the audit area. This means that the data are up to date as they are accessed from current files.

16.13 Statistical Sampling

Introduction
All auditors need knowledge of statistical sampling and it is advisable to adopt a clear policy regarding use. We summarise popular ways statistical sampling may be applied although a specialist textbook will provide a fuller understanding.

The role of sampling

Statistical sampling has a clear role and auditors make a decision during systems audits thus:

FIGURE 16.7 ROLE OF SAMPLING

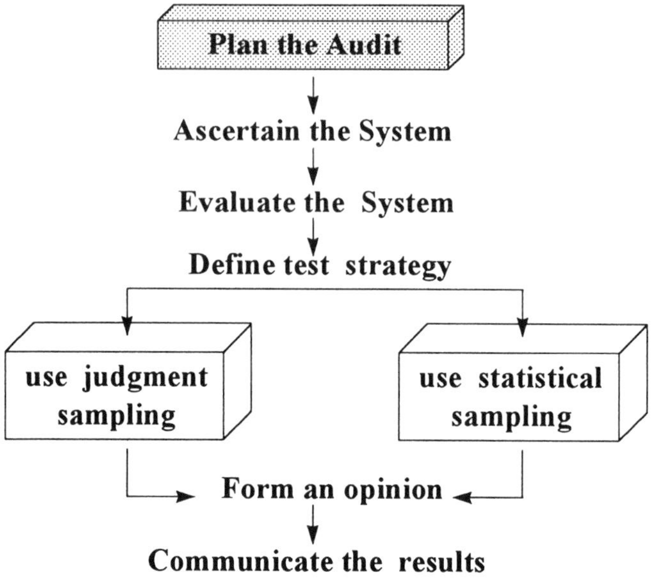

An auditor has to decide whether statistical sampling will be used based on knowledge and an appreciation of the technique and its application.

The external audit perspective

Most auditing textbooks have a chapter on sampling and so it might appear to be mandatory. One must consider the differences between the internal and external audit objectives before assessing the relative value to be derived. The external auditor is primarily concerned with:

1. Whether accounts show a true and fair view. Decisions may range from disagreement, qualification, through to a level of uncertainty and as such invite a yes/no response.

2. The reliance that can be placed on underlying financial systems of internal control. As a short-cut to checking all the figures in the final accounts there may be some reliance placed on controls, although there must be some direct testing to secure evidence to support the audit opinion.

3. Whether the level of errors found by examining selected transactions has a material effect on the accounts in terms of influencing the audit opinion. Materiality is a firm external audit concept that places emphasis on the impact of problems on the reliability of the final accounts.

4. Whether the level of testing carried out means that they have discharged their professional responsibilities. Substantive testing is fundamental to the external audit and the need for a defendable choice is uppermost. A method to determine sample size is useful. There are tests that can be applied to 100% of a database although this gives

a long list of items for further manual investigation, which will take time. The need to restrict the number of items examined remains.

The internal auditor is more concerned about:
1. Whether examining selected transactions confirms initial opinion on the systems of internal control. Samples are selected and examined to see whether the results coincide with the initial audit opinion.
2. Whether their findings are sufficient to convince management to act. Where management agrees that problems exist there is little point in extensive testing. It may be necessary to get an idea of the scale of the problems although the main objective is to get management to act. The internal auditor will use a consultancy based approach that emphasises the solutions and not the detailed errors that fall within a test based model. The audit report will then be based around the proposed changes.
3. Whether the extent of any losses or deficiencies may be quantified. This is where statistical sampling comes to the fore. This would apply more in investigative work than in systems auditing.

In conclusion, the external auditor is primarily concerned about accepting or rejecting a financial statement while internal audit work is geared to encourage management to act on defined control weaknesses. It is the external auditor who is more concerned with the use of statistical sampling in financial audits, although it does have a role in internal audit.

Reasons why statistical sampling may not be used
There are many internal auditors who do not use statistical sampling and audit departments that have no firm policy. There are many reasons why it may not be used:
1. Staff lack awareness and have had no training. This means that our diagram above suggests that the auditor does not necessarily make a conscious choice between statistical and judgemental sampling because of the lack of knowledge. The fact that statistical sampling can be complicated may discourage its use. It can be time consuming to master and cumbersome to use.
2. One needs knowledge of the population and this requires time consuming research. It may be difficult to tell exactly what is contained in the sample because of the nature of the audit. It is still advisable to analyse the populace as this gives an insight into an operation.
3. It may stifle the "audit nose" by not allowing the auditor to be guided by years of experience. Statistical sampling relies on randomness and does not allow the auditor to choose individual transactions. The auditor's "intuition" can be suppressed.
4. Quoting figures and probability ranges may not convince non-numeric managers to act. It depends on the perceptions of the client for the work, which vary. Some managers appreciate this approach while others feel intimidated. This factor should be balanced so as not to produce an audit report resisted by management although much depends on the terminology used by the auditor.
5. Statistical sampling is not readily applicable to small unusual populations. The real benefits come where population sizes are larger and samples relatively smaller.

16.14 Advantages of Statistical Sampling

There are advantages from using statistical sampling:

☐ **Results may be defended against bias**. Bias conjures up images of the auditor being subject to favouritism, narrow-mindedness, one-sidedness and partiality. Samples selected for no justifiable reason may foster accusations of auditor bias. Where there is a scientific method of defining sample sizes and selecting items we can assume the more appropriate stance of being objective, detached, dispassionate, fair, unemotional and above all, just.

☐ **A defined sample size is provided**. A close examination of statistical tables brings out the feature of larger populations requiring only relatively small increases in sample size to meet set parameters. A judgemental sample of say 5% becomes more difficult to handle for larger systems with thousands of accounts. Statistical methods permit smaller samples that are statistically valid.

☐ **One may safely extrapolate the results and apply them to the wider population**. This is a moot point in that there are many auditors who extend sample results to the entire data-field when the sample has not been obtained using statistical sampling. Although this prediction is usually accepted by management this is technically improper. The only professional prediction is one that sets the statistically significant results within the set parameters (e.g. 95% of cases will tend to fall within a defined range).

☐ **The technique is repeatable and one would expect a similar result from any repetition**. The exercise of tossing a hundred coins will tend to produce around 50% heads and 50% tails each time. With statistical sampling we would expect on average to find similar results each time the test procedure is applied.

☐ **It forces one to define and consider the attributes of the population**. We set as a disadvantage the need to research the data being tested from a holistic viewpoint and this is also seen as an advantage. The more that is learnt about an area, the better will be the auditor's ability to direct the audit. Unfortunately time is now seen as the most important component of the audit function that must be controlled and this does not promote extensive pre-planning. The balance to this last point is the growing trend whereby whole databases are downloaded and explored on a regular basis. This not only encourages a greater familiarisation but also allows one to generate global figures concerning the total number of records and other key facts.

☐ **Computers make statistical sampling more convenient to use**. It is simple to ask the computer to generate random numbers. Many interrogation packages have in-built statistical tables.

☐ **The level of confidence may be pre-defined**. Statistical sampling allows one to define predetermined risk parameters that the final opinion may be set within. This is factual and cannot be challenged as it states that a probable number of selections will follow a set pattern, but not all of them. This is a comfortable position for the auditor as it allows an authoritative opinion that in terms of logical presentation cannot be refuted, even if the precise interpretation may be.

Judgement, haphazard and statistical sampling

Some argue there are three types of sampling techniques:

□ **Judgement sampling**. The auditor uses knowledge of systems and people to select items more likely to exhibit certain features. The sample is purposely biased by the auditor to take on board matters that the auditor is aware of. For example, we may be concerned about our ordering system where an individual who left some months ago was known to be medically unwell and made known errors. We may look at orders he processed and skew the sample.

□ **Indiscriminate sampling**. This allows the selection of items at random but is not based on any defined statistical formula. The intention is to secure an unbiased sample although because the sample size is not mathematically based, it is not possible to formally extrapolate the results. The selected sample size may be too small or too large. It is best applied to smaller populations say under 100 items since statistical sampling is of no use at these levels.

□ **Statistical sampling**. The auditor has to define the population and set confidence levels. A predetermined sample size will be provided and one may indicate how reliable and accurate the results are. The results secured from testing the sample may be extrapolated to draw quantified conclusions about the population.

The normal distribution

The bell-shaped curve represents the normal distribution. The shape of the curve is determined by the mean and the standard deviation (SD) of the underlying values whereby the greater the range of values the flatter the curve. This feature is used in statistical sampling to allow the area under the curve to equate to 1. If the mean is seen as 0 then we can calculate that each SD from the mean will cover a defined portion of the normal distribution curve. This appears as:

FIGURE 16.8 THE NORMAL DISTRIBUTION

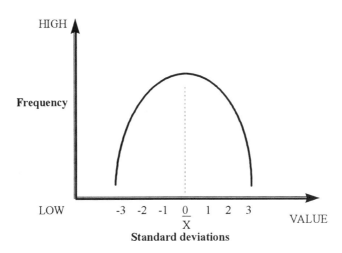

Area under the curve   + or - 1 SD = 68.3%

+ or - 2 SD = 95.4%

+ or - 3 SD = 99.7%

The relationships between the values and the SDs have been translated into statistical tables. These may be used to form conclusions about the population that are derived from an examination of a sample of the population. This is based on the theory that the mean of a distribution of sample means is equal to the mean of the population from which the sample is drawn. It is important to know the SD of the sample that is used and a formula may be used to calculate this figure. This is not reproduced here but it should be noted that the smaller the range of values the smaller the SD while the greater the range (i.e. variation from the mean) then the larger the SD.

16.15 Applying Statistical Sampling to the Audit Process

It is important that statistical sampling is considered in terms of its actual role in the audit process. It is used when performing the testing routines required to confirm or otherwise the initial evaluation of internal controls. To this end the samples and ensuing tests may be used for:

☐ **Quantifying the effects of control weaknesses**. Substantive testing reveals the implications of a lack of control. This is where statistical sampling may be used to allow a generalist comment based on the results of a predetermined number of transactions. We have already agreed that one can only give an overall opinion on the entire database where the sample has been statistically prepared.

☐ **Getting management to act on audit recommendations**. Ensuring that internal audit recommendations are supported by indicating the extent of risk in failing to take remedial action encourages management to adopt them. So where we find excessive levels of non-compliance with a key control, this must be quantified and set against the corresponding recommendation.

☐ **Highlighting implications of failure to act on identified control weaknesses**. We use statistical sampling to predict the extent of uncontrolled error. This need not be in terms of one-off examples that give no indication of the scale and extent of the problems as in some audit reports. Scientific sampling can result in matrix boxes in the report where the type of errors found can be given global values based on extrapolation, to increase the impact of the findings.

Statistical sampling is a means to an end. It assists in achieving defined test objectives, without examining the entire population. The role of statistical sampling within the testing routine is described in figure 16.9:

FIGURE 16.9 TESTING USING STATISTICAL SAMPLING

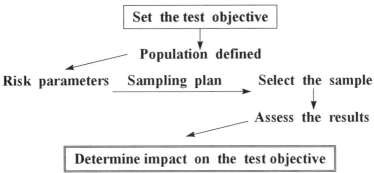

Sampling techniques
There are two main aspects to statistical sampling. One is how the number of items to be examined is defined. The other relates to the methods used to extract the required information. The latter is called the sampling method or selection technique. Methods used to define numbers tested are called sampling plans. This section deals with sampling methods and these may be set out as:

☐ **Random sampling**. This technique is used to select samples such that each item in the population has an equal chance of being chosen. Random number tables may be used to choose the required items and these may be generated by an appropriately programmed computer.

☐ **Stratified sampling**. If we recall that the normal distribution places values in the shape of a bell, then a skewed distribution will not appear symmetrical. This may mean that the auditor can divide the population into several segments that may consist of say a small number of high value invoices for revenue contracts and a large number of small value ones for one-off supplies. The auditor may wish to pay more attention to high value items and in so doing can split the population into two and apply statistical sampling plans with different confidence levels, to each one.

☐ **Cluster sampling**. This is a convenient way of selecting items for testing where once the number of transactions has been defined, they are then taken from one filing area. This may be a single drawer of a filing cabinet and is based on simple working practicalities.

☐ **Interval sampling**. Here the population should be homogeneous, with no cyclical bias or missing items. If we divide the population size by the sample size then the sampling interval is obtained and every nth item is chosen for testing. One might imagine a computer being asked to select say every 20th item from a particular file.

☐ **Automated sampling** may be seen as a selection technique where the auditor uses sampling software to set parameters, determine the number for testing, access the relevant file and then down-load the selected items into a separate spreadsheet for later analytical testing by the auditor.

Setting risk parameters

Statistical sampling is based on probability theory and as such one must set upper and lower limits within which the results may be placed. It is similar to saying that on average a die will fall on the number six on 1/6 occasions. With statistical sampling one has to set the criteria within which the results should be evaluated and this falls under three basic parameters:

☐ **Error rate**. This is the level of error that one may expect from the population being tested. Error may be seen as for example the number of invoices that are incorrect. This is normally set at 5% and most statistical sampling tables are based on this figure. If the actual error rate is different then a revision to the quoted risk boundaries has to be made. The rate is determined by the auditor and is based on pilot studies, discussions with management and the results of previous audits.

☐ **Confidence**. Confidence is the degree to which the results derived from the sample will follow the trend in the actual population. A 95% confidence means that 95 out of every 100 items examined will reflect the population. The position on confidence levels is:

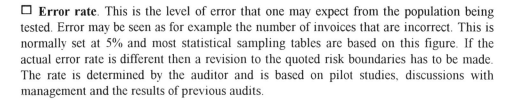

TABLE 16.1 CONFIDENCE LEVELS

LEVEL	PERCEPTION
Below 90%	is too low to be of any real value.
90%	is where the auditor knows a lot about the population but wishes to convince management.
95%	is the level that is generally used and is high enough to satisfy the auditor and management.
99%	is too high and will result in most of the population being selected.

☐ **Precision**. This shows the margin within which the results can be quoted and defines the degree of accuracy that is required. It may be in terms of the quoted error being expressed as a figure taken from testing the sample plus or minus the degree of precision, say 2%. The real result relative to the population will be somewhere within the lower and upper levels. If one needs to be accurate to 2% one may find an error in the sample of say £100, this may be quoted for the population as between £98 and £102. The level chosen will depend on the objective of the test and how the results are used.

☐ **Extrapolation** is when results taken from a sample are grossed up and applied to the whole population. The average result from the sample is multiplied by the value of the population to give the estimated total error. Risk parameters are set by the auditor and depend on the test objective. It is practice to use 5% error rate tables, with 95% confidence at plus or minus 2% precision. Using these standards, most statistically extrapolated results will be accepted by management.

Audit testing and statistical sampling

The two main types of audit testing are compliance and substantive testing although one may perform some walkthrough tests during the ascertainment stage. Note the following:

- **Compliance tests**. Here one is testing the existence or otherwise of a particular control. The test is of a yes/no nature where an attribute (i.e. control adherence) is either present or does not exist. An example may be a test to determine the number of purchase invoices that have not been authorised by a designated officer before being paid.
- **Substantive tests**. These tests are carried out to establish the extent to which the implications of a control weakness may be quantified. We may be concerned to discover the total value of purchase invoices incorrectly posted to the wrong year due to poor cut-off procedures.

These two testing conventions require different statistical sampling plans geared into the objectives of the tests. Compliance testing is concerned with specific attributes so that a frequency may be quoted. Substantive testing looks for variables and enables the auditor to quote a range of values from the test results. The sampling plans mentioned below may be placed in the following table:

TABLE 16.2 THE SAMPLING PLANS

COMPLIANCE TESTING	SUBSTANTIVE TESTING
Attribute Sampling	Variable Sampling
Stop-go Sampling	Difference Estimates
Discovery Sampling	Monetary Unit Sampling

Compliance testing requires variations of attribute sampling, while substantive testing is based on variations of variable sampling. These plans are expanded below.

The various sampling plans

Each of these sampling plans will be briefly dealt with. It is important to appreciate where each plan may be applied in determining the number of items to examine. Graham Westwood (1990) has suggested a criterion for selecting the most appropriate plan:

Quantitative features (substantive tests) :

is the book value of the population available?
if no - use variable sampling.
if yes - do we expect a difference?
if no - use MUS.
if yes - use difference estimates.

Qualitative features (compliance tests) :

is fraud suspected ?
if yes - use discovery sampling.

if no - do we expect a low error rate ?
if no - use fixed attribute sampling.
if yes - use stop-go sampling.

Substantive testing sampling

☐ **Variable sampling**. This plan enables one to take the average result from the sample and extrapolate this to arrive at an estimated error rate that applies to the entire population. A preliminary sample of 50 items is taken and the error rate calculated along with the SD from the sample. The error rate divided by the SD gives a proportion that can be used to determine sample sizes from the table for various confidence levels. For additional items the SD is re-calculated.

☐ **Difference estimates**. Where the book value (BV) is available one may take the difference between the BV and actuals for a preliminary sample of 100 items. The resulting SD is used to calculate the new sampling error rate that may be compared to the original. This technique provides a short-cut and can be very convenient. If there are many missing items then the differences may actually be bigger than the BV.

☐ **Monetary unit sampling (MUS)**. This plan is used by external auditors and incorporates an assessment of the strength of the particular internal control system. The poorer the internal controls the greater the degree of reliability required which in turn makes the sample size larger. One assumes that the population consists of a series of values and in so doing the larger (and more material) items are naturally selected once the sampling interval is determined. One is looking for an over or under statement of monetary values so that the auditor can decide whether the account may be accepted or not in an audit opinion. Accordingly one is able to sample say the debtor's figure and examine all the larger items before deciding if the balance sheet figure is correctly stated (i.e. not overstated). A MUS plan may give the result that out of a population size of £100,000; 60 items should be examined which are selected at intervals of £1,667.

There are **advantages** of this plan:
1. One only needs the value of the population and not the actual number or the SD.
2. The confidence level is determined by the reliability of the system of internal control.
3. High value items are always included in the sample.

There are also several **disadvantages**:
1. It is biased towards high value items that may in fact be better controlled than lower value ones.
2. No error can be defined for the population.
3. It will ignore nil value items.
4. It is only used for accept/reject decisions.
5. One needs to know the total value of the population.
6. A low confidence level will dilute the results.
7. It is a complicated technique to apply in practice.

Compliance test sampling

☐ **Attribute sampling**. One needs to set an error rate, confidence levels and precision limits. This may be a 5% error at 95% confidence plus or minus 2%. The error rate determines which statistical sampling table is used and this table will give the required sample size at a glance. When one determines the actual error rate then the precision is re-calculated for errors over the set rate. Additional error rate tables are used with the new error rate for the revised precision levels.

☐ **Stop-go sampling**. This is an incremental sampling plan that starts with smaller samples to save time once one sets an acceptable probability level. The plan assumes that all populations over 2,000 are the same. The sample will give a maximum acceptable error rate say 5% and if the actual results are higher, then further samples are taken until the results are acceptable and within the set limit.

☐ **Discovery sampling**. Discovery sampling is based on the notion of determining how many items must be examined if one has a fair chance of discovering a suspected fraud. The plan gives the sample size required to find the error and is useful for planning purposes although no conclusions may be drawn about the population itself. As with all sampling plans one must set a probability within which fall the chances of discovering the fraud with the sample size that the table provides.

16.16 Some Basic Rules for Applying Statistical Sampling

Some auditors never use statistical sampling while others have a policy of applying this technique whenever possible. External auditors are more prone to rely on mathematically based samples in deciding whether or not a financial statement is acceptable. While internal audit theory makes it clear that the use of statistical sampling is by no means mandatory, there are rules (Graham Westwood: 1990) that should be applied when deciding when it might be appropriate:

1. **Only use statistical sampling where it is appropriate**. The auditor makes a conscious decision at this stage rather than an instinctive view that it is not normally used. The audit unit should set out clear rules on the application of statistical sampling and these should be fully documented in the audit manual. Not only will this act as a source of guidance but it will also provide a mechanism by which audit management need explanation where the technique was not used when the audit manual indicates that it should be. By the same token, the rules should stop the auditor from exploring the statistical process where it is inappropriate say for smaller fields or where the population is unknown.

2. **Define and know the population**. Where the technique is applied there needs to be a formal process whereby the item that is being considered is fully researched by the auditor. This process will bring the audit to a higher level as this research will highlight what the auditor is reviewing, which in itself brings many benefits. It may well be that the act of getting to know the population (say a specific database) will bring findings relating to the quality of the information itself. If in a debtors system we could not extract the total value of debt at any one period, we may feel that the report generator may not have been properly established. Furthermore, management does not have access to high-level information fundamental to the control of the debtors system.

3. **Ensure that every item has an equal chance of selection**. Randomness is a main ingredient of statistical sampling as this supports the objective way that the technique should be applied. It is satisfying to be able to justify a sample that is selected through the principle of random selection. This can become an issue where the sample contains sensitive items that management may feel are being targeted by the auditor. Audits of payroll or personnel systems can experience this problem. It may be that the auditor is accused of missing out senior figures in the organisation or say, victimising named persons who have had some conflict with the audit service in the past. The random selection process defeats all these concerns as items are selected and examined with no in-built bias.

4. **Ensure that patterns do not affect the randomness**. The population should be capable of supporting random sampling in the way it is formed and maintained. Statistical sampling cannot fit all circumstances and this point should be fully recognised if it is to have any use at all. There are certain investigations relating to fraud, irregularity and breach of procedure where the auditor is looking for particular items and has to be very selective in the way the available information is analysed. Where the auditor wishes to inject his/her own supposition into the appraisal of data, this militates against the random methods that underpin statistical sampling.

5. **Where judgement sampling is used one may not form definite conclusions about the population**. The rules on the application of extrapolation mean, even where management is not aware of this, rough figures cannot be projected without a scientific base. Any such predictions should be qualified along the lines such as "a rough estimate of the effect of these errors on the entire system, although not statistically valid, would fall at a level of some £xyz". A formal projection would have to have a scientific base where the auditor would be able to state for example "there is a high probability that the extent of total error falls within the ranges £z to £y".

6. **Use an error rate that is reasonable**. The error rate is built into the statistical tables and is based on assumptions about the population. The required rate is based on the auditor's knowledge about this population and this should be assessed carefully.

7. **Stratify the population where this reduces variability**. We have touched upon the position where the auditor wishes to follow a certain line of enquiry, and is hindered by the need to assume a neutral stance by the use of statistical sampling. Stratification allows the auditor to profile the population in a way that suits the audit objective. If for example we are concerned about high value items in a certain system then we can divide the database and treat them to special attention by assigning a tight set of risk parameters that mean most of them are examined. The other transactions may be given less severe treatment (through the use of lower risk parameters). We can go on to suggest that low value (or low significance) matters, may be more or less ignored through the further use of stratification.

8. **Do not set needlessly high reliability goals**. There are accepted standards that reflect the general business environment. The use of 95% confidence, plus or minus 2% precision with a 5% error rate is normally sufficient to draw reasoned conclusions about the system under review and this may be used as a good starting place. The audit manual should provide suitable direction on this matter.

9. **Analyse the results carefully**. Statistical sampling is a means to an end and results must make sense and fit the audit objective. What comes out of the testing routines must make sense. One way of ensuring this happens is to keep in mind the report

format when applying any technique to promote basic questions relating to the way the resultant material contributes to the final audit opinion.

16.17 Conclusions

Testing secures material to support the audit findings and that can be of use when formulating the audit report. The results are used to confirm or not the auditor's opinion in a way that can be communicated to management. Compliance tests can be quite straightforward as long as one understands the control that is being tested. Substantive tests may pose problems. The auditor may set up as an expert in determining whether something has been successful. Care is required and the auditor should remember the overriding objective of securing adequate management action to solve real and material control weaknesses that affect the success of the operation/organisation. Working papers hold the documentation that results from the testing process which is why it is included here. The audit manual should establish standards for documenting audit work and retaining necessary information. There should be defined disposal dates for what will eventually be confidential waste. It is essential that these standards are high and contribute to the overall efficiency of the audit process. Moreover, the CIA should establish suitable reviewing mechanisms to ensure that these standards are being properly adhered to throughout the audit department. Statistical sampling is not a mandatory technique although it should not be ignored by the auditor as it can be used to comment on a system through the use of a relatively small sample. The audit department should define a clear policy on the use of this technique and where and how it should be applied, and this should appear in the audit manual. The use of automated statistical sampling via a suitable software package assists getting auditors to use statistical sampling. If judgement sampling is, in the main, being applied this should be stated as clear policy having reviewed the applicability of statistical sampling.

CHAPTER SEVENTEEN

INTERVIEWING

17.1 Introduction

Gathering information is a fundamental part of audit work as the auditor spends a great deal of time fact finding. The starting place for establishing facts is to simply ask, and herein lies the importance of interviewing. Some of the synonyms for interviewing are:

> *audience, conference, consultation, dialogue, meeting, talk, examine, interrogate, question*

We take a wider view of the concept and mean it simply to refer to "talking with" in a structured manner. The technique of interviewing should be mastered by the auditor and there is much material available on this topic that will contribute to this task. We see interviewing as a process, a task, a set structure, an audit standard and an exercise in understanding human behaviour. These components will be covered in the material below.

Types of interviews
There are many different types of interviews that the auditor will undertake and within each type there may be several different categories. One list may appear as:

☐ **Initial contact with the client**. This interview may set the whole tone of the ensuing audit and determine whether the client perceives the audit as a positive constructive matter or a basic inconvenience. The terms of reference of the audit and management's particular concerns may be defined and a clear path made for the field auditors. This interview will probably be carried out by the audit manager and/or the lead auditor. One key feature will be an attempt to explain the concept of independence to management, whereby the auditor works on its behalf but with the best interests of the organisation also firmly in mind. It is important that the promises made at this forum are followed up by the auditors who perform the work required. There is little point in having a highly skilled orator explain the audit objective, only to send trainees, who have a poor understanding of the important operational issues facing management, to perform the work.

☐ **Fact finding**. These interviews may be seen as the backbone of most audit work and will continue throughout the course of the audit. It is essential that each such interview leaves an opening for the auditor to follow up the findings and revisit the interviewee if required. One must maintain a balance between "getting the facts" and disrupting the auditees' work as these two forces will create some level of conflict. Negotiation skills and the ability to be firm while at the same time remaining diplomatic, come to the fore. Some interviews will go well while others will be less successful and this point will have to be accepted by the auditor.

☐ **General survey**. A general assessment of the main operational areas in an attempt to define those with the highest levels of risk requires talks with senior management. These interviews allow the auditor to build in the organisational and managerial needs before formal plans are published. This type of interview is a chance to listen to high-level concerns as well as marketing the audit service to an extent. One such meeting at senior management level can raise the entire profile of the audit service immensely, if done properly. We may take this opportunity to "sell" the audit product to managers who have had little or no contact with internal audit in the past.

☐ **Post-audit**. These potentially difficult interviews bring the main findings to the auditee's attention once the fieldwork has been completed. If the client has been kept informed throughout the course of the audit then we may avoid confrontational closure meetings. Our reporting standards generally mean that we should not present management with surprises in the formal audit report. As such a type of negotiation process may arise where the auditor retains the main audit points, but tones down others where the client is able to bring a new perspective to the initial audit findings. Personality factors may create a form of barrier to the effectiveness of the audit closure process if we seek to establish a win/lose position with the auditee. Again the interview should be handled with skill and care if these potential traps are to be avoided.

☐ **Audit marketing**. It is possible to interview new and existing clients solely to convey the audit role as part of a marketing strategy. Audit services may be "sold" to clients and one may enlighten managers on ways in which the wide ranging audit role may be used to improve services and performance.

☐ **Recruitment**. Audit management may be asked to perform recruitment selection interviews and these are critical to the selection and appointment of suitable new audit staff. This is dealt with elsewhere in the handbook and at this stage it should be noted that appropriate skills should be acquired and employed by the appointments panel.

☐ **Staff appraisal**. As with recruitment interviews, staff appraisals are covered as a separate topic in the handbook. Unfortunately poor appraisal schemes and lack of interviewing skills tend to undermine the entire appraisal process and in so doing demotivate staff.

☐ **Fraud**. Fraud interviews should also be very carefully planned since they are covered by the Police and Criminal Evidence Act 1984. In addition to abiding by the rules, one is also charged with securing the necessary information that may contribute to the investigation. Skill is required in these matters and a limited amount of guidance is contained in the notes below.

17.2 Structuring Interviews

Interviews are structured meetings where information is provided and obtained. The interviewee must understand what information is required and the interviewer must likewise understand the information that is being provided. It is generally advisable to structure the interview since this tends to assist the task of exchanging information. The process should involve the following key steps:

☐ **Background preparation on the subject area**. Whatever the interview it is always useful to do some background work related to the particular topic at hand. As a standard one would expect the auditor to at least consider material that has been provided to the internal audit unit. This involves reviewing files, talking to auditors who have some relevant knowledge and obtaining any previous written communications with the party in question. It is extremely embarrassing to meet with an individual who refers to correspondence that was sent to internal audit in the past, that the auditor is unaware of. The audit information systems should be capable of isolating all records of past contact with managers, and sections of the organisation. A suitable central database should be maintained by the audit administration officer that collects and indexes this information. The degree of preparation will be related to the importance of the interview. This may range from a basic internal search of the filing system (as indicated above) through to an extensive review of published material associated with the matters that will form the basis of the planned meeting. Most managers are greatly impressed by auditors who display some knowledge of the matters uppermost on management's mind.

☐ **Set convenient dates and times**. On the basis that an interview that is hurried with the constant pressure of other competing demands lowers the benefits that come from such a forum, it should be arranged properly. By this we mean that there should be sufficient notice given along with due regard for problems experienced by the auditee in finding the right time and place for the meeting. We obviously have to balance the need to complete our work promptly with the requirements of the auditee. Some leeway on our part is required if this balance is to be achieved.

☐ **Prepare checklist areas to cover**. This should entail a brief note of the areas that need to be covered as an aide-mémoire and as a way of thinking through the information gathering process beforehand. It is possible to provide this checklist to the interviewee beforehand so that any preparations may be made which will expedite the process. As a rule never list a series of detailed questions as this approach will come across as being far too mechanical in terms of reading the questions and repeating them in front of the interviewee. It also stops the auditor from using professional judgement to manage the interview process by changing the order and questions to fit the responses that are being provided by the interviewee.

☐ **Define objectives of the interview**. The next important stage is to state the precise objectives of the meeting. There are times that the auditor forgets the power of the audit right of access which forces managers to provide relevant information and explanation, as part of their managerial duties. This results in most requests from audit to attend an interview being readily accepted by managers who are aware of their special responsibilities in respect of auditor's requirements, which makes it easier to quickly convene meetings. There is nonetheless, the danger that managers are present simply because of their desire to discharge their duty and not with any belief that they may benefit from such a discussion. The act of explaining the basis of the meeting should be designed to remove this psychological barrier and allow a free flow of information in both directions. If this is not done then the level of efficiency may decline as the interviewee responds rigidly, as would someone who is forced to furnish information.

☐ **Set the tone of the interview that should normally be open, friendly and positive**. The opening comments are commonly known as "breaking the ice" and involve focusing on neutral topics such as the weather, so as to develop some form of immediate rapport. This is based to an extent on ritualistic behaviour that can indicate which social and political grouping each party belongs to, and set common standards of conduct. The point is made so as to provide a warning of some of the traps that the unwary auditor can fall into if this stage of the interview is overemphasised. To engage in idle social discussions can be very distracting for both sides to the meeting if this is not properly controlled. One might remark on general topics as a preamble to the real discussions but this should be contained as it will inevitably result in value judgements if too much depth is assumed. Seemingly harmless topics may hold a heavy political agenda; so for example a discussion on sporting events may end up in arguments about the relative attributes of cricket contrasted with football. The hidden agenda may be that one sport has a higher social status than the other (i.e. cricket is played by gentlemen). The conclusion then is that it is pointless becoming involved in discussing apparently neutral subjects as a way of setting the tone for an interview. It makes more sense to concentrate on the objectives in an informal manner and so avoid unnecessary complications. In this way it is safest to stay away from pointless social parleys.

☐ **Invite feedback on the audit objective and explain how the interview fits into the audit process**. It is one thing to state the audit objective and then break the ice with some opening remarks that show the human face of the auditor. Real progress occurs where the interviewee provides feedback by seeking further clarification where required. It is important that the auditor does not see this as a challenge to his/her position of independence but takes the view that all questions have a purpose and should be answered. If for example the auditee wishes to know why a different section with major operational problems has not been targeted for audit cover, this is a legitimate concern. The auditor must then provide a sensible answer and not just state that this is outside the terms of reference of the meeting. All legitimate questions from the interviewee should be addressed as best as possible, which is a guiding principle for positive points of contact between auditor and interviewee.

☐ **Ask the questions and direct the interviewee to the key issues without restricting the responses**. The real hard work comes in the main part of the interview. We have set the client at ease and explained clearly the purpose of the interview. We have encouraged feedback and where possible have provided explanation. This sets the tone for a good meeting of minds with full and open discussion on real matters of interest to both sides. The time then comes to secure the required information in order to progress the audit objective and it is here that the interviewer must take the initiative and maintain this throughout the interview process. As with an orchestra conductor, we must merge into the background and let the interviewee talk but at the same time direct and control the proceedings. The interview will be based mainly on encouraging the interviewee to talk and this becomes the main consideration. Talking and controlling are two different concepts but there is a link; the person who does the most talking tends to be the one who controls the discussions. We must reverse this principle by the use of techniques such as prompting and recapping that ensure the auditor is able to structure the discussions. These will be dealt with later. At this stage we must state that we can only direct and control the interview if in the process we have listened very carefully to the client. In this way we are able to fit what is being said onto the predetermined structure of the meeting. It is impossible to alter the course of a conversation in a natural manner, if we have not understood the point being made by the other party.

☐ **Run through matters dealt with during interview and clear up uncertainty**. It is frustrating to review interview records and pick out points that are unclear or ambiguous. These uncertainties should be resolved at the time that they are being discussed, i.e. during the live interview. This can be at the time a point is being made where we can ask for further clarification, so long as this does not involve constant interruption. Where there are many inconsistencies that would involve constant interjection from the interviewer, we may seek to summarise the points and so clarify these matters. There are some matters that are quite straightforward when first conveyed but clash with something that is said later. Which is why it is so important to listen carefully to what is being said. We may challenge diplomatically points as they are being made; or review our notes and pick up these conflicts towards the end of the meeting. One needs to ensure there is enough time to deal with the matters at hand and go through the notes at the end of the proceedings.

☐ **Conclude the interview with the usual courtesies**. We must retain a level of diplomacy at all times. Even where the interviewee has not been very forthcoming the auditor is expected to rise above this and remain polite to the last, which includes extending thanks at the end of the interview.

☐ **Ask for any questions**. There must be a clear stage at the end of the interview where the other party is allowed to reflect on what has been said and ask general questions. We have already said that all questions are asked for a reason and even where the auditor feels that they are immaterial, they nonetheless have to be responded to. Time should be allowed for this feedback and it should be encouraged. If for example the interviewee has no questions, we may give prompts by asking whether he/she is happy with certain of the points made, and in this way encourage a response. We do not want to leave a level of disquiet after the interview has ended.

☐ **Explain the next steps**. The last consideration is to explain clearly what will happen from here on. This should indicate the timing, who will be involved and how this fits into the overall audit process. The client is left in no doubt as to the value of the meeting and what may be reported by the interviewee to staff and other interested parties. It may be necessary to write to the interviewee and confirm points raised, although this can be a negative step that may lead to later disagreement on minor matters that detracts from the main concerns.

Based on much that we have already discussed, we may provide an outline illustration of how we might structure a typical audit interview.

FIGURE 17.1 INTERVIEW STRUCTURES

Introductions

Objectives

Questions and answers
(main part of the interview)

Wind up
(check communication)

Closure (next steps and thanks)

Explanations follow:

- **Introductions**. This involves introducing all parties present at the interview and explaining their role and position within the information gathering process.
- **Objectives**. What is hoped to be achieved from the interview is then fully communicated and further clarification provided if needs be.
- **Questions and answers**. The main body of the interview should then proceed in a way that flows naturally and promotes the achievement of the original objectives of the meeting.
- **Wind up**. The next stage is to re-check the information that has been given and any matters (such as the exchange of specific documents) that have already been agreed.
- **Closure**. An indication of next steps, further meetings and specific arrangements such as planned meetings with key staff should be given. Formal thanks (and possibly handshakes) should also be a feature of the last stage of the interview process.

17.3 Behavioural Aspects of Interviewing

What might appear a straight-forward interview may go badly wrong and leave the auditor and client confused. There are many reasons why people act in an unpredictable way which generally stems from a lack of appreciation by the auditor of the behavioural aspects of audit work. The actions of one aggressive auditor who may have left many years ago may still be foremost in many managers' minds whenever auditors call. There are many behavioural aspects that the auditor should bear in mind when conducting interviews and interviewees may possibly be asking themselves the following questions:

- What do they want from me?
- Are they human?
- Are they assessing me?
- Can I trust them?
- Should I tell them everything?
- What are they writing down?
- What about my problems?
- How can they help me?
- How will their work affect me?

- Who will be blamed if they find errors?
- Are they going to propose drastic changes?

The auditor poses a threat in terms of the potential for making changes to the working lives of everyone they meet. People generally dislike change particularly where they cannot be sure how it will affect them. Where these changes are possibly based on weaknesses that the auditor finds in the manager's area of responsibility they tend to start with negative connotations. These feelings can affect the way the interview progresses and the auditor needs to be sure that the audit objectives and how they should build into management's needs are carefully conveyed to the interviewee. The first few minutes of the interview may consist of a clear attempt by the auditor to explain the audit role and approach before a constructive dialogue may be entered into. It is also important to indicate the next steps that will be followed, after the interview is concluded. The auditor's actions must be consistent with his/her words and if he/she is seen as a spy for senior management, little or no co-operation will be received. The following records one difficult interview:

> *A senior auditor arrived at an interview with the Head of Personnel (HoP) to discuss a planned systems audit of recruitment procedures. During a strained interview the HoP made constant references to her files being available to audit at any time and she had nothing to hide. After a very difficult time, the auditor cut short the meeting and agreed to reconvene at a later date. The auditor later found that about a year ago, the HoP's files had been raided, in her presence, by a rather offensive audit manager (since left) during a fraud investigation and nothing was found. No reason for this raid was given, neither was an apology issued. At the next meeting with the HoP the senior auditor made reference to this raid. He dissociated himself from it, whereupon a more positive atmosphere reigned which resulted in progress being made on the audit.*

The mismatch between what auditors say they do and management's own understanding, can lead to fundamental conceptual problems. This has to be fought against at all times by the auditor to dispel myths, and build proper working relationships. Even where the auditor is involved in investigations into irregularity, there is still a view that the auditor is primarily examining the circumstances at issue and not the people concerned. Where a name can be fitted to a problem, then this should be a natural consequence of the proceedings and not a witch-hunt. One of the hardest challenges in the audit role is seeking to reconcile the systems and investigatory roles. We would hope that the image of the jackbooted "find the transgressor" auditor does not cross over into our main role in systems auditing and make constructive communications with management and staff impossible. Much resistance from auditees can be pre-empted by discussions on this point in a frank and open manner, so long as our actions coincide with our words.

Non-verbal communication

Non-verbal communication gives clues as to how each party to an interview really feels. We cannot say to an interviewee that we have plenty of time to discuss issues while continually checking the time and tapping the desk with a pencil. Examples of non-verbal communication include:

☐ **General body movement**. People who move around a lot are generally very busy or have nervous energy. Some people will move more when they become agitated and under pressure to make some form of decision, while others are more relaxed and give an air of command over the situation. There is not much that can be read into this as a nervous person may generate much work, while a laid back person may generate good control over a potentially chaotic situation. Medical conditions may mean the person cannot sit in one place for long, or appears to be hesitant in physical movements. Overactive glands can lead to a heightened state of readiness that may make the person appear to be over anxious, or overactive. The main point is that one must allow for many imponderables and not arrive at value judgements based on the way a person's body responds to the environment.

☐ **Eye contact**. This can be used to develop a working relationship with the interviewee. It is an oversimplification to suggest that people who cannot make eye contact have something to hide, as this ignores many other possibilities such as cultural bias and general tendencies to look elsewhere. The point about eye contact is more relevant to the auditor in reviewing their own behaviour. To this end it is generally advisable to make regular eye contact with the interviewee as this does tend to convey a feeling of openness and sincerity. At the same time excessive contact may be deemed intimidating or on the other hand, being excessively intimate, again posing a possible threat.

☐ **Physical position and posture**. The way the chairs are arranged in an interview room can impact on the proceedings and imply either a formal event or a less ceremonial attitude. Sometimes basic practical points come into play where there is no space for the interviewee to lay out working papers as this act is deemed to be the province of the auditor alone. One large chair behind a desk faced by a smaller one for the interviewee can represent the social (or working) status of the two sides to the discussions. Leaving a third person physically to one side and removed from the main proceeding can indicate that this person has less to contribute and so is isolated. Leaning back indicates boredom, withdrawal or an invitation to the other party to assume the initiative. It can also suggest that the person is in control and does not have to impose a greater physical presence on the proceedings. Leaning forward can be contrasted with this as it implies attentiveness or some anxiety. Words and actions should coincide; for example if a client says "can I tell you something in confidence?", the auditor could reinforce a co-operative stance by both leaning forward and refraining from taking notes. Much of this comes naturally and contributes to a smooth flow of information.

☐ **Touching**. This feature can be both positive and detrimental depending on how it is used. Firm handshakes tend to support a good working relationship, whilst a hand placed on the shoulder of someone sitting down can be patronising or even intimidating. Different cultures make varying use of intimate gestures such as hugging or kissing the cheek. The best approach is to assume a least offensive position, which translates to minimal contact if in any doubt.

☐ **Hand movement and facial expression.** Gesticulating with the hands is one way of getting points across and is used in most cultures where hand actions coincide with what is being said. The hand along with the face gives visual clues as to what is being said and the stress that is given to different parts of the presentation. Open hands tends to represent honesty and a drawing in, while chopping hands indicates a level of physical aggression that can be worrying if done excessively or at inappropriate moments. The auditor should watch for these clues and the idea will be to probe areas that are obviously stressed as being of concern to the interviewee.

☐ **Silences.** This can be used as an effective tool during an interview. Most people dislike silence as this creates a vacuum that they have no control over. It also focuses attention on the party that is most uncomfortable. Sometimes we may get more information on a sensitive issue by simply remaining silent as the interviewee gives guarded responses that are punctuated with constant pauses. Silences can be interpreted in many ways. They can imply that we are not satisfied with the answer and want it rephrased or that the meeting is overheating and both sides need time to re-position. If the auditor says "tell me about your role," and then sits backs in silence with pen and clipboard in hand, this may signal an important part of the interview where all is revealed. Further silences may be used to suggest that there is more to offer and encourage the interviewee to go into greater detail. Silence also underpins listening skills as one can only really take in material where the ears are in use and the mouth is resting. Silence should never be used to intimidate or manipulate the client as this will be seen as a bullying tactic, that has no place in the audit role.

Where the words spoken do not match other signals then the other party may not believe the representations and may be more willing to rely on the latter to guide them. Auditors need to check their own actions and also be sensitive to signals received from the interviewee. This is particularly relevant where certain issues need to be probed more deeply by the auditor. By the same token one should not attempt to manipulate the interviewee through an obsessive study of body talk. There is a view that we need to inject some degree of conflict into our role as auditors as this tends to support change programmes, in contrast to a cosy relationship where the status quo is maintained at all costs. Controlled aggression, annoyance and the considered use of some emotion may be seen as part of the process of challenging management to take up and resolve control issues. This approach can be used as a lead to "getting things done". However, it can have obvious disadvantages as it is based mainly on quick judgements by the auditor that do not really fit into the professional audit role. Nonetheless it does have a place particularly when dealing with people who can operate on a high stress plane (normally top management). Securing action at this level may require a less conservative mode by developing a more confrontational type environment, and non-verbal communication is a supportive device. The CIA should be involved in any decision to adopt this position.

17.4 Types of Questions

Some interviews go on for hours while others last a few moments and these two extremes do not necessarily coincide with the auditor obtaining full or limited information. The success of an interview is not only measured by length of time. Long discussions may be constructive but can result in inefficient use of time. The efficiency of interviews increases by the selective use of different types of questions. Interviewees are guided by skilful use of questioning so that material issues are expanded on while specifics are dealt with more quickly. Types of question include:

☐ **Open questions** such as "tell me about your job". There are times during an interview when we wish to give the interviewee a free hand in discussing a particular issue. It can open up a flood of material that can become uncontrollable if it is not structured at all, and in this way it should be used only where appropriate. It is best to set a scene by describing a set of circumstances and then asking the interviewee to comment on this. The answers can be structured to an extent by asking closed questions as the discussions progress, although this may involve an amount of interruption. The technique tends to stimulate a positive atmosphere on the basis that most people like to talk about their work area. If the answers become too long, or go in different directions, we may gently interrupt the proceedings by deferring specific matters for later coverage. The topics that we deal with using open questions must be related to matters that the interviewee has direct knowledge of, so that a value based opinion is not provided that delves not into facts but into pure conjecture. So we can ask questions like "tell me about your latest strategic goals", but not value questions such as "give me your views on whether the organisation treats people fairly".

☐ **Closed questions** such as "Do you work in the accounts department?" This requires a basic yes/no answer that can be recorded straight away. This is a useful way of getting precise responses to important factual questions that does not rely on judgemental material or long drawn out discussions. Name, post designation, start date, and specific factual matters can be dealt with in this way. Having said this, the extensive use of closed questions will elicit very limited information and can turn into an interrogation. It will also create a potentially confrontational mode as the interviewee is subject to a barrage of closed questions that result in the provision of substantial amounts of basic facts. It is best to use closed questions sparingly perhaps at the start of the interview and whenever we need basic detail, or need to check what has been said earlier. In general they should be avoided if we wish to develop a closer relationship and understand the real issues facing management.

☐ **Probing questions** such as "tell me more about xyz". These types of questions are used where the client starts a discussion but does not go into sufficient detail. Points raised by the interviewee can be highlighted and further details requested, as a way of directing the discussions. This requires an amount of recapping that makes the interview process longer and slightly less smooth. However it means that we get a complete picture of items important to the audit objectives. The problem arises where the auditor probes certain areas that the client is not comfortable with. Some people purposely avoid issues that they feel can leave them open to criticism. In this environment the auditor may find a reluctance to address these particular topics even where there is some probing. Rephrasing the question is another way of returning to a defined topic as will reviewing what has been said. At the end of the day it is difficult to get someone to talk about a topic that they wish to avoid without injecting some conflict into the occasion. It is here where interview skills should come to the fore through a mixture of gentle persuasion and firm perseverance. There is a need to achieve a fine balance between the auditor's right to information and explanations whilst recognising that we cannot really force people to talk openly.

☐ **Confirmatory questions** such as "Your job description refers to xyz, is this correct?" Compliance auditing recognises the realities of business life and the fact that not everything is always as it should be. Furthermore there are times when we need to double-check an assumption or official position as a way of getting to the truth. It is within this context that we will seek to confirm our understanding of events, systems, processes, circumstances and whatever else we have to research in the course of our work. The ability to re-check matters in a factual manner without causing offence, is useful where we need to obtain reliable information. Again we need to avoid the interrogation stance which is why the use of this approach should really be restricted.

☐ **Clarification** along the lines of "I thought you said that you worked for Mr. X?" when the interviewee has just contradicted himself. We are fast moving into the territory of manipulation where the auditor tries to squeeze otherwise classified information from a third party. Where there is an obvious inconsistency between the detail that is being provided it is best to place this problem directly in front of the interviewee and seek an explanation. There may be a straightforward reason for this and the opportunity to explain should always be provided. Where there is not then we will still need to obtain clarification as our record of the meeting will not be acceptable, if gaps and conflicts remained unresolved. Again the most efficient method of solving these "mysteries" is to simply ask.

In general one should not use the following types of questions:

☐ **Leading questions** such as "surely you check these invoices before approving them?" This category of question encourages a predefined response that has been invited or hinted at, whilst the interviewee tends to feel obliged to provide the acceptable answer. The problem is that it does not fit with the search for the truth, which is the main aim of the interview. In this way we can more or less ban the use of leading questions as a generally acceptable practice.

☐ **Loaded questions** such as "You appear to be more qualified than your boss". This incorporates a degree of emotion by being directed at a "soft spot". Some may feel that it will get the other party on the side of the auditor by implying a position that sides with them in favour of another outside party. Playing politics has no place in audit policy, not in terms of its usefulness but more in terms of the danger that comes with not saying what you mean or meaning what you say. Audit policy should rule loaded questions generally out of bounds.

☐ **Trick questions** along the lines "You say that you have worked here for three and a half years; what date did you start?" The auditor may appear to be clever by playing a game of "one-up-manship". This involves keeping one step ahead in terms of general knowledge and usually hiding certain pieces of information so as to rely on this extra insight for use at a later stage. There are many implications of taking a stance along these lines which have no place in the audit role. As with the other approaches there is little point in retaining the use of trick questions as part of audit standards on interviewing.

One principle that should be applied is that constant feedback should be obtained throughout the interview and matters double checked as far as possible. For more formal occasions the interviewee should be asked to comment on the documented interview record at the close of the meeting.

17.5 Conduct During an Interview

Auditors carry out interviews many times and tend to acquire the necessary skills as their level of experience increases. There are several points regarding how audit interviews are conducted that should be noted:

1. The interview should be planned. The tendency to rush headfirst into interviews should be dealt with by ensuring that the concept of defining a plan within which the interview will fall should be part of the conduct expected by audit management from their staff.

2. Auditors should familiarise themselves with the area under review. It is a necessary part of the preparation process and helps raise the auditor's credibility. It also means that answers can be understood and evaluated much more readily.

3. A structure should be aimed at so that there is introduction, fact-finding and winding-up. This involves formal introductions, getting the required information and explaining what happens next.

4. Observe the requirements of the auditor's code of conduct. Superimposed over the detailed code of conduct covering interviews, we have the general auditor code of conduct that also covers the way auditors interface with others during the course of their work. Basic rules on politeness, diplomacy and offensive behaviour should be firmly in place and apply to the interview situation as well as other points of contact with colleagues, clients, and members of the public.

5. Break the ice when starting the interview since a formal mode once entered into will probably be maintained throughout the interview. We would expect auditors to assume a working relationship with people they deal with in an interview situation. The world of internal auditing is becoming aware that the key to professional auditing lies in effective communication skills. Clearly, there is little room left for the auditor who is unable to develop the personal presentation skills so necessary to the art of successful communication. The days where the cold, obnoxious auditor, who is disliked by all he meets is allowed to remain in employment, are fast coming to an end.

6. Formally conclude the interview and do not leave any unresolved matters. Very often people meet, agree many things, and then depart without achieving anything in real terms. Many months later all that has been promised falls into a blurred memory with the passing of time. We expect auditors to avoid this unsatisfactory position by requiring them to tie up loose ends and ensure there is a proper conclusion to all that has been formally agreed.

7. Try to avoid making statements or giving opinions since although they might make the interview more interesting, they may be perceived as formal audit comment. They also tend to be based on an incomplete picture of the areas under review. Jumping to conclusions and/or providing the solve-all answers to complicated problems that have

not been researched to any extent, is a basic flaw exhibited by most new auditors. To allow such behaviour is unfair to the client, who cannot be sure whether a formal audit opinion is being given. It is also unfair to the auditor who assumes a know-it-all stance that defeats the audit objective in that conclusions are drawn without any supportive evidence or proper research. Fortunately, as we have suggested, this defect is found mainly in people new to the audit arena and not the more experienced audit professional.

8. Formulate specific objectives for the interview. Meetings and interviews are often held as a way of getting to know people who may have been mainly dealt with over the telephone. These face to face discussions may not have any real purpose as hours go by and an assortment of unrelated issues are chewed over by both sides to the conversation. To avoid this loss of time, we must set clear objectives for the interview and ensure that the checklist of areas to cover (drafted beforehand) reflects this objective. It is surprising how often an interview is brought back into focus by the technique of referring back to the original objectives, so that unrelated points can be side-lined before the direction of the discussions changes permanently.

9. Use negotiation skills where necessary. This means that one defines which points may be given up and which have to be preserved beforehand so that some flexibility can be assumed during the interview. A win-win position encourages each side to get something from the event and this can only be good in terms of its impact (perhaps we can call this a "feel good factor"). Giving ground is one way of arriving at this position and as such should be built into the code of conduct for interviews. The converse, where the auditor stands his/her ground in a rigid manner, oblivious to all that is being said, generates the opposite effect. This again can be addressed in a suitable code by making this approach generally unacceptable.

10. Ensure that audit brochures are available for the interviewee. It is important that the definitions and detail that appear in any brochure coincide with explanations provided during the interview. It is bad practice to force brochures on persons whom we come into contact with, as this engenders a feeling of "hard sell". Where it is appropriate, in that there is a request for further information expressed during an interview, then a suitable brochure will provide a positive response without going into too many details that detract from the real aims of the meeting. It also means that material put in front of the other party will have been carefully considered and planned by senior audit management.

11. One should list all the items that are not immediately available but have been requested by the auditor and this list should be checked at the end of the interview. This device saves time in the long run as it ensures a complete list of outstanding material.

12. Explain the purpose of note-taking and ensure that the notes reflect the information received. It is simple good manners to explain why one is writing all that is being said in an environment where this may not be the accepted norm.

13. Watch the human relations aspects and body movement. A suitable code of conduct will not allow the auditor to continue an interview where the other party is obviously distressed.

Above all listen, listen and listen. It is hard to set a standard on this but we must demand that our auditors have mastered the fundamental skill of being able to concentrate not on what they are saying (or plan to say) but more importantly on what is being said to them.

The significance is such that, if audit management is not able to train their staff in this skill, then these staff should be released and new people recruited.

17.6 Barriers to Good Interviews

Much can go wrong with an audit interview:

Guarded responses from the interviewee can give incomplete information. This may occur where there is mistrust between auditor and auditee. Explaining the purpose of the interview along with the use of open questions can help shift the interviewee's position. Probing questions can help so long as a working relationship has been established which allows the free flow of information between the two sides. A guarded response may create a reaction from the auditor that leads to a confrontation as the auditor becomes more insistent that all questions are fully answered. This elicits a greater defence from the interviewee and we approach the stage where the interview breaks down. The correct approach is to seek to understand why the interviewee is worried about giving complete information. We may then break down this barrier by explanation and probe points that need to be explored.

Poor timing can result in the interviewee being too busy to spend much time on each audit question. Most managers try to squeeze an interview into a busy work schedule and this can interfere with the free flow of information. The real-life practicalities of the working environment make this a norm rather than an exception that must be appreciated by the auditor. The key here is to base the discussions on the benefits that accrue from the interview, which in the main will be associated with an audit. Managers will assign time to matters that fit with their objectives and provide defined benefits for them. The fact that it is management who is responsible for installing and maintaining systems of internal control can be used to stress the need for audit cover. It will help generate the view that time spent assisting audit in this matter, provides good value for money. The auditor does not have to "sell" the audit service by the use of gimmicks and free gifts, but there is nonetheless a need to achieve support from management and the organisation generally. Actions must fit in with representations and the auditor cannot explain the importance of management spending time in audit interviews while engaging in idle conversation during these meetings. To this end the structure of the interview and the way it is managed should be designed to ensure it is an efficient use of time (for both sides). The onus is on audit to manage the time properly where the interview has been convened at the request of internal audit.

Defensiveness can result where the auditor poses a threat. A guarded response means that the client provides information that is politically acceptable while not necessarily addressing all relevant matters. Defensiveness is more proactive in that the interviewee will purposely seek to protect their position in the face of a perceived threat from the auditor. We have discussed the potential conflict between systems work and special investigations and this makes it difficult to reconcile the two approaches of policeman/advisor. This conflict can interfere with the interview process where audit's power to initiate proceedings that could end up with an officer being dismissed, does not allow a free flow of views. The worst case arises where the manager feels that audit is hiding behind the systems audit cover, to disguise the fact that they are actually investigating the manager. A study of the behavioural aspect of auditing that was discussed in part one will assist the auditor in managing this situation.

Personality clashes spoil the whole interview process. The first few seconds of contact between two people are crucial in that they will make fundamental conclusions about each other. These conclusions will be set and whatever happens next will be interpreted within the framework of these initial views. Some suggest that there is chemistry that interacts between two individuals that has an unknown quality. A further barrier to good interviews is a clash of personality where a win-lose position is assumed by both sides. The actual matters for discussion fall into the background against this "battle of minds" that is a feature of this type of situation. Auditors are bound by a strict code of conduct which bans them from engaging in heated argument and accusation and this is the first principle that should be applied. There is obviously the usual standard where we would seek to assume a working relationship and concentrate on the issues at hand and this must be explored as a possible solution. In the final analysis where there is an unresolvable clash of views with no logical basis, the auditor will have to withdraw from the interview and seek another way of getting the required information. This may be done by a more senior auditor, or through correspondence. If the interviewee fails to co-operate despite all efforts from internal audit then we would seek to have the matter resolved at a higher level. We can accept a personality clash with one particular auditor but not a general inability of an auditee to respond to legitimate audit enquiries.

If the auditor insists on jumping to conclusions, this may turn the meeting into a farce. If we turn the interview into a "who knows best?" battle, then little constructive work will be completed. These snap evaluations are sometimes made by an auditor as a short-cut to doing the necessary detailed audit work, which may destroy the credibility of the entire audit process. The auditor is there to secure relevant information and after having completed the necessary research, will furnish a suitable audit report. A know-it-all attitude by the auditor can also lower the quality of the interview. Here the auditor should realise that they can never know as much as the manager who actually runs the area under review. This task is easier if auditors remember that they are experts in control not operations. It is not the auditor's duty to second-guess management or show that audit knows more than managers about a particular work area. It is up to audit management to stop auditors who exhibit this disturbing trait.

Poor listening by the auditor will frustrate the interviewee. The client will sense lapses by the auditor particularly where the questions show a misunderstanding of what has been said earlier. It is a precise skill to alter the tone, content, and order of questions in line with information that is steadily provided during an interview. This skill depends wholly on the auditor having listened very carefully to the other party so that the required adjustments may be made as the interview progresses. Where the auditor is unable to take a back seat and listen, this proactive approach to information gathering will be impaired.

A general air of mistrust can result in constant checking and re-checking by the auditor and the conversation may eventually deteriorate. We have suggested that the auditor seeks confirmation of what has been said without using "trick questions". This is the correct approach but can become annoying if handled badly. Going over notes and re-checking everything can give the client the impression that they are not trusted by the auditor. It can be perceived as a trick question in that it may appear as if the auditor is looking for inconsistencies or encouraging the interviewee to change their mind as if the truth was not given earlier. Much is a matter of diplomacy and tact. The auditor can defeat this potential barrier by making it clear at the outset (along with explanation) that this device of re-checking what has been said, will be applied.

Polarisation may appear where the two parties take firm opposing views and place all issues within this narrow criterion of right or wrong. Working relationships may break down where this persists. Personality clashes result in differences that have no logical basis, whilst legitimate differences in opinion occur often without creating any real difficulty for the parties involved. In fact a healthy debate can result where we impart an honest belief in our position say in respect of the importance of good controls. The barrier arises where we cannot accept that there are different views that can each be respected. A "child-like state" makes a view right or wrong, and the person giving the view right or wrong (i.e. good or bad). Where this position is entrenched, we arrive at polarisation where everything the other party supports is classified as wrong. Without going into detail the simple solution to this is to assume a mature position (in contrast to childish) and ensure that all discussions are made on this level.

A poor reputation by auditors may lead the interviewee to take a flippant view of the audit process. The auditor is both a person and a representative of internal audit. Anything said or reported by internal audit has been done so in the name of the CIA. We cannot argue that an earlier encounter with an unprofessional auditor has nothing to do with us. We can overcome the poor reputation by an approach that is obviously based on high professional standards of work and objectivity.

Information overload results in one or both parties being unable to keep up with the information exchange and if the auditor does not own up and seek clarification much detail will be missed. Technical jargon is generally used to mislead. In practice, all matters can be conveyed in an understandable form as long as each party has been open and appreciates each other's level of knowledge on the subject discussed. Everything cannot be covered during one meeting particularly where the interviewee insists on going into great levels of detail. As such a common-sense approach must be assumed where general matters are dealt with first and specifics left for another occasion when the auditor has more knowledge of the systems under review. The other side of the coin is where the auditor is giving details of the audit performed and there is only so much detail that can be digested at any one session. Oral presentations using visual aids and handouts may replace the formal interview forum where it is important that complicated concepts are conveyed and understood. Most people switch off where great masses of data are thrown at them with no structure or order. These matters should be addressed before the interview is set up.

Noise occurs where external factors interfere with communication and this ranges from distorted perceptions through to low-flying aircraft. There are many times when it is best to remove someone from their work area to an environment that is controlled to ensure the effective exchange of information. The main disadvantage is the lack of ready access to relevant files and systems for demonstration purposes. This is along with the danger in removing the auditor from the work environment that may give many clues to control issues. One solution is to do an initial meeting away from the office and later more detailed discussions at the work place. Much depends on the objectives of the interview.

Unclear ideas lead to confusing thoughts being conveyed which will be difficult for the recipient to digest. This occurs where for example the auditor has a poor grasp of the issues that management faces or feel it is their duty to superimpose an artificial audit view on management that has not been well thought-out. Since the interview involves an exchange of information based around a structured series of questions, there is a need for common ground through which such a process should operate. Where this common ground is impaired by obscure ideas there will be a weaker structure through which the exchange of information can occur. Unclear ideas usually result from the auditor assuming an understanding that is not really there. It arises from a false sense of higher knowledge that the person in question feels they should possess. There is no real answer to this problem outside the need to base one's views on professional, well-researched audit work. Honesty is another important consideration based on the fact that there is nothing wrong with making it clear that the auditor has a limited amount of knowledge on the topic under consideration. Honesty also appears where the auditor admits that he/she cannot solve all problems that confront management. Bearing this in mind, the auditor may convene a useful discussion where each side has a clear understanding of the knowledge base of the other.

Language problems may arise where accents, terminology and speech patterns interfere with the information exchange. Constant feedback will be required to clarify any uncertainty. It is also the case that one quickly becomes used to accents as the conversation progresses. Tact and diplomacy should be fully applied in this situation along with a level of openness in explaining any difficulties, rather than a pretence of understanding with a view to saving embarrassment. Where language is a real problem, then the process of assigning a suitable auditor to the project should include a consideration of these concerns. It may also be wise to send two auditors to the interview on the basis that a joint effort in interpreting the interviewee may bring better rewards.

The auditor's perceptions and own personal bias may distort an interview. This is very dangerous ground and the auditor's independence, which is the cornerstone of the audit function, depends on objectivity of mind. It is only the professional auditor who can recognise and then rise above their personal views and bias, with a view to discharging the audit objective.

Where an interview is obviously not working it is generally better to cut short the meeting before it actually breaks down, and think of adopting a new strategy to secure the necessary information.

17.7 Fraud Interviews

Fraud interviews are based on the same underlying principles of exchanging information. There are special features dealt with in the chapter on fraud which are reproduced here in outline:

- The auditor is under a duty to take special care and secure as much relevant information as possible.
- The arrangements may be covered by legislation.
- The interview record may constitute a formal statement that may be read out in a court of law.
- The interview record may be formally submitted to the police.
- The matters dealt with in a fraud interview tend to be highly sensitive.

During a typical fraud investigation there may be three main types of interviews:
1. Informal background interviews that form part of the general fact-finding stage.
2. Formal witness interviews where an employee or member of the public may provide a statement on specific matters that form the basis of the investigation and provide evidence upon which to base a criminal prosecution.

3. Formal interviews of the possible perpetrator of the fraud where the allegations are clearly laid out and explanations sought.

Unexpected problems can arise during a fraud interview:

> *Two auditors interviewed a young woman whose mother worked for the organisation. The daughter was living in a house that belonged to her mother, now living elsewhere. She was claiming housing benefits on the basis she had no relationship with the landlady. During the interview the daughter claimed she paid rent to the landlady. After half an hour the auditor put the interview record to one side and said. "Let's start again with the truth". The interviewee started crying and was given tea and a tissue. A formal caution was applied and truthful answers provided and recorded. The interviewee refused to sign the interview record which was signed by the auditors.*

A confession is useful in that it can complete an enquiry by pointing straight to the perpetrators of a fraud or irregularity. Emphasis is now firmly placed on the evidence accumulated during an investigation. Whereas the interview is used to clarify any inconsistent points and seek explanations, and not to extract a confession. Each interview should be carefully planned and devised to provide the required information with the general approach being to give the interviewee an opportunity to impart full information. It is essential that the auditor does not intimidate, oppress or negotiate with the subject where this is the alleged perpetrator. We have agreed that the interview objective must be to seek clarification and not entrap. These types of interviews should normally be carried out in pairs. Further guidance on fraud interviews is found in the chapter on fraud investigations.

17.8 Standardised Procedures

IIA standard 500 requires the Chief Internal Auditor to establish written policies and procedures to direct the auditor's work and the audit manual should include a section on interview procedures. The procedures should cover these areas:

1. The level of preparation required and the type of matters that should be considered before the interview is held. A standardised checklist may be used to cover most of the key areas, bearing in mind many items may not be applicable depending on the type of interview that is being dealt with.
2. The way audit objectives are established for the interview. These should be formally set as a way of maintaining a clear direction over the process and not wasting time. The extent to which these objectives have been achieved may be documented after the event as part of auditing standards.
3. The various forms that should be used to document the interview. These will record the information that has been provided and also allows a review by the audit manager at a later date.

4. The way notes are maintained and checked with the interviewee before the meeting is concluded. Setting this process as a standard makes it a requirement to ensure that the notes are a fair representation of what has been said.

5. The fact that summaries of the interview should be included so that one need not re-read the entire record to appreciate the main issues. A front sheet may provide for a summary of the interview that lists the key points and the implications of the representations that have been made. This acts as a major convenience, particularly where the interview has taken a long time and covered much ground.

6. The way that representations should be verified by the auditor. We should seek to set standards on ways that information can be checked before it is deemed reportable. One useful technique is to secure copies of key documents that have been referred to by the interviewee. For example if we have been told by a manager that he sent a memorandum to staff instructing them not to install unofficial software onto their computers, we may ask for a copy of this document. This will then be attached to the interview record.

7. The way that outstanding documents referred to during the interview may be followed up. We would have to establish a standard on following up matters that had been promised during an interview and the review process should include a consideration of outstanding items.

8. Procedures for ensuring that excessive time is not spent in interviews. Even where we are in direct discussions with officers and others, this is not necessarily a good use of audit time. It still has to be justified as time charged to the job in hand. Procedures should require the auditor "to ensure that all interviews constitute an efficient use of time and contribute directly to the achievement of audit objectives". This would then be a consideration during the review process.

9. The way interview notes are reviewed by audit management. Any checklist for reviewing audit files should include the interview records. The usual problem is either there are no records of interviews with officers or there is a rough note that is very difficult to decipher after the event. Some auditors go to the other extreme and spend hours typing their notes when a carefully made hand written record on standardised documentation would have sufficed.

10. The way facts obtained in interviews are quoted in audit reports. Audit standards should cover this point so that any mention made of matters obtained from an interview is properly presented. Reporting devices such as "management has indicated that..." or, "we were advised that..." or, "the figure quoted by management is... although we have not been able to verify this in any way..." We must make an accurate account of the status of information that may be derived from a passing comment by a manager. This contrasts with a formal audit testing process from independently confirmed sources.

11. The way adverse reactions from the auditee may be dealt with. We have mentioned the possibility of a breakdown in relationships and here we suggest that formal standards should be in place to cater for auditor conduct where proceedings may otherwise become heated.

12. How to deal with an interviewee who appears to be withholding information or refuses to provide vital material. The auditor will probe, diplomatically repeat requests and restate any concerns about a lack of information forthcoming from the interviewee. Where these devices fail then standards will indicate next steps that should include referral to audit management, specific written requests, complaints to the interviewee's

line manager, and so on. The auditor will be expected to follow whatever has been established as the prescribed procedure in this case.

There should be clear policies on audit protocol covering the way auditors explain their role and conduct themselves. This should start with the wide privileges granted to the auditor and the need to avoid abusing this. These rules must apply even where the client adopts a less diplomatic stance. Furthermore a formal complaints procedure should be installed to pick up any problems resulting from the interview process. Standardised Forms 091 to 094 can be used to plan and document interviews (see diskette).

Recording the interview
It is good practice to record all interviews as part of auditing standards. What at first may seem to be bureaucracy in its purest sense does have an underlying reason so long as there are rules based on the sensible application of this requirement. Some of these rules are:
1. Apply different standards to different types of interview. Some may be limited notes on key points on one sheet of paper. Other more formal interviews may be fully recorded verbatim. It will depend on the circumstances although we should expect some form of record for all interviews.
2. Ensure that signatures applied are appropriate to the circumstances. Again this will depend on the circumstances as formal interviews may be fully signed and witnessed while others may not be signed by the interviewee but simply checked for accuracy then filed.
3. Provide a front summary sheet that contains objectives, results and conclusions that can be reviewed by the audit manager.
4. Use standardised documentation for all interview records. Remember different interviews will require different standards and we should have a batch of each type in our possession.
5. Type the record where necessary whilst retaining the original. This applies to formal interviews that may end up in court or at a disciplinary hearing or a forum involving an external review.
6. Retain documents referred to in the interviews with the record cross-referenced to the point where they are introduced by the interviewee.
7. Apply the usual standards of place, date, time, people present, audit job and reviewed by. Page numbering along the line page 1 of 5, 2 of 5 etc. ensures that documents are complete. It should be clear (from initials placed in the margin) exactly who said what during the interview.
8. Re-read notes for sense. We can apply the "six months later rule" and ensure that the record is understandable in six months time when the auditor may have left.

17.9 Conclusions

Interviewing is widely used to secure audit information. Interviews intrude into the interviewee's world and may be resisted or encouraged depending on the relationship established. Experienced auditors set up interviews and secure information in an efficient and effective manner. The interview is a two-way process and the auditor must convey audit objectives clearly and convincingly. There are many barriers to good interviews and these should be recognised and carefully managed with the aid of a comprehensive audit manual and training workshops.

CHAPTER EIGHTEEN

AUDIT REPORTING

18.1 Introduction
Some auditors argue that the audit report is the fundamental end-product of any audit and IIA standard 430 says that auditors should report the results of their audit work. In reality the impact of the audit should be the actual changes that are created as a result of the investment of audit resources and here the report forms just part of this process. Whatever the view, the fact is that audit reporting is one of those fundamental techniques that must be mastered by the auditor. There are many components and principles that underlie audit reporting, the most important of which is the quality of audit work that has been carried out prior to the reporting stage.

18.2 Types of Reports
Auditors are involved in many different types of report:

Annual audit reports
This annual report to the organisation may be presented to the audit committee and will have two main components. It should set out and discuss the audit achievements according to the annual plan. In addition it should provide a summary of key areas tackled and any material control issues that will affect the organisation but remain unresolved. In this respect, it acts not only as a control over the performance of internal audit but also as a major control over the entire organisation. This latter attribute means that major control issues that have not been adequately addressed will be isolated and brought to the attention of senior management of the organisation. Accordingly this should be used with great care since it represents the ultimate fail-safe mechanism where all other efforts to get the audit message across have failed. As well as the general areas that will be discussed, there might also have been specific failings that will be highlighted for action.

Quarterly audit reports
This is a more detailed version of the annual report and one would expect that most matters in the quarterly plan will have been dealt with. Accompanying statistics on chargeable hours and productivity should also be published and it is good practice to indicate how much each completed audit costs in terms of hours charged (times hourly rate). This is more a control over the audit function than a reflective statement on organisational controls that is a feature of the annual report. Again quarterly reports should be linked to the underlying plans. The current economic environment makes it much more difficult to plan and as such the quarterly period has greater significance than the annual one. An efficient auditor time monitoring system should provide information that can be incorporated directly into the quarterly report.

Monthly progress reports

Some chief internal auditors require a monthly progress report setting out the status of each main audit and this may be followed up by progress meetings to deal with potential delays and inefficiencies. This can be an important control that enables the CIA to keep tabs on audit work paying particular attention to aborted audits or those that appear to be in progress for an unduly long period. Suspended work creates additional problems and it is not advisable to have projects that are dealt with on a continuing stop-start basis. It is more difficult to find excuses on a monthly basis in contrast to the quarterly report where inefficiencies may be hidden by excessive details of completed audits. This monthly snapshot can expose problems and has a further advantage in that it can greatly assist resource re-scheduling where required. Armed with a monthly account of progress, the CIA may take comfort in the way that audit managers are deploying their resources.

Preliminary survey reports

Before formal terms of reference can be formulated and planned hours defined, we have to do an amount of background work. This is called a preliminary survey and the work should result in a preliminary survey report (PSR). Appendices to this report should include a draft assignment plan, audit approach and audit objectives. The PSR itself should be concise and normally not more than two pages long. This will allow the audit manager to formulate an assignment plan. Whilst the report itself cannot contain findings in terms of evidence of control weaknesses, it may outline "suppositions" which may be described as potential control weaknesses.

Interim audit reports

Before the full audit report is produced one would expect interim reports particularly on larger projects. These have three main uses:

It forces the auditor to build the report as work is progressed. As such the findings are fresh in the auditor's mind as they appear and are captured in written format. This allows a greater link between the audit report and underlying work that is being carried out by the auditor. Furthermore it should be possible to complete a draft audit report quite soon after the fieldwork is finished and not have to wait unduly long periods for the report to be made available.

It keeps the audit manager up-to-date and allows interim reviews of work performed. If the audit has to be aborted or suspended for any reason, then it is possible to report the results to date very quickly. This will act as a position statement that may be picked up again when the audit is being resumed. The worst case scenario occurs where the auditor introduces the audit to managers and heightens their expectations, carries out detailed audit work and after several weeks appears to disappear completely. Just when the managers have forgotten the audit, a draft report appears on their desk that contains many surprises. The correct model is where the auditor briefs management at the end of each week on findings to date and general progress on the audit. This is where the interim report comes to the auditor's aid as a useful communication device.

In this way it may be given to the client and so act as a continuous report clearance device as well as bringing the client into the audit process itself. Furthermore, it is possible to produce the final draft shortly after conclusion of the fieldwork. This approach will also allow audit to comply with the IIA reporting standards that suggest that nothing in the report should come as a surprise to management.

Audit assignment reports
This is what most auditors think of when considering the topic of audit reports and it is dealt with in some detail below.

Executive summaries
A two or three page summary can be attached to the front of the report or issued as a separate document. It provides a concise account of objectives, main conclusions and the steps that management should be taking. This recognises that managers are busy and wish to take a short-cut in getting to grips with any material issues that may result from an audit.

Follow-up reports
All audit work should be followed up and it is possible to establish a standardised reporting format to check on outstanding audit recommendations. These audits tend to be simple to perform but sensitive in nature. They involve forming a view on whether management has done all it promised to. It may be necessary to criticise management where it has failed to implement agreed recommendations while at the same time maintaining a degree of diplomacy. It is necessary to weigh up all excuses for a lack of action before deciding whether management has acted reasonably.

Fraud investigation reports
These reports detail the allegations, the work carried out and why, as well as the main findings. It is extremely frustrating to pick up a file on a fraud investigation and see no concluding audit report covering the case. This is a mistake that many auditors make and the audit standard that requires us to report the results of audits, applies equally to all types of work.

Oral reports
Auditors are charged with reporting the results of audit work and this may be in an oral format. Oral reports are designed to save time and can have a more direct impact on the recipient. They also allow the auditee to provide instant feedback to the lead auditor.

Staff appraisal reports
All auditors should have on file appraisal reports and these should flow from the performance appraisal scheme. It is generally advisable to link these reviews into individual development programmes. The audit manager will draft this report after discussions with the auditor in question.

18.3 Activity Reports
Activity reports are produced periodically by the CIA to formally report the activities of the internal audit department. These would typically go to the audit committee and may be based around an annual report and four separate quarterly reports.

Quarterly reporting cycle
The quarterly reports will tend to include:

☐ **Planning and control matters for the audit department**. This will explain whether there are issues and developments that affect the scope and effectiveness of the audit function now and in the near future. This may be seen as a form of self-audit and if an internal or external review of audit has been completed then this will also feature in the quarterly report.

☐ **An outline of audit's performance for the quarter**. This provides results of performance indicators that measure quality and quantity of audit work. These indicators include:
- Level of recoverable work.
- Number of reports issued.
- Number of audits within budget.

☐ **Statistics on types of work performed and departments charged** which will indicate the work that has been performed over each main Department/Section. These figures can be compared to planned profiles as a way of gauging the success and viability of the audit function. We would also expect statistical analysis to be carried out over periods as well as between components (e.g. types of work).

☐ **Brief summary of reports issued**. A brief account of the conclusions from final cleared reports may be provided for information. It may be possible to enclose the executive summaries of these reports as appendices to the quarterly audit report. The audit committee may take action where there are matters that remain unresolved arising from audits that have been carried out. However it should be noted that audit credibility may be damaged where we have "cried wolf" too often.

☐ **Details of staff turnover**. Information concerning starters, leavers, training programmes and exam success, transfers and any skills' gaps should be included since it may have a direct impact on the audit plans. Where additional resources are required to cover audit plans then this should be discussed before a formal bid is submitted via the agreed mechanism.

☐ **Overall productivity per output within time budgets**. This will be based on achieving the quarterly plan, the monthly plan and the requirements of the assignment plan. As such actuals will be set against plan and conclusions drawn about any variances that are so highlighted. Managerial concerns such as budget overruns, excessive unrecoverable time, and incomplete audits will have to be fully explained in the quarterly report, which will act as a high-level control over the audit function.

Annual reporting cycle

As well as recording the work carried out over the last year, reference will be made to the annual plan that will also be submitted for the coming year. As auditors we will be aware that reports can act as key controls so long as they are linked to a reference point in terms of expectations, that is, a form of plan. There is a timing problem in that the planning period will start before the report can be available and this gap has to be dealt with through interim measures. The main point is that the report will discuss the control problems of the organisation, while the plan will seek to address any continuing disorder.

The current audit strategy and how far audit plans, based on this strategy, have been accomplished will therefore be a feature of the report.

☐ **The annual report must be received by the highest levels of the organisation, ideally a suitably constituted audit committee**. We have argued that the annual audit report is the final device that ensures that audit's findings are published to the organisation. The problem arises where the report falls on deaf ears and is not properly dealt with by the organisation. The main safeguard is to ensure that it is received at the highest possible level in the organisation as a point of principle.

☐ **All comments relating to particular audits should be based on final audit reports i.e. not uncleared drafts that management has not yet been able to respond to**. There are several dangers if this factor is ignored. It is tempting to get newly drafted reports to the audit committee as a way of boosting the number of reportable items (which will tend to imply an increase in performance of the audit unit). Uncleared reports represent audit views that have not been answered by the people who are responsible for what is being reported. This is a fundamental point of principle designed to be fair for both sides which should be properly observed.

☐ **Where the annual reporting period has expired then the current position must be available in outline to members of the audit committee so that the information that is provided is up-to-date**. The technical fact that the formal reporting period relates to a date several months old should not prevent the CIA from providing a current position to the audit committee. This is because it can be frustrating for the organisation to dwell on the past when new problems are uppermost on their minds. The rush to get new data just before the relevant audit committee meeting should act as an inspiration to all audit staff, notwithstanding the additional stress that this might create.

☐ **Performance data covering internal audit should be based around comparing actual results to planned targets**. This should be presented in a suitable statistical table that encourages relevant questions from the audit committee. We need to "come clean" on audit's performance over the year in question. This will not be on a detailed level that is a feature of the quarterly audit report but must still indicate the general direction of the audit function based around defined expectations.

☐ **A view on the overall state of organisational controls (possibly over the five key control areas) should be expressed along with the main implications of any material weaknesses and how these might then be tackled**. We have an opportunity to paint a blanket picture of the control environment that can be understood by top management. This should be in the form of general statements in a suitable paragraph that has been carefully highlighted in the report. It should fall in line with the auditors' professional obligation to deliver a formal opinion derived from the detailed work undertaken within the organisation. Nothing short of this will suffice.

☐ **A suitable format for the annual report should be decided beforehand**. It is as well not to complicate issues by including an abundance of detail that will make the report unnecessarily long and possibly unreadable. The needs and demands of the audience should be firmly kept in mind when deciding the adopted approach. We must also consider the marketing angle where a hint of professional presentation will always be well received by the committees.

☐ **The annual report will be formed more at an overview level.** Some very poor reports appear to make global statements derived from basic management theory whilst quoting a stream of minor matters that have very little significance to senior management at all. Missing invoices are mentioned in the same sentence as major conclusions about controls generally in the organisation, which is a big mistake. We are only entitled to comment on important matters where work has been done at the same level or we risk an impaired credibility. Hopefully, we will have completed major reviews during the year to enable a sensible conclusion to be reported. If this is not the case we must go back to basic principles, and ask why this is not happening.

☐ **Problem areas encountered over the year**. This may be in terms of access to information, formulating audit plans and keeping up with developments within the organisation. We may have to use the powers of the audit committee to provide what in the final analysis will be a complaint that is brought to the attention of the organisation. Problems securing information (for example downloads of sensitive databases such as Personnel) should be brought before the audit committee as a way of stimulating discussions on resolving these concerns. Specific matters will have been dealt with at an earlier stage as problems arise. General problems such as a tendency for managers to fail to implement audit recommendations must also be exposed, if there has been no success resolving this difficulty beforehand. We would obviously use this technique carefully but it can be a powerful aid to the auditor where all else fails.

☐ **Pensive thoughts on the current state of the audit function and barriers to good performance**. All foreseeable barriers should be broken down by setting out ways that they may be dealt with. We would conclude with a look forward to the coming year in terms of the problems that the organisation faces and how the proposed audit strategy will take on board and deal with relevant control issues.

These reports may well help determine the level of support that audit receives and whether the internal audit function survives in times of budgetary constraint. They also remove the mystique behind audit and make it quite clear that, like all other functions, internal audit is also accountable for their resources and actions.

18.4 The Reporting Process

Audit reports are not published documents but are the result of a comprehensive audit reporting process that may be summarised in Figure 18.1.

FIGURE 18.1 AUDIT REPORTING PROCESS

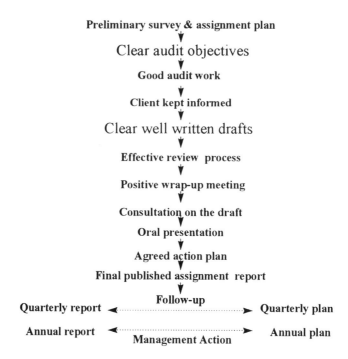

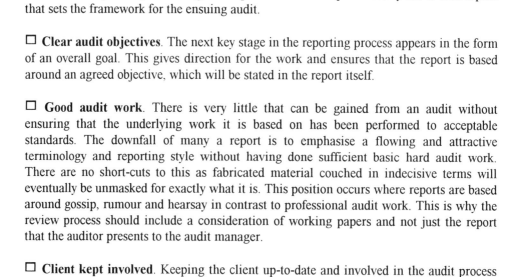

We discuss the above components:

☐ **Preliminary survey and assignment plan**. The audit report actually starts with a plan that sets the framework for the ensuing audit.

☐ **Clear audit objectives**. The next key stage in the reporting process appears in the form of an overall goal. This gives direction for the work and ensures that the report is based around an agreed objective, which will be stated in the report itself.

☐ **Good audit work**. There is very little that can be gained from an audit without ensuring that the underlying work it is based on has been performed to acceptable standards. The downfall of many a report is to emphasise a flowing and attractive terminology and reporting style without having done sufficient basic hard audit work. There are no short-cuts to this as fabricated material couched in indecisive terms will eventually be unmasked for exactly what it is. This position occurs where reports are based around gossip, rumour and hearsay in contrast to professional audit work. This is why the review process should include a consideration of working papers and not just the report that the auditor presents to the audit manager.

☐ **Client kept involved**. Keeping the client up-to-date and involved in the audit process leads to a better report. Some auditors feel that findings should be withheld from the auditee until the report is made available, for fear of action taken now by management "spoiling" the impact of the report. This is a distorted view of the audit role which is not to claim victories (i.e. findings) at management's expense. In reality it is to help and assist management in the discharge of its responsibilities. Any findings should be brought to the attention of management in regular progress meetings. These findings may nonetheless be quoted in the report, and the fact that management has already acted on them strengthens rather than weakens the impact of the audit.

☐ **Clear well-written drafts**. The way a report is written does affect the way the findings, conclusions and recommendations are received. Good audit work, based around close contact with the auditee provides a foundation for a well received report, but the actual words presented form a defined vehicle for communicating the findings. In this sense the report must be based on professional standards of presentation that lift the audit in the eyes of the reader.

☐ **Effective review process**. The two key points to the review stage of the reporting process are that firstly, this review should ensure that the report is prepared to professional standards, that fit with the underlying work that has been completed. Secondly, it should be completed without delaying the swift progress of the draft report. If these two principles are firmly in place, despite the fact that they conflict with each other to an extent, then the report process will tend to be successful.

☐ **Positive wrap-up meeting**. It must be said that one of the most stressful parts of an audit is the face to face closure meeting that is held once the field work has been completed. Much will depend on the relationship with the client that has been built up during the audit and the extent to which findings have been discussed as they arise. Whatever the scenario, we would hope that the auditor does not seek to avoid this stage, as it is an important component of successful reporting.

☐ **Consultation on the draft**. We would next wish to see a formal process whereby the draft report is sent to all parties affected by the recommendations. This is based on best practice and standards that ensure fair representation for all individuals that have a role to play in acting on audit findings.

☐ **Oral presentations**. It is as well to stage an oral presentation for audits that are more complicated and/or address sensitive matters. This provides an opportunity for feedback and promotes a process whereby the auditor justifies the assumed position. Both these factors have to be satisfied if we are to get effective action based around audit recommendations.

☐ **Agreed action plans**. We arrive at the negotiation/agreement stage that is also part of the reporting process. This will enable us to present management's proposals within the report so as to make it an active working document that has meaning to both audit and management.

☐ **Final published assignment report**. A final report should be prepared along with a clear definition of reporting lines and people who should be given copies. There are many audit units guilty of producing "draft" reports that remain in circulation without a final version much to the confusion of all involved with this document.

☐ **Follow-up**. The process is still not complete until we have set up a follow-up routine in line with best audit practice. These standards can be mentioned within the report or the accompanying letter.

☐ **Quarterly reports**. The audit report should feed into the quarterly reporting cycle that seeks to summarise what has been found and reported on in the relevant three month period. Reference to the quarterly plan makes this a dynamic process that is linked to a defined reference point.

☐ **Annual report**. The above is equally true for the annual reporting cycle that again should be set within the context of the plan for the year in question.

☐ **Management action**. We arrive at the true audit product in terms of management action based on the audit report. All else is simply to set a foundation within which this action may be stimulated by the auditor. The objective of the reporting process is to get management to act on audit's advice. A report that suggests no action is required is just as significant as one that asks for many changes. Assurances (of good control) allow management to channel resources into riskier areas

It is essential that the entire reporting process is carefully managed and controlled since a failing in any one component will impair the impact of the report. Note that the final result of this process may be defined as "management action" to secure changes and improvements to the way the organisation designs, implements, seeks compliance with and reviews its systems of internal control. There are auditors who complain that managers fail to implement audit recommendations and that they should be disciplined accordingly. In practice however most of the blame can be placed on a failure by audit management to implement a suitable reporting process based on the concepts set out above.

18.5 Defining the Client

The audit report should be directed at the client. This is not always easy to define and will be influenced by the organisation that the audit department is located in. For government auditors there may be a wide range of individuals that may benefit from effective audit cover including:

- **The finance officer**. This officer will probably be responsible for ensuring that suitable financial procedures are implemented and complied with across the organisation.
- **The taxpayer**. This may be seen as the ultimate client who is financing local and central public services. They will wish to be assured that value for money is being received from the organisations that they are funding.
- **Government Ministers**. Again these officials will expect and demand that public funds are being applied in a controlled fashion and that each department is fully accountable for their actions.
- **Directors of client directorates**. In the final analysis each director is ultimately responsible for what goes on in their particular Directorate. Reliance is placed on sound systems of control and if these are not working then the appropriate director should ensure that swift action ensues.

- **The organisation**. The corporate decision-making body of the organisation will wish to see an effective internal audit. As such all major control issues should be a fundamental concern of any corporate management team. Since internal audit is defined as a service to the organisation it is clear that the organisation must therefore be a principal client for audit services.
- **The eventual recipient of the services audited**. The current trend in marketing concepts sees the role of the client as paramount in strategic planning and decision making. The client will wish to see effective action taken in respect of audit recommendations. Service recipients are key players as they have most to lose where service objectives are not being achieved efficiently. The level of services impacts directly on the quality of life of those who rely on these services.
- **Middle management**. This group of people is placed between corporate management and line/operational managers. They oversee the operations at a level once removed from the supervisory role and will probably be responsible for more than one operation/service. Where the auditor has a problem with the operational manager, this officer becomes the next point of contact. Where the audit is going well with no fundamental disagreements with the operational manager, then it will not be necessary to involve middle management to any great extent. There are some senior managers who specifically get involved in an audit and maintain say a watching brief over the whole audit process. This should be encouraged but not to the detriment of the auditor/operational manager relationship. It may be audit practice to bring the senior manager into opening meetings and wash-up meetings or simply ensure that they receive a copy of the draft audit report when available.
- **Operational management**. This officer may be seen as the real client for audit services. The reasoning runs that the operational manager, by definition, runs the operation. This person is charged with delivering the defined end-product to the right standards of quality and quantity. Suitable controls are a necessary pre-requisite to this objective and the manager will wish to see these controls subject to audit reviews and any deficiencies isolated along with relevant recommendations. All things being equal, it is the line manager who will see the direct impact of audit reports and more importantly has to live with any changes as a result of audit recommendations. Furthermore it is this officer who will have the task of dealing with the field auditors and implementing any ensuing recommendations that may then be made. As long as the operational manager's objectives coincide with organisational objectives, goals, and policies then this is the main audit client.
- **Trade unions**. There is an argument that union officials have a right to know how well the organisation is controlled and managed. It is considered good practice to include staff representatives in change programmes that affect resources or working practices. There are audit reports that call for changes that will have a major impact on staff which therefore brings the unions into the picture.
- **Local politicians**. Councillors in a local authority set policy and rely on officers to ensure they are actioned. They will look for barriers to the efficient and effective use of resources in applying their policies which is where internal audit has a role.
- **The audit committee**. For longer term issues outside the individual audit report, this forum may be seen as the principal client for internal audit. As well as being a client in terms of audit reports, the audit committee will also assess the performance of the audit function. Accordingly internal audit "report" to the committee in the fullest sense of the word.

- **The Chief Executive**. In one sense this officer may also be seen as a principal client for internal audit. The CE is ultimately responsible for the performance of the organisation and this factor is affected by the adequacy of systems of control. It is quite probable that the CE will take a close interest in the internal audit service and the reports that they issue. It may be the case that audit report to the CE directly or via the audit committee. Returning to the view that audit provides services to the organisation, it may be argued that the CE is the ultimate decision maker concerned with these services and their impact on the organisation.

Much may be said about defining the client for audit services and this may vary according to the situation and arrangements made. The client concept has to be treated with flexibility. The guiding principle that should be applied to audit reports is that they should be addressed to the party who would be most effective in making the necessary changes required. This will depend on the type of organisation, the type of audit work performed and the circumstances of the audit. Ordinarily the report will go to the line manager for the area under review and the next tier up.

18.6 Objectives of the Audit Report

Extensive audit resources may be spent on performing an audit and the client may see as the end product, a published audit report. It is therefore important that the objectives of this final document are clearly established and this may be one or more of the following:

To recommend change
The audit report must be first and foremost about securing change in terms of new or improved controls. The technique of describing the current control failings should be used to help stimulate change by bringing home the problems that must be overcome. This concept can become somewhat blurred where the auditor/client relationship develops to a state of "one-up-manship". To criticise, to find fault, to expose and to search for the implications of control problems are subsidiary matters compared to the main point of getting something done about these problems. In short the audit report should primarily be aimed at this idea of change, with the recommendations being the single most important component of the document.

To provide an insight for management into control issues
It can be said that the audit report will highlight the importance of control issues and relate these to management's own business objectives. This places the need for control on the agenda. This is particularly relevant where there is a great deal of change in business operations due to environmental factors and where new systems and procedures are being developed. The audit report may help balance management's goals in driving through major new initiatives, by warning of the potential for danger where the control implications have not been properly addressed. Control requires resources which in turn must be prioritised by management. It is only by placing the need for control on an equal footing with other competing issues that adequate solutions will be provided and here the audit report can have a major role.

To secure action in response to audit advice

Action goes further than recommendation by moving an idea to the status of an actual event. This turns audit suggestion into real action by allowing management to claim the required changes as its own. This is a main goal of the audit report where one is able to report a management action plan agreed with the parties responsible for making it happen. One broad measure of internal audit performance is how much real action has resulted from audit reports.

> *Internal audit reviewed cashiering and the senior auditor had begun preliminary work. In the staff canteen, the Chief Cashier had an informal conversation with the audit manager responsible for the audit. He said he was urgently writing procedures to deal with cashiering operations so that he would not be "caught out" by the audit. The audit manager commended this, and said audit would be happy to contribute to developing sound procedures, which surprised the cashier.*

To bring problems to management's attention

Another view of the audit report suggests it is designed to ensure management is aware of material problems and their effect on systems objectives. These reports will feature the results of compliance and substantive testing, setting out the frequency of breaches and level of error. It may be possible to extrapolate these sample results to give an overall conclusion on the population. Client expectation will demand that error, irregularity and other problems are brought out in the report despite being based on misunderstanding of the audit role. It is only the brave auditor who will ignore these expectations when drafting an audit report. Some argue that a true management action plan is based on audit isolating the problem while management provides the most suitable solution.

To ensure that the results of audit work are clearly documented

Not all audit reports are published and some, particularly preliminary survey reports, are used as internal documents. Others contain no major findings but are still sent out to management. The report represents a formal record of work carried out and the results. It may be necessary to document findings when carrying out a fraud investigation even though these reports may not be sent outside the audit department. The main purpose of these reports is to document the audit. Where management decides not to take up audit recommendations then the auditor can point to the audit report as the formal device for conveying the audit opinion. This may be useful in the event of a dispute later. This appears at first sight a defensive approach but it is sound practice to use the report as a formal record of the audit.

To provide assurance to management on their activities

This part of the role of the audit report is based on the view that audit reviews controls, because they may have fallen into disrepair or misuse. There is a preventative approach that relies on the existence of sound controls in the first place. The audit may adopt the guise of providing comfort to management that controls are sound and are being applied in practice and as such many reports will have no major adverse findings. The lack of control problems should not be seen as a criticism of audit effectiveness or a failure to secure

"Brownie points" in terms of the number of errors/problems found. This would point more to the success of audit in getting the control message across to management who has then resourced the need for good systems. The audit report in this instance will be designed to support management in its drive for better controls. We have argued that assurances that controls are sound do in themselves promote effective management decisions. This is because resources may then be rightly directed towards other areas of higher risk in line with the knowledge provided by the auditor's report.

To show managers how their problems may be solved

Pointing the way forward is another objective of the audit report. There are many cases where managers are clear as to the nature of problems and sometimes the underlying causes. Their concerns are centred on securing help in solving these problems and it is here that the consultancy role of internal audit will comes in. Reports steeped in isolating the implications of control weaknesses will have little use in this scenario. The application of creative thinking applied to underlying barriers to value for money are the real products the client will be looking for.

To provide information to management

This is a valid objective as many audits will report new information that has been specially developed via the audit process. This may be needed to feed into a much wider management decision-making mechanism that may be considering a whole range of options. An example may be performance indicators that have been put together perhaps by a special analysis carried out by the auditors over a range of comparable operational units. This information may be used for many different purposes over a period of time, on the basis that it has been produced by an independent third party (i.e. the auditor) via professional audit techniques. In this case presentational matters will be important where schedules, tables and graphs would tend to be supplied within the report. For example, a list of large numbers of cheques drawn on the organisation that have been returned by the postal service because they could not be delivered. This may highlight a problem with the state of the creditors database (i.e. the address field) and so help direct management attention to this problem.

To protect the auditor

Many reports will have the subsidiary objective of documenting where audit resources were applied and where it was not possible to do detailed work. This indicates to the client that areas/issues have not been covered with an explanation. It may be used to protect the auditor against later accusations that certain matters were overlooked, which led to defined losses or exposure to high levels of risk. The audit terms of reference and clear qualifications set out within the report will clarify the extent of audit coverage. There is a variety of views and approaches adopted by audit report writers and each has justification. The audit role may be derived from these three objectives. The underlying goal may be to act as a catalyst for all material improvements to controls necessary to ensure that systems objectives are achieved. The three main functions of the audit report are:

- To **assure** management that operations are well controlled.
- To **alert** them to areas where this is not the case and there are defined weaknesses/problems.
- And to **advise** them on action necessary to remedy these weaknesses/problems.

18.7 Underlying Components of Action

The audit report is the result of a comprehensive process and is a means to an end. There are several clear parts of the audit process that directly impact on the audit report:

Record of control weakness

This working paper is called a record of control weakness (RCW) and contains details of each major control weakness that appears as an audit finding in the published report. The RCW should contain:

☐ **The operational objective.** This is the business objective i.e. that which the manager is required to achieve. It is essential that this concept is paramount in the search for suitable controls as it sets a frame within which all ensuing work can be contained.

☐ **The operational standard.** This provides the control model against which the current arrangements may be measured bearing in mind the fact that audit is about comparing what is with what should be. This may be seen as the appropriate control mechanism that we would expect to see in place in order to discharge the requirements of the aforementioned operational objective.

☐ **The risks of the current practice.** This constitutes the supposition that is being tested. By comparing existing controls to required controls, one may establish the type of dangers that should be guarded against and so assess the degree of risk derived from the current controls. Risks are expressed in terms of potential problems that should be quantified at some stage in the report.

☐ **The deficiency.** This is a concise statement of what is lacking. It is expressed in terms of control weaknesses and it is these weaknesses that the audit report will seek to remedy by drawing them to the attention of management. The audit report should feature an opinion that summarises the deficiency in control systems.

☐ **The cause of the deficiency.** Underlying causes must be clearly identified if any progress is to be made in rectifying problems. This is a moot point since it means that the auditor must probe the control weakness to discover why a fault or deficiency actually exists. Where a number of weaknesses can be related to a common fault we are getting closer to a position whereby these failings may be resolved. One such common cause may be a lack of concern by management for formal security arrangements and documentation, that lowers the effectiveness of overall controls. Another may be a view that senior manages are able to override procedures by virtue of their position in the organisation, again to the detriment of good control.

☐ **The effect of the deficiency.** Substantive testing is about defining the effect of control weaknesses. This information will bring home the importance of securing better control and allow management to undertake a form of cost benefit analysis before committing resources. This will feature as examples of how things can go wrong due to the lack of control and also an overall position, setting out the percentage of breach of procedure and/or error that was found during the audit. These findings should be arranged so they may feed into the draft audit report.

☐ **Conclusions**. An overall audit opinion forces the auditor to consider the wider implications and give a rounded view of the findings. It is possible to build in a discussion of the pros and cons behind management's current position and whether there are realistic options that may be considered.

☐ **A framework for the recommendations**. It is possible to set the boundaries within which recommendations will fall. Audit recommendations should flow from this process. Hopefully, not only will the audit view be professionally based, but it will also be derived from a systematic consideration of relevant material. The types of matters that fall into the change process animated by the report should appear in this, the final part of the RCW.

The aim is to lead the auditor into creative thinking so that problems may be solved. A logical foundation will have been built, which these ideas can be founded on. The RCW will form the main reference document for the wrap-up meeting where material issues will be discussed with the auditee. This working document will also feed directly into the draft audit report in that it will set out what was done, what was found, what it means and what now needs to be done. The stage at which the RCW appears in the report drafting process may be illustrated:

FIGURE 18.2 RECORD OF CONTROL WEAKNESS

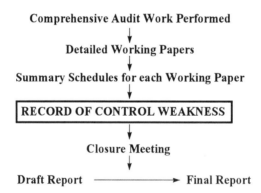

The RCW should form a high-level summary of the working papers (properly cross referenced) that lends itself to being fed directly into the audit report itself. Moreover relevant material that will enter into the report's standards, findings, conclusions and recommendations will be found in the RCW that promotes a structured approach to drafting the formal audit report.

Formulating the audit opinion

As well as identifying control weaknesses the auditor is charged with forming and publishing an opinion based on the audit work performed. This part of the audit report may be based on:

☐ **The results of control evaluation**. This will help identify the actual weaknesses that are being addressed via the audit report. As such control evaluation represents the process of establishing the key problem areas in the system under review.

☐ **The existing control culture**. The audit opinion must be set within the context of the management culture. Where there is a fundamental lack of control appreciation then this issue will feature in the report. Where there are sound controls but a lack of mechanisms to ensure compliance then again the audit opinion will reflect this factor. The tone of the report will be geared to the level and extent of change that is required to ensure good control which in turn depends on management's own perceptions of its control needs. The report can be reconciliatory and highlight all the positive steps taken by management to enhance control, or it may be hard hitting and seek to get entrenched managers to act on audit recommendations.

☐ **Basic problem areas**. The audit opinion will certainly highlight the outstanding problems. These may include for example a high level of defined error in the transactions that are processed, inconsistent information that cannot be properly reconciled and/or poor documentation.

☐ **The underlying causes of basic problems**. The audit opinion may operate on two levels whereby the detailed findings will be presented in terms of the type of problems mentioned above. It should also provide an overview where the principal causes may be discussed. In this way it may be possible to link isolated problems to a common cause. Examples may be a lack of clear procedures, staff absences and/or insufficient segregation of duties.

☐ **Whether controls are adhered to**. This is an important point in that regardless of how sound the controls may appear on paper, the auditor will be able to discover whether they are being applied in practice. The overall results of compliance testing should be referred to in the final audit opinion and if this is a material issue then the relevant facts should be disclosed.

☐ **Whether controls work**. Substantive tests seek to discover the net result of control weaknesses. This should appear in the audit opinion as the level of loss/error/inefficiency derived from these weaknesses.

☐ **The practicalities of available remedies**. The auditor must look at the available recommendations carefully before presenting them to management. If a great deal of effort will be required to effect any necessary changes then this should be noted in the audit report. Some form of reasoning must appear that justifies the recommended way forward. In some cases, reference may be made to any options that may have been placed in front of management as part of the various audit recommendations. The respective costs and benefits of each control option should be appraised and commented on. The audit opinion will hopefully put this issue into perspective.

☐ **Management's efforts to improve**. Specific improvements should be acknowledged. When dealing with the objectives of the audit report we noted that it is there to provide assurances to management on its systems of control. Where management has tackled control problems and put into action improvements, this should be an additional feature of the overall audit opinion. It may balance conclusions and stimulate a positive response from management.

☐ **The effects of any future changes planned**. In formulating the opinion the auditor can point to the future by outlining planned changes. This sets a framework for the report. Matters addressed and the auditor's approach to proposed developments should be included in the audit opinion. It enables the reader to judge how far the auditor has gone to relate audit findings to future plans.

☐ **Overall impressions on management's ability and willingness to address control issues**. We may be dealing with a follow-up audit that uncovers lack of effective management action to address problems identified in an earlier report. The audit opinion will reflect this barrier to change and perhaps be more critical than the normal tone used. If management has made great strides in meeting problems head-on, then the audit opinion will be directed towards supporting these moves and sympathising with management. The net result will vary according to circumstances.

☐ **Findings from unofficial sources**. The auditor may know of problems because staff have reported off the record without providing formal evidence. The "audit nose" may also have come to the fore and this may create a dilemma. The auditor may wish to refer to sensitive problems although there is no formal supporting basis that may be quoted. An example is where the line manager for the areas under review is nearing retirement and is not interested in making any major changes. Some argue that the tone of the audit opinion may be altered to reflect unspoken concerns although this must be used with great care. The CIA should have defined an appropriate reporting standard that will be in the audit manual. The audit opinion is formally communicated and here lies the importance of the tone of the written report. Reporting allows the auditor to convey professional opinion and make suggestions within the context of management's position.

Formulating recommendations
It is not enough to point out problems without providing guidance on required action. This is the positive part of the audit report and when formulating recommendations, we should consider:

☐ **The available options**. The audit opinion deals with available options in outline by describing different directions management may take. In the recommendations part of the report this will be dealt with in more detail. We may analyse the options outside the report by assessing them in the working papers. Alternatively, we may set out options within the recommendations. This approach may cause problems where an overload of advice may confuse management and blur the main issues. It is acceptable to give options when performing consultancy services commissioned by management. For audit work, a better approach would be to analyse options in the working papers and discuss these with management at the wash-up meeting before specifics are formally reported.

☐ **The need to remove barriers to good control**. Some recommendations are based on new resources, some seek to get management to do things differently while others seek to remove underlying problems. Where specific circumstances militate against good control, this needs to be dealt with. The recommendations should therefore take on board control barriers and seek to define ways in which they may be removed. The level of non-compliance with procedure may be related to the extent to which management perceives this compliance as important. A general lack of concern about staff adhering to procedures may act as a barrier to control that has to be addressed before we can start considering these controls. Another example of control obstacles may be in the form of poor staff that have been employed, despite failing to meet the requirements of the job specification. Again this factor must be tackled before we can have a constructive discussion on control systems. Remember our wider definition of control takes on board considerations such as sound recruitment procedures. The point is that an underlying foundation that supports good control may have to be referred to before the detailed control arrangements are featured in audit recommendations.

☐ **The exercise of creative thinking**. In many audits, managers are aware of control weaknesses and have noted the implication in terms of errors and/or inefficiencies. They need advice on solving these problems within resources available. The auditor has experience of similar problems and can stand outside the activity to create workable solutions. Creative thinking can be applied in formulating recommendations. This separates the professional auditor from the junior checker. New heights are achieved when the auditor enters the world of lateral thinking with ideas, inspiration and fresh thought. The important ability to associate problems with underlying causes underpins creative thinking. We would expect this exercise of creative thinking to consist of more than repetition of material found in ICQs. One lead into this is to define and assess these associated factors:

FIGURE 18.3 SEARCHING FOR RECOMMENDATIONS

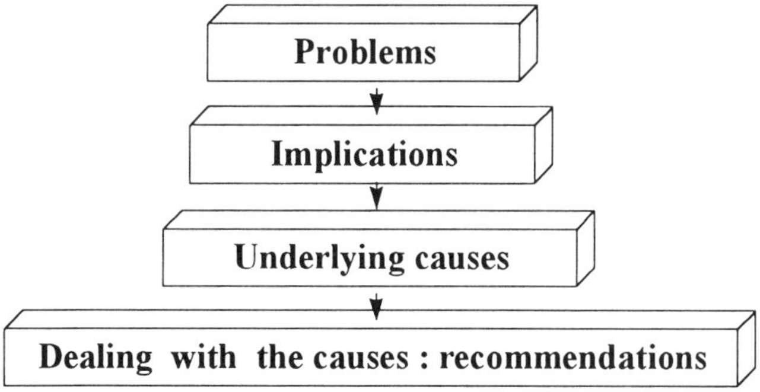

☐ **Value-for-money points**. The theory of VFM can be controversial in that some writers argue that it is good systems that will promote VFM. Others see an audit as an opportunity to identify new efficiency measures and possibly present a resultant figure for potential savings. The approach will depend on the adopted audit methodology. Where specific savings are being recommended then a level of discussion will have to appear in the main body of the report that justifies the required action. In this case it may be necessary to build up the actual recommendation itself so that it is more than a one liner. It is also as well to distinguish these matters from the other audit recommendations that may be directed towards controls perhaps by having them in a separate part of the recommendations.

☐ **The resource implications of recommended controls**. So that the report does not raise more questions than it answers, it is possible to indicate the cost of recommendations. This point is particularly relevant in a recession where new funds are not readily available. This feature need not be exaggerated to a great extent since management clearly has a role to play in assessing and taking on these recommendations. What needs to happen is that the report should acknowledge the fact that it may be necessary to secure additional funding to get improved controls. One way is to seek to minimise the need for actual new resources by setting the recommendations within this context.

> *An operational area consisted of three teams dealing with accounts by splitting the alphabet between them. A fourth temporary team had been employed to clear up backlogs. The manager had intended to assimilate this new team into a fourth team and spread the alphabet into four sections. A new computer system recently installed was causing disruption and contained poor and incomplete data. Operational procedures were inadequate and staff used inconsistent working methods. A key recommendation was to establish a quality and control team to support the computer system, formulate procedures and promote quality standards. This proposal was sold to management by using the temporary backlog team and transferring some of the duties of the three alpha teams to this new quality team. New resources were not required, it simply involved a change in direction for the current staff.*

One of the key flaws in audit recommendations centres on the assumption that control needs will be fully resourced by management. It is flawed because it fails to recognise the tremendous strain on resources that faces all organisations and all sections within these organisations.

☐ **Any bad management practices that impair control**. It is rare for audit reports to contain attacks on management and this approach sets up confrontation. It is essential that audit concerns are properly noted even if these include poor management practices. It is possible to do this in a constructive way that does not bring personalities into play and with careful drafting, an appropriately worded recommendation may be formulated. One factor that impairs control is distant managers who fail to communicate with staff. Problems such as this may be dealt with by ensuring the recommendations have a good chance of being implemented. We can suggest that managers issue the audit report to all staff and establish regular meetings to deal with the required changes. Where it is clear that managers are not acting as change agents then we can suggest that extra responsibility is given to a defined person to bring about recommended change. In terms of designing new systems (a role outside the audit remit) we may ask management to bring in a consultant where it is obvious that this task cannot be performed in-house. Much depends on the circumstances, and the extent to which audit needs to guide and direct management in its search for better controls.

☐ **The ideal solution**. The chapter on control evaluation addresses the concept of the ideal control system. This may be established to set a standard that may be aimed at over time. An example of an ideal would be to establish a fully automated operational process and convert staff areas into networked computer workstations. We would not expect recommendation to be too futuristic in that they are programmes to be applied over a long time period. There are some matters that can only be dealt with in incremental stages. Where there is a mismatch between skills required by management and staff and those that they actually possess, we can only seek to achieve so much through audit work. Far from being a solve-all situation, an audit is undertaken to leave the operational area in a better position in terms of suitable control systems. There is no definitive solution that can emanate from the audit report, and this is not the main objective of an audit. The ideal solution will be contained by the real-life practicalities that face all organisations.

☐ **The costs of poor control**. Recommended controls are put forward on the basis that the cost of control weaknesses, that they are meant to remedy, outweighs the cost of these new/improved controls. When designing suitable recommendations it is as well to consider this side of the cost equation by reviewing the implications of any lapses in control. It is a test that each recommendation will have to pass if it is to make it to the audit reporting stage. What makes this equation difficult is the view that "costs" encompass all negative influences that face the area under review, which includes qualitative factors, such as general reputation. The actual "cost" of a poor reputation within the organisation may be the closure or contracting out of the particular function.

☐ **Practical workability**. It is a failing of many auditors to make impractical recommendations. This "walk away" syndrome means that the auditor is satisfied to perform an audit, make numerous recommendations and then depart, blaming management for not taking a serious interest in the audit work. This can become dangerous where the auditor argues that management has something to hide. It may be that audit performance indicators are based on the number of recommendations made in published reports. The audit process must be accompanied by suitable audit standards that ensure this task of assessing the workability of recommendations is undertaken before they are put forward.

The auditor should point management in the right direction and stimulate effective management action. It is possible to adjust the tone of audit recommendations and choose from:
- **We recommend...**
- **We strongly recommend...**
- **It is advisable for management to...**
- **It is essential that management...**
- **Management needs to urgently address...**
- **Management should consider...**

Auditors may make many recommendations and these should be structured for maximum impact, the most important first. There should be a few enabling steps that management should take and these should be detailed in the opening part of the recommendations. They should be designed to place management in a position to effect the various recommendations. This would also appear in any executive summary and should not consist of more than two or three items in discussion mode. The remaining recommendations should follow in order of priority (See the section below on change management). One useful approach is to document a series of recommendations for each main section of the report and then repeat them as the final part of the executive summary (cross-referenced to the main report). Recommendations should be presented to create maximum impact. There are many busy executives who are primarily interested in what is being recommended, and why.

18.8 The Review Process

Audit work should be reviewed before a report is published and this should occur on two levels. First there should be a supervisory review of the underlying working papers where all audit findings should be supported by sound, evidenced audit work. The second level concentrates on the audit report and the way the work, conclusions and recommendations are expressed. The review should look at the quality as well as quantity of work. If work is reviewed as it progresses the draft report will not be delayed awaiting the audit managers' review. The report review may look for:

☐ **The structure**. The report should follow a defined format and reflect what may be called the house style. A major short cut to report drafting is to follow an agreed structure. If this has been automated (i.e. held on computer disk), one may imagine the ease by which the outline can be tailored for the particular report in hand. The review process should look for compliance with this standard and seek explanations where it has not been applied.

☐ **What the findings are based on**. There should be a clear link between the terms of reference, the work carried out, the findings and then the recommendations. The review will consider the appropriateness of audit findings expressed within the report. The draft report should be cross-referenced to the working papers and particular attention paid to factual quotations placed in the report. These should be accurate and represent sound evidence. Where a fact has been derived from an interview and not confirmed elsewhere, then terms such as "we have been advised by management that..." may be used. The importance of reviewing the findings cannot be over-emphasised and the audit manager will have a major role in this respect. As such, the review process cannot simply involve the report but must delve into the working papers themselves. This will consider the way the work was done, the extent of coverage, and the results of the tests applied. The working papers should be able to contain all this material in a simple and clear fashion. One useful test that can be applied by the audit manager is to suggest that it should be very easy to find supporting papers for each key point made in the report. If this is not the case, questions must be asked

☐ **How they are expressed**. Securing good findings is one consideration but the way they are presented is a separate matter. A major failing for some auditors is to exaggerate the findings or make generalised comments based on very limited information. The scale and significance of evidence uncovered should be properly reflected in the report and, as well as not suppressing major findings, one must also be reasonable in dealing with less material matters. The art of setting the findings within the context of the entire operation that has been reviewed is a difficult one to master. Reports that spend much time referring to a series of minor errors will make very boring reading and can lead to accusations of bias from the auditee. There is nothing wrong with using specific examples to illustrate a key point along the lines: "we found several instances where documentation was incomplete and in one case missing altogether..." At some stage however we would expect a summary of findings to appear that places our research against the entire population, using percentages where necessary. Such material would be presented along the lines; "over the hundred items examined, we found that around 15% were not authorised. Some 7% contained errors that would affect the resultant figures submitted to head office, to the extent of £x". If statistical sampling had been applied we can go on to quantify the implications for the entire database.

☐ **The tone of the report**. One important review point relates to the way the auditors have expressed their findings. The reviewer should aim to take out all emotive aspects of the report including underlining, exclamation marks, sarcasm, slang and other unprofessional techniques. This could be a sensitive part of the review process and the reviewer should ensure that time is set aside so that these points can be properly discussed. One should also aim at eradicating unacceptable drafting habits in future reports by explaining their use (or misuse). Internal reports are particularly susceptible to emotive drafting and it can be very embarrassing where these reports are eventually read by outsiders. It is best practice to stick to the policy of saying what needs to be said in a clear and concise fashion using standard terminology, so the problem of trying to read between the lines need not arise. The current trend is to give a degree of passion to the report so as to excite the reader by the use of terms such as "it is unprecedented..., we have a fundamental concern over..., management have clearly misdirected their efforts..., this is the worst case to come to our attention," and so on. This is an unwise position to adopt as each report competes with the previous one to be more dramatic, until they read more like tabloid newspapers, using a series of clichés. We must restate the view that auditors should resist this temptation and stick to the usual format whereby sensationalism is avoided.

☐ **Gaps**. The report must be read as a whole by the reviewer and obvious gaps isolated. This may include items in the terms of reference that have not been dealt with and findings that do not flow from the work carried out. The key here is to spot where the report leaves too many unanswered questions that lessen its overall impact. Where the report has been written over a period it may appear disjointed with repeated points and areas that have simply been left out. If one part of the report states that an issue will be expanded on later on, this should happen and a relevant section added to a later part of the report. If we have decided to restrict the terms of reference for an audit and leave one component to be covered in a separate audit then we must say so. We cannot assume that the report writer will always be available to explain apparent inconsistencies, which means that the report should be read as a complete document now and in the future. Gaps in the report will tend to annoy the reader, particularly where specific items have been left out with no explanation. Where for example we have found a major error, we must indicate whether management was made aware of this immediately and whether the matter has been put right and any losses recovered. To do otherwise would leave the reader in the dark, with many unanswered questions.

☐ **The terminology used**. The auditor is faced with a dilemma at times where although the line manager will be the main client for the report, it will also be read by others less familiar with the area under review. As such it is important that all terms used are explained and a list of abbreviations appears in the appendices. It is best to apply the policy that a report should be understood by all potential readers, and if audit is working to the highest professional standards then we would expect the Chief Executive, and top management to take an interest in our work. These senior officers will tend not to have an intimate knowledge of all operations, which should mean that audit reports are not only readable by operational management or technical experts. Excessive use of abbreviations may make a report incomprehensible.

☐ **The spelling and grammar**. This is a material point in that many audit reports contain excellent findings and crucial recommendations but are let down by poor spelling. This distracts the reader from the important points being made by allowing them to fall into a mode of active criticism whereby they look for further mistakes in the report. All word processors have spell checks and it should be a standard that no work is prepared without using this facility. Pocket-size automated spell checkers can be acquired to assist this process as will a general awareness of spelling and presentation. Grammatical checks are also available on better PC software and again we can set a standard where this facility is applied to all material published by internal audit.

☐ **Whether the house style has been applied**. Titles, colours, logos, binding and report covers should all follow the adopted format. Draft reports could be prepared to a lower presentation than the final versions which may be bound in expensive covers. If final reports have different colours then they will be distinguished from drafts. If there is in fact no house style then the CIA may be open to criticism as reports are published in an assortment of ways that do not promote a corporate view of the audit function. One simple standard is to set a procedure whereby different covers have been defined, for example:

1. **White** - internal use only.   **Pink** - confidential reports.
2. **Pale green** - all draft reports.   **Dark green** - final published reports.

☐ **Whether it appears as a professional job well done**. The reviewer should ensure that the report reflects a well done audit that has directed itself to the terms of reference. The overall "feel" of the report should be in line with audit standards and this is something that is achieved over time as the auditor becomes more and more experienced. If this test is not satisfied then the reviewer needs to go through the draft in greater detail so that it can be improved. It is always a good idea to read a report as a whole document and not as a series of separate sections to gauge this overall impression. We would look for this balance that recognises what we have found, what management is doing, where its needs to go and so on, so that the document reflects a considered view of the systems that have been audited. There are times when a fresh eye is needed to make this decision, removed from those who have been intimately involved in preparing the report.

☐ **Whether the client would be quite happy to pay for the resources invested in the audit**. One interesting feature of the review will be to ask whether the report is worth the cost in terms of audit hours. It is good practice to cost out audit hours so that audit management may then pose for example, the following question:

> *Does this report represent £5,000 worth of audit work?*

Again it is practice that allows us to make this judgement in terms of value for money. The old adage of *"Assure, Alert and Advise"* is foremost in this consideration where we deem our role as assuring management that all is well. If not we would alert them to any particular problems and then furnish some degree of advice to assist them. The report must offer this format in the search for value for money from the audit service.

18.9 The Clearance Process

The draft audit report, once reviewed has to be cleared and management given the opportunity to comment on the contents. The findings should not come as a surprise to management and it is advisable to bring them to the manager's attention as they arise. Regular progress reports (probably oral) and a brief meeting at the end of each week will assist this process. A wrap-up meeting with the line manager should be held at the end of the audit where the main findings are discussed. The reviewed draft should be sent to the line manager (only) and an informal meeting held to discuss this as soon as possible after completion of the work. Factual matters should be dealt with and the auditor may well revise the draft as a result. The auditors' conclusions will only change where the factual corrections materially affect audit findings. Once this has occurred a further draft should be formally sent to those affected by the work including the next tier of management. Formal written comments will be taken on board and a final report published. This is a useful technique for involving the actual operational manager as the report will be more reliable and we would have hopefully secured this officer's full support before it goes to a wider audience. Note that where management accepts without question all audit recommendations, this may mean they are not particularly interested in the results and wish to get rid of the auditor. Effective action normally starts with close discussions with management on each audit recommendation. Again see the section below on change management for a different perspective on this issue. Management is entitled to choose not to follow audit recommendations and in this instance it is the auditor's responsibility to ensure they understand the implications and are prepared to assume the associated risk. Management will then assume full responsibility for this documented decision and this issue may be brought to the attention of the audit committee.

18.10 Formulating the Action Plan

It is a good idea to form an agreed action plan with management based on the audit. This allows management to take over the audit recommendations and so be fully involved in implementing them. An action plan may be devised during the drafting procedure and once agreed may be included in the published report. Where management is allowed to form its own action plan, this becomes a very efficient way of getting audit recommendations implemented, although we would expect a degree of negotiation by both sides. Accordingly the auditor should work out which recommendations should be pursued and which may be partly given up for a greater good. The best solution is to include the action plan within the Executive Summary as part of the agreed solution and we would look for items such as work required, by whom, deadlines and reporting lines as a way of ensuring that the recommendations will come about. Once complete the action plan should belong to management as it seeks to embark on the necessary workload.

Supportive evidence

Recommendations must be based on sound evidence and the extent of this supporting material depends on the importance of establishing the effects of control weaknesses. Where internal auditors are required to attend management working parties which publish reports and make recommendations without comprehensive research then their views should be qualified as not being derived from the normal audit process. The formal audit reports in contrast must be based on sound evidence that has been derived from the audit process.

18.11 Change Management

Many auditors become demotivated when their audit reports are more or less ignored by the auditee. Some feel that line managers should be disciplined through failure to act on audit recommendations while others simply feel less enthusiastic about their work as a result. Where reports are not actioned there is always an underlying reason. Occasionally this is because management is acting negligently and against the best interest of the organisation. More often, it is because they can see no good reason to obey unrealistic recommendations made by people who do not understand the operation in question. Audit recommendations generally form part of a change process in that they tend to ask for something that is not already being done. As such they lead to some of the tensions that change itself creates and this in turn affects the client. Moreover the auditor may also be a source of management stress. When performing an audit the auditor should recognise the implication of the change process and ensure that where necessary these are taken on board particularly at the reporting stage. The chapter on behavioural aspects of auditing provide further insight. At this stage (there is a separate chapter on change management) it should be noted that on receipt of a draft audit report the auditee may exhibit some of the following reactions:

- **What does this mean?**
- **Will I lose out?**
- **Will I benefit at all?**
- **How should I play this?**
- **Will this lead to something bigger?**
- **Can I use this to get something?**
- **Is the auditor manipulating me?**
- **Is there a hidden motive behind all this?**
- **What are the costs of getting these recommendations actioned?**
- **Can I afford to ignore this report?**
- **Will my boss support me?**

Where these questions are left unanswered, the auditee may feel threatened and react negatively. If the audit has been professionally carried out with a clear understanding of management's systems objectives along with its close involvement at all stages of the review, then these fears may be reduced.

18.12 Logical Presentation

The flow of information contained in an audit report should follow a logical path that takes the reader through the audit process itself. The logic flow may appear as follows:

FIGURE 18.4 LOGICAL PRESENTATIONS

**SUBJECT
SCOPE
PLANNED COVER
ACTUAL COVER
MODE
EXISTING DEFICIENCY
UNDERLYING CAUSE
EFFECT/IMPLICATION
ENABLING STRUCTURE
REQUIRED CHANGES**

There are many ways that this information may be presented although the principle of providing a logical flow of problems' causes, effects and required action should stand.

Structuring the audit report

A defined structure for audit reports should be implemented by the CIA and this should be followed when drafting audit reports. This will vary from department to department depending on the nature of the work that is carried out and the type of officers who will be receiving the audit report. One example may be:

FIGURE 18.5 REPORT STRUCTURE

HEADINGS
title   date   auditors
level of confidentiality   distribution list

LIST OF CONTENTS

EXECUTIVE SUMMARY
audit objectives   conclusions
recommendations and action plan

MAIN BODY OF THE REPORT
detailed terms of reference   work carried out
background to the area under review   existing practices
list of control deficiencies and implications

APPENDICES
referred to in the report   required by the reader
glossary of terms

We can translate the above into sections e.g.;

TABLE 18.1 REPORT SECTIONS

SECTION	COVERAGE
One	This will contain the executive summary to the report.
Two	This will outline the objective, scope, approach and work done.
Three	This will contain a background to the area under review.
Appendices	Restrict these to the minimum.

The CIA should adopt a suitable policy on responses from the auditee and they may be:

☐ **Incorporated into the report**. Here adjustment is made throughout the report to reflect the comments received from management. A note to this effect may also appear in the report which is a technically correct approach, but can lead to delays in achieving a final draft for publication. There will also be some comments that the auditor does not agree with, and again the way that these are presented will have to be thought about.

☐ **Built into a management action plan**. The important part of the report is the action plan and it is possible to build management's views into this section without making numerous adjustments to the main body of the report.

☐ **Included as an appendix**. A convenient method for dealing with responses is to simply include them as an appendix to the report. The problem here is that they may be taken out of context if a form of audit responses to the comments is not also included. We may imagine however that a continuous exchange of memoranda based on responses to responses could become an embarrassment to all sides and this should be avoided.

Some audit departments send the draft for consultation without the Executive Summary and formulate recommendations after the auditee has been able to comment on the findings. The participative approach comes into its own where the auditor forms joint recommendations with the auditee after discussing the findings. This agreed action plan is then reported in the executive summary. Note that where there has been close co-operation throughout the audit, problems with formal responses will probably not arise.

Ongoing drafting
Most auditors are very efficient when performing the fieldwork and by working hard can give a good impression to clients. Back at the office, there is a tendency to slow down and spend much time on drafting the audit report and this may lead to delays in publishing the report. One solution is to encourage auditors to write reports as they carry out the audit and the outline structure may be drafted as soon as the audit is started. Portable PCs are essential to this process and as drafting occurs, any gaps may be spotted before the auditor leaves the client. Where a reporting structure has been agreed via the audit manual then one will be able to complete an outline when the audit is started. The terms of reference part of the report may be drafted from the assignment plan while a section on background to the operation will be available in the early part of the audit. It is not acceptable to

produce reports weeks after the audit and the reporting standard should set clear deadlines on this topic.

Reporting concepts

It is possible to build on much of the material that has already been mentioned and set out some of the wider concepts that come into play when dealing with audit reporting including:

☐ **Working papers**. These should be clear and suitably referenced. Evidence to support audit findings should be cross-referenced to the draft report and be quickly retrievable when required. One could imagine discussing the draft report with management and referring to the working papers when dealing with a particular audit point. The need to set standards for working papers cannot be over emphasised.

☐ **Model building**. We have agreed that systems auditing is about comparing what is, with what should be. One important component of an audit is the models that are built and described in the report as the basis of the audit opinion on the adequacy and effectiveness of controls. These models must be geared into systems objectives if they are to have any relevance to management and the audit report should not contain aspirational models that are unachievable in practice. One reporting technique is to define the outline model that is used to assess the operation early on in the report so that the reader can follow the comparisons and confirmation (testing) thereof.

☐ **Test findings**. The way that the results of testing are reported will affect the quality of the audit report. We accept that all audit findings should be supported by firm evidence and this is derived from testing procedures. In turn the implications of poor control should be determined and brought to management's attention as a basis on which to plan remedial action. The audit evidence may be reported in many different ways and this may range from providing all the technical detail through to generally summarising only the more important findings. The flow of the report will partly depend on this feature and this should be defined before drafting begins. Where statistical sampling has been used then extrapolation can be applied to the results to support specific statements. It is not a crime to use technical terms as long as they fit with the objectives of the audit and flow of the report. The main report will contain detailed test results while the conclusions and executive summary will be phrased in more general terms. It is possible to list relevant test results in a separate appendix in a matrix or graphic format for closer consideration if required.

☐ **Reporting status**. The level of confidentiality should be defined along with a list of recipients. It may be possible to use colour coding for different levels of confidentiality. It is as well to let each reader know who has seen the report and to whom they should allow access without being overly dramatic.

☐ **Results based**. Here the thrust of the report should be centred on the verifiable audit findings. The auditor must not go off in all directions when the findings can only support a certain number of conclusions. It is dangerous to act like a private detective and deduce from a whole series of findings a final view that comes close to pure conjecture.

Conclusions should be based on findings and not auditor intuition since this is really no different from mere speculation.

☐ **Style**. This should generally be positive and future-oriented. A discussion style can be used constructively although it depends on the targeted audience. Certainly dry facts listed one after another will not capture much attention from the reader and this should be avoided. Too much discussion will read like a novel, and this is the other extreme. The secret is to understand and use each reporting technique in the right way and achieve a sense of balance.

☐ **Structure**. The structure should flow from the audit objectives and follow a logical easily readable format. The audit standard on this should have foremost the needs of the reader. Managers are comfortable when reading a logical report that flows in a sensible fashion. At the same time it may be that one dips in and out of a report and again each main point should be separately understandable. A report that is confusing and unstructured will have the net result of frustrating the reader who may not even read the entire document.

☐ **Diplomacy**. Avoiding direct accusations and names is diplomatic and a well-balanced report is particularly important in special investigations. We should never refer to an employee by name (use designation) unless it is necessary, e.g. in a fraud investigation. Generally we are not concerned with the activities of individuals unless this is clearly required. Out-and-out criticism should only be applied where absolutely necessary. One must remember that auditors have a great deal of power through audit access privileges and as such we need to establish firm controls to guard against possible abuse.

☐ **Framework for recommendations**. Where the auditor wishes to formulate a whole series of recommendations it is best to take a tiered approach. In this way the Executive Summary may contain the underlying framework required to action the detailed recommendations that may then be placed in the main body of the report. Each recommendation should appear in descending order of importance with those that set an enabling structure, established as prerequisites to the more detailed specific recommendations.

☐ **Scope of internal audit**. It may be necessary to refer to the audit charter when setting out the scope of audit work since this may restrict the terms of reference. An example is where audit does not design and implement systems of control since this is management's role. The idea that audit provides a reviewing function that enables management to execute effective action may be explained as part of the report. Any comments made in the report must be consistent with other formal documents that relate to the audit function. As such the scope of an audit should coincide with the scope of audit work and if we are providing consultancy services then this should be indicated.

☐ **Overall conclusions**. The main body of the report should contain any detailed findings that should not be confused with conclusions. The executive summary at the front of the report should however, contain an overall conclusion on the state of the whole system of internal control or the matter that has been investigated. This should be a short concise note giving the auditor's opinion based on the underlying findings. Credit should be given where warranted and failings may be highlighted in an attempt to rectify them. The full scale of the auditor's experience will come to the fore since this opinion will attempt to capture within a succinct statement, the results of the audit. It may be argued that this aspect of the report will create the most impact and set the context for any ensuing recommendations. Standing outside the detailed findings that may have been quoted factually, the auditor is forced to sum up by indicating whether the state of controls is good, bad or indifferent.

☐ **Trading-off recommendations.** Management is entitled to resist specific internal audit recommendations as long as they have a reasonable documented reason. What should be avoided is a situation where management justifiably resists several recommendations and extends this decision to the essential ones as well. Audit should be prepared to give up some of the less material recommendations while at the same time sticking to the more important ones. In this way a limited amount of trade-off is possible as with any real business situation as long as it is justified by the final result. If recommendations are structured, then this will help differentiate crucial ones from less material matters. Management may also take a different course of action from the auditor's suggestions as long as the net result tackles identified control weaknesses. A certain level of tact and diplomacy is required in negotiating recommendations and this must be recognised by the auditor.

☐ **Executive summary.** All reports should start with an executive summary which may consist of one page for smaller reports and say three/four pages for the larger ones. This must tell senior management in a nutshell "what has happened and what needs doing!" The executive summary will give clues as to the extent to which the detailed reports should be studied depending on the seriousness of the issues that need to be addressed. Moreover this part of the report must be designed to be read as a stand-alone document that may be detached from the main body of the report.

☐ **Graphics.** Widely distributed reports that should have a lasting impact should be carefully constructed and graphs and diagrams may be used to break up the narrative and illustrate important points and concepts. The CIA should ensure that firstly, the facilities are available and secondly that they are used wherever necessary. The type of software that is being applied will have a major impact on this facility. Regular reviews should be made to ensure that the audit department is keeping up with trends in this direction. Make sure that graphs take up around one third of the page so that they are not too small to read, and do not consume the entire page, but are mixed with narrative.

☐ **Qualifications.** Whenever a report or piece of work is referred to in an audit report, its status should be qualified. The degree of objectivity and reliability should be defined since many reviews are commissioned by management for a specific purpose. As an example, we might imagine what a review by a trades union might say about the industry's rate of pay rises. Quotations made from reports should indicate the context within which they were commissioned. It should be pointed out that management consultants will operate to the terms of reference set by the client. For example a consultant's report may end up recommending closure of a department after having been set an objective of identifying which units may be dispensed with. As such this report may only be read within the context of the slimming-down strategy that was at that time adopted.

☐ **Ownership of controls**. The audit report should typically contain much information regarding the current state of controls and how they might be improved. This should certainly be used by management but at the same time it should be clear that management is wholly responsible for the arrangements that are employed to control operations. A review of controls does not pass on responsibility for discharging the five key control objectives to the internal auditors. The report writer may wish to clarify this point and reinforce the view that audit's role is advisory in nature.

☐ **Perception of internal audit**. Some audit departments are seen by management to be counter-productive and obsessed with identifying management's errors and failings. The final report may list a whole series of immaterial items from transactions processed many months ago. Audit may argue that these errors need to be corrected while at the same time, the major operational issues that management is trying to resolve are simply ignored. High-level constructive audit work is the most efficient way of employing audit resources and if this policy is adopted, the resulting audit reports will reflect this strategy and hopefully will be well received. Each report in this vein will improve management's perception of the auditors. Where the audit deals with extensive testing with narrow terms of reference then this factor should be disclosed in the section on audit approach. Quality assurance procedures should ensure that all reports promote the audit image partly by complying with professional audit standards. Always remember, a good report must be based on a good audit and the temptation to "draft oneself out of trouble" to cover sub-standard work should be avoided. If a report does not meet professional standards then it should not be published.

☐ **Standardisation**. Material audit findings tend to call for urgent action and if the auditor is able to present the audit report quickly, this again improves audit's impact and credibility. Standardisation will improve efficiency although at the extreme, it can make reports appear dogmatic and superficial. We must balance the technique of dropping standard text into a report with the need to ensure that it is linked directly into the audited area. Internal training workshops should be run to implement any suitable policy on this topic, along with standard report templates held on the hard disk of the auditor's personal computer.

☐ **Future orientation**. An audit report that does not talk of the future has little use for management since a problem is solved when management takes effective action to ensure that it does not occur again. Errors are sunk costs in that they have already occurred. What is important is that the defective control (or lack of controls) is identified and dealt with and it is here that audit can play a powerful role. The secret is to use past data to back up recommendations that are aimed at future improvements. A good report will be able to tie up these two concepts so that the timing differences are properly reconciled in the mind of the reader. It is however a fact that, if the data is too old, its relevance may decline. Planned changes may also be taken on board and again one may interface the past, present and future by careful report drafting.

☐ **Working paper references**. The file copy of the audit report should be cross-referenced to the underlying working papers so that everything that is reported can be instantly picked out in the working papers. It is advisable to hold such references in the margin. There is clearly a link between the standard of report and the adequacy of supportive working papers. References should refer to the file, enclosure number and enclosure page number.

☐ **Problem-solving approach**. The traditional approach emphasises the detailed findings as the main product that arises from the audit. Errors, problems, failings, control weaknesses and all matters that impact negatively on management are seen as the basis for the audit report, in that we have found out what is "wrong" with the system under review. A better approach that reflects the new breed of auditor is one that emphasises the recommendations as the key product from the audit in line with a consultancy based bias. This is a material consideration as it sets the tone and direction of the report and the way it is presented. The executive summary should contain a few words on the audit brief and opinion, but the main part of this (detachable), and most important section is the recommendations. These should describe and explain the required action. All else is secondary to this as errors and mistakes are simply there to support the recommendations and help gauge the extent to which action is now required from management. Any presentation of the report to management should reflect this position, i.e. be essentially based around the recommended action.

Good audit reports

The previous section dealt with general concepts behind audit reports. This section summarises features for good audit reports:

1. The client should be thanked for cooperation and assistance through a formal acknowledgement in the report. The auditor must be prepared to rise above negative management attitudes and even if the level of managerial support was not great, the acknowledgement should still be included in the report.
2. The report should normally not name names. One would refer to the designated posts wherever possible. Investigation into fraud and irregularity may be exempted from this requirement. Remember, we are not auditing people, we are auditing systems, procedures and circumstances. This principle also applies to any appendices that appear at the end of the report, where detail that identifies people should be removed from tables and schedules. Even where an officer is being commended we would still not wish to mention an actual name.
3. An action plan agreed with management should be set out in the Executive Summary. This represents the "agreements" reached based on the report and passes responsibility for the required changes from audit over to management.
4. We should always balance both good and poor features of the area under review so that we are seen to be fair. Recognition should be given to managers' efforts and any drives they have for improvement should be supported. We must also recognise pressures impacting on management's time and resources. Poor managerial practices may be seen more as barriers to these sought-after improvements, rather than disciplinary offences. If management has started to make changes as a result of an ongoing audit, it is not a question of who claims these improvements, but more a matter of mutual recognition on both sides. Any progress made on improving controls can be mentioned in the report, as well as reporting these changes as formal audit recommendations.
5. The auditees' views should be reflected within the report or their formal response set out as an additional appendix, to ensure that both sides to the audit have been fairly represented. This is particularly important where some degree of disagreement is present.

6. The whole style of the report should be positive and should not consist of a list of basic criticisms. If an audit is done well then the auditee will look forward to receiving the report as being a useful contribution to the management task.

7. The auditor should never blind the reader with science by using technical gibberish. This shows a flaw on the auditor's side in an inability to communicate effectively which is wholly unacceptable.

8. All reports should be professionally presented. If an unfinished draft is urgently required this should be quickly followed up with a final formal report that has been completed to professional standards. The first draft should state clearly the status of the document giving reasons.

9. The report should appear fresh and clear so that the reader might enjoy it. A well written discussion based style can assist this process with relevant summaries for quick consumption by busy executives. Factual discussion without recourse to emotive phrases is the best policy so long as this does not become too boring.

10. All facts should be quoted precisely. If part of the findings is based on limited information, or unconfirmed data then this should be clearly noted. If facts are conclusive then we are entitled to say so.

11. One may wish to use the audit "we" when describing the audit opinion. This personalises the work in one way by implying that it comes from the audit department, as opposed to some unseen force. On the other hand, it does not make it too intensive as it would be if it came from one individual (as would the use of "I").

12. The required action should be set out in a hierarchy of descending importance with the more important recommendations appearing first along with an appreciation of problems that may face management in implementing them. To this end the recommendations should be set within an enabling framework that may be described within the audit conclusions.

13. All excessive detail should be relegated to the appendices. These should be referred to in the report, but will not be essential reading. The operational manager might wish to study the appendices in detail whereas the director will probably concentrate on the executive summary. For this reason we would wish to see an amount of background information in the report that provides an insight into operational problems facing line management, and so make the report easier to follow.

14. Terms and structures should be consistent and follow logical processes. Where we refer to something in one way in the report, this term should be used through the document. Points made should support each other and contribute to the final audit opinion.

15. The work should flow logically with each point building up into a complete picture. Findings represent the culmination of this process. Without being too dramatic it is possible to take the reader through the system and how each part interlinks to form a whole system of internal controls. The reader should be reminded that these controls allow management to achieve its objectives and failings in one area rebound onto other areas and affect the overall quality of the end-product.

16. Reports should be well presented but not too "glossy". One has to be aware of the notion that the client is in effect financing the audit work and unnecessary waste and extravagance can be criticised. At the same time a final report should appear professional with the audit logo and card covers with cut-out windows, using desk-top publishing standards.

17. The report should be client-oriented in that it is directed at the needs of the reader. One useful technique is to use a standardised audit cover, white paper for the main body of

the report, a separate colour for the executive summary at the front of the report and another colour for the Appendices.

18. Reports should be produced quickly and one would expect the audit department to invest in computers, laser printers and a report binding device so that the draft does not spend weeks "at the printers/typist". The reports should be produced in-house to professional standards of desk top publishing quality. It is advisable to use an audit administration officer to help prepare the copies.

19. The work should recognise the various constraints that management faces and build these into the recommendations. An understanding of the pressures on managers and the criteria they apply will bring an element of realism to the audit.

20. We should state clearly the objectives, terms of reference and scope of the work and whether these were in fact achieved during the audit. All points on the terms of reference should be referred to in the findings and conclusions. If a participative style is assumed, then this should be reflected in the report, and the "we" might in fact refer to the auditor and management's joint efforts. If this is the case then we may not formulate audit recommendations, but instead agree and document a suitable action plan with management. This however, will depend, in part, on the role of audit in the organisation.

21. The report must address the real issues facing management if it is to have any relevance to organisational objectives. It is best practice to aim at the most material, sensitive aspects of the operation under review and so direct audit resources at real issues.

22. We must always remember that an ideal position is impossible to achieve and we have to work within the realities of the existing environment.

One fundamental truth the auditor must face is that a good audit report is based on the quality of the audit work and liaison with management that has to be done before one is able to report the results.

Audit expertise

When addressing the topic of audit reports it is vital that the auditor understands the actual role of audit. Managers are responsible for their operations and they will retain this right long after the auditor has done the review and departed to new fields. There are several points that should be mentioned to draw out this important concept:

Auditors should never assume that they know more than management about the particular operation. They are not paid to be experts in any one area. The auditor brings to bear an experience of controls and how these might be evaluated and tested. A "know-it-all" stance is off-putting and can only lead to problems when reporting the results of the audit. The audit must start from management's perspective and what it is seeking to achieve from the operations. The audit task is to feed into this process and examine the controls that have been provided to support the operation. What works in one organisation/department will not necessarily be appropriate in another and it is here that the auditor may fall down. The report must be drafted in line with this principle.

Audit is not there to "prop up management" and if it assumes this role, management will continue to require this service whilst the organisation will suffer. Assume management operates a sub-stores that holds local supplies that the central stores would take too long to provide. Management asks for an audit of these stores and it becomes clear it knows little about this unit. Audit then reports on the numerous problems that exist because no controls have been established whereupon management requests an audit and stocktake every six months. Audit is covering for management's failure to control the stores and the auditor's regular presence perpetuates this failing. A more common example is where management fails to define clear access procedures for computerised systems. They refer numerous cases of systems breaches to audit for advice on any action they may take against the employees. As long as we provide this service, management need not bother to plan and install suitable controls.

Audit is not employed to solve minor managerial problems since audit resources must be directed at material high-risk areas. Constant fire-fighting perpetuates the situation, particularly where resources are not available to deal with material control implications. Where audit responds to systems that have broken down without encouraging management to establish sounder controls this fire-fighting mode will continue. Audit may appear busy solving management's problems but this is a misdirection of resources.

Audit should not feel that it needs to show managers how to do their job. If management is unable to perform, then this is a control deficiency that needs resolving.

Audit should not second-guess management. If management does not know what it is doing, then the underlying causes must be addressed. There are many ways that services/products may be delivered and audit need not assume an executive role in this respect.

As the audit role moves away from inspection to consultancy the question of expertise will become increasingly sensitive. Computer specialists, human resource management, engineers, quantity surveyors and so on are now employed in the audit department. Despite this trend, it should be made clear that audit is above everything else, expert in control. The recommendations in the audit reports will reflect the relationship between audit and management and it is essential that these concepts are carefully portrayed in the way the audit report is drafted. The point is that audit must decide what it wishes to achieve before it can communicate these concerns in a formal audit report. If our role is to "check up on management" then so be it as long as this is a conscious decision rather than an individual auditor's whim.

The one minute manager
Research has shown that a typical manager will spend only a few minutes on each item of business before turning to another matter. Auditors who cannot identify with this point will find their work for all intents and purposes ignored. Managers may speak of the "audit books" to describe the detailed reports sent out by the audit department that are full of what appears to be insignificant facts and endless testing results. As well as using executive summaries, the auditor is well advised to give oral presentations to bring home audit points and in so doing save management much time and effort. The manager may need quickly to know:

- **What is the problem?**
- **What caused the problem?**
- **What are the implications?**
- **What is the best solution?**
- **What action should I take?**
- **What happens if I do nothing?**

An auditor who anticipates and answers all of these questions in say a brief meeting/presentation will be well received by senior management. Note that the formal comprehensive audit report should still be provided. The key is to anticipate unanswered questions and resolve them. If this does not happen then the impact of the audit report is lessened and a tendency not to act on the findings will arise. One only makes changes where there is a clear impetus based primarily on sound justifications and clear benefits. The realities of working life mean that management does not have time to deal with anything that fails this basic test.

18.13 Oral Presentations

Oral presentations can be used to break the mystique of internal audit and allow clients the instant feedback that audit reports cannot achieve. The consultancy role that may be adopted in contrast to the traditional policing role, gives audit a route into management's needs. To build on this relationship, one may arrange oral presentations to breathe life into audit reports. This happens to some extent at the winding-up meeting that is held on completion of the audit. The difference here is that a formal presentation applies all those visual aids and techniques that enable one to get the message across. For marketing audit services it is wise to ensure that some of the audit staff are experienced presenters and this skill can be extended across the audit department. One may only use oral presentations where a constructive atmosphere has been developed and management fully understands the audit role. The "OK CORRAL" model suggests that where all parties feel confident that the audit will be beneficial then a good working relationship will arise. This will not happen where audit's success is based on identifying management's failings and the auditor adopts an "I'm OK, you're not OK" policy. Likewise, oral presentations will not work where there are poor relationships between auditors and auditees and where this occurs, the room will simply become a battleground.

Managing oral presentations

From the previous section it is clear that oral presentations of audit reports can be great successes that lift the profile of the audit function, or they may be total disasters. They have to be managed and assuming a positive atmosphere has been established, we can refer to the work carried out by Steve Mandrell (1987) who suggests that one can address this subject on four levels:

1. **ANXIETY**
2. **PREPARATION**
3. **VISUAL AIDS**
4. **CONDUCTING THE PRESENTATION**

Anxiety

The starting place for would-be presenters is to determine where one is located (in respect of oral presentations) on the following scale:

FIGURE 18.6 THE ANXIETY SCALE

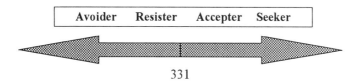

In other words an individual may enjoy and seek the task of performing presentations or, at the other extreme, avoid them altogether. In the middle fall those who will do them if pressed. Once the position has been identified then the required level of development can be determined. On the topic of managing anxiety the following should be noted:

☐ **Preparation is the key to success.** Where the auditor is comfortable with his/her material, we would expect a better performance. Not only does this engender greater confidence but preparation also makes sure all important matters have been considered and built into the presentation. This policy has a practical application within the audit unit, in that it depends on sufficient time to make arrangements for the event. Audit management and the CIA should encourage this, and view time spent developing acetates, setting up equipment and so on, as part of the legitimate chargeable time for the audit.

☐ **Practice makes perfect.** Following on from the above, one factor that tends to lower the overall level of anxiety is a foundation of past experience that should make each presentation easier. This consideration relates to previous presentations and also going through the motions of the current one beforehand. Trial runs enable one to time the event and iron out parts that do not readily flow. They also instill a sense of ease as the auditor now has to repeat what has already been performed (as a practice run) rather than undertake a completely new experience. We can bring in a volunteer auditor to assess the practice run or more appropriately, the audit manager should sit in to gauge the way the auditor performs.

☐ **Eye contact with the audience is essential.** Some nervous reactions are based on a fear of the audience who are perceived by the auditor as a potentially hostile group. To see the audience as individuals breaks down the conspiracy theory and it is through eye contact that this is made possible. The art of making contact naturally without fixing on any individuals should be practised by the auditor in the run-up to the presentation.

☐ **Muscle tension can be reduced** where the muscles are purposely tensed then released. Being aware of our muscles is a step in the right direction. Anxiety causes tension that can be translated into muscle tension, normally preparing the body for a state of alertness which militates against a relaxed state. Most presenters will tend to be nervous although this will be at varying states in line with the level of resistance/acceptance (as indicated on the chart above). The idea is to stop these nerves from interfering with the proceedings.

☐ **Breathing should be deep** as this helps relaxation and so allows the words to flow more freely. This is linked to the earlier point on muscle tension where poor breathing, because of anxiety, can interfere with the flow of words from the auditor. Trying to control breathing, by being aware of this problem, can help in solving this problem. This awareness is heightened by exaggerating our breathing then bringing it back in control, as a technique applied just before the event.

☐ **The presenter should move around slightly** as this releases tension although we should not exaggerate this action. Nerves can interfere with the smooth flow of information, which in turn can result in the delivery collapsing. The worst case is where the auditor feels tense, stands very still and starts to retreat into him or herself. Moving around from side to side in a considered manner, not only brings all parts of the audience into the proceedings but contributes to relaxation.

☐ **The presenter must know the subject well**. The auditor must have a detailed knowledge of the audit. It is better for the field auditor to perform the presentation, perhaps after an introduction from the audit manager. One feature that makes the presenter more comfortable is the ability to refer to examples to illustrate points. While most of these can be prepared in advance, there are some that will flow from discussion as the audience becomes involved interactively.

☐ **One may visualise the presenter's role** and the objective of getting a message across. Anxiety is based on a perception of oneself as the centre of the universe, where all eyes are set on the presenter. Where we are able to shift the focus from oneself to the subject at hand, we will perform the role of facilitator. By concentrating on the message, we may not have time to think about being nervous.

The above is concerned with reducing nerves and increasing relaxation so that the auditor may perform the presentation free from self-generated barriers. One of the key factors in a successful presentation is enthusiasm where the audience can be captured and the auditor acts as the change agent in terms of improved controls. This enthusiasm can feed from nervous energy and to an extent we may seek to encourage some adrenaline. We may construct a cycle to take this on board:

FIGURE 18.7 MANAGING ANXIETIES

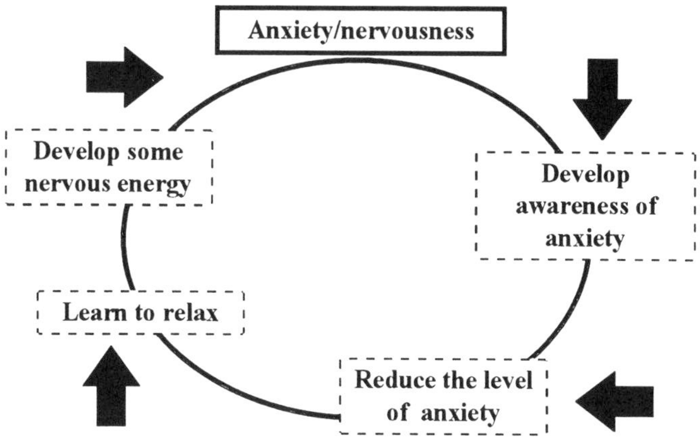

The idea is to manage anxiety by recognising and controlling it, rather than removing it altogether as a way of enhancing the impact of the presentation.

Preparation

We have referred to adequate preparations as a key requirement and this will involve:

☐ **Notifying the various parties in good time**. We will wish to invite the line manager and senior staff in the areas to attend. Anyone missed out will probably deem this to be a conscious decision and to avoid embarrassment we must ensure that invitations are properly issued.

☐ **Setting a clear audit objective**. For our purpose we will wish to present the results of the audit so as to introduce the draft audit report that will then be made available. It will not be to fully clear the report in detail as this will be impossible to do "on the spot".

☐ **Organising handouts**. Matters that will be referred to that cannot really be included in slides, should be given out in advance, or made available at the start.

☐ **Using visual aids**. These should be firmly in place in preparation for the presentation. The main problem is that the various devices such as an overhead projector may have been lent out to other sections. We would also want to test any such equipment beforehand.

☐ **Selecting a series of examples that may be used to illustrate specific points**. These should be taken from the audit and should consist of findings that were derived from testing. The audit standard that requires findings to be supported by sound evidence should also be applied in the presentation format. Charts and tables make ideal presentation tools as acetates.

☐ **Administrative arrangements so that delegates are not inconvenienced**. Coffee, biscuits, maps, handouts, seating arrangements and other administrative matters should be part of the preparation. A suitable checklist of items for consideration and action assists, as would an audit administration officer who is able to work at the highest levels.

☐ **Time should be carefully planned and rehearsals help clarify this**. At the start of the presentation it is a great benefit to be able to give an indication of how long it might take, so as to provide some form and structure. Once set we should try to stick to the timeframe.

☐ **The level of technical competence of the audience should be determined and the presentation format directed accordingly**. The managerial level should guide the detail provided. It is useful to go through a dress rehearsal in front of an audience with constructive feedback. To get a message across one suitable format appears as: Introduction, Work carried out, Findings, Conclusions, and Next steps.

Visual aids
There are many techniques that assist the presenter and turn what may be a very boring affair into an interesting and enlightening session.

Visual aids include:
- Dry wipe board. Remember to avoid the most common mistake of using permanent pens on the dry wipe board.
- Overhead projector with spare bulbs.
- Handouts that are linked to the acetates.
- Flip charts on a separate board where permanent markers may be used.
- Blue tack can be used to put up charts and standing data to be constantly referred to. With a list of material that will be covered during the presentation, it is as well to put

this up with blue tack (a sticky substance for binding papers to the wall) and tick each one as it is dealt with.

Visual aids should be used with care and here is some relevant guidance:

☐ **Use a pointer to highlight specific items** that are being spoken about on acetates. It is good practice to face the audience when speaking, which means it is better to refer to the images on the overhead projector rather than the screen.

☐ **Any slides should be carefully drawn to provide attractive images**. Professional standards require that they are printed via a suitable presentation package and not hand-written. Colour images are very useful as they hold the attention of the audience.

☐ **Use the illustration to focus attention**. Never fill the acetates with excess information or a copy of a detailed document. Slides should contain checklists or key pointers to expand on during the presentation. One approach is to use cartoons to pick up on key points. Humour should be used with care as we would seek to use neutral subjects that will not offend any sections of the audience.

☐ **Watch the positioning of equipment so that all can see**. There are many presentations that leave parts of the audience in the dark because of obstructions that block vision. A quick check from each side will make it clear whether there are obstructions. There are times when the presenter will have to move across the room and brief apologies should be provided.

☐ **Do not overload the audience with information and tables**. Some matters can be left for later consideration when the draft report can be read at leisure. This should be made clear during the presentation so that items such as schedules of errors found can be addressed at a later meeting.

Conducting the presentation
The physical environment for the oral presentation may be illustrated:

FIGURE 18.8 THE PRESENTATION'S PHYSICAL ENVIRONMENT

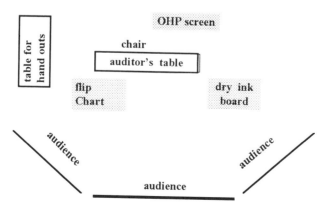

Practical considerations when conducting the presentation are:

☐ **Anticipate questions and ensure full answers are provided**. Some auditors see questions as flash points where possible confrontation may arise. The usual motive for questions is a search for more information on specific issues and this is the whole point in having presentations, where feedback can be generated. To avoid these questions defeats this objective. Where a delegate is seeking confrontation the person may be asked to meet separately to discuss any specific problems.

☐ **Use index cards as a guide**. An alternative is to use acetates as prompts throughout.

☐ **Ensure that eye contact is made with all in the audience**. It is more effective to include all in the room by looking at each person from time to time. Larger audiences make this more difficult. It is inexcusable to focus on a few key persons who appear to openly support the presenter.

☐ **Move around in a controlled fashion and use the various facilities properly**. The overhead projector may be used as the main focus of the presentation where acetates viewed in an ordered manner, represent the structure of the event. The flip chart may be used to set up diagrams and key pointers. The dry ink board may be used in a response to questions by setting out models and matrices to illustrate the answer that is provided. These diagrams will be erased as new ones are drawn so they should not be used for permanent items.

☐ **Speak clearly and always repeat what has been set out on an acetate**. This not only retains control but helps those with poor sight or concentration. It is good practice to summarise what has been said at regular intervals.

☐ **Negotiate and do not assume a fixed position where reasonable points are raised**. The auditor should not engage in heated discussion but must rise above the emotions present. Strong arguments can be smothered by simply noting them with no particular response. Another ploy is to get another person to respond to sensitive points by asking whether others agree.

☐ **Ensure that working papers are available for detailed queries although we may defer the response if further research is required**. Give overview answers but defer more detailed ones.

☐ **Relax and watch out for nervous gestures which distract**. Playing with keys or a watch creates an annoying distraction and this can become obsessive behaviour if left unchecked.

☐ **Control the audience and move them along when a point has been fully dealt with**. Most people recognise when one person is overreacting or making too many enquiries and they will not object if the auditor moves them along in a diplomatic fashion. If the structure is put up on the wall then we may tick each one off and suggest we move to the next as each matter is explored.

Further points may be noted on presentations that can be set within formal auditing standards.

☐ **Audit presentations are about bringing to management's attention the problem, its cause, the effect and required changes**. This can be done quickly and effectively where the facts are explained and brought to life. We need to refer to matters that affect management and the operational area; this may range from staff cuts or competition, to new computers. The idea is to capture the attention of those present in the opening few minutes. We can then go on to explain the control implications and how these may be met by improvements in line with the adopted recommendations.

☐ **Managers are entitled to assume risks where no action is taken although the implications should be carefully set out**. As long as they understand the significance of audit recommendations then management takes full responsibility for them. This understanding may be checked during a presentation. The audit position will be to advise and not instruct managers and this must be reflected during the presentation. We need to explain why recommended actions are important.

☐ **Professional presentations lift the audit image and get management on audit's side**. The auditor looks impressive if the presentation is well planned. The CIA must insist on preparation, audit manager input and standards governing the conduct of such meetings.

☐ **We may use the opportunity to educate management in both the role of internal audit and the importance of effective control mechanisms**. The questions and answers part of the presentation can be used to sell the audit product and pass over ideas to management such as self-audit. We will highlight the importance of the audit report by selling the role of controls as fundamental to the achievement of operational objectives. This educational role should be a theme throughout the presentation.

☐ **We may place alternatives in front of management and the resulting feedback may make evaluation and a final decision easier**. Negotiation skills come to the fore although it is not wise to simply throw away major audit findings as might occur if this is taken to the extreme. Do not ask managers for snap decisions as this is unfair and creates undue pressure. The presentation is to sell the audit report as a serious document worth considering and not to get instant agreement on complicated points.

☐ **Questions should be encouraged for a silent audience indicates the presentation has not been a success**. If questions are left unanswered or unasked then management and audit have not fully communicated. A skillful presenter will draw out questions from the audience without allowing one party to monopolise. Detailed questions that require review of the working papers should be deferred rather than hold up the entire presentation and this point should be made at the outset.

☐ **Generally the burden of proof falls on internal audit since management will not take action or redirect resources unless for good reason**. It is part of the audit role to persuade them by constructive reasoning. Change must be justified and cannot occur for its own sake. The presentation raises the profile of the audit and injects life into the report.

An approach to audit clearance procedures
One approach to audit presentations is to use them in the report drafting procedure to involve management and get an interactive response from them:
1. Complete fieldwork with ongoing discussion with management on findings as they arise.
2. Draft a report that sets out work done, findings and recommendations.
3. Hold a presentation where the report is discussed, concentrating on the outline recommendations as the most important part. Give out the draft report at this meeting and "sell the ideas".
4. Ask management to consider the detailed report and meet again for its response. An action plan should then be formulated.
5. Review the report to take on board any matters that management has brought to your attention.
6. Send the report out for wider consultation with all who feature.
7. Prepare final report for formal publication.

There is no point in convening a presentation where the relationship between internal audit and the auditee is impoverished or has broken down. The presentation then becomes point scoring with little constructive work possible. There is nothing to be gained from a presentation where the underlying audit has not been professionally done. Where findings are flawed, recommendations unworkable and/or the auditor has not been objective, the work cannot be defended in a presentation.

18.14 The Audit Manual

The audit manual is the forum for considering, evaluating and selecting the right reporting policy. In the manual we expect to see a reporting standard defining the most appropriate policies for:

☐ **The overall reporting process.** How reports are put together should be clearly defined. We expect this to promote progressive development with reports compiled during the audit and not just at the end of fieldwork. The issuing of interim reports will also feature in the reporting standard.

☐ **The review process.** The way draft reports are reviewed by audit management should be another matter for formal definition. Again we would expect a balance between expediency of the review (so as not to hold up the report) and depth of coverage (i.e. checks over quality). It may be that the CIA is required to sign off all reports or this may apply to sensitive reports only.

☐ **The draft clearance process.** Rules for providing for auditee comment in the report should be spelt-out. The adoption of a participative approach will tend to make this task smoother as clients are fully brought into the audit process.

☐ **Presentations.** We have discussed the role of oral presentations and this will be performed if adopted as part of the reporting standard. Many of the rules of best practice that have been outlined can readily be incorporated within the audit manual so long as auditors are sufficiently skilled in using this approach.

☐ **House style and colours**. The adopted colours and logos can be detailed in the audit manual as part of the marketing aspects of the audit function, and we would then expect to see these in place for audit reports.

☐ **Confidentiality**. Under the auditor's code of conduct we would wish to see material relating to rules of confidentiality, which will also apply to disclosure of the contents of the audit reports.

☐ **Terminology**. Rules on the style and approach to drafting the actual report should be conveyed through the audit manual. This will incorporate the various pointers that have been mentioned earlier on reporting concepts.

☐ **Level of detail**. A good item to include in the audit manual is guidance that will help the auditor in deciding the amount of background detail that should be included in reports. Some audit units publish reports that consist of brief numbered paragraphs going over the findings in detail with little or no introduction. Others contain much background material to set the context for the findings and comprehensively describe managerial practices and systems in operation. The adopted approach should be part of the audit manual as this is clearly a matter for the CIA to decide.

☐ **Appendices**. The extent to which supportive material is included as appendices or left in the files as working papers can vary, which is why some direction is required.

☐ **All other matters** bearing on audit reporting procedures should be subject to a reporting standard included in the audit manual.

☐ **Standardisation**. The audit manual should contain a specimen audit report. Having this on disk assists preparing audit reports and saves time. It may be necessary to have a number of specimens, for short reports, for longer ones and for reporting the results of fraud investigations. Another useful standard is to insist that each paragraph in the report is attached to a unique paragraph number from one onwards, for ease of reference.

18.15 Conclusions

Audit reporting procedures play a crucial role in the success of audits. The reporting mode should be geared into the culture of the organisation and the needs of management. We set out the minimum information that the auditor needs to consider when acquiring expertise on communicating the results of audit work as required under audit standards. We should also refer to the internal audit department's own reporting standard which will reflect the audit role agreed with the organisation.

CHAPTER NINETEEN

THE AUDIT MANUAL

19.1 Introduction

The topic of audit manuals touches upon a number of subsidiary issues including standardisation, procedures, controlling creativity and audit approaches. This chapter brings together the main topics that should be dealt with via the audit manual as well as discussing some models that help illustrate this all-important technique.

19.2 The Role of the Audit Manual

It is necessary to establish the role and objectives of the audit manual before considering appropriate models. Publications on internal audit procedures and performance bear on the topic and so a wide range of material has been considered. Our definition of the audit manual is:

> *"a process that accumulates and disseminates all those documents, guidance, direction and instructions issued by audit management that affect the way the audit function is discharged."*

The manual is a mechanism for channelling guidance for the auditor. The available material provides comments from many different sources and will give insight into the various issues that surround the design and implementation of audit manuals.

19.3 Relevant Sources of Information

General published material

Published research on audit manuals mentions the lack of cover provided by most internal auditing textbooks with the hope that this would alter in future. A publication called "Manual of internal audit practice" (Stearn and Impey 1990) does not discuss the audit manual as a concept although there are sections on policies, procedures and working papers. There are textbooks that make mention of the audit manual including Willson and Root (1989) which has a separate section covering definition, role and contents. The overall feeling from reviewing the major texts on internal audit published in the UK and the USA is that the audit manual is considered mundane. By considering published material of a more general nature, many principles derived from the topic of managing internal audit can be applied to the expanded definition used above. Heeschen and Sawyer (1984) have produced detailed guidance on audit procedures and list the contents of several specimen audit manuals. It is only by adopting an extended view of the role of the audit manual that the available material on internal auditing can be applied to building suitable models.

Government Internal Audit Manual

The Government Internal Audit Manual (GIAM) was issued by the UK Treasury in 1983 to government departments and non-departmental public bodies in response to growing pressures to improve central government internal auditing. It is interesting to note that this publication establishes a set of standards that are set out in section B of the manual. Furthermore, the material in the manual was specifically selected to meet the needs of government auditors. The concept of a manual as setting tailor-made standards of performance and the link to developing the audit function is clearly illustrated by the process behind the implementation of the latest (1996) edition of GIAM.

CIPFA/ILEA Manual

The Greater London Council (GLC)/Inner London Education Authority (ILEA) audit manual has been adopted by CIPFA and was published in 1985 and hereafter this will be referred to as the CIPFA manual. This was the first readily available local government audit manual. As well as its formal use within the old GLC and ILEA (they have since been abolished) many local authorities have based their own versions on this model. CIPFA have also produced a guide to preparing audit manuals which contains their various statements and an illustration outline audit manual.

NHS Audit Manual

The UK's National Health Service (NHS) audit manual was first produced in May 1987, and as with GIAM was geared to supporting the development of a more effective audit service. It sets down standards, in this case, minimum standards as both targets and performance benchmarks. The manual is divided into a managerial part (volume 1) and an operational part (volume 2). The latter was designed to be used on a day-to-day basis covering a number of operational areas that are audited within the NHS. The guidance provided through the audit manual mechanism in the NHS model is at a comprehensive level in that a methodology is established and detailed control matters are isolated for use by the auditor. One difficulty in this level of detail is that it would have to be fully understood and supported by audit management and also carefully implemented throughout the various audit departments. Although the audit manual is a document, it is also a process for enhancing the delivery of audit services.

19.4 Main Issues

Objectives

Most material on the role of the audit manual highlights the need to define standards and approaches to work and communicate this to audit staff. This is both as a guide to what is required from them and consequently what will be used to measure their performance. Sawyer (1988) brings in the link between establishing standards and securing assurances regarding the quality of audit's final product. GIAM stresses the advisory nature of the manual although we might imagine that each individual department would construct a local version based on GIAM. The manual has been described as in part an invisible manager setting out the methodology as well as acceptable standards of performance and a quality control device. We are moving closer to viewing the manual as a means of controlling the audit function rather than a bound document relegated to the filing cabinet. The GIAM and NHS versions recognise this important aspect of its role. The CIPFA manual emphasises the need for uniformity and consistency, relying more on the existing CIPFA standards to deal with the issue of performance. APB guidelines view GIAM and the NHS manual as standards and guidelines for specific organisations although they contain no specific requirement to publish a formal audit manual. The IIA standards are firmer on this matter and talk of the need for written policies and procedures from the Chief Internal Auditor for larger audit departments. Manuals fulfil the following roles:

☐ **Defining standards and methods of work**. This is the first and foremost task of the audit manual as the vehicle for defining auditing standards. The way audit will be managed and audit resources employed are matters that have to be decided by audit management in seeking to discharge its responsibility for delivering a quality audit service.

☐ **Communicating this to auditors**. The second role of the manual is to bring the requisite standards to the attention of audit staff. By including relevant material in the manual we can argue that this means they have to be adhered to by all staff by virtue of their position. Assorted memos, advice and documents issued to auditors have no real status if they are not delivered in a co-ordinated manner and it is here that the audit manual is of great assistance.

☐ **Establishing a base from which to measure the expected standards of performance**. So long as management has set standards and communicated these to staff (along with training if required) the auditors can then be expected to apply the standard. We then use this to determine whether audit staff are able to perform. Herein lies the third role of the manual in enabling management to consider and judge the performance of their staff.

In using this model we return to the concept of the manual as a framework for processes that lift the quality of audit work. The question that then arises is what mechanisms are used to establish an acceptable audit service in audit departments that have inadequate audit manuals? Although the main objectives of the manual may be clearly defined, the degree to which audit requirements are specified will vary, and the adopted manual may be more or less prescriptive depending on a number of factors. One might view the actual task of the manual as falling on the following continuum:

•   To provide a range of reference material for auditors.
•   To provide a general framework for the audit function.
•   To provide a comprehensive guide to audit work.

These three definitions move from a basic through to a more comprehensive view of the manual with increasing degrees of guidance provided. The precise function of the audit manual will vary. A conscious decision must be made by audit management regarding which model to select based on the circumstances and an understanding of available models.

Contents
Heeschen and Sawyer (1984) set out examples of the contents of audit manuals and list six different illustrations from a variety of industries including a bank, a chemical company, and a university. Each is formulated to suit the particular type of audit service. Many of

the manuals mentioned in textbooks are centred around standards. The example used by Willson and Root for a corporate audit manual includes standards on independence, training, fieldwork and four separate reporting standards. One of Heeschen and Sawyer's examples is in fact a reproduction of the heading for the IIA's general and specific standards. After considering the contents of many audit manuals, Henrietta Stewart (1989) felt that they should concentrate on managerial aspects and specific audit areas rather than audit procedures. The final contents of a manual depend on the model adopted and the degree to which auditors are directed and controlled. Sawyer (1984) divides the audit manual into three main sections: Technical, Administrative and Miscellaneous. Considering the CIPFA, GIAM and NHS manuals, it is possible to relate each topic to these three main sections with standards falling into the Administrative section. We can draw from this three section model by separating the managerial aspects from basic administration and adjust it to appear as follows:

TABLE 19.1 SECTIONS OF AN AUDIT MANUAL

SECTION	CONTENTS
Managerial	concerning the management of the audit function
Operational	concerning the performance of audit work
Administrative	all other procedural matters

It is not possible to be more precise than this. The great diversity in style and format of audit manuals is a natural result of the diversity in audit work, approaches and quality assurance mechanisms that are applied by chief internal auditors. What we can say in addition to the managerial, operational, administrative headings is that, firstly the objectives of the manual must be clearly defined and secondly, the resultant document must be sufficient to achieve these objectives.

Standardised forms

One issue is the concept of standardised documentation and the associated role of the audit manual. Before we touch on the topic of standard forms it should be clearly established that our definition of audit manuals is as a managerial vehicle for directing auditors. This means that standardised procedures form part of the formal standards that have to be achieved. To have documentation standards as ad-hoc forms without co-ordinating them as a manual will necessarily cause inconsistency and inefficiencies in their application. There is an abundance of material on the advantages of standardisation and a number of features can be highlighted:

1. The most familiar standardised procedures are in the form of internal control questionnaires and audit programmes that are developed by many audit departments. The general view is that what in effect are checklists must be tailored by the auditor or the audit objective can become immersed in the sole task of completing these documents. In many cases this can lead to low-level audit work carried out by junior or inexperienced staff and a corresponding poor image for internal audit.

2. Flowcharts should follow a uniform pattern that should be consistently applied throughout the audit department. This enables one to direct training at a particular model that is in use and also ensures that different auditors are able to understand flowcharts prepared by their colleagues. This also applies to block diagrams and other simplified graphical models.

3. Standardisation leads to consistency and report writing can have a "house style". We would expect audit functions to publish reports in line with an adopted standard, that is well known throughout the organisation. Audit reports may end up anywhere within (or outside) the organisation and it is right that they follow a prescribed format.

4. Standardisation can lead to auditors giving less attention to format and procedures and more attention to the actual objectives of the task at hand. We need not re-invent the wheel each time an audit is performed since standards once applied are used whenever the set criterion applies. Auditors should be more concerned with the underlying messages that are provided via the audit process and not the documentation and procedures applied to arriving at this position. The argument runs that audit management can give detailed consideration to a standard that can then be used by auditors as an efficient vehicle for performing their work.

5. Standardisation can constitute a vital control over each audit assignment. The act of setting a standard also provides direction over the relevant parts of the audit and this helps give it form and direction. For example, we may state that all interview records will include a summary that indicates what impact the information has on the audit at hand. In this way we will have forced the auditor to make this consideration which in turn will give better direction to the interview. This acts as a control over the interview process that stops them from drifting aimlessly if the audit objectives are not held in mind.

Despite the obvious advantages, there are many dangers, and Heeschen and Sawyer (1984) warn that standardised procedures can do more harm than good in restricting the auditors in the approach that is applied. The position we have reached in defining a model audit manual is that all moves to standardise procedures should be channelled through the audit manual. This might be the biggest single benefit from resourcing the implementation of a comprehensive and up-to-date manual. Lastly the task of progressing an audit automation strategy depends largely on having standardised procedures that might be automated and a formal vehicle for implementing these procedures i.e. an audit manual. Note that the accompanying diskette contains examples of standardised documents that may be applied to managing and performing internal audits.

Procedures and working papers
Auditing standards are quite specific on the topic of working papers with the APB guidelines suggesting that:
Para 39 - "In order to demonstrate that due care has been exercised the internal auditor should be able to show that work has been performed which is consistent with this guideline."

The IIA version has similar requirements in their standard on performance of audit work:
420.02.8 - "The CIA should establish policies for the type of working paper files maintained, stationery used, indexes and other related matters."

The IIA also requires compliance with the standards although in this instance the Code of Ethics establishes this point. The audit manual is the device that allows audit management to consider, formulate and apply suitable audit procedures aimed at ensuring efficiency as well as compliance with standards. It is difficult to visualise any other way that this could be achieved. It must be remembered that audit procedures cannot simply be extracted from audit textbooks but have to be adapted to suit the particular audit approach.

Audit approach and methodology

We are concerned with the manual as a projection of the audit personality or the voice of the director of auditing on the basis that in practice, auditing can be performed in a variety of ways. The APB and IIA standards recognise this issue and have framed their requirements in a generalised way with two main implications. Firstly, differences in audit approaches and methodology are seen as inevitable and secondly, it is not enough to simply declare that a certain set of standards are being adopted. The precise audit philosophy must be agreed and documented for application throughout the audit department. Chambers, Selim and Vinten (1987) argue that there are three main audit approaches; verification, vouching and systems whereas Sawyer (1988) speaks of accounting orientation, operational, managerial and participative auditing. Courtemanche (1986) has provided a vivid illustration of different styles of auditing that affect the way independence is achieved by audit and categorises them into four distinct types. Over and above this question of individual approaches there is a general consensus that internal auditing, as a function, is moving from a transactions based style to a systems based approach that touches on managerial processes as fundamental aspects of the overall control mechanism. To further complicate this maze of change, auditing is now achieving higher professional status. Also, with the widening scope, the consultancy aspects of a client based (or even partnership) role is developing at the same time. Courtemanche (1986) describes the interesting case of the newly qualified accountant who enters internal auditing with little understanding of its real role far removed from the verification of financial statements. The point that we are moving towards is that experienced, as well as new auditors, need firm direction on what is expected from them in terms of discharging the particular audit role. In this respect, the audit manual is the ideal device for placing the agreed solution on record. Each audit department must offer a defined product that is the result of the "contract" struck between audit and the organisation. Views from the world of management consultants can provide an insight into the need to assume a suitable methodology and offer a differentiated product. The ability to engage in less structured activities and move freely from project to project can be developed with a carefully thought out methodology. This may be set out in the audit manual but not from the generalised set of audit procedures found in audit textbooks.

Impact on creativity

Most writers on audit manuals and procedures mention the problem of stifling initiative. We might therefore imagine audit managers following defined routines that are found only in their memory banks so that a flexible and dynamic application of audit techniques may be freely applied with no restrictions. The argument against resourcing the audit manual is centred on the fear of creating a robot-like audit workforce with little flair or imagination. Chambers, Selim and Vinten (1987) comment on the potential for autonomy of action of the auditor, unless restricted by tedious work programmes. Courtemanche (1986) underlines the initiative and creativity required and argues that the obsession with audit working papers as a measure of productivity is unwarranted. Venables and Impey (1988) consider initiative and mature judgement in interpreting evidence an important audit skill. They view the manager's role as providing the framework that allows the auditor to contribute to achieving objectives. There appears to be a direct conflict between the extent of direction and standardisation that a comprehensive audit manual provides, and the auditor's professional autonomy. Both are essential for enhancing audit productivity. This conflict is akin to the perennial problem of reconciling managerial control and autonomy, where autonomy is defined as the freedom to succeed or fail. Auditors cannot perform if they are unclear as to what is considered successful performance while at the same time little commitment can be achieved within a bureaucratic straitjacket. Audit manuals must recognise this inherent conflict.

19.5 Building a Conceptual Model of the Audit Manual

Wide definition

This section builds a conceptual framework that promotes understanding of audit manuals. The manual is a device for formulating and communicating the audit role in conceptual, managerial and operational terms. We can make several firm statements:

- All audit departments have some type of audit manual although the contents may be dispersed and consist of uncoordinated items of guidance. According to our definition, manuals should cater for all types of relevant material. This requires a mechanism by which all published guidance can be collected and documented. The worst run internal audit section may still produce a manual by locating all memos that management has sent to audit staff in one file, along with a copy of standards. There is no excuse for failing to prepare a manual, even if a formal version is not possible.
- The manual should provide an avenue for establishing mechanisms crucial to audit performance ranging from quality assurance, standards, performance appraisal, methodology, approach, standardisation, automation and generally controlling the audit function. The ongoing search for excellence should be reflected in additions and alterations to the manual as a vital process.
- If the manual is not carefully conceived, formulated, implemented, reviewed and maintained it is difficult to see how an audit department can achieve successful service delivery.

The three main elements

We would expect to see the following aspects covered in any "adequate" audit manual:

1. **The management of internal audit**. We expect to see coverage of objectives, standards, code of conduct, structure, policies, strategic plans and control of the audit function. It is deficient to omit material on audit management from manuals.
2. **The operational aspects of internal audit**. This covers guidance on how the audit role is discharged in terms of planning, approaches, procedures, methodology, conduct and the techniques to be applied, as well as guidance on specific audit risk areas with related controls, and different types of audits ranging from systems work through to fraud investigations.
3. **Administrative matters concerning the audit function**. This catch-all section would include matters such as timesheets, subsistence, timekeeping and absences, job descriptions, health and safety, data protection, and equal opportunities.

Applying the management control system

Systems based auditing depends on systems theory and auditors who apply this approach should accept the implications of viewing activities as consisting of a series of managerial systems and sub-systems. The management control system is a conceptual system of control that follows the logical order of managerial processes that enable resources to generate services in an efficient and effective manner. Each part of the control loop should be considered, designed and implemented to achieve optimal control. Each aspect of the managerial control system should be decided via the manual (note that this is illustrated in chapter one) and we can assess the adequacy of current manuals by how far they incorporate the various control components.

The dynamism of currency

The extent to which the audit manual is kept up-to-date is one measure of efficiency. Procedures must be completely relevant or they will not be complied with. If not:

1. It gives out signals that the manual is not considered important by audit management and lowers its status. The objective of the document is to reflect and reinforce changing best professional practice.

2. It is difficult to insist on compliance and auditors drift into their own interpretations of the audit role.

3. It becomes a procedures document held in a rarely used filing cabinet. Important new events that affect the future of internal audit will certainly be addressed by audit management. If they are left out of the manual, it sends the message that the manual is not meant for real issues. Dusty old rules on timesheets and travel claims may be held unchanged in the manual and we return to the old view of the manual as a set of basic administrative procedures.

4. It means newly appointed audit staff, particularly at manager level, will have no firm commitment to adopt the audit style and methodology or to view the internal standards before accepting appointment. Conflict may arise that leads to a disjointed and uncoordinated service. The role of the manual in pulling together the audit resource around professional standards is lost.

A continual appraisal of the manual to keep it up-to-date and vibrant requires a firm policy of resourcing this. This can only happen where the manual is seen as an audit product to be successfully accomplished and the task is built into performance indicators for both individual auditors and the department. Our model requires current material to be part of the dynamic process of directing audit resources effectively. Dowden (1986) comments that reviewing the manual provides an opportunity to also carry out an objective review of audit practices and methodology.

19.6 Using Models

It is difficult to devise models that can be used to evaluate audit manuals since the content of each manual is determined by many factors including the perceived function of such a document. The content, style, degree of detail and length of each manual will be influenced by:

1. How important is the manual, i.e. how much audit resources should it consume and at what level? The type and size of the audit function will impact on the profile it achieves and this should be decided beforehand.

2. What functional model is most appropriate in terms of the manual being a compilation of reference material, a general framework for the audit department or a more comprehensive guide to managing and doing the audit? The level of detail must be established.
3. How prescriptive should the manual be, and how much autonomy should auditors have?
4. How far can audit formulate its own policies or must it adopt general organisational policies? The organisation will have established clear policies in many areas such as staffing, promotion, and training, and these will have to be recognised in the manual. In other areas audit may set its own direction. The business unit concept devolves many corporate roles down to local manager level. This may mean the manual can set its own rules for auditors in the search for quality services.
5. Is it necessary to document all guidance or can we leave some matters in conversational mode where audit management makes decisions based on the individual circumstances of each problem? This can be easily catered for by inserting in the manual considerations such as "audit management will determine the precise level of testing having regard to the circumstances of each case".

Managing the audit function

Documenting management's decisions on how the audit function will be managed and performed will be reflected in the manual and will form the basis for strategic review. The principles in the model are based on managerial concepts and derive from systems thinking.

Other attributes of an audit manual

Some associated problems need to be solved:

*   Objectives must be clarified. The point in a continuum should be selected ranging from a simple list of reference material, a general overview framework through to a comprehensive operational guide to controlling an auditor's performance.
*   The contents of the manual, in terms of topics for inclusion and degree of detail, should relate to the need to fulfil the chosen objectives. This depends on the size and type of audit service provided.
*   Standardised forms are advised and care should be directed to their design and use and the potential for automating the audit process.
*   The adopted procedures and working papers should be based on the assumed standards in terms of ensuring that the requirements of the standards have been adequately discharged. It is not good practice to simply use forms and standards taken from other organisations' audit manuals.
*   A clear audit methodology should be selected and applied based on the needs of the organisation, the audit charter and the level of skill and experience of the auditors.
*   The creativity and initiative of auditors will not prosper if their professional autonomy is curtailed. "Auditing by numbers" is unproductive.

Applying the conceptual framework

The final product is not the manual but successful implementation of standards and methodologies. We need to define and formulate a framework that incorporates the main principles behind successful manuals. The diagram below is based on four main planks of the audit manual process:

- The task has to be properly resourced (A).
- The wide concept of the manual has to be supported (B).
- The manual has to be used by auditors (C).
- It must play a role in evaluating auditor's performance (D).

FIGURE 19.1 FRAMEWORK FOR SUCCESSFUL AUDIT MANUALS

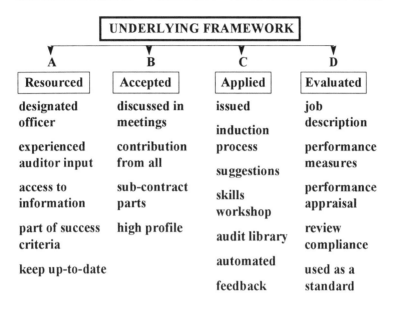

Explanations follow:

(A) **Resourced** - An experienced audit manager should produce and maintain the manual.

(B) **Accepted** -The manual should be brought into mainline audit management and managers' meetings should include discussions on "implications for the audit manual" for all decisions made. Parts of the manual should be subcontracted to auditors (mainly managers) and again this should be part of performance targets. The chief internal auditor should ensure that the manual maintains a high profile and is a constant discussion topic. It is possible to rotate the task of maintaining the manual between auditors and introduce an element of competition in improving it.

(C) **Application** - It has to be used by auditors based on understanding and acceptance. Firstly it is essential that all auditors have a copy and a process for inserting amendments. All new auditors should go through induction training based around the manual. Specially tailored skills workshops may be regularly held either internally or externally to cover separate topics in the manual on say flowcharting, systems based auditing, report writing, statistical sampling, and interviewing. Convenience in design and use encourages auditors to keep their manuals close to hand and if PC notebooks are provided it would be sensible to hold the audit manual on hard disk. The ability to copy standardised working papers from the manual for use during the audit will feed into the process of automating the audit.

Feedback should be obtained from auditors particularly where there are inconsistent or difficult parts of the manual along with suggested improvements.

(D) **Evaluation** - Auditors should use the manual to guide performance and quality assurance. The requirement to comply with the manual must be included in job descriptions and the manual should establish how performance will be measured. A formal performance appraisal scheme should be geared to meeting the standards set out by the manual. Supervisory review of auditors' work should look for compliance with the manual and audit managers have a major role. It is possible to use the manual as the standard for the performance of audit work and develop a career development scheme based on the manual. We might devise levels of ability to perform to the manual's requirements:

TABLE 19.2 ABILITY LEVELS: UNDERSTANDING THE AUDIT MANUAL

ABILITY LEVEL	UNDERSTANDING OF THE MANUAL
level 1	General understanding of the principles and techniques in the audit manual.
level 2	Comprehensive understanding of the principles and techniques in the audit manual.
level 3	Excellent understanding of the principles and techniques in the audit manual.

The performance appraisal programme may be based on the requirements of the manual. This can be extended so that junior auditors fall at level 1, senior auditors at level 2 and promotion to audit manager grade depends (in part) on achieving level 3 performance.

19.7 Selecting the Right Model

The three models:
1. **Compilation of reference material**. This contains basic rules developed over the years governing audit staff. Managerial policies, operational concerns and other high-level issues would not appear.
2. **General framework for the audit function**. We move now to a more developed format where the manual sets frames within which the audit work is contained. The approach to planning, systems based audits, reporting and so on will feature in this version of the audit manual. The guidance will be in outline form that will set general policy rather than fine detail.
3. **Comprehensive guide to audit work**. This seeks to cater for most of the situations that the auditor will experience. The proactive use of standardised documentation and checklists is the main feature. The manual will be self-contained in that it should include material that the auditor will require on a day-to-day basis. There will be extensive reference to documents in the audit library.

Impact of the services
The model below assesses the impact of the type of audit service on the type of guidance that should be given to auditors:

FIGURE 19.2 FLOW OF AUDIT SERVICES

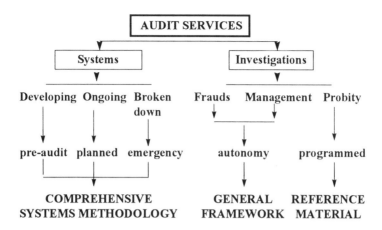

Reference material should generally not be included within the audit manual. A series of audit programmes might be referred to in the manual but the documents held separately in the audit library. Comprehensive guides will be appropriate where there is a clear methodology that would take on board all types of operations including computerised systems, capital contracts, and financial systems. Investigations require more autonomy, and consistency can only arise in a generalised fashion since each investigation will be different. Probity work tends to require a detailed programmed approach, which is less of a methodology than a process of completing a number of checklists. Parts of manuals involve a comprehensive methodology controlled through say standard documentation, while other aspects can only be contained within a general framework.

Other factors

These include the type of auditor employed and the size of the audit function. More guidance is required where auditors are less qualified/experienced or in a large audit department. More experienced auditors can be given more autonomy than less experienced. This can be highlighted:

FIGURE 19.3 IMPACT OF THE NUMBER AND TYPE OF AUDITORS

```
                    ┌─────────────────┐
                    │  LARGE AUDIT    │
                    │    SECTION      │
                    └─────────────────┘
                              ▲
              general      │  comprehensive
              framework    │  guidance
  ┌──────────────┐                    ┌────────────────┐
  │ EXPERIENCED  │◄──────────────────►│ INEXPERIENCED  │
  │  AUDITORS    │                    │   AUDITORS     │
  └──────────────┘                    └────────────────┘
              freelance    │  reference
              autonomy     │  material &
                           ▼  supervision
                    ┌─────────────────┐
                    │  SMALL AUDIT    │
                    │    SECTION      │
                    └─────────────────┘
```

19.8 Overcoming the Creativity Problem

There is a contradiction in the underlying objectives of the manual in providing direction throughout the audit function, and the need to maintain professional autonomy. The greater the degree of guidance provided, the more the auditor's efforts are restricted by standardised audit procedures. It is necessary to reconcile the two opposing forces of autonomy and control. The model below sets out the relationship between these two main factors:

FIGURE 19.4 AUTONOMY VERSUS CONTROL

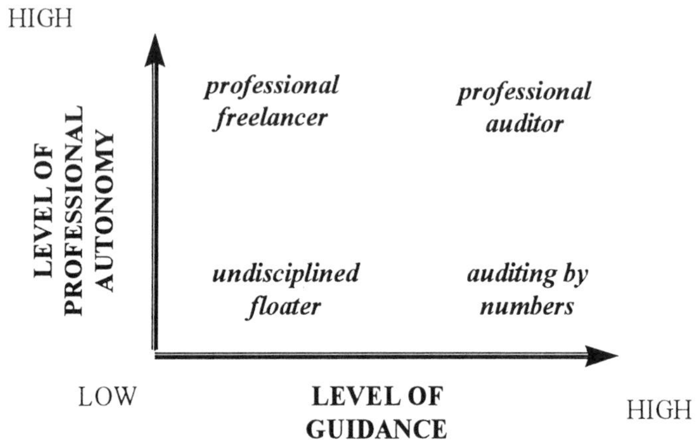

The point that we must arrive at is where auditors retain their professional flair and imagination but direct effort in the way that is required by the chief internal auditor, in line with the existing audit strategy and organisational culture. In this way we would move towards the target position shown in the far right hand corner of the above diagram by developing the "professional auditor":

[1] **Ensure that more comprehensive guidance is only provided where it is required**, e.g. where a particular methodology is required rather than a basic textbook approach. It is not necessary to cover common-sense points that the auditor will know anyway. We will seek to concentrate more on areas where there are different options that the auditor may adopt, and so promote a degree of consistency.

[2] **Leave general reference material outside the main audit manual.** We may make extensive references to the audit library and documentation published by the organisation itself. These factual matters can be explored at leisure without clogging up the manual with unnecessary detail. At times, it may be necessary to repeat pointers from key documents such as the purchasing code of practice. Here a brief summary of limits and rules may be mentioned and reference made to the full document which will be held in the audit library.

[3] **Indicate whether a particular procedure is optional.** It is good practice to state clearly where auditors are expected to carry out certain defined routines in contrast to those parts of the manual for guidance only. A suitable code may be applied (e.g. bold or

set in a box) to make this clear. Where it is possible to leave matters to professional judgement, then this approach should be pursued.

[4] **Explain why a procedure has been selected**. Resistance arises where an auditor does not feel it necessary to follow a rigid routine. Explanations can help break down this barrier by demonstrating why it is required. For example if we insist on the manager signing each working paper when it has been reviewed, this potentially cumbersome process can be justified as part of the quality assurance practices. If auditors are required to note (in their diary) any decisions they have made over the telephone, again the reason may be stated.

[5] **Allow departures as long as they are documented and justified**. We can avoid treating people as children by setting standards that allow some discretion where required. The terminology used can promote this approach by allowing departures in defined circumstances. The key is to encourage some discretion while stopping all-out anarchy, by careful drafting of the audit manual.

[6] **Encourage all auditors to participate in improving the manual and consider rotating the task of maintaining it**. The manual should develop from within the audit function and not be imposed from above (or outside). This will bring some degree of consensus and involvement into the process of establishing and maintaining the manual, and so generate a feeling of teamwork. This is in contrast to an elitist approach where the manual is given to a "high flier" for development as a form of wholly theoretical model building, far removed from the practicalities of working life. Note that this is just as bad as giving the manual to an administration officer and so lowering its profile.

[7] **Do not appoint an auditor until the approach and standards are explained and he/she can work within them**. We may place the requirements of the audit manual in front of newcomers before they sign the formal contract of employment. Our model suggests that the manual will be a detailed document that creates many demands on senior and junior auditors as they strive to meet the high professional standards embodied within the audit manual. This position should be made clear to all persons who are considering an offer of employment as we will require full commitment from staff. This "opt out clause" may save discontent as new staff feel unable to work within the confines of comprehensive managerial and operational standards that they may be experiencing for the first time.

[8] **Where a requirement in the manual has been overridden consider whether an amendment is required**. The most frustrating feature of the audit manual is where elements are no longer appropriate or lead to unnecessary work. Non-compliance can be deemed to be basic breach of procedure or indicative of a problem with the manual itself. The first point of call is an assessment of the adequacy of the manual, particularly where the breach is frequent and spread across the audit function. Unrealistic parts of the manual must be removed or revised and this is a matter that should be under constant review by the CIA.

[9] **Ensure that auditors who refuse to perform to the requirements of the manual are moved out of the audit department**. The approach adopted above was to stand back and

consider the manual in the event of non-compliance. After this issue has been dealt with we will turn our attention to acting on unjustified breaches of audit standards. This is a simple matter and requires audit management to reprimand the culprit immediately a problem arises and seek dismissal where there is continual or serious case of non-adherence. So long as the manual has been properly drafted and implemented, nothing short of this action is required to retain the credibility of the manual as an important management tool.

[10] **Test each section that is drafted to ensure that it is not unnecessarily cumbersome and bureaucratic**. Nothing should enter the audit manual until it has passed the "sensibility test". This requires a considered process whereby proposed changes are dealt with by audit management and reviewed in detail before it appears as a formal revision to the manual.

[11] **Watch out for auditors who appear demotivated and investigate underlying reasons**. Where staff are demotivated and/or seek resignation we must find out if this is the result of inappropriate auditing procedures. Group meetings may highlight this problem as will exit meetings for auditors who leave.

[12] **Ensure that there is a continuous programme to search for and amend all faults**. We should keep a watchful eye on anything that impacts on the manual. It is as well to make the audit manual a part of the agenda on all audit management meetings that address developmental issues.

19.9 Structuring the Audit Manual

As with other features of a manual the structure and content depend on the particular circumstances although it is possible to set out a four tier model for structuring the manual:

FIGURE 19.5 STRUCTURING THE MANUAL

STRUCTURING THE AUDIT MANUAL			
Managing audit	**Performing the audit**	**General admin**	**Reference material**
role & objectives	audit planning	conditions of work	control mechanisms
standards	audit services	equipment	audit library
strategy	methodology	filing systems	
structure	reporting	sundry	
HRM	techniques		
information systems & control			

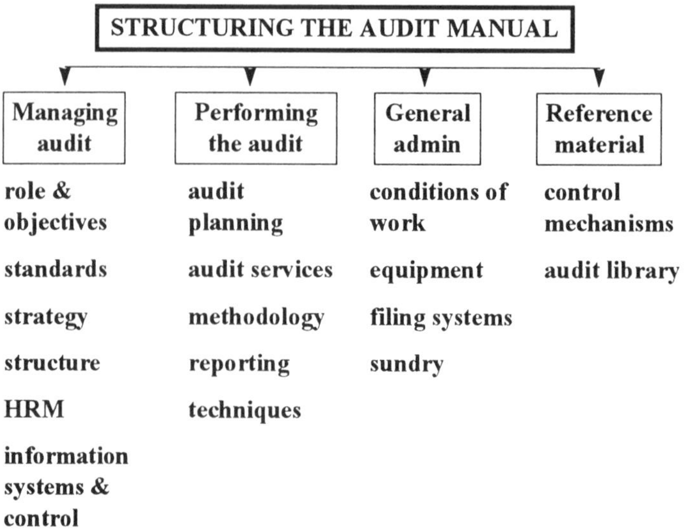

1. It is generally better to have a few main sections as with the above model so as to generate some degree of form and structure. Accordingly each main section should have a focus that sets the tone for the material that it contains.

2. Keep basic reference material outside the audit manual. Reference material can consist of many pages of detailed information that is generally applicable to officers of an organisation. Auditing standards on the other hand deal with professional approaches to discharging the audit objective, which should be the main thrust of the manual. These two types of guidance should be differentiated and as we suggest, the former is best held outside the main body of the manual.

3. Maintain an extensive up-to-date audit library and cross-reference this to the audit manual. The audit manual should contain a list of contents of the audit library and an indication of other relevant material held elsewhere. This standard however depends on a comprehensive library that meets the requirements of most day-to-day audit work, as a considered investment. The library complements the manual as the manual will act as a funnel that invites the reader to explore useful detail held outside the manual. In short if the manual is to work, the library must also work, which as a resource issue must be fully funded by the CIA.

4. Ensure that all the topics mentioned in figure 19.5 are fully dealt with in the manual so as to promote a complete and worthwhile document.

19.10 Implementing the Manual

The process of formulating and implementing a new or revised audit manual is:

FIGURE 19.6 IMPLEMENTING THE AUDIT MANUAL

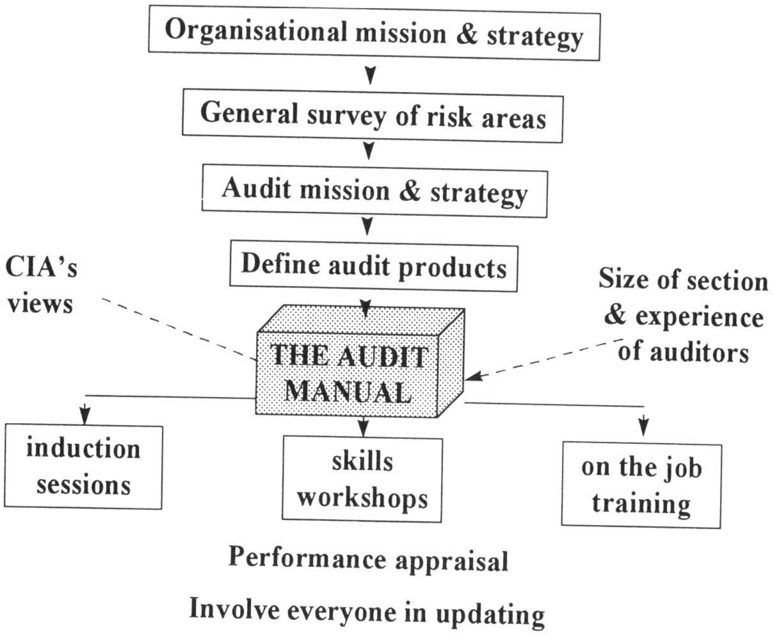

Performance appraisal

Involve everyone in updating

We hope that the resulting manual would be linked into the audit strategy which in turn is based on the organisation's need. In addition it also takes account of the specific needs of the auditors as well as the chief internal auditor's views on the way the audit role should be discharged. Lastly, it is hoped that after developing the auditors to enable them to apply the methodology and techniques as required by the manual, they will in turn be appraised in accordance with their success, or otherwise, in this task. The implementation process should include skills training workshops that explain and expand upon the contents of the manual as an ongoing process. Desk (on the job) training seeks to bring the manual to life by relating it to the actual work that is being performed. The onus is on audit management to have much expertise in understanding and applying the requirements of the audit manual. The other key point is to try to assimilate the audit manual into formal managerial mechanisms such as audit strategy, performance appraisal, marketing, quality assurance routines and so on. Where this is successful, the manual will perform its main role in providing the very foundation of the audit service.

Maintaining the manual
It should be a dynamic mechanism for directing auditors and as such is ever-changing to reflect the latest circumstances and strategy. Accordingly there should be regular changes either adding to the material in the manual or amending sections, and all should participate. A useful technique used by one audit department provides that whenever an auditor attends a conference or training session, they would give a brief presentation to the audit department and draft a summary of any relevant matters for inclusion into the manual. One would imagine that the manual might be updated/amended every week and weekly or bi-weekly staff meetings might be a good forum for this process and in addition quarterly comprehensive reviews might also occur. It should be a constant challenge for dedicated auditors to keep up with the manual and we would expect audit management to acknowledge those who undertake this task successfully. The culture of audit should be such that it becomes a compliment to be asked to be responsible for the manual and this could be rotated say quarterly. Most of what happens that impacts on the auditor's work should also be deemed to have an effect on the audit manual. If this principle is applied as a rule, we should see no problems with maintaining the manual in the fullest sense of the word.

19.11 Conclusions

The chief internal auditor has a clear responsibility to provide formal guidance and direction to auditors and if this is not done, audit can become an uncoordinated, undisciplined affair relying on word-of-mouth and isolated comments from audit management. Research has shown that the audit world does not generally assign a high profile to audit manuals and they have been somewhat neglected particularly in the 1990s. If we are prepared to commit resources, build supporting frameworks and consider the potential role of the manual, then many models can be devised to assist in promoting the manual as a vital control mechanism. Where the CIA is not wholly sold on the idea of using the manual as the key managerial control, then nothing will be achieved via this document. One final point to note is the inherent hypocrisy in commenting on an auditee's failure to establish suitable operational procedures as part of the control systems that have been audited. Especially when the reporting auditor is not able to point to a sensible audit manual that performs this very role for the audit service.

PART THREE

MANAGEMENT OF INTERNAL AUDIT

INTRODUCTION TO PART THREE

Management of internal audit conjures up an assortment of managerial concepts that include:

- Strategic planning.
- Quality assurance.
- Marketing audit services.
- Management liaison.
- Structuring audit resources.
- Performance appraisal.
- Budgetary control.
- Staff motivation.
- Improving the audit service.
- Disciplining staff.
- Recruitment and selection.
- Training.
- Project management.
- Risk analysis.

It is possible to extend this list by using the Institute of Internal Auditor's standard 500 on managing internal audit which in summary is:

500 Management of the internal audit department
The chief internal auditor should properly manage the internal audit department.

510 Purpose, authority and responsibility
The chief internal auditor should have a statement of purpose, authority and responsibility for the internal auditing department.

520 Planning
The chief internal auditor should establish plans to carry out the responsibilities of the internal auditing department.

530 Policies and procedures
The chief internal auditor should provide written policies and procedures.

540 Personnel management and development
The chief internal auditor should establish a programme for selecting and developing the staff of the internal audit department.

550 External auditors
The chief internal auditor should ensure that internal and external audit are properly co-ordinated.

560 Quality assurance
The chief internal auditor should establish a quality assurance programme to evaluate the operations of the auditing department.

Another approach is to perceive management theory as a body of knowledge that goes to fill up a large academic library of texts, papers and research articles as an open-ended list of related topics. It is impossible to write notes based around this as there would be no natural start or finish. A third option is to isolate the audit process and suggest that this needs to be managed.

This process is:

FIGURE PART 3.1 MANAGING THE AUDIT FUNCTION

Each item is dealt with as a specific topic in other parts of the handbook. A fourth approach is to develop a boundary of management theory that can be conveniently used to decide what items to include within this part of the handbook. This may be based on the systems school of management and is the approach assumed here. The relevant managerial processes may be placed together to form what we have already referred to as the managerial control system (see chapter one). Components of the managerial control system are featured below, as well as other related topics on managing internal audit. Several topics are dealt with in greater detail elsewhere. Accordingly, part three covers:
• Setting objectives.
• Audit strategy.
• Audit structures.
• Resourcing the unit.
• Quality assurance.
• Information systems.

- Marketing internal audit.
- Establishing a new audit function.
- Dealing with managerial problems.
- Combating threats.
- Delegating audit work.
- Training.
- Managing change.

Reference is made to various standardised documents in the accompanying diskette. In addition there are a number of assignments (along with suggested answers) in the accompanying diskettes that are case-study based. These may be attempted as a way of thinking through issues involved. The diskette also contains supplementary notes covering:

- **Establishing internal audit.**
- **Dealing with managerial problems.**
- **Delegating audit work.**

CHAPTER TWENTY

AUDIT OBJECTIVES AND STRATEGIES

20.1 Setting Audit Objectives

Introduction
Deciding clear objectives is the starting place for internal audit management. Directing resources towards accepted objectives sets the frame for success. The process of setting clear audit objectives is:

FIGURE 20.1 SETTING AUDIT OBJECTIVES

There is no one way of defining audit objectives as they result from the changing influences of competing forces. There are a number of key points:

Clear objectives
This sounds straightforward but clarity of objectives is not always present. A basic test is to ask each auditor what they see as their main objective. It is not enough to compose a formal document entitled "audit objectives". There is need for a mission for the audit function. This should guide the whole department. The variety of audit services is not a problem so long as an appropriate model is defined and applied. An example is:

> *A small internal audit section in a large private sector manufacturing company consisted of three staff. As a result of restructuring, a new manager was transferred from the sales department to head internal audit. On arrival he promptly announced he was unhappy with the dated term "internal audit" and was changing the name to "financial management".*

Scope of audit work
There is need to decide what is included within the scope of audit work. It is possible to provide services outside the formal scope so long as we make a conscious decision. The

361

scope of internal audit should be based on a professional framework. IIA standards dictate that "The scope of internal audits should encompass the examination and evaluation of the adequacy and effectiveness of the organisation's systems of internal control and the quality of performance in carrying out assigned responsibilities". Anything else is consultancy. A discussion of scope allows opportunity to agree on the important distinction between audit's role in contrast to management's. There are various forces that impact on the final model adopted. These range from the CIA's views, the needs of management and the type of staff employed.

Communicated
There is little point setting formal objectives for the audit function if these are not properly publicised across the organisation. Communication may take the following forms:
- Objectives embodied within an audit charter.
- Suitable correspondence that repeats the objective.
- The annual audit report.
- Regular meetings with management on this topic.
- Formal presentations to the audit committee.
- Some mention within major audit reports.

This is a continual process as strategy does not arise as a one-off event but changes and adjusts over time, in response to the environment.

Understood by all
Passing formal documents out to auditors and management is not enough. There is need to ensure auditors understand and work to agreed objectives. For audit staff this may involve internally organised induction training and skills workshops. We may make a formal presentation to senior management that might be used to dispel myths and misunderstanding. It is essential that members of the audit committee have a clear understanding. We will have to turn to the audit charter to set the record straight. It may be best to present this and any later amendments as an oral presentation using slides, flip charts and other facilities.

Types of services required
The scope of internal audit sets a clear frame within which audit may operate. This will be designed to be widely applicable to most types of audit activities. The adopted scope of internal auditing can determine which services fall within the audit role. Those services that come under the audit head may be categorised. We select an overall range within which services would tend to fall:

FIGURE 20.2 TYPES OF AUDIT SERVICE

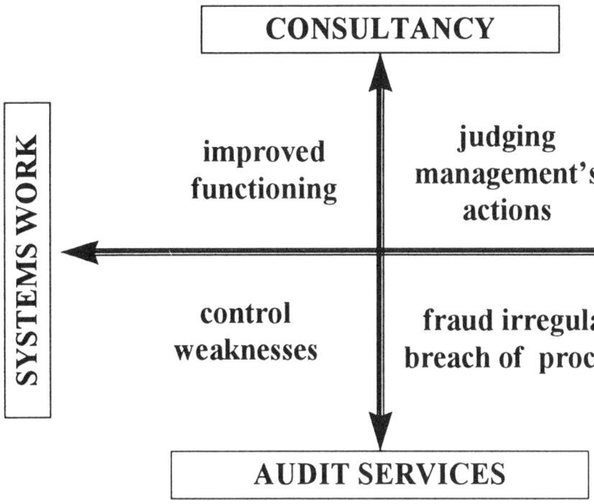

These four scenarios represent different areas for review available to audit management. It does not matter which model is chosen as this depends on how best audit resources might be applied, which depends on organisational needs. More important is for audit management to plan and decide the type of services, armed with a good understanding of alternatives.

Policy on fraud work
The topic of fraud holds a special place when discussing audit objectives. Auditors understand the control cycle that dictates that fraud is caused by poor controls. This does not detract from the need to set out our role in relation to fraud detection and investigation. The CIA must not only ensure that the audit role in frauds against the organisation is documented, but also that audit is in a position to discharge this role. It is better to place a caveat by stating that the organisation should provide additional resources for large projects. Management is ultimately responsible for investigating frauds.

Geared into the organisation
Any audit objective must be linked directly into the organisation's own objectives (or mission). The starting place for setting audit's role is to isolate what the organisation is trying to achieve and then see how audit resources can assist this. So long as we accept that our role is located in control issues, then the final audit product may take different guises in addressing control-related matters. Controls must be set within the culture of the organisation and its success criteria. Organisations range between tightly bureaucratic entities through to loosely based project teams.

Approved
Any objective must be approved by the organisation. This in most cases will be the audit committee where a formally signed audit charter will be agreed along with any changes.

20.2 Defining Audit Strategy

The audit strategic process is a continuing cycle of events that must be properly controlled by audit management. The context is:

FIGURE 20.3 ESTABLISHING AN AUDIT STRATEGY 1

This diagram highlights the link between the audit charter, the organisation's control need (as isolated through the General Survey) and the resultant strategy. This strategy helps determine what needs to be done (scope), by whom (resources), and how (methodology). It is then possible to set standards for the key issues of audit automation, quality assurance, human resource management policies and the audit manual. A confidential business plan would accompany the published strategy. The above may be addressed when formulating an audit strategy. An alternative strategic process is:

FIGURE 20.4 ESTABLISHING AN AUDIT STRATEGY 2

```
            ┌──────────────────────────────┐
            │  Organisational objectives   │
            └──────────────────────────────┘
                          │
                Organisational strategy
                          │
                   General survey
                          │
        ◄─────────Required audit products─────────►
 ┌──────────────┐         │          ┌──────────────┐
 │   Existing   │         │          │   Existing   │
 │  resources   │         │          │  procedures  │
 └──────────────┘         │          └──────────────┘
        └───────► PESTL & SWOT Analysis ◄──────┘
                          │
                   Strategic gap
                          │
            ┌──────────────────────────────┐
            │   Required strategic plan     │
            └──────────────────────────────┘
                          │
     Implementation ──────┴──────► Review
```

General points relevant to strategic analysis are now addressed.

The general survey
A cornerstone of audit strategy is the general survey. This establishes an organisation's control needs. It involves the ongoing task of capturing the key systems that underpin an organisation so that material control needs may be isolated and addressed. Whilst audit objectives set out what we wish to achieve, control needs dictate how much work needs doing and the type of resources most appropriate. A general survey necessitates discussion with middle management and involves:
1. A definition of the audit unit.
2. An assessment of the relative importance of each unit.
3. Research into the type of problems units attract.
4. Ranking related to resources subsequently assigned via an audit plan.

Risk analysis
We would construct a methodology that caters for different activities being associated with different types and levels of risk. There is no universal formula but we need to ensure:
- The methodology is accepted by the organisation.
- It is applied to the audit field in a consistent fashion.

Management participation
A further aspect of audit strategy relates to the need to involve management in the process. There is a temptation to become trapped inside the struggle to preserve audit independence, wherein contact with the outside world is avoided. Our plans and strategies are then based entirely on audit's perception of organisational needs on a "we know best" basis. What may have been acceptable in the past can no longer be defended when all expenditure (including audit costs) must be justified to front-line managers whose budgets bear the eventual re-charges. There is the need to explain the audit process and demonstrate why resources should be directed at one area as opposed to another. Bringing management into the process means additional pressure on audit management. This derives from the need to perform one's job while at the same time communicate what is being done. A strategy not based on organisational needs and supported throughout the organisation will be hard to implement. Management participation includes:
- Explaining that audit operates to a defined strategy.
- Ensuring that this strategy is based primarily on addressing organisational control needs.
- Publicising the link between risk and resource allocation.
- Keeping management informed as to changes to the existing strategies.
- Securing avenues whereby relevant information may be imparted to and from management.
- Clarifying the agreed cut-off points between management and internal audit's roles.
- Retaining a degree of independence that gives audit the final say in strategy and planning.

20.3 PESTL and SWOT Analysis
Audit management is like any other management process in that all relevant techniques should be applied in the course of developing a clear strategy. Two such techniques are

PESTL (an assessment of political, economical, social, technical and legal factors) and SWOT (consideration of strengths, weaknesses, opportunities and threats). These assist audit management in determining the current relative position of the audit function, along with some of the forces that may influence its future progress. The factors that might be pertinent to internal audit are:

☐ **Political**. The factors relating to government policy might affect the audit function. The government may turn towards internal audit as a safeguard against financial impropriety particularly where large-scale scandals receive press coverage. Where government policy calls for quality control over public services or controls over executive directors for enhanced corporate governance in the private sector audit implications have to be considered.

☐ **Economic**. Economic factors will affect the development of the organisation, and might lead to growth, retrenchment or a basic maintenance strategy that should affect the audit style. Growth calls for expansion and aggressive policies with audit advising on the control aspects of take-overs and new systems. Rationalising may require closing down parts of the organisation's activities and audit recommendations involving extra resources may not be appropriate. Economic factors may affect the audit budget and the supply of new auditors. Audit will consider whether a growth, retrenchment, or maintenance strategy should be pursued in internal audit.

☐ **Social**. Social factors must be recognised since they affect the culture of the organisation. These include moral aspects relating to business ethics and wider issues like environmental protection. The rate of unemployment and supply of auditors should be appreciated along with the availability of training schemes. National opinion on fraud, VFM, accountability and business practices affect the role of audit.

☐ **Technology**. New technology has a dual role for internal audit for it will affect systems and processes used by the organisation, and also expand the range of IT available for use in audit work. Audit strategy must keep up with IT developments and if possible stay a step ahead particularly in automating audit work. It is important that audit's IT strategy flows from that of the organisation.

☐ **Legal**. Audit must always keep up-to-date with legislation not only relating to the audit function itself but also legislation that requires compliance based controls. Examples are health and safety, data protection, employee protection, equal opportunities, environmental issues, and accounting practices. New legislation on contracting-out public sector internal audit has a major impact.

☐ **Strengths**. The positive factors may be developed and used to defend against threats and seize opportunities. Strong features may relate to the quality of staff, degree of automation, special skills, a clear methodology and good client relationships.

☐ **Weaknesses**. Areas that need attention might jeopardise the welfare of audit. It is vital these are identified and dealt with via the strategy. Common problems are:

Excessive non-recoverable hours	Low staff morale
Lack of audit procedures	Out-of-date audit manual

High staff turnover   Poor client relationships
Low-level audit work   Recommendations ignored
Poor quality of work   Assignments overrunning budget
No career development   Poor reputation

Each of the above problems must be addressed or the audit function will fail to fulfil its full potential. It is through a carefully planned integrated audit strategy that weaknesses may be tackled. There is a strong link between staff morale and career development programmes. Client relationships affect the success in getting recommendations accepted.

☐ **Opportunities**. The audit function should seize opportunities. Failure may cause the downfall of the audit department in total terms or in the level of respect that it attracts. If the organisation requires new services that might be provided through the audit function, it is important that this issue is considered. If there is a gap in control in developing new computerised information systems and audit is unable to respond to this problem, then the organisation will find this expertise from elsewhere. If opportunities are not seized, they may pose threats in the future. The new computer experts may compete for other audit-type services. The audit strategy should ensure that strengths are developed to maximise available opportunities.

☐ **Threats**. Threats can come in many guises and may affect the status of the audit function. The obvious threats come as competition, and this can arise on many fronts including external audit, management consultants, and internal control teams. Developments within the organisation may affect the level of independence acquired by audit and these must be countered. If the existing audit reporting line is stifling audit findings and recommendations, moves to find a direct link to the organisation's power-base through say, an audit committee, may be part of the strategy. If audit states its intention to perform high-level audit work it must also have an additional strategy to ensure that its staff and procedures are sufficient to meet these new demands. A SWOT analysis is:

FIGURE 20.5 ILLUSTRATION OF THE SWOT ANALYSIS

	STRENGTHS	WEAKNESSES
OPPORTUNITIES	max opportunities max strengths	max opportunities min weaknesses
THREATS	min threats max strengths	min threats min weaknesses

20.4 Features of Audit Strategy

Resource allocation
The bottom line in audit strategy is to assign resources to key areas. A parallel issue is whether the existing resources are sufficient to drive the required strategy. There exists an option to apply a "push-or-pull" formula where strategy is either determined by the existing resources, or vice versa:

FIGURE 20.6 AUDIT RESOURCE APPLICATION

The key question is are we trying to do too much? The answer depends on:
- The profile of audit.
- The financial constraints facing the organisation.
- The procedure for approving additional bids against the revenue budget.
- The perceived importance of organisational control issues.
- The level of support that audit has from line management and the organisation generally.

The above process is a continuing one that should seek to constantly re-assess audit resources in support of the desired strategy. Strategy is about keeping pace with developments to assume an advantageous position by anticipating and catering for the changes that naturally occur:

FIGURE 20.7 STRATEGIC AND ENVIRONMENTAL CHANGE

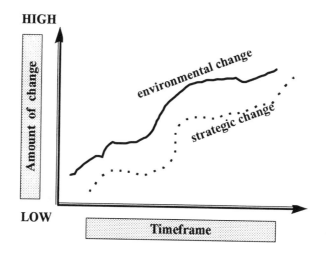

Achievable

The audit strategy must be realistic. It is possible to set high goals that motivated people may achieve. It is not business-like to produce papers that cannot be executed. The result will be the relegation of such papers to the waste-paper basket, or an obscure file that is never looked at. Early successes in achieving adopted strategies have an inspirational impact on the audit team. If we are currently training computer auditors, this takes time. It would be inappropriate to suggest that fully equipped computer auditors would be on-line in a short period. There is a temptation for audit management, led by a distanced CIA, to develop a whole set of strategies and plans not discussed with staff which are unrealistic. There is a fundamental imbalance in the equation:

Does what we can do = what we need to do?

It is incumbent on the CIA to reconcile this equation and not only promise a great deal, but also ensure that what is promised is subsequently delivered.

Communicated

If an employee starts work in a new department and wishes to enquire into the strategy that management have adopted to develop and run the department, he or she may ask one question:

Am I aware of any particular strategy?

If the answer is no, then enquire no further. We cannot have a strategy without communicating this to all those who are expected to discharge it. This basic point is overlooked by many managers who see the strategic process as a form of undercover operation. The confusion comes about because some aspects of a strategy are confidential to outsiders. This may relate to unit costs of the services provided or how competition will be tackled, or how audit might seek to take over various associated functions such as quality assurance or data protection. These issues may be dealt with via a confidential business plan. This does not mean the staff within the audit department are not advised. We may involve all auditors in the strategic process. They must not only be sold the ideas, but should help produce them by the practice of active involvement. Group meetings, regular consultation, and vibrant discussion sessions all help to establish this principle. Away days, seminars held at suitable hotels, away from work, help produce this sense of involvement. Ensuring objectives cascade downwards is a component of implementing strategy:

FIGURE 20.8 CASCADING OBJECTIVES

Long-term plans
The link between audit strategy and audit planning is:

FIGURE 20.9 STRATEGY AND LONG-TERM PLANS

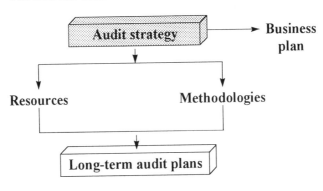

Whatever audit strategy seeks to achieve must be secondary to the resulting formal audit plans that are produced as a result. These plans set out the audits that will be performed over a defined period that constitutes the substantive work of the audit function. The strategic process allows these plans to be prepared through a mechanism derived from best management practice. We cannot move straight into the planning process without first setting the correct context by applying formal strategies.

Preliminary surveys

How much detail should long-term plans provide? Risk analysis allows one to judge which areas should be subject to audit cover. This feeds into the strategic process and along with other things, results in a long-term plan of work that will help direct the activities of the audit function. The question then arises as to how an audit can be picked up from these plans and performed without a great deal of additional effort. We may feel pressured into conceding that long-term planning must establish formal terms of reference for these planned audits. Fortunately the preliminary survey comes to the rescue since we need not provide detailed plans for each audit over and above the act of selecting those areas that attract a high level of risk. The preliminary survey allows us to take an audit area and carry out some background work with a view to setting formal terms of reference for the ensuing audit. We have shown that audit strategy must operate at the highest possible conceptual level over and above the day-to-day workload of individual auditors. The preliminary survey helps interface the resulting audit work with these generalised issues.

Contingency allowances

It is sensible to set aside resources for matters outside the general work of the audit function. There are emergencies and unexpected events that call for change in strategy or short-term additional resources. This must be accommodated by audit management. Audit strategy must assign resources to audit work, but it must also allow resources to deal with unforeseeable problems. There are two ways to avoid installing contingency allowances into strategic resource planning:

1. Provide a mechanism whereby additional short-term resources may be taken on and dropped at short notice. Internally funded project teams, external consultants, agency staff and staff employed on fixed-term contracts can all be used to secure these additional resources as and when required. The secret is to be able to shed these extra resources at short notice, once the project/problem has been completed/resolved.

2. Construct a strategic process that operates on a short-term basis and is subject to continual and constant review. Where this is implemented we would be in a state of constant change, where resources were continually changing to meet new demands on the audit function. This task is high-risk, and must be closely controlled by audit management. One might imagine weekly audit manager meetings driven by the CIA, where resources are switched, secured and terminated at short notice. This will tend to have an unsettling effect on staff and the constant change will not promote much personal development or consistency. In times of recession and major change, it can be used to keep in touch with the fluctuating demands on the audit service.

20.5 Successful Strategic Implementation

Strategic development is getting auditors to work together proactively to drive the audit service forward in the right direction. The need to rally round a clear goal is fundamental to the success of any strategy. A chain may be established by the CIA that represents the flow required for successful strategic implementation.

FIGURE 20.10 SUCCESSFUL STRATEGIC FLOW

This is an important factor for audit management to acknowledge since it is based on strong leadership that drives a powerful message (such as "quality control provides quality services"), throughout the audit function.

CHAPTER TWENTY-ONE

AUDIT STRUCTURES

21.1 Introduction

Once a clear audit strategy is in place audit management must then turn its attention to the way resources are organised. This will have a crucial effect on the delivery of audit services. Furthermore, there are many options underpinning the type of structure that should be in place, which have to be considered and decided on. Some of these options are:

☐ **De-centralised** departments may arise where the audit field consists of geographically isolated segments when it may be advisable to place an audit unit in each one. This can cover a region, country or even a whole continent, where the differences in local customs are so great that a centralised audit role would be inappropriate.

☐ **Where this is not the case then one centralised** audit department may be preferable. In contrast, the current trends to devolve financial management to line managers can also affect internal audit, who may be swept up in this strategy. Unfortunately this will tend to dilute the power-base of the CIA as stronger reporting lines are established with each department.

☐ **Service based** functions may be divided into groups that provide specialised audit services such as computer, contracts, financial, consultancy, investigatory, regularity, systems based and so on. The idea is to develop a level of expertise in particular audit services, in the search for enhanced professionalism. The setback is the degree of cross-over that will arise where several auditors may emerge in the same work area, but with different objectives. It is also more difficult to establish a client based view, as audit teams service the entire organisation and not specified departments.

☐ **Client based** groups are each responsible for a defined range of audit fields providing audit services for their main clients. Once an audit group has been assigned to a client (say a director) then we would expect a range of services to be provided as a contribution to developing the client/auditor relationship.

☐ **Mixed structures** arise where a combination of client and service based approaches is applied, and the audit field is allocated to groups that also provide some specialised services. This may reflect the practicalities of working life where clients are established for each audit manager, while there are some specialist audit services (such as fraud investigations) that will run across the organisation.

☐ **A project based approach** allows auditors to fall into a resource pool which forms into teams when audit projects demand. This is designed to provide a quick response based service made up of floating expertise, and mirrors the multi-disciplinary team approach where resources tackle problems as and when they arise. This can be an excellent solution but requires great skills to manage properly.

☐ **Consultancy based** models are similar to the project based one although auditors would work separately rather than in teams. This flat structure provides no client affiliation but can give a fast response time, particularly for unplanned work. An assignment is obtained, an audit brief and budget provided and an auditor is sent out, to return with a draft report completed within budgeted hours.

☐ **Hierarchical structures** involve several tiers of auditors with a range of different grades each placed within defined audit groups. We may find an audit manager, principal auditors, senior auditors, audit assistants and then trainees. This traditional approach deems control to be inherent in all staff knowing their position in the audit unit and reporting lines clearly set and applied.

☐ **Project teaming** involves fixed audit groups but also selects individual auditors to form project teams for temporary assignments. Over and above this policy, auditors may be rotated between groups, say every three months, or have fixed-term secondments to specialised areas. Note that many groups that were originally set up as project teams become a permanent fixture.

21.2 Factors Influencing Structures

There are many choices and combinations of methods that may be applied and again, as with most of the material on audit management, a suitable decision must be made. This decision should be positive, based on the available options and founded on the overriding need to achieve a quality audit service. In practice there is no one solution. Although there are firm principles that should be applied along with a need to obtain a degree of in-built flexibility on the basis that change is now the norm. Furthermore, the audit structure should flow naturally from the agreed audit strategy. Once the CIA has set an agreed structure for the audit function and defined procedures and standards for the performance of audit work, then one might argue that staff should be able to deliver audit services:

FIGURE 21.1 STRUCTURING INTERNAL AUDIT

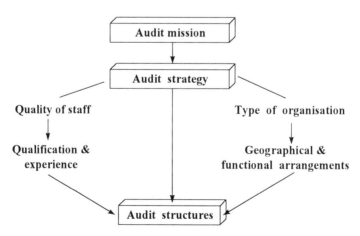

The quality of staff can be adjusted through the audit strategy but can depend on company policy.

Status of internal audit

The status of internal audit has a knock-on effect on the level of independence that is secured. In an ideal world one would argue that the higher the audit status, in terms of grades of staff, the better. This however does impose additional burdens on the CIA not least being the high costs of running the services that will have to be recharged. Nonetheless, structuring must start with the actual position of internal audit in the organisation and adopted reporting lines. There is also a link with status:

FIGURE 21.2 AUDIT STATUS AND STRUCTURES

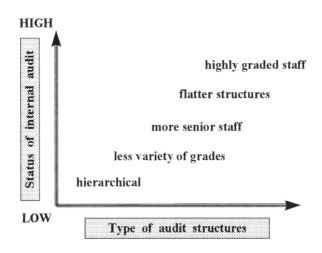

Low-level audit work reporting to a fairly junior CIA (or audit manager) will result from low status and hierarchical structures will be the norm. High-level complicated audits of direct interest to the Chief Executive require the flatter, more response-based services provided by higher graded staff.

Individual work

There is a conflict between the traditional auditor and the new style of working that has to be managed. The conventional working model is based on audit teams assigned to one project that could take several weeks. The team would consist of a senior auditor (or lead auditor) and one or more junior staff. The lead auditor would undertake systems evaluation and ascertainment while the juniors would tend to carry out the resultant testing programmes. A sense of team spirit would prevail and valuable experience in supervising may be gained by the senior auditors. The juniors would meanwhile learn on the job and develop the necessary auditing skills as they moved up through the grades. In many audit departments, this model has given way to the new consultancy based approach:

1. High-level audit work de-prioritises the detailed testing that used to be carried out. Financial systems testing is done via interrogation software applied to downloaded databases.
2. Tight budgets are assigned to each audit to reflect the need for efficient use of resources. Clients pay directly for audit work and there is no excuse for assigning large teams to one audit.

3. One auditor would constitute the team and be required to complete the work within tight timeframes. This person would have a great deal of control over the assignment, although the report would be cleared by audit management before publication.

4. This auditor works more or less alone and only use juniors for specific testing when required. Additional staff arrive for say testing routines, and depart after the few days it would take to complete. The assigned auditor would be responsible for the results of this extra input.

5. In this way the team concept is lost, but each audit is well delivered with the minimum costs and a focus retained by the assigned auditor.

One way in which some team spirit may be retained, alongside the application of the consultancy model, is for the audit manager to be a sounding board by discussing the project with the auditor. Another is to hold regular group meetings where each auditor may mention his/her project for limited debate. Finally one might permit some exchange of views between staff as they discuss their specific audit (and any associated problems) when they are in the office. Unfortunately, the high cost of audit hours tends to mean that each auditor will have to perform his/her own audits from start to finish.

Project teams
Project teaming is a useful way in which the audit department may build flexibility into its structure. This involves reassigning staff so that they group into a small team for a specific major project or series of projects. Alternatively, additional resources may be brought in to complement the existing staff, again for specific projects. This can be powerful particularly where additional consultancy services are being provided. Where management wants a particular exercise carried out, we may preserve our planned systems work and use project teams to resource an anti-fraud exercise or a major management investigation. If the project is so important, management will not mind funding these extra resources. A key auditor, say an audit manager, will have to direct the team's work so that it remains in control. Project teams can be resourced as follows:

☐ **Existing audit staff**. They will be reliable but will not then be available to carry out planned audits. This approach may be perceived as treating audit as waiting around for real work to do, which does not promote a professional image. It will also be very difficult to plan work when staff are constantly being reassigned to project teams, unless the teams are part of the plans in the first place.

☐ **Employ consultants**. This is a very expensive option although there will be less time spent reviewing their work. We would tend to use consultants for individual short-term projects and not for team based work, that may last some time.

☐ **Employ agency staff**. This is a useful model as these additional resources may contribute directly to the project that would be managed by in-house auditors. Audit plans would remain intact and we can use the temporary staff for some time as they should not be charged at premium rates.

☐ **Second staff from elsewhere in the organisation**. An excellent hand-picked team may be secured although we must ensure that members' loyalties lie with the project. A training need may arise where this approach is applied and non-audit staff are used to any extent.

☐ **Employ people on short-term contracts**. The disadvantage is that confidentiality may become an issue where people who will not be staying with the organisation are used on sensitive work. The main advantage is the flexibility that this creates where we may release staff as soon as their contract expires. We would be careful about investing excessive resources in training and development as this resource may be terminated in due course.

☐ **Allow the managers commissioning the project to supply the resources from their own establishment**. Here one may lose a degree of independence where, in the event of a conflict, loyalties may lie with the managers and not the organisation. It is as well to set clear controls over the project team revolving around firm terms of reference, good review procedures and a tight budget for the work required. Remember that some staff may wish to engineer a permanent role for something that was only meant to be temporary.

Service based

It is possible to set up audit teams or groups on the basis of the type of services that each group provides. This can be simplified in an example of five main audit groups specialising in:

Investigations; Contracts; Financial systems; Computer audit; Probity audits.

This is one way of developing expertise in specific audit areas. It is also possible to use the investigations team to avoid interrupting planned systems and probity work. One criticism of this approach is that client affiliation may be difficult to maintain where there is no one group responsible for one department. A contrasting approach is to set up groups for each of the main departments across the organisation. This may be illustrated:

FIGURE 21.3 CLIENT VERSUS SERVICE BASED TEAMS

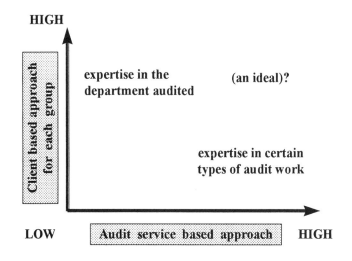

We would have to consider the pros and cons of each approach and make a reasoned decision. It is possible to develop a mixed solution whereby audit groups are departmentally based but have an in-built specialism. This may appear as:

FIGURE 21.4 DEPARTMENTALLY BASED TEAMS

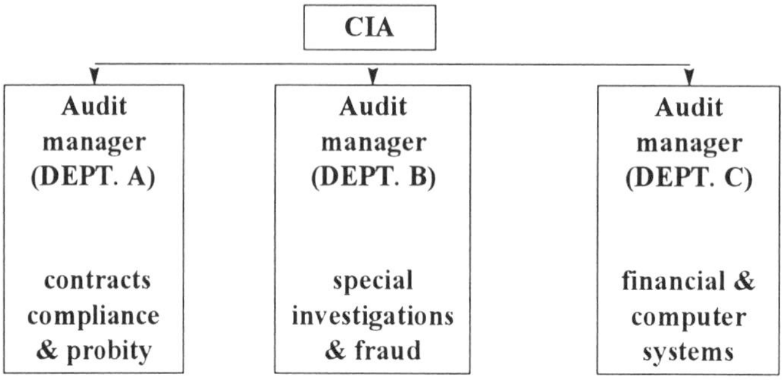

Audit groups may be assigned to departments whilst also being responsible for a defined type of audit service. This is made easier by relating the service to the department where this type of approach is most appropriate. The group would also be responsible for providing this service across departments. The investigations team would not be assigned to a department as problems of this nature could occur anywhere in the organisation.

Minimum numbers

A discussion on how many staff need to be employed to support the audit mission was outlined above in the section on audit strategy. This is not repeated here. What we have to address however is the fact that any audit structure will be determined by considering many factors; one of which is the number of auditors available to discharge the audit role. The larger the number of auditors the more temptation there is to develop a bureaucratic audit department with many tiers of staff and varying grades. As the number of staff increases over a certain limit, say five or six, one would have to consider developing the concept of audit groups. These groups would enable the CIA to divide the unit into manageable proportions headed by an audit manager (or group auditor). The freedom from staffing problems would then enable the CIA to deal with strategic matters that move the function from their existing position towards their targets/goals. The CIA in contrast who has a section of less than five staff, will tend to assume a less strategic and more managerial role. The key point to note is that no fundamental answer to the question of how to structure the audit function can be provided. This is because the ideal position will depend on a variety of competing factors, including the audit strategy and the number of staff. If we are asked whether there is a minimum number of auditors that should be employed then one answer is:

> *"What is the minimum number of staff that should be employed to enable the Head of Audit to hold senior management status and have a real impact on the organisation?"*

An ideal position is reached where the audit function is seen as a major force in terms of its formal designation as a Division or Department rather than a small section or group. There is one caveat to this in terms of the need to ensure the audit budget does not become so large as to make this an excessively costly overhead to service managers.

Reporting lines

The chosen structure should ensure a degree of flexibility in the way audit services are delivered. At the same time there has to be some consistency in the defined reporting lines that have been established. These two concepts do create some conflict in that firm reporting lines tend to set boundaries of responsibility which in turn can militate against quick responses to changing demands for audit services. The key is to set reporting lines that allow a degree of autonomy. The consultancy based approach to audit structuring promotes a great deal of freedom for the auditors where at the extreme they are simply given terms of reference for the project along with a fixed budget. The auditor then disappears for the requisite period and brings back a draft report. Using this model, there may be very little contact between the audit manager and field auditor but the responsibilities of the audit manager nonetheless remain. In fact, the final audit report is still formally issued in the name of the CIA. A decision to set reporting lines may result in defining the audit structure by default. There are several points to note when setting an appropriate structure:

1. All auditors should report to someone in audit management. This point sounds simple enough but should be set within the context of employing contract, agency and other temporary staff. It is not unknown for temporary staff or trainee auditors to end up without a line manager and this can lead to abuse and a general lack of control. Making one temporary member of staff manage other temps can also be a dangerous practice which again may lead to loose control.
2. It is good practice to promote the autonomous auditor who is equipped with the necessary skills and facilities (e.g. PC notebook and printer) to perform the audit with little input from audit management. The idea of an audit manager being in a position to co-ordinate ongoing audits depends on a level of autonomy from the assigned auditors, as a workable solution.
3. The technique of delegation should be employed to the full. This should be based on developing each auditor's role, although the audit manager/CIA is ultimately responsible for all the activities of the department. We must seek to employ auditors who are able to solve problems as they arise and only in the extreme require direct intervention from the audit manager.
4. It is as well to employ a clerical assistant who can act as a personal assistant for the CIA as well as filtering direct contact from clients and other outsiders. This should be aimed at keeping the CIA free to deal with important matters.
5. There should be in place suitable arrangements to cover the absence of the CIA wherever this occurs. In short, one of the audit managers needs to be designated as the deputy CIA and to act in this capacity whenever necessary.
6. It is advisable to give one of the audit managers special responsibility for training and development so that this aspect of audit management can be given due consideration. It allows a consistent approach to training as a major management device for achieving value for money from audit.

Independence

Independence is an important concept for the internal auditor. The two cornerstones of independence are firstly, the audit staff and their procedures, and secondly, the position of the audit function within the organisation. Dealing with the second point, there are again two key factors in the structuring equation that impact on audit independence as follows:

1. The officer to whom the CIA reports;
2. The forum at which formal audit activity reports (e.g. the annual reports) are dealt with.

We refer to the problem when the CIA reports to the Director of Finance. This does not promote audit independence since there is an increasing reliance on financial management/systems for the successful running of any organisation. These cannot be objectively appraised where the Director of Finance "owns" internal audit, and is trying to hold onto a fixed term performance-related contract that cannot withstand criticism. It is also important that the CIA reports to an officer who is sufficiently senior to support the audit service. The recipients of audit activity reports should have sufficient authority and ideally there should be a formal audit committee. Independence is enhanced where audit managers have direct contact with the corporate management team or the Board of Directors without necessarily having to refer to the CIA. This will help lessen the impact of those political forces that apply primarily to the CIA, not the audit managers. Audit independence is reliant on audit staff being able to work at the highest levels, in contrast to a basic probity approach.

> *An internal audit unit of twenty-five staff who held senior grades worked on high-level operational reviews that exposed poor management practices and inefficiency. A newly established audit committee asked that internal audit be reviewed and restructured to secure budget cuts through staff reductions. The new structure reduced the audit staff to fifteen, the majority in junior grades. As a result the audit function could only undertake low-level regularity audits with little impact on the impoverished management and lack of suitable controls continued to impair service delivery.*

The problem identified results because restructuring was driven by budget cuts rather than service delivery. If the review started with the organisation's control problems and the type of audit services that would be required to tackle these problems, there would be a much better chance of any new structure promoting a positive rather than inefficient audit service.

Supervisors

The audit structuring process cascades down from the CIA, audit managers through to senior auditors and other audit staff. The lead auditor/supervisor is a key officer in the audit world as it is this person who, above all, produces the actual audit work. This fact should be fully recognised and catered for. Under the direction of an audit manager, the senior auditors should form the main unit that is assigned to the project either individually or as head of a small audit team.

Trainees

The bottom tier of the audit structure should ideally consist of trainees. These individuals will have limited experience in auditing matters but should be enthusiastic and form an inexpensive resource. It is good practice to use trainees as a source of future auditors and to ensure that we are up-to-date on new developments and research that comes with training programmes. Some audit departments do not necessarily employ "trainees" but nonetheless encourage the less senior staff to undergo formal professional training. This is then built into their career development programmes.

21.3 Conclusions

We need to develop a sound model of the internal audit service with each auditor contributing to the work programme appropriately. Audit cannot be managed unless there are people working at the right level in the right capacity. The CIA has to keep a clear desk to formulate strategy and develop new and existing client bases. The audit manager should be able to run many projects at the same time while ensuring that each one meets quality standards that have been formally adopted. Auditors should be able to complete their audits in a competent manner to professional standards in line with the audit manual, and so generate the important fee income for the audit function. The structuring decision and underlying arrangements all contribute to the implementation of the most appropriate model that promotes the above position.

CHAPTER TWENTY-TWO

RESOURCING THE AUDIT UNIT

22.1 Introduction

Human resource management (HRM) is a major component of the management process. This area of the handbook on managing the internal audit function necessarily assumes a key position. We include here the main issues that impact on HRM within the context of internal auditing.

Management's role

Audit management must ensure that HRM issues are adequately considered and dealt with. This sets the stage for defining management's role as one of managing (not performing) the audit work. There are potential complications, since managers may find it hard to stop auditing and start managing. The fact that the type of work that auditors tend to handle can be very sensitive provides a convenient excuse for audit managers not to refer the work down to their staff. The position we need to reach is where audit managers appreciate the need to employ staff whom they can trust and rely on to discharge the audit role. They need to ensure the staff are properly developed and directed so that they are able to perform to accepted standards. The only way that this can be achieved is through the application of suitable HRM techniques. A further complication is that HRM matters must be set within the overall framework of the organisation's own HRM policies. Audit management is restricted by the autonomy it has in the application of policies specific to internal audit. Having said this, everything that auditors do or fail to do, is the direct responsibility of audit management.

Traditional weaknesses in management

Management may actually impose barriers to audit performance:

1. A failure to appreciate the principles of good HRM can undermine the whole audit department. We have the truism that it is only good managers who are able to apply good HRM policies. An old-fashioned CIA who is stuck in old ways will make little progress.
2. There is a temptation to refer all matters on HRM to the Personnel department for them to deal with. This is a failing as it is only audit managers who really appreciate the audit role and what is needed by their staff to discharge it. Recruitment, selection, training, development, appraisals, discipline, and codes of conduct are matters that cannot simply be referred to Personnel.
3. Progress can be made by enlightened management where new ways of developing staff are devised and motivation is managed professionally. Managers who perceive their staff as a problem are less likely to inspire excellent performance.

If audit management is not able to lead from the front, it will not inspire confidence:

> *A Chief Internal Auditor spent much time reviewing reports produced by his senior auditors. He would ask for changes and alter the way a basic point was expressed, although the point remained the same. This was a drawn-out process suffered in silence by each group auditor. Over the years this continued until the CIA prepared a short report on an audit he was personally involved in. This report was of poor quality and contained repetition and woolly terms. The group auditors got sight of it and lost confidence in the CIA whom they began to openly criticise.*

The human resource management cycle

It is as well to define what we mean by HRM. Personnel issues are unrelated matters that concern staff, which are dealt with partly by Personnel and partly by line management. These can relate to travel claims, overtime, sickness records, timesheets, timekeeping and so on. Their impact on the relationship of the employees and employer are but single issue topics. HRM on the other hand is concerned with a whole system of management that is designed so that the right people are doing the right things at the right time, to ensure organisational objectives are achieved:

FIGURE 22.1 THE HUMAN RESOURCE MANAGEMENT CYCLE

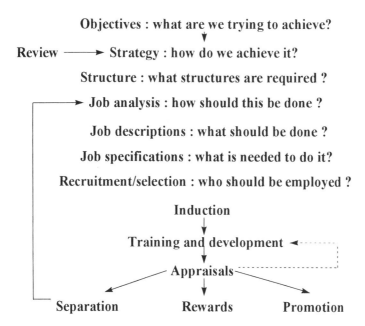

22.2 Attributes of Auditors

Why attributes?
Auditors will be able to deliver quality services where the following hold true:
1. The objectives are clear.
2. What is expected of them is made clear.
3. The standards of performance are made clear.
4. They have the ability to perform to the requisite standards.
5. They are motivated to do so.
6. Management removes any barriers to performance.

There is an un-stated assumption that the auditor has the right attributes to perform to the requisite standards. This can only arise where audit management has defined these attributes so that recruitment and development programmes can be directed towards them. If this definition has not been carried out then it becomes guesswork. At worst, auditors may guess wrongly and behave in an inappropriate way because this is what they assume is required. Important attributes are discussed below.

Ability to deal with people
The old saying "internal control is people..." holds true. A short story illustrates:

> *A junior auditor passed an auditing examination. He was advised to apply for senior auditor posts. Unfortunately he found it very difficult to talk to strangers and would not leave the audit offices unless absolutely necessary. His manager understood this and assigned him to a senior auditor who did all the talking and PR work. As a result the junior auditor never applied for promotion as it was clear that he could not perform as a senior auditor.*

The ability to communicate can make the difference between a successful audit and a complete disaster. There are many times where it is a misunderstanding of the audit role that creates poor communicators who feel that they are spying on management. They assume a "cloak-and-dagger" approach to their work that results in impaired communications with the auditee. Audit management may tackle this issue so long as they are not the main perpetrators of this attitude.

Ability to persuade
This is another important skill although linked to communication skills. There are a number of levels on which persuasion skills are required by the auditor, such as negotiation of start dates to coincide with the availability of staff from the auditee's office. This can set the tone of the ensuing audit. The fact is that everyone is busy at all times and there really is no good time for an audit. Persuasion skills may be applied to convince the client that auditors are used to working in this environment, where they are interrupting work. Moreover the benefits of the audit can be used as an additional selling point. The auditor will meet some resistance throughout the audit process which again can be minimised through the use of careful persuasion based on the audit being for a worthwhile purpose. A concentration on systems and not people can assist this process,

notwithstanding the fact that in the final analysis it is really people who instigate controls. The need to implement audit recommendations is where this technique can be applied to the fullest. It is far better to persuade management to strengthen controls than have to threaten retribution if they fail to take the necessary action. Unfortunately persuasion is based on a bottom-line remedy if the other party does not waver, and there needs to be a careful balance between the "carrot and stick". The ability to persuade can be taught to auditors, although it appears in its more forthright form as part of negotiation skills. Blustering through an audit using threats and a menacing stance produces auditors who quickly burn out over the years. This contrasts with the more subtle and professionally based ones who will not suffer this emotional overheating.

Ethics and integrity

Ethics should not be taken for granted and there are situations where the ethical stance is not clear:

> *The CIA had recently advertised for a contracts auditor who would report to the audit manager (contracts). This audit manager had a good friend who had applied for the position after seeking advice from the same audit manager. It is policy to have the line manager on the interview panel and the audit manager was worried that he might experience a conflict of interests when interviewing his friend. At first, he felt that he could be objective but after thinking about it decided to talk to the Personnel officer. She advised him to withdraw from the selection panel although this would have to be his decision. The audit manager did, in the event, inform the CIA and withdraw from the panel.*

The question of ethics then is not necessarily one of compliance with procedures but may be a matter of professional judgement. This imposes a clear responsibility on the individual auditor which to some extent is greater than other staff. This is because of the inherent hypocrisy in reporting on matters of conduct concerning other employees (if this is necessary) whilst at the same time one's own standards are far from perfect. The assumption for the report reader is that one who criticises must be above criticism. We cannot always teach ethics, it is only possible to set a framework within which standards can operate and then stress the importance of observing personal and professional codes of conduct. However, the mysterious world of subsistence claims and expense allowances can cause major problems for the careless auditor. History records at least one example of two senior auditors in a large organisation who were disciplined for irregular expense claims.

Physical and mental state

Auditors should in the main be fit and well enough to perform their duties. Disabled people can perform just as well as able-bodied auditors, even where there is extensive travelling involved. Equal opportunities should provide for fair treatment for all groups of people whatever their circumstances, as long as they are able to meet the job specification. A medical examination before an appointment is made is one way of ensuring the right physical condition. This may be built into the selection process although we would look for clues in the information that is provided (e.g. "are you on prescribed medication?") before a full scale medical examination is commissioned. Mental health can be affected by lifestyle. For a fast moving audit department with tight budgets and a large workload, anti-stress training/counselling is one way of promoting well-balanced staff. We would seek to employ staff able to perform in a stressful environment. Suitable policies on smoking and alcohol consumption at work can contribute to this drive for healthier lifestyles at work. There is a vicious cycle where hard work leads to after work drinking sessions which tend to make the next working day more difficult. This in turn leads to hard work (i.e. difficulties in meeting time budgets) and so the cycle continues. It is important to catch signs of mental disorder and depression at an early stage although work itself can be a form of therapy. Unusual behaviour where the auditor overreacts to minor problems or treats irrelevant issues as problems, can give out signals that the person needs treatment. We would expect audit managers to be aware of these types of problems, which may be picked up in the first instance, through the performance appraisal scheme.

Competence in internal audit techniques
The requirement that all auditors should be competent in auditing techniques is important. This underlies the work that forms the basis of internal auditing and is a prerequisite to the success of the audit function. The main problem is that what should be a foregone conclusion is sometimes not fully achieved. The level of expertise should cascade downwards from the chief auditor, through to the audit managers and the rest of the staff. One caveat to this arises from the need to create some degree of specialism depending on the type of organisation. It is unrealistic to expect all auditors to have great expertise in contracts, legislative matters, automated systems, fraud investigations, production management and so on. It is more appropriate to define what may be termed "basic audit skills" and ensure that these are acquired and maintained. This may be achieved via the following process:

1. Define the basic audit skills. This may be based on specific work requirements or general measures such as a professionally examined syllabus.
2. Set these out in the job specifications which means that a decision must be made as to which grades should be capable of mastering which skills, and to what extent.
3. Build these skills-requirements into the recruitment/selection system and the performance appraisal scheme. We would wish to buy in the basic skills required and then seek to develop them, although the latest trend is to capture them at the recruitment stage.
4. Document in the audit manual the underlying procedures that provide for the application of the various audit techniques. Audit skills and techniques should not float above the real workload of the field auditor but must be assimilated into this day-to-day work (via the audit manual).
5. Keep them under review and ensure that training programmes are based around relevant auditing skills. Training should have a direct application to the defined skills base required.
6. Keep these techniques up-to-date and ensure that any poor performance resulting from a skills deficiency and/or the misapplication of audit techniques is rectified. It is one thing to define skills and recruit and train staff within this context. It is quite another to insist that these are mastered by all auditors and we must have suitable mechanisms for addressing this issue.

Personal drive and initiative

The modern view of internal auditing sees this discipline as a long-term career. This is not to say that there is not room for the career accountant or manager who spends some time in internal audit as part of their development. The key point is that the core audit team should comprise individuals who are professional internal auditors. For this model to work, auditors must possess the necessary drive and ambition that underpins the sacrifices required to pursue a career as a professional auditor. This must however be put into context in that, what may be a positive attribute in one person, may become a hindrance in another. Generally speaking, the CIA will wish to recruit lively, ambitious people who are striving towards promotion and success in their chosen field. But, as the following illustration brings out, this needs to be treated with care:

> *During a job interview, one particularly over-bearing candidate was asked by the CIA what his career goal was. He promptly replied "my goal is to become deputy CIA as soon as possible..." The CIA just as quickly replied, "not while I work here...". Needless to say he did not get the job.*

One looks for some modesty within which ambition would be contained. Eagerness, zeal, drive and yearning are positive traits so long as they take second place to the auditor's professional code of conduct. Ideally we would look for:

A long-term view of internal auditing that means that any training and development will be a useful investment and be taken seriously by the postholder. Most recruiters will look for a "linear progression" where the person in question is obviously headed for a clear career path in the chosen field, i.e. internal auditing. There is an obvious risk attached to giving someone a chance, who changes direction mid-way through a career.

A commitment to pass professional auditing examinations. We would look for this quality on the basis that the only way to success in professional examinations is a commitment to assign time and direction to this task. We will arrive at an imbalance within the audit unit where some staff have no intention of securing professional qualifications, despite a policy where auditors are expected to qualify. It is best to clear this point at the recruitment stage.

An honest belief in the work undertaken that is seen as more than a 9 - 5 job. The CIA should not require staff to put in extra effort to get to the audit product. It should be an in-built desire from the auditors themselves to perform at this level, without cajoling from management. Where the auditors have a belief in their work we can arrive at a convenient position where this effort is ever-present.

A degree of self-belief mixed with a desire to progress in an auditing career that has no short-cuts apart from sheer hard work and dedication. Auditing should be seen as hard work and not an opt-out from a more demanding discipline such as accountancy.

A realistic understanding of one's abilities and strengths where development is readily accepted. This is a dilemma in that on the one hand we wish to see great confidence while at the same time some reserve, where personal weaknesses are recognised. This is the same as suggesting that the auditor should be positive without being conceited, which does require some careful balancing.

A fresh outlook on work that is not tainted with cynicism and a lack of respect for management. We do not want auditors who feel that one audit is much the same as another, as they move from assignment to assignment. What is needed is a proactive approach that sees each project as a new challenge, and not a repetition of the last time it was done. Certainly there is no room for complacency in discharging the audit role or for people who do not accept this.

Emotional maturity

This is a necessary attribute that should attach to staff working in internal auditing. We should look for this when recruiting auditors and considering their development programmes. Internal audit has a special place within an organisation with its rights of access and ability to report on management's systems of control. These privileges must be exercised with due professional care as they represent a source of potential power. Power must be controlled or there may be repercussions. Emotional stability enables one to exercise this power for the best interests of the organisation and not for some hidden purpose derived from an insecure personality. We would not expect auditors to view certain managers as enemies and see their work as a chance to "get" certain individuals who have upset them. We must be able to rise above feelings that are not unheard of amongst sometimes senior managers, who enjoy playing the point-scoring "organisational game" against each other. Emotional maturity can come with age but tends to come more with a feeling of being comfortable with oneself based on:

1. A professional approach to work where the audit objective is seen as paramount.
2. Audit managers who set good examples in the way they control their emotions and deal with fellow colleagues and members of the organisation generally.
3. Performing in a competent fashion within one's skills-limits with the support of managers wherever necessary. Most insecure employees become aggressive because of an inability to work at the required level of competency, with the aggression covering for this deficiency. They see all outsiders as threats to their position, who may expose their incompetence. This can be avoided if the recruitment policies stop this type of individual from entering the organisation. Unfortunately many organisations promote internal employees beyond their skills base and so encourage the very same thing.
4. A culture promoted by the CIA which requires a clear standard of conduct and professional objectivity in the performance of audit work. There are certain things that the CIA should not be prepared to tolerate and this includes conduct unbecoming to an employee, bias, childish behaviour, and inappropriate language.
5. An internal audit department that stresses teamwork and common goals based on the organisation's mission. Audit does not service key individuals, but the organisation, which is a bigger vision.

Understanding internal audit concepts

There are internal auditors skilled in techniques such as flowcharting, computer interrogation, statistical sampling, and risk assessment but with poor grasp of the real audit role. They may see their job in many different ways with the most common mistake being to feel that they are responsible for doing management's work for them. Whilst one may make many friends if this approach is applied, it is professionally incorrect to misconstrue the audit role. Take an example:

> *A senior auditor developed a powerful interrogation programme that enabled him to download databases and check for duplicate accounts, gaps in sequential numbering and credits over an authorised level. His audit manager recommended that he give this package to management (in this case the database administrators) so that they could make regular checks on the integrity of their databases. The auditor became disillusioned and complained that this was an audit tool and much mileage could have been achieved by the internal audit department, if he could use this facility and make regular reports to management on their errors. His manager tried to convince him that he misunderstood the audit role.*

A good appreciation of audit concepts can be so crucial as to render some audit work impoverished if this understanding is not achieved.

Intelligence

Synonyms for intelligence include:

acumen	*alertness*	*brightness*
capacity	*cleverness*	*discernment*
perception	*quickness*	*understanding*

We should expect all auditors to be reasonably intelligent. Intelligence must be bought in at the recruitment stage as it cannot readily be developed. It is hard to find one acceptable definition as it covers a range of abilities. We set out some of the features relevant to internal auditing:

1. An insight into what is important and what should, in contrast, be relegated as minor issues. This involves more than appears at first sight. Auditing can result in an abundance of detail acquired over the course of the fieldwork. There are many auditors who have secured files full of information/documents only to find that it is difficult to get a sensible report from the masses of data obtained. The ability to get real issues from this mass is a great skill not to be underestimated.

2. An ability to see the association between two or more key factors in terms of a cause and effect relationship. Understanding the link between problems and underlying causes leads one naturally into the process of formulating recommendations. Unfortunately to arrive at this point is no mean feat.

3. An ability to rise above the matter at hand and appreciate the "big picture". Building on the above point, there must be a place for the appreciation of the "bottom line" in contrast to the maze of facts that appear in front of the auditor. Many audits miss the mark in that they fail to capture the real concerns of line management. The resultant report is not well received by these managers and the auditor finds it difficult to understand why there is a reluctance from management to respond.

4. An ability to juggle several different concepts at the same time and prioritise between them in line with an overall objective. There is no clear line from audit field work to audit report that represents an uninterrupted course of work. Many subsidiary factors

interfere with this process and can lead the auditor to stray from time to time. The ability to focus on the matters at hand and decide what should be dealt with and what can be left, is a desirable feature that should be sought in auditors.

5. An ability to compartmentalise various facts and recall them when required. We do not ask that auditors have a photographic memory, but they do need a basic skill in recalling important matters. The experienced auditor may end up being exposed to most parts of a large organisation and this aggregate knowledge is extremely useful so long as it can be retained to an extent.

6. An aptitude for skills relevant to the internal audit function. There is a natural affiliation that some people have for the type of work that the auditor has to deal with in a typical assignment. Applying techniques to huge databases of information and extracting the items that are of concern to the audit objective, cannot be done by all-comers. Some will feel that this task is either very daunting or boring in the extreme, feelings that the professional auditor has to rise above.

7. An understanding of the political implications of audit activities and how different parties will be affected and might then react. There is no hiding from power structures in any organisation and although we do not ask the auditor to play politics, there must be a basic understanding of this.

22.3 The Importance of Clear Personnel Policies

Link to organisational policies
The Chief Internal Auditor has a clear responsibility to install suitable arrangements for managing human resources and this is a feature of this chapter. However these procedures must be set firmly within the context of the organisation's personnel policies. There are two extremes that may be used to formulate a suitable model to deal with this issue:

FIGURE 22.2 AUTONOMY VERSUS COMPLIANCE

The CIA should try to move the department towards the right. Here audit managers become responsible for recruiting, training, developing, appraising, promoting, counselling, disciplining and dismissing their own staff. Where the organisation has adopted good employer policies designed to create a balanced and stable workforce, the general principles should ideally be retained. It is advisable to use the Personnel officers as consultants where considering changes to staffing. The role of the organisation's personnel policies is important since the CIA must ensure that the internal audit department complies with relevant procedures. Divergence must either be allowed or specially approved by the organisation.

The internal audit angle

Internal audit should ensure that all human resource management policies are clearly documented and made known to staff. The ideal vehicle for this is the audit manual where internal audit policies and procedures are considered, designed and detailed. We would look for clearly defined policies over a range of audit-related issues (and not just the ever sensitive issue of auditors' expense claims). The best approach is to hold the organisation's personnel policies in the audit library for ready reference. These would be general in nature and the CIA would then redefine them in greater detail to incorporate specific internal audit matters. An example follows:

> *The organisational policies on selection interviews state that each candidate will undergo a formal interview carried out by a suitably constituted panel which includes a personnel officer. The CIA then set out an internal audit policy based on this which states that the panel will consist of the CIA, relevant audit manager and the personnel officer. Each candidate for an audit post will be required to undergo an hour-long written test based on an in-tray situation, that will be assessed before the formal interview is carried out. The interview will include questions concerning the submitted test paper.*

Here organisational policies are complied with whilst specific audit related matters are taken on board via more detailed procedures. This should be recorded in the audit manual.

22.4 Recruitment Selection

Job analysis

In theory the recruitment process starts with a manpower planning exercise that seeks to identify which resources will be required and how they will be secured. This however moves us into the world of audit strategy that is dealt with elsewhere in the handbook. For our purposes we start with the analysis of a post that has fallen vacant. Job analysis involves the following procedures:

1. The structuring process (following strategic analysis) will result in a number of defined roles within the internal audit function. An outline budget should have been approved to appoint to these roles.
2. These roles along with any vacated posts will be made available for job analysis which will assess the way a post will be defined in line with the required work duties.
3. The type of work that is needed to discharge the defined roles will be applied to these funded positions. This is defined through a consideration of several matters including the funds available, whether the vacant post should actually be filled, the existing levels of expertise within the audit department and the changing needs of the audit unit (as captured through the strategic analysis).
4. An outline statement of objectives will be defined that attaches to the vacant post. This will set out the job title of the post and a brief description of its role along with a view of reporting lines within the internal audit unit.

Job descriptions

The next stage in the recruitment procedure is to formally define the requirements of the post. The process of setting the job description is one of considering the ensuing contract of employment that will be entered into by the incoming appointee. This process may be documented as:

1. Define the key responsibilities of the post having regard to other jobs in the section.
2. Include the main components that apply to all audit staff in line with the level of responsibility of the post.
3. Set out the categories of activities that will be required from this job in distinct groups such as:
   - Managerial responsibilities.
   - Internal audit responsibilities.
   - Organisational responsibilities.
   - Compliance with defined procedures.
   - Compliance with relevant legislation.
   - Compliance with professional code of conduct.
4. Write out a formal job description and ensure that it is consistent with the others across the audit department. Remember that we may wish to promote the use of generic grades where movement between auditors may be readily arranged to promote a flexible workforce and career development.
5. Carry out a formal job evaluation and assign an appropriate grade to the post that fits with the requirements as defined via the job description.

Job specification

We can now define the type of person who would discharge the requirements of the job description. This is known as specifying the job. Not only will the final version provide a basis on which to select a suitable individual but it also has the key role of forming the foundation for any performance appraisal scheme. There are different ways that the specification may be achieved:

1. Establish the essential requirements for the postholder in terms of formal physical attributes, qualifications and years/levels of experience.
2. Establish the desirable requirements across a range of factors including managerial skills, supervisory skills, auditing skills, specialist skills, personal attributes, relevant experience over a range of audit-related areas and other material factors.
3. Review the specification to ensure that the needs of the job description would be fully catered for by the detailed skills that have been agreed.
4. Review the specification to ensure that it falls in line with other job specifications for other audit posts and complies with the spirit of personnel policies particularly relating to formal qualifications.

Recruitment

Much of the above material falls under the recruitment procedures that precede the selection of actual staff. However we must also address all the other pre-selection matters including:

1. The compilation of a suitable advertisement for the post. It is good practice to mention essential requirements from the job specification so as not to mislead applicants who may not realise that they will not qualify for the position. The advert is also a marketing device in that it may contain a public commentary on the audit department

with well-chosen phrases such as "a progressive department", "a highly successful audit service", and "in line with the highest professional standards".

2. The selection of a suitable medium depending on the grade of auditor being appointed. It may be advisable to adopt the policy which states that the more senior the audit post, the greater the effort to find a suitable candidate. Thus audit managers and the CIA may be selected via a formal recruitment consultant whilst junior posts may simply be advertised in an appropriate journal/newspaper.

3. Arrange a package of pertinent material that should be made available to applicants. This will include the job description, job specification, material on the audit department and a brief background to the organisation in question. Some provide the name of a person within the audit department who can be contacted for an informal conversation concerning the vacant post. This is time consuming but can be useful in helping to vet potential applicants and ensure that applicants are really sure they wish to be considered for the post.

4. Define a convenient recruitment process that allows potential applicants to make contact, receive papers, submit an application and receive confirmation of receipt of their forms. Professional arrangements will add to the overall image of the organisation/internal audit function.

Selection

The final stage is to establish a formal selection panel for the entire process. This may consist of the CIA, an audit manager and a personnel officer who review the completed applications to shortlist for interview. The audit manager has managerial responsibility for the appointee. Shortlisting should be carried out by the selection panel soon after the advertised closing date. Applications may pass through a variety of stages depending on the number of responses:

FIGURE 22.3 JOB APPLICATION SHORTLISTING

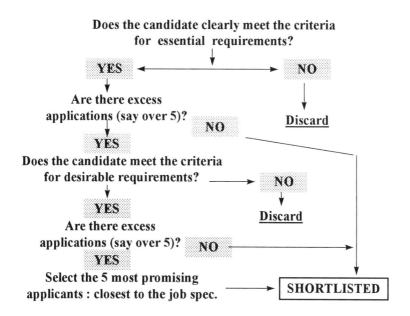

The maximum number (five in our example) should be decided beforehand. It is impracticable to interview dozens of people and then seek to select the best one as this leads to an information overload. The final decision on maximum numbers must fall in line with organisational policy.

There is debate as to whether personal references should be secured at this stage. The application form may ask for the name and address of say two referees. If references are taken up beforehand this may well delay the entire process and if they are persons nominated by the applicant, then they serve little real purpose in terms of providing an independent appraisal of the person concerned. The only useful reference is a questionnaire that is sent direct to the personnel department of the applicant's current or last employer. It is good practice to check professional qualifications as it is not unheard of for these to be falsified. There can be many anomalies in application forms. A candidate may claim to be a member of a professional body and it may be unclear whether this is by examination. There is an example of one application form which set out details of the various stages of an MBA that was studied at a particular University. Unfortunately, it was not clear from this form that the person had withdrawn from the programme without completing it. Any question marks over the reliability of personal data must be resolved when appointing auditors and the CIA must adopt the view that we can never be too careful.

There are professional interviewees who are very comfortable in what should be a highly pressurised situation. They give off a relaxed charm that can persuade the panel to appoint on the basis of the candidate being a very pleasant person. Good inter-personal skills are a very useful attribute but have little use if auditing skills have not been mastered. An extremely pertinent skill that may be tested as part of the selection process is that relating to report writing. Poor reporting skills are very hard to rectify, particularly where the auditor is on a senior grade. A way around this problem is to give each candidate a written piece of work ("test" is an emotive word) that should be completed say, within an hour, and handed in to the selection panel before the interview is started. It is better to interview a small number of candidates and have extended interviews in contrast to meeting large numbers of hopefuls for a short time each. The candidate may be asked to present the work which would ideally be in a report format. This work will be assessed along with the performance in the interview as part of the decision process. An example helps:

> *An auditor was appointed to fill a general audit post as a semi-senior. She did not have an audit background but was very enthusiastic at the interview. Furthermore she had a good sense of humour and a very nice presentation. After several months her manager realised that her report writing skills were very poor and not only did she fail her internal audit examinations several times but she found it impossible to draft a sensible report even after much training. She was eventually disciplined and dismissed as the result of an inability to perform to acceptable standards.*

The main part of the selection process has traditionally been the formal interview. Although this technique has been much criticised, it would appear to be the most convenient way of getting to know the candidate and making a reasoned assessment of their potential ability. In fact, we can make two levels of assessment in an interview involving the understanding displayed by the candidate and secondly, the way he/she handles an interview situation. The latter point is related to the view that interviewing/communications skills is, in itself, an important attribute for the auditor. The interview format provides an opportunity to ask relevant questions and in this way test the candidate with a series of pre-planned questions. It is important to ensure that each interviewee gets the same questions and that they are directly linked into the job specification. It must be said that the interview also gives clues as to whether the person will "fit in" although this may well be part of a hidden agenda. As a final point, the selection panel must ensure that there are no outstanding queries after the interview has been concluded. All relevant issues should be voiced even where they are sensitive. There is one example on record of an auditor being appointed to a post when, unknown to the panel, he had already resigned from his current employer "under a cloud".

The assessment process must as far as possible be applied in a consistent fashion to all the interviewees. There is only one question that the panel should ask and this must be "how far does this person meet the job specification?" This must be the overriding factor. Note that a controversial candidate who has much initiative may create some conflict with the panel but this is not necessarily a bad thing. It is sometimes necessary to break the cosy world of internal audit where everyone agrees with each other, and seek to bring in some new ideas. A fresh appointment can promote this situation so long as this new-found conflict can be managed by the CIA to provide a constructive debate to the overall benefit of the internal audit function.

Selection is the next stage where a suitable appointee is selected to fill the vacant post. The criteria for selecting the right auditor should be clearly set in the minds of the panel members. Firstly a selection should only be made if the best candidate is appointable. If this is not the case the post should be re-advertised and the previous applicants should not be invited to re-apply. If there is more than one person suitable for the job, one must then go through a process of elimination that allows the person who most closely meets the job specification to be chosen. A point-scoring format may be applied that, whilst not being wholly scientific, does impart a level of consistency for the process. An alternative approach is to "free-float" with open discussion of the key points so that a picture is painted rather than a points-scale filled in. It is also possible to set each person off against the others and so seek to eliminate them one by one until a choice is made by default. Whatever the approach, the CIA should ensure that there is a clear method through which such a selection may be made and that this is properly applied by the interview panel. The final point to note is that it is not always possible to contain the process of gathering information on the candidate within a set framework. Even where standard questions have been designed there will always be a level of discussion that may lead into other related areas. A good interviewee may, in practice, gently lead the panel into topics that they are happy to discuss that reflect well on them.

Most auditors find it comfortable working with checklists and procedures and this is how it should be. Once a selection has been made it is a good idea to go through a formal checklist of matters that have to be dealt with before the appointee turns up for work. This checklist will cover important steps that must be taken such as references, start dates, probationary periods, payroll, new starter routines, medical examinations, contracts of employment, induction training, security passes, facilities such as desks etc. At some stage, and this should ideally have been done at short-listing, the information contained on application forms should be verified including qualifications, past employment, residential status etc.

The formal contract of employment will have to be signed before the auditor is taken on. This may appear to be a formality at first sight but in the event of a dispute can be very important. For audit staff there are several special matters that should be incorporated into the contract of employment. These provisions should cater for travelling and overnight stays, subsistence allowances, unsocial working hours, compliance with professional auditing standards/code of conduct, meeting time-budgets and so on. As a word of warning, it is not unheard of to review a selection of personnel files and find that some of them do not contain signed contracts of employment.

Once the auditor is in post there should be a suitable introduction process. This is a matter of acclimatising the newcomer into the audit department in terms of management's expectation of him/her. There is a misunderstanding of induction in that it is not only necessarily for junior staff, but is all about explaining how this (as opposed to other) internal audit departments operate. Some warning of expectations should be outlined in the selection interview since selection is about both offering a job and having that offer accepted by the candidate. Both sides must be satisfied with the arrangements before they are finalised. If the requirements of the audit manual are made clear to the candidate between the time of selection and signing the contract of employment, they will have a chance to withdraw if not happy with the procedures that are applied in the particular internal audit department. Induction should be based around the audit manual although one would also cover the wider organisation and any important policies that are in use. This induction could be on two levels. One may be a half-day consisting of general organisational matters on a one-to-one basis. A formal programme may be arranged for a batch of new auditors that may last several days and, as already mentioned, should consist of material taken from the audit manual. This may be presented by a senior audit manager.

22.5 The Career Development Profile

The audit career debate
The world of internal audit is, in fact, fast-moving and going through a process of continual change, generally to the advantage of the profession. One such development is related to the view that we may now have a career in internal audit. Not so long ago organisations felt it necessary, when advertising for audit staff, to promise a transfer to line management after a spell in internal audit. As such it was seen as good training in a function that potentially came into contact with all aspects of organisational activities. Good all-round general managers who had, as it were, a helicopter view of the organisation, could in this way be developed. There are two main arguments located in this view of the audit function. Firstly, the fact that internal audit provided a good training ground for managers is a valid concept. However the perception that one must use bribes to encourage people to join internal audit, which is the second implication, is misguided. Furthermore, the management career development programmes that use secondments to internal audit can run hand in hand with separate programmes for career internal auditors. So long as audit careers are respected in their own right, there should be no problems. This chapter is based firmly on the concept of internal audit as a formal professional career.

Staff appraisals

Staff appraisal is a management control that audit would tend to recommend when undertaking an audit where staffing is included in the terms of reference for the work. As such one may argue that we, as auditors, should apply this technique to the management of the internal audit function. However, staff appraisal schemes can be positive motivators or complete demotivators depending on how they are designed and implemented. The theory of staff appraisals is based on telling people what is expected of them and then telling them how far they are achieving these standards, as a way of motivating them. The other benefit is the positive steps that may be taken where performance is not on par. Appraisal schemes also underpin career development programmes that again may be used to direct the activities of staff and ensure there is good progression so that good staff are retained and poor staff improved. This may be illustrated in a simple diagram:

FIGURE 22.4 THE AUDITOR APPRAISAL PROCESS

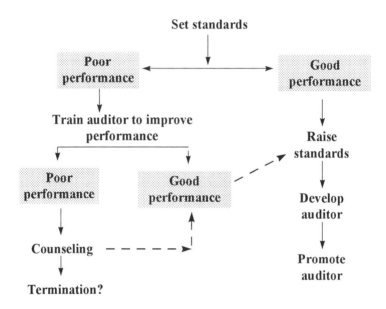

An alternative approach to the appraisal process is to separate performance appraisal from procedures for dealing with unacceptable poor performance and particular problems. The latter would come into operation where there are obvious flaws in performance which cannot be addressed through traditional training and development programmes. Figure 22.8 is based on the organisation distinguishing between different management procedures for dealing with a variety of performance related issues. As such where the auditor breaches procedure, this is dealt with through the disciplinary procedure. Where the employee is often sick the frequent sickness procedure comes into action; and poor performance is handled by special action that may result in dismissal of the auditor in question. In this way the performance appraisal scheme can be operated in a positive mode at all times. Special staffing problems are handled by distinct and separate arrangements outside performance appraisal. Special attention will be directed towards the auditor and this will not wait for or be dependent on the performance appraisal programme. In this way these types of problems can be fast tracked before they get out of hand. Meanwhile the appraisal scheme may continue in its positive mode. The words "performance, development, advancement, excellence, and quality" may each promote a positive environment. The counter argument is that this positive environment has to be firmly in place before any performance appraisal can be planned. Whatever the view, it is essential that auditors are appraised in a positive fashion. This in turn depends on:

1. Keeping the accent on praise.
2. Not using the appraisal scheme to criticise but using it to develop.
3. Using performance appraisal to engender good communications and listening skills.
4. Seeking to promote a win-win environment where all sides gain.

Appraisal criteria

There is no way that auditors can be appraised without reference to a formal appraisal criterion. This would be based on the types of skills, abilities and attributes required to discharge the audit role. The idea is to employ, teach, develop and improve each of these factors through a formal process of appraising each auditor's ability to achieve these standards. These performance standards may cover:

- Basic auditing skills that all auditors should possess.
- Advanced auditing skills that should attach to more senior auditors.
- Managerial skills for auditors with staff responsibilities.
- Skills in related specialist areas such as computing, accounting, engineering, law and so on.
- Other skills as required.

We are moving closer to defining a job specification that may be used to appoint audit staff. The same personal requirements may be applied to appraising the staff along with a series of personal targets. Higher levels of audit management need to acquire different types of skills:

FIGURE 22.5 DIFFERENT SKILLS LEVELS

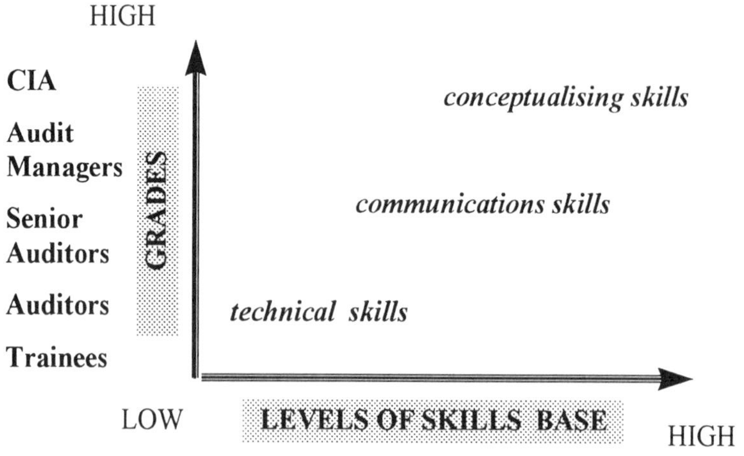

The performance appraisal scheme must cater for the above factors if it is to have any relevance to the internal audit function. Superimposed on this are special projects which may be developed by the auditor and one such typical basket of targets may be defined below.

TABLE 22.1 RANGE OF PERFORMANCE TARGETS

SOURCE	TARGETS (EXAMPLES)
Job description	completing audits to budget & quality standards (audit manual)
Delegated tasks	implement a new time monitoring system
Special projects	restructuring exercise for the audit department
Personal development	better communication skills e.g. making oral presentations

22.6 Factors for Implementing an Auditor Appraisal Scheme

It is one thing to design an auditor performance-appraisal scheme but quite another to implement it in such a way that it produces the desired results. What looks good on paper may be different in practice. There are several matters to be considered including:

The scheme must in fact address the auditor's performance. It should not be an alternative method of getting rid of problem staff or simply a paper exercise. The key objectives must be to assess and then seek to improve the performance of auditors at all levels in the internal audit department.

The scheme should attempt to meet employees' needs that should be based around a desire to obtain feedback on their achievements and approach to work. It can be sold to staff as a mechanism for providing this all-important feedback as opposed to just another management technique to increase the work-rate.

The scheme should represent a source of challenge to the auditor. The process of working to one's own personal targets engenders a form of maturity from staff but can lead to an assortment of soft targets being defined. Extremes can occur where parts of these personal targets may have already been achieved before they are applied. This positive approach can only be used in audit departments that employ highly motivated staff and use team-building approaches to work.

The scheme must incorporate the concept of regular progress reporting. This is much better than an annual scheme whereby reports "appear out of the blue" every twelve months. Ongoing assessment makes it easier to assimilate the scheme into everyday work that the auditor carries out.

An auditor can compile a career plan so long as there is an awareness of the areas that have been developed and those that need further developing. A short-cut to this process is via the performance appraisal scheme that isolates one's strengths and weaknesses. To be valid the scheme must incorporate this feature rather than simply result in a finite category in the ranges of say 1 - 5. We have shown that auditors bring to their work a whole range of skills that together comprise a unique package. To simply classify a person as a category 1 (very poor) or 5 (very good), or a range between these two figures is bad management practice. Unfortunately there are many audit sections that do just this and still have difficulty working out why their particular scheme appears to demotivate their auditors.

We can build on this idea of motivation by suggesting that any valid scheme should be geared directly into this concept of releasing "people power". Performance appraisal must as the bottom line exist to improve performance. As such it must then feed into a suitable development plan that gives a sense of direction and purpose to staff as they work for an organisation over the years. This simple notion is sometimes forgotten when a scheme is introduced and fast becomes a weapon of terror in the wrong manager's hands. Note that what may be acceptable in a recession where the supply of auditors exceeds demand, may be resented in times of high economic growth.

The scheme should acknowledge the personal goals of each auditor. In this way we should seek to establish a bridge between the organisation's and the auditor's own targets. If the performance targets can become personal targets then the appraisal scheme will run automatically as it is driven by the auditor's motivation, as opposed to an obscure set of goals.

The appraisal scheme should ideally feed into a suitable training programme. This being the case, the scheme will hopefully be used to isolate any training needs that must be met to fill gaps in the skills required to perform at the appropriate level. There is little point in identifying skills gaps without seeking then to close them. Such an approach whereby training is applied to problems, makes the scheme more dynamic as a positive technique rather than concentrating merely on the perceived weaknesses.

Performance appraisal should be sophisticated enough to define an auditor's potential to work at a defined level. This requires extrapolation to move the historical achievements into projected areas. The only imponderable is the impact of training and development plans. A learning rate may also be estimated so that one uses three key factors to arrive at the auditor's potential performance:

FIGURE 22.6 AUDITOR DEVELOPMENT RATES

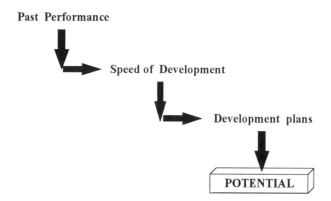

Using the bridge between performance appraisal and auditor development plans we can go on to consider the future of each auditor in terms of promoting their management skills, existing job, and future potential. Again the idea is to get the scheme into a positive mode that is well received by staff.

Counselling is also an important component of an appraisal scheme. Where the scheme isolates poor performance this can lead to a great deal of stress for the auditor in question. One final implication of poor performance may be transfer/removal/dismissal. This is necessary as a final remedy that hopefully will never have to be applied so long as staff are willing to work and possess the basic skills that underpin this work. If we have to follow a line from the performance appraisal scheme to the poor performance procedures that may result in the removal of the auditor, there needs to be an interim stage based on counselling. This will seek to uncover barriers to performance that may be dealt with in addressing an inability to perform to required standards. Where these barriers can be eliminated then the final transfer decision may be delayed and the auditor given what may be seen as a second chance. Here special support programmes should be in place to address this problem. Note that counselling should not be left entirely to audit management but must include a professional input from say the Personnel department. The CIA should always remember that some employees perform badly because of their managers and this factor is often hidden from view as an interpretation of events is provided by the same manager. Again a level of sophistication built into the scheme is the keyword.

We arrive at the final point of principle underpinning performance appraisal which is the key ingredient: feedback. Performance appraisal provides an opportunity for the manager and audit staff to discuss performance as an issue and so develop the necessary mechanism for this feedback. Without stating the obvious, this feedback is a two-way affair. It requires both sides to listen to each other and develop a meaningful rapport along the following lines:

FIGURE 22.7 FEEDBACK AND APPRAISALS

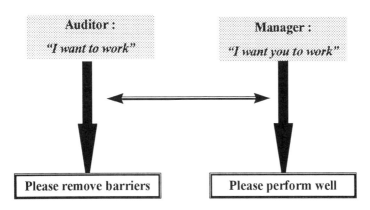

Performance appraisal is less of a bureaucratic management technique. It is more of a vehicle through which performance can be addressed and developed by way of a close working relationship between the auditor and audit management.

22.7 Methods of Staff Appraisal

There are a variety of methods that are used to assess performance. Fortunately the internal audit arena, because of the nature of the work, provides a ready-made avenue through which auditors may be assessed. This is based around the audit review procedure where audit work is considered by audit management before it is signed off. Ways that auditors may have their performance assessed are:

The audit review process. Here we can use a standardised form to allow the manager to comment on the way the auditor carried out a piece of work that can then be copied onto the person's personnel file. This brings appraisal naturally into the review process based on the hands-on work that the auditor performs rather than vague concepts.

A periodic review may be undertaken that deals with the auditor's performance say on a quarterly basis. Here one might simply take each item from the auditor's job specification along with special projects that have been assigned, and indicate the extent to which the required standards have been achieved. The manager must have reference to valid material to form the basis of this assessment and to this end one may refer to the jobs that have been charged on the auditor's timesheet.

It is possible to set performance targets for each auditor based around the annual/quarterly plans. This will be based on completing defined audits, keeping within budgets, performing special tasks such as the audit manual, achieving a percentage of chargeable to non-chargeable hours. Where these targets flow from the overall organisational/departmental targets, a form of management by achievement ensues and hierarchies may be developed so that goals cascade downwards. Examples of some specific and team performance targets may be listed:

- Extent to which the annual and quarterly plan has been achieved.
- The percentage of recoverable hours charged.
- Time taken to respond to management requests for assistance.
- Staff turnover.
- Absenteeism rate.
- Number of improvements to the audit manual.
- Time taken by auditors to get access to audit management.
- Level of managerial agreement to audit-risk criteria.
- Level of involvement of auditee in the audit terms of reference.
- Number of recommendations agreed.
- Level of complaints.
- Level of staff grievances against management.
- Time taken to issue audit reports after completion of the audit.
- Level of suggestions from staff to audit management.
- Level of compliance with the audit manual.
- Regularity of group and departmental meetings.
- The percentage of staff with poor timekeeping.
- Number of aborted audits.
- Level of problems found during work reviews.
- Extent to which audit objectives have been met.
- Number of audits completed on time.
- Level of audits within time budget.
- Number of auditors passing professional exams.
- Number of audits delegated by the audit manager.
- Level of draft reports requiring re-writes.
- Extent to which developmental plans have been achieved.
- Extent of audit automation.
- Rate of production of audit products.
- Currency of time-monitoring information.
- Currency of timesheets submitted and authorised.
- Level of satisfaction from the clients.
- Extent to which desks are kept clear.

- Extent to which files hold all relevant information.
- Time taken to find specific files.
- Extent to which follow-up audits find that recommendations from previous reports have been implemented.

There are drawbacks in defining auditors as belonging to a certain performance group or category. It is nonetheless possible to rate each range of the performance factors by assigning a figure. It is the final overall figure that creates the problems and as such this average or aggregate need not be calculated. The auditor's job specification has been quoted as one way of setting a suitable framework for the performance-appraisal scheme. Some of the relevant items on such a specification that relate to auditing skills only may include the following:

Responsible for systems based auditing of:
- Computer applications.
- Systems developments.
- Corporate functions.
- Managerial functions.
- Operational functions.

Application of audit techniques such as:
- Interviewing.
- Flowcharting.
- Statistical sampling.
- Risk analysis.
- Audit planning.
- Oral presentations.
- Report writing.
- Preliminary surveys.
- Compliance testing.
- Substantive testing.
- Assignment control.
- Audit work review.
- Formulating recommendations.
- Following up audit work.

Responsible for investigations into fraud and irregularities including:
- Strategy for the investigation.
- Fact finding.
- Surveillance techniques.
- Interviewing techniques.
- Preparing evidence for disciplinaries and courts.
- Attending as a witness at disciplinaries and courts.
- Liaising with the police and other regulatory agencies.
- Preparing suitable reports and dealing with the implications of control weaknesses.

Responsible for consultancy projects that would include:
- VFM projects.
- Preparation and audit of financial accounts.
- Advising on resource rationalisation programmes.
- Advising on take-overs and mergers.
- Advising on efficiency savings.
- Restructuring.
- General problem-solving exercises.

For each of the above a rating of say 1 - 5 may be assigned with 1 "excellent" and 5 "very poor". Note the natural tendency of managers to stick to the norm when assigning a rating. When using the 1 - 5 scale, this ends up with either 2 or 3 being assigned to all assessed items. One way to counter this is to provide that the way audit managers administer their performance appraisal scheme becomes one of the items assessed in their own appraisal.

22.8 Pros and Cons of Performance Appraisal

These may be listed as:

Advantages
1. A database of audit skills is compiled as staff that excel in certain areas are readily identified.
2. It is possible to set a policy on promotion to fit in with the way auditors are developing and so provide a link between reward and performance in terms of career enhancement.
3. It is possible to link part of remuneration into the appraisal scheme and so pay by results although this has to be very carefully planned.
4. A training-needs analysis will flow from the scheme and this can be used to establish a suitable training programme. We must be careful about rewarding poor performers with extra training while good workers are ignored by the training programme.
5. Managers and their staff may discuss objectives and goals that are considered in a programmed way as the scheme is implemented. These discussions will probably improve motivation and overall communication between audit managers and their staff.
6. Good schemes help promote highly motivated staff who have a clear sense of direction and excel under pressure.
7. The all-important feedback is developed based on the performance criteria. Auditors are told what is expected from them and then they are told to what extent they are achieving these standards.

Disadvantages
1. All performance-appraisal schemes are subjective and there is no hiding from this factor. We would hope that despite this, they were applied in a systematic fashion, setting clear standards for all staff. Where they are not linked to salary or disciplinary action (for poor performance) then they simply become a way of developing staff and so acquire a less emotive role in managing the internal audit function.

2. One absolute drawback of all performance appraisal schemes is the fact they depend on a foundation of mutual trust and respect between all staff. This point cannot be overemphasised since there are many schemes that simply fail because management has failed to install sound managerial standards. The types of standards that are required include: clear policies and procedures, career development, strategic planning, automated systems, management information, training programmes, mechanisms for upwards and downwards communication and so on. Where management is impoverished and has no clear idea of its role and goals, then any appraisal scheme is doomed from the start. Not only will it have a negative impact but it will tend to foster the child/parent relationship common in badly run organisations.

3. Unprofessional managers will allow schemes to become bogged down with negative features:
   - Manipulative management.
   - Inconsistent application.
   - Bias introduced.
   - Defensive subordinates.
   - Manager's drinking partners promoted.
   - Not linked to training.
   - Top management not involved.
   - Bad industrial relations.
   - The old adage that failure generates failure will apply fully in this type of environment.

4. Another disadvantage is that data used to support the scheme may be out-of-date and not reflect the current position. This can be overcome where appraisal is continuous and occurs every time an auditor completes an audit or related piece of work.

5. There is an inherent conflict in the Judge/Helper role that may arise in a poorly managed scheme. Here the manager sees him/herself as a helper whilst the perception of staff is that of a judge whose main role is to criticise them. Again the feedback system that allows a two-way communication will help avert this problem.

6. We have already mentioned the difficulty in installing a scheme that looks good on paper. The only point that is relevant here is the need for it to be driven by top management (i.e. the CIA/Head of Audit) for this most difficult task to be achieved. Not least of the problems is the excessive paperwork that can result from many schemes.

7. Most argue that performance appraisal tends to highlight existing problems rather than cause them. The concept of appraisal must be set within a mechanism to codify what should be best management practice in dealing with staff. There are many things that could go wrong with performance appraisal schemes where they are applied in an inappropriate fashion. It is important that there is a control over this process not in terms of an appeal, but in terms of referring matters for review. For this reason, it is possible to allow auditors to have specific concerns referred to the CIA to seek reconciliation or any amendments (if required). This review should revolve around the annual report and should be related only to matters connected with setting targets, reviewing performance and/or defining the resultant career development action plans.

22.9 Good Appraisal Schemes

Additional factors to consider when devising and implementing an appraisal scheme for the internal audit function:

1. They should be continuous and not periodical.
2. They should be accepted by the vast majority of auditors. Where this is not the case the scheme will probably lower motivation levels rather than have a positive impact on the audit service.
3. The audit managers should also be subject to appraisal and this may be on the basis of the overall performance of their audit groups.
4. Training is required before any sensible scheme can be applied or the "stick to the norm" tendency will arise.
5. Targets may cascade downwards to ensure that they are linked into organisational goals.
6. They should be linked into the underlying culture of the audit department and depend on whether a group basis is applied or one is seeking to promote individual working rather than teamwork.
7. Appraisal interviews should be carefully managed and used as a positive vehicle for open discussions in a confidential but structured format.
8. The scheme should result in at least a formal annual report that is held on file for future reference.
9. The underlying documentation to support the scheme should be devised and standardised as much as possible.
10. The scheme should be directed towards professional auditing standards.
11. They may be linked into financial rewards although it is best to allow the scheme to operate for a while (at least a year), before it is amended to impact on the auditor's remuneration.
12. The CIA must be on guard for prejudice and must insist that audit managers bring to his/her attention any issues that may interfere with the smooth running of the scheme. Furthermore the way the audit manager has operated the scheme should be reviewed by the CIA.
13. Each scheme should contain clear objectives that have been derived from a systematically applied procedure. In general the more senior the job, the more demanding the targets.
14. One way of forcing managers to make clear decisions is to use alternative categories that one must select. This must however be accompanied by a suitable narrative that supports this choice. No overall mark should be assigned.
15. One should avoid using personality measures unless this is specifically asked for in the job specification. Even where this is the case it is notoriously difficult to measure them if they are not linked into a specific skill.

Link into career development

The concept of appraising staff must attach to some form of professional foundation for it to have any real meaning. If it is not seen as part of a career development programme then we return once more to the view that appraisals can have a de-motivating effect on the auditor. Appraisals should be founded on a two-sided agreement that seeks to assess the auditor and then help him/her address any identified deficiencies. Training, rotations, secondment, work assignments, staff assignment, skills-workshops, special projects and so on are all valid techniques for developing staff based on their appraised needs. The key is to apply the right method, to the right auditor, for the right reasons.

Training and development
There is a separate chapter on audit training that deals with this topic in some detail. Here we can simply state that there are different types of training that may be applied to meeting skills-gaps identified through the performance appraisal scheme. Not only is it important to select the right training scheme to meet skills deficiencies, but there should also be a formal method through which the results of such training can be assessed. Development, on the other hand, is a wider concept that entails many different activities. Development programmes are aimed at getting the auditor to maximise his/her potential within the internal audit function. Once performance targets have been set, there are many different ways in which an auditor may be developed to meet these targets including:

- Rotation between audit groups.
- Secondment to other departments/organisations.
- Assignment to increasingly more difficult projects.
- Assignment to specialist areas of audit work.
- Additional managerial responsibility.
- Special tasks such as the audit manual, audit planning, the IT strategy, risk appraisal etc.
- Attendance at external groups such as an inter-organisational computer audit working group.
- Opportunities to deputise for a more senior auditor.

The idea is to develop and extend the skills database and so set the scene for career progression. In this way the auditor's promotion is not derived from the performance appraisal scheme but uses personal development to seek and obtain promotion. Training and development which is geared to poorer performers is equally important, to simply get the auditor's skills up to a sufficiently high standard. In this way no member of internal audit is left out of the equation that caters for all performance levels (so long as they meet basic minimum standards).

Client feedback
There is a growing view that internal audit is primarily about providing a service to management. The more one is in tune with client needs, the better the final impact of the audit product. Client contact is the result of the many meetings and discussions between individual auditors and individual line managers, as well as the formal presentations by the CIA to the audit committee. The auditor's individual development programme should incorporate a consideration of client relationships, both in terms of appraising the adequacy of existing skills and with a view to developing them wherever possible. The section below on quality assurance outlines the use of client questionnaires that should follow the completion of each audit. The information contained therein should also flow into the auditor's development programme. The CIA should seek to develop the relevant communications skills in members of staff, for example:

1. An ability to appreciate the needs of auditees and seek to incorporate these into the audit work that is performed.
2. Good interpersonal skills and an ability to communicate in an open and friendly fashion. We could dedicate an entire book to this subject in view of the importance it

holds for the success of the audit service. It is no exaggeration to suggest that this may be the single most important skill in any auditor, on the assumption that basic audit skills are in place. The excellent auditor will display these communication skills and a naturally acquired capacity to converse with all levels of client management.

3. An ability to work with managers in tackling control deficiencies. We have discussed the participative approach to auditing early on in the handbook and this requires a basic ability where the auditor is able to bring this practice to life and work in a joint problem-solving mode.

4. Lastly we should note that there must be a mechanism for receiving and dealing with complaints from clients that is independent of the auditor being complained about.

Counselling

Most of management's input into an auditor's career development programme will be quite positive, based on helping the auditor grow and progress. However, there will be times when management has to address staffing issues arising from poor performance or behavioural problems and this will impact on the person's development. One model that may be applied breaks down staffing issues as:

FIGURE 22.8 THE APPLICATION OF STAFF COUNSELLING

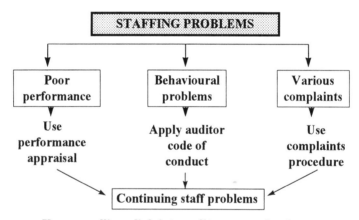

Use counselling : link into auditor career development

When applying counselling, audit management should take expert advice (from Personnel) and ensure that they address the underlying problem and cause. It is an opportunity to discuss personal issues in confidence and understand how and why they are impacting on the auditor's performance at work.

Productivity

Productivity is a fairly simple concept that suggests inputs produce outputs via a suitably controlled process. One measure of the effectiveness of this control is to set standards for the output, based on the defined level of inputs. These standards become targets and so long as mechanisms for measuring the work have been installed, productivity can be assessed in terms of the extent to which these targets have been achieved. Career development uses performance measures as one way of measuring the way the auditor is developing and productivity factors are one feature of such a system. In this way audit management may gauge an auditor's progress through quantifiable factors as well as more subjective considerations. We must always appreciate the limitations of productivity measures, which may appear scientific, but are based on underlying (and subjective) principles that have been agreed by management. The only real feature is that they may promote a degree of consistency across staff if they are applied in a systematic fashion. They may also provide a sense of direction for development plans by highlighting some of the targets towards which we are seeking to develop staff. There are many factors that may form part of such a productivity profile and these will vary depending on the type of work performed. They may include:

- Number of audit reports issued.
- Amount of alteration as a result of management review.
- Level of recoverable hours to non-recoverable hours charged in the period.
- Degree to which one keeps within the budget hours for each audit.
- Extent to which work plan has been completed.
- Level of positive comments from clients via satisfaction questionnaire.
- Level of absences from work.

The standard SMART test applied to target setting is based on the following model (subject to variations):

S :	Specific
M :	Measurable
A :	Achievable
R :	Results oriented
T :	Time based

For example a target for a senior auditor may be:

> **To prepare and implement a new and revised audit manual that complies with best practice and adopted audit standards by date X (using 100 audit hours).**

Attached to this would be various performance measures that could form the basis of reviewing the extent to which the targets have been achieved. These measures could include:

1. Time budget - 1/3 of work should be done by 33 hours, 1/2 by 50 hours etc.
2. Timeframe - the due date should be kept under review.
3. Qualitative - all key areas in line with professional audit standards should be covered.
4. Acceptable - the draft manual should be accepted by audit management.
5. Implemented - plan to get the document implemented should be drawn up and achieved.

Accomplishments

A career development programme will assume the auditor is being taken along a clearly defined path:

FIGURE 22.9 THE CAREER DEVELOPMENT PATH

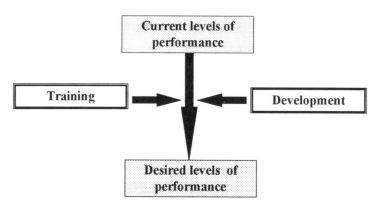

This is straightforward in that management simply helps and encourages its staff to meet target performance levels and hopefully receive promotion and greater respect at work. There are times when the auditor does not follow this linear progression and excels in a particular matter. The career development scheme must be able to cater for this additional factor by recognising specific accomplishments. So for example an auditor may be asked to draft a section of the audit manual covering a new risk appraisal criterion that is being developed. If the person produces an excellent draft that brings in new ideas and makes the internal audit function better placed to deliver a successful service, this will be an achievement above and beyond expected targets. Unfortunately professional jealousy may tempt some audit managers to suppress this work, but a better position will be reached where it is recognised and suitably rewarded, perhaps by increasing the speed of the development programme and possible ensuing promotion. We can now re-write our illustration:

FIGURE 22.10 THE CAREER ACHIEVEMENT/DEVELOPMENT PATH

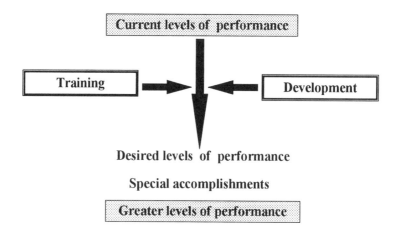

Single audit evaluation

One key factor in any development programme must be the ability to perform an audit. This may be seen as the basis of success in that, if each audit is performed well, we have a good chance of delivering a quality audit service. The management review process that is applied to an audit before it is signed-off provides an opportunity to assess the auditor's performance and so build this into the various career development programmes. As such the review process should incorporate a judgement as to the adequacy of the application of auditing procedures by using the following approach:

1. Audit manager reviews each aspect of the audit, both as it progresses and after it has been done. Compliance with the standards established through the audit manual would feature in this review as will the overall "feel" of the audit.
2. Any deficiencies should be highlighted for action and correction by the auditor in question.
3. Relevant points arising from the above should be assimilated into individual auditors' development programmes where there are obvious problems dealing with some aspects of the audit.
4. A suitable document should be extracted from the audit file for inclusion into the personal performance appraisal file for the auditor/s in question, based on the review points. This will address the question "how did the auditor perform in this piece of work?"
5. They should then be linked to the audit post specification in terms of defined audit skills and attributes that should be seen in action during the audit.
6. Action should be taken to address any auditor weaknesses. Remember to look out for any special accomplishments as well as problems.

SWOT analysis

One useful technique that may be applied to developing auditors is SWOT analysis whereby strengths, weaknesses, opportunities and threats can be isolated and assessed. This then feeds into the individual's development process. This is a confidential building exercise that is performed by the auditor in question with the help of their manager. As with most managerial techniques, this can either be done well and act as a major aid to efficiency, or be done badly and marginalise the employee in question.

Continuous appraisals

An annual appraisal scheme should be established for each auditor that seeks to assign an assessment along with suitable comments. It is an administrative convenience in that a manager would only need to consider this issue once a year, so saving much time and trouble. However, this is a misconception since an annual procedure that has no link into the ongoing work of the auditor has little or no real use. Appraisal needs to be carried out as part and parcel of the manager's responsibilities throughout the year and not only at one point in time. The problem can in part be solved by installing quarterly assessments but in truth the process of discussing and resolving performance issues should arise whenever it is necessary. This ongoing debate will be aimed at tackling performance problems as they arise as well as the formal quarterly/annual procedures that are also required.

Leavers

Career development programmes give direction to staff and help them achieve a sense of purpose in their work and their plans for the future. It tends to create a positive culture where auditors in the main wish to stay with the organisation and do not necessarily have to leave to achieve their career goals. This is not to say that staff should not leave and pursue career adventures outside their current employment. We should however be concerned about auditors who leave because they are unhappy about their development in the internal audit department. As such, audit management should establish a mechanism whereby it may identify any problems with development plans that have led to staff resignations. Exit interviews are one way that this may be carried out so long as the right questions are asked and management acts on any information obtained from this source.

Implementing an auditor appraisal scheme

The illustration set out below follows a possible performance appraisal implementation process for internal audit:

FIGURE 22.11 AUDITOR PERFORMANCE APPRAISAL SCHEME

It is clear that the scheme should be based on the organisational format and this is the correct starting place. A suitable draft document should be implemented through the use of audit management meetings, staff briefings, formal training for appraisers and relevant insertions in the audit manual. The actual annual appraisal scheme itself will call for an initial meeting where the audit manager will set targets for each member of staff. Regular review meetings should take place throughout the year and a formal progress meeting should be held either six monthly or quarterly. The annual appraisal report should document what has been agreed at the formal annual meeting and copies held by the line manager, personnel and the auditor being appraised. A copy should also go to the CIA, who will sign the report off (which will also be signed by the appraisee and appraiser).

22.10 Dealing with Problem Staff

Standards
Clearly the CIA has to establish sound codes of conduct and performance measures based on professional auditing standards. These are targets that are constantly sought-after in terms of the entire audit service and each individual auditor. Effort is directed towards moving the internal audit function closer to these targets as all levels of auditor contribute to this process. This is the upside of development where the push from all staff is in the same direction. The downside occurs where there are cracks in this model that, if left unattended, will impair the efficiency of the audit service. These cracks may result from problems created by that most unreliable of resources, people. Staffing problems must be resolved as quickly as possible and the best way to isolate them is by contrasting this behaviour with defined standards that are demanded from all staff. Hopefully, most staffing problems can be perceived as breaches of procedure and dealt with by management as such. There are unfortunately many problems that are caused by managers, particularly where they fail to deal with an issue in a timely way. Standards nonetheless are important. As an example there is little action management can take against any employee who takes excessive sick leave, if the organisation has not bothered to defined exactly what is considered to be excessive.

Grievances
All large organisations should install suitable procedures to deal with staff grievances to ensure that policies are being applied in a consistent fashion and problems are resolved as close to the source as possible. Typical examples of grievances are provided below:

> *After the resignation of an audit team leader (ATL), the assistant audit team leader (AATL) for the audit group was asked to act up for six months until the vacancy was permanently filled. The Director of Finance (DF) allowed this acting up to continue for two years unbeknown to Personnel. During this period the seven other AATLs complained that this was unfair as they would like a chance to "act up". The DF had promised them he would advertise the ATL post. After the two years the AATL who was acting up wrote to Personnel to clarify his position and was advised that, according to organisational policy, he was now assimilated into the post because he had done the work for two years. The seven AATL took out a grievance against the DF on the basis that they had not been given a chance to compete for this post.*

> *The CIA decided to advertise a vacant Contract Auditor (CA) post. He altered the job specification so that the applicants would have to be fully qualified accountants, a provision that does not apply to any other post in internal audit. Three general auditors, who were not qualified, were advised by the CIA that they could apply for the post since Personnel did not accept that this CA post-holder needed to be fully qualified. A fourth auditor took out a grievance against the CIA on the basis that he did not apply for the job because he did not know this qualification was not an essential requirement.*

> *A junior auditor applied to the CIA in August for support for a training course due to start in October. She asked for assistance on three levels; time off (on day release), the tuition fees and the costs of a revision course (May the following year). The CIA ignored this request despite repeated reminders from the junior auditor's line manager. Meanwhile the internal audit department was supposed to be implementing a positive action programme designed to develop female auditors who were under-represented at senior grades. In December the junior auditor was advised by the Union representative to take out a grievance on the basis that staff in other departments had had their training considered and approved.*

> *In the past three auditors had attended assessment interviews on successful completion of their accounting examinations. As a result they were given an upgrading. Two newly qualified auditors submitted similar applications to a new CIA, who simply ignored them for two years. They proceeded to take out a grievance against the CIA for failing to deal with their applications.*

The above-mentioned situations place the CIA/audit management in a tenuous position since most result from a breach of procedure and/or managerial inefficiency. There are key points that can be learnt from the problems highlighted by the examples:

1. Audit management must abide by organisational policies when dealing with staffing issues. One way to address this is to build these policies into the audit manual and if there are any different interpretations of these policies, they should be agreed through the official channels.
2. All staffing issues should be dealt with in a timely fashion. Many grievances do not arise because management does not approve various applications, but are based on management's failure to deal with the issue at hand.
3. It is better to treat staff in a fair way as this not only promotes team spirit, but also enhances the reputation of internal audit management. The CIA should act as a control over the audit managers.
4. The CIA and audit managers need to be aware of relevant organisational policies before they make decisions that require an understanding of these policies. If this is a problem then advice from the appropriate officers (e.g. Personnel or Legal) should be sought.
5. The CIA should always remember that he/she is ultimately responsible for all decisions made by audit managers and other staff, and as such should review these decisions where necessary (e.g. where they are controversial).
6. Grievance procedures are always designed to resolve problems at a local level by discussion and reasoned consideration of all the relevant factors. It is only where this breaks down that a formal grievance arises. Most problems result from poor communication or a failure by management to deal with staffing problems expediently.

There are many different ways that a grievance procedure may be implemented, for example:

FIGURE 22.12 OUTLINE GRIEVANCE PROCEDURE

```
┌─────────────────────────────────┐
│  Staff experiences a problem    │
└─────────────────────────────────┘
                 ▼
   Attempts to resolve with line manager
                 ▼
           Writes formally to line
        manager seeking a solution
                 ▼
   Appeals formally to line manager's manager
                 ▼
     Appeals to Personnel who will consider
      whether there is a case to answer
                 ▼
 If there is : a formal grievance panel will be set up to look
  into the problem and make relevant recommendations
                 ▼
┌─────────────────────────────────┐
│  Director acts on recommendations │
└─────────────────────────────────┘
```

Counselling revisited

Counselling was discussed earlier in the context of career development where we considered any relevant barriers that needed to be removed. When dealing with problem staff this becomes a most important technique. We can go on to suggest that if counselling is missed from the array of developments when dealing with a problem, then management will have left themselves open to severe criticism. Counselling in this case is an attempt to discover the underlying cause of problems that are affecting the auditor's recurrent adverse behaviour at work. It is also a way of persuading the person in question to change or make any necessary arrangements as a way of tackling the defined problems. All counselling should be formally recorded on the officer's personal file whilst most of the other key points have already been dealt with.

22.11 Disciplinaries

In an ideal world we would spend only a short amount of time on internal disciplinaries when tackling the topic of management of internal audit. Unfortunately, this is not to be. The CIA must be prepared to take disciplinary action against audit staff whenever this is appropriate and there are many real-life examples where this has been necessary. Internal disciplinaries may be seen as a last option decision when all else has failed. There are also times where this arises from a one-off event as opposed to the culmination of a developing situation. An example is where the auditor has been convicted of a criminal offence and on his return to work is immediately suspended, disciplined and dismissed. For organisations that need to adopt fairly bureaucratic staffing procedures the entire disciplinary procedure may be illustrated.

FIGURE 22.13 DISCIPLINARY PROCEDURE

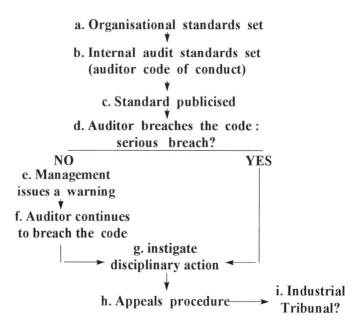

Each of the above points (a to i) is dealt with in more detail below.

(a) **Organisational standards set**. The internal audit department operates within the sponsoring organisation unless it is a contracted-out service provided by an external supplier. It is right and proper for the auditors to be bound by the same standards of conduct that cover all employees. This sets the ethical framework for the performance of the employees' relevant work duties. One argument runs that the internal auditor should operate to higher standards than others. This is debatable, since the underlying factor for internal audit is related to the increased scope for breaching standards of conduct that is inherent in the audit role. The standards are the same, it is simply that having more freedom in turn makes this a more sensitive issue.

(b) **Internal audit standards set**. Building on the point outlined above, we arrive at the need for tailored auditing standards. These should be based on two key concepts, the first being professional standards of conduct that are derived from a body such as the Institute of Internal Auditors. The second would be defined within an internal set of standards that would be contained in say the audit manual, and referred to in the contract of employment. They may simply be a repetition of the organisational standards or a version specially tailored to meet internal audit's needs. One useful approach is to refer to the professional standards within the internal code so that the following relationship is established.

FIGURE 22.14 CODES OF CONDUCT

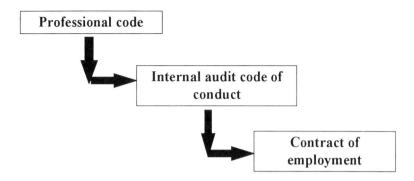

(c) Standard publicised. One crucial feature of the disciplinary process is based on ensuring that each auditor is wholly aware of the standards of conduct that are expected. This is not as simple as it sounds as it must include at least the following action by audit management:

- Making newcomers aware of these standards before they accept a position within the audit department.
- Carrying out induction training that includes a clear explanation of the standards.
- Formally documenting them in the audit manual and ensuring that they are made available, read and understood by all audit staff.
- Installing a procedure for updating the standards and communicating any changes to staff.
- Providing a suitable means through which auditors may seek clarification of matters that impact on codes of conduct.
- Publishing reminders of important matters pertaining to the standards particularly where there may be minor breaches that may be seen as acceptable by some staff.
- Most important of all, defining in a clear and concise fashion exactly what would be the consequences of any intentional breach of the standards.

(d) Auditor breaches the code. Once the above matters are firmly in place, audit management must establish clear mechanisms that enable them to isolate any individual breaches. Before this point is reached, the managers must behave in a way that reinforces the standards and is conducive to promoting behaviour that corresponds to the requirements of the organisation. So for example there is little point in putting up "no smoking" signs and then allowing one particularly stubborn audit manager to smoke in the office. A more powerful example relates to the use of profanities; if audit management swears at work then one must expect all other staff to conduct themselves in a similar fashion. This applies also to the consumption of alcohol during office hours. The key point is that we must not only lead by example but also develop a culture where standards are seen as important and respected by internal audit at all levels. Turning to the issue of breach of procedure, where this arises, we must make reference to the following factors:

☐ **Whether the breach represents a material issue or is simply a minor affair that does not interfere with the delivery of audit services.** In this instance it may be best to have an informal discussion with the person. An example of this would be an auditor who steps out of line with a dress code, by turning up for work in clothes that are too casual.

☐ **Whether the breach is a one-off or continuing matter**. Where it may have occurred in the past it may be necessary to carry out some form of investigation. If for example an auditor is accused of harassing a female member of staff this should be further explored. Harassment involves continued, unwanted advances that presumes a degree of continuity. Formal interviews will be required to complete this type of enquiry.

☐ **Find out whether the breach was unintentional or deliberate**. If for example a mileage claim-form is incorrectly filled out then this may be a mere error or an attempted fraud depending on the particular circumstances. All relevant matters should be fully investigated although the possibility of error must not be ignored.

☐ **Substandard performance also falls under breach of acceptable standards rather than breach of procedure**. Here one is concerned with the formal results of performance appraisal schemes that would measure the work carried out by each auditor. It is only in the last instance when the impact of training, developing and counselling schemes have been dealt with, that management would turn to the possibility of intentional breach of standards, or a basic inability to perform. This matter is dealt with under the topic of performance appraisal.

☐ **One very common breach of procedure relates to timekeeping and attendance at work**. The less time that is spent on audit work, the less will be the chargeable hours that can be directly recovered from clients. Timesheets must always be in use in the internal audit office and these will record the amount of time at work and the various jobs that are worked on. Where budgeted hours are regularly overrun, the possibility of fabricated hours charged to these jobs should be considered. We have agreed that short days result in less time spent on the job and if the full days/hours are nonetheless charged, this will inflate the final time allocation. These fabricated hours are in fact "stolen" from the organisation and are a form of fraud as well as falsification of official records (timesheets). This must be dealt with firmly by audit management. A culture where auditors wander around the offices making general conversation and appearing to have all the time in the world, will probably result in a lax view of official timekeeping and time-recording. This would represent a potentially disastrous situation that interferes with the delivery of a successful audit service.

☐ **Sick-leave is another contentious issue**. Generally, no one can help falling sick (unless this results from an inappropriate lifestyle), but the level of sick leave still has to be managed. If a limit is imposed after which the auditor will be investigated, this figure may be seen as "the sick-leave entitlement". Alternatively, if it is left undefined, then it will be hard to form a consistent approach to this problem. Without going into great detail it is best to set standards on the acceptable levels based on their frequency, history and whether the time off is certificated or not. Audit management would then be charged with keeping a close eye on any potential offenders. There are several useful techniques that may be applied including counselling, referral to the company doctor and insisting that a certificate is obtained for all periods of sick leave, if a poor record has been established.

☐ **The final point to note in respect of breach of procedure is that not one of us is perfect**. People do make mistakes and bad practices can increase as management turns a blind eye when it suits them. What might have been acceptable some time ago may be treated with the utmost severity for many reasons. A good example is sexual harassment whereby offensive calendars may have been the norm several years ago only to become dismissible offences if they are now displayed at work. Some organisations may ban them altogether or allow women and men to have calendars of their choice. We must look for a degree of reasonableness and once again as we have already said, audit is not on a higher plane than others. It is just that there is more scope for hypocrisy where an audit report asks for high standards from management, based on the assumption that audit already meets these same standards. An example is opportune at this stage:

> *A news broadcaster informs the general public that there has been a serious accident on a particular motorway. He goes on to say that drivers are slowing down to see what has happened and criticises these drivers and asks them not to be nosy. The assumption then is that the newsreader is not nosy and would not dream of slowing down in these circumstances.*

(e) **Management issues a warning**. Audit managers like all other managers are bound by the principles of natural justice when they are required to deal with staffing problems. These principles will demand a level of reasonableness from the organisation as it tackles issues that may go on to affect an employee's career. One such principle is embodied in the concept of "a second chance" whereby people are allowed to make one mistake. This appears in the process of issuing warnings to staff where there has been, or is likely to be, a breach of procedure. This is particularly appropriate where the breach is of a general nature involving more than one auditor. A balance must be struck in that one should not pursue one individual for failings that are apparent in many of the employees. This is in contrast to criminal law where each offence is a distinct matter even where other offenders have not been prosecuted. A speeding motorist cannot use as a defence the view that other drivers, who were not stopped by the police, were also exceeding the speed limit. A general reminder to all internal audit staff may be an efficient way of dealing with a particular problem such as delays in completing timesheets. Where there is only one main offender a specific instruction may be issued. Warnings can operate on increasing levels of severity as follows:

FIGURE 22.15 DEGREES OF SEVERITY OF ACTION

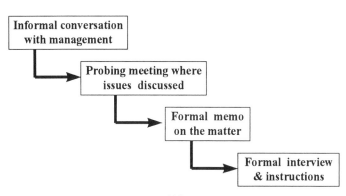

The questions to ask are;

> *Does the officer understand the issue at hand and the need to adjust his/her behaviour? Are there any barriers that mean this change in behaviour is not possible?*

Never forget that there are times where management is to blame for not providing clear advice or dealing with a problem before it accelerates and gets out of hand.

(f) **Auditor continues to breach the code**. We now arrive at the first key stage of the disciplinary procedure where there is a clear breach of procedure that may not be justified. We have to start with the premise that our auditors are adults and as such are fully responsible for their behaviour. The proper running of the internal audit function is impaired when staff engage in activities that are unacceptable and management must take a firm line when dealing with this. This notional distinction between staff and management is not always appropriate as real-life examples can be quoted where audit managers and assistant audit managers have been disciplined in the past for breach of procedure. There are some auditors who enjoy "testing" the system in what sometimes appears to be akin to a death wish. There are others who are very vocal and aggressive and feel that they are exempted from the rules. For example:

> *One such employee, an audit manager, spent a great deal of time working at home on "special audit projects" that he had engineered, to the detriment of his staff who were left with little direction. Meanwhile the Chief Executive gave a formal instruction that this practice of senior officers working from home is now banned. This particular audit manager continued this practice despite constant reminders from his manager, the CIA. To cut a long story short, the audit manager resigned soon after this episode to take up an entirely new career.*

Again we must stress the dangers of ignoring slack discipline even though this may be the easiest option for audit management. It is much more difficult to take firm action against your own staff. Where internal audit has engendered much team spirit the CIA may feel that staff may rebel as he/she acts against one particular person. This fear is unfounded since, as long as management has been fair and follows the correct procedure, most right thinking auditors will accept its right to act. In fact, the members of the audit department will tend to become demotivated where management allows problems to continue unabated. There must be an ultimate audit mission and this must be based on professional standards and codes of conduct while preserving this concept should be uppermost in the mind of the CIA.

(g) **Instigate disciplinary action**. The stage is now set for a formal disciplinary. These proceedings are unfortunate, regrettable and can create a major source of stress for audit management. Nonetheless, if this procedure has to be applied it is better to do so properly and ensure that one has clear standards within which to operate. The formal disciplinary procedure applicable to the final stage may appear as follows:

FIGURE 22.16 DISCIPLINARY PROCEDURE

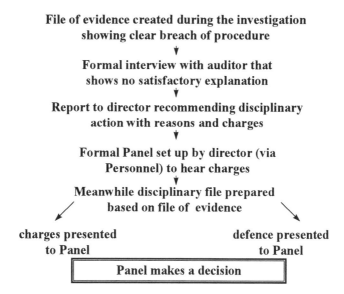

**File of evidence created during the investigation
showing clear breach of procedure**
▼
**Formal interview with auditor that
shows no satisfactory explanation**
▼
**Report to director recommending disciplinary
action with reasons and charges**
▼
**Formal Panel set up by director (via
Personnel) to hear charges**
▼
**Meanwhile disciplinary file prepared
based on file of evidence**

**charges presented
to Panel**   **defence presented
to Panel**

Panel makes a decision

There are a number of points that should be noted in respect of audit disciplinaries:

The CIA must be seen to fully support and direct activities that impact directly on a member of the internal audit department. Accepting that any detailed work and/or analysis may be delegated to a defined auditor, the results must nevertheless be reported directly to the CIA. All disciplinary action is serious even if it does not result in the dismissal of the auditor concerned. Any disciplinary offence must be proved on the "balance of probabilities" and not the more severe "beyond reasonable doubt" test, that is applied to criminal cases. Audit management need only show that there is sufficient evidence to support the defined charges. Much depends on the question of reasonableness and this should be uppermost in the mind of the CIA where any formal action is being considered. The arrangements to hear disciplinary charges should follow the organisation's policies. One useful model requires a panel of say three senior officers with one being the Chair. The appropriate management would present the case whilst the employee would defend the charges accompanied by a representative (usually a union member):

FIGURE 22.17 DISCIPLINARY HEARINGS

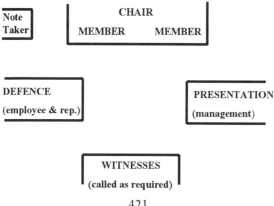

Note Taker

CHAIR

MEMBER   MEMBER

DEFENCE

(employee & rep.)

PRESENTATION

(management)

WITNESSES

(called as required)

Audit management should take on board the implications of the disciplinary arrangements and try to manage them as well as possible. One issue that has to be addressed is "who does what" in terms of a planned disciplinary. The ideal model is for the CIA to personally present the charges as this has the following implications:

- The voice of the CIA will tend to be highly respected in the organisation.
- One would avoid the view that there might be an appeal to the CIA, who might not support the action being taken.
- The CIA will be able to show clear support for the audit managers.

It is also a good idea to get the audit manager of the auditor being disciplined to assist the CIA in the presentation. This will avert the situation where the line manager is called as a witness and blamed for the employee's activities that resulted in him/her being disciplined. It is a standard defence to blame the person's manager. The presentation of the case may be scheduled in the following way:

FIGURE 22.18 PRESENTING A DISCIPLINARY CASE

Opening statement

↓

Address the charges

Discuss the disciplinary report

Explain detailed figures/evidence

Call witnesses

Cross examine employee's witnesses

Sum up: refer again to charges

↓

Ask for a remedy: e.g. dismissal

The idea is to present the case in a clear and sensible way that brings out the key points and the implications of the breach of procedure for internal audit. Meanwhile the panel will want to ensure that they hear and understand all the relevant evidence. The panel may assist either side in presenting their facts so long as this is designed to bring out the truth and is in the best interests of the organisation. Moreover they will want to ensure that all sides have had a fair hearing and that management has acted in a reasonable fashion bearing in mind all the circumstances of the case. Also:

1. The CIA should provide a confidential report covering the disciplinary investigation and resulting charges for submission to the hearing. This is crucial since it is notoriously difficult to bring home the real issues in any case. Panels take a long time to assimilate the facts and build a clear picture of management's concerns regarding an individual auditor's behaviour.
2. The CIA must ensure that the evidence provided to support the case meets certain standards. It must be relevant and the best that is available. If these relate to procedures

then they must have been published and communicated to the employee in question. The panel will be concerned over any new evidence that is introduced by either side. They may choose not to view it if its source is unclear or it provides an unfair disadvantage to management or the employee.

3. The auditor will seek to defend the case and may use a union representative or lawyer (if this is permitted under the rules). The defence may wish to challenge the evidence presented in terms of its accuracy or interpretation. Alternatively, the defence may set out mitigating circumstances and ask the panel to be lenient. Whilst audit management must pursue the charges in a positive way, it is best not to go for a win/lose position. If the auditor is reinstated, it will be necessary to build a way forward in terms of future working relationships. It is however possible to direct the panel by suggesting that the person is question should not be returned to the internal audit department.

4. One final point to note is that the progress of internal disciplinaries should not be dependent on any criminal investigations and associated court proceedings. One must push ahead with the disciplinaries by dealing with them as breach of internal procedure even where related matters will be discussed in a court of law. One technique is to get the internal matters resolved very quickly before any case reaches the courts. If this does not suit the employee who may refuse to attend the disciplinary, the case may be heard in his/her absence, so long as there is no good reason for non-attendance.

(h) **Appeals procedure**. Most disciplinary procedures allow the employee to appeal against the decision of the panel. This acts as a safety valve and as such strengthens the procedure. Audit management must prepare for an appeal where charges have been proven and the auditor being disciplined is not satisfied with the outcome. The precise arrangements vary from organisation to organisation. Having said this, one good model is for a fresh panel to consider the principles that form the basis of the appeal and make a decision in the light of all the relevant circumstances. An inefficient model asks for a re-run of the entire disciplinary hearing as this simply encourages employees to appeal automatically for no good reason. Again a suitable model would require the Chair of the original panel to present the grounds of the decision to the appeals panel in contrast to asking management to present the case again.

(i) **Industrial Tribunal**. There is a final appeal to the Industrial Tribunal (before litigation is considered) where an employee feels that he/she has been unfairly dismissed and/or the organisation did not comply with laid down procedure. The CIA must ensure that the evidence files are well maintained and in a suitable condition to be presented to an external body.

CHAPTER TWENTY-THREE

QUALITY ASSURANCE AND PROCEDURES

23.1 CIA's Responsibilities

There is a lot being said about quality assurance, as this appears to be one of the new buzzwords for the 1990s. Without going into great detail, the key point that emerges from the latest research is that checking done at the end of a system (i.e. an operation) is an inefficient way of promoting quality. What is more relevant is to ensure that the systems themselves are steeped in a culture of quality from start to finish. This concept is, in truth, not new as it should underpin the whole thrust of internal audit's efforts in promoting better systems and systems' controls. Nonetheless, internal audit like any other activity must set and meet quality standards under the direction of the CIA. The other feature of the drive towards quality assurance is the principle of getting the client to set these quality standards, as the ultimate recipient of audit services. One might argue that quality is simply a matter of applying good management practices in line with the human resource management techniques that have already been discussed in chapter twenty-two. For convenience we may deal with several topics that have a direct impact on quality issues along with the IIA standards on quality. A contrasting argument views the CIA as primarily responsible for quality assurance and procedures, and all the resources that should be directed towards the various related initiatives. The latter view is gaining support as one might view the CIA as directly responsible for all audit reports and the overall quality of audit services that are provided to any organisation.

ISO 9000

The British Standards Institute's standard 5750 (now superseded by ISO 9000) deals with quality assurance. This allows an internal audit department to register under this standard so long as the department has been organised to meet audit procedures and controls devised to:

- Achieve and sustain the quality product or service produced so as to meet continually the purchaser's stated or implied needs.
- Provide assurance to its own management that the intended quality is being achieved and sustained.
- Provide confidence to its purchaser that the intended quality is being, or will be, achieved in the delivered product or service provided.

(See BS5750, Part 0, Section 0.1, Para 4.)

The internal audit department has to show that it had installed the required procedures and controls to meet the above requirements. In addition, these controls would also be reviewed by BSI officers before registration would be approved. There is an expense involved and registration is in no way mandatory. There may come a time however, when we might question why audit has failed to secure such a status particularly where activities that are being audited have already been fully accredited. It clearly is a matter that should remain high on the agenda of audit management team meetings.

23.2 Features of Quality Assurance

Poor products

One key benefit from quality assurance is that poor products are seen in a different light. A poor audit report is not simply a matter of blaming the authors and bearing down on them. Substandard work becomes part of the learning process, where management seeks to address the underlying causes with a view to rectifying poor performance. Because audit work is primarily human resource intensive, then problems can normally be traced back to poor procedures. However, in limited cases there can be other causes relating to say outdated information technology or a lack of facilities. Again we return to the view that the CIA is responsible for all audit work and it is only through clearly thought out procedures that this role can be fully accepted. Quality depends on a formal method of identifying poor products that relates problems back to systems. One has heard of the chef who never cooks at home. This image may run parallel to the auditor who never reviews his/her own systems or adopts a systems approach to solving service delivery problems. In truth there is no excuse for this stance, as in the long run it will impair the integrity of the internal audit function. Poor audits result from poor systems so long as we use systems in their widest form to include all those activities that are carried out to achieve business objectives.

Barriers and constraints

Effective quality assurance does not come about without much work and commitment. There are many barriers and constraints that act against the successful implementation of formal quality systems and these can represent major obstacles. Quality is a concept while quality assurance is a collection of well planned management systems that take time and effort to apply. Some of the barriers to good quality include:

1. A failure by audit management to recognise (and/or understand) the importance of quality assurance systems. Quality systems have to be driven from above and they will not take effect if the required regimes do not attach to audit management as part of the commitment to good services. Where QA has been assimilated into management practices we are well on the road to a successful audit service.

2. Poor management information systems that fail to provide feedback on performance targets. QA thrives on information since standards once established must be used to measure the efficiency of operations and services. Suitable information systems should be designed to spot defects at a minimum. Proper QA systems are based on guiding the way resources are employed so as to minimise the incidence of any defects.

3. A redundant audit manual that is not able to act as the vehicle for defining and using audit procedures. A quality manual is required to set the frame for QA as a way of defining formal procedures. Where this is not in place we need first to set a change in the audit culture before the required documentation can be installed.

4. Internal audit departments that have failed to adopt good change management techniques which means that new procedures become very difficult to install. Serious QA programmes tackle the actual foundation of audit work by requiring a position of excellence wherever possible. This may depend on total quality management policies being adopted so as to provide a clear impetus to the search for quality. We are fast arriving at the far reaching culture-change environment that is dealt with in the chapter on change management.

5. An absence of formal audit strategy leading to a lack of direction. Quality systems will have to be attached to the current strategy to be of any real use, and where this does not exist, little or nothing will be achieved over and above mere statements of intent.

6. An absence of human resource management practices, such as formal training programmes, leaving staff to "sink or swim". Management cannot insist on quality if they have not established support systems to underpin this venture. In this way there is a meeting of both sides where auditors and audit management both express a commitment to quality services.

7. A failure to appreciate the need for client-based systems that enable service recipients to specify their needs and expectations in respect of internal audit services. The reconciliation of independence and client needs should be undertaken with due regard to the need to formulate a model of audit service that duly takes on board both factors.

Improvements

Quality assurance consolidates and stimulates the formal auditing procedures that underpin quality initiatives. A further concept that sits with the quality approach is one of continual improvement. This results from the feedback loops that are essential, where we seek to discover why things go wrong, with a view to putting right any controllable problems. Again, there is no excuse for auditors not being in tune with the view that management must be about a constant drive for improvements to systems and controls that impact on performance. Internal audit management must be fully conversant with the following practice:

FIGURE 23.1 QUALITY AND SYSTEMS

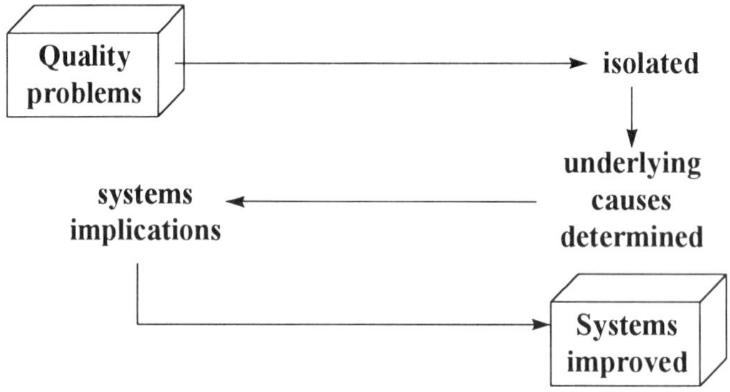

This may be seen as the single most important benefit of good quality practices.

The appropriate approach

One perplexing question that should come to the fore through quality assurance systems, is that relating to the type of audit services that are being provided. Poor performance should not be confused with inappropriate audit services. Quality starts with asking the client for their view of the type of services that are required. This model is correctly applied to the vast majority of support services within an organisation. There is a problem however for internal audit where we cannot always simply provide what management wants. There are times when we have to deliver a professional audit service, based on assessing management's control systems and criticising them where necessary. This may not be precisely what managers want particularly where they are insecure and have not properly resourced relevant control issues. Where the client is defined as the audit committee, rather than management per se, we move closer to an acceptable platform upon which to build quality systems. We must still ask whether the services that are provided by internal audit are suitable and match the organisation's control needs. Quality assurance should enable us to assess, re-assess and further assess our audit services on an ongoing basis. So long as we have defined our client this assessment process should enable us to preserve the audit service as a long-term resource that is respected throughout the organisation.

Appropriate structures
Once we have determined the "right" audit services we must re-appraise the resources that are used to discharge the audit role. One of the main considerations is the type of structure that is adopted. In practice, many quality problems concerning the final audit product may be traced back to inappropriate structures where there is a mismatch between the required audit services and the way the audit function is organised.

Compliance with code of conduct and standards
One further point to note in respect of quality assurance is the due reliance that is placed on professional standards. Quality systems must, above all, be able to distinguish non-compliance with professional standards be they personal (i.e. relating to conduct) or operational. We would look to our systems to tell us whether internal audit is meeting the requirements of these standards. This entails the following:
1. Adopt suitable professional standards (e.g. IIA) as part of the formal mission statement that drives and directs the audit service.
2. Re-define the above as local standards via suitable enclosures in the audit manual. This creates an assimilation of outline standards into working practices as a necessary step towards fully integrating them into the audit role.
3. Implement them via a formal procedure whereby staff are advised as to the requirements of these standards and so understand all that this entails.
4. Train and develop staff to meet them.
5. Review compliance with standards via suitable control mechanisms.
6. Deal with any non-compliance as high profile serious issues.
7. Review these standards to ensure that they make sense and fit with the audit work that is performed.
8. Seek to relate quality problems with these standards in terms of gaps therein or non-compliance. This is in full recognition of the systems approach to problem solving where all operational defects are related to deficiencies in the underlying systems.

23.3 IIA Standard 500
The Institute of Internal Auditors has produced a standard on quality assurance (Standard 560) that deals with this issue within the material on managing internal audit. The key areas that are covered include the following topics:

☐ **Supervision**. The main feature here is that auditors should be able to discharge their audit role in a professional manner. On the one side this requires compliance with agreed standards and procedures. While the other factor is that they should be provided with sufficient guidance and advice from audit management including clear terms of reference and any assistance where required. The team leader, audit manager and CIA each have a duty to ensure that they are available to direct staff as the audit is being conducted.

☐ **Internal review**. This may operate at a number of levels including reviewing the working papers and draft audit reports. One should develop a programme of audit reviews where audit management will carry out comprehensive reviews of say the bigger audits that have been completed. Spot checks may be undertaken at random on various audits to establish whether they are meeting acceptable standards. It is advisable to appoint one manager responsible for quality assurance throughout the audit department. This person will report periodically, (say annually) to the CIA on the overall position and indicate whether any changes to current practices are required.

☐ **External review**. The IIA recommends that these should be commissioned every three years although this will depend on the level of supervision and extent to which internal reviews are used. They may be carried out by:

> *External audit - Here an over-emphasis on financial systems and support for the external audit role may bias the work.*
> *Internal audit departments in groups of companies - An informal policy of not criticising each other may invalidate the work. Or fierce competition may make the review less than objective.*
> *Reciprocal arrangements - Here companies may review each other although confidentiality may be a real problem.*
> *Other external auditors - Using other companies' external auditors helps reduce bias but they would still tend to have a financial orientation.*
> *Consultant - A consultant who specialises in internal audit reviews will probably be the best choice in terms of skills, independence and final result.*

The CIA should use the results of the external review to help form a strategy for improving the audit function and producing an effective quality programme. We can use the model in figure 23.2 to illustrate the more traditional view of quality which starts at the end of the management cycle, i.e. at the end of the audit. The issues that arise as a result of the quality assurance process are then fed into the strategic analysis, and staff development exercises whereby any problems may be resolved. An alternative way of dealing with quality is to try to ensure that these problems do not arise in the first place, by establishing sound management and operational practices within the entire audit function. We have explained the three-point procedure of supervision, internal review and the occasional external reviews that feed into the quality process. The QA programme should be built into the strategic development process as a high profile item. In turn the strategy should then ensure that quality impacts directly onto staff development programmes in recognition of the far reaching effects of moves in this direction.

FIGURE 23.2 AN AUDIT QUALITY ASSURANCE PROGRAMME

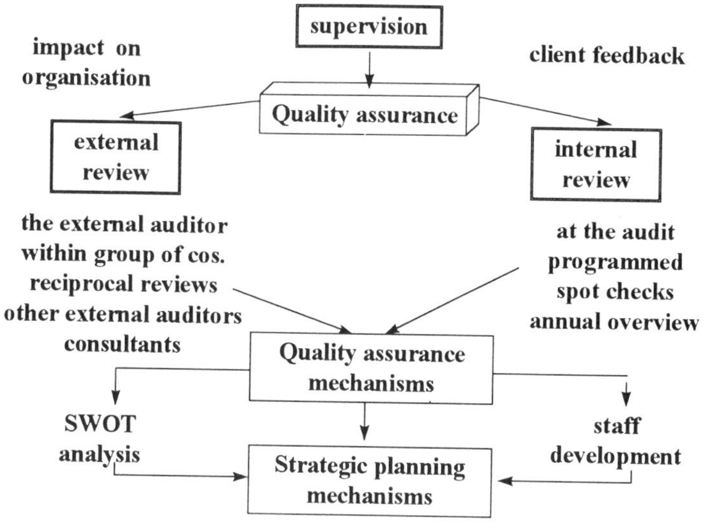

23.4 Audit Procedures

The topic of auditing procedures must fall under any material covering the management of the internal audit function and quality assurance. Auditing procedures are covered in the chapter on the audit manual since the manual is simply the aggregation of these procedures. In this section we deal with auditing procedures in outline, from a managerial point of view.

Directing internal audit

Procedures are part of the process of directing the work of staff, which falls in line with management's responsibilities. This responsibility consists of more than conversation and the occasional comment. It should result in formal documented material that can be held up as recorded evidence of management's requirements. Audit procedures cover:

1. Preparing long-term plans.
2. Recruiting, training and developing staff.
3. Acquiring information technology.
4. Setting audit objectives.
5. Assigning budgets to jobs.
6. Applying relevant auditing techniques.
7. Investigating frauds.
8. Recording information on audit files.
9. Reviewing audit work.

Audit methodology

One important matter that should be addressed through the process of issuing formal procedures is the adopted audit methodology. This point is important because of the wide diversity of approaches to internal audit work. Following on from this we can also argue that procedures are not simply there for junior/new staff, but are equally applicable to experienced auditors who may be used to a different way of discharging the audit role. As such one cannot by-pass the need for establishing clear procedures by simply employing experienced staff.

Instructions
Procedures direct the work of audit staff and this is the basis upon which they are issued. This operates on a number of different levels that provide increasing detail and less flexibility:

FIGURE 23.3 AUDIT DIRECTION

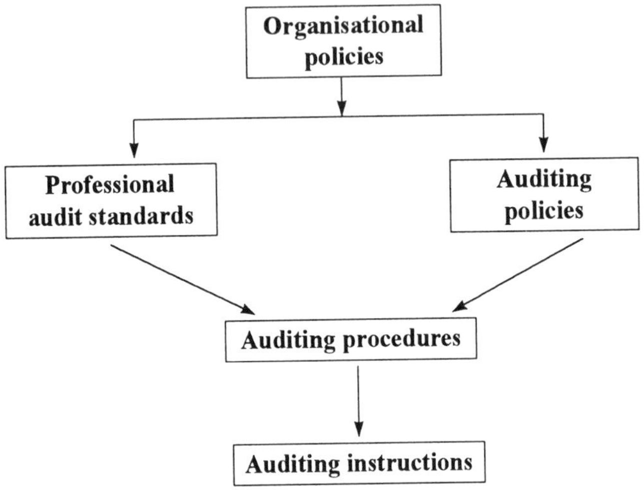

There are areas where audit management needs to define a requirement in an explicit and inflexible way, that fall under the term "instruction". These cater for decisions that must be followed in all circumstances such as the need to set an initial time-budget for an audit job before it can be set up on the time recording system. Instructions must be used with care since there are dangers in management being too inflexible.

Standards
The best type of auditing procedures are those linked into professional standards. Procedures, if used properly, can become standards in their own right, hence their importance. Standards are set up as benchmarks against which performance can be judged and this should be the same for procedures. Despite this, procedures have a bad reputation as being boring. Auditors are partly to blame for this reputation where a standard clause in the typical audit report reads "there is a lack of formal and up-to-date procedures...". This is not enough. We should talk about standards, quality, management direction and formal recording systems and how these may best be achieved.

Standardised working papers
A good way of developing formal standards is by standardised documentation. This implies:
1. The process of developing documentation forces management to consider what is being asked for as these papers are completed which in itself sets standards.

2. Standardisation also allows management to set parameters within which work can be contained. This should result in only the right amount of work being performed, rather than an excess of paper-work (which is the main criticism of standard forms).

3. The act of standardisation, instils a level of discipline and provides a foundation upon which increasing degrees of automation can be built.

There are examples of standardised documents in the accompanying diskette.

Decision-making mechanisms

A major benefit of designing and applying formal procedures is the act of deciding what should be done and how. This is part of establishing a clear set of routines that cover areas that are being catered for. Suitable decision-making mechanisms should be built in. The type of decision-making culture will affect the way procedures are applied, ranging from consensus management through to the autocratic. We can superimpose over this, a system ranging from the position whereby staff are asked to submit their own procedures for approval, through to procedures being issued as complete documents by management. Where audit management fails to establish clear procedures, an opportunity to make clear decisions and set direction for staff is missed.

Supervision and review of audit work

Supervision is fundamental to audit management that seeks to isolate potential problems before they arise. This requires ongoing involvement of senior auditors in their staff's work, providing advice and guidance. A sure way of making this consistent and workable is to base the audit management input around the use of audit procedures, rather than ad-hoc tips. The audit review should be based around ensuring the auditor complied with procedures. These procedures play the key role when audit management is considering the quality of an audit. The reviewer must ask questions such as:

1. What were the procedures relevant to this audit? The answer will vary according to the type of work performed and the experience of the auditor in question.

2. Have these procedures been fully communicated to the auditor who carried out the work?

3. Is there sufficient evidence of compliance with these procedures?

4. Is there any evidence of non-compliance with these procedures?

5. Is there any explanation for apparent non-compliance?

6. Has the audit been a success, i.e. achieved its objectives? If this is not the case, do procedures, or the way they are used (or not used), need revising in any way?

We should try to move to a position where a cause-and-effect relationship is established, so that poor performance can be related to the underlying procedures that form the basis of audit work.

Induction training

Induction training operates on two fronts. Firstly, it should be applied to new starters to set out procedures and how they should be applied. Secondly, training can be used to introduce new or revised procedures through appropriately tailored sessions. It is possible to use an open management style where procedures can be tested on staff in a training format and altered where needs be. This is in line with management's responsibilities to ensure that procedures are workable, efficient and understood by all. Staff should also be able to operate to the requirements of the adopted procedures in terms of the performance standards deemed to be achievable. When interviewing a potential new appointee, it is well to discover whether the person would be comfortable with the demands of auditing procedures which can be determined through an assessment of attitude and past work experiences. Not everything can be taught at induction and we would look for as little culture acclimatisation needs as possible from applicants, before they are formally appointed.

Staff meetings
Meetings of audit management and staff are ideal to promote the design, appraisal and implementation of auditing procedures. It is good practice to hold on the agenda for all staff meetings a permanent item "Any need to review existing procedures". This item would be at the end.

> *"If something is wrong (or needs changing) in internal audit we must first review adopted procedures."*

If audit managers do not hold meetings between themselves or with their staff then this is a recipe for disaster. Any procedures in this instance will remain formal documents that have little impact or meaning to the field auditors in their day-to-day work.

Controlling internal audit
Auditing procedures can form a process that helps control the internal audit function. This dynamic concept relies on a systems approach to setting and using procedures so that they form a complete cycle of events, with distinct components:

FIGURE 23.4 PROCEDURES CYCLE

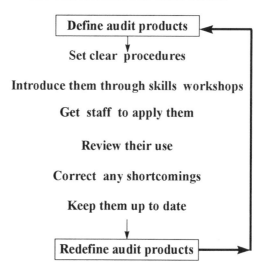

This depends on audit management considering many issues when dealing with procedures which is a far cry from issuing an obscure memo to staff in the distant past.

Link into quality assurance

In a previous section we discussed quality assurance and agreed that it depends on clear and workable procedures. Much of the distinction is a matter of terminology since some of the available synonyms for the word "procedure" include the following alternatives:

Action	*Conduct*	*Course*	*Custom*	*Form*
Method	*Performance*	*Policy*	*Practice*	*Process*
Routine	*Scheme*	*Step*	*Strategy*	*System*

The terms "quality, standards and controls" also conjure up a similar picture as is painted by the use of the word "procedures". In one sense they are much the same way of describing the concept of formal management direction that is fundamental to the provision of quality assurance. They are kept apart for convenience although the clear links must always be appreciated by audit managers.

Staff discipline

A final point is the potential use of the concept of procedures in staff discipline, particularly where a formal disciplinary is being held against a member of the internal audit function department. In this instance, best practice concerning the use of procedures that have been breached should make them comply with several criteria before they may be used in a disciplinary:

1. Procedures must be clear and concise.
2. They must be fully communicated to staff.
3. Their status should be set out: whether they constitute instructions, rules, advice, or explanations.
4. The people who are affected should be clearly identified along with any measures to deal with further information or guidance that may be required.
5. They should explain how compliance will be monitored and what staff's responsibilities are in assisting this process.
6. The role of any warnings that will be given for instances of non-compliance.
7. The consequences of non-compliance must be defined, particularly where this is serious e.g. a disciplinary and possible summary dismissal.
8. Important procedures should be re-issued regularly and meetings used to convey their importance.
9. They may form part of the induction training for new starters.
10. Any non-compliance should be deliberate for it to have a role in a formal disciplinary.
11. They should be fair, consistently applied and meaningful.

CHAPTER TWENTY-FOUR

AUDIT INFORMATION SYSTEMS

24.1 The Effect on Audit Work

The computer has major implications for audit work. Effects range from impact on the audit field, the way audit work is performed and how audit itself uses computers to improve productivity. This chapter provides an introduction to the impact of computers in internal auditing:

FIGURE 24.1 IMPACT OF INFORMATION

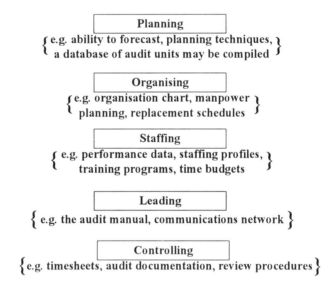

Planning
{ e.g. ability to forecast, planning techniques,
a database of audit units may be compiled }

Organising
{ e.g. organisation chart, manpower
planning, replacement schedules }

Staffing
{ e.g. performance data, staffing profiles,
training programs, time budgets }

Leading
{ e.g. the audit manual, communications network }

Controlling
{ e.g. timesheets, audit documentation, review procedures }

Another way of considering the effect on audit work is to break up the main work areas into:

☐ **Managing generally**. Management should be undertaking a constant search for ways that computers can be used to improve the audit service. This may mean employing computer personnel to promote computer skills through the department. An information technology strategy should be developed to ensure that efficient information systems are developed to support the overall audit strategy. The strategy should also be geared into developing overall computer literacy so that auditors may be confident in the way they approach automated systems. This may allow a step into computer audit whereby advanced computing skills may eventually be acquired. Public systems such as the Internet may be accessed and form an almost limitless database of reference information. In-house information databases may be built up over time as a complement to the audit library. In fact, it is difficult to explain how an audit department could prioritise systems based auditing without developing a database on available control mechanisms. Direct information links between the auditor and the audit office can arise via the PC notebook, which can send data to the audit based terminals. It is then possible to promote the free lancing auditor whose motto is "Have notebook will travel". Furthermore time-monitoring systems can account for audit hours and be linked into a planning and control system. In addition they can be used as a billing and accounting system.

☐ **The audit manual**. This is an example of how management may set formal documented standards for the way audit work is performed. In an ideal situation each auditor will have the audit manual on the notebook's hard disk and this will build up into an invaluable source of reference material and guidance on operational matters. The audit manual is the medium for providing information on accessing the organisation's information systems. Standardised forms in line with a clear methodology may be promoted by automating them. This allows one to develop the "paperless audit" where automated audit documentation is used to perform the audit and all mainframe data is downloaded for later testing on pre-designed spreadsheets.

☐ **Long-term planning**. It is possible to set up models of the organisation's main systems so that audit plans may be derived and altered as the circumstances change. In effect, the whole audit field is captured on the computer for analysis and management decisions. Risk analysis models may be computerised and one may set up a risk profile in such a way that changes in risk factors produce an automatically re-prioritised long-term audit plan.

☐ **Assignment planning**. The planning and control system may be developed which sets out planned hours, progress checklists, target dates and so on for each assignment. This then feeds into the time monitoring system with relevant variances being thrown out for management action.

☐ **Ascertaining systems**. Block charts, flowcharting, and systems notes may be produced on the computer. This allows easy updating and editing.

☐ **Audit programmes**. A whole range of audit programmes may be held on disk and this may be amended as required and each programme tailored to suit an individual audit. Note that audit programmes are not wholly suited to the system based approach but may be useful in other circumstances. What may have been particularly boring audit techniques such as statistical sampling, flowcharting and transaction sorting may be automated with minimal effort.

☐ **Evaluating systems**. Where a matrix approach to control evaluation is applied then a computerised spreadsheet format may be readily used.

☐ **Testing systems**. Testing data held on main-frame systems can be facilitated by downloading the samples onto the auditors' computer and carrying out analytical work and other calculations. File enquiry is an example of using computers to talk to computers and an interrogation package for the main operating systems that are used by the organisation, may be used to extract data. Information may be accumulated during the course of an audit and wherever possible, this should be automated.

☐ **Audit reporting**. Standardised reporting is one option and the use of word processing facilities is widely practised by most audit departments. Predetermined structures may be held on the system and so aid consistency in report presentation as well as saving time.

☐ **Following up audit work**. Reporting dates and follow-up periods may be defined to ensure that the implementation of audit recommendations is properly monitored. Follow-up periods may be set out in an appropriately designed spreadsheet.

24.2 The Development of Information Systems

Introduction

Part of internal audit management's task is to formulate and install a suitable information systems strategy and we cover here some of the matters that should be addressed. It is possible to set the terms of reference for computer audit to include responsibility for assisting with this information strategy as part of their everyday work. The use of in-house information technology (IT) staff to support IT initiatives should also be considered in line with the fact that auditors are also IT users. There are a number of strategies that the audit manager may adopt including:

☐ **No impact**. Here IT is not seen as an important resource and a no-development strategy ensues. This will mean that machines will be replaced as and when they breakdown, no budget for IT will be secured and there will be little or no development in the type of software used in audit work. This position occurs where there is no one person given designated responsibility for IT development and it is therefore not seen as important.

☐ **Automation in current form**. A more progressive strategy appears where audit management seeks to automate existing activities by the application of new and/or enhanced IT. Audit management may ask basic questions such as:

> *"How can IT help us perform our existing functions in an automated fashion?"*

Greater development will arise where management optimises activity through greater levels of automation. These strategies are still confined by the consideration of IT's application to existing activities.

☐ **Enhance functions performed by activities**. Higher planes of performance can be achieved where audit management asks:

> *"What new functions can be performed through use of IT to promote achievement of audit objectives?"*

What may be seen as the final phase of IT assimilation occurs where we seek new activities through the use of new technology. Existing applications may be reconfigured into an "audit IT network" where shared information enhances communications throughout the audit function. New audit tasks such as matching and merging different systems databases can be developed as an aid to management in ensuring the integrity of automated information. This format is however wholly dependent on the continuing search for new and improved systems for use within the audit function, which in turn is dependent on resourcing this initiative. One such role fundamental to this objective is the ongoing study of newly released software that brings an ability to perform more powerful functions. Software is now becoming more flexible, user-friendly and integrated. Taking advantage of these developments is a major task that requires the implementation of the following process:

FIGURE 24.2 USING IT DEVELOPMENTS

Isolate the audit objectives

Consider the type of work that is required to achieve these objectives

Define the type of information that is required to support the audit workload

Define the type of technology that underpins the information identified above

Research the market to determine the latest developments that might help produce the underlying information needed

We need not only understand the audit role and types of work products that support this role, but we must also appreciate how new IT can fit into this scenario. New releases of software represent new systems and it is these systems that are important. The operating systems and environment simply support the systems and again represent a major purchase decision. Unfortunately many newer systems require a certain type of environment (e.g. the latest version of Windows). The machines in use may in practice be seen merely as potential obstacles in terms of providing the skeleton upon which the system sits. The problems arise where the machines are not fast enough, powerful enough or have insufficient RAM and/or hard disk capacity. Audit management must ensure that the machines keep pace with the systems and in this context "upgradeability" will be the buzzword. We must keep an eye on other business units within the organisation to ensure parity in IT development.

IT as a strategic resource

We are moving closer to the concept of IT as a strategic resource for the internal audit unit. The key questions asked by audit management become more urgent and will be framed more in terms of:

> *"What are others doing with IT? Have we got state of the art printers? Are we fully into desk-top publishing? Have we got an edge on similar audit units? Are the External Auditors ahead in the IT stakes? Can we download, manipulate, analyse, utilise and maximise our use of organisational databases? Is there anything else we should be doing? Who should I be talking to?"*

Strategic IT considerations must move to a high level where major related concepts are addressed at audit management meetings and reported regularly. These matters will include:

☐ **Added value**. We would expect the investment in new IT to add speed and vitality to the work product and so increase the overall value of the audit service. IT does cost a lot and needs replacing regularly as new software makes increasing demands on machine capacity.

☐ **Competitive position**. What is done elsewhere should be done in internal audit and the idea of "keeping up with the Jones" applies in this environment. This is particularly appropriate for presentation purposes and database interrogation. Where parts of the organisation are producing colour reports, we must consider also our position in this regard, so as not to fall behind.

☐ **Better information**. New IT is primarily about getting better information and this must be an important consideration for audit management. For example our time monitoring system may be outdated and not able to provide a sophisticated package of reports as well as providing a client-charging system. IT is about buying in improved facilities but should also act as a stimulus for considering the adequacy of existing information and how it can be improved.

☐ **Cost containment**. Information is about improved services as a result of better decision-making abilities. Another concern is the possibility of reducing the costs of the audit service in terms of reports produced. The biggest audit cost is time charged to jobs and it is here that we would expect vital information on weekly charging profiles to contribute to the task of keeping these charges contained within budget. Exception reporting is applicable to audit as well as other parts of the organisation, and this should direct the CIA to key areas of concern that may be falling out of control.

☐ **Managerial effectiveness**. We have set out a number of performance indicators applicable to internal audit earlier on. The information systems that are used by audit should be geared to furnishing the required feedback for each of the key measures. For example audit management should be able to tell how many reports have been issued, how may audits have been aborted, how many audits are over budget and so on in line with the adopted performance measures.

☐ **Link back to head office**. We should be developing the communications model where auditors are able to plug into corporate systems from anywhere in the organisation (or from home). The main consideration for audit management is the need to keep sensitive information confidential. So if a UNIX platform is in use, the systems administrator may have access to audit directories and this will determine what may be safely held on this system.

☐ **Better flexibility**. Having the ability to set vast databases of reference material onto audit notebooks can create a real freedom from the paper based environment. This added flexibility should contribute to the efficiency of the audit service as a major benefit.

☐ **Real time working**. The move from past data (say many months old) to on-line up-to-date information can have many benefits in terms of the vibrancy of audit reports. The ability to address current data as part of our audit findings moves us from the past into the present-day environment.

☐ **Better control**. An overall improved state of control can be promoted through increased use of new information technology. This must be a key consideration of audit management as the in-house organisational experts in control.

Data is a resource that makes a vital contribution to service delivery. Being at the front of this development is important.

24.3 Resourcing IT

The costs of new IT can be great and it is commonplace to buy-in new systems only to find that they have become obsolete, with new and improved facilities on the market. This constant struggle to keep up can be frustrating which is why it must be derived from a clear vision. This vision should drive and direct the CIA towards a constant search for excellence. It may be based on establishing a paperless environment whereby paper files are frowned on and manual working schedules are positively discouraged. The relevant model is:

FIGURE 24.3 TRANSLATING VISION INTO REALITY

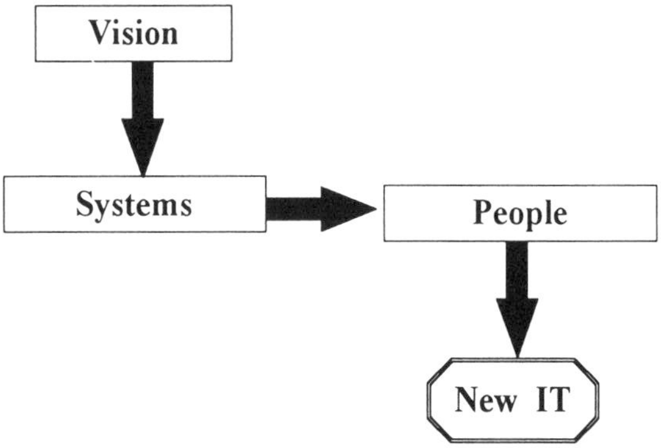

Audit management must set aside time to develop this vision and ensure it is filtered down into control systems, how auditors work and the necessary facilities (IT) to support this model. The main question to address is: "what information is required to support this vision?" The greater the impact of IT the greater the level of resources set aside to buy-in the new facilities. Where this impact is deemed material we need to implement a systems architecture in support. This architecture should cover the entire audit function and all existing computer facilities and new requirements in a programmed manner. It is here that we may arrive at a global solution to cover the whole audit unit. The vision we speak of is more than a general statement of intent but is a work based condition that looks for progress in all fields of work. In terms of the application of new IT, during the course of a working day, the CIA may ask basic questions such as *"why are these files lying on desks?...why are we still preparing manual spreadsheets?...why are we not downloading*

data from the corporate personnel system?...why are we not producing colour graphics in our brochure?...why are we still sending audit reports to the print shop?...why does this auditor not use a PC?".

24.4 A Hierarchical Structure

When developing suitable information systems we must take an overview in considering the precise information requirements of internal audit. It is amazing how many IT development projects are formulated without a systems analysis. This process should ideally utilise a top-downwards approach where we start with a "Big Picture" before moving down through the function to isolate where IT is best located. The starting place is important, in that it sets the tone for the rest of the exercise. Physically we start from the Chief Auditor, through audit management and work downwards, while conceptually we must start with the basic process of:

FIGURE 24.4 GENERATING USEFUL INFORMATION

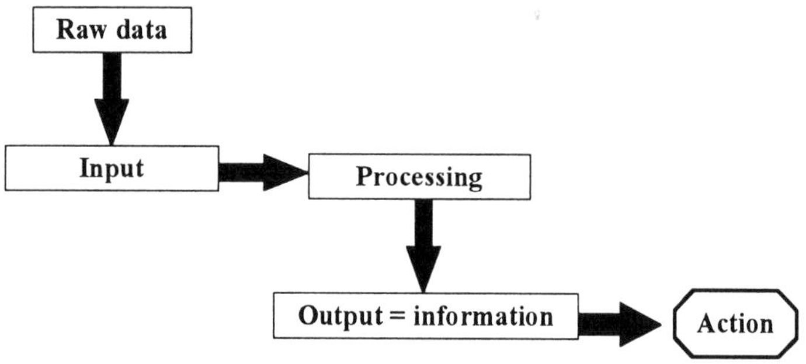

It is the action that is important since information is of little use unless it is converted into suitable action. This brings into play the second problem with many IT developments where there is no full recognition of the types of actions that management must pursue in furtherance of audit objectives. Which is why it is best to generate the project internally through audit staff (say the computer auditor) as opposed to external consultants. The final view of information is one based on the type of action that it is meant to stimulate which may be classified in the following manner:

☐ **Strategic**. Audit management require aggregate information, say monthly, that sets the global position over the entire audit function for long-term planning. This "big picture" will assist in the overall direction of audit and help develop a futuristic strategy to cater for the next months or years.

☐ **Managerial**. Weekly timesheets, if processed properly will generate weekly reports that may be used to get a fix on the performance of audits and auditors. These reports will be more detailed and give the narrow and more accurate picture that is required to make quick decisions on resourcing all current audits. We may wish to abort audits, extend them, transfer resources and/or seek explanation from the field auditor on receipt of this type of information as part of the management process.

☐ **Operational**. Daily feedback on what is going on in internal audit is one way of controlling resources. This may be related to information on who is doing what, where, for how long and why, so that relevant decisions may be made as required.

Attributes of good information are:

1. Timeliness.
2. Quantity.
3. Efficiency.
4. Effectiveness.
5. Documented.
6. Accepted.
7. Security catered for.
8. Flexible.
9. Relevant.
10. Accurate.

Audit management would be advised to review the reports they receive to determine whether they adhere to the above mentioned standards. Bearing in mind the emphasis we have placed on the importance of information as opposed to IT, we can list here examples of some of the reports that will typically be prepared by internal audit for use by audit management:

- Summary of reports issued and findings.
- Summary of chargeable hours to projects.
- Breakdown of non-chargeable hours such as general administration.
- Summary of auditor performance appraisal reports.
- Level of sick leave and other absences.
- Current status of all outstanding audits.
- Audits over their time budget.

24.5 End-user Computing

Within any organisation there will appear the much vexed issue appertaining to the extent to which corporate systems should be centralised/decentralised. There are advantages to either approach and trends alter with time as the weight of opinion swings from one to the other much the same as power might change hands over time between two major political parties. Many an auditor has reviewed systems such as stores, transport and office security while wrestling with the question of centralisation. Control processes tend to work more efficiently in a centralised arrangement whilst the common consensus is that most corporate systems/services are becoming de-centralised with a force that is hard to resist. This is particularly true for IT systems, even where they are located on a large mainframe. Distributed systems are now the norm, whilst the proliferation of PC-based systems has meant that end-user computing has grown considerably. Internal audit must recognise this trend and ensure that its needs as an end-user are fully recognised. Specialist IT staff have a newer (and perhaps uncomfortable) role of communicating with front-line staff and supporting their IT drives. This need to disseminate IT skills goes against the traditional view of IT specialists who retain their skills so as to help preserve their status in the organisation. The Chief Auditor must arrange a solid interface between IT specialists and the internal audit function, ideally through the use of IT-based audit staff (say computer auditors) who could take on this role. The development of IT products should be as close as possible to the front-line activity. Bringing IT to everyone and having it driven by the user (in line with the user's real needs) is a process that must be carefully managed. Just as auditors would advise controls over this matter, it is equally important that audit IT developments also work to best practice. End-user computing is here to stay and there are points to note:

Decision support systems should be used by audit management to help them direct the course of the audit service. It is a question of asking: what types of matters need to be decided at audit team meetings and what information is therefore required to make these decisions? The answer sets the parameters of the decision support system which includes information relating to audit plans, staff performance, fee income, budget position, general performance indicators, and skills database.

Executive information systems. We can move a step further and suggest that the CIA should be able to access the organisation's corporate systems and extract reports that are required to manage the audit function. These would typically comprise high-level aggregate reports that cover areas such as budget profiling, summary committee decisions, and snapshot of outstanding audits.

Download concept. The CIA should be concerned that auditors are moving away from paper printouts towards local information derived from the main organisational computer systems. The trend has altered from learning the utilities that relate to each system, to simply extracting the data from these systems and setting them onto audit PCs.

Role for computer audit. The computer auditor is ideally placed to help develop the end-user concept, which should be recognised by the CIA. The fact that we have an on-line computer expert within the audit unit can be used to bridge the needs of audit management and the services of the corporate IT function. This aspect of the computer auditor's work should be in the job description.

24.6 The Workstation Concept

The workstation model is another concept that the Chief Auditor must hold in mind when developing audit strategies. Workstations link the worker into the information systems that are maintained by the organisation and provide at the touch of a button (or two) all the material that is required to perform daily work. The work environment has as a result, changed from one where the day was spent trying to get the information that was needed to work. The organisation now has all relevant data on line for use by staff and the important activities are centred around making things happen with this information, i.e. action and decisions that move one towards achieving organisational objectives. Furthermore the information must be available in the format that best suits the individual users' needs, which in practice, may change from time to time. The internal auditor is no different in this respect since we may argue that most of his/her time is spent analysing information from a variety of sources and producing oral and written reports that address the state of control systems within the organisation. Some of the points to note in this respect are:

The mobile auditor. We would wish each auditor to become a workstation in the sense they are completely on-line to all relevant systems they have at their disposal. The best solution is to issue each auditor with a notebook for use in the field and at home, along with making several office based workstations (i.e. a quality screen and keyboard) generally available, so as to fall in line with European directives.

Display screens. We will have to ensure compliance with the legislation relating to display screens if the workstation concept is to be fully adopted. This is essentially based around obtaining sufficient comfort and ease of use for the user. Without going into detail, this requires that the chair, desk, foot rest, screen angle of rotation, and light levels are all controlled so as to minimise discomfort. There must also be suitable policies on taking breaks away from the computer. The main problem for internal audit is the tendency to use notebooks as the main PC facility. As we have suggested, having several screens and keyboards in the office will solve this problem when staff are in the office.

Multimedia working using fax, text, video, sound, images, and graphics is a move that should be encouraged as we turn to a CD-based environment. By linking systems into networks we seek to avoid the problem of information islands where staff set up isolated PCs that cannot share information. The main problem is fragmented PC standards where some machines are better than others in terms of speed and power. Audit management must encourage a degree of sharing between auditors where high specification machines are available for all to use as required.

There are a number of practical considerations that must be addressed when designating users as workstations. One key factor is access to print facilities where an appropriate solution should be sought. In an ideal world the auditor would be issued with a notebook and printer, or a portable PC with an in-built printer as another option. We would also need to ensure all auditors are able to access organisational computer systems and also that the required software solution is available.

24.7 An IT Strategy

When devising an IT strategy for the internal audit unit there are a number of matters that should be given due attention:

Rooted in business strategy. The first point to note is that the information solutions must be based around a clear business strategy if they are to have any use at all. This means that the CIA needs to formulate a clear plan of action to cater for the next few years to drive the audit service forward. One key matter that should be addressed in this respect is whether the CIA is seeking fresh markets in line with an expansion policy. The converse is where audit wishes to become "lean and mean" in preparation for being more competitive, and so intends to release staff over the coming months. The position of computer audit will also have an impact on the IT strategy where we may choose between centralised computer audit teams or devolved models where all auditors are deemed IT literate. Again the type of facilities applied will depend on the adopted model.

Prioritise applications. Part of the IT strategy will be based on a determination of the types of systems access that are required by the auditors. In general, we would want all auditors to have on line access to all key computer applications run by the organisation. The way this is brought about should be firmly built into the IT strategy.

An effective IT strategy will tend to take a global view of the main considerations that are required to progress the audit service in the information arena. In one sense we are required to make information a high profile issue as it forms the lifeblood of the audit service in the following way:

FIGURE 24.5 INFORMATION NEEDS OF AUDIT

The solution should be seen as an entire package which will take on board factors such as audit plans, the IT budget, and IT standards.

One of the most common failings of audit management is an approach to IT developments that does not recognise that a formal project is actually being established. An organic approach to IT has the advantage of ensuring resources are attracted to areas of most need (or people with the loudest voice). The setback is the absence of the important controls that appear over projects. These controls involve defined resources, deadlines, specific products and tasks, regular review, monitoring reports, documented meetings and so on. Auditors are excellent at auditing defined parts of the organisation but sometimes fail to install in their own section, the very controls that they recommend elsewhere. We will spend a great deal of money on IT and this will probably be the next most significant item of expenditure after staffing costs. It is a fundamental part of audit management's responsibility to install adequate controls over this expenditure.

The importance of people involvement
There are many people who have a role in IT developments, who will have an opinion on the types of solutions required. This will include corporate IT officers, hardware suppliers, consultants, computer audit, field auditors and even the auditee (who will promote their own systems). The CIA will reconcile these competing influences and work out who is offering the best advice. It is good practice to pass all proposals through audit management meetings. People give different advice, and there are many reasons why certain systems are supported by certain people. Some of the "people considerations" that relate to IT can be listed:

Human resource planning is required to ensure that auditors have the necessary skills to administer the systems that are required to discharge the audit role. We need to consider training needs, staff development, and the way audits are undertaken. Computer boredom is an additional concern where it is not always easy to get staff to use new systems unless they are motivated. It is as well to have a requirement that auditors use new IT built into job descriptions in case there is some dispute in this matter (in terms of co-operation).

The other side of human resource planning is a more proactive approach where we need to fast track the required skills by considering interactive training (CD based), recruitment policies, scarcity allowances, redeployment, redundancies and dismissal where the skills are not present.

The final side of the equation is the power play that comes with new IT. Resources may be deemed to relate to the level of status of the officer in question. So for example instead of resources attracting to staff on a needs basis, it will be assigned on the basis of grade. This is unfortunately part of human nature that can result in the misapplication of IT resources.

24.8 Managing IT Acquisitions

There is a lot that can go wrong with IT developments, and as an audit issue this can create much embarrassment to all parties on the basis that we should know better (we should practice what we preach). Some of the guidelines that have been established as important and which should be uppermost in the mind of audit management in terms of managing IT can be noted:

1. Set realistic deadlines for implementing new systems. This is particularly true where we are changing over from one software package to another. This will always take longer than planned as some auditors stick to the old version longer than others. The existence of old PCs, say 286 and 386 processors, also leads to continued reliance on older software, on the basis that newer software tends to require more powerful machines.

2. Make sure that the main consideration is not costs. PCs, printers, scanners, interrogation software, presentation software and so on all subscribe to the basic equation that quality relates to costs. This is particularly the case with PCs where cheaper models are simply not designed for the great demands of business use.

3. Consider the training needs of staff. This should be ongoing and incremental since the "big bang" approach never works, as staff will tend to learn, practice and then learn some more. Training is a hands-on cost as it takes time away from front-line audit work, although we should seek to revise this view to read that training is an investment in people, rather than a basic cost.

4. Do not introduce new systems at peak times. One basic drawback to new systems is the learning curve whereby it takes longer to do things on the new system. This factor may be high-jacked by sceptics who use it as an excuse to stay away from the new systems, as it interferes with work.

5. When bringing in new systems check all options and go for the low-risk ones. When considering a new system such as auditor time monitoring, or a flowcharting package the first two questions to ask a supplier are, "how long has it been out and who else uses it?" If it has been shown to work for others there is no reason why it should not work elsewhere.

6. We have already dealt with the workstation concept.

7. We need to treat what is being said by sales personnel very carefully and seek to verify information that is provided. To this end we may talk to other users and seek independent advice wherever possible. Before we arrive at this point it will be necessary to undertake extensive fact finding based on a market research approach. Another factor that needs to be reviewed is support service costs and a policy of buying extended warranties may be seen as good value for money. Wherever possible we should try to control the contract that is on offer although this is obviously difficult with larger and more powerful suppliers.

8. When implementing the new systems we must have due regard to the views of users i.e. the auditors themselves. Problems such as slow response times may call for action

(say increased memory) or this will make the success of new developments less attainable.

9. To avoid an obsession with state of the art systems, audit management should make sure they ban 100% solutions. Computer facilities should be reviewed annually and we will naturally migrate to newer more powerful systems, but this should not mean we need to buy in the most expensive machines on the market. The software solution is more of an issue since it is helpful if we can choose a package that will be in place for some time, so as to avoid the need for retraining.

10. We need to ensure that all acquisitions are firmly linked into the defined IT strategy. One way of ensuring this is to ban spot purchases (i.e. an auditor asks for a new system that is then bought). As such all proposed purchases should be supported by a feasibility report which will explain how it fits into the IT strategy and contributes to service delivery. This document may then be considered at the next audit management team meeting, where it may be considered and agreed (or rejected). This will also bring into play the concept of accountability for the expenditure.

11. We have mentioned the need to apply basic project management techniques wherever possible. This is assisted where we break down IT acquisitions into smaller projects and try to shorten the development time as far as possible, within the remit of the overall IT strategy.

12. The final point to note is the need to achieve a focused innovation whereby new ideas are encouraged so long as they fit into the vision of delivering quality audit services within cost confines.

Storage
We must set basic rules of data storage as part of our auditing standards:

☐ **Rules of evidence**. We need to consider the adequacy of evidence that is stored in supporting the audit findings. Document imaging may be used to store original papers that may be reproduced on an as-and-when basis. There are times when paper files may be required to hold certain categories of information and this is one area where clear standards would be required from audit management.

☐ **Retention periods**. The organisation will have produced rules of time periods for the retention of documents. These should also be applied by internal audit although the format, which can cover say microfiche or automation, can vary according to agreed policy. Fraud investigations may result in files that will be used for many years in disciplinaries, industrial tribunals, and court cases.

☐ **Media**. The way information is stored should also be agreed on, as part of formal audit policy. We tend to use diskettes although there are other storage media such as tape or CD. There should also be rules on using the PC hard disk to store information.

☐ **Security**. We need to install suitable procedures for ensuring that information obtained and used by internal audit is secure. Lockable diskette boxes, a safe based in the audit offices, and rules covering the transportation of diskettes need to be considered. Passwords placed over PCs can assist this task so long as other auditors and audit management are capable of accessing audit PCs. In practice however, a simple test of reviewing the contents of the top right side drawer to any auditor's desk will probably reveal a bundle of unmarked diskettes. This situation should be deemed unacceptable and suitable measures put in place to guard against it.

□ **Protection off site**. Building on the above, we also need to define rules covering the protection of diskettes off site. This may involve for example procedures whereby diskettes must be stored in briefcases with combination locks, and that they should not be left lying around either at home or in the office. A suitable coding scheme may ensure that each diskette can be fully identified.

□ **Ownership**. All data generated during the course of the auditor's work should be clearly designated as belonging to the organisation. This means that all diskettes are owned by the organisation as will the contents, and as a policy this should be communicated to audit staff. To this end it is good practice to rule that only diskettes formally issued by audit can be used on audit's PCs.

□ **Backing up**. This is a common problem with many auditors having experienced the task of retyping work that has been lost. Audit management can establish clear rules on this whereby a back-up is held on the hard disk (to be deleted when the audit is complete), copies made to a back-up audit diskette each night that is then held in the safe. This is in addition to the diskette held by the auditor. An additional provision is to produce a paper draft when the document becomes large, as this is a back-up albeit not in an automated format.

24.9 The Need for Computer Standards

With the implementation of computerised processing within the audit department, an additional responsibility for ensuring that the facilities are adequately controlled arises. It is essential that the chief internal auditor defines and implements standards that cover many of the areas that we have already made reference to, which may be categorised along the following lines:

□ **Acquiring hardware**. The way new computers are acquired must be controlled covering compatibility, cost, evaluation, use of tendering, specifications and so on.

□ **Acquiring software**. This most important aspect of computerisation should be carefully planned. As such procedures are required for selecting and implementing audit software. There may be a conflict between organisational policies on standardised software and the type of programmes that audit as opposed to other departments require. Staff training is also a crucial factor along with the rules on who can set up new software and how we can avoid pirated material.

□ **Pirated software**. Rules on using unlicensed software must be firmly in place. This problem can be tackled through suitable hardware and software registers and regular checks on audit machines, particularly portables.

□ **Protecting computer equipment**. A policy of assigning PCs (e.g. notebooks) to auditors is designed to increase the autonomy and operational efficiency of auditors as they work in the field. Clear policies on controlling the movement of computer equipment used by auditors should be defined along with mechanisms to ensure that they are all accounted for. Current records showing who has each machine are the least requirement and one would encourage a regular inventory check on all items. We must also address the vexing question of private work being carried out on audit computers and whether this may be controlled to acceptable proportions so as not to interfere with official audit work. It is generally best to assign responsibility for audit computers to a designated auditor, with support from the audit administration officer (if there is one).

☐ **Inputting information**. The CIA must set out rules for data input. This should be aimed at providing a disciplined approach to getting information onto data files in an accurate fashion so that any resultant audit report is based on correct and complete information. Verification procedures usually involve an element of double checking with the extent dependent on the sensitivity of the input data. Some form of compliance check linked to the audit review process should then accompany these procedures. We must also consider the use of passwords to protect the automated information.

☐ **Processing data**. Regular checks need to be applied to the software that is used to ensure that files are not being corrupted, viruses are not introduced and the system is operating as intended. Standardised software and training will assist this aspect of control.

☐ **Using printers**. The audit department should establish standards on output in terms of the type of printers to be used for draft and final reports, the font types and the format used. VFM issues must be considered and generally cheaper quicker printers are used for draft reports while final versions need the more expensive (say laser) output.

☐ **Files and diskettes**. In many audit departments, one might observe an abundance of disks and diskettes lying around some carrying an obscure marking and others with no label at all. The CIA must define standards for files on:
- Issuing diskettes.
- Labelling diskettes.
- Locking them away when not in use.
- Storing data on diskettes and the hard disk.
- Backing up files and storing the copy in a secured manner (perhaps in a fire-proof safe).
- Ensuring that confidential information is not seen by unauthorised persons.

☐ **Computer assisted audit techniques**. Auditors need guidance on interrogating the organisation's main-frames and the procedures to be adopted when applying test data to these systems.

☐ **Documentation**. The standard and level of documentation covering computerised information should be defined and suitable procedures applied.

☐ **Referencing reports**. All computerised material should be traceable to the originator and a suitable referencing standard should be used throughout the audit department that is displayed on hard copies.

The Data Protection Act
Procedures that ensure compliance with the DP Act should be in place. This means that auditors should take care with the way personal data is collected, stored and protected, and that it is properly registered with the DP officer.

24.10 Time Monitoring Systems

Time management systems will tend to feature in most internal audit units and this will be an important information based system. This should enable audit management to receive regular reports on the way their staff are working. It will be used to support performance measures that relate to a variety of performance targets that would ideally have been set for both auditors and audit teams. They should cover each of the defined information needs that derive from the management of audit time. This will involve periodic reports as well as specially requested items. The reports should revolve around the time-frame, types of work, auditors, audit groups and the entire audit unit. As such it should report on:

- Time spent on audits.
- Audits over budget.
- Non-recoverable time charged (such as training).
- Breakdown between systems and investigations.
- Audits that should have been completed.
- And so on.

The inputs of a suitable time monitoring system may be illustrated as follows:

FIGURE 24.6 TIME MONITORING SYSTEM INPUTS

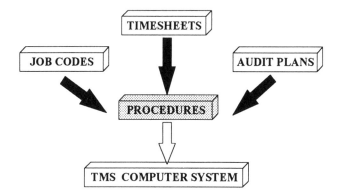

The various roles of time management information should be duly recognised and catered for. Here we would expect any such system to cover the following functions:
1. A method of charging time to specific audit jobs.
2. A way of identifying variances from planned to actual hours though incorporating budgeted hours to each chargeable job.
3. A method of charging clients for work carried out and generating the supporting schedules and covering invoice if needs be. Accordingly, it is important to identify a client for each job that is set up on the system.

4. A method of establishing the status of each job. Suitable booknote messages may be used in any good system to compile a form of database of audit jobs, that will provide summary information. This may range from terms of reference, assigned auditor, special features, stage indicators (say planning, fieldwork or reporting) and so on.

The time management system will typically be a computerised package that performs the function of recording and reporting auditors' time. There are three main components that must enter the system for it to work. This is the auditor's weekly timesheet, the job coding (and clients) and the planned hours. This may be illustrated as follows:

FIGURE 24.7 THE AUDIT TIME MONITORING SYSTEM

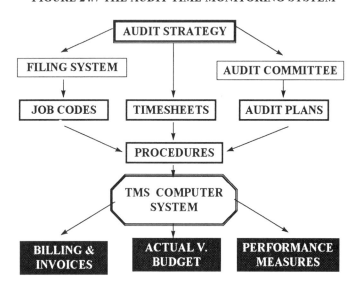

As such it is not just a matter of buying a time management system and installing it on a PC or network. The underlying procedures must be carefully thought through and addressed before a suitable reporting system can come on line and be of any use to audit management. Building on the point mentioned above, it is as well to resource any time management work as a proper systems development project. Here the task is not just left to the audit administration officer but is assigned a high profile and given the status of a formal computer project. To this end, for larger audit units, we may designate the following key officers:

☐ **A systems controller**. This might be a senior auditor who would be responsible for job code structures, technical detail on the system including archiving, data input standards, enhancements, and rules regarding who has access to the system and how the integrity of the database is maintained. This person may have to write procedures for timesheets, the input data and reporting functions.

☐ **A systems manager**. This may be an audit manager who will have overall control over the system and set general strategy for its use, review, procedures and the way staff interface with it.

☐ **An input officer**. This may either be decentralised, with each auditor inputting their own figures (with controls over accuracy say managerial review of figures) or one person may hold this responsibility.

☐ **The data owner**. The CIA will have overall responsibility for ensuring the data is correct, the reports adequate and the system is sound. The systems manager would be required to provide assurances on these and other related matters.

Again time management will not work if the role is simply delegated to the audit admin. officer and nothing more. It should be a regular feature of audit management meetings and a key concern of the CIA. We have suggested that the job code structure is seen as a separate consideration before the computer system is established. Ideally this should reflect the way the systems based approach and investigations role are perceived in terms of audit work and audit consultancy respectively. Any coding system must be based on clear rules which will vary between different audit sections. We may however make some general observations:

1. Code the work in line with the adopted reporting framework. The audit committee may have a view on this. In this way we may secure reports that feed naturally into our monthly, quarterly, and annual reporting structures.
2. Do not allow auditors to set up individual codes for small jobs that will mean the system becomes overloaded. A general code of "advice and information" may be used to record these one-off tasks. We may set a time standard and require jobs under say one or two days long to go to this code. If this approach is adopted it is important that timesheets record full details of the work and are retained for later review, if there is a query from the client.
3. Following this line it is as well to have small number of fixed codes for non-recoverable (or non-chargeable) time such as annual leave, training, sickness and so on.
4. Have strict rules on who can set up codes and budget hours. This should be restricted to senior staff (say audit manager or the CIA in smaller audit units).
5. Ensure that timesheets are signed on a weekly basis by audit management before submission to the system.

We may set out an example of a coding structure where systems and investigations work have been separated.

TABLE 24.1 JOB CODING SYSTEM

DESCRIPTION	JOB CODE RANGE
RECOVERABLE	
A. SYSTEMS	
1. Corporate & Operational	1001 - 1500
2. Financial systems	1501 - 2000
3. Systems development	2001 - 2500
4. Computer audits	2501 - 3000
5. Contract audits	3001 - 3500
B. INVESTIGATIONS	
1. Management investigations	3501 - 4500
2. General probity audits	4501 - 5500

3. Fraud investigations	5501 - 6500
4. Other investigations	6501 - 7000
C. CONSULTANCY SERVICES	7001 - 8000
D. AUDIT PROFESSIONAL ADVICE	(8001 - 80020)
1. Department A	8001
2. Department B	8002
3. Department C etc.	8003
E. NON-RECOVERABLE	(8021 - 8041)
General management	8021
Audit admin.	8022
Audit strategy, plans & risk appraisal	8023
Activity reports	8024
Client relations & marketing	8025
Audit meetings	8026
IT strategy & enhancements	8027
Seminars etc.	8028
Professional training	8029
IT training	8030
Non-audit training	8031
Other training	8032
Delivery of training	8033
Staffing issues	8034
Recruitment of auditors	8035
Performance appraisal	8036
Audit manual, procedures & quality assurance	8037
Audit library	8038
Liaison with external audit	8039
Non-audit work	8040
Other	8041
F. ABSENCES	(8042 - 8049)
Annual leave	8042
Sick leave - certificated	8043
Sick leave - uncertificated	8044
Hospital, doctor & dentist	8045
Bank holidays	8046
Special leave	8047
Unauthorised absences	8048
Miscellaneous	8049

24.11 Conclusions

Managers rely on the progressive use of information technology and this means more computerisation. This is also true for the internal audit department and suitable standards must be applied to controlling these developments in line with organisational policies. Automation is a fact of life and the audit department must have the same level of controls that it expects from the departments that it audits.

CHAPTER TWENTY-FIVE

MARKETING AUDIT SERVICES

25.1 Introduction

Marketing identifies, anticipates and satisfies consumer requirements profitably. It is included within managing internal audit as this is a relevant management technique that forms part of the array of methods for ensuring that audit objectives are achieved. Internal audit must be properly marketed if it is to be of any use to an organisation. The audit client includes:

- Line management.
- Middle management.
- Directors.
- The Chief Executive.
- The Director of Finance.
- The Audit Committee.
- The Shareholders (private companies).
- The Taxpayer (public bodies).
- The Organisation itself.

25.2 Should Internal Audit Adopt a Marketing Profile?

There are those who argue that the unique feature of the internal audit function that relates to its independence, in some way means that there is no need to adopt a market based orientation in the way services are delivered. They may go on to suggest that if we let managers define the way internal audit works then we become little more than consultants. This view is misconceived as it fails to recognise that internal audit is a service to the organisation and not to itself, although there are some considerations that impact on a purist view of marketing. There are several key factors that make it an advantage to undertake market analysis:

☐ **The need to define internal audit's role in the organisation**. There are many different types of auditing services that may be provided and within this equation there are different degrees to which each type of service may be resourced. We have considered the differences between systems work and investigations along with specialist work such as fraud investigations and value for money studies. The way that these services interface with the needs of the organisation must be seen as a prime factor in the marketing process. As a result, firm decisions must be made as to how services will be provided and the mix of types.

☐ **The importance of top management support**. The chapter on the behavioural aspects of auditing made it quite clear that in the final analysis, a lack of support from top management will be detrimental to the audit profile. Marketing involves securing this support proactively, through a process of determining and meeting control needs.

☐ **The opportunities for development**. One advantage of marketing is that gaps in service provision may be spotted either by identifying obvious new openings or by developing more of an existing service. So for example we may find out that there is a great demand for presentations by internal audit of "control appreciation" seminars. This may be a good way of promoting good control and selling the concept of internal audit reviews.

☐ **The different roles and models for internal audit**. Based on the service-mix considerations we have mentioned above we can go on to develop new models for the delivery of audit services. This in turn impacts on the type of structure that we define for the audit function. The importance of client feedback cannot be underestimated as a source of useful information.

☐ **The threats that may be faced**. Marketing should also isolate potential problems for the audit service, in terms of poor performance and/or direct threats. Actual discontent from managers is a good indicator of problems and can give an indication of areas that need to be improved as a matter of urgency. Threats to audit can come in many guises although one main problem is competition from other providers of internal audit services. The need to fit into a defined specification that has been set by the organisation, gives the CIA a firm advantage over competitors who may be seeking to meet such a level of service.

☐ **The impact of change management**. The process of carrying out market research and feeding the results back to audit management will have a knock-on effect to any change programme that may be in place. Strategic change needs information to act as a source of guidance as it develops and changes. Marketing information is an important part of the database that is used to underpin management decisions.

☐ **The image of internal audit**. We may uncover vital information relating to the actual image and reputation of the audit service from our work on marketing. This should be quickly acted on by audit management in line with a clear policy that justified criticism is unacceptable.

☐ **Distinguishing between management's and audit's roles**. Marketing is a two-way process in that it seeks to find out what the client wants while at the same time making it clear what is already available. Many problems with audit/management relationships are based on a misunderstanding of the audit role vis à vis management's responsibilities. In general, managers will view audit as being responsible for systems of internal control rather than themselves. The opportunity to clarify this and related issues can be built into the marketing process.

☐ **Providing advice and assistance**. Marketing will also uncover the extent to which a "control help desk" should be provided by internal audit. The ability to provide on the spot advice in terms of control/compliance issues may be seen as an additional service that could enhance the profile of the audit role in the organisation. As such this should be given serious consideration by the CIA.

Defining and meeting client's needs should be done within the context of professional independence and in this respect the audit committee may be seen as the ultimate client. It is nevertheless the case that if operational management does not support the audit function and sees no value in its services, it will probably lose status and in so doing its independence. Accordingly a failure to recognise management's needs will lead to many problems for internal audit.

Audit services

As a start to the marketing process we list different types of audit services. These services represent conscious decisions by audit management as to selected types and mixes of available services:

- Financial systems reviews.
- Financial systems testing.
- Management audits.
- Operational audits.
- Compliance programmes.
- Procedures reviews.
- Computer audits.
- Quality audits.
- Inventory, cash and stock checks.
- Value-for-money studies.
- Fraud investigations.
- Special investigations.
- Probity investigations.
- Training and development support.
- Security reviews.
- Systems consultancy - e.g. new systems.
- Systems development role.

Audit roles

We can formulate distinct audit roles that should be derived from a formal marketing strategy:

☐ **Getting management more control oriented**. Audit may decide to target managers rather than systems in the search for better control. The idea is to get management thinking about controls and how they can be better used to promote the achievement of operational objectives. Presentations to key managers may be a feature of this approach to audit work.

☐ **Ensuring the organisation understands the review concept**. Another approach is to encourage a positive approach to the audit process as a fundamental part of securing better control. So for example we may encourage managers to seek audits whenever they face a particular problem such as competition, budget reductions, poor performance and so on.

☐ **Getting procedures up and running**. Many audit reports state that operational procedures are inadequate and then move on to other findings. An alternative approach is to resource an additional component of the audit service which involves reviewing current procedures and providing comprehensive advice on making improvements.

☐ **Promoting a systems solution to all problems**. The systems philosophy states that all problems have underlying causes and it is these causes that must be put right if a long-term view of success is to be promoted. This means that our audit work is sold as being based on this principle. For example if we need to audit an organisation which has twenty warehouses, among other things, we will start at head office by asking what controls have they established over the warehouses, rather than treat each one as a separate entity.

☐ **Promoting change**. We may argue that the audit role includes supporting the various change programmes that are in place to ensure that they have proper controls. If this is the case then we would require all proposals for restructuring, reorganising, developments and so on, to be sent to internal audit for detailed comments before they can be approved. An extension of this view sees the audit role as recommending change where this is not happening and there is poor performance.

☐ **Designing control teams and training them**. One version of the audit role is that of a corporate control that directs and co-ordinates teams based in each department. Since audit functions appear in larger organisations that involve thousands of employees, the need for locally based control teams can probably be justified. In this environment audit would spend time ensuring that these teams work properly, and to this end we might see a functional reporting line from the teams to the CIA.

☐ **Teaching management self-audit**. This version of the audit role is based on extensive devolution whereby management seeks advice from audit on ways that they might audit themselves. This consultancy type role seeks to spread control expertise across the organisation and so provide an ongoing audit type process supported by real audits that are carried out in conjunction with this practice.

☐ **Helping to set control standards**. The idea here is to spread best practice on many areas that impact on managers covering for example topics such as purchasing, systems development, recruitment, quality assurance, security, systems administrators and performance appraisal.

☐ **Checking standards across the organisation e.g. financial regulations**. We may support corporate standards across the organisation in respect of financial regulations, financial management, IT security and quality assurance. Internal audit will then promote these procedures and ensure that there is full compliance in the organisation as one way of delivering better control. This moves us closer to the vision of audit as an inspection function that regulates managerial activities.

☐ **Issuing ad-hoc advice on control matters**. This help-desk model is based on a vast database of knowledge about organisational policies and procedures located within the audit unit by virtue of its centralist location. Advice and assistance is provided by audit one-off via the established "hot line".

We would expect an ongoing process of research and development to be funded by the CIA to assess and make recommendations on the applicability of the types of audit services that have been mentioned above. This is far better than the usual practice where different types of services appear by chance as a result of the judgement of individual auditors. As such an auditor may spend hours giving advice to a line manager on a concern over breach of procedure, without realising that this is a new and important audit role that is being assumed.

Revisiting the acid test

One useful way of assessing whether our marketing efforts have interfered with the levels of independence that we should have achieved is to apply the basic acid test:

> *"If internal audit were instantly removed from the organisation,*
> *would certain operations collapse?"*

A purist's view would insist that this question receives a negative answer to reinforce the concept of the audit services being free from operational involvement. The dilemma, from a marketing angle, is that this exposes the audit role and makes it akin to a dispensable commodity. This problem warrants further exploration since there is an inherent conflict between the marketing concept and the independence test that must be recognised and managed by the CIA.

25.3 Different Approaches to Marketing

We move to marketing as it impacts on the internal audit role. This may be set within an illustration of the marketing approach contrasted with other managerial standpoints:

FIGURE 25.1 THE MARKETING CONCEPT

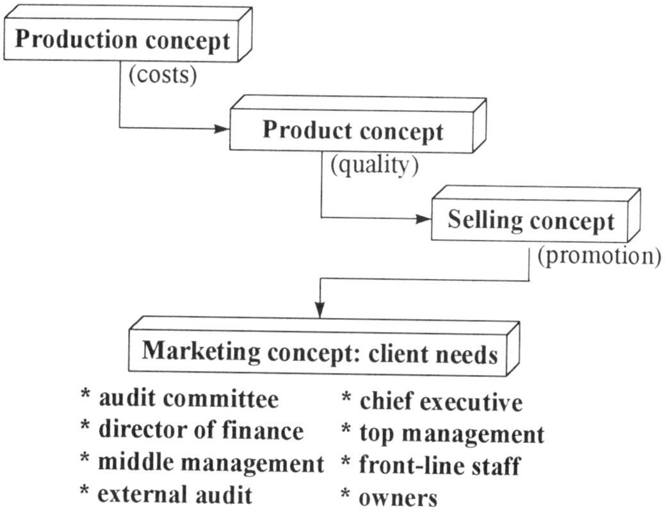

The IIA.UK have suggested that audit clients fall into three groups: those it reports to (e.g. audit committee), those it reports on (e.g. middle management) and those it reports with (e.g. external audit and internal control teams). **The production concept** seeks to minimise the costs of the audit, which translates to the number of hours spent on each individual project. **The product concept** will on the other hand concentrate on the audit itself and suggests that so long as the work is good and the report is done to quality standards everything will be fine. **The selling concept** is particularly relevant to internal audit in that it suggests we need only ensure that the client pays for our services, which may be mandatory in most organisations who resource an audit function. **The marketing approach**, on the other hand, takes the view that we must first find out what is required by the organisation and then seek to meet these requirements. No matter how efficient or professional the audit work is, so long as we have not fed our work into client expectations then our future is not assured. This may come as a surprise to many auditors who do not believe that they (or the CIA) work for anyone.

The marketing mix:

☐ **The product**. Here we consider whether the audit work that is being provided fits with the requirements of the organisation. The Boston Box comes to our aid in making this consideration when deciding our product strategy. This may consist of doing nothing, seeking new developments, seeking market developments, diversification and/or going for new markets.

FIGURE 25.2 BOSTON BOX - ASSESSING AUDIT SERVICE

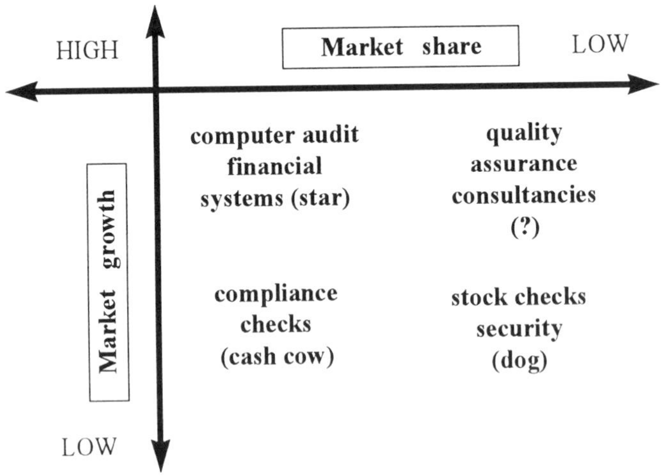

We may aim at a balanced portfolio of audit work in line with the classifications of the Boston Box:

☐ **The price**. The costs of the audit work should be subject to ongoing review so as to work to an optimum profile. Different types of audit work take different timeframes to complete and different types of auditor, some expensive (e.g. a computer auditor) and others relatively cheap (e.g. a junior auditor). The starting place is to ensure that costing systems are sound and that they differentiate between different grades of auditor. Premium work that may have to be done on overtime or require additional consultants to be brought in, will be charged at higher rates than standard audits.

☐ **Promotion**. This may be seen more as being built into the public relations function as a way of selling the audit image and underlying services. Where we have adopted a push strategy we will be seeking new fields of work and promote the audit service. A formal complaints procedure will help identify the state of the audit image and it may be necessary to create defined messages to reinforce the profile of the audit service. The annual report is a useful vehicle for promoting the audit presence.

Audit feedback questionnaire

One way of achieving a degree of feedback from the auditee is to obtain a response to a formal questionnaire that makes enquiries about the audit service. We have already outlined the survey of auditees as part of the quality assurance programme and a major control that the CIA may use to assess the success of internal audit. The auditee survey also has a role in the marketing plan since it constitutes a formal mechanism for obtaining independent evidence of audit's successes and problems when dealing with clients. The survey has to be carefully administered since it should not give the impression that audit management does not trust its staff, neither should it be an opportunity for line managers to undermine the field auditors. Accordingly the purpose of the survey should be explained in a covering memo from the CIA and the main objectives are:

- To obtain the client's view on the benefits secured from the audit.
- To isolate any communication problems that may have been experienced by the client.
- To assess whether the client's perceived needs have been met.
- To identify any adjustments to marketing strategy and audit methodologies that may be required.

The auditee surveys operate at two levels; one as an assignment follow-up while the other looks for more general comments that are not linked to any particular audit. An Audit Effectiveness Questionnaire, along with a covering memorandum from the CIA, may be given to the client by the lead field auditor and once the audit has been completed it will be returned direct to the CIA. It is felt that by allowing the field auditors to distribute and explain the survey, this dispels the view that the CIA does not trust them. The arrangement whereby the form is filled in by the client and returned direct to the CIA ensures that the auditees may be quite open in their views. Audit working papers will note any disagreement that the auditors may have had with the client and this point should be taken on board when reviewing the survey results. A wider survey may also be carried out from time to time, which can be used to provide feedback on audit's overall impact on management, for use in formulating audit marketing plans.

The audit information brochure

This is a standing document that provides much of the detail that clients might require along with details of audit services and contact names. It should be a brief, colourful, foldable brochure possibly with several photographs. Reference can be made to the published annual report for more comprehensive information, on the basis that a brochure with excessive detail will tend not to be read. It is advisable to have the brochure produced professionally from a print-shop where a glossy, conveniently sized pamphlet may be commissioned without appearing excessively flamboyant. It should be given to employees on those occasions when auditors feel this would be appropriate. The brochure may be structured along the following lines:

- What is internal audit?

- What can internal audit do for you?
- Who do you contact?

The audit department should ideally follow a house-style with an appropriate logo that projects the basic image that audit wishes to present. The audit name and logo will appear on all correspondence and reports, and a suitable "house colour" will also be used for all published documents, including the brochure. We may go on to contact management where it requires further information on the internal audit services. This correspondence may be structured in the following manner:

1. Introduction. General background to the audit role, audit standards and how work is undertaken. Independence, audit approach, fraud and other relevant issues can be briefly described.
2. Summary of year's achievements. The particularly major reviews will be mentioned along with the real benefits that accrued.
3. Available audit services. Here the main services will be set out and the type of control-related problems that can be solved.
4. The service level agreement. Audit plans, contingency work, special requests and the audit scheduling process will be outlined along with mention of the fee charging system. The complaints procedure may be defined which involves direct representation to the CIA.
5. Understanding internal controls. Management's responsibilities may be highlighted in this section which will discuss the general concept of control and ways that management may discharge their responsibilities in this matter.
6. Contacts. A brief list of the main contacts will be set out. The group structure and responsibility levels will be provided to ensure that management is able to contact the right audit manager wherever necessary.

Auditors' business cards
Each auditor may be issued with a business card that will set out:
- The auditor's name.
- The designation.
- Any professional/academic titles.
- Their areas of responsibility.
- The contact phone number.

Again the audit logo would appear on this document.

A complaints procedure
A formal complaints procedure should be applied whereby management is advised of a clear process for submitting their concerns.

The introductory memoranda to management may include the following paragraph:

> *"We hope that you will not experience any problems with the audit work since all auditors work to the highest professional standards. However should you have any particular concerns please voice them to X who is the team leader for this project. In the event that you are still not satisfied please contact the CIA."*

Marketing information

Marketing decisions must be based on sufficient information and some of the main sources of this information are:

- General feedback from auditors on management's views. Here the CIA should have regular contact with senior management to discuss general audit-related matters.
- Level of complaints from clients.
- Formal responses from the audit committee.
- Results of the formal auditee survey.
- Surveys of competitors.
- Internal reports produced by the organisation that mention internal audit.
- Feedback from auditors.
- Informal contacts with officers and people associated with the organisation.

Each source provides an insight into the success or otherwise of the marketing plan and they need to be carefully monitored.

Marketing plans

There is a link between marketing and audit strategy, and many strategic decisions will have an impact on the marketing plan. As a result, the strategic plan should also incorporate the marketing plan and revisions to strategy may well affect the way internal audit is marketed.

FIGURE 25.3 MARKETING PLAN STRUCTURE

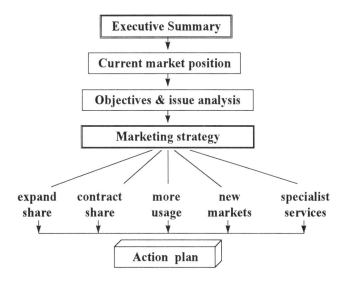

These plans should be assimilated into audit strategies and form the basis of discussions at the audit manager meetings that should be held regularly.

Analysis of competitors

The public sector is now facing the direct threat of competition from external providers of audit services. There is a need for extensive preparation in this environment, since much of the drive is about allowing the in-house team to bid for the contract in competition with other suppliers. There are many examples of public sector audit functions that are now being performed by private sector firms. To this end an analysis of the current market can be a useful exercise and provide important information that can be fed into the marketing strategy. We would be concerned with:

- Entry barriers that stop new suppliers entering the market for internal audit services.
- Competitors' reactions to the contracts that may become available for competition and whether they have expressed an interest in submitting a bid.
- Competitors' strengths and weaknesses in comparison to what may be provided by the existing audit unit.

It may be possible to develop a competitors' intelligence system or subscribe to a service that regularly provides this type of analysis. Essentially the results will provide an insight into the types of decisions (i.e. improvements) that are required to make the in-house service better placed than competitors' services.

Consumer behaviour
It is as well to research the attitudes of clients and seek to understand their behaviour. Independence can be used to strengthen the audit role and ensure our reports are heard at the highest levels. If however we are not satisfying the needs of auditees generally, we cannot simply hide behind the cloak of independence, and ignore this factor. We should be concerned about auditees' attitudes towards internal audit and how they use audit services. We need to pay particular attention to unsatisfied needs, and how these may be met through a revision to the service provision profiles that we have discussed above.

The audit budget
Clients pay for audit services through the quarterly fee-charging system, and it is essential that the charges are linked into the audit budget. We need to recover whatever it costs to provide the audit service and the main annual cost components will be:

TABLE 25.1 AUDIT COST PROFILE

ITEM	£
SALARIES	
STAFF EXPENSES	
OFFICE ACCOMMODATION	
GENERAL ADMIN. OVERHEADS	
EQUIPMENT	
OTHER EXPENSES	
TOTAL COST	

By dividing the total annual costs over the projected number of chargeable audit hours for the year (normally 214), we can arrive at a recovery hourly rate. By increasing this hourly rate we may achieve a trading surplus as a contribution to non-recoverable time and purchases such as expenditure on computer equipment. The hourly charge-out rate will vary by grade of auditor and this factor will be entered into the time monitoring system. Alternatively, a rough indicator of the hourly rate may be calculated by using the following formula:

ANNUAL SALARY ($\times$ 1.5)
CHARGEABLE HOURS FOR THE YEAR   =   HOURLY RATE

Service level agreements
Service level agreements (SLAs) may be defined for each department audited and involve the following:
1. Define the audit strategy based on the wider organisational strategy.
2. Carry out a general survey of audit risk areas.
3. Discuss the results with management.
4. Agree an annual plan as a result.
5. Take the draft annual plan to the audit committee.
6. Cost out the financial implications of the agreed audit services.
7. Produce a costed service level agreement for formal confirmation by the various directors.
8. Take the agreed and priced annual plan to the audit committee.

The time charging system will allow audit management to monitor the extent to which the budgeted income is being achieved and this will be reported quarterly to audit management. The audit committee, as well as having a general overseeing role, may also request certain reviews and will be charged accordingly. The CIA will probably advise the audit committee on any necessary corporate reviews. Note that management should not generally be able to refuse a planned audit review, but may negotiate the timing or ask to negotiate additional work where there are sufficient audit resources available. Managers may in addition request details of audit's planning, risk analysis and time charging mechanisms.

Creating the audit image
Audit needs to formulate and maintain an appropriate image and one auditor who breaches professional behaviour may tarnish the reputation of the whole department. The audit image is based around the standards set out in the audit manual and the auditor code of conduct. In addition it requires the following features of the internal auditor:
- Politeness, having regard to the need to respect fellow officers at whatever grade.
- Being positive by building constructive working relations with management.
- Sensitivity to management's needs.
- Respect for confidentiality with an understanding of the damage that idle gossip can do.
- A team based audit approach working with and alongside management.
- A hard working attitude with a constant mission to encourage management to promote good controls.
- A desire to explain the role of audit and promote the audit service wherever possible.

The published annual report
The internal audit department will publish an annual report after the confidential annual activity report has been considered by the audit committee. This will cover the work carried out and services provided, and has the role of a general information document. It should be written in a public relations style to communicate the services audit may provide and how management may participate and incorporate its views into audit planning.

Important concepts such as independence, behavioural aspects, audit approach, different perspective of external audit and so on will also be mentioned. This should be sent to senior management and be available on request, to all employees.

25.4 Conclusions

Marketing audit services starts with being able to offer professional services. Services should be publicised and arrangements set out for first identifying and secondly addressing any concerns that clients may have with the quality and delivery of audit services. Marketing helps extend the audit role beyond the point where the final report is issued and brings home the undeniably important concept of effective client based service delivery. The following types of questions should be addressed via a carefully planned marketing strategy:

1. What kind of audit services should be provided?
2. What should be the balance of unplanned (response based) work to planned audits?
3. How much time should be spent on consultancy projects as opposed to systems audits?
4. What should be the mix of senior/junior auditors?
5. Following on from the above, what level of hourly charge-out rate should be aimed at?
6. How do we promote the audit image?
7. Are our clients satisfied with the services that we are providing?
8. How are we placed vis à vis our potential competitors?

CHAPTER TWENTY-SIX

TRAINING AND DEVELOPMENT

26.1 Introduction

Training is an important aspect of developing internal auditors which has to be carefully planned in line with a career developmental programme. Several issues should be noted:

☐ **Mautz (1984)**. This research suggested that most internal auditors do not see internal auditing as a long-term career. Many organisations used the audit experience as only one part of a management development programme for staff who would return to line management after a brief spell in internal auditing. This is the "short-stay syndrome".

☐ **Sawyer (1988)**. Sawyer suggests that auditing qualifications would hold more credence if there was a requirement that only certified internal auditors could sign off audit reports. As it stands there are no regulatory barriers that mean all auditors have to be professionally qualified.

☐ **Spooner (1976)**. Spooner considered the extent to which the IIA.INC (in the USA) examinations were transferable to the UK. He concluded that this was not the case and as a result the IIA.UK examinations are based on a separate syllabus examined twice a year.

☐ **CBOK**. There is a common body of knowledge (CBOK) relevant to the work of internal auditors that should be mastered by all practising auditors. This CBOK forms the basis for the syllabus to the formal IIA qualification.

☐ **MIS**. The role of management information systems (MIS) is becoming increasingly important and training in this area is almost a prerequisite to the performance of audit work.

☐ **New IIA syllabus**. 1995 saw the introduction of a new syllabus for the IIA.UK that sought a wider coverage of the audit world and related areas. This now provides for two levels of qualification, the practitioner level and the more advanced professional level. The professional level builds on and extends the subjects that are covered at practitioner stage. There is more emphasis on financial management, information systems and a new paper dedicated to the topic of control. The advanced internal auditing paper is based around a case study that is available before the examination date, so reflecting the growing trend towards assignment-based work.

We will establish a clear link between training and the development of individual auditors and point out pitfalls, where training has not been properly managed. We will suggest that training is not simply sending staff away on the occasional seminar.

26.2 Benefits of Training

☐ **Increase in the quantity of work done by auditors**. Audit training is not carried out for its own sake but should be designed to secure defined benefits. There should be an increased efficiency in the way audit work is carried out which is then translated into increased output. A suitable training programme may have as an objective the reduction of audit hours charged to planned audits so that in any one year, more audits may be completed. Better techniques and more efficient procedures should lead to higher turnover.

☐ **Better quality of work**. It is one thing to churn out audits and performance indicators based on this sole factor will be misleading. Audit training should achieve a higher standard of quality from auditors. Training may have a firm objective to produce excellence. There should be a direct link between the level of training and the increasing ability to audit at higher managerial levels.

☐ **Cost savings in terms of better overall performance**. Becoming more efficient can be translated into the number of audits performed in any one period. On the other hand it may also be seen in terms of the potential to effect cost savings. An example might be in training auditors to prepare their own reports on a suitable word-processing package as opposed to sending them to a typing pool. This may mean that in future no overheads will be apportioned from central administration (i.e. the typing pool) and so provide savings on the audit budget. It is also possible to get more junior staff to operate unsupervised through effective training so that the overall charge to an audit will include less time from the audit managers. One useful technique is to move away from audit teams and get each individual auditor to perform his/her own audit project.

☐ **Better standard of report writing**. This is more a process for change than a mere document. Some argue that the report is the "window" to the audit department as a formally published item widely read. There is no short-cut to performing good audit work and this should be the main concern of audit management. Much will be lost if this professionalism is not wholly reflected in the final product, i.e. the audit report. It is here that additional effort must be expended to complete the circle of performing good work and then reporting it. Audit training will certainly include report writing and inconsistencies between individual auditors will arise. Some of these are not only attributable to junior staffs but will also cover different reporting styles acquired over time that need to be harmonised. Reference to the audit manual will help define the reporting standards that have been adopted bearing in mind the fact that there are many different models that may be applied.

☐ **Better quality of working papers**. We are moving to a position where the working papers that are prepared by auditors are acquiring a clear status. The rules on advance disclosure of evidence, and public enquiries that may be commissioned in the public sector as well as by the regulatory agencies in the financial services arena, mean that audit findings may be subject to an independent third party review. Audit's quality assurance provisions will also require formal standards that cover audit working papers and these should be properly implemented. Whatever the scenario, there is a need to ensure that auditors are preparing suitable working papers. It is frustrating to review a report that is well presented and based on sound evidence but the underlying evidence cannot be readily gleaned from the working paper file. It is here that many auditors let themselves down. A formal standard on audit documentation must form part of the audit procedures and its implementation will necessarily include training sessions on this topic, again based around the audit manual.

☐ **Less audit staff required in the long term**. This is a sensitive topic but one may assume the stance that training will help produce a higher standard of auditor which in turn should generate better work. One useful model is to employ a smaller number of auditors, working to higher standards. This does depend on the type of work being carried out although if facing competition as is the case in the public sector, then this "downsizing" is a fact of life. Training facilitates this process as skills are spread, greater efficiency is encouraged and the training process itself may be used to filter out those staff who are not able to readily transfer to these higher standards. If one has to be cynical, it should be noted that it is not best practice to take action against staff who are not performing unless relevant training programmes have already been directed at these staff. The process of defining a training programme necessarily involves setting performance standards and if an auditor is not able to meet these after all available assistance, management must then review this individual's position.

☐ **Smaller training gap in terms of skills shortages**. The audit manual will set standards covering the way that the audit role is discharged in a particular organisation. This will be designed to promote efficiency and effectiveness and so help guarantee the future of internal audit. Within this thinking is the presumption that all audit staff are able to function to the various standards that have been adopted and there will be obvious problems where this is not the case. A skills gap exists when auditors are not able to meet management's expectations and again if this is the case, the audit manual may fail. It is essential that all skills gaps are systematically identified and closed through a suitable training programme. All training should have this clear objective and so runs the argument that as these gaps are closed, audit will be better able to succeed.

☐ **Greater degree of professionalism**. Throughout the handbook we have developed a model that views audit as assuming a greater degree of professionalism with the passing of time. This is a conceptual matter that runs across the whole discipline of internal auditing. In practice, however it has to be translated into the work being carried out in each individual audit department and it is here that training comes into the frame. Training will play a major role in making progress towards this model of smaller numbers of more professional auditors. This is in contrast to vast armies of junior checkers that was a feature of the old days of internal auditing. Training is seen not only as a way of effecting development but can also comprise a set of basic targets that must be achieved before we can start to talk of this development. Herein lies the argument for using qualified staff.

☐ **Better motivated workforce with career development programmes**. Training means more than mere courses, seminars and days out. It indicates commitment from audit management to staff and injection of resources for each employee. Where training is linked into individual career development programmes, which is really a necessity, then it will have a motivating effect all round. It is possible to build team association into training by working on case studies in small groups and so enhancing the ability of staff to work together on real-life audits. Whenever a course is organised, the impact on motivation should be considered and catered for in the course wherever possible. For external courses an example would be to arrange them at a scenic location and have staff travel there together (say in one car). In this way it acts as a team-building day out in addition to the dissemination of information. Without a suitable training programme, performance appraisal has little use as there is no point identifying a skills gap and then not seeking to close it. In this instance an appraisal scheme would probably act to de-motivate participants and lower performance.

26.3 The Common Body of Knowledge (CBOK)

The CBOK is of interest to auditors, audit management, trainers and clients. This determines topics that will be covered during audit training. This should include all items in the handbook. It is possible to break these down into several main categories:

☐ **Underlying principles of internal audit**. The meaning of internal audit and the foundations upon which it is built. Even experienced auditors may misconstrue basic principles such as:
- Role of internal audit.
- Formal definitions.
- Auditing standards.
- Independence.
- Dealing with people.
- Audit committees.
- Audit charters.
- Relevant legislation.
- Relationships with the external auditor.
- Difference between public and private sector auditing.

☐ **Audit concepts covering different approaches and types of audit work**. There are many ways internal audits may be carried out, some based around testing routines while others move into evaluation. Each needs to be understood and used where relevant. An all-round auditor will master each approach and apply appropriate styles. Approaches to internal auditing will cover:
- Systems based auditing.
- Operational auditing.
- Management audits.
- Value for money studies.
- Fraud investigations.
- Contract audit.
- Management information systems reviews.
- Compliance audits.
- Environmental auditing.
- Final accounts work.

☐ **Basic audit skills required to administer the range of audit techniques**. There is a level of internal audit that is basic in that it requires no specialist skills. Standards achieved are minimum auditing skills that should be in place for the most junior staff.

Auditors who cannot achieve these standards may not be suited to audit work. Basic audit skills cover:

- Long-term audit planning.
- Risk assessment.
- Assignment planning.
- Systems flowcharting.
- Systems evaluation.
- Formal interviews.
- Statistical sampling.
- Compliance and substantive testing.
- Audit reporting.
- Oral presentations.

☐ **Advanced audit techniques relating to operational audits and computer audit**. Depending on the organisation, there will be certain audits that require specialist skills because of the nature of the operations or the sensitivity of the services/products. We will have to develop these skills within the audit unit to enable us to deal with these types of audit projects. This may be via a special audit group or through specialist individual auditors attached to the audit group. The skills may be brought in or developed and some of the advanced audit techniques will cover subjects such as:

- Computer interrogation and downloading.
- Formal fraud interviews under caution.
- Automated working papers.
- Computer test data.
- Project management.
- Financial modelling.
- Analytical review.
- Surveillance techniques.
- Contract tendering and compliance.
- Formulating recommendations.

☐ **Management of internal audit**. The CIA, audit managers and more senior audit staff will need exposure to audit management techniques and practices that allow them to provide the necessary direction and control to carry the audit unit through a formal strategy. The success of internal audit is mainly dependent on this factor. Management of internal auditing will cover subjects such as:

- Audit strategies.
- Formal business planning.
- Quality assurance.
- Structuring audit resources.
- Audit IT strategies and audit automation.
- Control and review of audit work.
- Marketing audit services.
- Performance appraisal.
- Dealing with clients.
- Training and developing audit staff - teambuilding, coaching and mentoring.

☐ **General management topics that have a direct or indirect bearing on internal auditing**. Auditors review controls, and experienced auditors will agree that over 80% of the components of a formal system of internal control are located in the managerial aspects of this system. As such, a typical auditor will need to have mastered the basic material that is taught in general management courses. The range of this material can be quite wide although basic management will cover:

- Schools of management thought.
- Structuring resources.
- Strategic management and planning.
- Controlling.
- Decision making and communications.
- Policies and procedures.
- Marketing.
- Operations management.
- Total quality management.
- Personal skills development such as inter-personal communication skills, negotiating skills, time-management, motivating staff, problem solving and so on.
- Financial management.

The all-round performer will be expected to master this common body of knowledge and also the way that particular methodologies are applied in his/her audit department. Training should therefore be directed towards these components and if a topic is not within the CBOK it is questionable whether it will have any relevance for the internal audit unit.

26.4 Training Auditors

Specialist skills training via internal or external skills workshops
These can be extremely efficient in terms of auditor development as long as the following rules are adhered to:

1. They are tailored to the exact requirements of the internal audit department in question and not framed as general developmental courses. There is little point having a trainer stand in front of an audit team who has no idea what specialist work this team is involved in.
2. They form part of an individual auditor's career development programme and can be geared towards tackling known weaknesses, identified from the performance appraisal scheme.
3. They are based around a needs analysis that has formally identified the training needs of the department.
4. The matters set out in the course are immediately put to use in a practical way in current audit work. This is a major benefit in that the real training goal is achieved not when participants listen to a trainer, but when they actually perform the new techniques learnt.
5. There is a clear link into the performance standards as set out in the audit manual. Skills workshops may be used to reinforce the standards required by the audit manual, which will encompass the defined working methodologies that have been adopted by the audit unit in question.

6. They form part of a formal ongoing programme that falls within the strategic goals of the audit department, as a way of ensuring that staff understand and work within the frame established by the strategy.

7. The workshops may be supported by audit management who may assume a key role in delivering the training modules.

8. The policy may be to utilise all available in-house skills before external sources are applied to this programme. This is why the skills database that was discussed in the chapter on human resource management is useful in isolating in-house skills and ensuring that they are shared.

9. If the skills workshops are performed by external resources, they should be based on a tailored programme specifically designed by audit management.

10. The CIA takes a personal interest in these programmes and ensures that they are given a high profile in the audit strategy. One major benefit of the skills workshop approach is that they may be contained within the working day. So for example we would expect audit management to introduce a two hour session to cover a new development that will consume very little audit hours, or interfere with ongoing audit work. This means there is no excuse why this type of training should not be undertaken frequently, whenever there is a need.

11. Value for money is achieved from them in terms of their transition from classroom to their successful application to audit work.

Professional training

This may be based on passing examinations of a defined professional body such as the Institute of Internal Auditors that is a completely different form of training from skills based courses. As such the rules here are different:

1. This must form part of a long-term strategy underpinning the entire staffing policy of the audit department. It takes years to put staff through professional courses and a long-term approach is essential for this policy to become successful.

2. A formal budget must attach to this programme that caters for subscription fees, books, travelling, college fees, time off, exam fees and so on. The CIA must be wary about depending on corporate training budgets as these tend to suffer in times of budget reduction exercises. As such the CIA may wish to set aside a separate fund for this activity financed by fees from additional areas such as consultancy services.

3. The requirement to secure a professional qualification should form part of the staffing policy. Real success is achieved when auditors are required to pass the internal audit qualification, to remain with the organisation or at least obtain internal promotion. Unfortunately it is only by placing this severe pressure over the career auditor, that one can guarantee that studies will be prioritised, so making success in the ensuing exams more probable. Without this pressure much is left to chance and many auditors will not study sufficiently hard to pass the exams.

4. Professional exams cannot replace skills workshops for a number of reasons. Firstly they are based on general concepts and not geared towards any particular audit methodology. Secondly it does not train individual auditors based on their special training needs but simply conveys the basic principles of best audit practice. Lastly an auditor who is well-versed in "question spotting" can pass a variety of exams without really understanding much about the topic in question.

5. Audit management must have a mechanism to enable any elements of best professional practice that is learnt in a classroom and brought back to work, to be considered and

catered for within the audit department. An example may be statistical sampling which may or may not be applied by the CIA, but cannot simply be ignored.

6. The policy on audit textbooks should ensure that they are acquired for the department and not the individual, and sufficient copies are made available to all audit staff. This applies equally to research papers and other relevant material.

The training co-ordinator

Appointing a training co-ordinator is a positive way of promoting various training programmes, particularly where the co-ordinator can undertake some of the actual training. All larger internal audit departments should designate an audit manager as having responsibility for staff training. If this responsibility is extended to cover auditors' career development in line with a suitable programme of individual SWOT analysis then one is well on the way towards quality training. In fact it is a good idea to make one audit manager responsible for implementing all human resource management policies and procedures. Where this manager is able to carry out in-house skills training personally, great progress may be made with audit training. Whatever the adopted format, it is clearly essential that all training is properly co-ordinated, or one might fall into the trap of staff attending a variety of courses with the sole objective of making themselves more marketable so that they might leave the organisation for a better paid job. The other problem is where training has no relevance to the audit work being performed and is not being applied once learnt. The final drawback in not resourcing a training co-ordinator is that this might lead to a low pass rate for professional exams because insufficient support is made available.

Continuing professional education (CPE)

CPE keeps qualified auditors up-to-date on technical and other matters. Some departments find they have employed senior staff who passed examinations years ago but have failed to keep up-to-date. They cannot respond to new ideas from younger auditors in the middle of their study programmes. This rift can lead to inefficiency, frustration and de-motivate staff. It is essential that all auditors attend regular training courses. For qualified staff this may be classified under CPE although many of the skills workshops will be equally relevant. Qualified staff should also have career development.

Directed reading

This is one way of encouraging auditors to research aspects of internal audit. The department should subscribe to all relevant journals and publications. It is possible to assign specific topics to auditors so that each member of the department will research designated audit topics as a contribution to the audit information database (i.e. the audit library). The auditor responsible for (as an example) "systems interrogation" will research any articles or material that impact on this subject. This falls under "training" since it involves the assimilation of new information.

Training through work

Programmed audits enable audit management to ensure auditors are rotated and exposed to a variety of audits and experiences. It is possible to designate smaller audits as "training audits" where they form part of the auditors' personal development programme. This applies to all audits to an extent. For a training audit, additional budgeted hours will be assigned and extra assistance made available. This is the best type of on-the-job training so long as high standards have been adopted, supervision is good and monitoring and feedback is properly used.

The audit review

The audit review process enables audit managers and team leaders to direct the work of junior staff and also provides experience in staff management. The process should form part of the training programme by building in the concept of staff development. As such we are not looking for errors and/or poor performance, but merely providing advice to junior staff on how they might comply with the requirements of auditing standards. This allows a positive interface between audit management and more junior staff and should be seen as such. The review process also provides some training in management techniques primarily based around communication skills where the audit work that has been performed is considered and discussed. A good manager will use the review as an opportunity to provide vital on-the-job training. Whilst being wholly relevant to the task in hand, it should also make reference to best audit practice and the underlying principles. This obviously depends on the presence of "good" audit managers.

Professional affiliations

These can be part of CPE and stimulate group discussions. Membership of professional working groups should be encouraged as another way of keeping up-to-date. Seminars, meetings and presentations all contribute to bringing new thinking into the audit department as long as participants provide feedback once they return to work.

The audit library

As an important source of reference material it should be kept up-to-date and time allowed for its use. It may be policy that all relevant audit material is centrally held in the library thereby allowing unrestricted access. Such a policy will have a major impact on audit efficiency. This contrasts to the situation where each auditor jealously guards a personal store of audit related documents. The CIA ought to keep a tight rein on this.

The audit manual

This sets out the defined methods and procedures required to discharge the audit mission. To feed into the auditor's personal development, this should be assimilated with accompanying skills workshops and training programmes. It is possible to compile a training manual that represents a basic minimum level of expertise required across the department. The manual defines how these skills will be applied. The audit manual has a wider role in addressing human resource policies on audit training and links into individual career development. The manual should cover:

- The type of training that is available.
- The link into career development.
- The link into performance appraisal.
- How the training needs analysis is carried out.
- How the training budget is managed and controlled.
- The rules on sponsorship for particular courses.
- The rules covering official time-off for training.
- How the audit department interfaces with local colleges and other local training organisations.
- A policy on qualifications and whether they are mandatory for specified audit posts.

26.5 The Role of the Institute of Internal Auditors

The Institute of Internal Auditors (IIA) has a major role in training and development:

☐ **Professional examinations**. These ensure the student has covered a defined series of subjects, and has shown competence in relevant examinations. Some pass without understanding the subject while experienced and capable auditors may perform badly in the circumstances of the examinations hall. A factor is the amount of time one is able to devote to professional studies. A cynic might argue that staff who concentrate on their studies as opposed to their audits may succeed if exam results are the principal performance indicators. Others may prioritise their audit work and fail their examinations. Employing qualified audit staff (or trainees) is the only way to promote professionalism.

☐ **Conferences**. The IIA organises seminars and conferences. This provides an avenue for meeting people in the auditing arena and allows open exchange of views.

☐ **Periodicals**. We may subscribe to all relevant periodicals that contribute to the audit database of relevant information. These may include statistical services or other indicators that have a bearing on the organisation's particular industry although it does depend on having a procedure for assimilating this new information into the audit database.

☐ **Research publications**. The IIA publishes specialist research papers that may be used by the CIA to develop audit practice. These range from computer audit material through to marketing surveys and they add to the level of knowledge accumulated over the years by the audit department.

☐ **District societies**. The IIA.UK are organised geographically into District Societies with each member being located in one. They meet regularly and organise events and seminars that may be used in developing the audit function. Keeping up with fellow members in different audit departments can help measure the degree to which they are in line with these trends. Open exchange of views is useful in the search for excellence that forms the cornerstone of the CIA's efforts.

☐ **Committee meetings**. A more pro-active approach is applied where one is actively involved in the various committees that help shape the overall direction of the profession of internal auditing. This not only ensures that one is up to date with current developments but also allows an input into the actual development process itself so that one is not a mere bystander. Time spent at committee must however be controlled since it may mean less time spent on audit work.

☐ **Journals and articles**. Up-to-date and precise articles breathe life into the audit arena and can act as a real-life translation of audit theory. We may keep up with topical debates by reading the latest articles from the IIA journal. It is also possible to build a library covering many specialist areas by using current articles as one very useful source of new material. Technical updates are vitally important to audit management as they may impact on the current audit strategy.

26.6 Action Learning

Action learning is a concept originally developed by Reg Revans. This has a role in training since it is based on the argument that learning is derived from:

$$L = P + Q$$

L: is learning   **P:** is programmed (or rote) learning   **Q:** is questioning insight

Questioning insight provides skill and perception and asks fundamental questions from first principles. People are encouraged to bring new experiences to a situation by transferring skills from other areas. This is relevant to internal audit as clear justification for resourcing an audit function:

FIGURE 26.1 APPLYING KNOWLEDGE 1

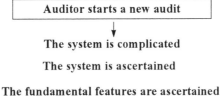

The question arises how auditors form opinions on complicated operations with no expertise. The audit may cover, for example, very high-level technical research and development programmes administered by experienced scientists. If the chief scientist puts this question we can provide a suitable response:

FIGURE 26.2 APPLYING KNOWLEDGE 2

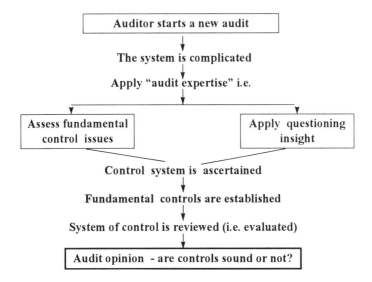

This approach depends on concentrating on the system of control, in terms of audit assessment. Applying questioning insight allows us to question the chief scientist on fundamental controls such as "How do you measure the performance of your staff?" However technical the work, this question can still be applied. It is better to develop the auditor in applying questioning insight than seek to make the auditor an expert in the many operations in a large organisation. The transfer of training skills to real-life work is an issue that can affect overall efficiency and effectiveness of audit.

26.7 Monitoring Training

Training may be funded and implemented but often there is little follow-up and benefits are not secured. Training not assimilated into the audit role has no benefit and management is responsible for monitoring the effects of training. Available monitoring techniques are:

☐ **Examination results with a good pass rate**. This is an interesting indicator in that good results are a sign of a progressive department that is able to produce qualified staff. However this has to be used with care as there are good audit staff who are not able to master the examination system. Having said this, exam passes are prima facie evidence that the people in question have reached a defined standard of technical competence. As such they should make a positive contribution to the audit function. It is important to find out where an auditor has gone wrong where performance in the examinations is poor. It is wrong to simply leave each auditor to struggle through the exams with no support.

☐ **Defined improvements in work performance**. This in one sense is the ultimate goal of most training. If after organising a series of training workshops on report writing, one finds that the general quality of audit reports is still poor then it may be argued that the programme was not a success. Mechanisms for measuring the performance of staff should always be employed and built into the policy on staff training. It should be possible to plot the progress of each auditor's training programme by making a direct reference to performance appraisal reports.

☐ **Better quality of work**. Auditors can generally be very productive and well versed in the audit process. Some of the training should be targeted at the quality of audit work in conjunction with a quality programme that seeks to improve the various work products. We must then define ways that quality can be measured as a way of gauging the success of any such training. Checks on a sample of audits may be commissioned by the CIA as part of this process and if quality standards do not improve in line with the training then questions must be asked.

☐ **Candidates' views on the success or otherwise of the training**. It is surprising how much can be learnt simply by asking the participant to describe a training course that they have recently attended. There is some correlation between enjoyment and internalisation when it comes to courses, since we are more likely to remember events that were enjoyable as opposed to boring. As such any feedback of this nature can act as a general guide to the success or otherwise of a training session and whether it should be used again in the future.

☐ **Informal reviews by general discussion**. The extent to which a person has progressed as a result of attending a particular training course may also be assessed by reviewing what has been learnt. This is best done on an informal basis. Where this policy has been clearly laid out one might expect a greater motivation from staff who know that they might be "tested" on the course contents at a later date. One useful way to promote this technique is to ask the participant to give a short presentation of the main points on returning to the office, for the benefit of the rest of the staff. It is also possible to ask the individual to draft a short note for the audit manual where new material impacts on the existing policies and procedures that are applied in the department.

☐ **Peer reviews that assess the audit service**. If there is a shortage of formal training in an audit department this will be commented on in any external review of the audit function. Accordingly we should expect any training that is carried out to have a positive impact such as to affect the results of any subsequent external review where additional training has been provided. The position on auditor competence with each review will help to establish whether the trend is towards improvements on this front. This in turn will provide an indication of whether training has in fact led to any noticeable improvement so long as these reviews are carried out regularly.

☐ **Weekly reviews on progress on quality matters**. Suitable performance indicators can be used to monitor progress on quality targets. A weekly review of these pointers can help determine whether training is having the desired impact. An increase in training should therefore be accompanied by a corresponding increase in achieving quality targets. This may include meeting audit time budgets, sending out draft reports quickly, restricting the time on non-recoverable work and so on.

☐ **Client feedback on the quality of the audits that have been recently carried out**. Quality assurance procedures require that the client provides feedback on whether audit objectives have been achieved. The information that may be gleaned from a suitable questionnaire sent to auditees which can be used to assess the efficiency and effectiveness of auditors and isolate any particular trends. Any training needs relating to, say, communications skills will be quickly identified via this technique and one may direct training towards this area or discover whether relevant past training has been effective.

☐ **Increase in the overall level of auditors' morale**. This is a more general indicator that is based on the premise that staff who are well trained and developed are more motivated and content than staff who have been ignored in this respect. This need not be overly scientific as one may sense very quickly whether there is constant complaining about the lack of support from management, where this is the case. On the other hand an atmosphere where staff are eager to discuss the latest technical developments does indicate a positive culture and can also be readily identified.

26.8 The Link into Development

Training is part of the managerial process and as such forms only one constituent of the overall system of human resource management. It cannot be seen in isolation from the other techniques for developing audit staff. Training must be set clearly within a formal auditor-development programme that tracks the progress of each auditor throughout their career with the organisation. There are several relevant points that may be made in this respect:

- Each auditor should have a personal development programme that is carefully reviewed and monitored, particularly in terms of training needs.
- The development programme should be linked into a formal performance appraisal system that seeks to set standards and judge whether these are being achieved.
- Audit training must be linked into this programme as one way of closing any skills gaps that will have been identified via the above mechanisms.
- The development programme should also be capable of reviewing the extent to which training has improved the auditors' performance.
- The training co-ordinator, whose role was mentioned earlier should ideally have a wider function in monitoring each auditor's personal development programme.

The "short-stay syndrome" results because organisations view internal audit as an ideal place to train managers. There are many who do not view internal audit as a career in its own right and, for example, trainee accountants may wish to return to main line accountancy after a spell in audit. This poses a problem in that extensive training is lost on audit staff who will not remain with the department for long. All staff should be developed and those who may wish eventually to leave auditing will simply be replaced by other auditors. Vacancies create scope for internal promotions for auditors who excel via their development programmes. The only concern is that short-stay staff should not be placed on professional qualification programmes as these last several years and require a major commitment to a career in internal auditing.

26.9 National Vocational Qualification (NVQ)

An interesting development is the growth in NVQ courses where the student is developed to the requisite level of technical competence through work based training. In the United Kingdom the Lead Body for Accounting has led the way to develop areas where NVQ can be applied. Its role in auditing has been noted by bodies such as the Association of Accounting Technicians, where it applies to the auditing unit of their syllabus. Implications for internal auditing are:

1. Employers are expected to forge links with local colleges to support NVQ programmes.
2. Auditors can achieve accreditation for their work so long as they meet required levels of professional competencies.
3. Audit training will become more "hands-on". This may bridge the gap between the long-serving auditor who has no formal qualifications and the newly qualified but inexperienced newcomer. NVQ recognises past achievements and seeks to assess these within a structured environment where levels of technical competency can be formally obtained.
4. The CIA will be advised to nominate an audit training co-ordinator. This will probably be an audit manager who has special responsibilities for audit training. As such it will no longer be possible to leave audit training as something that is dealt with solely by the universities and colleges. The audit unit has a clear role in building the new two-way relationship with the local colleges.

A good CIA will take the initiative and become involved in current NVQ projects.

26.10 Building on Existing Knowledge

Training is a developing process with no natural start and finish. The auditor should build on existing skills and knowledge to achieve higher levels as they acquire increasing degrees of expertise. This model of audit training can be illustrated diagrammatically:

FIGURE 26.3 BUILDING ON EXISTING SKILLS

```
        ┌─────────────────────────────────────┐
        │     Current levels of performance    │
        └─────────────────────────────────────┘
                         ↓
              existing skills and knowledge
                         ↓
        ┌───────────────────┐        ┌─────────────────────────────┐
   ▼    │  new perspectives  │   ▼    │  some new skills &  knowledge │
        └───────────────────┘        └─────────────────────────────┘

                       Codification
                          ↓
                      Development
                          ↓
        ┌─────────────────────────────────────┐
        │     Improved levels of performance   │
        └─────────────────────────────────────┘
```

The idea is to direct training at skill areas that the auditor is familiar with, and uses in day-to-day work. Training consists of setting a clear perspective within which existing skills and knowledge may be re-appraised by the auditor. An ongoing process of codifying these skills so that they may be better directed at the achievement of audit objectives, is established as a key role for the trainer, while new knowledge may also be imparted. The secret is not to try to teach new skills, but to build on existing skills and develop a sensible framework within which they may be better applied. This recognises how difficult it is to teach new knowledge that has no base to which it may attach itself. It acknowledges the need to link training into real-life experiences. The handbook seeks to set a conceptual framework that will be translated by auditors according to their work environment.

26.11 Conclusions

Training costs money and must be properly managed. This means developing individual auditor-training profiles and linking this to a developmental programme. It must be co-ordinated and carefully monitored and, ideally, integrated into a formal quality assurance programme. Training must not only be funded and applied. It must also be managed and controlled as part of wider human resources management that should underpin resourcing the audit function.

CHAPTER TWENTY-SEVEN

MANAGING CHANGE

27.1 Introduction

Change management is a discipline in itself alongside a growing recognition of the crucial role of clearly defined change strategies. Auditors are likewise primarily involved in the change process, through their concern for seeking improvements in controls. A careful study of the basic principles of change management will certainly pay dividends for the internal auditor, which is why it is included as a separate topic in the handbook. It is clear that managers are beginning to adopt the view that poor performance can be rectified through positive and planned change. The public sector is one area that is going through a major and ongoing change exercise in an attempt to promote efficiency, effectiveness and quality in the delivery of public services. By studying change as a topic, the auditor may be able to promote the use of change techniques by management within a specially devised strategy that allows them to manage and control the change process. In fact there is one view that suggests that the auditor may become the change agent that underpins the fundamental process of change. Within this context audit recommendations may be a key part of management's attempts to engineer change, a point that must be fully recognised if these recommendations are to have any great impact. To place this topic into perspective, note that Scott and Jaffe (*Managing organisational change*; Kogan 1989) have listed the results of studies:

1. Companies expect to cut an average of 15% of their workforce.
2. The hundred biggest mergers in the USA recently affected four and a half million workers.
3. The take-over trend is increasing. It is more than double what it was three years ago.
4. British manufacturing needs to increase productivity to remain competitive with foreign industry.

27.2 The Need for Change

There is a growing trend to the adaptive organic organisation which has the ability to change as competing factors alter and affect it. Key features are:

☐ **The availability of specialist experts who can advise on specific changes**. The ability to recognise the need for specific change programmes and properly cater for this can be spotted by suitably trained personnel. These may be staff employed by the organisation and/or management consultants brought in on contract work. As long as competing organisations are using skills in change management, then other organisations within the same sector will have to keep up with this trend. On the other hand, organisations who have not resourced this function will not be able to control the change process to any great degree. Internal auditors also fall into the category of change consultants by virtue of their work.

☐ **Knowledge and general skills located throughout the organisation**. When experts as noted above are able to advise the organisation on change management, the organisation should ideally build on these ideas to develop and implement the various required change programmes. Where the recruitment/selection process is inadequate this will tend to result in a lack of relevant knowledge and skills. This in turn will militate against effective change management which does depend on a high degree of skills across the organisation. The trend now is to employ trained managers who have undergone say the MBA programme and again this provides one of the planks upon which change management is based. As such, the auditor may view the applied recruitment policies as a major control if this type of development potential is fostered. In contrast a policy of employing unqualified staff with no management training (pre- or post-selection) creates an inward looking organisation that may well stagnate.

The auditor's first control concern must be:

> *"Whether the existing recruitment policy promotes the required skills-base to drive the organisation forward in times of great change."*

☐ **More advisory communication as opposed to direct instructions**. Many organisations increasingly rely on advisory functions such as Personnel, Finance and Legal staff. Internal audit falls wholly into this all-important category. Some organisations employ project managers and in-house management consultants who again are able to furnish top management with ongoing professional advice. Change management does require a strategic approach where one is able to step back from front-line operational matters in a co-ordinated fashion. Even within the operational field there is still an element of advisory communications. An example is the use of quality circles to make recommendations to management that arise from the work area.

☐ **More commitment from employees**. Most agree that successful organisations rely increasingly on a firm commitment from their employees. Recruitment and development mechanisms should be redesigned to promote this feature. In times of financial constraint most employees recognise that their future is tied into their employers' future viability and this "goal congruence" does set the positive mode within which change management should be set. In fact where competition is fierce, which now tends to be the norm, staff may actually insist that major changes are made to meet the challenges. Contrary to popular belief, auditees may actually look forward to positive changes coming out of an audit review to help them establish a position to meet future challenges. It is the wise auditor who recognises that this may become a basic expectation from clients.

☐ **Individual tasks resourced as and when required**. By definition change management requires that things do not remain the same. This then calls for a situation where operational processes are not static with a fixed management perspective that seeks only to contain these operations. New approaches should be developed and explored in a constant search for improvement. This promotes a project-based style where management resources tasks (projects) whenever this fits into the applied strategy. Staff are now more willing to work on this basis in furtherance of organisational objectives.

There are other practical reasons why organisations need to change:

1. Increasing competition means the flexible, ever-changing organisation is now the norm.
2. More participation by employees and therefore increased innovation forms a firm foundation upon which change initiatives may be developed.
3. Pressures on financial resources provides the impetus for slimming-down and restructuring periodically.
4. Problems interfacing different departments may generate a change formula.
5. Greater levels of professionalism provide access to expertise on change management. This may be seen as the "MBA phenomenon" whereby newly qualified staff join organisations with a view to doing things in new and improved ways.
6. Better performance review mechanisms allow management to monitor performance and target resources in a way that is most conducive to the achievement of organisational objectives. This however is dependent on good underlying information systems.
7. The tendency to differentiate activities paves the way for process re-engineering to be applied. The business unit concept encourages a client based approach to work where local managers can make most business decisions without reference to corporate approval mechanisms.
8. Better forecasting techniques again assist the forward-planning process which in turn promotes management action that matches the activities with probable changes in the environment.
9. Technological changes and improved decision support information systems are also relevant to this overall trend.

The drive is towards greater efficiency and performance and the much sought after "competitive edge". It may be argued that the manager must now be an expert in change management regardless of the field they operate within. Furthermore the internal auditor should, as a minimum, understand and support this expertise if he/she is not already a change consultant.

27.3 Implications of Change

The implications of change and the HRM programme

Change will tend to affect three main areas of the organisation:

- **The structure** - With a trend towards changing, flatter organisations with decentralised chains of command and better work flows, along with closer contact with clients and customers.
- **The technology** - Capital equipment and tasks combined. The link between organisational structure and underlying technology is featured in the socio-technological systems school of thought. New technology is quickly brought in if it is thought that there is a service delivery advantage that may be secured, without being seen as a major issue.
- **The people** - Selection, training and reward schemes are being given increasing attention in the search for the right people. Organisations in the past have tried to "fit" systems into people, but are now increasingly buying in people who fit into the

systems. People are now required to change to survive, as jobs are no longer guaranteed.

It is possible to extend this model to cover evaluating major options with a material affect on the organisation. In the past management has considered options via two-dimensional criteria:
1. **Economic feasibility.**
2. **Social acceptability.**

Change management requires management to consider a third dimension:
3. **The human relations implications.** Here each individual (and group of individuals) may be affected in terms of economical, social, personal and political implications. The worker now has an additional role over and above the operational functions, as they must now become a positive, interactive component of the change programme.

Management may react to signs of change by piecemeal modification. Alternatively, it may develop and resource a programme of change in line with a clear human resource management programme over and above mere training. A change agent should be appointed to facilitate this.

The internal audit angle
There are several ways that the internal auditor may apply a knowledge of the change process. They range through degrees of involvement in change as a concept. At the most moderate level, change management may simply involve an understanding of the basic principles to add to the overall body of common knowledge that relates to the work of the internal auditor. At the other extreme, the auditor may actually drive the change process across the organisation by advocating those controls that need to be in place to make things happen. This level of contact with change practices may constitute the highest possible level of internal auditing.

> *A public sector organisation had suffered from poor performance for many years with a reputation for unsatisfactory services in regular press coverage. Internal auditors recommended better recruitment policies, performance indicators, information systems and management development. Packaged in a total quality management initiative it led to major improvements in service delivery.*

The change programme advocated by internal audit became the single most important event in the organisation. This is internal audit at its best, where significant organisational issues are tackled and addressed. This can only evolve from deep understanding of change management with the equation:

> *The internal audit process = The change management process*

Using consultants in strategic development change programmes
- They are outsiders and may be seen as such by staff.
- They will need to build links across the organisation.

- They will have to work to clear terms of reference.
- They must appreciate the barriers to communication and the culture that they must operate in.
- They must form joint working relations with management.
- They help manage projects but not provide main support without which programmes may fail.
- Their activities must be linked directly into the overall strategy.
- They may cut across organisational boundaries including physical, cultural and political ones.
- They may provide the required expertise to enable the changes to be planned and applied.

Consultants may assume a level of power but must be very carefully controlled. The internal audit role in this respect may be to recommend various controls over the way consultants are employed and used. It is a well-known fact that some consulting firms adopt a "hard-sell" approach whereby they entrench themselves into their client organisations in a way that it is hard to get released from. This is one reason why it is sometimes safer to use internal audit consultancy services to support strategic development as an alternative to bringing in too many external professionals.

The role of Personnel
Personnel assume a major role in the drive to change culture. The internal auditor may seek advice from these professionals when considering issues, such as large-scale non-compliance with procedures, that depend on a culture change approach. Personnel staff may be involved in:
- Recruitment and selection policies.
- Organisational restructuring.
- Counselling and redundancy directed at affected staff.
- Social activities that help with team building.
- Redrafting the terms and conditions of employment.
- Employee relations.
- Staff performance appraisals.
- Payment and reward systems.
- Staff based communications systems.
- Training and development programmes.
- Formal induction training.

Computerisation
Much of the impetus for planned change management is derived from experiences when work areas are computerised or existing systems enhanced. Some relevant factors concerning an IT driven strategy are listed:
1. Technical efficiency becomes the overriding objective that is used to drive many related operational activities.
2. Power bases may shift as the control of information systems is defined. In this instance, the old adage "information is power" comes to the fore.
3. Computers may assume a strategic position within the organisation as its profile is raised and top management becomes involved.

4. Systems implementers may assume a central role in the organisation as a result of this shift in power.
5. Political factors come into play in terms of defining who holds what information.

The much neglected "people factor" must be carefully managed as a level of resistance may develop and the project could then run out of control. The simple concept of information efficiency must be viewed in relation to the complicated interaction of power bases, which shift position to take advantage of the control and use of key management information systems. If internal auditors are to act as change agents in this type of scenario then they must recognise and cater for these factors.

27.4 Strategic Development

The role of strategic development
Change strategies have to be resourced to be effective and one approach that was used in the past was to use people who specialise in strategic development. Nowadays there are many different branches of management consultancy that are provided to help improve organisational performance. The internal auditor has a key role in this respect and as we have mentioned many times in the handbook, this role may vary in the degree of direct involvement. We may recommend strategic development or seek to provide much of the necessary services under our consultancy (as opposed to systems) arm of audit services. Whatever the formula, it is a foolhardy CIA who would ignore the organisational ten year development plan when devising an audit strategy. Strategic development may be applied to help structure the required programme of changes and some of the main features of this type of development may be set out as follows:

- Resources are applied to long-range efforts in the knowledge that it has been possible to project into the future.
- The thrust is in solving organisational problems. Here crucial and material issues are considered over and above the day-to-day operational matters that management has to deal with.
- Much research is based on detailed analysis and techniques specially designed to assist.
- Behavioural science concepts may be applied since, by their nature, the resultant changes will tend to have a major impact on the workforce.
- Complicated areas are tackled.
- Questionnaires tend to be used to elicit new information.
- Employee participation is encouraged.
- External consultants may be brought in to assist the process.
- Inter-group cultures are recognised and used to stimulate strategic development.
- The effectiveness of work teams may be examined and improved.
- Top management must fully support the initiative.

One way of applying strategic development is to perform an organisational review at the highest level. This may be carried out by internal audit under the consultancy role that may be part of the services provided to management.

A formal methodology for such a project may appear:

FIGURE 27.1 A METHODOLOGY FOR STRATEGIC DEVELOPMENT

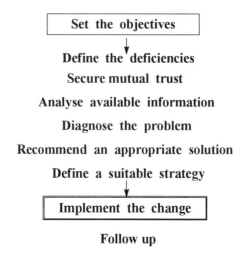

Strategic development appears under many different names and guises. These include Total Quality Management; Business Process Re-engineering; Organisational Development; Corporate Review; Organisational Restructuring and so on. The main point is that these initiatives involve a major review process followed by the implementation of a suitable change programme designed to move the organisation closer to its corporate goals. So long as this holds true then we may treat such events under the generic term "Strategic Development". A book by Colin Carnall entitled *Managing Change* (Routledge 1991) contains a workshop approach to developing and implementing change programmes using specially prepared forms. In this way it is possible to analyse and organise, develop areas for improvement and then implement these improvements. A detailed case study is provided based around a fictional company "Money Matters PLC". Areas addressed are:

- People issues.
- Finance.
- Marketing.
- Operations/services.
- Corporate/business development.

With strengths and weaknesses isolated for future use, the change implementation programme covers:

- Dealing with resistance to change.
- Clarifying effects of change.
- Identifying ownership of change.
- Ensuring that top management support it.
- Creating acceptance of the required changes.
- Building an effective team to implement change.
- Clarifying plans for change.
- Building new systems and practices into the organisation.
- Providing training and support.

- Building commitment to change.
- Providing feedback to those involved.
- Managing the stress induced by change.

Individual management skills are important and these once identified may be subject to a change programme. A sample of 215 firms highlighted ten traps in corporate planning:

1. Top management assumption that it can delegate the planning function to a planner.
2. Top management becomes so engrossed in current problems that it spends insufficient time on long-range planning and the process becomes discredited among other managers and staff.
3. Failure to develop company goals that are suitable as a basis for formulating long-range plans.
4. Failure to obtain the necessary involvement of major line personnel in the planning process.
5. Failure to use the plan as a standard for measuring managerial performance.
6. Failure to create a climate in the company that is congenial and not resistant to planning.
7. Assuming corporate planning is separate from the management process.
8. Injecting so much formality into the system that it lacks flexibility, looseness and simplicity and restrains creativity.
9. Failure of top management to review with departmental and divisional heads the long-range plans they have developed.
10. Top management consistently rejects the formal planning mechanism by making intuitive decisions which conflict with formal plans.

27.5 Change Problems

The individual cost benefit analysis

Some writers argue that when a major change exercise is undertaken, each member of the organisation tends to carry out individual cost benefit analysis to identify gains and losses:

TABLE 27.1 INDIVIDUAL COST BENEFIT ANALYSIS

PERCEIVED GAINS	PERCEIVED LOSSES
more convenience	personal inconvenience
social gains in status	social fears
job satisfaction	less job satisfaction
more security (more skills)	insecurity
economic gains	economic losses
better conditions	longer hours

After weighing up each of these factors the individual will decide whether their support for the changes will be high or low. Remember that the above equation will vary depending on whether the person is part of top management, middle management or front-line staff. It is not unusual for a sense of loss to be experienced as a result of a planned change even where defined benefits will be received. In essence this may be seen as a loss of the security that many people need that is derived from a steady-state environment. The problem is that while security is sought after in times of turbulence, it is these same times that demand great change from an organisation and herein lies the potential conflict. This factor may well dictate the degree to which the employee is involved in, or distanced from, the change decisions. Many senior managers make the mistake of assuming that changes will be temporary and not disruptive. As such they fail to install effective controls at an early stage in the process, in anticipation of these types of problems. Internal audit is ideally placed by being removed from the operational detail, to define the types of control requirements that arise from a programme, as well as pointing out barriers to effective performance.

Resistance to change and other associated problems

Where members of the organisation have adopted a change resistance strategy there will be problems in implementing the changes. Justified resistance to change may derive from:

☐ **Uncertainty as to the effects of the changes through lack of information**. When new things emerge without any warning or information to put them into perspective, there is a natural tendency towards apprehension. The unknown holds fear for many people who do not thrive on uncertainty, but prefer to work in a controlled environment. This is why it is so important to keep management advised about audit findings before a formal draft report is put before them.

☐ **Unwillingness to give up existing benefits that are threatened by the planned changes**. We may seek to alter the balance of power through planned changes and there is a level of resistance that derives from protectionalism in terms of these powers. For example, the auditor may be concerned about the fact that only one IT support specialist has experience of a particular corporate application and an audit report may comment on this as constituting poor control. This is the correct position in terms of the welfare of the organisation, but can lead to great resistance from the IT officer as it removes him from a position of great power.

☐ **Awareness of specific weaknesses/loopholes in the proposed changes**. There are times when operatives know far more about a particular work area than the people who are developing the change programmes. What appears at first sight to be resistance from front line staff, may in practice be concerns about problems inherent in the changes themselves. For example a new computer system that gives a very slow response time may create problems from operational staff that have not been fully appreciated by the project team responsible for implementing the new system.

There are many problems that can arise where there is a high level of resistance to planned changes that may threaten the entire change process if left unattended. The ensuing problems can result from a poorly planned change programme that can lead to many problems:
1. Poor quality of work that impairs productivity, service delivery and performance.
2. Strikes and other forms of overt industrial action.
3. Persistent quarrelling amongst the workforce leading to a volatile atmosphere.
4. Earnest hostility towards management akin to a "work-to-rule" type of environment.
5. Sabotage.

6. Token support with no meaning or depth.
7. Reduction in output affecting productivity levels.
8. Computerphobia where new systems are rejected and manual methods held on to.
9. Requests for transfers out of the affected areas and resignations.
10. Anger from the workforce.
11. Significant increase in the level of absences due to illness and stress.
12. Increase in complaints from both staff and clients.
13. Accident levels increasing.
14. Insufficient leadership resulting in a lack of key decisions.
15. Key tasks not properly defined resulting in insufficient co-ordination.
16. Poor MIS that do not show feedback on progress on planned changes.
17. Inadequate training leading again to performance problems.
18. Competing crises that divert resources to operational problems which means that the change programme then takes a back seat as "real-life" problems are addressed.
19. Unforeseen problems that make the task much more difficult. The fact that it is very hard work may have been overlooked by all those involved.
20. Delays in progress leading to frustration and demotivation. Where this continues there is a tendency for top management to withdraw their support where the programme is not working, and disassociate themselves from a potential disaster.

Stemming from the individual cost benefit analysis, many members of the organisation may be convinced that the planned changes will not work. This can turn into confrontation with a destructive win-lose stance. Confrontation with uncooperative staff is valid but is risky and may result in long-lasting lowering of morale. Management will have to decide whether the potential conflict can be managed through the existing machinery or whether new processes have to be devised. This should be kept under close review as, if the required mechanisms are not put into place, the programme may fail. There is nothing wrong with internal audit providing advice so long as it is conducive to the achievement of organisational objectives. We have stretched our definition of controls to cover arrangements to ensure objectives are achieved. We illustrate the need to manage change:

FIGURE 27.2 EFFICIENCY LEVELS AND CHANGE

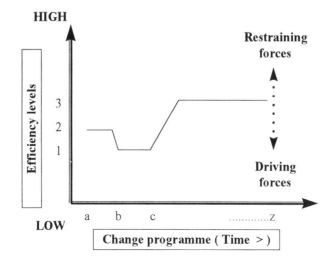

This illustrates how the organisation must be prepared to suffer a temporary drop in efficiency from level 2 to level 1 before level 3 is achieved. This problem will last from period b to c although the longer and deeper this curve, the longer the period and the more of a challenge the change programme will represent. In fact the precise shape of the curve will be determined by the combination of both driving and restraining forces (see below). If change programmes are not carefully devised and managed they will be difficult to implement. Many organisations try to achieve too much over too short a timeframe and this may cause an environment of unmanageable chaos.

> *A large organisation brought in a new top management team. Their first initiatives were to implement a 25% staff downsizing programme and introduce performance appraisal for all staff. Most posts were deleted and the more capable officers applied for redundancy and left to pursue new careers. Staff with no qualifications had no option but to remain. Performance targets set just before the job cuts fell into disuse as turmoil and chaos resulted from the restructuring. The performance appraisal scheme was abandoned and the quality of services declined noticeably.*

The power audit

There is much that occurs within an organisation that is not set out in formal policies and procedures. Herman (1984) used as an illustration, an organisational iceberg where formal overt goals, structures, technologies, policies, procedures and resources are defined. However this represents only the tip of the iceberg where a whole sea of informal covert perceptions, attitudes, feelings, values and group norms may be found below the surface. Any change strategy will have to recognise these hidden parts of the organisational iceberg for it to be effective. Kurt Lewin (1951) has developed the force field as one way of analysing the competing pressures that drive and stop changes occurring. The idea is that the driving forces push for change so that the organisation advances to a better position. The resisting forces on the other hand, maintain an equilibrium by negating the power of these driving forces. Some of these driving forces are:

- New IT and better systems create an almost unlimited scope to spot and develop change routines.
- Better materials can lead to faster and leaner production.
- Competition forces change and is perhaps the single most important driving factor.
- Supervisors' pressures for better performance in line with a suitable strategic direction.

Resisting forces are:

- Group norms for group performance that restrict the push for change.
- A genuine fear of change can add to this resistance.
- Complacency is a real dampener. The "two years to retirement" syndrome is not conducive to any real change as a key manager seeks a containment position until he/she retires.
- Well-learned skills that may become redundant and this may fall on the wrong side of the individual cost benefit equation.

This model may be used to devise a master plan based on a strategy of enhancing the power of the driving forces while at the same time minimising the impact of any resisting forces. A power audit may be used to isolate and so cater for the power bases that are affected by a change situation, particularly where an enhanced corporate computer system is being implemented. There is nothing wrong with the internal auditor performing such an exercise before embarking on the main change programme, as a way of weighing up the practicalities of a particular recommended course of action, before it is reported. The five stages of this power audit are:

1. Analyse the existing political and cultural systems.
2. Assess likely changes in these power bases.
3. Consider the range of possible new operations and each one's effect on the power bases.
4. Assess the political and cultural problems in implementing each option.
5. Develop strategies for making a successful combination of options in terms of their political and cultural acceptability.

This may be seen as an ongoing process whereby particular problems are sensed and appropriate solutions then defined. The force field may be used to work on the driving and resisting forces. Where the power audit isolates attitudes that form resisting forces, a careful process of unfreezing the old and installing the required new attitudes must be actioned. The idea is that the old attitude is unfrozen, changed, then re-frozen as new attitudes. There are critics of the unfreeze/freeze/re-freeze argument who see this as an artificial concept and this point must also be observed. Meanwhile if we accept that old attitudes must be changed, we can set out a number of ways for unfreezing them:

- Show the effects of the existing problems to add an in-built acceptance of the need to change.
- Impress on staff the need for a competitive edge again as a forerunner to pending reforms.
- Gear the changes into a clear strategy that is known about and understood by staff.
- Provide suitable training programmes attaching to the required changes.
- Use staff counselling and ensure the required expertise is included within the change programme.
- Provide clear information on the proposed reforms.
- Define the necessity for all major changes to justify the need to secure improvement.

Controls and change

The auditor will be concerned with the ability of defined controls (including structures, culture, procedures, technology and HRM) to keep pace with the operations they seek to shadow:

FIGURE 27.3 CHANGE AND CONTROLS

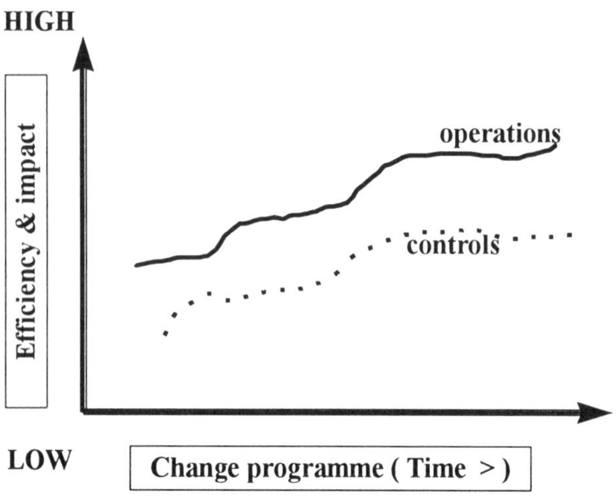

There are two approaches that the auditor may adopt in that it may involve recommending change strategies to underpin agreed recommendations for improvement. Alternatively, the audit work may focus on recommending suitable controls over the change process that is adopted by management. It is possible to address both concerns by promoting change (i.e. better performance) and also advising on controls over these changes.

27.6 The Change Strategy

The change strategy

So far the change process has been built up using models and techniques that have been devised over the years. By spending resources on assessing the likely impact of proposed changes, we may then define an appropriate change strategy. First and foremost we may refer to the required changes and then ensure that the change strategy covers:

- How the structure may be changed; with restructuring, decentralisation and modified work flows.
- How the technology may be changed; redesign work operations in line with good database and networking strategies.
- How both may be changed (i.e. techno-structural change). Here structure and operations are re-designed together.
- How people may be changed; in terms of their skills, attitudes and perceptions. Alternatively, as a final option where all else fails, it may be necessary to change the actual people themselves.

The change strategy may move from a "soft" through to a "hard" approach depending on the degree of change, time available and the level of support secured. Where the anticipated level of resistance is high, one may wish to forgo the usual "selling" techniques. Management may select a rigid, confrontational approach as a short-cut to getting the changes implemented. Starting from the soft end, models have been developed to assess how confrontation moves through levels of severity.

FIGURE 27.4 DEGREES OF CONFRONTATION

1. Education & communication
2. Participation & involvement
3. Facilitation & support
4. Negotiation & agreement
5. Manipulation
6. Explicit & implicit coercion

Management must remember that the selected change strategy sets a precedent for future programmes.

27.7 Implementing Change

Ten problems with strategy implementation are set out by Colin Carnall (1991). This was derived from a sample of 93 firms (the percentage of firms is in brackets):

- Implementation took more time than originally allocated (76%).
- Major problems surfaced during implementation that had not been identified beforehand (74%).
- Co-ordination of implementation activities was not effective enough (66%).
- Competing activities and crises distracted management from implementing the decision (64%).
- Capabilities of employees involved were not sufficient (63%).
- Training and instruction given to lower level employees was inadequate (62%).
- Uncontrollable factors in the external environment had adverse impact on implementation (60%).
- Leadership and direction provided by department managers were not effective (59%).
- Key implementation tasks and activities were not defined in sufficient detail (56%).
- Information systems used to monitor implementation were inadequate (56%).

Carnall has described some of the attributes of a sound project management approach to managing change based around the following main requirements:

1. Establish a management structure to implement change.
2. More extensive planning for the implementation of change.
3. Effective leadership at all levels.
4. Use long-term criteria in change planning and implementation.
5. Use flexible controls.
6. Develop a communications plan.

Successful strategic development
The auditor may encourage management to deal with the people problem by applying some of the change techniques that are available to management. These include the basic tools of successful strategic development that are fundamental to the process of making ideas happen:

FIGURE 27.5 CONVERTING IDEAS INTO ACTION

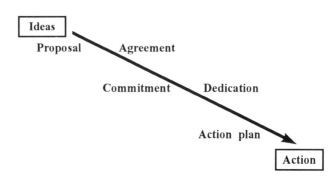

Many techniques have been developed over the years which are now established as a fundamental part of the change process. They are based on the following key policies:

1. **Define the strategic development programme**. A clear start and finish must be agreed since we do not want to embark on a never-ending series of studies that has no direction.

2. **Understand the basic principles of strategic development** and its link into change management.

3. **Reconcile quality and productivity**. These two forces are normally in conflict. One solution is to re-interpret quality in line with new perceptions that see this concept as a process rather than an end product. In this way we would seek to install clear procedures that promote productivity and good output and so replace productivity programmes with quality systems.

4. **Promote communications and trust**. Unfortunately strategic development programmes depend heavily on a mutual trust between managers, staff and departments. There is little scope for significant, wide ranging development, if these bridges are not in place. The internal auditor must remember that a proposal that looks good on paper must be translated into action which in turn is founded on people power.

5. **Select a dynamic change agent**. There are important lessons for the internal auditor. Action requires a positive movement directed at a clear objective that stimulates additional action from within the organisation. Many projects fail because the wrong people have been assigned to them and more importantly, the people that count have been left out. There is a crucial debate on the role of internal audit in this respect. If we have developed many key proposals that may move the organisation towards its goals, then is it right to simply step back, under the cover of audit independence and have no further role? Or should we become the all-important "change agents" that underpin big developments?

Unfortunately, the only correct answer is "it depends...". It depends on the audit charter, the consultancy role, the needs of the organisation and whether new resources can be seconded into audit to protect our audit plans. If, in the event, we cannot provide this change agent role, then we must ensure that it is secured and applied from other sources within the organisation.

6. **Ensure changes are consistent with power bases and culture**. Internal auditors are used to sending their reports out for consultation and using this process to secure feedback on what may be a detailed and long document. What should happen is that those individuals who are most affected by the work along with those who are best placed to authorise the required changes must be brought into the review process. This involvement should be well before the reporting process and should ideally happen at the formation of the terms of reference for the work. The reality of organisational life is:

> *"The organisation will get what the people in power want it to get."*

7. **All things are possible under the consultancy role of internal audit** so long as this does not interfere with the planned systems reviews that should run side-by-side with consultancy services. Strategic development projects must start by seeking out and understanding the power structure and finding out where its members stand. Note that a well researched strategic document that sits on a shelf gathering dust will have little impact on changing the direction of a major organisation.

8. **Make sure that the strategic development programme is goal related**. One must ensure activities that result from the review are derived from goals defined through the development process. Visualise a newly founded performance appraisal scheme that seeks to promote discussion between managers and their staff. There is little point setting performance measures on the basis of stimulating this discussion, if these measures are not directly keyed into clear organisational objectives. Some development programmes that are prepared by external consultants fall into the trap whereby they operate to goals that are vague and not supported by top management. They may aim at increasing worker satisfaction without relating this concept to more relevant concerns such as efficiency or service delivery. Herein lies the need to retain a balanced view and ensure that the programme does not drift into an artificial view of organisational intentions.

9. **Ensure that strategic development grows from real needs** and that it is seen as wholly relevant. There is no point practising new techniques as an end in themselves. There is also nothing that can be gained by copying other organisations who have introduced new concepts when this is not relevant to the working conditions under review. These fabrications will not add credence to the programme. Strategic development must bring about changes that have a real purpose and create firm advances for the organisation. One useful test of reasonableness, is whether the recommendations from the reports that appear as progress takes place, are workable, reasonable and add value to the organisation. Where the authors walk away from the situation and have nothing more to do with progressing the development, there is a temptation to produce material that does not really contribute to the future welfare of the organisation. This situation should be avoided at all costs. Note that the above is equally applicable to internal audit reports.

10. **Use behavioural scientists as consultants**. The flavour of modern strategic development brings in the human angle wherever possible. This is in recognition of the "people factor" as the single most important determining force that distinguishes the successful from impoverished organisations. New IT, restructuring, better procedures and state-of-the art machinery are all subsidiary matters that depend on the drive and ambition of the people who operate them. If the necessary expertise is not found within an organisation, it must be acquired either on a temporary or permanent basis.

11. **Apply human resource management procedures**. Linked to the earlier recommendation to use behavioural scientists, it is as well to apply the main principles of good HRM. This is based on clear recruitment, training, development, and motivational techniques to ensure that the staff are geared into the change process.

12. **Get support and involve top management**. We may assess the likely degree of acceptability (via the cost benefit analysis) and therefore the degree of resistance that may be met. Where there will be a high degree of resistance, top management may fail to pursue the required course of action because of the obvious difficulties that will have to be faced. The auditor must seek to understand this viewpoint that makes what should be simple decisions appear to be very complicated.

13. **Secure early successes**. Development programmes seek long-term changes that cater for the changing needs of the organisation as it reacts to external forces. This wide ranging stance takes up all material issues that impact on the products and services now and in the future. Long-range planning must be applauded but can have drawbacks where goals are based too far into the future. Good programmes create this feeling of longevity but also allow for short-term improvements that can be held up in support of the programme. It makes sense to get a few quick results as soon as possible. They may well be the more obvious changes that are agreed by everyone so long as they fit in with the direction of the overall programme. There is no harm in providing some instant benefits to staff as long as one avoids establishing a new negotiation process and/or making it appear akin to manipulation. The use of "staff sweeteners" has to be controlled because of these two factors.

14. **Educate management in strategic development**. The drive and support for major developments can be encouraged by providing a level of training to senior managers. If done properly this may generate further interest which in turn generates more demands for training and so on.

15. **Ensure the programme is managed**. Management is about assigning resources, setting standards, making someone responsible for results and ensuring there is constant pressure for success, applied in a positive way. These principles should be followed when establishing a strategic development programme. The programme should be managed and a dilemma arises for the internal auditor: how far do we take part in this management process? How do we balance the equation:

FIGURE 27.6 AUDIT CONFLICTS

We refer the reader back to the rules of consultancy versus audit services where they are differentiated and applied to the way the internal audit function operates. All things are possible in the consultancy role so long as they do not impair the ability to deliver good audit services.

16. **Make sure that the results are measurable**. An organisational project must be result-oriented and quantifiable. It is possible to perceive the key features of systems development that we are now describing as controls. If this is done then the audit role can be immersed in recommending these project management controls to management, as being wholly applicable to the change programme.

17. **Acknowledge managers' strengths**. It is best practice to build on the abilities of management and ensure that the culture of the organisation is used to maximum effect. Flexible, fast-changing entities can cope with quick change and perceive most things as challenges. Slower, more traditional ones may be encouraged to develop formal, well planned policies that allow for a cautious incremental approach. As internal auditors we must never put forward unrealistic recommendations, which means that we cannot propose new practices that management cannot cope with. Training is not the key to all evils as it is better to assess and apply the existing skills of the management team as part of the strategic development process.

18. **Involve work-group leaders**. Just as we have tried to build on management's strengths, we must also seek to channel enthusiasm wherever it is found. One key organisational component is the work-group and it is from here that much commitment and drive may appear. Getting team leaders involved in the development strategy is one way of releasing these energies and securing firm support for the change programme.

19. **Recognise the scale of existing problems**. Strategic development programmes must have as one goal, the resolution of major problems that affect the welfare of the organisation. There is little point resourcing a review and change programme that does not deal with real concerns that face members of the organisation as this will lower the credibility of the proposed changes. At worst they may be seen (by cynics) as an artificial exercise engineered by external consultants who are driven by the available fee income.

20. **Promote an open leadership style and obtain feedback from participants**. There is no alternative to communication when designing and installing a wide-ranging change programme. Internal auditors who have poor communications skills will be unable to contribute to this process. Our study of change management has shown how important it is to take staff along with the process by involving them at the outset. This is best done by simply talking to them and keeping them up-to-date with all relevant information. Whilst this sounds straightforward enough it does in fact depend on a distinctive management

style that stresses openness and two way communications. Unfortunately the old school of management still persists (and positively flourishes in times of recession) whereby the old adage "management knows best" is firmly applied. These managers are not hard to spot as they walk around with hand on hip stating that "they (i.e. their staff) must learn to do as they are told, and stop moaning every time we (i.e. managers) have to make a decision". Any major change management programme will tend to flounder in this type of environment.

21. **Use consultants if required but also develop internal strategic resources**. Use external consultants as facilitators, working alongside staff to help them assimilate strategic development skills. Consultants who jealously guard their special skills will leave a vacuum when they leave.

> *A consultant assigned to a development project designed a complicated Gantt Chart that no one on the project team understood. He said this would help them keep control of project deadlines. When he left the team abandoned the chart as they were unsure how to use it as they revised their project plan.*

22. **Make sure change is welcomed and be prepared to change yourself**. The short answer to this point is to ensure that internal audit staff who work on these programmes understand the principles of change management and are able to apply them in their everyday work. This may be an argument for a new breed of auditor who adopts a proactive view of the organisation.

23. **Stay in touch with reality by discouraging an "Ivory Tower" attitude** that is out of touch with day-to-day operational problems. There is need to allow freedom to fail in a way that does not impair the entire change process. It may be used as a learning exercise that provides a foundation for further development. It will be necessary to allow sufficient time and effort to ensure that the change programme has a chance of success, that means we must work to realistic expectations and deadlines. Allowing a degree of experimentation is generally advised as is some degree of failure. We should not perceive some failure as a negative influence that engenders frustration all round. Failure is more part of the practical problems in the search for success, and as such is fundamental to the learning process. There is little point in rejecting high-fliers when things are not going well. It is far better to support them and clear up problems quickly so that success may be the next experience.

24. **Gear change strategies into the power structure** as a way of loosening any resistance from top management who should be encouraged to demonstrate a commitment to change that runs across the organisation in a consistent fashion. It is best to secure broad political support that will help drive the initiatives by establishing tight pockets of commitment and building on them. There should be consistency between words and action, which may so engender a degree of mutual trust between management and staff. It may be necessary to balance hard and soft management styles in an appropriate formula. We would hope to encourage support and also deal firmly with unjustified resistance. We would need to ensure that the Chief Executive provides a linchpin for the strategy and stimulates top-level approval at all stages in the development plans. Since top

management must be involved it is as well to create management teams that can be directed at problem areas as identified.

25. **Formally list all interested parties** including trades unions and note their areas of interest. Participation may be stimulated by good all-round communications. The next step is to anticipate problems experienced by these interested parties as a result of the planned changes, and try to get them addressed through the various communication mechanisms.

26. **Apply careful pre-planning and give advance warning**. Group meetings, so long as feedback is encouraged, are a useful forum to deal with change issues. Linking the changes into the people-value systems through suitable rewards and justifications can assist the process. Also make sure that the plans are action-oriented with clear results.

27. **Ensure that there are clear objectives which are fully communicated to those involved**. The recommended changes must be based around stated goals and not matters of personality or personal ambition by providing a no-lose situation where all parties gain to some extent.

28. **Share satisfaction for project success with staff and management**. Turning a "them and us" situation into "our" project requires some skill along with a recognition that it takes involvement from all parties to make changes work.

29. **Provide suitable rewards and incentives** that reflect the level of additional work/pressures that will ensue from implementing the change process. People are certainly motivated by success and the knowledge that they have achieved a difficult task. Likewise personal pride will make them work hard to ensure a new procedure achieves its objectives. This however does not mean we can ignore straightforward rewards as part of the compensation package, such as a promotion and a higher salary.

30. **Establish alternatives so that some level of negotiation may be applied if required**. Teambuilding requires an ability to compromise and understand the needs of each side of the team. Having options to play with provides some scope for flexibility and is a good way of recognising these constraints over the change process. The auditor may require certain changes but should be mature enough to accept that these improvements may be obtained in different ways. There are times where management is best placed to make these decisions having due regard to the "big picture". It may be possible to assess the likely reactions to these alternatives by testing them to an extent.

31. **Mobilise the social groups by giving them a defined role in the change programme**. Vocal people generally feel that they need a role in society and group dynamics. Their behaviour can be unpredictable if not controlled at all, which is why it is a good idea to give these people a defined role. This is not to say that they should be rewarded for disruptive actions while responsible employees are ignored. It is more based on directing special energies towards the end product and using leadership qualities in the process.

32. **Define how the new power will be shared and anticipate shifts in the power base**. This is a technique that should be used at the outset as we judge what position will be

sought by each group. We have to accept that some groups will not survive this process and we will have to remove them before real change can arise. The harsh realities of business life make this a real consideration as we clear the "dead wood".

33. **Provide clear lines of communications** and explain/justify important decisions that have been made by examining relevant issues and determining a suitable response/approach. It is good practice to respond to all concerns and not assume that this is part of a wider conspiracy to stall the project. Any unanswered questions raise many subsidiary questions that could spiral out of control. There is no reason why audit reports should be given to staff in the areas affected by the work as a way of promoting this policy.

34. **Emphasise personal development and challenges along with the need for teamwork**. It is extremely important to get people working to a common goal that is both challenging and rewarding at the same time. Nonetheless it is amazing what people will accept so long as there is a common unity and one is able to share the experience in an enjoyable way.

35. **Link the strategy into the culture of the organisation** so as to give it a better chance of working and monitor the way the strategy is working. It is possible to establish milestones for the change programme and so ensure that there are clear success stories along the way. One way of supporting such an approach is to identify specific action plans where required. There should be moves to apply structured organic development that adapts and flows with the organisation and its environment.

36. **Project teams may be used** to apply available skills to solving new problems as a way of releasing energies of key people. All change programmes have to be resourced and the typical "lets bring in a consultant" solution cannot be relied on to address all problems. Consultants may be better used to help point strategy in the right direction but not as hands-on people. This also applies to the internal auditor, who cannot become too tightly linked into the operations they audit, for obvious reasons. We need also to ensure that both hidden and obvious talents of the workforce are released and directed at the changes.

37. **Resource the change agent at the right level, expertise and personality**. Where we are able to allocate responsibility and accountability for success there is a better chance of encouraging change agents. There is an additional need to monitor performances of staff and define and meet training needs in a co-ordinated manner.

38. **Strategies not supported end up as dusty documents**. A suitable project management methodology may also be applied which is one technique that most auditors would be familiar with.

39. **It may be possible to use SMART objectives** throughout the project management process:
- **S**: Specific about what is to be accomplished.
- **M**: Measurable.
- **A**: Attainable.
- **R**: Results or output orientated.
- **T**: Time limited.

Bottom-up change

McGregor's (1960) theory X assumes employees have little to offer in terms of developing the organisation. Using this model, change is a matter for senior management to define and pass downwards. Theory Y in contrast, promotes bottom-up management where the individual is encouraged to feed into the organisational development process where:

- Management moves away from the classical school and looks to new approaches to managing staff that involve an interactive team building model.
- Theory Y is applied as staff are given a chance to show what they can do in an open and honest manner.
- The Blake and Moulton's (1981) management grid 9.9 manager is promoted who is concerned about both work and their staff.
- The organisation moves towards HRM in contrast to a traditional man-management approach. The whole cycle of human resource management forms a system in its own right and this composite approach gives the "people factor" a higher profile.
- Upwards communication is encouraged in all relevant matters so as to allow front-line employees a feeling of involvement and the chance to make real contributions to the change process.
- Questions from staff are positively encouraged and as far as possible, fully answered. This is particularly relevant to sensitive areas such as staff reductions or downgrading, that affect an individual's actual welfare.
- Constructive criticism is encouraged as part of the communications process. The art of conflict management can be used to get people to put opposing views to good use and so enhance performance.
- Staff are fully involved in the planning process and not just the implementation thereof. Giving people the solution without making them part of the process of arriving at this stage, does not promote teamwork. The involvement should start much earlier and continue throughout the programme.

27.8 Changing culture

The question of changing culture is relevant as an additional means of improving organisational performance. Culture has been described as commonly held and relatively stable beliefs and values that exist within an organisation. It results in many common features such as behaviour, beliefs, symbols, and attitudes. These may be learnt, or acquired partly subconsciously. They are commonly held rather than shared and influence action in that once adopted they are self-reinforcing and we may see heterogeneous sub-cultures in one organisation or department which could have arisen for historical reasons. Culture may have a major effect on the organisation by impacting on the level of motivation, the agreed strategy, goals pursued and types of decisions made by management. Let us not forget that the internal auditor is concerned with systems of internal control. Controls are in place to ensure that system (i.e. organisational) objectives are achieved and this is then translated into performance issues. Culture then affects performance and as such culture change techniques are in fact types of controls that may be applied to enhance the welfare of the organisation. We return once more to the role of the internal auditor in both front-line audit and consultancy work. Here, an appreciation of culture and its implications adds to the overall expertise that the auditor will bring to audit work. Culture provides a defined set of attitudes, values and behaviour and the type of culture will affect the internal and external stakeholders and their perceived needs. It pervades the whole organisation and flows through the structures, systems, technology, tasks and most of all, the people. In this respect it will have a major role in defining the level of performance that is achieved. The ability to change culture into a model that promotes the achievement of organisational objectives may be crucial to the success or otherwise of the organisation. One may have to change:

- People's position in the organisation.
- Beliefs, attitudes and values.
- Behaviour.
- Corporate image.
- Technology.
- Structures.
- Systems.
- And in the extreme, the actual people themselves.

This should be carefully planned and based on a defined culture-change strategy. These conceptual changes may be achieved by the use of the appropriate culture change techniques. These techniques include:

1. **Redundancies**. We sometimes overlook the simple technique of getting rid of staff who perpetuate the type of culture that militates against change. This obviously assumes a confrontational stance and a level of trades union resistance may well ensue.

2. **Reshuffles**. Changing people around is another way of getting things done. This may create new challenges, new ideas and may help differentiate between good performers and those employees who show little or no interest in their work.

3. **Rotation of staff**. As part of a management development programme, staff may be exposed to different parts of the organisation and so help nullify a culture that emphasises artificial departmental barriers.

4. **Management training** is another useful technique in promoting the "new and improved manager".

5. **Participation** can lead to culture change although this does depend on secure and respected top managers who are able to communicate and share values at all levels.

6. **Role models can also help**. Here one promotes and publicises those few individuals who encompass the new culture in the hope that they will set standards that others will want to follow. The concept of popular heroes may be applied to lead staff in a clear direction with a view to securing excellent performance.

7. **Quality circles** have been used to provide an additional drive and release energies of those who know most about the day-to-day operational matters that together make up the real output.

8. **Group discussion** is a less formal version of the quality circle that may stimulate communications.

9. **Targets are all-important**. They can change culture by encouraging a new direction to the workforce that is based on moving from one position to another. If all activities work to clear targets, this may provide a sense of direction and unity amongst employees that otherwise may not exist.

10. **Logos** tend to be evidence of a culture change although they may in part help this process by becoming a form of target. This may be embodied in a new question being asked: "can we live up to our new image?"

11. **Promoting high fliers** is one sure way of getting people used to the concept of performance and its associated rewards. Conversely, promoting poor performers for perhaps long service may well send out the wrong messages across the organisation.

12. **Developing a success orientation** is a positive technique that may be applied. Viewing organisational performance in a competitive way can emphasise the win-lose equation of commercial realism. Again this presupposes a culture where challenge is viewed in a positive way as opposed to a stress inducing threat.

13. **Regular seminars** and conferences all help develop a sense of unity and direction that impacts on culture.

14. **Open communications** have already been described as all-important.

15. **Social events** can assist the team-building and networking process.

16. **Computerisation** and a growing reliance on management information systems also has a role where the new IT literate manager is developed.

17. **Publicity** sets a tone by stating what we have achieved in the hope that this will bring about greater achievements and place activities under a spotlight where one can enjoy being a performer (so long as one is successful).

18. **Training** can never be overlooked.

19. **Project-teaming** builds experience and can be exciting.

20. **Recruitment and selection** may in fact be the most important techniques in that we may be able to buy-in the right types of culture.

Review techniques

There are many powerful techniques available to the consultants/internal auditors that can be used when generating strategic development, including:

- Sensitivity training (for interpersonal skills).
- Team building (to develop a sense of unity).
- Transaction analysis (communication games).
- Process consultation (group dynamics).

Each of these techniques is a separate subject in its own right and may be found in any good management textbook. The key point to note is that they all involve a level of socio/psychological interaction between individuals and as such a specialist should be consulted when considering their use. If this type of project is required by the organisation it may provide an ideal, high profile opportunity for internal audit to show what it can do. Note that this can be a high-risk policy since, once we have promised to deliver important results, the pressures are on to succeed. The counter argument is found embedded throughout the handbook, where internal auditors are encouraged to work on top level projects that are of major concern to the organisation. We have the techniques in performing objective work based on firm evidence, it is only the process for doing this work and capabilities of audit staff that must then be in place for it to succeed. This is a far cry to the low-level probity audits that are the feature of many internal audit functions. Herein lies the need to understand and master the principles of change management as a basis for raising the audit profile.

27.9 Stress and Change

Dealing with stress

Change and stress are intimately linked in that one may well lead to the other particularly where the full impact of the changes has not been fully catered for. This then has a knock-on effect on the change programme and the ensuing performance of the staff involved. Colin Carnall (1991) using the work of Cooper (1981) and Miller and de Vries (1985) has noted that:

- New systems and processes have to be learnt and this takes time.
- New systems do not work perfectly at first but need modifying to improve performance.
- There is then an effect on self esteem which may decline in times of change.

There is a view that performance will decline shortly after the changes are introduced as a result of the above mentioned factors. The process of re-building the self esteem then leads the drive for better performance and this task should be directed by senior management. Carnall goes on to describe a five stage process where the changes are in time fully taken on board:

1. **Denial**, where the need for change is denied.
2. **Defence**, where one starts to face up to reality.
3. **Discarding**, where one now looks to the future.
4. **Adaptation**, where the challenges are met by building performance and overcoming setbacks.
5. **Internalisation**, where new systems are created and new relationships accepted.

It is here that self esteem can then be re-built as a foundation for improved performance by sound communications and understanding. The role of the manager is fundamental to the task of leading change and retaining the underlying sense of direction.

Scott & Jaffe (1989) see this moving between:

FIGURE 27.7 MOVING FROM DENIAL

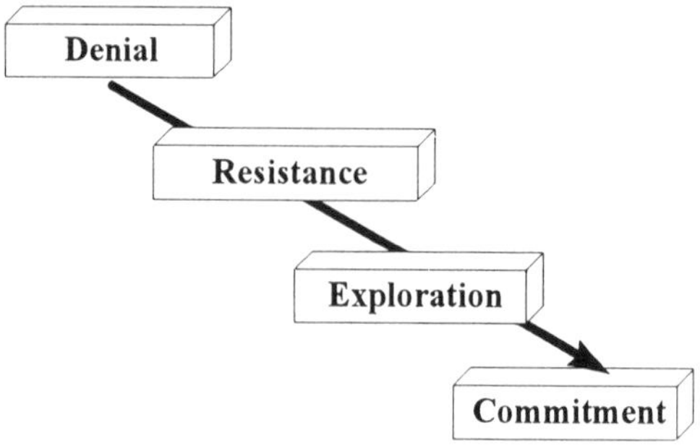

Denial and resistance are the two main stages where stress may well develop and potentially lead to medical complications and it is here that support and reassurance is most required. Certainly we cannot turn to the issue of productivity until these early stages have been overcome and we have moved into the commitment arena.

Consequences

The principles, practices and techniques underlying organisational change should be studied and applied by management. The more resources applied to researching and using these techniques, the better placed the organisation will be to meet competition. The auditor likewise must be prepared to become involved in this process as the audit presence can also contribute to the overall level of managerial stress, as an added pressure on both operational and senior management.

27.10 The Impact on Managing Internal Audit

The entire topic of change management has important implications for managing internal audit and the CIA must ensure that:

1. Change management techniques are applied to the internal audit service to be in the forefront of developments.
2. A formal change strategy is published that auditors may subscribe to. Defining where we are and where we need to be are simple but important concepts that imply that there is a great deal of work to bring about. The best way to understand change is to become involved in the change process as it affects all parts of an organisation.
3. He/she communicates fully with staff the above principles and bring them inside the change programme. This is a two-way process that should generate as much feedback as possible.
4. Audit management implements all the change management devices that have been discussed above with a view to promoting excellence in the audit service.
5. As an associated policy, audit will also seek to recommend to senior executives all the change management devices that have been discussed above. This should be done with a view to supporting excellence in the areas that are being audited.

We will need to assimilate good change management practices into our audit work. As well as providing direct recommendations for improving control, we should also indicate the enabling framework that must be in place to support the required improvements. This enabling framework is based entirely on all those policies and practices that we have earlier discussed as change techniques. There is no reason why internal audit cannot embark on a review of the corporate change management process and consider whether it is adequately managed and controlled. Where suitable supporting practices and procedures are not in place, this fact will feature in the resultant CIA's report to the audit committee. This should be the case even where the chief executive is personally directing the change programme.

PART FOUR

SPECIALIST AUDITING

Introduction to Part Four

Part four of the handbook reflects practical aspects of tackling specialist audit work. We have dealt with the theoretical aspects of performing audit work, including the different approaches in part one. Fundamental techniques were featured in part two and these may be tailored to the different approaches. They provide the ammunition for the auditor as problems are isolated and tackled through the application of appropriate techniques. Part three addresses the role and responsibilities of audit management and draws on management theory. Here we discuss the way different types of audits may be conducted covering:

- Computer auditing.
- Fraud investigations.
- **A formal investigations procedure is found in the accompanying diskette**.

As such we draw on audit theory, audit techniques and the way audit work may be managed, and apply these concepts to the performance of audit work. There are a number of assignments (along with suggested answers) in the accompanying diskettes that are case-study based. These may be attempted as a way of thinking through issues involved.

CHAPTER TWENTY-EIGHT

MANAGING COMPUTER AUDIT

28.1 Introduction to Computer Audit

Advanced computerised systems have major implications for the internal auditor. The audit response must take on board changes in computerisation otherwise audit is left behind. One response is to define an audit role that specialises in reviewing computerised applications as "computer audit" and this is the subject of this chapter. There are differing views of computer audit with many believing that all audit sections should employ specialist computer auditors. Others feel there is no such animal as the computer auditor since tackling computerised applications is part of everyday audit life. Such views meet in the goal to ensure that control objectives are met.

The computerised environment

Automated procedures affect the way audit work is planned and performed. Computerised data is held on magnetic files which cannot be read without accessing the computer. The traditional manual audit trail is no longer available and transactions cannot be read without knowledge of how the system operates. We cannot rely on the tried and trusted control in books and records. The organisation will depend on technical staff who have acquired skills and associated terminology. This may lock out auditors who cannot communicate on the technical level. The end result is that the auditor is not able to provide independent audit cover. The software makes systems work and has major control implications for the accuracy of resultant information and significant impact on questions of operational efficiency and effectiveness. Software is a management tool to ensure objectives are achieved and it is essential that this is properly fulfilled. The auditor cannot assess the software unless there is an understanding of what it does and how it may be controlled. We may seek assistance from the computer department and they may provide input to audit's cover of organisational systems, although where the computer department is a client, some independence may be undermined. Access arrangements will play a crucial role in system controls, particularly for networking systems where the database may be accessed from many remote terminals.

Problems with computerised systems

1. The computer system may reject certain input documents and a failure to investigate the cause and then re-submit the item may lead to a backlog of unprocessed transactions.
2. The system may produce exception reports where rules have been breached and a failure to investigate problems highlighted by these reports may lead to poor control.
3. Inadequate controls over standing data may mean that certain transactions are subject to routine errors until the master files (standing data) are corrected.
4. Inefficient authorisation procedures may mean that transactions are processed as long as they are coded without being cleared by the relevant person. This may introduce erroneous data.
5. A lack of supervisory control may mean that incorrect data enters the system.

6. A lack of visual checks over the reasonableness of the output may lead to unnoticed errors. There is a view that material produced by the computer must be right and no common-sense considerations are required.

7. Unrealistic exception reporting criteria may lead to report blindness where, because most of the output is useless, all of it is ignored.

8. Inadequate segregation of duties may mean that transactions are considered by one person only before being processed.

9. Indigestible reports may lead to managerial inefficiency where the right information is not readily obvious. The whole output may be put to one side in this situation.

10. There may be inadequate restrictions over files in the computer centre library creating security problems.

11. Lack of access controls can be very dangerous with little restriction on enquiry and updating. Slack use of password controls may make systems vulnerable to unauthorised penetration. Unprotected communication lines may lead to vulnerability with files that can be hacked into.

12. While tight control may normally reign over computer operators, they may become very slack during evenings and weekends where little or no supervision may be available. This may allow breach of procedure or abuse of facilities where private work may be carried out.

13. Lack of control over programme changes may mean no supervision, with no clear documentation on the current programmes. Note that most software is now bought from software suppliers.

14. With no review of the extent of computer facility use, the efficiency of equipment cannot be measured.

15. The whole issue of the proliferation of PC-based systems is prone to control problems and if not carefully considered, may result in uncoordinated growth that becomes dysfunctional.

16. Where systems are inadequately tested, this may lead to weakness or complete failure in the future.

17. Where standing data is given a low priority, errors may appear.

18. Reconciliation routines may be by-passed where the transaction has to be processed in a hurry. Where most processing is designated as urgent, timely control procedures may become obsolete.

19. Systems may be developed haphazardly and so not meet organisational objectives.

20. Systems may not be enhanced and as a result may become less efficient with the passing of time.

The role of audit in computerised systems is vital to the continuing welfare of the organisation. The high cost of investing in information technology in terms of set up costs and its impact on achieving objectives results in an abundance of control implications. The biggest task may be to control this aspect of the organisation and if audit is kept out of these issues, their role will be relegated to minor matters only.

28.2 Approaches to Computer Auditing

Introduction

This section places the audit objectives into perspective and relates these to the approach to audit work. We can become immersed in the technicalities of automated controls and how these may be tested and lose sight of principal audit objectives. This is where it is important for computer auditors to be auditors at heart since without clear objectives, little constructive work can be performed.

Audit objectives

The audit objectives are set out in IIA standard 300 that deals with the scope of audit work:

310 - Reliability and integrity of information - Internal auditors should review the reliability and integrity of financial and operating information and the means used to identify, measure, classify and report such information.

320 - Compliance with policies, plans, procedures, laws and regulations - Internal auditors should review the systems established to ensure compliance with those policies, plans, procedures, laws and regulations which could have a significant impact on operations and reports, and should determine whether the organisation is in compliance.

330 - Safeguarding assets - Internal auditors should review the means of safeguarding and, as appropriate, verify the existence of such assets.

340 - Economical and efficient use of resources - Internal auditors should appraise the economy and efficiency with which resources are employed.

350 - Accomplishment of established objectives and goals for operations and programmes - Internal auditors should review operations or programmes to ascertain whether results are consistent with established objectives and goals and whether the operations are being carried out as planned.

These objectives must be achieved by any operation whatever the nature of the underlying systems that are used to guide the activities. Information is an important part of the control cycle where management continuously directs and adjusts its activities. Systems for collecting income, disbursements and preparation of financial statements are primarily information based systems. It is possible to list subsidiary objectives that arise in computerised systems:

- The information should be clear, complete, relevant, consistent, sufficient, useful and timely.
- Information should be accurate and based on correct processing of data.
- Information should be secured and distributed according to defined criteria.
- It should be produced economically.
- It should be effective in meeting the objectives that have been established in the first place.
- Someone should be responsible for the information and the above controls.
- There should be a process of continual review and adjustment.

The traditional approach

Auditing around the computer described the traditional approach to auditing computer based systems. This meant adjusting the usual audit approach without applying additional expertise in computerised applications. Another term was the black box approach where the computer was seen as a foreign object to be ignored by the auditor:

1. The auditor does not attempt to acquire any specific expertise in computerised applications.
2. The auditor uses the result of the computerised processes as printouts and accepts their correctness.
3. Where the printouts mainly appear as exception reports, no one complete list of transactions may be available and the audit work is restricted accordingly.
4. The emphasis is based on manual controls and many computerised control processes are ignored.
5. The auditor assumes that as long as the output is correct (or at least the selected sample), the system is working. The reports may be provided by computer staff and not secured independently.
6. The auditor's scope may become limited and major issues such as hacking, data protection, software piracy, IT strategies, network security, and contingency arrangements may be outside the audit.
7. The ability to tackle complicated de-centralised network based systems may be limited and the dis-aggregation of computer facilities down to end-users may be more or less ignored.

Compliance auditing
This approach is an extension of the vouching principle and may follow these steps:

FIGURE 28.1 COMPLIANCE AUDIT APPROACH

Define objectives

Gather basic information

Isolate system

Identify controls

Design audit tests

Test for compliance with control requirements

Evaluate findings

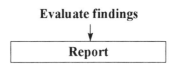

Report

Management information systems
A view of computer audit is that it is the audit cover for management information systems. The reliability of information systems is one of the five items of IIA Standard 300. All operational reviews should consider the role of information systems in operational efficiency and this may be dealt with during the review or as a special exercise. If dealt with separately it may be carried out by the MIS auditors who review all aspects of input, processing and output controls. This moves away from the standard computer audit role and takes on mainline audit work that links into an operational area. Where all auditors

review the MIS routinely, we revert to general audit work with perhaps a computer expert (auditor) as advisor. We may argue there is little point in developing the concept of computer objectives and controls to promote the achievement thereof. The emphasis is now directed towards business objectives, which IT has to support. The key components of the audit approach are:

FIGURE 28.2 ANALYSING THE COMPUTER AUDIT APPROACH

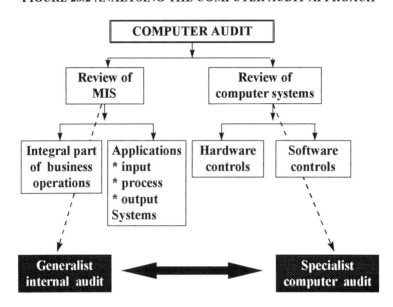

Computerised systems affect the applied audit approach and there are many control features. Systems auditing can be used for any activity and depends on an understanding of the system being reviewed.

28.3 Controlling Information Technology (IT)

The impact of computers
Many features of computerised systems affect the audit approach and the main stages of systems auditing along with the implications are:

☐ **Long-term planning.** New and improved systems must be planned for and the long-term audit plans will allocate resources for any major new systems and systems enhancements. Where existing operations are planned for enhancement, audit cover might be postponed and attention directed at the proposed changes.

☐ **Assignment planning.** The assignment will indicate the type of audit resources that will be required for the project and the scope and approach to the audit. This stage will also consider the type of information systems used and the way they will be tackled.

☐ **Ascertain the system**. Computerised systems may be ascertained in different ways and systems documentation may contain comprehensive diagrams that can be used for the audit.

☐ **Evaluate controls**. Some of the controls may be built into the software to act on the data as it is being processed. It is not possible to consider the adequacy and effectiveness of these controls unless their role and costs are fully understood by the auditor.

☐ **Test controls**. Testing the controls is where a great deal of computer expertise comes into play and the ability to get into systems and check the way they are operating without corrupting the files has to be carefully planned. Expertise is essential at this stage of the audit.

☐ **Evaluate findings**. The implications of the findings have to be considered in the context of automated operations. So for example, weak access controls may make files vulnerable to unauthorised access or changes. Processing controls tend to work on large numbers of routine transactions and this may make a minor control important in the long term.

☐ **Audit report**. The recommendations and report will be geared to the recipient. The level of technical content will vary depending on the reporting objectives.

☐ **Follow-up**. The follow-up routines are also affected and one might carry out a post implementation review where a system is recently installed. Follow-up may consist of a series of testing routines after the main evaluation work has been finalised and reported. Computerised controls may be tested and re-tested periodically and in some cases 100% checks can be carried out using suitable software. It is advisable to encourage management to conduct these tests if the auditor uncovers continuing errors.

The control cycle
Any review of controls should mention the control cycle and this applies equally to information based systems. The control cycle is a fundamental process that has to be followed for controlling an operation. The computer comes into play in two ways. Firstly the information that it generates may be a part of the control cycle by providing feedback on performance. Secondly, computerised operations must likewise be subject to their own control cycles where any necessary adjustment may be made. The basic control cycle might appear:

FIGURE 28.3 APPLICATION CONTROL CYCLE

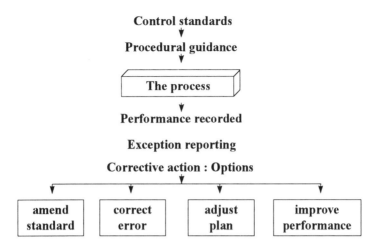

The layering of controls assists the entire control process:

FIGURE 28.4 A CONTROL FRAMEWORK

This suggests that one should avoid errors in the first place and if they do occur, the systems should pick them up and ensure that they are put right. Preventive controls are cost effective and attention should always be directed here. Some argue that another way of categorising computer controls is:

FIGURE 28.5 CATEGORISING COMPUTER CONTROLS

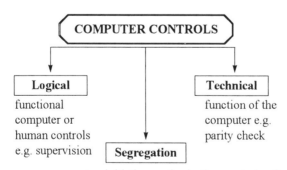

The rule with computerisation is that, due to the many users, overall control will tend to rise to higher managerial levels throughout the organisation. This is promoted by the use of IT steering groups (ITSG) chaired by the chief executive. The general impact of computers on controls does then affect internal audit. This is because auditors are nothing if not experts on control and they need to be aware of both the available controls and how they might be applied in practice.

28.4 Staffing and Planning Computer Audit

Introduction
We describe how the auditor might approach the audit of computerised applications and tackle the growing impact of automated operations. The acquisition of relevant computer expertise is a major issue facing audit management since little progress will be made without the required specialist skills and knowledge. The problems are not simply related to employing computer auditors but more about finding, developing and retaining the specialist expertise.

Computer audit skills
Computer audit work covers a wide remit and may include:
- Personal computers.
- Computer bureaux.
- Live applications.
- Computer assisted audit techniques.
- Information technology generally.
- Complicated high-tech issues such as integrated communications solutions.
- Acquisition of computer facilities.
- Computer fraud and abuse.
- Operating systems.
- UNIX platforms.
- Corporate IT security.
- Data protection.
- Systems under development.
- Software piracy and viruses.
- Database management.
- Networking systems.
- Supporting audit IT developments.

Computer audit expertise may be seen to operate on a number of levels as advanced, intermediate and primary skills each moving to a more sophisticated level. One available model supports a "guru type" individual who oversees the development of audit expertise. Necessary skills should be defined by the CIA and made available to support the audit role.

Establishing computer audit
The starting place is to translate the skills base into the organisational structure of the audit department since this will help define the relationship. There are a number of options:
1. Use a consortium to provide the necessary skills.
2. Use a small number of computer auditors (perhaps one computer expert) to assist the other auditors as they tackle computerised systems.

3. Train general auditors in computer audit techniques.
4. Rotate auditors between groups with one group specialising in computerised systems.
5. Use consultants either to perform certain computer audit projects or to assist the general auditors.
6. View computer audit as the audit of MIS and apply a wider base to computer audit projects covering managerial controls as well as computerised ones.

Selecting an appropriate option from the above will ensure that this aspect of audit work is properly covered. If this issue is ignored the resulting credibility gap may lead to competitive disadvantage.

Securing computer audit expertise

Setting out a policy and structure is still not enough to deliver the required audit product. There are additional points to be considered:

- Whether to have a separate computer audit group. This may become elitist and isolated from mainline auditors.
- If a consortium is used an appropriate arrangement must be defined and agreed.
- The expectations of the organisation must be considered and if they rely entirely on external computer consultants then their interests may need protecting by say internal audit. If the in-house computer staff are control oriented then audit may take a less high profile role.
- The status of computer auditors should be considered and if they are generally more powerful than main auditors this could create management problems.
- An experienced computer auditor may be hard to find and we would have to decide whether the individual should have a finance, engineering, audit or computer orientation/qualification.
- When considering the personal attributes of the computer auditor, openness and an ability (and willingness) to communicate would come above pure technical skills.
- The training needs of general auditors are a material issue and generally the more computer experience they have then the less pressure on computer audit.
- Scarcity allowances may be paid to computer auditors and this may bring them a greater salary than other audit staff. This will not necessarily create a problem, unless the computer auditors are not seen to be working at a higher level by their colleagues.
- A suitable policy on secondments may help spread computer expertise across the audit function.
- The level of independence of computer auditors is an issue particularly where they are employed/seconded from computer department staff. The option to use expertise from the computer department has to be carefully managed.
- Computer auditors must also have management skills which again may be in short supply.

Training computer auditors

In addition to buying-in computer audit skills it is necessary to train and develop auditors involved in this aspect of audit work. All auditors should go through a continuous process of acquiring computer audit expertise so that they become computer auditors. Note:

- Avoid isolating the computer audit staff from the rest of the audit department. As one guideline for success one could measure the extent to which computer audit interacts with other auditors. An incompetent computer auditor is generally one who speaks in terms that no other auditor understands and attempts to create an air of mystique around the whole function.

- Encourage auditors to take professional auditing examinations since a computer auditor who does not understand the principles of auditing is a liability.
- Programming courses can be very useful.
- There are computer audit training courses available but these must relate to the day-to-day work being performed or little value will be obtained.
- Computer auditors can train other auditors in computer audit techniques.
- One-off seminars and lectures may bring staff up-to-date with the academic research.
- Computer audit work-groups particularly where they specialise in relevant types of operating systems and networks can impart knowledge across audit departments.
- Directed reading can keep auditors up-to-date with current developments in the fast-changing world of computers. Subscriptions to monthly and weekly computer journals should be established.
- Courses on advanced computer audit techniques can build on existing skills.
- All training must be linked to career development and the costs of this training must always be worth the defined resulting benefits to the audit service.

Well planned training programmes, alongside field experience on relevant projects lead to highly skilled computer auditors although the better individuals are mobile and may leave at short notice.

Managing computer audit resources

Points relevant to managing computer audit resources:

- A cycle of audits may be planned to cover all of the main computerised applications.
- It will be necessary to set up a constructive liaison with the computer department managers.
- The difficulties in recruiting good quality computer auditors have already been mentioned.
- The depth of technical expertise should be defined an appropriately worded job specification.
- The timing of computer audit work has to be planned as systems tend to take turns in securing a high profile as the organisation's strategy alters.
- A budget for computer audit should include high-specification computer facilities along with notebooks, scanners, quality printers and so on, for use by auditors.
- The audit manager must carry out or arrange a technical review of the computer auditor's work. Work must be properly supervised.
- The work that computer audit performs on systems development may become part of the systems of internal control. As such the role should be clearly defined at the outset.
- Computer auditors may spend time supporting the audit function by developing computer assisted audit techniques and the way this is resourced has to be agreed via the audit plan.
- Developing a comprehensive range of control matrices covering automated systems can aid control evaluation and this may well be a computer audit task.
- Computer auditors should be encouraged to become operational auditors and acquire a good understanding of managerial systems of internal control as well as the computer based controls.

- A compliance audit approach may lead to extensive testing being the main thrust of audit work.
- The scope of audit work should follow key control objectives.
- Liaison with computer bureaux or external contractors for computer facilities may have to be arranged. Also liaison with external audit and consultants is an important part of computer audit.

Planning computer audit work

The work of computer audit must be properly planned and managed. Unplanned work is difficult to control. Once the role has been defined and a policy on the interaction with general auditors is in place, formal plans may be published. Some work will be internal and provide a support to the audit function on individual projects, automation and computer assisted audit techniques (CAATs). The way computer equipment is acquired, used and maintained is another issue on which direction must be provided and audit standards play a vital role. It is necessary to set out the audit field before assessing each individual component. A useful way of analysing the audit field is:

FIGURE 28.6 COMPONENTS OF COMPUTER AUDITING

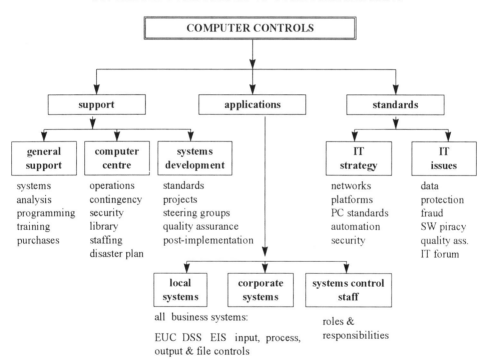

The main issues within an automated environment range from the three main components of computerisation: applications, IT support and IT/IS standards. Risk analysis may be applied so that high profile sensitive areas may be targeted. Computer audit work must be planned and audit management needs to define the audit approach, the type of work carried out, and the areas that will be audited. An appropriate methodology will flow from the professional principles of auditing and the guidance provided to the audit function should be documented in the audit manual. The way computer audit is organised and staffed should be carefully planned since the computer department may set up artificial barriers of obfuscation. If audit mirrors this by setting up a mysterious free-floating group of technical auditors with higher status than the rest of audit, the same dysfunctional factors arise, which may make them a separate uncontrollable function. The trend is now executive information systems and local expertise at operational level which also applies to internal audit as users of corporate information systems. If the computer auditors do not spend most of their time developing internal resources to get auditors inside complicated systems then there may be little scope for delivering a comprehensive and professional audit service.

28.5 Dealing with the PC Environment

Controlling micro-computers is relevant to computer audit since we look for good controls both across the organisation and in the audit department. The audit manual should set out the standards covering the use of computer equipment by auditors. Stand-alone PCs are common although the trend is to use PCs as remote intelligent terminals that link into a networked system. Portables are stand-alone PCs that can also be used to access compatible main-frame systems. PC-based systems users can become responsible for their own systems, and decentralised processing can be quicker and more efficient, with low start-up costs. The explosion in PC-based systems brings the user into the foreground with powerful machines at his/her fingertips at low cost. It is not sufficient to have an IT budget since many control risks have to be addressed before a system is installed and goes live. The auditor recognises these control risks and the available precautions that may be applied to ensure an adequate level of control. This control revolves around a formal IT strategy and associated purchasing procedures.

28.6 The Audit Role in Systems Development

Systems development is probably the most important aspect of any computerisation programme and the success with which an organisation controls new and enhanced systems directly affects the success of resulting systems. The accepted definition of controls covers all those arrangements management establishes to ensure objectives are achieved efficiently. Audit resources directed at the systems development process are well used. The new system has to meet competing needs as does the systems development process. These must be fully taken on board since all of these parties are users and their various expectations should be met. Most new systems are enhancements or replacements where new software releases extend the existing system. Smaller more compact solutions tend to be based around PC-based systems. The computer auditor will look for the systems development life cycle that is an established procedure for managing new systems.

FIGURE 28.7 THE SYSTEMS DEVELOPMENT CYCLE (SDLC)

initial investigation into feasibility ————————▶ systems analysis - user requirements

outline systems design & specification

detailed specification of technical requirements

order & purchase system

testing

implementation planning

user training

conversion & implementation

post-implementation review ————————▶ ongoing maintenance & enhancement

Poor developments

The programming element of the systems development cycle is replaced by purchase decisions where the new system is bought from a supplier. The associated machines may form a separate contract. As such the contracts auditor may have as high a profile as the computer auditor in computer acquisitions. Potential problems with badly managed new systems result from poor controls:

- Substandard systems coming on line.
- Unauthorised changes to the system.
- Systems that are inflexible and difficult to amend as circumstances change.
- Business interruptions and general loss of client confidence may result from system failures.
- A general loss of confidence among management and staff may also result.
- Fraud is another well-known danger.
- Excessive costs may mean that investment in computer facilities overshoots budget and perhaps the whole computerisation programme.
- Laws may be violated by poor systems particularly relating to data protection legislation.

User withdrawal results from poor systems and may set back the whole organisational computer strategy. Users will find it difficult to lead on new systems where the existing ones coming on line are substandard. The computer auditor will promote the use of good project management principles. For the audit role in systems development there are two main approaches:

1. **To review the way that the organisation controls developments generally**. Project management techniques should be applied along with a defined methodology that suits the organisation. We are concerned here with the process itself and the way that it is used. To test compliance, a number of actual past or ongoing developments would be selected and examined in order to test the extent to which the defined systems development process has been applied in practice. This may be an effective way of using scarce audit resources.

2. **The other option is to ensure that audit is present on all major development projects.** We would advise on any control implications relevant to the system under development. The audit role would be as watchdogs picking up on any control loopholes. This can be very useful for major, sensitive systems that are working to tight timetables. Potential control problems could be rectified before it is too late and possible disaster thereby avoided. There is a point of principle that arises here in that it places responsibility for ensuring systems have sound controls at audit's feet. Management is responsible for controls and audit's role is to review and advise on possible control weaknesses. By taking this task away from management it deprives them of an opportunity to acquire a control orientation. In practice urgent short-term problems call for all parties to get involved in seeking solutions and points of principle tend to be placed to one side. However it is only by taking a long-term strategic view that the audit role can be directed to the real welfare of the organisation.

Auditor's involvement in developing systems
When reviewing either the systems development process or individual developments note:
1. The auditor is one of the systems users and can ask for certain requirements such as an audit-based link into the system or a remote testing facility.
2. The auditor must remove the mystique behind computers. Basic project management techniques are applicable to all types of development regardless of the level of technical complexity.
3. Audit may be seen as "wet blankets" who look for problems rather than become caught up in the excitement of "making the system work".
4. An imbedded audit module may be built into the new system and allow unrestricted access to files for audit testing (note that this does cost money).
5. Audit independence should be watched and it should be made clear that SD involvement does not mean that the system now belongs to internal audit.
6. The amount of testing that audit will perform should fit into the systems development plans and audit should be careful not to unreasonably hold up progress.
7. There is some debate as to whether the auditor should "sign off" the system before it goes live. It is not the auditor's system but at the same time the auditor does have a professional obligation to give an opinion where called to, without assuming operational responsibilities.
8. If the auditor acts to check on the work of the project team this may lead to the auditor being perceived as a negative force perhaps as some type of management spy.
9. The auditor should have sufficient training before tackling a complicated development. Newer auditors may rely on the goodwill of computer staff, which depends on the relationship with the computer manager.
10. There is a link between audit and quality assurance and if there is a suitable quality programme for systems development that is arranged by the computer department, this should receive audit attention. If quality assurance works this acts as a major control over the development process.
11. Controls cost money and time and the auditor should appreciate that all systems have a "Rolls Royce" control option and a more realistic one. The organisation cannot operate a zero-risk policy for all operations and a business-like approach must always reign. The criteria should be that controls should be adequate and effective.
12. Auditors need to go through familiarisation before any systems development is reviewed and systems documentation should be obtained and reviewed beforehand.

13. An important role auditors may adopt is to present a series of searching questions to external consultants who may be managing the projects. Consultants work on individual projects within an agreed fee budget and not necessarily for the welfare of the organisation.
14. Audit input into individual projects may uncover weaknesses in the systems development process.

Audit must be involved in the development process, although the nature of this involvement will depend on the audit and the organisation's policies. Whatever the role it should be well defined and publicised.

Recognising the interface issues

We have limited our discussions of systems development to the need to implement a defined technological solution to business problems. The main consideration is the concept of "getting the systems going", where data, IT, terminals, and software are established along with an amount of staff training on the new system. The systems development life cycle revolves around these fixed tasks in a mechanical order. History has recorded the number of important computer projects that have failed, despite some of the principles of good systems development methodologies being firmly applied. The auditor, in this situation has a difficult task. Formal methodologies may be in place and the system has good control features, but the project still falls behind. This could be for a number of reasons:

1. Steering group fails to focus on key issues.
2. Project team does not include the right representatives.
3. No one takes responsibility for the system.
4. Deadlines are set too tightly.
5. The system's supplier (hardware and software) provides a substandard product.
6. Systems interfaces are not addressed.
7. The existing database is unrealisable.
8. The project team fails to take on board quality issues.

The most damaging problem is a failure to interface the information, technology, and operational implications of the new development. A one dimensional view of the system as simply information and supporting technology, will provide an inadequate view of the development. New or enhanced systems consist of three main business components:

FIGURE 28.8 THREE PART SD MODEL

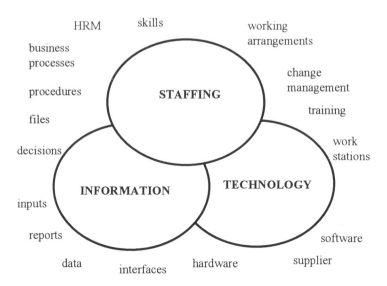

We expect a systems development project to consider within the project terms of reference:

Staffing
1. The way staff are deployed.
2. The skills and aptitude of staff.
3. The way the new system is sold to them.
4. The way new working arrangements are determined.
5. The need to rationalise the operational processes, particularly regarding the flow of information files through the processing procedures. Also the way information is extracted and delivered to enquirers both internal and outside the organisation.

Information
1. The type of standard reports required. The decision support system model requires this feature to be flexible and controlled by the user.
2. The type of data that is already available and its general state.
3. The new data that is required and how it might be captured.
4. The extent to which information will be either automated or held on manual files.

Technology
1. The strains and stresses on the system and the capacity required to deal with this.
2. The type of operating system and actual machine configuration that is required.
3. The number of terminals and whether these should be dumb or PC-based.
4. Benchmarking arrangements for the new machine.
5. The interface between the existing IT architecture, including networks and communications.
6. The skills of in house IT staff and degree of dependency on suppliers.

These three components are inter-linked. The staffing/operational issues determine the information solution which in turn determines the technological requirements. Many systems projects have a main focus on the IT part and make passing reference only to the other two at feasibility stage. The main implementation stage is then driven by the need to get the hardware in place, the data converted and the computer running smoothly, which is component three. The first two are simply fitted into the project if there is time. More importantly the project team may not have the necessary skills to deal with high-level human resource management and business process re-engineering problems. The auditor will need to consider these issues since they impact on the likely success of the system. Our view of controls may have to be expanded to take on board these wider concepts in viewing the systems development life cycle. A large proportion of control is located in the overall managerial arrangements for a business. This also applies to IT projects and as such, any consideration of controls must be applied by the auditor within this context.

Pre-event auditing
Audit involvement in developing systems is termed pre-event auditing:
1. The auditor should ensure that the development process itself is sound.
2. The defined development process should also be seen to be applied in practice.
3. Adequate controls should be built into the new system at development stage.
4. Independence cannot be guarded at all costs and it is worthwhile becoming involved in developing systems.
5. The auditor must be prepared to give professional advice although if this is not based on firm evidence then the opinion must be qualified accordingly.
6. The systems development should be consistent with the organisation's corporate policies.
7. The required control evaluation should be carried out before the contract is signed.

The idea behind pre-event auditing is to minimise the need for subsequent changes and the auditor must be prepared to provide practical advice.

Maintaining the audit objective
The audit role in the organisation is to:
- **ASSURE**: Assure management that systems development (SD) mechanisms work.
- **ALERT**: Alert management where there are problems.
- **ADVISE**: Advise management on how these problems might be resolved.

This is the case whatever the approach to auditing systems under development. We have gone full circle in that the responsibility to establish suitable systems of internal control moved from audit to the computer staff, and is now seen to belong entirely to systems users. Users want good systems and will turn to all the available professional help in this struggle. This must include internal audit and we must meet these expectations in providing the professional support. Attention directed towards quality assurance arrangements over the adopted systems development methodology may be the best way to use audit resources. Work on individual systems becomes part of the way audit tests the adequacy and effectiveness of the adopted corporate project methodology.

28.7 Controlling Applications

All operations use information systems as a fundamental part of their systems of internal controls by providing feedback to operational management. Suitable information systems will ensure accountability, performance measures and information for strategic and operational planning. Operatives, line management, middle management and corporate management have different information needs although the common factor is that they rely on regular, reliable information. Most information systems are computerised and new systems developments are generally geared towards updating systems that have already been computerised. The auditor needs a rounded knowledge of systems of internal control and where controls over the informational aspects of an operation are in part computerised, they cannot be ignored. There are issues that affect both the reliability of control and the auditor's ability to review these controls. The systems development process and the preparations by the computer centre should ensure each new application coming on line has acceptable standards of control and is able to operate successfully. Control problems that relate to computerised in contrast to manual systems:

- Where data is centrally held, this can lead to less supervision over this data.
- Computers may themselves initiate transactions and make the transaction trail difficult to follow.
- Magnetic data may be easily destroyed.
- Many error conditions may lead to a continual repetition of errors.
- Compliance with the Data Protection Act will have to be resourced and checked.
- The definition of responsibility may become blurred between the computer centre and the users.

The audit problems will have to be solved by the application of auditing skills and computer expertise into which falls the definition of the computer auditor.

Specific controls over applications

Specific problems may be:

1. **Input** - May be delayed, unauthorised, inaccurate, lost or duplicated.
2. **Process** - Wrong files may be used, processing may be incorrect, lost files, delays, or inappropriate treatment of transactions may occur.
3. **Output** - May be late, lost, incorrect, unreadable, or sent to the wrong person.
4. **Other** - The system may be inefficient, it may give unlimited access and management may override controls.

These and associated problems give major concerns for the organisation and may result in:

- Incorrect records.
- Misleading accounts.
- Excessive costs.
- Competitive disadvantage.
- Statutory breaches.

These are many stakeholders in any business application and likewise there are parties with defined control responsibilities. The basic principles of control require that control features are owned by someone and the usual position is:

1. **Systems designers** - Responsible for design, procedures and manuals.
2. **Computer centre** - Responsible for inputting, processing and output.

3. **Input source department** - Source documents and input correct, and errors corrected.
4. **Users** - Information is reasonable and can be used.
5. **User control group** - Input properly equates to output and procedures are being complied with.

Each party should be satisfied with the reasonableness of control covering all material aspects of the application. There are a number of important points that should be noted which relate to the principles of controlling computerised applications. Some of these are:

1. Internal audit is entitled to review individual applications even where it had previously had an input into the systems development process.
2. Not every conceivable control that the auditor may think of needs to be in place.
3. Controls should be established at the earliest possible point. A macro control framework will cover the major managerial areas from which the operational aspects of control will flow.
4. Manual controls are just as important as automated ones and together they form the system of internal controls.
5. There is no such thing as an audit control - only management controls. The auditor has a duty to persuade management that certain controls are required and this is achieved by reporting the verified implications of poor controls.
6. Information systems must give a product that is based on information being authorised, accurate, complete, timely, not previously processed, genuine and continuous. As such, the auditor must appreciate that the computer is only a mere tool in this process. The information is the end product.

There are several basic **input controls**:
- User procedures.
- Double keying and verification.
- Authorisation.
- Completeness e.g. batch numbers.
- Batch control.
- Well designed input documents.
- Turnaround documents.
- Validation (display the data after routine).

Note that there is no such thing as 100% accuracy.

Processing controls are set within the underlying software and include:
- Overflow flags that indicate where excess digits have been used.
- Range checks - so that a transaction must be between say £0 and £200.
- Validity checks - say checking that a correct code has been used.
- Format checks - that ensure the item is either alpha or numeric.
- Compatibility checks - consistent field used.
- Exception checks - e.g. overtime only given to certain grades of officers.
- Systems failure controls.
- File identification controls.
- Run to run controls - e.g. total gross pay from the Gross Pay programme should be the input to the Net Pay programme.

- Duplicate input checks.
- Sequence checks on consecutive numbering.
- Check digits.
- Completeness checks e.g. all fields covered and all data is accounted for.
- The whole validation programme.
- Reconciliation of related fields.

Output controls includes:
- Suitable reports.
- Working documents.
- Reference documents.
- Error reports.
- Good security arrangements for reports in line with Data Protection rules.
- Manual procedures to ensure all reports reach their destination.
- VDU access viewing restricted.
- Prioritisation of output.
- Security over valuable stationery.
- Independent check on all output.
- Confidential waste shredded.
- Reports only sent to authorised users.
- Mechanisms to ensure that the output is received in a timely fashion.
- The appropriate media used.
- Appropriate format.
- Well planned error and exception reports.
- User feedback to ensure that reports are no longer sent where they are not used.
- Completeness schedules of expected output.
- Data is quickly re-submitted wherever necessary.
- Exceptions are investigated by a responsible officer.
- All expected output is received.
- An adequate transaction trail should be available so that data may be traced to the originator and through the system.

The computer audit role in applications

There is debate on the precise role of computer audit vis à vis operational/financial systems auditors. An audit plan may include an audit twice, once as a financial system (e.g. payroll) and again as a computerised system (i.e. the payroll application). There is scope for discussion around where each audit role starts and stops:

1. The role of computer audit versus generalist internal audit.
2. There is emphasis of business systems in contrast to computerised systems.
3. There is growing stress on end-user orientations where the information is considered more important than the technology.

The computer auditor may review a system, e.g. creditors, and must be able to bring into play important operational matters such as set out terms of reference for the audit clearly.
- Start with the business objectives.
- Recognise that many controls are operational and interface with automated controls.
- Plan computer auditor's work with this in mind.

FIGURE 28.9 BUSINESS OBJECTIVES AND INFORMATION SYSTEMS

```
                    ┌──────────────────────────┐
                    │    Business objectives    │
                    └──────────────────────────┘
                                  │
                                  ▼
          ┌───────►┌──────────────────────────┐
          │        │    Managers and staff     │
          │        └──────────────────────────┘
          │        ┌──────────────────────────┐
          │        │   Operational procedures  │· · · ►  SERVICES
          │        └──────────────────────────┘
  INPUTS  │        ┌──────────────────────────┐
  · · · ► │        │      Computerised         │ ◄· · ►  FILES
          │        │        systems            │
          │        └──────────────────────────┘
          │                      │
          │                      ▼
          │        ┌──────────────────────────┐
          └────────│      Information          │
                   └──────────────────────────┘
```

The new computer auditor must recognise the link between the business activity and the computerised systems used to facilitate this process of setting and achieving business objectives. The computer auditor will concentrate on the input, process and output aspects of the system (below operational procedures), while the operational auditor will pay more attention to the controls located in the upper section. Both audit approaches must acknowledge each other in a supportive and communicative manner. Application controls have to be tested by the auditor in line with the requirement that all audit findings should be supported by suitable evidence. Auditing around the computer means relying on management to provide all the necessary testing information and schedules and this does not promote audit independence or enhance the audit knowledge of the systems under review. The auditor may incorporate a systems control review file within the software to extract interesting information. In addition, parallel simulation may be used to set up the auditor's own model of the programmes that are being run. Interrogation software may also be used to obtain suitable audit samples for analysis while test data may be used to test the correct functioning of the documented controls. Internal audit may use application audits to establish a level of credibility within the organisation and amongst computer specialists. This process may be illustrated:

FIGURE 28.10 ESTABLISHING APPLICATIONS AUDITING

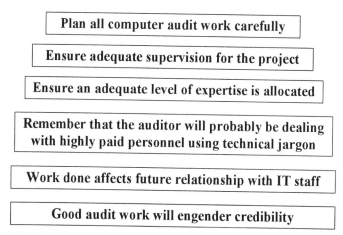

Plan all computer audit work carefully
Ensure adequate supervision for the project
Ensure an adequate level of expertise is allocated
Remember that the auditor will probably be dealing with highly paid personnel using technical jargon
Work done affects future relationship with IT staff
Good audit work will engender credibility

The auditor must earn respect and the computer auditor must bring to the audit function the level of computer expertise that auditors will require to fulfil their audit objectives. However difficult, the auditor is charged with forming an opinion on key control objectives that cover:

- Adequacy of information systems.
- Compliance with laws and procedures.
- Safeguarding assets (including information).
- The efficiency with which resources are used.
- Systems objectives being achieved.

Applying the systems based approach

The systems based approach requires the auditor to go through defined stages before formulating conclusions on the state of control and suitable recommendations:

1. **Plan the audit**. The right staff with the required level of computer skills will be assigned to the audit and the various interrogation techniques will be available.
2. **Define the systems objectives**. The systems objectives and the various control objectives will be defined.
3. **Ascertain the system**. Systems flowcharts and documentation will be reviewed along with manuals. The hardware will also have to be defined.
4. **Identify the key controls**. Controls over the flows from input, processing and output will be ascertained and evaluated.
5. **Evaluate the system of controls**. The auditor should consider the existing controls and determine the level of exposure to risk. The control evaluation will have to be directed at those controls that will achieve systems objectives.
6. **Test the controls and weak areas**. This part of the audit requires planning of which technique to use and how they should be applied. It is essential that the auditor uses testing to meet test objectives, be they compliance or substantive tests. File structures and layouts will have to be identified if interrogation is to be used, while a short-cut may be taken by using the existing utilities software. Test data will have to be carefully constructed and used to check programme controls and the auditor should keep the level of testing under review since this can be time consuming. The computer auditor's skills come to the fore at this stage.
7. **Evaluate the results**. The auditor will look at the quality of management information, sensitive areas, costs of control, management trails, risks, benefits of control, the quality of documentation and the results of testing.
8. **Communicate the results**. A number of parties may be interested in the results of application audits including systems designers, users, user control groups, the computer centre and others. The IT steering group may also wish to consider larger application reviews.
9. **Follow-up**. There may be implications for other related applications and documents that use information from the system. There may also be implications for the systems development procedures particularly where there are major control deficiencies.

Lessons for the audit approach may be learnt and this might affect plans for developing audit expertise, software packages and review techniques. The auditor should ensure audit objectives are met and there are no "no-go areas" where the auditor is locked out of the system. Computer skills will be required so that systems controls may be identified and tested without undue reliance on the computer department. Applications audits follow the same principles as other system audits and have the same audit objectives. The main difference is the nature of information systems that are reviewed and the type of controls that management needs to implement. All auditors should be able to review computerised applications and information systems may be a major component of an operation's system of internal controls. If an MIS approach is adopted the auditor may wish to trace information systems through to the decision makers who rely on the information. The computer auditor is best used advising other auditors on how to develop and apply a suitable level of computer expertise. As such, the chief auditor may decide to assign computer audit time to main operational audits so that input, processing, output, file controls and security issues are addressed and incorporated into the overall audit. The difficulty in interfacing computer based controls with the whole system of controls is more a conceptual matter that will impact on the audit approach. One model calls for the computer auditor's work to be interfaced with general auditor's work and there is a growing support for the development of all round auditors with the requisite skills.

28.8 Controlling the Computer Centre

A principal function of the computer department is to administer the organisation's computer centre where centralised processing is carried out. Processing transactions and providing suitable output on a routine basis may be fundamental to the continuing success of the organisation and a trading account may allow the costs of this activity to be re-charged to users. Charging for computer services creates added pressure on the computer centre for an efficient and effective service and systems of internal control must be designed and implemented by management. The audit role is to review these systems and ensure they promote objectives. The precise role of the computer centre will vary and will reflect the degree of IT centralisation/decentralisation and the extent to which applications are loaded onto the mainframe. Because of the high profile of IT, the computer manager may report to a top-level IT steering group. This is in line with the growing trend to viewing the computing function as an information service. One model of the structure of the computer centre is:

FIGURE 28.11 THE COMPUTER CENTRE

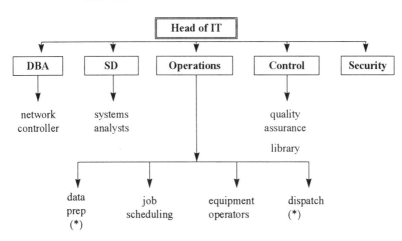

Data preparation and dispatch will be limited in an end-user environment (*). The database administrator and systems development staff may be located outside the computer centre. For audit purposes the computer centre review may also be called an EDP review, or installation review or a review of facilities management. There are at least three different models of the IT function:

FIGURE 28.12 MODELS OF THE IT FUNCTION

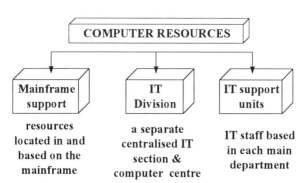

resources located in and based on the mainframe

a separate centralised IT section & computer centre

IT staff based in each main department

The great mainframe debate

Whether the organisation supports a substantial mainframe or not will affect the way the computer centre is managed. There is one model of IT facilities that is based on the organisation being locked into a supplier driven cycle which promotes the use of one mainframe to provide processing power:

FIGURE 28.13 SUPPLIER BOUND CYCLE

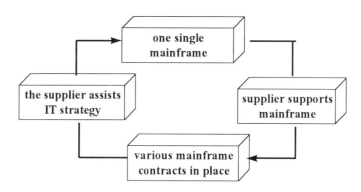

The problem is the continuing dependence on one supplier who provides support and upgrades for the mainframe. Where the supplier has developed a close relationship with the IT manager, which is good business practice, there is a temptation for the organisation to rely on the consultancy, support and other services that will promote the continuing use of their systems. This is an important point for the auditor in that a full downsizing policy may mean that there will not be a computer centre. The emphasis will be on local, department based systems based around corporate networks. As with any other operation, the computer centre management is charged with managing resources entrusted to provide the defined services. There are many points of principle that should not be obscured by the idea that aspects of the computer centre's operations are technically complicated and unauditable.

Controlling the computer centre
Controls have a wide definition and include all arrangements required to achieve objectives. It is not possible to identify a suitable control without first defining the associated control objective. Control features that might be found in a well-run computer centre:

1. Defined budget and related management accounting system.
2. Up-to-date and regularly tested disaster recovery plan with in-built environmental controls linked into the plan.
3. Regular hardware utilisation checks and a resourced maintenance programme.
4. Appropriate output controls.
5. Standards manual.
6. Separation of duties.
7. Resource planning.
8. Good security arrangements.
9. Controls over programmes and programme change.
10. Human resource management policies.
11. Well defined organisational structure.
12. Controls over the operations themselves.
13. Well run media library.
14. Appropriate insurance policies.

It is possible to build further control frameworks and set the main control aspects as follows:

FIGURE 28.14 FRAMEWORK OF CONTROLS

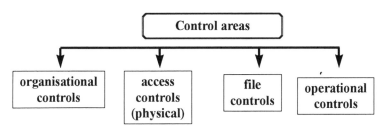

The review of the computer centre is like any other audit review and should follow defined stages:

FIGURE 28.15 REVIEWING THE COMPUTER CENTRE

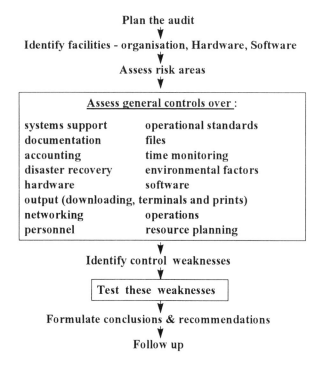

Plan the audit

Identify facilities - organisation, Hardware, Software

Assess risk areas

<u>Assess general controls over :</u>

systems support	operational standards
documentation	files
accounting	time monitoring
disaster recovery	environmental factors
hardware	software
output (downloading, terminals and prints)	
networking	operations
personnel	resource planning

Identify control weaknesses

Test these weaknesses

Formulate conclusions & recommendations

Follow up

It is advisable to break down each key component under general controls above, and treat them as separate reviews rather than an overall audit. Standards should cover:
- File access.
- Supervisory review.
- Downtime.
- Data preparation.
- Stand-by facilities.
- Recruitment vetting and termination procedures.
- Training.
- Budgets.
- Shift working.
- Management reports.
- Personnel evaluation.
- Terminal connection.
- Software documentation.
- Systems development procedures.
- Care and maintenance of files.
- Charging for computer time.

28.9 Disaster planning

The investment in computers should lead to greater efficiencies and that much sought after competitive edge. The organisation's commitment to information technology creates dependence on computer systems. The organisation will have to face the possibility of a disaster hitting the main computer systems and where this involves client-ordering, income, payroll, stock control, payments and other sensitive systems that impact on the profit and loss account, then the effects may be great. This should be subject to a suitable system of internal controls. Some of the effects of a disaster are:

- Effect on the customer in terms of information and orders received.
- Cost of damage to the equipment.
- Direct effect on the profit and loss account.
- Loss of equipment.
- Effect on the investors and the share price.
- Effect on sales, production and purchases.
- Knock-on effects.
- Breach of legislation.
- Damage to the image of the organisation.

Types of disasters
The type of information lost and the length of the interruption will impact on the extent of damage done. Some of the disasters that an organisation might face include:

- Terrorist attacks.
- Sabotage.
- Strike.
- Fire and explosion.
- Natural disaster.
- Systems failures.
- Corrupt database.

Reducing risks
There are techniques that can be used to reduce the level of risk at the computer centre:
1. Good maintenance programmes for equipment.
2. Access restrictions.
3. Remove any fire and flood hazards.
4. Ensure that the computer centre can withstand the impact of an aeroplane crash.
5. Provide a back-up power source that can take over for uninterrupted power.
6. Install humidifiers.
7. Install fire detection devices.
8. Careful positioning of the computer centre.
9. Careful positioning of the rooms.

Disaster planning
The normal disaster planning process is set out below.

FIGURE 28.16 DISASTER PLANNING PROCESS

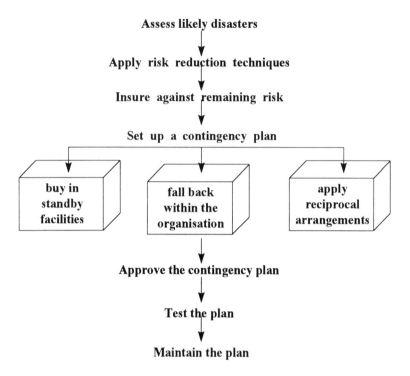

Stand-by facilities

The organisation should ensure that it has a contract for stand-by facilities to take over processing in the event of the computer centre becoming unusable. There may be three main types of contracts:

□ **Cold stand-by centres**. One might either:
- Maintain an in-house computer room into which replacement equipment might be moved.
- Subscribe to an existing stand-by room.
- Subscribe to a portable computer room that would be available at a few days' notice.

□ **Warm stand-by centres**. Here the room would be readily available and be functional within a fairly short time.

□ **Hot stand-by centres**. This facility, being the most expensive method, is set up with copies of the files dedicated to the system in question and may be operational at a moment's notice.

Hot and Warm centres may be provided by a suitable supplier and again the response rate will depend on the degree to which processing is critical to the organisation. The centre itself must be protected from unauthorised access and it is generally advisable to set up security borders:

Level 1 - The computer centre ground would be a restricted area and appropriate measures taken to stop entry including the use of barriers, walls, alarms etc.

Level 2 - Here access to the computer room is restricted by suitable measures including badges, swipe cards, videos and a 24 hour staffed reception area.

Level 3 - This level protects the data files and passwords and read-write controls and library procedures would assist this process.

Whenever a disaster occurs consideration should be paid to contacting each of the relevant parties and one may establish a formal disaster committee that has been well briefed and rehearsed. The resources expended in recovering the information will depend on many factors since the information may be critical, important or merely useful. Relevant factors:

Restoration speed.	Frequency of use.	Relative importance.
Cost of recovery.	Impact of legislation.	Available recovery methods.
Sources of information.		

The standard disaster plan should cover:

FIGURE 28.17 DISASTER PLAN

Introduction
↓
Staffing profiles : skills requirements & contact numbers
↓
Equipment & facilities (normally a contract)
↓
Physical requirements
↓
Operational procedures (emergency scheduling plans)
↓
Software (copies, back up, datafiles)
↓
Transportation arrangements (to the new site)
↓
Suppliers : disks, stationery, power etc.
↓
Other : e.g. DP Act)
↓

> **The action plan : in the event of an emergency**

The disaster co-ordinator

It is necessary to appoint a disaster co-ordinator to devise the plan, test it and oversee arrangements. This requirement should be built into the job description of the computer manager and form part of performance appraisal. The disaster action plan should be tested periodically and participants should meet at least once a year to discuss current arrangements and issues. The plan should be directed primarily at high priority systems that have been identified through a formal process of risk assessment. The computer auditor's role in disaster planning is to:

- Recommend that a plan is in place.
- Independently test this plan.
- Review the contract with the facility's supplier along with any tendering arrangements.
- Review the extent to which the plan is understood by all participants.
- Advise the disaster committee on any security implications that may need to be addressed.

In any emergency, operational expediency tends to take precedence over control matters and short-cuts may be taken by management. The principal control in this situation is the presence of key officers who can be responsible for authorising any required action. This may include the release of large creditor system cheques from a remote stand-by location, or for that matter, hand-written cheques. Another key consideration is the way responsibility is located throughout the organisation. The computer manager should be required to establish a contingency plan. The participants will include those who authorise use of important applications such as payroll, creditors, and income systems. With distributed systems, many applications are controlled by end-users who should be represented on the disaster planning committee. To force decisions on roles and responsibilities, there must be a higher level forum that would drive the plan linked into the executive decision-making mechanism, led by the chief executive. It is good practice for internal audit to present reports to this forum which may be a high-level IT steering group. Another technique is to ensure the audit committee is made aware of anything that may impair the emergency arrangements. In times of financial constraints subsidiary matters such as disaster planning may take a back seat. This does not mean that disasters will not occur and the systems for managing them should be subject to audit cover.

28.10 Data Protection

There is a direct link between data protection and computer controls and so this falls within the computer auditor's work. Since it involves legislation, the question of compliance comes into play and the auditor needs to review arrangements for dealing with the requirements. The Council of Europe held a convention on data protection in 1981 and a number of articles were developed:

- **Article 5**: Data should be obtained legally, be accurate and stored properly.
- **Article 6**: There should be adequate safeguards over sensitive data.
- **Article 7**: Security measures should be taken.
- **Article 8**: Access rights should be devised.
- **Article 9**: There should be certain exemptions for matters of national interest.

These articles have to be adopted by members of the European Union and the response in Great Britain was The Data Protection Act 1984 that covers data held on computers, and highlights the issues that need to be addressed.

DP terminology
The Data Protection (DP) Act uses terms that have precise meaning:
- **Data User** - this is the party who holds the data.
- **Processing** - this includes amending or deleting the data.

- **Personal Data** - this covers data from which a living individual may be identified. It includes an expression of opinion, e.g. X is a bad debt, but not a statement of intent, e.g. we will not be giving credit to X.

The eight principles
The DP Act requires compliance with eight basic principles of data protection:
1. Personal data should be obtained lawfully and fairly.
2. Personal data should be held for a lawful purpose.
3. Personal data should be only disseminated according to the Act.
4. Personal data should be accurate and relevant and not excessive for the purpose held.
5. Personal data should be kept accurate and up-to-date.
6. Personal data should be discarded when no longer required.
7. Data subjects have access to information on them and may have it corrected or erased.
8. Personal data should be kept secure against unauthorised access, alteration, disclosure, accidental loss or destruction. This eighth principle is the only one that applies to data held by a computer bureau and data held for back-up purposes only.

The Act established a DP Register to:
- Promote data protection.
- Publicise the Act.
- Encourage a code of practice on DP.
- Maintain a DP register of data users.
- Maintain a DP office.
- Supervise the users of Bureaux.
- Institute proceedings for an offence under the Act.

The Registrar
The Registrar has to prepare an annual report to both Houses of Parliament. Each data user has to register the following:
- Name and address of data users.
- Name and address of the officer that the data subject should apply to.
- A description of the data.
- The source of the data.
- The purpose held.
- Where the data is disclosed.

Rights of data subjects
- Access to the Register.
- Access to personal data within 40 days.
- To receive compensation for damage suffered due to inaccurate information.

The subject may be asked to pay an access fee set by the organisation and the subject may complain to the Registrar.

Exemptions from access
Personal data may be accessed in certain circumstances:

For national security.	For the national interests.
For tax collection.	Department of Social Security records.

Research statistics with no names. With the sanction of the Home Secretary.
For back-up purposes.   Legal and professional privileges.
Un-incorporated clubs.   For accounting purposes.
For pay and pensions.

Exemption from disclosure
Personal data may be disclosed in certain circumstances:

National security.   With the permission of the data subject.
To computer Bureaux (and internal audit) as part of their work.
To prevent or detect a crime.   Research statistics - no names mentioned.
Payroll and accountancy.   As required by law or by court order.
To prevent damage or injury to a person.

Offences under the Act:
1. Giving false or misleading information.
2. Obstructing a person who has a warrant for entry and inspection.
3. Not complying with an enforcement notice.
4. Not maintaining a current register address.
5. Contravening registration requirements.

The enforcement process goes through degrees of severity:

FIGURE 28.18 DP ENFORCEMENT PROCESS

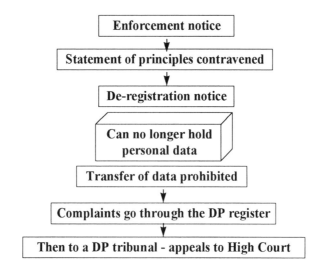

Security measures and the DP role
Adequate security measures should be established to protect personal data from:
- Unauthorised destruction.
- Unauthorised disclosure.
- Unauthorised alteration.
- Actual loss or destruction.

The degree of security measures will take into consideration various factors:
- Nature of the data.
- The degree of harm that could result.
- The place that the data is stored.
- The reliability of staff with access.

The security measures attaching to data protection will depend on the type of role assumed by the DP officer. This can vary between two extremes:

FIGURE 28.19 DP: PROACTIVE VERSUS REACTIVE ROLES

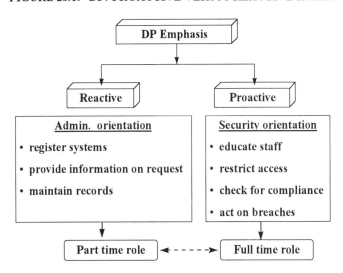

Here the DP officer can adopt either stance where they would simply record DP activities and provide information whenever required. Alternatively the DP officer could assume a more interactive role of implementing the legislation and installing mechanisms whereby the process of DP is properly managed and controlled. The computer auditor should consider the arrangements and review certain aspects of complying with the DP Act and these may include:
- Written procedures for disclosing information.
- Recruitment of DP staff.
- Confirm the registered address.
- Review requests to correct data.
- Review file contents.
- Review the responsible DP officer.
- Review overall DP arrangements.
- Review compliance with the act.
- Review library controls.
- Review access controls.
- Look at amended data.
- Look at back up procedures.

Applying a systems based approach
A systems based approach may be applied to reviewing the DP function:

FIGURE 28.20 SYSTEMS BASED AUDITING AND DP

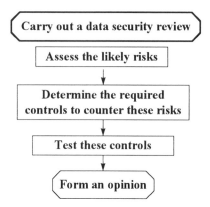

The idea would be to ascertain the existing DP arrangements and determine whether the existing controls are sufficient. Testing would provide evidence of the operation of the controls and one might recommend additional controls or better compliance with existing ones. Data protection is required by law and organisations should ensure compliance. The auditor will review these arrangements and identify security lapses that make sensitive data vulnerable. This has the dual objective of examining the question of compliance with legislation while at the same time protecting valuable information.

28.11 Computer Assisted Audit Techniques (CAATS)

Internal auditors are charged with securing sufficient evidence to support their audit findings and to be of any use, this evidence must be reliable. Auditors need to test automated controls and select and test transactions held on computer files. To extract the necessary evidence and meet these two objectives it is necessary for the auditor to get inside the system (i.e. the computer) and secure all automated data. This occurs during testing routines where controls are being tested either for compliance or for effectiveness. Because of the auditors' special position in the organisation and the need to assume a level of independence, it is inadvisable to rely on management to provide all the required evidence. It should ideally be extracted by the auditor and the fact that it may be held on magnetic media should not affect this. The auditor must then use automated facilities to assist the audit of computerised operations and these are computer assisted audit techniques (CAAT).

Audit interrogation process
The process for applying audit interrogation packages is as follows:

FIGURE 28.21 COMPUTER INTERROGATION PROCESS

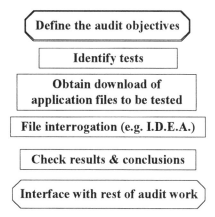

Audit testing

Internal audit should ensure that they have full access to all organisational systems and that this access is available from within their offices. Terminals linked into corporate networks are essential along with the necessary passwords and training. Local print facilities are also required, ideally mainframe printers that can handle A4 and A3 format reports (or screen dumps). Downloading is another facility that should be available where data is sent to audit terminal/PCs in ASCII coma-delimited format for importation into a suitable PC spreadsheet package. Automated data should be subject to audit testing just as other sources of information are. The link between test data and enquiry facilities may be illustrated:

FIGURE 28.22 AUDIT TESTING

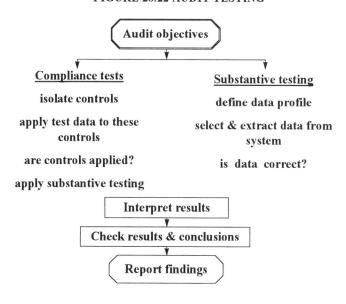

Achieving control objectives

CAATs must be used to achieve a control objective and this tends to be applicable to the various testing routines that the auditor may have designed. We should never construct or acquire a set of sophisticated techniques looking for suitable problems to solve. In selecting the most appropriate technique to use the auditor may consider a number of factors:

- The level of assurance that the auditor requires.
- The level of technical expertise available to the audit department.
- The importance of the system.
- Whether the review is one-off or a continuing matter.
- The set up time and cost.
- The adopted audit approach.
- The level of independence required.
- The time and cost of maintaining the technique.
- The complexity of the audit test.

Interrogation software, as the name suggests, may be used to analyse downloaded data from computer files. This is important when applying walk-through tests, compliance tests and substantive tests. Where a package such as I.D.E.A. is applied the computer auditor may:

1. Select transactions from a file as a download in ASCII coma-delimited or a dB file.
2. Extract exceptions for special attention. We may look for oddities, items outside a defined range, duplications, items missing from a number sequence, irregularities, invalid fields and so on.
3. Analysis of frequencies and patterns with a view to isolating areas of concern.
4. Stratify data.
5. Validate data.
6. Recreate audit trails.
7. Highlight items not conforming to systems rules, not sensible, of audit interest, or duplicated processing.
8. This may be used to confirm that the system is not working, the input is wrong, or that the processing is wrong.

This is useful with high volumes of data, lack of an audit trail, computer generated transactions, lack of printouts, or a paper-less environment. The auditor may question whether management should have access and be using such specially generated information and this may become an audit finding.

Using test data

Test data may be used to re-create the type of transactions that the system will process and so test the correct functioning of systems controls. Points to note:

- Tests processing logic.
- Tests correct operation of controls.
- Tests algorithms in programmes.
- No need to rely on the normal production run.
- Can only test pre-conceived controls that are documented.

There are alternative ways that test data may be applied:

1. **Live processing/live data** - Data that conforms to the test requirements will have to be found by sifting the input data.
2. **Dummy data/live processing** - A higher level of assurance but will need to negate corruption by manual adjustments and journals. Should be discussed with the computer centre beforehand.
3. **Dummy data/dummy processing** - This may cover all features of data. It is run against copies of files and programmes and so does not disrupt processing. The dummy programmes may however become out of date and so need to be maintained.
4. **Test data generator** - Creates large volumes of test data through the utility software.

Computer-generated evidence

Computer-generated evidence may be used in court if certain rules are complied with:

1. **Civil cases:**
   - The information is derived from data supplied to the computer.
   - The computer is working properly and is regularly used for the purpose.
   - Data is regularly provided.
   - The evidence must be legally admissible.
2. **Criminal cases:**
   - No grounds for the computer being inaccurate and any errors in the computer do not affect data.
   - A certificate is required which identifies the data and the computer which is signed by the responsible officer.
   - Complies with relevant law.

Moving from the black box approach

The "Black Box Approach" is typified by the auditor analysing reams of computer printouts. It ignores the existence of the computer and client management is relied on to provide information the auditor requires. In circumstances where audit is operating on a consultancy basis, this can be acceptable. In the normal course of business it is necessary to preserve a level of independence and so adopt a more pro-active line. The auditor must be able to stand back from management and be able to secure the information required. This may either be done through liaison with the computer centre and building special audit facilities into systems at development stage. Alternatively the audit department may develop its own suite of software to extract data and test controls. Computer audit then comes into its own, but if this is not being addressed the audit function will eventually become locked out of the organisation's computerised systems. The computer auditor should spend time working with other auditors on their interrogation needs and how test data will be developed and applied. The chief auditor should ensure that this happens and that audit policies build in this important issue.

28.12 Acquiring Computer Facilities

Computer facilities may be acquired as part of a major main-frame or mini-based systems developments but increasingly may be part of an ad-hoc growth in PC based developments. With the falling costs of computer equipment and accompanying software, smaller stand alone systems are readily available to line managers and a small budget provision for equipment can represent the required authorisation to go out and purchase.

IT acquisitions are governed by the organisation's rules on purchasing. This means that compliance with procedures also has a place in computer audit objectives. The acquisition process has to be understood and reviewed by the computer auditor and this activity also falls within the audit field. We can set out a more realistic model of buying patterns:

FIGURE 28.23 REAL LIFE IT ACQUISITIONS

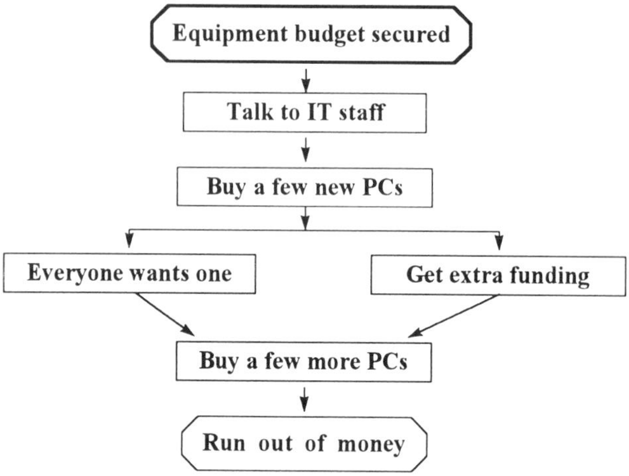

Equipment budget secured
Talk to IT staff
Buy a few new PCs
Everyone wants one
Get extra funding
Buy a few more PCs
Run out of money

Acquisition problems

There are many problems with this approach:

- No clear PC standards are adopted.
- Acquisitions are based around who shouts loudest.
- Everyone has a different idea of what is the best system.
- Each PC arrives with its own pre-packaged software.
- The above promotes an atmosphere of chaos management.

Controlling the acquisition process

In contrast to the above, a suitable well-controlled acquisition process may be shown:

FIGURE 28.24 THE ACQUISITION PROCESS

Computer policy & strategy
Establish the need
Feasibility study
Specify the requirements
Appraise the tenders/market
Installation
Post-installation review

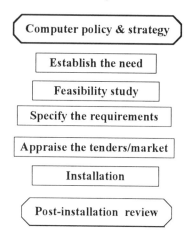

If adopted, this process should always be followed and be built into the IT strategy. The sections that follow cover some of these stages in more detail. Before a purchase decision is possible the case for the acquisition must be proven and the areas to be covered during feasibility include:

- Finance required should be clearly quantified.
- The proposed course of action should be set out.
- Alternative solutions should be detailed.
- A formal feasibility report should be issued.
- The feasibility report should be formally presented for approval.
- The features of the proposed solution should be outlined.
- Business problems should be defined and solutions geared towards them.
- The feasibility should be in stages and start with an initial feasibility outline.
- The study should be based on an information gathering process.
- The feasibility report should contain planning data such as an outline implementation schedule and resource implications.

Specifying requirements

To meet the needs of the proposed solution, a precise specification must be defined and the market tested for the best supplier rather than ad-hoc purchases. The IT world is fiercely competitive and the organisation should take advantage of this in allowing suppliers to compete for the contract:

- The specification should be based on the approved feasibility study.
- Work loads should be defined.
- Capacity requirements (including peak periods) should be fully set out.
- Processing needs should be defined.
- Testing requirements should also be established.
- Delivery schedules and timetables should be set out.
- A full timetable for implementation should be part of the contract.
- The useful life of the equipment is another factor to be evaluated during the tendering process.
- All matters connected with implementation should be built into the contract specification.
- It should be possible to identify all incidental costs so that a fair comparison may be made between competing suppliers.
- The evaluation should include a technical appraisal and a financial appraisal.
- Future changes that might be required should be indicated and systems that can be upgraded on a modular basis may be preferred.
- The conditions of supply should be part of the contract terms.
- One feature of the contract may relate to what can be done with existing hardware since most computer acquisitions replace existing, outmoded computerised systems.

The installation process

The installation process must be properly controlled:

- The whole implementation process should be scheduled and assigned to a responsible officer.
- The delivery of facilities must be carefully planned.
- All the affected areas should be defined at an early stage.

- Staffing matters regarding job descriptions and training should be addressed.
- Maintenance and insurance should be agreed.
- Feedback on user satisfaction should be reviewed regularly as this is a crucial success criterion.
- The implementation should be followed up and a formal report published.
- Health and safety considerations regarding display screen standards should be in place.

Software acquisitions

Software should be supplied to drive each system and this may be the most important part of the acquisition process. Software may be:

1. **Developed in house** - This again will require a separate feasibility study although most organisations have moved away from this approach.
2. **Bought off the shelf** - This is cheaper and will require little testing. However it will be less flexible and may not meet all defined user needs. Modularised systems may in part be fitted together to form a suitable solution.
3. **Tailor made** - This is very expensive and will match user needs exactly. It can be a risky option and will need extensive testing although the final result should meet all user requirements.

Management needs to establish a firm policy on using illegal software firstly because a virus may be transferred and secondly because all copyright rules should be complied with. It may be possible to secure a site license to use software on additional machines. When evaluating software note:

- It should be well specified.
- It should have built-in controls.
- It is best to have menu driven options rather than commands.
- All software should be bought according to a common acquisition methodology.
- Suitable arrangements need to be in place if the supplier goes out of business.
- Testing arrangements should be in place.
- We may secure comments from other users.
- Site licences may provide additional copies.
- The software should be suited to the operational environment.
- It should produce good readable reports.
- Error reports should be made automatically.
- The cost of the software is an important factor.
- We should review the financial stability of the software house.
- Also look for good after-sales support.
- Manuals and good documentation should be provided. (These may be automated.)
- It should be user-friendly.
- An audit trail should be available to trace transactions.
- It should be compatible with the existing printers and screens.
- Back-up copies should be available.
- It should be reliable.
- It should meet user needs and be flexible.
- If the supplier is not working on the next release then the system is in practice obsolete.

The points to look for are:
1. Obscure errors will be investigated and corrected.
2. Any necessary changes can be catered for.
3. Technical enhancement is possible.
4. Changing user requirements are (and will be) met.
5. Operational changes are possible.
6. Control needs are fully met.
7. Increased capacities are possible.
8. Maintenance may be catered for.

As well as considering the extent to which the principles mentioned above have been applied the auditor will look for other basic controls:
- There should be a clear policy and strategy that the acquisition fits (e.g. Windows).
- The criteria for approval should be well defined.
- The system should be able to be operated by existing staff.
- Each department that is affected by the acquisition should be properly co-ordinated.
- The system should have an approved budget.
- The tendering procedure should be clearly defined and adhered to by all parties.
- Each acquisition should be processed within a consistent policy.
- For larger developments a project control team should be set up led by a suitable project manager.
- Each member of the team should have a defined role with accompanying performance indicators.
- Progress on the project should be reviewed regularly.
- Watch out for excessive entertaining by prospective suppliers.

The auditor should look out for the one-person syndrome where the project relies entirely on one officer. One powerful manager should not be able to override agreed procedures. The above material would apply to the smaller one-off acquisitions comprising typically of autonomous stand-alone PC based systems. These smaller applications may be difficult to control particularly where they are driven by a senior manager who wants the system quickly installed and is not concerned about official procedures. IT acquisitions need to be co-ordinated via a clear IT strategy based on overall organisational strategy. A high-level IT steering group is essential to set and maintain corporate IT standards. Audit involvement in this area will be rewarded and we may be the only review facility that is able to consider the position on IT purchases organisation-wide, and determine whether they fall in line with a defined project management standard.

CHAPTER TWENTY-NINE

INVESTIGATING FRAUD

29.1 Background to Fraud

Introduction

This chapter covers the investigation of fraud. It is equally applicable to the investigation of internal breach of procedure and irregularity. Many allegations of fraud turn out to be internal disciplinary matters outside the criminal law and so do not involve the police. Unfortunately, enquiries into internal procedure may uncover major fraud. It is best to adopt the same standards when investigating internal breach of procedure as are applied to formal fraud investigations. Frauds arise when "things go wrong" and this has implications for the system of internal control. Because it is so sensitive, management becomes desperate to investigate and solve alleged frauds. They need as much support as possible and generally turn to internal audit for guidance. The audit function should have extensive knowledge of frauds and how they are investigated, if the service is demanded by management. This chapter summarises the minimum knowledge for the auditor.

Defining fraud:

> *"Any behaviour by which one person intends to gain a dishonest advantage over another."*

The Chartered Institute of Public Finance and Accountancy (CIPFA) has used the following definitions:

> *Fraud* - *"Those intentional distortions of financial statements and other records which are carried out to conceal the misappropriation of assets or otherwise for gain."*
>
> *Irregularities* - *"Intentional distortions of financial statements or other records for whatever purpose."*

Fraud can develop where an innocent error has gone undetected so that the ability to breach a system's security becomes evident. Once a member of staff spots a system weakness, it can be used to perpetrate fraud. This weakness may consist of unclear procedures covering access privileges to a computerised system where there is little distinction between authorised and unauthorised work. Some argue that this equation is important:

> *Motive + Means + Opportunity = Fraud*

Here the person with:

A reason say paying large amounts of alimony
ability in that the technical or other skills are present
and, access possibly with the chance to conceal the fraudulent act

may be prepared to perpetrate fraud against an organisation.

Fraud may be perpetrated internally by employees or externally by third parties. It may consist of a conspiracy between outsiders and an employee as with many contract frauds. Fraud is generally:

☐ **Complicated**. It may be perpetrated by someone with particular expertise in an area. An individual's actions may appear normal to an outsider with no experience. An example is when fuel is transported, it expands and would appear to be of greater volume. The mere act of selling fuel based on its value after transportation may not be viewed as an actual fraud.

☐ **Simple**. Some frauds may be very simple and involve basic adjustments to documents. One fraud was based on the use of Tipp-Ex erasing fluid on a photocopied document that fooled a US bank into parting with £6.7 million, via a transfer to an overseas bank.

☐ **May be one-off or continuous**. A criminal may steal a cheque, forge the amount to make it greater in value and then pay it into a specially opened bank account. The offender will hope to be gone before the loss is discovered. An employee may fabricate petty cash claims of reasonable value over a long period of time such that the aggregate amount becomes material. In the first case, time is an essential factor to catch the culprit. In the second case a painstaking exercise may be required to put together all fraudulent claims so that the clear weight of evidence accumulates throughout the investigation.

☐ **May be carefully planned**. A fraud may be planned over a long period where all loopholes are considered before it is carried out. It may be that in the normal course of events it will not be uncovered and only comes to light when additional checks are made. An outsider will have a great deal of difficulty in uncovering these types of frauds without being tipped-off.

☐ **It may involve regular amounts**. Some frauds are used to top up salaries and involve regular amounts. Misappropriation of stores may fit into this category so that each theft is unnoticed. The main problem is that management information may have been for some time based on deflated figures and so give no clues to any under-declaration. The sums received may then appear to be what is expected and all sides are content. Some see this as a perk of the job. Local traders may prefer to pay refuse collectors cash sums rather than official (and more expensive) accounts raised by the local authority for the removal of trade refuse. The Bank of Credit and Commerce International scandal of the 1990s exposed an organisation that was involved in fraud on a day-to-day basis.

☐ **It may be perpetrated by senior officers**. The scenario of the long serving senior manager who has a dislike for the internal auditor is seen in many departments. Answers that do not make sense may be provided to a junior auditor who feels unable to challenge the manager. The manager may then insist that "getting things done" is more important than complying with official procedures and this argument may be used time and time again. If this employee does perform well then superiors may not delve too deeply into their activities and control breaks down. Senior staff have greater access privileges and may be able to authorise discretionary transactions without challenge. The view that all senior staff are naturally trustworthy is not always correct. Frauds perpetrated by the late Robert Maxwell were based around an organisation where staff felt they could not challenge him.

☐ **It may involve large amounts**. One type of fraud that is high profile relates to Euro-subsidies. The European Commission has disallowed over £1 billion as expenditure improperly incurred.

The four components
Fraud is an act of deceit to gain advantage or property of another with four main components:

1. **Motive**. There should be a motive for the fraud. This may be that the employee is dissatisfied or is in financial difficulties. In the case of non-employees there should be a reason why the fraud is perpetrated. Good human resource management keeps employees satisfied and lowers non-financial motives for engaging in frauds.

2. **Attraction**. The gain or advantage secured must have an attraction for the perpetrator. This varies and may provide a gain for an associated person e.g. a mortgage applicant.

3. **Opportunity**. There must be adequate opportunity. Someone may wish to defraud an organisation and know exactly what is to be gained but with no opportunity, it may never occur. Preventative control should be used to guard against the possibility of fraud by reducing opportunities.

4. **Concealment**. In contrast to theft, fraud has an element of concealment. It can be by false accounting which is a criminal offence. This makes it difficult to uncover and allows the fraud to be repeated.

Types of fraud
There is no legal definition of fraud. The fraud may be carried out by insiders or outsiders and an organisation may carry out fraud by, say, overstating its earnings. Acts associated with fraud are:

☐ **Theft**. This includes obtaining property by deception and false accounting. It is defined as "Dishonestly appropriating property belonging to another with the intention of permanently depriving the other of it". The Theft Act 1968 Section 17 covers false accounting which may be the most common charge of fraud: "Where a person dishonestly with a view to gain for himself or another or with the intent to cause loss to another (a) destroys, defaces, conceals or falsifies any account or any record or document made or required for any accounting purposes; or (b) in furnishing information for any purposes, produces or makes use of any such record or document as aforesaid, which to his knowledge is or may be misleading, false or deceptive in a material way". The Theft Act

1968 Section 22 covers stolen goods and provides that "A person handles stolen goods if (otherwise than in the course of stealing) knowingly or believing them to be stolen he dishonestly receives the goods, or dishonestly undertakes or assists in their retention, removal, disposal or realisation by or for the benefit of another person, or if he arranges to do so".

☐ **Bribery and corruption**. The Prevention of Corruption Acts 1889 to 1916 apply to local government and provide that "any money, gift or consideration paid or received shall be deemed to have been paid or received corruptly as an inducement or reward unless the contrary is proved". The Local Government Act 1972 S.117(2) provides that an officer should not under colour of his office or employment accept any fee or reward whatsoever other than his proper remuneration. The Local Government Act 1972 Section 117(1) states that: "If it comes to the knowledge of any officer employed, whether under this act or any other enactment, by a local authority that a pecuniary interest, whether direct or indirect (not being a contract to which he is himself a party), has been, or is proposed to be, entered into by the authority or any committee thereof, he shall as soon as practicable give notice in writing to the authority of the fact that he is interested therein". The Audit Commission defines corruption as "the offering, giving, soliciting or acceptance of an inducement or reward which may influence the actions taken by the authority."

☐ **Forgery**. "A person is guilty of forgery if he makes a false instrument with the intention that he or another shall use it to induce someone to accept it as genuine and by reason of so accepting it, to do, or not to do some act to his own or some other person's prejudice."

☐ **Conspiracy**. This involves the unlawful agreement by two or more persons to carry out an unlawful common purpose or a lawful common purpose by unlawful means. This would cover collusion to override internal controls.

There are other actions that fall under the generic category of fraud, including:
- Perjury.
- Concealment (of information).
- Fraudulent trading (e.g. unable to pay creditors).
- Conversion (fraudulently endorsing a cheque).

Unauthorised removal and breach of internal procedures may also be investigated but these are seen as internal disciplinary matters with no criminal implications.

Why fraud occurs
Michael Cromer (1985) has provided useful illustrations of the moral state of society:
1. An internal report by fidelity insurance underwriters suggested that the work-force of an average commercial enterprise could be divided as follows:

TABLE 29.1 WHY FRAUD OCCURS

DEGREE OF HONESTY	% PEOPLE
As honest as controls and personal motivation dictates	50%
Totally dishonest wherever possible	25%
Totally honest at all times	25%

2. Polygraph tests on American Banks and retail shop employees showed that 40-70 % had stolen from their employers.

3. In the UK 33% of men have been convicted of an offence.

4. In the UK 12.5% of women have been convicted of an offence.

5. Nine out of ten schoolboys admitted stealing by the time they had left school:
   - 88% had stolen from school.
   - 70% had stolen from a shop.
   - 33% had stolen from a store or barrow.
   - 25% had stolen from a car or lorry.

To test this, ask whether you have ever done anything dishonest such as:
- Paying less than the correct fair on a public transportation system.
- Failing to renew the certificate of vehicle roadworthiness before it expires.
- Claiming expenses based on standard rates that are higher than actual expenditure.
- Overstating one's abilities at a job interview.
- Using the company photocopier for private work.
- Finding money in the street and keeping it.
- Getting undercharged at a shop and keeping the change.
- Rounding up mileage claims.
- Not recording long lunches.
- Selling a car without disclosing its faults.

People are not completely honest all the time. Responsibility for the prevention of fraud should start with senior management and it is essential they see this as important. This will only happen if the risks are fully understood and the value of effective controls is fully appreciated at the highest level in the organisation. Slack attitudes will cascade down through the organisation and adversely influence every member of staff.

Audit Commission research 1994
Research on Protecting the Public Purse in local government and the National Health Service was reported in 1994. For local authorities it was found that:
- Little reported fraud was shown.
- The value of frauds remains low.
- Few council members or employees are involved in fraud.
- There is a fall in the number of proven cases of corruption.

However the Audit Commission warned about complacency since:
- The number and value of fraud are rising.
- In 1993/94 there were 83,000 cases involving some £34m losses.
- The frauds were mainly related to benefits cases.
- There was also an increase in student awards and renovation grant frauds.

For the National Health Service:
- The incidence of detected fraud was low.
- Over the last 3 years some 960 cases were reported.
- Losses came to £6m (out of £80 billion expenditure).
- There are some risk areas.

Frauds were concentrated in several high-risk areas and those reported were not spiralling out of control as is public perception.

Main risk areas
- Debtors.
- Cash.
- Payroll.
- Large capital contracts.
- Revenue contracts.
- Major computer acquisitions.
- Computer access.
- Portable attractive items (say notebook computers).
- Housing benefits and other public sector benefits.
- Government grants and grants to voluntary organisations.
- Expenses.
- Stock.
- Cheques drawn by the organisation.
- Creditors and payments.
- Mortgages.
- Pensions.
- Petty cash.
- Recruitment references: false qualifications, personal references, earnings records and employment histories.
- Overtime and extra employee claims and allowances.
- Confidential information that has a value to third parties.
- Subsidy claims.
- Credit cards.
- Computer memory chips.

Indicators of fraud
Frauds are normally found through luck or third party information while some are discovered during audit reviews, or through controls or by line management. Indicators of fraud are:

1. Strange trends where comparative figures move in an unexplained fashion. For example spending patterns on attractive portable items may suddenly increase over the Christmas season or unexplained drops in income may appear on income returns. It is not unknown for spending against revenue budgets heads to increase towards the end of the financial year.
2. Rewritten and/or amended documents may evidence unauthorised alteration to cover up fraud.
3. Missing documents may signal a fraud where items are sensitive such as unused cheques or order forms. Computers can print out missing items by isolating gaps in sequential numbering.
4. Tipp-Ex (erasing fluid) applied to documents may indicate unauthorised alterations. This can be readily used with photocopies to create distorted file documents. We can normally see the original entries by holding up the reverse side of the original document against the light.

5. Photocopies substituted for originals can be readily tampered with since the photocopy may make it impossible to uncover alterations to the original.

6. Complaints from suppliers that do not tie in with the records should alert one to a potential problem. So if a supplier claims that their payment was not received, although the cheque has been cashed, this may mean that the money has been diverted to the wrong account.

7. Social habits of staff are sometimes used as an example of a fraud indicator particularly where they appear to be living beyond their means. This should be used carefully since it is not uncommon for people to have more than one source of income. Some fraudsters arrive at work very early in the morning or stay late at night when they may alter records unobserved. Others have obsessive jealousy over their work and resent any intrusion.

Many indicators go unnoticed and the problem arises when, after a fraud has been uncovered, there are criticisms that there was obviously something wrong that should have been spotted. There are employees who are alert to these signs and as long as the organisation promotes alert behaviour this becomes an additional control. The only real remedy is effective control.

Defining officer roles
The organisation will have to agree on roles in respect of fraud investigations:

☐ **Management** is directly responsible for ensuring all actual or suspected frauds and irregularities are investigated and resolved. It is achieved by recognising the risks involved and establishing suitable controls. Management is responsible for making sure fraud does not happen.

☐ **Internal audit** is responsible for reviewing the way systems minimise the incidence of waste, inefficiency, poor value for money and fraud. Audit should be informed whenever there is a fraud and will support management in investigations. They are responsible for advising management of any required action to remedy system breakdowns.

☐ **The external auditor** must ensure that management has taken reasonable steps to control fraud, and where this is insufficient it may be referred to in a management letter. The external auditor will ensure that fraud is considered when planning the audit and reviewing internal controls. They will follow up indicators of fraud and report the results to management. The external auditor may advise management on the prevention of fraud. The local government external auditor will:
• Look at minutes and agenda.
• Have discussions.
• Maintain general awareness.
• Monitor compliance with new legislation.
• Review applicability of relevant national issues.
• Review compliance with statutory requirements for the accounts.

☐ **Internal control teams.** Management may set up internal control teams to assist in promoting compliance with procedures. These teams do not relieve it of its responsibilities, since management must still be prepared to make executive decisions, even where based on recommendations made by internal auditors. The teams may be used to investigate frauds and irregularities and should have a level of independence so that they may work objectively. They may be applied to investigating minor frauds. Managers are responsible for resolving frauds and resource this through the control team.

☐ **Personnel**. Personnel may be seen as an independent function that may be used to formally communicate between the alleged perpetrator/s and management and ensure that personnel polices are being adhered to. This is relevant where management is investigating and taking action against the parties involved. Personnel have a dual role of advising management on their actions and ensuring that the rights of the employee are protected. Personnel disciplinary procedures must be observed by management.

☐ **Others**. There is a growing recognition of the need to fight fraud and teams such as London Team Against Fraud (LTAF) have come on-line. This is an intelligence unit, gathering data on cross boundary fraud that affects the London Boroughs. LTAF exchanges information and carries out data matching exercises in all 33 London Boroughs. They have a network of contacts and prepare good practice guidelines in high-risk areas such as student grants and housing benefits claims.

Claiming losses
A schedule of losses should be presented to the court and insurers. We may apply for an order blocking a potential defendant's assets (Mareva injunctions) so that they cannot be moved beyond the jurisdiction of the court. An Anton Pillar order allows the plaintiff's lawyers to enter, search for and seize documents and other evidence specified in the order. When carrying out a fraud investigation try to isolate the quantified extent of the fraud so that this schedule of losses may be built up as the work progresses. This will be used as the basis of insurance claims.

Court Trial
The Criminal Law Act 1977 provides that offences triable on indictment (and serious cases) are heard at Crown Court. Meanwhile offences triable only summarily are heard at Magistrates' Court. Where they are triable either way then they may be tried in either court. In this instance the case goes to magistrates first for a committal hearing to decide whether it should be heard in there, or go to Crown Court. If it goes for summary trial the defendant can opt for trial by jury in the Crown Court.

APB guidelines
The Auditing Practices Board (APB) has guidelines on fraud. These are aimed at external auditors:
- The organisation needs good systems of internal controls.
- An employee code of conduct should be in place.
- External auditors should advise management where they have found evidence of a fraud.
- The external auditor has a role in investigating frauds with a material effect on the accounts.
- Management is responsible for investigating frauds.
- Where there are indicators of a possible fraud then audit tests should be extended.

An APB standard on fraud and irregularity, Statement of Auditing Standard 110, was issued in February 1995. Key features for consideration when auditing financial statements are:

Para 2. Auditors should plan and perform their audit procedures and evaluate and report the results thereof, recognising that fraud or error may materially affect the financial statements.

Para 10. It is the responsibility of the directors to take such steps as are reasonably open to them to prevent and detect fraud.

Para 13. In order to assist them in achieving the objectives in para 10, directors of larger entities will often assign particular responsibility to:

- An internal audit function
- A legal department
- A compliance function and/or
- An audit committee

Para 17. It is not the auditors' function to prevent fraud and error. The fact that an audit is carried out may, however, act as a deterrent.

Para 24. When planning the audit, the auditor should assess the risk that fraud or error may cause the financial statements to contain material misstatements.

Para 25. Based on their risk assessment, the auditors should design audit procedures so as to have a reasonable expectation of detecting misstatement arising from fraud or error which are material to the financial statements.

Para 50. Where the auditors become aware of a suspected or actual instance of fraud they should:

- Consider whether the matter may be one that ought to be reported to a proper authority in the public interest.
- Except in the circumstances covered in SAS 110.12, discuss the matter with the board of directors including any audit committee.

Para 51. Where, having considered any views expressed on behalf of the entity and in the light of any legal advice obtained, the auditors conclude that the matter ought to be reported to an appropriate authority in the public interest, they should notify the directors in writing of their view and, if the entity does not voluntarily do so itself or is unable to provide evidence that the matter has been reported, they should report it themselves.

Para 52. When a suspected or actual instance of fraud casts doubt on the integrity of the directors, auditors should make a report direct to the proper authority in the public interest without delay and without informing the directors in advance.

This guidance provides for greater involvement in fraud by the external auditor which is now ingrained within the adopted auditing procedures. The ability to report to third parties also creates an additional control over frauds that implicate top management. The criticism that has been levied at external audit in failing to deal with organisations where fraud is prevalent has been met, in part, by this new standard.

29.2 The Concept of Evidence

Introduction

There are a number of techniques applied to fraud investigations and these revolve around securing relevant evidence. All investigations should be undertaken to acceptable standards since the findings may be presented to senior management, a disciplinary panel, an industrial tribunal or a court of law. We outline below the importance of evidence and then cover interviewing, surveillance and recording.

The importance of evidence

A fraud needs evidence to prove it. Evidence is information by which facts tend to be proved. The courts will reach a decision based on evidence presented to it even if inadequate or inconclusive. A fraud investigation secures evidence that is both relevant and sufficient. Relevance is determined by the scale of the investigation in that the search for evidence will spread into parts of the organisation that become implicated. Sufficiency depends on the importance of the investigation and the extent to which allegations have to be supported. Political sensitivity is another factor that may affect the investigation.

Legal aspects of evidence

The modern law of evidence remains largely case law based. Important terms are set out below.

Testimony. This is an oral statement under oath made in open court.

Hearsay evidence. This covers all statements other than one made by a witness in the course of giving evidence in the proceedings in question. It can only be received in exceptional cases. An example may be used to illustrate this point where:

HEARSAY

> *Mr. F killed Mr. B*
> *Miss X was an eye witness*
> *Miss X told Mrs. Y that she saw Mr. F kill Mr. B*
> *Mrs Y repeated Miss. X's statement to Mr. Z*
>
> *Mrs Y or Mr. Z could not narrate to the court Miss X's statement as proof of the killing.*
>
> *Neither could Miss X narrate to the courts that she told Mrs. Y as proof of the killing.*

Another example of exclusion would be an out-of-court assertion by a third party that he committed the offence with which the accused is charged. This would be excluded under the rule against hearsay since this third party cannot be cross examined and may have been misunderstood.

Documentary evidence

This covers documents produced for inspection by the courts and includes maps, plans, drawings, discs, tapes, video-tapes, graphs, photos and negatives. Primary evidence is the best that is available whereas secondary evidence may be a copy where the original is not available. The best evidence rule is largely defunct in that it may not mean that inferior evidence is excluded, although the absence of best evidence may result in adverse judicial comment. The underlying principle of documentary evidence is that the person relying on the contents of a document must adduce primary evidence of those contents. PACE 1984 S.71 provides that the contents of a document may (whether or not the document is still in existence) be proved by production of an enlargement of a microfilm copy of that document, or of any material part of it authenticated in such manner as the court may approve. There are limited cases where one may prove a fact without evidence: e.g. where there is no acceptable affirmative evidence that a person was alive during a continuous period of 7 years or more, where persons who would be likely to have heard of him have not, and that all due enquiries have been made, then the person is presumed dead.

Real evidence

This applies to material objects produced for inspection where inferences may be drawn about their existence, condition or value. They should be accompanied by a testimony and include items such as a person's physical appearance or the intonation of voices on a tape recorder.

Circumstantial evidence

This is defined as the existence of relevant facts (from which the existence or non-existence of facts in issue may be drawn) which may be oral or documentary or real. The cumulative weight of this type of evidence may be great but it must be used with care since it can be fabricated to cast suspicion on another. An example of this would be the fact that an alleged murderer purchased a gun prior to a shooting or the fact that the defendant had the opportunity to perform a criminal act.

Admissibility

All evidence that is sufficiently relevant to prove a fact in issue, which is not excluded by any rule of law, is admissible. A fact in issue is a fact that the plaintiff (or prosecutor) must prove in order to succeed in the claim (prosecution) together with those facts that the defendant (accused) must prove to succeed in the defence.

Relevancy

Stephen's Digest of Law states that:

> *"any two facts to which it is applied are so related to each other that according to the common course of events one either taken by itself or in connection with other facts proves or renders probable the past, present or future existence or non-existence of the other."*

When performing an investigation, it is pointless pursuing evidence that will not be deemed relevant.

The weight of evidence

Factors that will be examined to assess the weight of evidence include:

1. The extent to which it is supported or contradicted by other evidence.
2. For direct testimony, the demeanour, plausibility and credibility of the witness and all the circumstances in which he/she claims to have perceived a fact in issue. This is important for auditors who may have to present evidence to the court.
3. The general rule is that questions of law are decided by the judge and questions of fact by the jury.

Sufficiency

The party needs to adduce sufficient evidence for the issue to be submitted to a jury. Sufficiency is a question of law for the judge and there needs to be enough evidence to justify, as a possibility, a favourable finding by the jury. If not the judge will withdraw the issue from the jury and direct them.

Closing

After the evidence and closing speeches the judge sums up the case to the jury. The judge indicates which party is obliged to prove the facts and the standard of proof required, and reminds them of the evidence and warns of any special need for caution. A trial judge has a duty to secure a fair trial.

Securing evidence

It is difficult to design hard and fast rules for securing evidence over and above the fact that it must be sufficient and relevant. This depends on the circumstances and in the real world, each investigation requires a different level of sufficiency and relevancy. Internal auditing standards require that the information to support the results of an investigation should be:

1. **Sufficient** - factual, adequate and convincing so that a prudent, informed person would reach the same conclusions.
2. **Competent** - Information should be reliable and the best obtainable through the use of appropriate audit techniques.
3. **Relevant** - It should relate to the matters in question.
4. **Practical** - One would weigh up the extent of evidence required, the cost and time taken to obtain it and sensitivity. This is the case for statements required where the witness resides overseas.

These standards may also be applied to the investigation of fraud. Where there is sufficient evidence to bring internal charges (or any other management action), or refer the matter to the police then the investigation should be concluded. We all live in the real world and it is a fact that an investigation must have a cut-off point and not go on forever. Resources are always an additional constraint as is the time factor, which makes it essential that both resources and time are used efficiently.

Types of Evidence

There are many different types of evidence that will be secured during a typical fraud investigation:

☐ **Documents**. This is the "bread and butter" material of most fraud investigations. Accumulation of vast amounts of documentation is time consuming and makes the case complicated. Suitable audit house rules are essential and these are listed below:

1. Clear filing arrangement with full indexes.
2. Documents indicating date and time of removal.
3. Originals extracted and signed copies put in their place.
4. Important documents held in plastic wallets.
5. Copies of documents should be provided to the police until the originals are required.
6. Statement should be made as to how the documents were obtained i.e. source and method.

☐ **Re-performance of calculations/processing**. An example would be to re-do a bank reconciliation to make sure that no figures have been altered. This may be used to isolate false accounting.

☐ **Analysis of figures** can extract trends and patterns as well as aggregate figures that may be used during the investigation. Where one is looking at a series of suspect transactions this may be crucial for arriving at global figures to determine the extent of the fraud. Major findings can be ascertained from plotting items of income/expenditure over time and assessing them for reasonableness.

☐ **Reconciliations**. It is possible to balance two related accounts and reconcile them or expose a material difference. It may be that the difference is an indication of a fraud or irregularity and may be used to indicate the extent of losses suffered by the organisation.

☐ **Third-party confirmation** secures independent information from outsiders by asking them to confirm facts or figures. So long as these have not been altered or people have a motive for lying, then the resultant information may be used to confront a suspect who has provided inconsistent details. The major problem is a reluctance to provide such information and it may be necessary to visit the party in question. Where information is forthcoming it is as well to secure the confirmation as a written witness statement.

☐ **Reports that deal with the area under review**. It may be necessary to secure important reports that document decisions made or confirm figures being examined. The source and status of the report should be noted, particularly if it will be quoted in a subsequent audit report on the investigation.

☐ **Vouching checks**. A great deal of basic work may revolve around vouching where one record is checked against another. This involves invoices being checked against payments or travel claims ticked against supporting vouchers. If one source of data has been tampered with while another is not affected, this may be the only method of obtaining a true picture of a person's activities. It must be done methodically so that the resulting schedules may be presented to a court of law.

☐ **Verification**. This is similar to vouching but involves tests to establish that assets or liabilities exist, belong to the right person/party and have been accurately recorded in the books. An example would be a stock-take that is then checked against the stock records. Again not an exciting prospect but it may nevertheless produce valuable results.

☐ **Testimonials**. A witness statement should be obtained for all material matters that are being confirmed by an individual who has knowledge of the events being examined. This should be taken formally in line with a laid-down procedure where the person's comments are formally recorded, signed and witnessed on pro forma witness statement forms. These may be presented in court and/or a disciplinary at a later date. They should be hand-written and signed although a typed version may be attached at a later date.

☐ **Physical material** e.g. photographs. It is possible to photograph (or video) relevant occurrences even to the extent of recording a crime as it is committed. This creates a short-cut for the investigation by providing what can be irrefutable evidence. This evidence tends to be secondary as the surveillance record is the prime evidence, with the photograph simply confirming what the witness has seen and recorded in formal notes. Rules covering the use of photographs are:

- Use a camera with date and time displays.
- Make sure it has a powerful zoom lens.
- Take relevant pictures and get them processed after each day's filming.
- Relate photographs to surveillance records as exhibits with unique sequential reference numbers.
- Store negatives in a safe place.
- Store photographs, back-up copies and records in a safe place.

Make sure the movement of the unprocessed film can be accounted for at all times so that it is protected from tampering. The film must be under the control of the auditor up to the time it is submitted for processing.

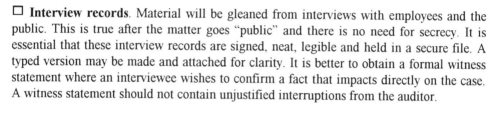 **Interview records**. Material will be gleaned from interviews with employees and the public. This is true after the matter goes "public" and there is no need for secrecy. It is essential that these interview records are signed, neat, legible and held in a secure file. A typed version may be made and attached for clarity. It is better to obtain a formal witness statement where an interviewee wishes to confirm a fact that impacts directly on the case. A witness statement should not contain unjustified interruptions from the auditor.

☐ **Computer records**. This is a major source of evidence and may be the only way to prove that a transaction occurred. There are people who will have to review computer records who hold a deep-seated mistrust for them, and it may be best to create a clear table derived from the records as a covering schedule for presentation purposes. One common fault with computer records is to make any copies of screen prints too faint so that they become unreadable. The auditor should be able to show which system they came from and when they were produced. They will have to be registered under the Data Protection Act 1984 for use in management investigations and internal disciplinaries. PACE 1984 provides further direction on computer generated records.

Cases of fraud may be investigated by internal audit and then passed over to the police. They will prepare a case for the Crown Prosecution Service (CPS) who will decide on whether to prosecute. CPS will consider the reliability and sufficiency of evidence and whether it is in the public interest to prosecute. Weaknesses in evidence will be exploited by defence lawyers and the only way that this can be averted is to install precise standards on how evidence is secured and recorded. The need for formally documented standards (say in the audit manual) cannot be over emphasised.

Witnesses

When acting as a witness there are certain guidelines that should be observed by the auditor:

1. **Make sure you are familiar with court procedure**. There is a separation of prosecutor and witnesses so that no undue pressure is applied. Rules cover contact with other witnesses during the course of giving evidence and court protocol guides the witness when in court. If these matters are not in the audit manual, advice should be

provided by the organisation's legal officer. Any person representing the organisation should be briefed about court procedure before attending a hearing.

2. **Refresh your memory by reading your statements**. An auditor may ask to refer to their notes when giving evidence.

3. **Do not discuss your evidence** with other auditors who may also be called as witnesses, as the defence may argue that there has been fabrication.

4. **Think before answering questions**. The golden rule is to be honest; if the witness cannot remember precisely what happened then simply say so. If the statement is inaccurate this should be admitted. If something is a matter of opinion then say so. If a request is made by the prosecution (say to see an audit report) and the auditor is unsure whether it should be entertained, it should be referred to the CIA.

5. **It is not the witness's job to please anyone in court**, only to present evidence in a fair and open fashion.

6. **Keep calm if the defence seeks to discredit your evidence**. It is the role of defence lawyers to influence the jury. A weak defence relies on spotting gaps in the evidence and if any level of doubt/error can be brought out, no matter how immaterial, this may be used to cast doubt on the rest of the evidence. The tactic is either to discredit the documents presented by the witness (e.g. by the auditor) or discredit the auditor. The defence may sum up the case by asking the jury whether they are convinced that the investigation was professional after suggesting not. Resilience is necessary where a witness can remain calm and composed and keep hold of the vital rule of thinking before answering while keeping to the truth, the whole truth and nothing but the truth.

It may be possible to seek a restitution order to recover losses from the fraud. The Judge should be advised of this during the hearing and may make a ruling if the defendant is found guilty.

29.3 Interviewing Techniques

Objectives

Interviewing is useful for obtaining information relevant to the investigation. The Police and Criminal Evidence Act 1984 (PACE) states that the purpose of an interview is to obtain from the person concerned explanation of the facts, and not necessarily to obtain an admission. Formal interviews held during a fraud investigation should be carried out in accordance with the provisions of PACE. There is debate as to the applicability of PACE to persons not police officers although Code C, that deals with interviewing, does apply to persons who are responsible for investigating frauds. Since PACE is based around best practice it is as well to apply it.

Strategies

Some writers argue that there are a variety of strategies that may be used when interviewing a suspect ranging from the friendly approach ("tell me all about it"), the solution approach ("we can work it out") through to the sustained strategy (clinical, objective and unshockable). They feel that a strategy mix should be adopted to suit the situation. The best approach is to set out a clear standard for the conduct of interviews possibly based on being fair but firm. This is extremely important, bearing in mind that an aggressive approach to interviewing can affect the audit image tremendously. We may agree a policy whereby no auditor is allowed to conduct a fraud interview unless they have attended an appropriate training workshop where the adopted approach would be presented. A further policy may be that all fraud interviews should be conducted in the presence of at least two auditors. Audit management then needs to install suitable policies whereby all audit interviews are reviewed against agreed quality standards.

Conducting the interview
The different types of interviews that may have to be conducted are:

☐ **Fact-finding interviews with staff generally to secure background information relating to the matters being investigated**. The audit right of access may be used here to secure the relevant information. In this case it can be argued that the employee has a duty to respond to the questions. An employee may be interviewed at this stage and later on enter into the frame as a main suspect as more information is obtained. Where there has been a theft at an office/building, all employees who work in this area may be interviewed by audit as part of the fact-finding stage of the investigation. These may be seen as relatively informal meetings and exchanges of information, rather than formal fraud interviews and the auditor should adopt a diplomatic approach that reflects this view.

☐ **Confidential interviews with an informant where the investigation has not yet become public knowledge**. These interviews are different in that the success or otherwise of the investigation may well hinge on the type of information that is secured in this meeting. A "sit back and listen" mode should be adopted by the auditor. The main problem for the auditor is that information relating to the area where the fraud is being carried out will have to be secured. At the same time the actual allegations must be captured and understood. If for example information is provided on the activities of a particular individual, then the extent to which these activities are authorised (and comply with procedure) must be made clear. If then the informant states that the suspect has signed a purchase order, then we must be clear as to who the authorised signatories are. A further problem is that we may have to deal with information that falls somewhere between two extremes:

FIGURE 29.1 ALLEGATIONS

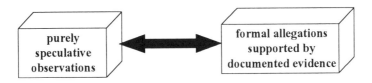

The speculative comments may be unfounded and will have to be fully investigated before a case may be put to the party who is the subject of the allegations. On the other hand, where the informant has produced a solid case with supporting documents, this will make things much easier. In the latter case however, one must ask why someone might go to some lengths to prepare a case against what may be a fellow worker. As such great care must be taken in vetting any documents that purport to confirm that a fraud has taken place. At the same time vague accusations must be treated with equal care as the informant's real motives may not have been isolated. An overriding factor is that on no account should informants be discouraged from providing relevant information to the auditor.

☐ **Interviews with potential witnesses to the matters being investigated**. This type of interview requires time spent on explaining the objectives of the investigation. Most potential witnesses feel threatened by an investigating auditor and would rather do nothing than become actively involved. It may be that information needs to be coaxed from the interviewee. One rule that may be applied is that the more uncomfortable the witness, the less forthcoming they will be. It is also advisable to get the required details perhaps as a witness statement, at the first interview where a potential witness may not have been put under pressure from anyone implicated in the fraud/irregularity. These interviews can be difficult where much time may be spent going over the detail and writing a formal record. As well as the matters that the auditor knows about there may be other facts that impact on the investigation. Accordingly, the auditor must not be obsessed with "getting the statement" but must also keep the conversation open enough so that new information may also be provided. The interviewee's only responsibility is to tell the truth and not please the auditor and any undue pressures applied by the auditor may well pervert the course of justice. In addition, a statement prepared after the witness has been "led" by the auditor will be exposed by any good defence lawyers in court (or representative in an internal disciplinary). This may throw the reliability of the whole case in doubt.

☐ **Interviews with senior management for the areas under review**. Managers may feel that they may pass an allegation over to internal audit for investigation. They are still however responsible for resolving the fraud and this fact should be kept at the forefront of the auditor's mind during the investigation. Line and senior managers must co-operate with audit by providing formal statements on what activities they have authorised or delegated to defined officers. They must also state their formal procedures for the area where the fraud had occurred. The important point to note is that it is the manager, not the auditor, who must make formal statements on these matters for the court, industrial tribunals and/or internal disciplinaries. The auditor may find the relevant management reluctant to make these formal statements and this issue should be pursued if necessary. The reasoning behind this view is that internal audit is not an executive function and cannot dictate procedure. This is management's role and audit may only provide an advisory input into this.

☐ **Interviews with the suspect or potential suspect**. This is probably the most difficult interview to perform as well as being crucial to the investigation. The auditor has to balance the need to secure information with the competing need to be fair to the individual concerned and there is much misconception on this matter. Interviewing suspects is dealt with later on. There are several ways that the interview process may be broken down:

1. **Preparation**. It is tempting to compile a list of pre-arranged questions and then go through each one in their strict order. This however will make the interview appear somewhat mechanical and may inhibit both the interviewer and the interviewee. A checklist of areas to cover should be devised along with any specific questions that must be tackled. The interviewer may then be able to float through the proceedings, adjusting the questions to suit the responses. Preparation is the key to a successful interview and the

more one knows about the circumstances under review then the better the ensuing conversation. Remember the types of interviews outlined above and differing objectives.

2. **Arrangements**. The domestic arrangements should be dealt with, including location, notification, refreshments, timing etc. It is best for the Personnel section to communicate with the officer who is being formally interviewed particularly where the person is a suspect. There should be a formal process for instructing officers to attend formal interviews that may result in a disciplinary and Personnel will provide advice on this, in line with a standardised letter that should be used for this purpose. For example the officer facing the allegations may be entitled to bring a trade union representative or friend and should be given details of the general areas that are the subject of the interview. In addition adequate notice of the interview should be provided ideally on standardised documentation. It is always advisable to have two officers carrying out the interview where one would ask the questions with the other taking notes. The location should be arranged to suit the particular circumstances. An informant may be interviewed away from the work environment where they may feel sure that they are not being observed. Note that the auditor should try not to meet informants in bars as this conjures up an image of shady deals and underground activities. Witnesses may be seen at the audit offices or in their line manager's office so as to reinforce the view that it is their official duty to provide full information to the investigators. A suspect may be seen away from his/her place of work to reduce any embarrassment factor that would be present if done at their place of work. It is possible to arrange to reimburse witnesses for any reasonable travel expenses.

3. **Structure**. It is good practice to structure an interview as a logically flowing process:

FIGURE 29.2 INTERVIEW STRUCTURE

Introductions

▼

Explain the objective of the interview and the procedure for note taking

▼

Ask for any queries/concerns

▼

Go through the various areas and ask relevant questions

▼

As each part is clarified, make a formal written record

▼

Sum up what has been said

▼

Check the accuracy of the interview record

▼

Explain the next steps as far as they have been determined

▼

Provide a copy of the record to the interviewee

▼

Thank the interviewee for attending

▼

Obtain a typed version of the interview record

Interviewing suspects

Most interviews will be of a general fact-finding nature and as such they will be low keyed and not unnecessarily formal. In contrast to this, Cromer (1985) has listed tips for interviewing suspects:

- Stress that there is limitless time to find the truth.
- Do not use emotive words.
- Maintain a logical and calm approach at all times.
- Never underestimate the suspect.
- Do not engage in humour or sarcasm.
- Use language that is understood by the suspect.
- Give the impression that the truth will be discovered.
- Be as frank as possible.
- Indicate if you feel the truth is not being told.
- Maintain the initiative.
- Never try to rush through the interview.
- Keep pens and paper out of sight as this is distracting.
- Try to get admissions repeated frequently throughout the interview.

Some interviewers use body language where for example they pursue a line of questioning where the interviewee is obviously uncomfortable. A study of this topic can pay dividends although the detailed psychological implications go beyond the remit of this chapter. What can be said however, is that where the interviewee becomes disturbed, then the area of conversation that creates this reaction needs to be probed by the interviewer.

A new approach

During 1992 the Metropolitan police (in the United Kingdom) developed a new approach to interviewing that stresses the need to put the suspect interview within the context of the entire investigation. In the past interviews were seen as the most important part of an investigation, where it was deemed good practice to extract a confession. The pressures applied to suspects, e.g. asking the same question repeatedly, were designed to get them to relieve the pressure by confessing. The aim now is to get to the truth by seeking accurate and reliable information. The interviewer will go through events with the interviewee and use free recall to get the person to talk about the issues at hand. They are then invited to go through this free recall process several times, changing the order of topics and clearing up discrepancies. Meanwhile the interviewer will draw out any inconsistencies with information that has already been secured and invite clarification. Once the correct position has been established it will be possible to write a formal statement. The principles behind this interesting new approach may be listed:

1. The role of the investigative interview is to obtain accurate and reliable information from suspects, witnesses or victims in order to discover the truth about matters under police investigation.
2. Investigative interviewing should be approached with an open mind. Information obtained from the person who is being interviewed should be tested against what the interviewing officer already knows or what can reasonably be established.
3. When questioning anyone, a police officer must act fairly in the circumstances of each individual case.
4. The police interviewer is not bound to accept the first answer given. Questioning is not unfair merely because it is persistent.

5. Even where the right to silence is exercised by a suspect, the police still have a right to put questions.
6. When conducting an interview, police officers are free to ask questions in order to establish the truth.
7. Vulnerable people, whether victims, witnesses or suspects must be treated with particular consideration at all times.

The above guidelines are equally applicable to the internal auditor. One particularly useful issue that was also brought out was the need to ensure that interviews are reviewed for quality and correct procedure after they have been completed. This gives an added pressure for the interviewer to comply fully with the agreed standards of conduct, which in itself is a control. It was felt that false confessions were given voluntarily (which are normally discounted) or through coercion by the interviewer. While true confessions tended to be because of the strength of evidence, applied pressures or a feeling of remorse. It is essential that the auditor undertakes the interview with an open mind. One final point that the auditor would do well to note is environmental factors including the condition of the interview room, which if dirty and oppressive, contributes to the overall stress applied to the interviewee.

PACE 1984

PACE 1984 has resulted in four codes of practice issued by the Home Secretary:

CODE A - The exercise by police officers of statutory powers of stop and search.

CODE B - The searching of premises by police officers and the seizure of property found by police officers on persons or premises.

CODE C - The detention, treatment and questioning of persons by police officers.

CODE D - The identification of persons by police officers.

CODE E - The tape recording of interviews.

CODE C provides guidance on interviewing suspects where the results of the interview may be admitted as evidence by the courts. This covers the following:

1. General.
2. Custody records.
3. Initial action: detained persons.
4. Detained persons' property.
5. Right not to be held incommunicado.
6. Right to legal advice.
7. Citizens of independent commonwealth countries or foreign nationals.
8. Conditions of detention.
9. Treatment of detained persons.
10. Cautions.
11. Interviews generally.
12. Interviews at police stations.
13. Interpreters.
14. Questioning: special restrictions.
15. Review and extensions of detention.
16. Charging of detained persons.

There are a number of general points regarding PACE that should be noted as follows:

1. A caution should be given to a person of whom there are grounds to suspect an offence before any questions about it are put to him for the purposes of obtaining evidence which may be given to a court (10.1). The caution used before 1995 was as follows:

> *"You do not have to say anything unless you wish to do so, but what you say may be given in evidence."*

(but see new PACE caution below)

2. Where there is a break in the interview make sure that the person is aware that he remains under caution (10.5).
3. Make sure the person understands the caution.
4. One must not use oppression to obtain answers to questions (11.3).
5. As soon as there is enough evidence to bring a prosecution, the interview should be terminated (11.4).
6. Breaks should be provided at recognised meal times along with short breaks for refreshment at approximately two hourly intervals (12.7).
7. Generally, persons at risk (juveniles, mentally disordered or mentally handicapped) will not be interviewed unless an appropriate adult is present to advise them (11.14). "Appropriate adult" means (3.7): A parent, guardian or some other person responsible for his care or custody.
8. An interpreter should be used where (13.2):
   - The person has difficulty in understanding English;
   - The interviewing officer cannot himself speak the person's own language; and
   - The person wishes an interpreter to be present.
9. An official English translation should be made in due course (13.4).
10. Normally a deaf person will not be interviewed without an interpreter unless he agrees in writing (13.5).

In relation to PACE 1984 several points relate to the maintenance of suitable documentation:
1. The interview record must be made of each interview (11.5) or as soon as practicable after its completion (11.7).
2. Any refusal to sign should itself be recorded (11.12).
3. The person shall be given the opportunity to read the interview record and sign it as correct or to indicate the respects in which he considers it to be incorrect (11.10).

Code C

Annex D covers statements written under caution and provides that a person shall always be invited to write down himself what he wants to say. Where the person wishes to write it himself, he shall be asked to write out and sign before writing what he wants to:

> *"I make this statement of my own free will. I understand that I do not have to say anything but it may harm my defence if I do not mention when questioned something which I later rely on in court. This statement may be given in evidence."*

Any person writing his own statement shall be allowed to do so without any prompting except that a police officer may indicate which matters are material or question any ambiguity in the statement. If a person would like someone to write it for him, a police officer shall write the statement, but, before starting, he must ask him to sign:

> *"I, ..., wish to make a statement. I want someone to write down what I say. I understand that I do not have to say anything but it may harm my defence if I do not mention when questioned something which I later rely on in court. This statement may be given in evidence."*

Where a police officer writes the statement, he must take down the exact words spoken by the person making it and he must not edit or paraphrase it. Any questions that are necessary (e.g. to make it more intelligible) and the answers given must be recorded contemporaneously on the statement form. When the writing of a statement by a police officer is finished the person making it shall be asked to read it and to make any corrections, alterations or additions. When he has finished reading it he shall be asked to make his mark on the following certificate at the end of the statement:

> *"I have read the above statement, and I have been able to correct, alter or add anything I wish. This statement is true. I have made it of my own free will."*

If the person making the statement cannot read, or refuses to read it, or to write the above mentioned certificate at the end of it or sign it, the senior police officer present shall read it to him and ask him whether he would like to correct, alter or add anything and to put his signature or his mark at the end. The police officer shall then certify on the statement itself what has occurred.

The new PACE codes

The new Criminal Justice Act and Public Order Act 1994 and the new PACE codes of practice make changes to the auditor's work. We are primarily concerned about new provisions relating to interviewing and cautioning suspects. In the new code an interview is defined as follows:

> *"An interview is the questioning of a person regarding his involvement or suspected involvement in a criminal offence or offences which by virtue of paragraph 10.1 of code C, is required to be carried out under caution."*

Cautions must be administered where a person is not under arrest in the following circumstances:

> *"Para 10.1 A person whom there are grounds to suspect of an offence must be cautioned before any questions about it (or further questions if it is his answers to previous questions which provide the grounds for suspicion) are put to him regarding his involvement in that offence if his answers or his silence (i.e. failure or refusal to answer a question or to answer satisfactorily) may be given in evidence to a court in a prosecution."*

It should also be made clear that the suspect is not under arrest and is not obliged to remain with the interviewer. Where a caution is issued and the person remains then the person's replies (or silence) may be given to a court in prosecution. The new words used from April 1995 as a caution are:

> *"You do not have to say anything. But it may harm your defence if you do not mention something which you may later rely on in court. Anything you do say may be given in evidence."*

The old caution is still used in certain circumstances, for example where questions are being put to a person who has been relating an offence that he has already been charged with. It should also be made clear to the interviewee that the interview can be delayed so that he can obtain legal advice. The main reasoning behind the new arrangements is not to abolish the right to silence, but to open the possibility of bringing this factor before the court as part of the prosecution. This is particularly relevant where the suspect presents a clear explanation (e.g. an alibi) to the court that was not provided to the police (or prosecution team), despite ample opportunity. The possibility that this has been fabricated may then be explored by the prosecution.

Taped interviews
It is possible to follow the procedures used by the police and use taped interviews when recording fraud interviews. This should be a carefully planned process as it will result in the replacement of contemporaneous notes with a taped record. The emphasis is then removed from the note-taking process and all parties will concentrate on the actual questions and answers, as the centrepiece of the interview. Research has shown that interviews using tape recorder are much shorter. In one exercise a 30 minute interview was found to take 10 minutes when notes were replaced by a tape recording. This may result in a substantial saving in audit hours used on a typical fraud investigation. There are costs associated with buying the required equipment (it may have to be portable) and this would have to be justified by the frequency of use and the advantages. There is an overall impression of professionalism when tape recorders are used in fraud interviews. There are setbacks, not least the need to ensure all words are audible, which requires a private room for this purpose. It is also more difficult to review what has been said, as a way of checking for consistency and this may mean that a further interview may be required. For presentation to a court or disciplinary we would be required to produce a typed transcript, and this is time consuming. It is a matter of weighing up the advantages and disadvantages. There is greater scope for using one auditor, as opposed to the usual two, on fraud interviews where a tape recorder is used. It is possible to set clear standards for

the application of this technique through additions to the fraud section of the audit manual:

- Use should comply with legislation.
- The interviewee should be advised that the recording is being made.
- The date, time and people present should be recorded at the start of the interview.
- The tape should be kept secure and not made vulnerable to interference.
- A copy should be made (use a twin tape machine) and kept secure in the audit safe.
- All tapes should be properly labelled.
- A transcript should be made from the tape and signed by the auditor.
- The interviewee should not be given a copy of the tape but may be given a copy of the typed transcript.

Note that Code E of PACE 1984 contains a code of practice for taped interviews.

Documentation
Each fraud investigation must be recorded in a formal file that contains all the relevant documents that have been secured during the course of the investigation. There are a number of general attributes of good working papers that should be applied to these files:

1. **Clarity**. It is good practice to insist that files are legible and can be understood by all potential readers. Neat writing with clear headings that guide the reader through the papers is essential particularly since the files may have to be read without assistance from the auditor who performed the work.
2. **Indexed**. Each item in the file should be referenced and noted in a main index at the front of the file. As such it should be possible to go directly to a specific document with ease.
3. **Support the audit decisions/opinion**. The findings and decisions made in the resultant report by the auditor will each have to be fully supported by firm evidence. The entire investigation will be driven by this factor in terms of securing evidence to refute or support the allegations in question. When compiling the working papers the auditor, in turn must recognise and cater for this factor.
4. **Defend conclusions**. This builds on the previous point. One feature of fraud investigations is that as they progress, one may need to exclude defined individuals from the enquiries. This is a material decision bearing in mind that the auditor may personally know some of the people implicated by the fraud. At all stages, the working papers should clearly indicate why major decisions were made by investigating staff and what evidence was available to support these decisions. This may become an important factor if at a later stage the defendant claims that he/she has been victimised by management, which is a defence that is commonly used.
5. **The use of pro formas**. These can provide short-cuts to what may be a fairly bureaucratic process of collecting and filing evidence. Interviews, meetings, analysis of documents and many other exercises may be recorded in a standardised format via the use of pro formas and this should ensure a more efficient approach to an investigation.
6. **Cross referenced**. It goes without saying that the working paper file must be properly cross referenced. The ability to retrieve documents instantly gives a good impression as well as being very efficient. The police authority will be more positive in their response to audit findings if the papers are obviously readily accessible. Inadequate cross referencing on the other hand will lead to embarrassing gaps as the evidence is presented by the auditor to management and/or the police.

7. **Economically used**. The realities of resource utilisation mean that an investigation cannot go on indefinitely and this is also the case for the accumulation of evidence. Rules must be applied in terms of securing material for the working paper files based on practicality and the available resources. Each item must therefore meet this criterion before it is entered into the files. A decision may have to be made on how far the auditor should go back when accumulating evidence of a fraud.

8. **Headed up**. The principle that each paper must be properly headed must be applied. The idea is that each item must be separately identifiable if it became separated from the main file. We should be able to tell which investigation the paper belongs to and who compiled it (along with the date).

9. **Clearly shows the impact on the investigation**. Every fraud investigation changes as it develops and as new information comes to light. Throughout this process the auditor, in conjunction with management, will make decisions that will affect the form and direction of the investigation. This process should be evident from a study of the working papers and each new document should be set within a defined time frame. One approach is to prepare progress reports on a regular basis that refer to the documents that have been obtained. It is possible to date, stamp and sign each document (via a label) as it is discovered by the auditor. Lastly, the auditor may draft a file note that indicates the significance of any new material that has been secured. This might alter the objectives of the investigation, the resources required and/or add or delete a suspect from the enquiries.

10. **Signed by the officer and the reviewer**. This tends to be a standard audit requirement in that the file indicates who has carried out the work and the role of audit management in reviewing it.

11. **Show the work carried out**. The way this requirement is met will vary. It may consist of a brief note setting out what has been done perhaps in terms of analysing expenditure in the area under review. At the other extreme the auditor may construct a witness statement that describes in detail the steps taken to formulate a specific document. The status and reliability of the evidence may be affected by the absence of this detail. It will reduce the possibility of any defence challenging the evidence in court or at an internal disciplinary. It is frustrating for an audit manager to pick up a file that contains lists of figures scribbled down by the auditor with no indication of what they represent.

12. **Set out the objectives of the work**. Much of the material that forms the basis of a fraud investigation is derived from the use of extensive testing routines. In this respect, it is useful to have for each test, a clear objective statement possibly signed by the audit manager, that sets out exactly the aim of the test and how the ensuing results may be applied to the investigation. As well as forming a formal record for the file, this approach should provide for greater efficiency in the work carried out.

13. **Indicate which matters are outstanding**. For completeness, it is a good idea to indicate whether there are gaps in the work carried out. An example would be a strategy whereby all staff working in a particular unit are interviewed as potential witnesses to the fraud. Where one individual has not been available then this should be clear from an analysis of the relevant documentation. It will be difficult to explain months after the event why one person was left out particularly if the auditor in question has left the organisation. It may be that a certain exercise was planned but for some reason, was no longer required. Again the working papers should contain a suitable note to this effect.

14. **Dated**. This rule should be strictly applied.

15. **Show any impact on the next stage of the investigation**. Bearing in mind that we would have planned an investigation perhaps based on a planning document that has been submitted to management for discussion and action. Where the direction of the original plan changes as the investigation progresses, this needs to be recorded so that the working papers reflect the changing path of the investigation.

16. **Complete**. All relevant documents must end up on the definitive audit files which means that this should be the only file (or set of files) that is maintained. It is bad practice to hold many files in the office with each one containing copies of some evidence without making it quite clear which is the original and complete file(s).

17. **Set out in a neat and orderly fashion**. Sloppy work should never be accepted.

18. **Consistent**. If interviews are typed after the event then this should be applied to all cases where an interview has taken place. Post designations and terminology should coincide which is particularly relevant where more than one auditor is working on the investigation.

19. **Simple**. A great criticism of some fraud investigations is that they can become extremely complicated. This can create major problems for all parties involved, apart from the defendant. The state of the working papers can add to this state of confusion or make the whole matter manageable. The rule here is to keep it simple by having clear objectives, good evidence and ensuring that too many issues are not dealt with at the same time.

20. **Required**. A document/working paper should be secured only if it is required. This point is related to the level of resources that are applied to an investigation as the main benefit of using senior auditors is their ability to apply greater discretion when building up a file of evidence. Junior staff tend to apply the policy of "when in doubt put it in".

21. **Includes summaries**. There is little point in accumulating a vast store of documents on the basis that they each have a link to the allegations however vague. The investigative process requires one to sift through the available material and extract only that which is necessary to prove the issues at hand and this does rely on some skill and experience. This concept is assisted when summaries are used to isolate the key features of documents that have been filed. This technique should be used wherever possible. It is certainly not acceptable to file large reports and schedules without indicating which parts are material to the investigation.

22. **Reviewed**. As per normal audit practice, the working papers should be reviewed by an appropriate level of audit management. This review should also be documented.

23. **Shows the source of information/data**. This is vital, and all sources should be clearly quoted so that any schedules may be re-produced if necessary. The date is also relevant as information particularly financial data does change over time as accounts are updated by the system.

24. **Logically arranged**. The information may be arranged to coincide with the progress of the investigation and this will help take the reviewer through the various stages as a case is put together.

Verification of documents

The Laboratory of the Government Board (LGB) is an executive agency within the UK's Department of Trade and Industry. The document examiner of the LGB is able to:

1. Identify the author of disputed handwriting by comparison with reference handwriting.

2. Determine whether two or more documents have been typed on the same typewriter/printer.
3. Identify the make/model of typewriter/printer, and even the individual machine used to produce a given typed text.
4. Provide a hard-copy transcript of the details in a single-strike carbon-film typewriter/printer ribbon.
5. Identify alterations to document entries.
6. Reveal the sites of erasures.
7. Reveal the original writing/typewriting under obliterations.
8. Reveal indented impressions of writing.
9. Compare inks on documents by non-destructive means and by chemical tests.
10. Compare watermarks, postmarks and seal impressions.
11. Determine whether envelopes have been opened and resealed.
12. Reassemble and preserve torn or damaged documents.
13. Bring together documents seized at different locations.
14. Say whether two or more photocopy documents have been produced on the same photocopier.

When securing and storing documents from a fraud investigation:
1. Handle all documents with care and protect them by placing them in polythene pockets. Preserve fingerprints by using forceps.
2. Label all documents carefully (i.e. the pocket) and note date, time and location. Where a person admits using or having an association with a document, record this; e.g. a diary belongs to them.
3. Do not write on the documents or attach any sticky labels.
4. Do not attempt to re-assemble documents by using adhesive.
5. Make sure the original documents are retained.
6. Secure all ribbons in typewriters/printers significant to the investigation. Take a sample from the typewriter after the ribbon is removed, and replaced. Take samples from the complete keyboard, lower and upper case.
7. Try to obtain samples of handwriting from all suspects. The sample should match what it is being compared with.

29.4 Surveillance

Surveillance involves observing the activities of defined individuals without their knowledge. Watching, looking and gathering evidence does not generally breach privacy standards and is a useful way of securing information in a fraud investigation. It is sensitive and must be handled with care. One approach is to formulate a formal policy based on the premise that it should only be used when absolutely necessary. Some argue surveillance should only be carried out by experts. Simple under-cover operations can yield results particularly where this is the only way of obtaining proof of a fraud. To carry out surveillance:

☐ **Plan the operation carefully**. Start with a clear objective based on the nature of the investigation. Surveillance is time consuming and resource intensive. It may be policy that senior management is informed and that an audit manager authorise it and brief the CIA beforehand.

☐ **Do a trial run**. One auditor will check the area for feasibility before resources are allocated. This provides information on the location, description, timing and useful tips for the full operation. A detailed map of the area should be constructed and copied to the team. The auditor assigned to the trial run must be experienced and look out for significant factors and interpret them.

☐ **Prepare by deciding resources and approach**. A briefing session with those taking part is a useful way to plan the work. A brief file may be made up for all team members with a report on the case, relevant personal descriptions, photographs, a map, specific instructions and blank surveillance records. Observation may be fixed point (static) or mobile and may involve tailing cars (or people). A motor bike is useful for mobile observation although cars are more comfortable in bad weather. Cameras, videos, dictaphones, watches, mobile phones, and CB links may be used. These should be signed for and batteries checked. On the move it is difficult to buy fresh films, petrol or batteries. At least two people should be allocated to each team. There are practical arrangements such as the supply of sandwiches and drinks as well as the possibility of spending a long time on the job outside office hours. A home base should be designated that vehicles/auditors will return to when the suspect falls out of the frame. A phone or CB link should be arranged and one senior auditor should co-ordinate the activities ideally from a static point.

☐ **Action should be anticipated and authorised activity distinguished from the unauthorised**. Permission may be sought when using buildings for observation. Ensure vehicles are carefully positioned. It is a breach of privacy to follow someone into their house or gardens. It is best to call the local police in the area under surveillance to let them know what is going on. Information from a surveillance exercise may not make sense until all the observations are put together.

☐ **If confronted during a surveillance initially try to deny it while avoiding a conflict situation**. Avoid declaring the real reason unless the threat of injury is apparent. Keep the exercise secret on a need-to-know basis. There are tailored excuses that may be rehearsed for being in an area. This can range from carrying out market research through to waiting for a late partner. One cover is a couple who stand around for hours making small talk. On one occasion a couple who appeared to be in a series of long embraces recorded fraudulent activities using a camcorder. Useful aids to the exercise include newspapers (held the right way up), a football or running in a jogging suit. Dictaphones may be used to record detail where a notepad would look out of place. Great care must be taken and the auditor should withdraw immediately if there is any chance of being spotted by the suspect.

☐ **Always carry an ID card** and take notes contemporaneously on a formal surveillance record. It is possible to write up formal notes after the event as long as this is done as soon as practicable and the rough notes are retained. The clothes worn should be chosen to suit the occasion. Anything out of the ordinary will arouse suspicion although there is no point in wearing a boiler suit to merge in with workers if strangers who appear on site are challenged.

☐ **Simple matters may be resolved through surveillance** such as the movements and whereabouts of an individual throughout a defined period. It is more difficult to determine why a person goes to a particular place or what the significance is for more complicated frauds. Simple breaches of procedure covering overtime, sick leave, work attendance and locations visited during the day are easier to prove. A court appearance will mean cross examination of surveillance and other evidence. The auditor should only record what was seen and not make guesses or assumptions. If the exercise results in nothing of significance then this is a finding in itself and not a cause for embarrassment.

29.5 Advance Disclosure of Evidence

Introduction
Strict rules allow defence lawyers in the UK to view material relevant to their case. These rules are issued by the Attorney General and form part of the current arrangements now being reviewed by the Royal Commission on Law and Order. They are under review since they are cumbersome and have resulted in some prosecutions being dropped. The rules have solved one problem whereby defence would plead not guilty at Magistrates' Court as the only way of getting the committal papers to see whether there was a case to answer. If there was, defendants would then change their plea to guilty at Crown Court, wasting court time and expense.

Terminology
For the new rules, it was agreed that the police would reveal to the Crown Prosecution Service (CPS) everything related to the case. The CPS will then disclose relevant material to the defence. The question of what is, and what is not, deemed relevant will be decided by the Trial Judge if necessary. Unused material consists of that which has not been served on the defence but has an impact on the case. Parties to the case include defence, the prosecution team and third parties. The prosecution team currently consists of:
1. The police.
2. The prosecution counsel.
3. Forensic scientists.
4. Psychiatrists.

Auditors may fall under the third party category in that we hold unused material. The police will advise an organisation to retain information relating to the case and to notify them of its existence. This is then revealed to the CPS.

The rules
1. The police provide copies of a specimen form to any third parties. This form asks for details of all material that forms part of the papers to the investigation. This includes for example:
- Witness statements and rough notes.
- All other statements and rough notes.
- Correspondence relating to the case.
- Material that may cast doubt on the reliability of a witness (e.g. rough notes show continual change of mind).
- Material that casts doubt on a confession.

The term "material" covers that held manually and on computer.

2. The completed form is sent to the CPS for disclosure to defence representatives.

3. Defence may then ask to view (and copy) any material on this list that they consider relevant to the case. They will contact the third party directly.

4. If permission to view and copy is refused by a third party, then defence may take their case to the Trial Judge for a ruling on whether the material is relevant or not.

5. There is an exemption for "sensitive material" that is dealt with under the Attorney General's guidelines that covers matters such as:

- To protect national security.
- To protect the identity of an informant whose family would be in danger.
- To protect the identity of a witness whose family would be in danger.
- If it would disclose an important method of surveillance.
- If it would alert someone to the fact that he/she is a suspect.
- If it might allow someone to be blackmailed.

Audit would have to inform defence that the information is held but that it is sensitive. If challenged, the CPS will have to convince the Trial Judge that this is the case. On rare occasions (e.g. a murder case), this application may be made in private without informing the defence.

Main implications

Internal audit should attempt to keep up-to-date with this development since there are many audit investigations that result in a police case and criminal prosecution. There are wider ranging implications where a case is worked on by an auditor that later forms the basis of criminal charges:

1. Working papers covering investigations that may be referred to the police must be maintained to acceptable standards so that documents may be readily retrievable. There should be standards on note-taking, recording meetings, interviewing and evidence gathering along with any in-house training that may be required to implement them.

2. The organisation will need to adopt a policy on whether to respond to requests for unused material, although any refusal could be overturned by a Trial Judge. The defence may ask for excessive amounts of material as part of a "fishing expedition". New rules on legal aid mean that fixed fees are now payable to defence lawyers which may result in fewer demands for material in an attempt to reduce workload that can no longer be charged for.

3. Where viewing is agreed, it will be necessary to adopt a policy covering supervising the visitor, charging for copies, recording items that have been requested, advising the CPS, defining sensitive material and any other related issues.

4. If the status of any material is considered by a Trial Judge, then the organisation would have to be represented at this hearing where its internal policies and the particular case would be discussed.

5. The organisation will need to designate an officer who would be responsible for completing the pro forma on unused material in line with the adopted policies on this matter.

All large organisations should publish policies on the disclosure of evidence which should be kept up-to-date with any changes in this area of law.

29.6 Investigating the Fraud

Courses of action
When employee fraud or irregularity comes to the attention of the auditor there are a number of alternative courses of action. It is essential that each course is carefully weighed up and the most appropriate action selected, based on the circumstances and the strength of evidence so far secured. These options should be kept under review:

☐ **Call the police**. This will be necessary where there is strong evidence of a fraud. Policy should be that the police are informed at the earliest opportunity. For more complicated concealed crimes, the police would expect the organisation to have done some basic background work beforehand.

☐ **Commence a management enquiry**. This may involve a manager or management team being assigned to formally enquire into the circumstances of the case. This represents a responsible approach by management that acknowledges the importance of resolving frauds at once say by interviewing all staff working in the area in question. It can spoil an investigation where those responsible are alerted and so are able to cover their tracks. If management, through lack of experience, do not cover all eventualities then records could go missing, potential witnesses may be pressured and the investigation thwarted.

☐ **Commence an audit investigation**. The matter may be referred to internal audit for formal investigation. It may be kept confidential while a suitable strategy is formulated. An issue that is increasingly relevant is securing data held on PCs. If a suspect is alerted the files may be irretrievably wiped clean or destroyed.

☐ **Commence a joint management/internal audit investigation**. This is normally the best approach since it combines audit expertise with management's local knowledge in a suitable strategy. It also recognises that management is responsible for investigating frauds.

☐ **Interview the officer in question**. There are times when this is the simplest option. It is possible to spend weeks investigating a matter which when presented to the culprit, he/she admits to straight away. Some fraudsters seek attention and want to be caught. It also allows simple explanations to be presented before the investigation has gone too far, for example a case of mistaken identity or someone using another's computer access ID and password. The problem here is that, if little work has been done on the investigation, suspects may cover their tracks before any real evidence has been secured.

☐ **Suspend the suspect**. Where the evidence is strong and there is a real risk that losses may ensue if action is not taken straight away, then the suspect may be suspended. There needs to be a clear case and the decision should be reasonable and in line with the organisation's disciplinary policy. The main difficulty is that while suspension does not imply guilt, an assumption of guilt tends to be made by others. Suspension means that evidence cannot be tampered with. It also makes a stronger case for dismissal at a later disciplinary where one may be arguing that the person's presence at work can no longer be tolerated. It will stop audit catching the person as the fraud is being perpetrated. Another disadvantage is that it may make it difficult to quickly convene an interview with the suspect who may resign before a case has been built up.

☐ **Instruct disciplinary proceedings.** We may wish to move straight into a formal disciplinary based on the facts that are available. This is possible where we find that an employee has been convicted for fraud at court and this affects his/her position at work. It is better to carry out a full investigation beforehand and base the disciplinary on the findings.

☐ **Check the system of internal control.** This is an important step and there are times when there is little that may be done. If a cheque has been stolen and fraudulently encashed then apart from advising the police there may not be much more that can be done. On the control side we might wish to issue a strict instruction that cheques issued by the organisation should not be left out on desks and should be locked away overnight.

☐ **Issue a formal instruction to staff.** This may sometimes be the most appropriate response. If it is clear that staff are over-enthusiastic in, say, travel or overtime claims then it may be necessary to remind them that this is unacceptable and further distortion may constitute a disciplinary offence. We must be sure of the facts before making general comments and there are varying degrees of severity. Best practice suggests that employees should be told what constitutes a disciplinary offence and given sufficient warnings before a formal disciplinary is applied.

☐ **Do nothing.** This depends on policy. It is possible to have a policy where anonymous phone calls making allegations where the person refuses to be seen (in confidence) are not followed up. This must be justified and arises where there are resource constraints and excessive levels of unfounded allegations.

The above options should be considered with care as soon as information is received on possible fraud and irregularity. A process of assessing the circumstances and selecting the right response should be established so that a sound decision may be made. Each of these options should be reconsidered periodically as an investigation progresses. It is possible to establish a formal policy whereby internal audit is informed immediately of all frauds, actual or alleged. Some argue that there is no one way to investigate a fraud since each one varies depending on the circumstances. This does not preclude us from developing principles for the investigation of fraud.

One framework is as follows:

FIGURE 29.3 A PROCESS FOR INVESTIGATING FRAUDS

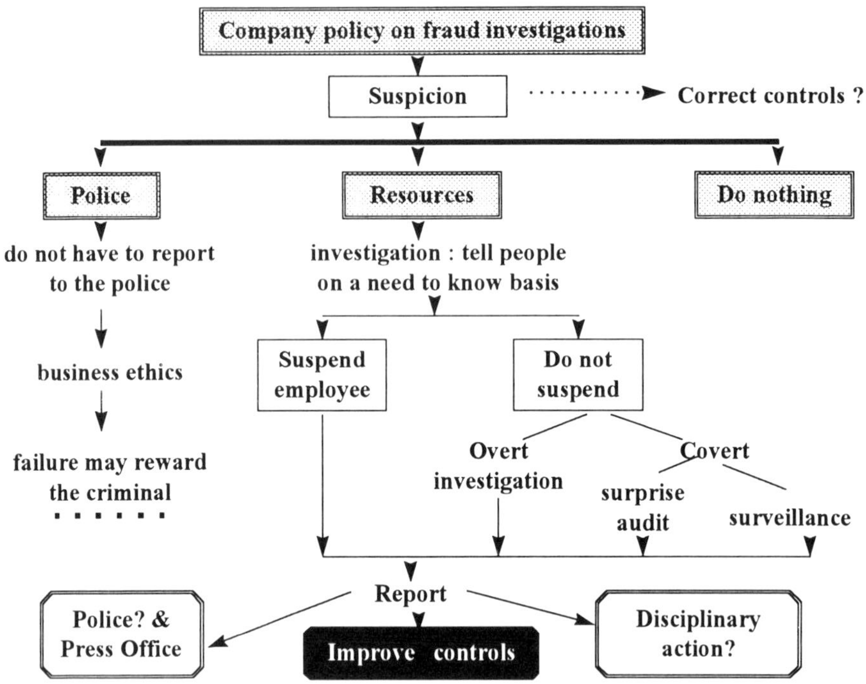

Main considerations

Parts of the IIA standards comment on fraud and these provide some interesting guidance (IIA 280, 330, 410 and 430). During a fraud investigation consider:

1. **Planning the investigation**. The adopted strategy will have to be carefully selected, taking on board all relevant factors.

2. **Surveillance**. The use of this technique should be considered.

3. **Resources required**. The need to re-assign resources will be high on the agenda.

4. **Recovering any lost funds**. At the outset of the investigation, identifying the extent of losses should be a major concern. This will affect the way that the ensuing work is carried out so that a confirmed "schedule of losses" may be documented at the conclusion of the investigation.

5. **Legal status of the allegation**. Is it theft or simply breach of procedure? The police may be able to have an input on this matter. We have already suggested that a simple breach of procedure may turn out to be a major fraud.

6. **The level of evidence that has to be secured**. This will depend on the materiality of the fraud and the degree of difficulty in securing the available evidence.

7. **Limiting access to required documents**. It may be necessary to take immediate steps to protect files, documents and computerised records that contain evidence of the fraud. Where there is a clear suspect then this may be the best course of action.

8. **Management's role and the way that it will support the investigation**. This will vary depending on organisational policies. Where management shows no interest at all then the fraud will be very difficult to penetrate. Where management is over-

enthusiastic then mistakes may occur, and a sensible middle ground needs to be achieved.

9. **The need to refrain from unfounded accusations**. Shooting from the hip is unacceptable. Even if we are sure who perpetrated the fraud, the case will rest on the evidence that supports our views and this can only be gathered through a careful process of investigation.

10. **Police involvement and advice**. Having a key contact at the local police station is very useful and this may be the first place for advice when the allegations first come to light.

11. **Staff interviews**. It may be necessary to meet with staff from the area in question as soon as possible. This may provide good leads to the culprit and who may, unknown to the auditor, be one of the interviewees. It also has a deterrent affect as staff see that the problem is being taken seriously by management.

12. **The need for tight confidentiality**. One of the biggest questions that needs to be addressed is who to see. It is as well to keep the enquiries one step removed from the area of the fraud and work with a more senior level of management. Much information can be secured from sources that are accessed centrally and it is here that the auditor's right of access becomes very useful. This also means that people outside the investigation's team need not be alerted to the fact that the investigation is taking place.

13. **Surprise audit**. This technique may be used where there is a history of audit carrying out unannounced checks at organisational locations. Where this is possible much inside information may be secured as well as checks made on relevant records without alerting the suspect(s).

The investigative process

Although every fraud investigation will be unique it is nonetheless possible to devise certain key stages and standardised procedures that may be applied to each one. These may be summarised:

1. Allegation received. A clear policy should be established. One may place limited reliance on anonymous accusations where the informant refuses to give name and contact number. If allegations come from several reliable sources their status is higher. Line managers' concerns over a member of staff may be given close attention and members of the public satisfied their concerns are being properly dealt with. Auditors may come across unexplained discrepancies. All allegations should be documented and full details, including action taken, kept in a confidential file. This is particularly relevant since claims that the problems will be covered up may later accompany allegations. There are many sources of information on illegal activities including routine audits, conversations, observations, MIS, systems of internal check, letters and phone calls. It is essential that the policy allows all allegations of fraud to be filtered through to internal audit so that centralised records may be maintained. Allegations could be the result of a grudge and/or incorrect information.

2. Establish the basic facts before firm action is taken. Interview the person supplying information at their convenience. This gives the auditor a good idea as to the validity of the allegations as well as providing necessary background information. Contact names should be taken and a full write-up of the allegation made. A personal profile may be drawn up where there are defined suspects and information such as payroll, pension records, personnel, creditors, income, electoral register, and Companies House may be used. It is possible to establish a defined list of details that relate to a suspect which may be placed on a check list. This will include description, age, address, car, grade, length of services, marital status, and sick record without alerting anyone to the investigation.

3. Carry out background research. This includes securing all information available to the auditor without entering the area where the fraud is located. It involves reviewing previous audit files and documents that relate to the location. A brief fact sheet may be compiled setting out an organisation chart and background details. An auditor cannot without permission search a person, car, personal bags or home address. However it is possible to search the suspect's office desk, and filing cabinets.

4. The preliminary report indicates whether the allegation may be true and should be investigated. An overall strategy should be defined. Management should be shown the report and a meeting held to discuss the implications. This is important because if it is shown there is no foundation for the allegations, then time is saved by avoiding a full scale investigation. Alternatively, it may be more efficient to send a memo to staff where wide-scale minor abuse is evident such as high levels of private phone calls or private photocopying as a form of amnesty after which action will be taken against continuing offenders. This may be the best solution and save audit time. The preliminary report will address how best the problem should be tackled and by whom.

5. Investigation plan. This plan should be derived from discussions with management and will indicate the approach, work required, resources, and any contact with the police or other authorities. The preliminary report outlined above will be used to derive a plan of action and may set the tone for relevant meetings with senior managers. The plan should set in motion the agreed approach so that all parties to the matter have a clear role with timescales attached to each task.

6. Managerial support. The level of managerial support will depend on the fraud and level at which it is alleged to have occurred. It is best to link with the level of management twice removed from the allegations. This ensures the manager is outside the range of the fraud. A decision will be made on audit/management roles and whether it will be a joint investigation. The reporting mode will be defined and how frequently these reports will be made. It is advisable to draft brief reports and present them orally to management since time is a prime factor in most fraud investigations. These reports should be made at least once a week and more frequently for high-risk investigations that need urgent action. It is good practice to keep the CIA informed by providing copies of the reports.

7. Defining barriers. Throughout the investigation it is necessary to work out possible barriers to the investigation such as missing documents, sources of evidence, the culprit's presence, close associates of the culprit, the need for confidentiality, and records being tampered with. Where any of the evidence is at risk, swift action must be taken. An organisation can assist by making the intentional and unauthorised destruction/removal of documentation a disciplinary offence. Computerised information, particularly that which is held on a PC, can contain valuable evidence and is at risk.

8. Initial strategy. New information will come to light and the adopted strategy will alter as necessary. The idea will be to cover all angles and find the best way of securing relevant evidence. The options of suspension, interview, notifying the police and so on should be continually reviewed. Some investigations have a funnel approach where they start out with a broad base and narrow down the relevant issues as new facts come to light. The strategy changes to become increasingly focused on key areas. These will be where there are outstanding queries or inconsistencies that cannot be explained without implicating defined individuals. Meanwhile occurrences that at first sight appear suspicious may be explained as the investigation gets going.

9. The full investigation. Most of the investigation will involve obtaining confirmatory evidence in whatever form it is available. This may include reviewing documents, interviews, photographs, surveillance, analysis, and/or tracing transactions. It is here that the real art of applying auditing techniques comes to the fore. We must seek to prove guilt by carefully compiling relevant evidence although we should be careful not to be seen as acting as an agent provocateur. The resource issue must be resolved and this will alter as the investigation takes shape and changes direction. It will be linked to sensitivity and overall impact on the organisation.

10. Interim reports. Throughout the investigation interim reports should be issued setting out findings to date, implications and further work recommended. It is for management to suspend staff, instruct the police, search desks, confiscate books and records and the internal auditor should act in an advisory capacity. All major decisions should be made by management under advice from internal audit. These reports will represent a formal record of the progress of the investigation and used in conjunction with the minutes of meetings held with management. They provide an account of decisions made through to conclusion.

11. The final report covers the necessary action that should be taken and this may treat the activity as an internal matter or seek referral to the police. The report should address any immediate action on control weaknesses and may recommend a full systems review once the fraud has been dealt with. The recommendations should be sensitive to the welfare of the organisation and if staff have to be interviewed, this should be done through management in a carefully planned manner with a minimum of disturbance to the services provided by the affected area. When reporting it may be practice to name individuals implicated or use a coding system with detachable keys that are kept confidential. All reports should be clearly marked confidential. The number of copies should be restricted and it is best to present them on a need-to-know basis.

Practical points
All frauds are different and fixed rules cannot be applied to unpredictable circumstances. A disciplined approach is based on compiling sound evidence from reliable and confirmed sources with the resulting documents put together in a systematic fashion. Practical points to note:
1. The police prefer cases to be well presented with the evidence clearly compiled. This enables them to resource the investigation and assign to it a degree of importance. If a case is poorly put together with obvious gaps, this will make it more difficult for the police to deal with it in an efficient manner. The ideal position is reached where a good

relationship has been built up over the years between internal audit and the local police. In dealing with cases, the police will have defined their requirements and a level of trust will exist where the auditor's work is deemed wholly reliable.

2. We should determine whether the enquiry is an internal disciplinary matter or a case for the police. It is good policy to refer all criminal cases to the police or at least seek their advice. On the other hand, the implications for the organisation must be considered for all cases even those that are being dealt with by the police. It is important that a separate case is developed for use in an internal disciplinary that does not depend on the results of the police case.

3. The police should be assigned a liaison officer which may be an internal auditor who will be in contact with them throughout the investigation. Auditors may assist where say a whole group of staff has to be interviewed since a heavy police presence may disturb the services that are being provided. In this respect it may be advisable for audit to undertake these interviews and present the results to the police. Again these and other issues should be discussed with the liaison officer.

4. When an allegation first comes to light, it is essential that the affected area is defined since any initial covert enquiries will have to be performed outside this area. This is particularly true where through lack of evidence it is necessary to allow the fraud to continue and capture current evidence. Surveillance is an example of securing concurrent evidence to support the allegations. Secrecy must be preserved and this point should be repeated to all involved at every opportunity. Sometimes it is better to take a case away from management, and report only to a senior manager so this element of secrecy may be maintained. An investigation will eventually become public knowledge.

5. Where an employee is being investigated by the police as a result of an internal investigation, it is still possible to discipline this person. The person can be interviewed and disciplined without waiting for the outcome of the police case as long as the charges relate to internal matters, e.g. breach of procedure as opposed to a criminal act such as theft. It is difficult to see how a fraud could be perpetrated against an organisation without an accompanying breach of procedure. It is the breach that should be dealt with and this matter should be addressed in the disciplinary code of practice and job descriptions. It is a good idea to interview a suspect before he/she is arrested by the police. This is because a defence lawyer may recommend that any employee arrested in respect of a criminal offence should not discuss the case with the employer. We may go further and suggest that a disciplinary hearing may be held in the absence of the employee although it is better to hear a representation from the employee before the disciplinary panel make their decision.

6. When an employee is accused of stealing the organisation's assets it is important that the situation is quite clear. Theft requires an intention to permanently remove the goods and one defence is that items are held at home for later use at work. If there is no clear policy the courts may find it difficult to give a guilty verdict. A formal document should spell out exactly what is entitled to be kept at home and what must not be removed. A formal inventory should be devised with signatures for each item removed. It should be possible to show in court that an officer had no right to hold defined objects or use them for unauthorised purposes. If the policy is slack, vague or not applied, then any subsequent investigation will be hindered.

7. The standard of evidence will be high since it will be scrutinised in detail at any later court hearing or internal disciplinary. Defence will attempt to find fault with prosecution evidence and any minor error may be used to call into doubt remaining evidence however accurate. The standard defence is to engender doubt into a jury's mind. If junior auditors are being used, they must be given clear instructions. The audit manager may organise the case so that he/she will present an item of evidence even if it was compiled by a junior auditor. On no account should an inexperienced auditor be left to the mercy of the defence lawyer at court, where the audit work is unreliable, not reviewed and un-checked. Regular team briefings will promote a consistent approach. It is advisable to give junior staff a clear insight into the nature of the fraud enquiry before they undertake their work on the basis that a better understanding of the objectives will encourage better results.

8. It is best for management to present disciplinaries and represent the organisation in court while the audit role may be reserved as that of principal witnesses. Management are responsible for investigating fraud. Audit may act as advisors and compile evidence in support. Audit may become experts in presenting evidence to court as reliable witnesses, while management will stand up in court and explain their procedures and describe how they were breached. Management would also present the case to a disciplinary for a formal consideration and decision, while auditors will attend as witnesses. It helps if the precise roles of each party have been properly defined at the outset.

9. Under the Data Protection Act 1984, non-disclosure does not apply where the information is needed to detect crime or apprehend or prosecute offenders. Internal audit should have access to all information and explanations necessary for the performance of their work and an appropriate audit warrant will be issued to reflect this. There is a view that the Data Protection Act is infringed where one embarks on a "fishing expedition" with no clear suspects in mind. This might occur where one is seeking to compare two computer files as a general fraud detection exercise.

10. The Advance Disclosure of Evidence Act allows defence the right to look at evidence before it comes to trial. This has an impact on internal audit since it will cover the original documents that were used to arrive at the audit opinion. Defence may also view material that was never published in the audit report but may have been used in the investigation. This applies to audit working papers, primary documents and related documents. The defence will make requests through the relevant police officer who will then make necessary arrangements. The auditor should always take the name and address of the person visiting and be present when documents are examined. The defendant is not entitled to see the documents, only the lawyers. Where photocopies are requested the auditor should note these requests and supply them at a later date with a covering letter and accompanying invoice set at a reasonable rate. It is essential that the organisation publishes a suitable policy on the arrangements for complying with the legislation.

When conducting an investigation always open a file and adhere to the in-house standards on the following:

*   Always use indexes in all files.
*   Placing original documents in plastic wallets.
*   Using photocopies (with the words "I certify that this is a true and fair copy taken this day"; signed and dated).

- Using interview notes and photographs (marked with dates, times, places).
- Ensuring that all information is recorded and all documents kept secure. Particularly sensitive material may be held under lock and key in the audit safe.
- Retaining the original documents and giving copies to third parties, including the police.

29.7 Computer Abuse

Introduction
Fraud and computer abuse are problems that have to be adequately controlled and this requires much audit attention. When computers were first introduced it was felt that they were prone to fraud and well publicised cases confirmed these fears. This was not strictly correct as it became clear that a whole assortment of controls has to be established to ensure that the sensitive systems are protected. The ability of controls to keep up with the development of software and the potential for abuse is a major factor in this constant battle to keep computer abuse in check.

Types of abuse
There are different types of problems that may fall under the term computer abuse:

☐ **Sabotage**. This may be carried out by a disgruntled employee or ex-employee. There may be political reasons that may underpin computer sabotage as it is now recognised that an attack on an organisation's main computerised systems is the single most effective way to disrupt business.

☐ **Data protection principles contravened**. Here data that relates to a living person may be interfered with such that the relevant legislation (Data Protection Act 1984) is breached. This would typically involve accessing files that contain confidential information relating to a specific individual. Some feel that because there is no defined loss to the organisation, then one may legitimately breach systems security and secure unauthorised access to information.

☐ **Actual computer-related theft**. This covers the straightforward theft of computer equipment. Computerisation, particularly for distributed systems, may bring with it an abundance of terminals and printers that sit on numerous office desks. These will have a re-sale value and are vulnerable if not properly protected. Software theft is more sophisticated in that it generally involves making unauthorised copies of programmes for business or private use. Alternatively these programmes may be legitimate copies since, if a computer is stolen, we have lost the machine and any software that is resident on the hard disk. An increasingly common problem relates to the theft of PC microchips.

☐ **Misuse of computer equipment and processing time**. This could range from playing computer games or developing personal software through to running one's own business on company machines. In some respects, this is the most difficult type of abuse to control as most portable machines are used, to some extent, for private purposes. The important issue that should be considered is any loss in terms of business time that is mis-applied where the abuse occurs during office hours. Unfortunately, if the PC can only be used at work, i.e. is not taken home, then any private/unauthorised use may consume business hours unlike work done at home on portable PCs. It may be good practice to allow employees to purchase redundant PCs for use at home to help avert this.

☐ **Misuse of computer files and programmes**. This may consist of deleting and manipulating files, planting time bombs, introducing viruses, or generally embarking on criminal activities. This type of abuse may have long-lasting effects that cause severe problems for the organisation. A comprehensive package of controls will be required to combat these threats. The greater the level of access that the perpetrator has, the greater the risk and this along with technical knowledge and motive can be the single biggest worry that an organisation may face in terms of computer abuse.

☐ **Computer fraud**. Fraud is perpetrated through the use of a computer so that detection is made more difficult if not impossible. Dormant accounts with credit balances may be used to generate refunds to the internal fraudster who may also purge audit logs that would otherwise disclose these.

The Audit Commission has defined computer fraud as:

> *"Any fraudulent behaviour connected with computerisation by which someone gains a dishonest advantage."*

Another convenient way to analyse computer abuse is:

FIGURE 29.4 COMPUTER ABUSE

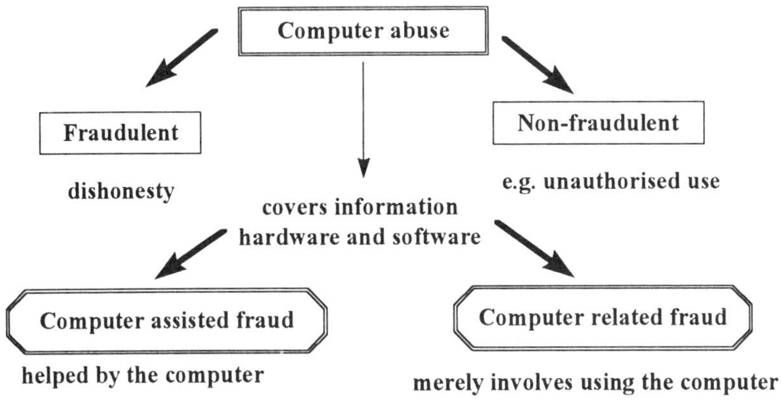

One estimated breakdown of cause of losses may be:

TABLE 29.2 CAUSE OF LOSSES

CAUSE	% OF LOSSES
Human error	50%
Malicious damage	15%
Fire and Flood	20%
Fraud and theft	15%

Audit Commission research

Audit Commission research (1981) in local authorities found that frauds were increasing and many were undetected or not disclosed to the authorities. They argued that there is a need to promote a well-managed organisation with less risk of fraud that involves:

Vision	**To minimise risks**
Style	**Management reviews the computer**
Strategy	**Identify risks, plans and strategy**
Structure	**Responsibility for security and reviewing the arrangements should be well defined**
Systems	**Systems for controlling computers**
Skills	**Trained staff aware of risks**
Staffing	**Suggest improvements**

The next local authority based Audit Commission research (1990) updated this and concluded:

- Few organisations recognise that part of the cost of IT is its security. As desktop computing becomes an everyday part of business life so the need for better security measures will increase.
- Because the cost of computing is falling, more staff are being given computing facilities to perform daily tasks and yet comparatively few are given training in protecting the data on which they rely.
- With so many more users of microcomputers which are linked to networks, there is a need to ensure that access is restricted and control becomes more important.
- Keep it simple. Basic controls implemented successfully could reduce the exposure to risk.
- Audit has a vital role to play in advising upon and helping to design controls and security measures. More computer-literate auditors are needed, to appreciate the increasing risks which computing presents.

IIA and Chartered Institute of Management Accountants Survey

This 1988 survey on computer fraud found:

- Pressure of work meant that preventative controls were given a low priority.
- There was a general lack of sophistication in access and other controls.
- Organisations felt that external audit should have an advisory role.
- The audit team should include an IT specialist.
- There was little attention directed at personnel recruitment as a control.
- Audit enquiry software was not really used by finance managers.

The report recommended:

- Steps should be taken to ensure that controls are adhered to.
- Make extensive use of password controls.
- Carry out random tracking of individual transactions.
- Use human resource management techniques including recruitment, performance control, segregation of duties, motivation and awareness training.
- Formulate a well defined policy on fraud.
- Do not rely on the computer always being correct.
- Software packages make it more difficult to manipulate software.

National Computing Centre, ICL, Department of Trade Survey on Computer Misuse 1992
This survey showed that computer misuse-related losses amounted to £1 billion for 1991 and highlighted business and industry's lack of awareness and concern:
- Over a quarter of small business and nearly a half of businesses with over 10,000 employees had suffered a serious security breach involving the unauthorised use of computer systems in the last five years.
- Only a quarter of businesses had taken any precautions in the light of the Computer Misuse Act 1990.

They concluded that organisations need to adopt clear policies on computer abuse that includes formal links with the police.

Further Audit Commission research
October 1994 saw the release of the latest Audit Commission research on computer abuse ("Opportunity makes a thief"). Based on 1,000 private and public sector organisations, the Audit Commission found that reported incidents trebled. Reported frauds were up by 38% and the value of reported fraud increased by 183%. The role of controls (particularly for financial systems) was once again highlighted with the need to recognise the risks inherent in computerised systems. They found that nearly half of fraud was discovered by pure accident. In terms of prevention it is unfortunate that:
- Nearly a quarter of organisations had no internal audit.
- About half had no computer audit skills.
- Two-thirds had no security awareness training in place.
- Four-fifths practised no risk analysis.

A lack of basic controls along with ineffective monitoring arrangements were pointed to as the main problems. Interestingly the research brought out the new problem of unauthorised access to personal data which breaches both the DP Act and the Computer Misuse Act.

Features of computer fraud
Some argue that the computer makes it easier to perpetrate fraud:
1. **The records tend to be centralised**. For centralised in contrast to distributed systems, the records may be located away from the operational staff who would have some insight into their reliability. As a result, obvious errors may well be missed.
2. **Small repeated frauds may go unnoticed**. If a loophole in the system allows less material frauds to occur these may then be repeated over a long period. The system will accept these are the norm and any management information will not readily isolate adverse trends. Many systems apply looser controls to smaller amounts so that a creditors' system for example may allow small amounts to be paid without an accompanying official order.
3. **Concealment is easier**. It is possible to use the system to hide a fraud. This is particularly true where it is possible to alter programmed controls related for example to an exception reporting facility. The system will only report data that has been deemed important and unlike manual records, the unreported items cannot be viewed in the normal course of events. Armed with the knowledge of what is regularly reported a fraudster can plan a crime.

591

4. **There may be no human monitoring**. Many frauds are picked up because "something is wrong". Many organisations rely on this natural ability for sensing inconsistencies to keep matters in check. Computerisation may mean that this technique is no longer relevant. Duplicate names will not be picked up where the account number is the key field and only one record is shown on screen for each enquiry (where names are entered in different formats). In the past a clerk who manually recorded each transaction might have been able to spot any such errors or falsifications.

Computer fraud may be carried out in many ways
- At the computer centre.
- By manipulating software.
- By manipulating computer input.

The defrauder may be:
- A non-technical in-house system user.
- A computer specialist.
- An outsider; for example an ex-employee.

Computer hacking
- Conspiracy to defraud is a common law offence.
- Fraud requires a degree of permanency and a VDU screen is not a permanent medium.
- Access controls are essential.
- The fraud squad now employ computer experts.
- Under the Data Protection Act 1984, an organisation is liable where personal data is subject to unauthorised access.
- The state of social and business ethics impacts on the acceptability of hacking.
- Various British attitude surveys indicate that white collar crime is not generally seen as serious.

Gerald Vinten (1990) mentions arguments adduced in favour of hacking:
- Industry benefits where hackers try to break into systems by identifying control weaknesses.
- We can learn about the system as part of a training programme.
- It brings forward research into the problem.
- Systems can be tested by the consumer before a purchase decision is made.
- It may be legitimate when one is inadvertently locked out of a system.
- It may promote public order when used by the police.
- It may be part of a national defence strategy to infiltrate foreign governments' systems.

Computer hackers are now being jailed in a move to address this problem. In one case two such hackers, operating from home with a basic terminal, modems and phone lines, were jailed for six months in June 1993 for hacking into databases of the American space agency, NASA, and defence systems run by Britain and the European Community.

The Computer Misuse Act 1990
An Act has now been passed providing for three new criminal offences:
- Unauthorised access to computer systems.

- Unauthorised access to computer systems with intent to commit or facilitate the commission of a serious crime.
- Unauthorised modification of computer material (this covers viruses and time bombs).

These offences are prosecutable if conducted from or directed against the UK. An organisation should adapt its policies to include notifying the police and must decide beforehand exactly what is included under the formal definition of authorised access for each employee.

Software piracy

Some mention must be made of the special problems associated with software piracy. The Copyright, Design and Patents Act 1988 states that "the owner of the copyright has the exclusive right to copy the work". In the context of software, the copyright owner is the software developer. The legal penalties for breaking this law include unlimited fines and up to two years imprisonment. There are the obvious ethical issues of right and wrong and one must ask the basic question of whether it is right to steal someone's work for your own personal gain with no intention of rewarding the author. There are those who feel that all other questions are subsidiary to this.

☐ **The scale of the problem**. The scale of this problem is great and a survey commissioned by Apple, Claris and Microsoft (1989-1992) revealed that approximately £20m was lost as a result of unauthorised software copying. There are many points that should be noted concerning software piracy:
1. It is associated with the spread of PCs (particularly portables) and may appear to be an attractive option at first sight.
2. There are many ways that this unauthorised copying can arise and illicit copies may be:
   - Brought into the organisation by an over enthusiastic user.
   - Duplicated from elsewhere in the organisation.
   - Pirated from the organisation and then taken home.
   - It may result from too many users on a network.
   - The software may be "inherited" from a PC that has been in use for many years.
   - Software may have been borrowed from colleagues in an emergency and never removed from the system.
   - It may have been copied for a training session and never deleted.
3. Some users feel justified in using unauthorised software as long as it is being applied to organisational objectives. A drawn-out software acquisition approval process may hinder and frustrate users who simply want specific software to do their work. The available direction from senior management may suggest that copying is allowed as long as they do not know about it and this will set the tone throughout the organisation. The fact that this is an offence may conveniently pass over the heads of many staff.
4. Software piracy should become a personalised issue covered within the disciplinary code of practice. The task of raising awareness of illegal software copying is a major issue and the advice is that it should be based on a clear understanding from all levels of the organisation aided by staff presentations and regular bulletins.

☐ **The software audit**. Most argue that they cannot afford a software policy and the necessary tracking procedure, although breaking down procedures into departmental level for manageability can greatly assist this task. Up-to-date records are essential and as a start many problems may be tackled by firstly defining where the organisation stands in terms of its software (and hardware). A software audit can pay dividends in this respect and this is recommended by the Federation Against Software Theft (FAST) as having the following benefits:

1. Identifies what licenses exist.
2. Ensures software is used for the right task.
3. Helps rationalise training needs.
4. Reduces any upgrade costs.
5. Increases bargaining power with suppliers.
6. Eliminates security risks from viruses.
7. We may recover hard disk space that is being inappropriately used.
8. And most importantly it will enable the organisation to minimise any risk of legal action.

☐ **The organisational culture.** There is a need to place what typically is the widespread practice of software copying into context. Even if the software is being applied to organisational objectives the practice is still unacceptable. An organisation that condones this practice by failing to guard against it in a pro-active fashion may be openly criticised. Software copying is also associated with a lack of training and support from the organisation and a failure to establish close supplier contact. It is also indicative of the absence of a clear software policy where a "free for all" attitude becomes the order of the day. In practice, software piracy is generally symptomatic of an overall lack of controls over the software and also the various machines in use. The benefits that flow from tighter controls therefore have a wider impact on the way an organisation might manage IT and whether value for money is achieved therein. To tackle these issues, a simple code of conduct may be introduced that would cover the following matters:

1. Unauthorised software copying is asking for trouble.
2. Ensuring that proper licenses are obtained.
3. Checking whether back-ups are permitted.
4. Keeping programme disks secure.
5. Keeping hold of original manuals and disks.
6. Keeping a record of software resident on PCs.
7. Unauthorised software may contain viruses and specific rules must be introduced:
   - Do not copy software.
   - Do not share software or make copies with colleagues.
   - Do not make additional copies for the network.
   - Do not make copies of software to take home.
   - Do not accept free software from colleagues and friends.

☐ **Establishing responsibility.** Most organisations suffer from software piracy because they fail to define managerial responsibility for this issue. Where software is acquired it must either be centrally registered or recorded locally, depending on the type of organisation. Where there is a central purchasing function in place for all software, then this central register may be feasible. Decentralised organisations will adhere to local arrangements and here designated officers should be responsible for each section/division so that system disks are held in a secure location and suitable records maintained.

☐ **The Federation Against Software Theft (FAST)**. FAST is an independent organisation set up to raise awareness of software copying. In this respect there are several points that should be publicised:
1. It is illegal to copy software.
2. Senior management is responsible for the actions of its employees.
3. In 1992 FAST took proceedings against 200 companies.
4. Adverse publicity can result for the company in question.
5. FAST have not yet lost a single case.
6. Companies prosecuted have been forced to pay legal costs and damages to the copyright holder, remove all illegal software and legally purchase new copies.
7. FAST is now working on the problems caused by car boot sales and office equipment auctions.

☐ **The European directive on software**. This is effective from January 1993 and provides that the license holder cannot restrict the user's right to back up their copies. Error correction may also be made by the user and some de-compilation and copying may be allowed during reverse engineering.

☐ **Computer viruses**. These present further problems that are linked to the wider issue of software control. Viruses can be introduced from a number of sources and pirated software is one way that they might appear on an organisation's systems. Viruses are programmes that act in an unpredictable or damaging way. A tighter definition of a virus is a self-contained sequence of machine code which when run, can insert executable copies of itself into other executable codes. Suitable controls need to be implemented to guard against the threat of computer viruses and these may include:
1. Booting only from original write protect diskette.
2. Purchase only film-wrapped or securely contained software.
3. Backing up new software immediately and storing the original securely.
4. Treating all new software with caution.
5. Prohibiting staff from using unauthorised diskettes on computers in the organisation.
6. Testing all new software for viruses on a stand-alone machine with virus identification software prior to its wider use in conjunction with suitable anti-virus programmes.
7. Vigilance with symptoms that suggest a virus has struck e.g. reduced memory space or files disappearing for no good reason.
8. Formal procedure for backing up data files.
9. Publicise any particular problems.
10. Formal contingency plans for action where a virus is suspected.
11. Rehearsal of these contingency plans.

Policies on personal computing facilities
Computer equipment may be misused although if adequate supervision is applied and staff are motivated to meet targets, they should be too busy to spend unauthorised time. One special problem is controlling staff provided with portable equipment for use on location or at home. We have suggested that applying computers to private work is not in itself a major problem; it is more the time diverted that represents the real cost. Where staff only have access to computers (and printers) at work this may result in private work being carried out in office time. It may be impossible to stop staff doing private work on portable

office PCs used at home, although a firm policy covering this matter should be published. The following issues are noted below.

☐ **Publish a clear IT policy and ensure that staff are aware of it**. Best practice suggests that an organisation must make people aware of what is expected from them and the consequences of breaching these procedures. This should not be simply a paper exercise but must involve clear procedures supported by management and applied consistently across the board. It is best to explain the special rules regarding IT soft/hardware and not leave this issue as part of the general procedures covering organisational assets. Remember procedures must apply to all regardless of how senior.

☐ **Make a clear statement that private work is not allowed and may result in disciplinary action**. It is possible to work within this rule by allowing an immaterial level of private work as long as it does not interfere with the business at hand. What must be avoided is excessive levels that become a complete distraction. This will arise where there are no rules at all.

☐ **Make sure that staff working at home are given deadlines for work products**. Encouraging home working in line with the use of notebooks can lead to greater efficiencies. On the other hand the temptation to misapply these resources is great, although this will only arise where the authorised work has not been controlled through either deadlines or time budgets. There is an additional link with the use of timesheets for staff whose work is project based.

☐ **Establish procedures for protecting personal data under the Data Protection legislation** including passwords, locks and controls over the diskettes. Security is the keyword that should be foremost on all IT managers' minds. This extremely simple concept requires an enormous amount of planning and the application of specific resources and is dealt with later on.

☐ **Carry out occasional spot checks** to look for abuse of facilities and follow up with the necessary action. One problem with controlling computer facilities is a lack of definition of ownership for the underlying equipment. The task of specifying and acquiring computer equipment can be quite simple with the downward trends in costs over the last few years. Once in place, the various PCs, terminals and portables can become lost in the vast assortment of machines. Some of these will become redundant very quickly and may be seen to have little value on the open market. Local printers are prone to becoming lost/misplaced and/or misappropriated. It is essential to ensure a defined officer is responsible for accounting for IT equipment with a further link officer located in all relevant departments. Once this is in place it will be necessary to check the items periodically not only for existence but also for the software that is held on each machine. Effective follow-up action depends on the presence of clear procedures where the spot check reveals problems.

☐ **Watch for the level of maintenance of equipment** and whether employees have been taking good care of items. It is advisable to have staff responsible for defined machines and also have PCs and printers assigned to individual officers. These officers will then be responsible for applying good housekeeping practices to their equipment in conjunction with servicing/maintenance work that should also be carried out possibly under contract. The careful use of dust caps, cleaners, hard disk locks, and once again good housekeeping should be required from all PC users.

☐ **Ensure that a record is maintained** so that all computer equipment may be traced to a defined officer. Hardware and software registers are a fundamental part of controlling PC facilities. This is more complicated than it sounds and once again we can turn to the view that a manager may feel that, as the budget holder, he/she owns the machines that are purchased over the years. Functional responsibility must be established via a clear IT register that may be centrally held and kept up-to-date via a suitable reporting mechanism.

☐ **Ensure that the equipment is being used efficiently** and that more urgent needs are given priority. IT acquisitions can result from a form of "one-up-manship" where items are purchased primarily to keep up with other managers. Ideally IT should be attracted to those areas that have an urgent need for it. As such it is as well to monitor how equipment is being used and whether there is a greater need elsewhere in the organisation. One may not necessarily aim to take back equipment from users, but this information will assist when planning budgets for additional acquisitions. These and other relevant factors should be taken on board during this monitoring. Reports may be presented to an appropriate decision-making forum such as an Information Technology Strategy Group who would consider and authorise IT budgets and individual IT acquisitions.

☐ **Call back all items periodically**, say bi-annually, for checking and avoid the scenario where staff feel that they have their own specific PCs. The point is re-stated here to emphasise the importance of keeping a check on equipment. Working from home and/or on location using organisational facilities is convenient but must be controlled. As well as checking the inventory say every six months we may also carry out routine cleaning and servicing at the same time. We would aim to check the hard disk, the resident software and the machine itself and if necessary view files that have been deleted from the hard disk.

☐ **Take out the required insurance policies** and provide guidance to staff about securing the items covering conspicuous behaviour, locking car boots, security at home etc. Portable PCs should be carried in such a way that it is not obvious that they are computers. Good practice guidelines should be established covering the way portable PCs may be protected when out of the office.

☐ **Appoint an individual to take overall responsibility for the equipment.**

☐ **Adopt a code of conduct** that requires high standards and ensure that it is followed to the letter. If IT issues are built into the employee code of conduct then this will give them a high profile. Efficient procedures are aimed at encouraging, assisting and promoting good practice. Where these are ignored despite reminders and staff training, then a second level control is to establish disciplinary action if procedures are not followed.

☐ **Ensure that managers talk to their staff and set good examples**. Control must start at the highest possible levels. If a manager has no regard for IT security then it is not possible to expect better standards from staff. Keeping IT on the agenda as an ongoing topic for discussion provides a firm foundation from which good systems of control may be built. The disciplinary code of practice should therefore be more rigidly applied to more senior staff.

Controlling computer abuse

There are additional practical measures that may be taken to control computer fraud:

☐ **Physical security**. As mentioned earlier, security is very important. There are varying levels of security that range from locks and keys, swipe cards, alarm systems through to full-time security staff.

☐ **Suitable recruitment procedures**. Employ the right staff in the first place.

☐ **Adequate supervision**. Managers should be concerned over the way staff are applying their computers and how this contributes to the achievement of organisational objectives. They must keep an eye on what is going on. A good example is where new software appears to be in use that in effect locks out the line manager. The activities of computer centre staff should be supervised even where they are working on night shifts. Staff involved in data keying should also be subject to adequate supervision. Even more sensitive are staff designated as systems managers (or systems controllers) who may have access to update files and other people's passwords. The way these staff interface with the system must be supervised as the scope to defraud the organisation for high-risk systems is great.

☐ **Withdraw access rights from leavers immediately**. IT staff who no longer have an affiliation to the organisation can cause harm with their inside knowledge of particular systems and controls. It is best to lock leavers out of the systems as soon as they resign by withdrawing physical and password access.

☐ **Encourage a general awareness of the risks**. A good place to start with control awareness in line with the risks from systems abuse, is the systems development process. Suitable controls should be designed at this stage where a new or enhanced computer system is being developed and implemented. Policies covering computer abuse and Data Protection should be well publicised throughout the organisation.

☐ **Resource the problem**. One vexed question that continually rears its head is who is responsible for controlling computer abuse? The answer not only addresses this issue but will by default, define the type of resources that are dedicated to this task. These resources should be adequate, trained, sufficiently independent and properly applied. Moreover, this may be the single most important factor in the success or otherwise of controlling computer abuse.

☐ **Encourage management trails**. A management trail shows who did what, when and to which records. All high-risk systems should address this issue. There are many systems where trails are available but are not put in place by management. In addition, even where the detailed information is available, it may not be used in any respect. The final problem that may occur is where the data that the trail is based on is incorrect in the first place. This will happen where staff are using each other's Passwords/IDs. By replacing the term "audit trail" with "management trail" we would hope to bring out the need for management (and/or systems control staff) to view the logs and not file them, on the chance that internal audit may review them at some stage.

☐ **Use terminal controls - passwords, locks, ID etc.** The use of passwords is dealt with extensively in the notes on computer input controls. It is possible to apply physical keyboard locks that block access to a system (or terminal) without the right key. Rules to be applied to passwords are:
1. All users should be uniquely identified.
2. Users should only have one user ID on a machine.
3. All users should have a log-in password that should be changed periodically.
4. Users should log-out whenever they leave their terminals.
5. As soon as someone leaves, their password should be removed.
6. Any user inactive from a system for a specified period should be locked out or removed.
7. Passwords should not be changed to a previously used one.
8. Do not use passwords that are easily guessed, e.g. family names, car registration, phone number, date of birth and so on.
9. For distributed UNIX based systems, root password privileges should be restricted to as few people as possible. Never allow a system password to expire or have them without password protection. Use log files to monitor failed log-in attempts; users who have left should immediately be removed from the electronic mail system; the initial password must be set by the local systems administrator and changed immediately to a personal one.
10. Use passwords that are long enough, as the length of the password is directly proportional to the ease of guessing the password. This is because some hackers use randomly generated guesses to crack the password.
11. Do not allow others to observe the operator keying in a password. It is possible to observe and follow the keystrokes used when standing over someone who uses their password. It is a matter of increased awareness that must be used to guard against this type of problem.
12. Ensure that the whole topic of password protection assumes a high profile within the organisation.

☐ **Install environment controls** over fire, power failures, alarms, back-up and insurance. This not only protects against accidents but also possible sabotage.

☐ **Trace all unauthorised attempts at access.** Instead of assuming a laid-back reactive approach, the systems manager may be more active in fraud prevention. The systems manager or network controller may receive reports on all unsuccessful attempts to access data files and take action in investigating them. This will act as a strong control against unauthorised access as any systems breaches are checked. It does however depend on a change in emphasis on the role of the systems manager to one of a systems controller.

☐ **Investigate suspense accounts items.** The Suspense Account facility is a convenient way to avoid interruptions in processing where most input is accepted even if there are coding problems. This may be abused where used excessively. It should only be used in exceptional cases and not regularly in the normal course of processing. Where a balance accrues, it must be investigated and all queries resolved before the balance grows too large and too much time has passed. Fraud is aided where it is known that items that fail the systems input criteria will stay in suspense for long periods. Standards must be established to cover the use of this account.

☐ **Define a policy on prosecuting fraudsters**. The classic situation is where a company does not want the publicity that arises when an employee who has breached its system's security is prosecuted. Best professional practice requires that the company uses the full extent of the law to punish offenders regardless of the consequences. It is necessary to define and publish a formal policy on prosecuting fraudsters that is used to guide management. Publication implies that the policy should be well understood throughout the organisation and that it is followed in practice.

☐ **Appoint a responsible officer**.   Security starts with clear responsibility and this is located with all managers in an organisation. To enforce this principle an officer must be appointed to define and implement appropriate policies and procedures as well as ensure compliance. The absence of a responsible officer will lower the overall consciousness of management on matters relating to systems security and take away a potential source of guidance and advice. A security policy may also be established that covers the organisation's IT arrangements. This should include security procedures for access, systems development, networks, asset registers, personnel issues, physical security and so on, in line with the Department of Trade and Industry and British Standards Institution codes.

☐ **Define standards of good practice**. The officer responsible for information systems should issue guides to good practice on important IT related matters. Parts of these guidelines may have mandatory status for important topics such as passwords and ID control. The point is that the IT officer must take the lead in this issue with clearly documented standards.

☐ **Set up traceable bait records**. The most up-front technique for combating computer fraud is to actually invite the fraudster to come into a system. We may leave credits suspended on accounts that may prove attractive to someone who can divert this for their own use. These "bait" records may then be traced back to the terminal that is intercepting them and so lead one to the culprit. This is an expensive technique that should only be used where specific frauds are expected.

☐ **Use computer usage logs**. Most systems allow the systems manager to read a log that shows who has been interfacing with what systems. The problem is that these logs may be very detailed and not used to any extent. By specifying the types of interfaces to be reported one may carry out spot checks on a sample to ensure that this use is consistent with what has been authorised. The role of the systems manager would have to be expanded to take on board this issue in line with direction from the IT security officer.

☐ **Transactions profiling**. It is possible to profile items that meet a defined criterion which seeks to isolate fraud. These items are then separately reported for later investigation. As an example, a creditors' system may profile possible duplicate payments or amounts without official orders for subsequent review.

☐ **Establish clear plans and investigation practices**. The organisation should decide exactly how alleged frauds will be dealt with. This policy will help define officer responsibilities and investigative methodologies so that a tried and trusted process may be put into motion as and when required.

☐ **Concentrate on access controls**. Much of the work done to safeguard computerised systems will revolve around access controls. These should be designed in line with the level of risk associated with the systems in question so that the more sensitive the system, the greater the degree of access controls. A careful study of the available controls will pay dividends bearing in mind that passwords may be guessed and that simple locks and keys can be very effective. An organisational review of access controls, their use and whether they are working should be carried out on a regular basis.

☐ **Use authorisation**. The Computer Misuse Act 1990 relies on the organisation to define whether an activity carried out on their systems is authorised or not. This is a crucial point and can make the difference between a criminal offence and an acceptable act. Any failing in this area will make it very difficult to discipline an employee for systems breaches, or for that matter initiate a criminal prosecution. Once an activity is deemed as unauthorised there must then be swift remedies where it occurs. This reinforces the policies and allows them to stand up to scrutiny in court/disciplinaries at a later date.

☐ **Consider staff morale**. Fraud directed against an organisation may be initiated by disgruntled or bored employees who have channelled their energies to work against business interests. In the fast changing world of IT, it is important to ensure that employees can keep up with the demanding pace. This requires a high motivation which can be either stimulated or hindered by the approach adopted by management.

☐ **Use call-back to check authenticity**. Wherever possible, users who access systems over telephone networks, should be called back to check whether they are authorised users. Building in these types of basic checks can deter many would-be fraudsters.

☐ **Segregate duties by rotation and watch vacation leave**. The principle whereby one person should not be the sole party involved in a transaction from start to finish should always be applied. It is possible to rotate staff from time to time so that any systems flaws that may be abused will be identified via an officer newly assigned. This could be applied to those responsible for initiating purchase orders. Making sure that officers in sensitive positions take their annual leave is another way of getting inside a system that may be based around one person. This is a valid approach as long as the duties are carried out by someone else when this person is on leave. Concealment is more difficult where one's duties are taken over by another person from time to time.

☐ **Use confidential document shredders**. Some frauds are based on using information obtained from systems printouts. For example one may apply for a credit card using bank and other details obtained from a printout from the payroll system. The rule must be that data should always be kept secure.

☐ **Use file control procedures**. Running the right files against the right system requires organising suitable controls to ensure this is done in a controlled environment.

The fraud control project
It is possible to carry out a special review of controls over computer abuse/fraud planned using an established model:

FIGURE 29.5 THE FRAUD CONTROL PROJECT

```
┌─────────────────────────────────────────┐
│      Identify corporate assets at risk   │
└─────────────────────────────────────────┘

      ┌───────────────────────────────┐
      │        Analyse threats        │
      └───────────────────────────────┘

      ┌───────────────────────────────┐
   ╱  │      Look at personal policies │
  ↙   └───────────────────────────────┘

┌──────────────────────────────┐      ┌──────────────────────────────┐
│   Apply preventive controls  │ ───► │   Apply detective controls   │
└──────────────────────────────┘      └──────────────────────────────┘

      ┌─────────────────────────────────────────────┐
      │  Have a plan for dealing with any frauds that│
      │      may be uncovered by the audit           │
      └─────────────────────────────────────────────┘
```

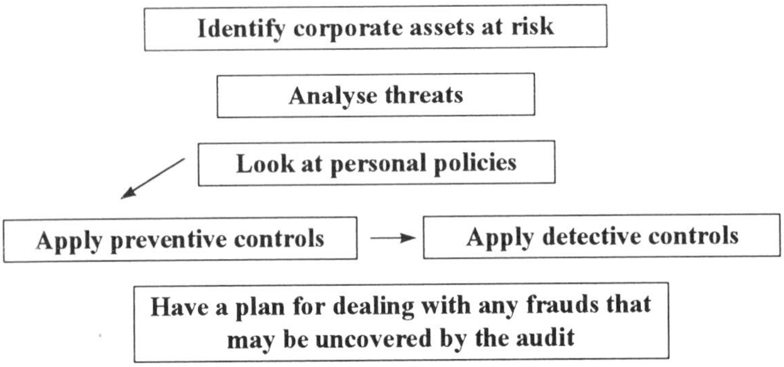

We would look for suitable controls over assets and information at risk. These would be evaluated to discover whether they were adequate and applied in practice and steps recommended to address failings found as a result of the project. It is essential that the project team report to a high corporate level within the organisation with decision-making powers that can be used to action recommendations. Much of the work will revolve around the IT security officer although if there is no such person then this may well be the first major recommendation. Fraud is not a natural consequence of using computerised systems although there are differing views on this issue. Research has been carried out but there are many organisations who protect their credibility by not reporting frauds and attempted frauds. Suitable controls have to be applied and audit's role remains the same in reviewing adequacy and effectiveness. The only supplementary issue is where internal audit makes a bid to perform a systems security role in the organisation although this is a matter that the chief internal auditor should consider and resolve.

29.8 Cheques: Fraudulent Encashment

Introduction
Fraudulently encashed cheques have always been a major problem. Once a dishonest person gets hold of a negotiable instrument there are many things that he/she can do including opening a bank/building society account in the name of the payee. Alternatively, the name of the payee may be altered as may be the value of the cheque. Bank accounts may be more difficult to open than building society accounts as they usually require more references. Bank cheques take three working days to clear in comparison to ten days for building society accounts. Whenever someone claims not to have received a cheque or giro then the possibility of fraudulent encashment should be considered.

Examples of fraudulent encashment
Cheques left unattended on a desk may be stolen by someone with access to the building whereupon they may be paid into a fictitious bank account, the funds drawn out and

account closed before the theft is noticed. Where a cheque is made out to a payee in an abbreviated fashion this may cause problems:

> *A cheque made payable to IBM may be altered to read I.B. Miller and then paid into a suitable account.*
> *A cheque may be altered to read a much higher amount and a new payee inserted above the original payee name and paid into a specially opened bank account.*
> *Details of payee and value can be erased from a cheque and a new name and value inserted.*

The investigative procedure
The organisation should define procedures for the investigation of fraudulent cheques:

1. Initial notification. Once an organisation has released a negotiable instrument say to a supplier, then it will assume that it has been paid in by the correct party. The payee will have to notify the organisation that it was not received. Where a payee complains that they have not received a cheque that should have been sent to them (or collected by them) then this information should be notified to a central point within the organisation. This might be internal audit, if this service is provided by them. The information should initially be phoned across and then confirmation of details immediately sent in a fax signed by the manager for the area. In some cases a bank may be suspicious and so contact the organisation. The bank reconciliation system will also isolate frauds where the cheque value or number has been altered.

2. Stopping cheques. The next step is to place an immediate stop on the cheque.

3. Third party contact. Once it is clear the cheque has been paid we will need to contact the receiving bank/building society immediately, and advise them that a fraud has been attempted. They should be told to freeze the account (where funds are still held) and as much information as possible should be secured about the account holder. A contact name and number should be taken. It will be necessary to sign an indemnity for the receiving bank which may read:

> *"In consideration of the XYZ bank, address, agreeing to pay abc company the sum of £X, being the amount paid to the XYZ bank by the JMP bank representing the balance of the account of Mr. A at the JMP bank. We the abc company undertake to indemnify the XYZ bank against all actions and proceedings, costs, damages, expenses, claims and demands whatsoever which may be brought against, incurred or sustained by the XYZ bank by reason of this payment.*
>
> *Signed...............................   Dated..............*
> *abc Company Ltd."*

4. Police contact. It may be possible to arrange for the local police to liaise with the receiving bank and seek to arrest the account holder. As such police contact should occur as quickly as possible. Note that most of these frauds involve account holders who cannot be traced.

5. Initial enquiries. Once the information has been received then it will be necessary to take several steps:

- Identify cheque number and type of payment.
- Extract the returned cheque and insert a signed copy back into the system. Note that this original cheque will probably not be returned to the filing system but held in audit files.
- Extract any available vouchers that support the payment.
- Determine if possible how it could have been intercepted.

6. Payee interview. Where the payee is an individual who receives cheques from the organisation say an employee, or a public sector benefits claimant then he/she should be advised that they may have to be interviewed (depending on the circumstances) and a contact phone number should be taken. The process for this should be as follows:

- A checklist of questions should be compiled.
- A formal interview record may be made out and the payee should agree to have their statement released to the police.
- The payee should complete a signed indemnity.
- Any signatures on the back of the cheque should if possible be compared to the rightful payee's signature.
- Identify if possible who may be responsible.
- Establish whether the payee has "lost" a cheque before.
- Can the payee convince us that they have no knowledge of the cheque/giro?
- The payee should then agree to collect the replacement cheque and provide ID.
- We will need to establish whether this was an inside job. A fraud file should be opened up for each case that is investigated.

7. Replacement. The payee will invariably request a replacement cheque and if the cheque has been successfully stopped then a replacement can be arranged immediately. If however the cheque has been paid then there are additional complications. Once we are satisfied that the original payee is not implicated (the police can advise here) and has signed an official indemnity then we may arrange a replacement. It is important that any account payment that is written off ("fraudulent encashment") is properly cross referenced to the frauds database. This should ensure that any write off, and newly generated replacement payment, is authorised and correct. As such the use of the write-off code should be authorised by a senior manager. We must avoid the position where an account appears to have been credited twice (once with the misappropriated cheque and then with the replacement). In short, the fraudulent cheques database must be reconciled with the payments system. Note there are some payment types (such as social security claims) where we can ask the original payee to report the crime to their local police and so place some responsibility with the payee before any replacement is agreed. This will help deter payees seeking to submit false claims.

Police referral

As soon as it is clear that a fraud has occurred the local police should be notified and we would need to establish the following:

*   The case number assigned by the police.
*   Whether the case is being pursued and by whom.
*   Whether the payee is implicated.
*   Whether an offender has been apprehended.
*   Whether the offender has been involved in additional thefts.
*   Whether any of the organisation's officers are implicated.
*   Court appearance date and charges which may include theft, false accounting, forgery and/or handling stolen goods.
*   Outcome of the court hearing.

Regular meetings with the local police are suggested say at monthly intervals to secure details of progress on all outstanding cases.

Recovery

All efforts should be made to seek recovery to the value of the cheque/giro. If stopped then it should be cancelled. If frozen in an account then the appropriate bank/building society should be contacted and they will require a signed indemnity form. They will then refund the value of the cheque which should be posted to an appropriate income code. Any such cheque should be banked and the receipt held on file. If the funds have been withdrawn and the culprit apprehended and charged then this should be referred to the organisation's Legal Officer.

Reports

A comprehensive database of each fraudulent encashment, the investigation and result should be established and maintained. This should show:

*   The name of payee.
*   The amount.
*   The value.
*   The cheque number.
*   Bank account.
*   Where paid in.
*   The bank/building society to contact.
*   The action taken.
*   Any recovery of funds.
*   The insurance claim number.
*   The department that authorised the cheque.
*   The type of payment.
*   The investigating officer.
*   The resultant police action.

It may be possible to build a sophisticated PC based system that would generate various standardised forms/memo/letters that would be used in the investigation so that most information is actually held on the system. Having said this, it will nevertheless be necessary to maintain individual manual files containing:

*   Returned cheque (or copy if with the police).

- Copies of payment vouchers.
- Signed statements.
- Checklist of action with dates and signatures.
- Receipts for any replacement cheques.
- Pro-forma documents if not held on the system.

Each file should have a unique reference number used for the manual files, the database and entered into a case register.

Systems implications
The auditor should consider whether the organisation has taken sufficient steps to guard against fraudulent encashment and avoid being a target for the gangs that are now active in this field. Some of these controls include the following:

1. Defined person (e.g. chief cashier) responsible for dealing with fraudulent encashment. To this end there should be in place adequate procedures covering notification, bank contact, police contact, recovering funds and replacing cheques. Employees should be able to refer all possible cases of non-receipt to this key officer.
2. Clear rules on sending cheques through the post. This should be done in a way that reduces the risk of interception by not making it obvious that the contents of a letter include a cheque. Three part fold-over cheques that become envelopes as well, are obviously cheques and although generated by the computer printer are vulnerable.
3. Clear rules that ban collection of cheques by originators. This is a breach of the principles of segregating duties. If correspondence must be included with the cheque this may be sent separately with an indication that the cheque will follow in due course. Cheques should be sent out directly from the computer print section and not returned to sections of the organisation (e.g. the originator).
4. Proactive bank reconciliation system that means all alterations to amount and/or cheque number will be acted on immediately (i.e. cheque stopped).
5. Close contact with the organisation's bank that means problems can be notified to them immediately over the phone, and action taken.
6. Close contact with the local police (or specialist cheque fraud unit such as that run by the City of London Police). Patterns may be spotted and fingerprint tests can be run on paid cheques. Criminals will tend to target a number of organisations and it may be possible to establish similar cheque frauds carried out against other organisations.
7. An arrangement whereby all paid cheques are returned to the organisation once paid. These will form part of the evidence in the event of a prosecution. Where an organisation is being targeted it is possible for all returned paid cheques to be reviewed for alteration. The receiving bank's account may be frozen if forged cheques are found quickly.
8. Good security built into the cheques whereby they fall in line with the Association for Payment and Clearing Services (APACS) standard 3.
9. Tamper proof devices may be applied whereby alterations are obvious either on the face of the cheque or via the use of ultra violet light.
10. Hologram and other anti-copying devices such as "Fraud" appearing in all colour copies.
11. Arrangements so that non-standard and bold print fonts are used making it harder to remove print and insert alterations.
12. A value restriction can be placed on some cheques.

13. It is possible to arrange a call-back facility with the organisation's bank for cheques over a certain amount, whereby verification is sought before a cheque is paid.
14. A thick black box around the payee details makes additions above the payee line difficult.
15. Standards of data input on the payments system. Where the full name and words "limited" appear it is harder to erase and more difficult to pay into a private account (limited: requires a business account). Abbreviations of company names must be banned.
16. A cheque signing machine means that pre-signed cheques do not have to be stored. Raised multi-colour signatures make it harder to copy.
17. Security warning messages printed on the cheques can help deter potential fraudsters.
18. The professional fraudster is one who does not alter a cheque but is able to manufacture identification on the original name, and use an established bank account for money laundering. Here we have to rely on the supplier to notify non-receipt and it may be possible to request that the supplier provide a receipt confirmation on high value cheques. This also means that extra security should be applied to high value cheques. We can rely on the bank reconciliation to enable us to spot alterations (on amount and account number) quickly, and the officer performing this task must have cover in his/her absence.
19. One high-risk area is returned cheques sent back to the organisation because the address is wrong or the payee has moved away. In this instance all incoming cheques should be logged in the post room (staffed by at least two people) and cancelled immediately.

The best control is to move away from cheques and use bank transfers (BACS).

In most cases time is of the essence in intercepting attempted fraudulent conversion and can make the difference between a successful fraud and loss to the organisation, and a mere attempt that has been thwarted. To this end, internal audit may resource a fraudulent cheque service as part of the consultancy role. If this is the case, it is as well to have on-line access to the bank account's reconciliation system so that cheque presentation dates can be obtained and stops placed on un-presented cheques. This is in addition to an enquiry access to the creditors system so that original details (before alteration) can be obtained.

29.9 Dealing with Public Sector Benefits Fraud

Introduction
This section deals with some of the general issues that are relevant to the investigation of benefits frauds. Note that the figures and rules set out below are those prevailing during 1994. It is important to distinguish between the various available benefit claims that are available from public sources in the United Kingdom. These may be categorised as follows:

☐ **Social Security Benefits.** There are a variety of benefits that can be claimed and these depend on one's personal circumstances. They cover people on low incomes, unemployed people, women expecting babies, people bringing up babies, young people, sick injured or disabled people, people going into hospital or residential care, war pensioners and women over 60 and men over 65. For our purposes we are primarily concerned with Income Support which is paid to people over 18 years old, on low incomes. Where a person's capital is under a certain limit and less than 16 hours a week are worked, income support may be available. It is not normally payable if the claimant or the claimant's partner is working over 16 hours a week. Savings (again of claimant or partner) must not exceed £8,000. There are many factors that affect the final amount payable for income support including the earnings of the claimant and partner. This is why it is important for all claimants to disclose their earnings from employment along with details of the hours worked each week.

☐ **Housing Benefits (HB)**. This is paid by the local authority to people who need help with paying their rent. A person can qualify for HB whether employed, self employed, unemployed or retired. The savings limit for this benefit is currently £16,000. Note that a claimant may get HB and not qualify for income support. Someone getting income support and paying rent will normally qualify for maximum HB and a claim form is given to all those currently claiming income support.

☐ **Council Tax Benefits (CTB)**. CT is paid by most owner-occupiers or tenants from 1 April 1993 (including joint-tenants and council tenants). The rules that apply to qualifying for HB are more or less the same for CTB and again a CTB claim form is given to all those currently claiming income support. It is possible to obtain 100% CT benefits and one may claim it at the same time as claiming income support.

☐ **Poll Tax Benefits (PTB)**. PTB is similar to CTB although Poll Tax applied to all residents in the local authority and the benefits are limited to 80% and not 100%. PTB operated for three years for 1990/91, 1991/92 through to 1992/93.

There is clearly a direct link between the various benefits systems which is designed to minimise the level of means testing that needs to be carried out by the local authority. So long as the claimant is able to convince the Benefits Agency (BA) that income support is due and payable, then there is a good chance that an associated HB and CTB claim will also be accepted. If someone has been claiming income support for some time then PTB may have been secured for the three years that this local tax was in operation. The Government recognises the importance of benefits systems and the need to combat any attempts to make fraudulent claims. In response, each BA district has a fraud team that seeks to detect and investigate benefits frauds. In fact, the need to co-ordinate the efforts of both the BA and the local authority has led to several initiatives including the latest one called "finders keepers". This seeks to encourage the BA and associated local authority to enter into a formal service level agreement between the local authority's fraud section and the Benefits Agency's Sector Fraud Team.

Background to the Benefits Agency
The Department of Social Security administers several agencies including the Benefits Agency and the Contributions Agency. The BA has a main section in charge of administering the various benefits and a separate section covering the detection and prevention of fraud. There are some twelve main categories of fraud although most local authorities are primarily interested in frauds relating to working whilst in receipt of

undisclosed income. When the fraud team discover what is termed a possible "overpayment" they instigate an investigation. This involves:

1. Securing the order books that are cashed at the local Post Office.
2. Securing any details of earning from employment via a QB.9 return that is made by the employer.
3. Securing a formal statement from the employer which confirms the claimant's earnings, employment dates and job title.
4. Carrying out an interview under caution (IUC) where an explanation is sought from the claimant.
5. Passing the papers to the area lawyers who submit these to the local magistrate's court for prosecution. These cases have to be brought to court within 12 months of the offence and so can become "time-barred" if there are any undue delays.
6. Before the court date, the fraudulent claim is notified to the local authority via a form QB.64. This requests details of any overpayment on HB that may be added to the DSS benefits overpayments (normally income support) and so form part of the overall losses that are used to support the criminal charges. Note that the charges presented to the courts are made under social security legislation, whilst any HB implications merely add to the amount overpaid.

Prosecution policies

The BA seeks to achieve a high success rate when prosecuting claimants under the relevant legislation. As such a formal vetting procedure tends to be applied to cases before they are sent to the area lawyers for prosecution. The service level agreement sets out some of the factors that are given due consideration when making this decision including:

- The amount of money obtained and the duration of the offence.
- The suspect's physical and mental condition.
- Voluntary disclosure.
- Social factors.
- How clear-cut the evidence is.
- Any failure in the investigation.
- Any failure in the benefits administration including delays.

From the above it is quite clear that there are many cases where a prosecution is not pursued despite the fact that a fraudulent claim has been established. Furthermore there are cases where the offence is admitted at an interview under caution, which is also not sent for prosecution.

Local authority benefit fraud investigators

Local authorities also tend to employ specialist teams of fraud investigators who will concentrate on Housing Benefit and Council Tax Benefit fraud investigations. These may be separate teams which may be located inside the internal audit function, and it is advisable to ensure that they have sufficient status to carry out wide ranging reviews of the integrity of payments made. Some local authorities do not have a clear prosecutions' policy and are in this respect held back in terms of installing a deterrent and securing compensation. The Audit Commission research into HB and CT benefits fraud (Protecting the Public Purse, 1995) highlighted 81,000 fraudulent cases involving losses of some £26 million, making this the bulk of local government fraud. Figures indicate that this is one of the fastest growing areas of fraud, although this may be partly the result of better detection.

London-wide fraud initiative

The whole concept of fraud detection and investigation is now on the agenda of the Society of London Treasurers who are actively involved in progressing an anti-fraud initiative for local authorities across London. In conjunction with the Audit Commission (who are embarking on a comprehensive review of fraud), London Boroughs are currently involved in a fraud detection exercise that seeks to isolate cross-boundary frauds. The London boroughs subscribe to this initiative and seek to investigate benefits frauds as part of this drive towards controlling public sector fraud by employees and others.

Types of fraud that can arise

There are several different ways that a local authority can be defrauded in respect of benefits claims. They each result in a financial advantage being secured through dishonestly misrepresenting the facts at hand. It can arise from presenting false or misleading information or simply failing to disclose relevant information. In practice some frauds are perpetrated through a negative action in failing to disclose a change in circumstances that would impact on the existing benefits claim. Having regard to the benefits legislation, some of the types of frauds may be listed as follows:

- Failing to fully disclose one's income from employment.
- Failing to disclose one's capital accumulation.
- Failing to disclose a non-dependant who resides with the claimant.
- Failing to disclose a relevant change of circumstance.
- Making multiple claims using false identities.
- Fraudulently cashing benefits cheques/giros by forging the amount due and/or intercepting the instrument and diverting it to someone other than the correct payee.

Added to this list may be internal fraud where housing benefit payments are diverted to an employee through the use of false accounts set up on the computer system. This may involve the use of previously redundant accounts of people who no longer qualify for benefits. Systems may use BACS, giros or a combination of both and it is not surprising that a process that typically generates thousands of small payments each week to landlords and tenants is extremely vulnerable.

Controlling benefits frauds

It is wholly recognised that benefits administration is about getting the right payments to the right people, and this single factor drives staff who operate the relevant systems. The fact that HB is subsidised by the government may also lead local authorities to prioritise the distribution and not the control aspects of this facility. There are however ways that HB administration may be controlled so as to minimise the incidence of fraud that are listed below.

Structures

Sensible organisational structures that separate three key HB functions:

- Assessing the benefit.
- Setting up accounts.
- Paying the benefits.

In addition, there needs to be a continuous review of the above three operations along with suitable controls over the computer system.

Main controls
Some of the general controls that should be established over benefits administration are:
1. Suitable management trails (linked to password controls) that make it quite clear who processed and authorised the transactions that affect benefit entitlement and payment.
2. A specialist, high profile, HB fraud investigations unit that seeks to uncover and investigate irregular payments.
3. Application forms that make it quite clear that all information is provided in good faith and will be the subject of criminal prosecutions if it is knowingly incorrect. It should also require any change of circumstances to be notified as part of the conditions for claiming benefits.
4. A clear procedure for independently verifying the information that the benefits claim is based on. This may range from confirming employment through to actual visits to HB clients.
5. Confidential hot line for tip-off from members of the public.
6. Comprehensive operational procedures that seek to restrict the level of discretion that is available to any one officer. These procedures should also set standards and lead to consistency in the way benefits are dealt with by staff.
7. Regular audit of these systems by internal audit, that seeks to review the systems used and whether they are being properly complied with by staff.
8. Close correlation between the HB systems and other link systems such as Council Tax, housing rents, electoral register, bank reconciliation, payments and so on. A one-off hand delivery of cheques and giros can bring useful results in terms of tenancy arrangements.
9. Close and regular liaison with the Benefits Agency. Best practice calls for a service level agreement to be signed between the BA's fraud unit and the corresponding local authorities HB fraud team. The relationship should be based around the regular exchange of information and confirmation of facts between these two parties. The weekly benefit savings scheme set up by central government in 1993 seeks to set targets for savings through identifying benefits frauds, and sharing these savings between the two organisations on a "finders keepers" basis.
10. A special prosecutions team that can bring criminal action in court against perpetrators of benefits fraud. They would also seek compensation once the magistrate has found the defendant guilty. This will be agreed with the defence with the award being made payable to the courts and passed over to the organisation. Working in conjunction with the prosecutions team a local firm of solicitors can be used to present the cases to court.

Other controls
There are many lower level controls that should be applied, based around standardised documentation, supervision, authorisation and review. Note that the importance of good recruitment and training and development practices along with targets and other incentives is obviously equally applicable to the HB arena. A full internal audit of these controls is a good way of ensuring that they are in place and actually work. In addition to reviewing controls, an audit may also decide to target risk areas for extensive testing. This may include areas such as:
•   Returned giros.

- Post diverted by the Post Office.
- HB claimants who are not also claiming income support.
- Newly activated accounts.
- Self employed.
- Long-term claimants.
- Right To Buy mortgage applications.

Special project - employee benefits fraud
It is possible to establish a special fraud detection project covering all employees by exchanging payroll details with the fraud unit of the local Benefits Agency. This can be run against records that they hold and will identify employees who are claiming benefits and those with national insurance numbers that do not relate to details held by the Contributions Agency. Once the matches have been obtained a great deal of work will be required to investigate each case, and weekly meetings with BA staff are advised. The dual objectives will be to prosecute employees committing benefits fraud and also discipline (and dismiss) them. Likewise all wrong national insurance numbers would also have to be resolved by the organisation. It is best to set up a key contact person in both organisations. Internal audit can volunteer a proactive role in this matter as facilitators and/or co-ordinators, on the basis that an organisation can never seriously combat fraud while at the same time employing fraudsters. To implement such a project the following steps should be taken:

1. Draft a project proposal for attention of the chief executive, personnel, legal and other relevant senior officers. It is essential that support is obtained from the highest levels and oral presentations to a specially convened steering group of senior officers may be used to assist this task.
2. Review the organisation's disciplinary procedures and ensure that they cater for wide-scale benefits fraud. This should be a dismissable offence and one may establish a fast tracked procedure say with a specially convened panel to hear these types of cases. The status of benefits fraud should be specifically established. It may be that this constitutes a prima facie disciplinary offence or it may be dependent on the nature of the postholder's duties. Benefits fraud will tend to relate to lower paid employees who seek to top up their earnings. It is probably best to make this a dismissable offence on the basis that all jobs are sensitive.
3. Get suitable input from the organisation's data protection officer and ensure that payroll and personnel data can be provided to the Benefits Agency as registered users.
4. Identify a suitable officer who will lead the project and ensure that this person is experienced and senior enough to drive through the underlying tasks.
5. Obtain a download from the payroll database that should include (at minimum) all relevant data such as name, payroll reference number, national insurance number, start date, address, post title, grade, and gender. We will need to keep a close eye on starters and leavers and it is a good idea to secure this information for periods after the download has been obtained.
6. Compile a special database of employees to hold this data. This will form the basis of the exchange of information between the BA and the organisation. Note that the BA will tend to use the national insurance number as the key reference field whilst the employer will use the payroll (or employee reference) number. Make sure that these two references are catered for. There are many fields that may be set up on the database although, when constructing it, think of the type of reports that will be required as

progress on the project is monitored. We may wish to report benefits frauds over gender, grade, department, start dates and so on. The database should include items for each case covering at least:

- Basic personal information.
- Status of case.
- Interview under caution.
- Court appearances (there will be a number of hearings over several months).
- Court verdicts.
- Disciplinary position.
- Any appeal dates and results.
- Any further action.

7. Ensure that a link officer is nominated by the Benefits Agency. It may be necessary to liaise with several district offices who cover the various areas where employees may be claiming benefits. As such is it always useful to ensure that this exercise is centrally co-ordinated by a relevant district, to avoid excessive fragmentation.

8. Establish a two-way flow of information with the Benefits Agency on at least a weekly basis where further payroll data, witness statements and other matters may be discussed and dealt with. It is best to make personal visits where paperwork can be discussed and exchanged. Also hold regular review meetings where high-level issues can be discussed among more senior representatives.

9. Make it clear that an employee who appears on the data-matching exercise is not necessarily involved in fraud. Part-time staff and older benefits claims may mean that the claimant has fully disclosed their pay details. It is only where a positive fraud has been identified that we may consider action against the person in question. It is good policy to allow staff to resign when they realise the fraud has been uncovered, and so save time disciplining them.

10. There may be an associated housing benefits claim that can be added to the overpayment in court that will also have to be taken on board. Alternatively the relevant local authority may seek their own criminal prosecution, if this is the adopted policy.

11. As the project progresses the scale of the problem will become evident. In line with this information will be a move to resource the project depending on the number of employees who appear to be working and claiming (i.e. submitting fraudulent claims). Since each individual case has to be established we would need a level of experienced staff who would secure documentation for the Benefits Agency and put together cases for disciplinary. Much will depend on the outcome of court hearings and personal attendance by a member of the project team at each one is preferable.

12. The project will isolate staff who are defrauding the government and therefore should result in two remedies. The benefits agency will seek to bring a prosecution where this falls in line with their policies on this matter. The employer will seek to bring disciplinary action against the same individuals. Note that it is possible to agree an "amnesty" where staff will be given strict warnings as opposed to instigating dismissals. Alternatively a more serious stance may be assumed. In the latter case it is a good idea to prioritise certain employees for disciplinary action, which may include senior staff, and staff in sensitive positions (such as payroll officers).

The above exercise will also highlight staff who have no recognised national insurance number, or whose number appears to belong to someone else. We may set up a separate project in conjunction with the Contributions Agency to determine the correct insurance numbers. This may involve the exchange of personal data, a formal letter to the employees in question, and in the final analysis a formal interview where we can seek to uncover the person's work status. The above will be required to ensure that the payroll database holds correct information and that contributions are going to the right accounts. It may also uncover fraud, and/or breach of employment regulations where this is present. In terms of involvement in benefits fraud, this will have to be proved in a court of law to represent a fraud. The employer will have to wait for this to happen before a disciplinary can be held. We can take action pending the outcome of the court case ranging from removal to a less sensitive position through to being sent home on suspension from duties. Unfortunately court cases may take some time to complete with a number of adjournments before they are concluded.

29.10 Preventative Techniques

Introduction
The investigative process is reactive in that it is initiated as a result of an alleged fraud. Steps may be taken to guard against fraud. The importance of establishing sound control cannot be over-emphasised as most frauds could have been avoided with proper controls. We must also question an organisation which fully resources the investigation of fraud whilst ignoring the control implications. Unfortunately those charged with performing these investigations may have little incentive to push the control angle if it will result in less work being available for them. Key controls include:

☐ **Good recruitment procedures**. Fraud prevention starts with good recruitment procedures. If poor staff are employed, they will give poor performances. This leads to under-achievement and pressures from management, which is the ideal climate for de-motivated staff. Impoverished management will employ staff who are not competent to question them and so the cycle continues. Enthusiastic staff with a career in the organisation will not generally promote the atmosphere in which fraud thrives. The determined delinquent who has carefully worked a way into the organisation always poses a problem difficult to counter even with efficient recruitment procedures. Corruption exists at all levels in the organisation with varying degrees of severity where staff are taken on without reference to a clear assessment standard. Careful and independent confirmation of references and career facts before an appointment is offered is part of this good practice. One should always request a reference from the applicant's Personnel Officer and not someone that they nominate. All qualifications and membership of professional bodies should be checked. Employing the right people is the starting place for good controls and this is the foundation for organisational efficiency and effectiveness.

☐ **Independent checks over work**. We cannot assume all employees are honest and this must be recognised when designing control systems. One feature that must be present is to ensure that work is checked by an independent source. This source has to be at a more senior level to achieve independence. There must also be an avenue through which one may act on any discrepancy. The more senior the officer, the greater the level of discretion in decision making and therefore the greater the need for a check on these powers. No one person should control systems that are able to generate a valuable commodity and this rule should be firmly applied throughout the organisation.

☐ **Supervision**. There must also be checks on what an employee is doing. It cannot be assumed that an employee will necessarily be committed to work related matters during the working day. Supervision is based on management accepting that they are responsible for the activities of their staff. Where this supervision is not provided, this can only be because the manager has deemed it unnecessary. Matters cannot simply be left to chance. Effective supervision will help identify poor performance and also unauthorised activities as a contribution to fraud prevention. When considering this, the question to ask is, if unauthorised activity is taking place, how can it be spotted? A manager should know where staff are, what they are doing and how this contributes to their work objectives.

☐ **Regular staff meetings**. As part of the communication process regular staff meetings serve a useful purpose. This not only helps keep the manager up-to-date with progress on outstanding tasks but as a two-way process, keeps staff informed of current developments. If a team spirit can be engendered, each member of staff will feel that they should not let the others down and so operate on this basis. Being involved in fraud may in this respect be seen as one way of letting colleagues down. Team meetings also tend to increase the level of motivation and this also acts as an additional pressure to encourage staff to adhere to organisational standards of conduct. This feeling of mutual trust and co-operation between staff and their managers helps create the right environment that in turn acts as an additional preventative control to guard against fraud and irregularity.

☐ **System of management accounts**. A good management accounting system will contribute to fraud prevention. Firm budgetary control mechanisms secure tight procedures within which spending decisions will operate. This is a key feature of financial control and there are many situations where corruption occurs due to a lack of accountability. In extreme cases incompetent corporate management will decline to resource a drive towards good accounting systems knowing that any systems efficiencies will expose their inefficiency. Reckless spending with no regard for organisational objectives and unlimited discretion to enter into contracts would be inhibited by sound management accountability systems. Inadequate accounting staff may be employed on purpose by such managers to avoid financial controls. The first major symptom is failure to recognise the finance director's responsibilities for financial control throughout the organisation. This leads to a lack of compliance with written procedures on financial regulation which leads to a state of chaos, where anything goes. This typifies organisations where corruption is rife. Management accounting systems where budgets are controlled and cost variances isolated and assigned to defined staff for explanation, rely on clear penalties for under-performance. The essential ingredient for the budgetary control system will be to locate responsibility for an approved level of expenditure. Everything that happens in this cost centre becomes the direct responsibility of the relevant manager, and herein lies the important concept of accountability for the decision maker.

☐ **An employee code of conduct**. The code of conduct appears both at the start and towards the end of the fraud prevention cycle. These standards set the ethical frame within which organisational business is conducted. They define unacceptable behaviour that may be the subject of a formal disciplinary. They have both a pro-active and reactive effect throughout the organisation, promoting high standards whilst punishing persistent offenders. The code should be reviewed and updated regularly including any reference to the code in the contract of employment.

☐ **Up-to-date accounts**. A way of neutralising the impact of the external auditor is to file accounts late and so maintain out-of-date accounting records. External audit work becomes located in past periods while the current business activities escape external scrutiny. The gap between a financial transaction and its recording can be used by fraudsters. Tendering depends on the time factor in terms of receiving bids, assessing and selecting them. Dates are extremely important when reviewing whether the process has been interfered with by corrupt employees. There are many other examples and we must always pose the question: who benefits if records are not properly maintained?

☐ **Good management information systems (MIS)**. Information is there to help tell management where to direct their efforts. Information in itself cannot make decisions or answer all questions but it can stimulate discussion and force choice where it would otherwise not occur. Good MIS will assist this task of fraud prevention by providing information that will help identify inconsistency or irregularity which are symptoms of fraud. The knowledge that this is the case will also add to the preventative nature of effective control. Reconciliation, exception reporting and reports on systems breaches will all add to the ability of management to ensure that its organisation is properly run. This is not to suggest that management does not perpetrate frauds; which means that this information must report on the activities of all levels of staff. Good information is a prerequisite to good control and this is becoming increasingly important as information assumes a higher profile in the organisation. Some systems are implemented without adequate management reporting facilities. Or if these facilities are available, they are not taken up and applied by systems users which may result in a lack of basic control information. A management control orientation is required before the significance of management reports is appreciated at the systems design stage of any new computerised development. An organisation that supports an information strategy group, chaired by the chief executive, will be better placed to recognise the importance of good MIS.

☐ **Clear lines of authority**. Many controls depend on defining who does what, when and how. The need for some clarity of role underpins the concept of control. Blurred lines of responsibility, roles and reporting arrangements will all add to a feeling of chaos. This sets the environment for fraud and corruption to flourish as people are unclear as to who has authority to do what. This confusion hinders any resultant internal disciplinary or court case where defence may use this state of disarray to cloud issues and challenge any case against someone who has abused the lack of clarity in lines of authority. Someone can only be shown to have done something wrong where the organisation has made it clear that he/she is not authorised to do it. The burden of proof falls on the prosecution. When an organisation allows its management to avoid making decisions or respond to outstanding operational issues then chaos management will be the norm.

☐ **Publicised policy on fraud**. A bold and effective approach is to publish a firm statement on fraud and corruption. This explains what is expected from staff, what to do if fraud is suspected and what type of action will then take place. No-one should be exempt from this clear standard. Posters may appear at convenient locations reminding employees of the policy and its application.

☐ **Controlled profit margins**. Tightly controlled profit margins can be used to contain managers' performance within prescribed limits. This acts as a control as long as used in conjunction with other controls. What must not happen is for short-term profit making measures to be used without regard for longer-term issues and knock-on effects. Other factors such as the level of staffing, the time period, capital employed, and level of waste must be accounted for when assessing performance.

☐ **Good documentation**. We have dealt with up-to-date records above and here we note the need for concise records as another relevant factor. Moreover good documentation is increasingly dependent on good systems that have well-planned input documents and well-presented management reports. Ideally all documents should indicate the name of the originator.

☐ **Good staff discipline procedures**. Staff need to be advised of what is expected from them and what will happen if these expectations are ignored without justification. It should be kept as a live topic on the agenda. Unfortunately a comprehensive disciplinary procedure that is used regularly to dismiss staff indicates that all is not well. Proper controls should mean that this measure would be reserved for rare situations where preventative controls have broken down or been by-passed. One needs to strike the right balance and not rely on sacking staff as the main control.

☐ **Financial procedures**. Clear corporate procedures in financial regulations or directives should be firmly in place to set rules on how finances should be managed and controlled. A formal purchasing code of practice that covers regular supplies as well as major contracts is a good way of setting a framework against which compliance may be measured. The various codes should contain a fraud awareness flavour and once in place, form a key component of the disciplinary code of practice that binds all staff. Documented operational procedures should then flow from the corporate arrangements as local standards that staff subscribe to in day-to-day work. Unfortunately the only way to make this work is to either employ professional managers, or make the design and maintenance of formal procedures a requirement of each manager's post, with disciplinary action for persistent failure.

☐ **Management trails that identify transaction initiators**. Accountability is based on people being responsible for actions. This is based on systems that locate actions to individuals with the end result being a need to have a record of these activities. Many transactions will be actioned through computerised systems and it is here that good trails are essential. If one has a full record defining the actual person who initiated the transaction then this is prima facie evidence that will have to be challenged by the person in question. It does depend on good password/ID control procedures. Sound archiving practices and a follow-up routine to isolate suspicious items are also important.

☐ **Good communications**. An organisation is as effective as its internal systems of communication and this is true for fraud prevention also. Much fraud is committed by staff who feel isolated from the main activities that drive the organisation. It is only the professional criminal who appears to be totally immersed in his/her work while at the same time planning a fraud. Good communication can bring a sense of belonging to staff who may then feel responsible for preserving the organisation's assets as they identify with business objectives. Goal congruence can be established through regular meetings, briefing papers, staff newsletters and other media. It certainly will not solve all problems but will go some way towards motivating staff and getting them committed to work related issues.

☐ **Effective internal audit service**. This may be seen as a mechanism for promoting controls that help guard against fraud. An organisation cannot fall into the trap of depending on internal audit to catch the fraudster. The real answer is to depend on internal audit to provide advice on strengthening the various safeguards against fraud. This assumes that these controls are already in place and that management has recognised the importance of this. Where the auditor tackles frauds after the event and does not consider the control implications then an even greater danger may arise where the auditor's existence is dependent on a high level of fraud. The incentive to direct audit towards recommending preventative controls may become lost. This can be averted if the respective roles of management, personnel and audit have been properly defined in line with professional standards. There now exists a lucrative fraud detection industry which supplies staff and consultants to resource investigations and not prevention.

☐ **Good controls over cash sales/income**. One-off high-risk areas should be tackled by applying particularly stringent controls. This applies to many areas including pension funds and creditors systems. Cash sales is another example where there is an obvious temptation for dishonest employees. An organisation is being unfair if it allows its staff access to cash without installing adequate controls as this may provide undue stress by assuming that the person will resist any temptation. The employee is not so much dishonest as weak willed. An employee may be completely honest for many years only to experience lapses that may come as a surprise to management. It may be that as time passes, the extent to which this person's activities are checked may be reduced as time after time he/she has been shown to be trustworthy. The final position may be reached where little or no controls are applied and this may prove to be fatal. We arrive full circle back to the essential need for sufficient controls for sensitive areas that must be in place.

☐ **Segregation of duties**. This feature is fundamental to many systems of internal control, using the basic principle that a person cannot self-check. Where one person's work outputs flow naturally to another person as inputs whereupon certain checks are made as this work is received, then control is enhanced. Many frauds are allowed to happen because one person has excessive levels of unrestricted discretion which are not checked by anyone else. The problem here is that there is a tendency for more senior officers to have greater discretion which must be controlled. At more senior levels there are fewer people who may provide this effective check on activities. When implementing a computerised system this concept of breaking down an activity over several staff should be considered along with adequate supervision and monitoring. Each transaction should be associated with the originator, the authoriser and the inputter in conjunction with suitable reports.

☐ **Stores control**. Stores, inventories, equipment and other attractive and portable items should, like cash, be subject to special controls. An organisation should have suitable mechanisms for identifying exactly where its portable property is located at all times. This is particularly the case for computer equipment that may be taken home or on site. It depends on making defined staff responsible for specific items. This is important for it is generally impracticable to have centralised control that does not involve staff from each main department in record keeping and monitoring. To set no standards for protecting these items may be disastrous. Records must be supported by regular physical checks.

☐ **Anti-corruption measures.** This involves controlling the relationship between employees and key third parties such as suppliers or the public. There should be clear guidelines on contact with suppliers as well as specific rules on any matters that could affect buying decisions. Registers of gifts and pecuniary interests should be in place to require all such occurrences to be registered. It is necessary to formally register all offers refused. The definition of gifts should be wide and include hospitality, free gifts for use in the office and inappropriate business meetings such as held at a sporting venue or expensive hotel. Policies on pressure selling and direct targeting of key staff should be adopted to cover where the employee is placed under undue pressure from third parties.

☐ **Fraud hot line.** One interesting control is to provide a facility whereby employees may report a concern direct to an independent party, such as internal audit or the chief executive. History records that whistleblowers tend to suffer in the long run as a result of their actions and a policy of encouraging legitimate disclosure may act as an extra guard against fraud and irregularity.

☐ **Good all-round systems of internal control.** This factor sums up most of the main controls that are mentioned in this part of the handbook. The essential point being that the controls must operate as a system with each one having as well as an individual significance, a role in the overall control process. So we may only rely on firm disciplinary procedures where they have been publicised and applied to all staff across the board and have a clear link into organisation procedures. In this way the success of each factor is in part dependent on the success of other associated factors. Here, as with all systems, the drive and commitment must start at the very top of the organisation. One way to reinforce this is to provide that managers are responsible for installing suitable controls that guard against fraud and will be held liable if these are found to be deficient.

☐ **Well trained and alert management.** Major control is embedded in a management culture where a turning a blind eye is shunned.

Wide-scale fraud may occur as a result of:

FIGURE 29.6 UNCARING MANAGEMENT

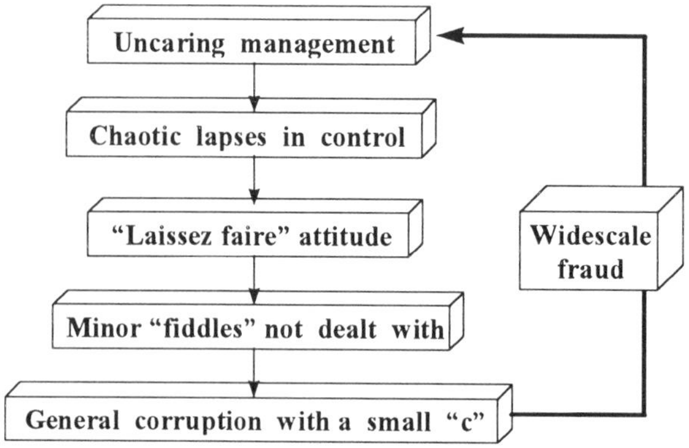

This places responsibility firmly with management. Management may promote a well-balanced organisation by resourcing controls or it can fall within the uncaring management bracket. Resourcing the investigation of the frauds that regularly arise is still a failing by management, who may feel absolved by their actions in dealing firmly with dishonest employees. Although management may sound dramatic and reassuring, this is nevertheless inadequate in that it does not recognise managers' need to admit to their failure to install preventative controls. Audit must not get caught up in this flawed approach where fraud investigations are wholly centralised. The best approach is to get all managers to take responsibility for their own resources. Audit may support them in their efforts in guarding against fraud, detecting it and acting on allegations/suspicions.

Fraud control process
Most frauds are the result of weaknesses in systems of internal control. Management needs to establish an overall process for controlling fraud which includes:

☐ **Preventative controls**. These are the most important controls that seek to prevent frauds. We have noted that these cover policies on fraud, segregation of duties, internal audit reviews, good control environment, good overall systems and many of the other points dealt with earlier. These are the most efficient types of control in that they are aimed at averting any potential frauds before they occur. Effort directed at this stage of the business systems will pay great rewards even if this is negatively expressed as a lack of fraudulent activity. These controls provide assurances to management that they might concentrate on achieving business objectives without risking losses in those organisational assets that they are responsible for. Management, rather than being responsible for the assets, are more accurately described as being responsible for establishing adequate controls over these assets. This brings the concept of preventative controls to a higher profile so allowing them to attract sufficient resources to be operationally successful.

☐ **Detective controls**. These controls are based on the need to pick up any irregularities as quickly as possible. These include techniques such as alert management, trend analysis, spot checks, supervision, exception reports and probity audits. The question to ask is "can any frauds have slipped through our systems and if so how can they be picked up?" We must accept that not all potential problems/frauds can be dealt with via preventative controls and there will be occasions where irregularity is almost unavoidable. Detective controls are designed to pick up any systems offenders and are an essential ingredient in the control cycle.

☐ **Corrective controls**. Once a fraud has been picked up it must be corrected. These include defined fraud investigators, management action, insurance policies, systems rectification and effective disciplinary action. There should be clear procedures covering the topic of restitution and insurance. As such if a fraud is picked up, there needs to be an effective method of dealing with it in contrast to a hit or miss approach. Management must know who to contact, what will be done and how they can support this process of investigating the fraud. The diagram illustrates how some of the major controls may be arranged to form an effective system for controlling fraud and irregularity by addressing the need for:

- High-level corporate standards.
- A nominated fraud investigation officer.
- Associated resources and budgets.
- A fraud manual.
- Management information on frauds.
- Security over resources and IT system.
- Procedures for key areas such as purchasing.
- A clear link into staff discipline.

FIGURE 29.7 OVERVIEW OF THE FRAUD CONTROL PROCESS

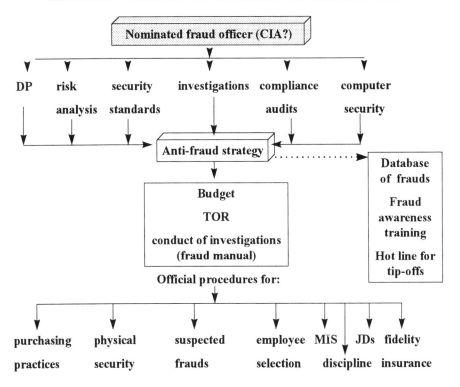

In this way a whole system of controls can be devised across the organisation to promote good security over organisational assets and resources. This is part of management's responsibilities which cannot be abrogated, although internal audit may assume a pivotal role.

Fraud detection

It is possible to adopt a pro-active approach to fraud by carrying out audit projects to seek out and eradicate specific frauds. This might be done in conjunction with the police who would provide advice and become involved where there is a clear case of criminal activities. Plan the audit with reference to:

1. The probability of fraud occurring within high-risk areas of the organisation.
2. The staff required to resource such an important project including qualifications, experience, skills and personal attributes as the team should be hand-picked, based on a demanding job specification.
3. The extent, terms of reference and scope of the audit should be very carefully defined as this will have a major impact on the work done and direction of the audit. This factor should be kept under review since the scope may well change during the course of the work. This may also have a knock-on effect on the type of resources that are being used. One important feature may be the need to secure computer skills for the project.

This work must be done in conjunction with management who remain responsible for dealing with fraud and irregularity.

The internal audit role

Within the audit terms of reference, under scope of audit, appears the issue of safeguarding the organisation's assets. The question then arises as to whether this is in terms of reviewing controls over assets or examining whether they are properly accounted for and taking action if not. The first approach is systems based while the latter is geared into transactions testing or is probity based. A systems based audit approach provides a more effective use of audit resources but the problem is that management does have an expectation that audit will help uncover major error/irregularity. Legislators hold the view that audit will check up on management. In some organisations the audit role and the fraud investigators' role are separated and in other audit departments a great deal of time is spent on frauds as opposed to planned systems reviews. The extreme occurs where cases are referred wholesale to internal audit. They are investigated and audit reports them to the police as well as presenting any resultant disciplinary against the employee in question. The organisation should negotiate the audit role in respect of frauds. Principles to be applied are:

1. The audit charter should establish the audit role in frauds.
2. The organisation should define a clear policy on fraud and if this involves internal audit then it should say so. It may be that all frauds are reported in the first instance to internal audit.
3. Within the organisational policies, internal audit should establish a service level agreement that will describe the role in frauds. This should be agreed at audit committee.

4. Whatever is agreed, it is clear that management is wholly responsible for investigating and resolving their frauds and any internal audit involvement is in reality, consultancy work.

5. The most effective model is where management resolves their own frauds while internal audit provides an advisory role. If properly directed, management can use their close knowledge of the affected area to speed up the investigation while audit has a learning curve before the work can be performed. If management is kept out of investigations because of a lack of skills then they are being deprived of this experience that once acquired will enable them to deal with fraud. The main exception is where the report is going to an outside body or the nature of the fraud implicates all tiers of management and an independent investigation is required.

6. Executive decisions should be made by management who should implement action required to solve the fraud. Even where audit carries out investigatory work, it is essential that management issue any resulting instructions.

7. Where audit investigates the fraud they should be careful not to become manipulated by management. If it is clear that, because of their behaviour, the managers whom audit is working for are partly responsible for the irregularity then audit needs to clear a reporting line to the next tier of management. The party under suspicion must be given the full opportunity to explain their actions and management should not apply oppression. Managers have been known to dismiss innocent staff and pay them any consequential compensation at industrial tribunal.

8. Once a fraud is resolved, audit must ensure that management recognises its responsibilities to close internal control loopholes. One must be careful that audit is not used to regularly discipline staff because management cannot be bothered to install effective internal controls.

9. Auditors who are skilled in dealing with frauds will not necessarily be developing into professional auditors and system work, which is of more value, cannot simply be ignored.

29.11 Conclusions

Fraud can be a very exciting topic and may be greatly stimulating for the auditor. There is much to learn and many audit techniques, particularly relating to testing, may be applied to securing the underlying evidence that any case will be based on. There is however little developmental value in this role and audit theory directs one towards operational reviews of systems of internal control as the true audit goal. Fraud takes a high level of resources and much planned audit work may fall to one side. A consultancy role, advising managers on how they might solve their frauds may be an efficient working relationship and this will have to be negotiated with the audit committee. If planned audit work is seen as a secondary issue, then the risk assessment process that identified these projects for the audit plan is obviously not working and should be reviewed. Systems weaknesses that allow frauds to occur should however be programmed into the audit plans and appropriate systems of preventative controls properly established. On no account should responsibility for guarding against and resolving fraud and irregularity be taken away from management.

References

Auditing Guideline. (1990). 'Guidance for Internal Auditors' CCAB.

Barret, M. J., Brink, V. Z. (1980) 'Evaluating Internal/External Audit Services and Relationships', *Research Report 24*, IIA, Inc.

Blake, R. R., and Moulton, J. S. (1969) *Building a Dynamic Organisation Through Grid Organisation Development*, Addison-Wesley Publishing Company, Ltd.

Carnall, C. (1991) *Managing Change*, Routledge.

Chambers, A. D., Selim, G. G., and Vinten, G. (1987) *Internal Auditing, 2nd edn*, Pitman Publishing.

Courtemanche, G. (1986) *The New Internal Auditing*, John Wiley and Sons, Inc.

Churchill, N. C., and Cooper, W. W. (1965) 'A Field Study of Internal Auditing' *The Accounting Review* Vol XL, No. 4.

Cromer, M. J. (1985) *Corporate Fraud, 2nd edn*, McGraw Hill Books.

Dittenhofer, M. A., and Klem, R. (1983) *Ethics and the Internal Auditor*, IIA, Inc.

Downden, T. (1986) 'Reviewing an Audit Manual', *PFA Magazine*.

Fern, R. H. (1985) 'Independence, an Incomplete Standard', *The Internal Auditor* Vol XLII, No. 5.

Gobeil, R. E. (1972) 'The Common Body of Knowledge for Internal Auditors', *The Internal Auditor* Nov/Dec.

Heeschen, P., and Sawyer, L. B. (1984) *Internal Auditors Handbook*, IIA, Inc.

Keane, A. (1986) *Modern Law of Evidence*, Professional Books Ltd.

Lewin, K. (1951) *Field Theory in Social Science, Selected Theoretical Papers*, Harper and Brothers.

Likert, R. (1961) *New Patterns of Management*, McGraw Hill Books.

Mandrel, S. (1987) *Effective Presentation Skills*, Kogan Page.

Mautz, R. K., Tielson, P. and Colson, R. H. (1984) *Internal Auditing Directions and Opportunities*, IIA, Inc.

Mautz and Sharaf (1961) *The Philosophy of Auditing*, American Accounting Association.

McGregor, D. (1960) *The Human Side of Enterprise*, McGraw Hill.

Mints, F. E. (1972) 'Behavioural Patterns in Internal Audit Relationships', IIA Research Paper 17.

Rittenberg, L. (1977) *Audit Independence and Systems Design*, IIA, Inc.

Sawyer, L. B. (1988) *Sawyer's Internal Auditing,* 3rd edn, IIA, Inc.

Sayle, A. J. (1988) *Management Audits*, 2nd edn, Allen J. Sayle Ltd.

Scott, C. D., and Jaffe, D. T. (1989) *Managing Organisational Change*, Kogan Page.

Standards and Guidelines for the Professional Practice of Internal Auditing (1984), The Institute of Internal Auditors.

Stern, H. J., and Impey, K. W. (1990) *Manual of Internal Audit Practice*, ICSA Publishing.

Stewart, H. (1989) *The Contents and Production of Audit Manuals*, CUBS.

Venables, J. S. R., and Impey, K. W. (1988) *Internal Audit,* 2nd edn, Butterworths.

Vinten, G. (1991) unpublished course notes from Master program, City University Business School.

Wade, K. (1991) unpublished course notes from Master program, City University Business School.

Wilcox, L. (1991) unpublished course notes from Master program, City University Business School.

Willson, J. D., and Root, S. J. (1989) *Internal Auditing Manual,* 2nd edn, Warren Gorham and Lamont, Inc.

Index

Note: Page references in *italics* refer to Figures; those in **bold** refer to Tables

ability levels 350
ACCA 44
acid test 457
action learning 475
action plan 319
activity reports 298
advisor/inspector conflict 84
allegations 565, 583
allocation of audit resources 56
analysis of information 134
analytical review 244
Anderson 213
anxiety 331
APB 140, 141, 147, 182
applications auditing 529
appraisals 401
approaches to internal audit 53–7, 468
  and methodology 345
ascertaining systems 210–16
  balancing the level of details required 215
  narrative 211, **212**
  securing the required information 211
attributes of auditors 384
audit agenda 147
Audit Commission 38, 143, 554, 589
audit committees 22, 24, 26, 68, 84, 97, 105–15,
    121, 134, 364
  abuse from 108
  constitution 106
  independence 113
  internal audit perspective 110
  introduction 105
  need for a clear focus 111
  pros and cons 106
  relative reporting lines 111
  role of 105
  utilising 106
audit field 33, 181

audit manual *see* manual
audit methodology 21, 37, 189
audit nose 181, 312
audit opinion 310
audit programme 194, 240
audit representatives **77**
audit review 87
audit risk *see* risk
audit service, types of 363
audit snoop 83
audit stamp 26
audit styles 88, **92**
audit testing *see* testing
audit theory 27
audit variety 53
audit warrant 13
auditing skills 403
authorisation 159
authority, audit 117, 159
automation 263
autonomous auditor 379
autonomy
    v compliance 390
    v control 352

backing-off 60
BACS 607, 610
BCCI 31, 125
behavioural aspects of auditing
    75–104
Benefits Agency 608
black box approach 545
Blake 501
block diagram 212, *212*, 216
Boston box 458
bottom-up change 501
Brink and Barratt survey 146
brochures 459

budgets
  for audits 197
  control 93, 462
business cards 460
business objectives 529
business plan 189

Cadbury 31, 148, 169
Canadian experience 105
career development 396, 406, 410
Carnell, Colin 486, 493, 504
carrot and stick 385
cascading objectives 370
CCAB 3, 44, 139
central government 45
Chambers 66, 345
change and change management 320, 480–505
  basic planning 92
  bottom-up change 501
  changing culture 501
  consequences 505
  controls and 491, 492
  converting ideas into action 494
  efficiency and 489
  HRM and 482
  impact on managing IA 505
  implementing change 493
  implications of 482
  management style 93
  moving from denial 504
  need for 480
  problems with 487
  resistance to change 488
  review techniques 503
  strategy 492, 494
  stress and 504
chaos management 157
charter, audit 3, 15, 116–23, 362
  1986 survey 117
  attributes 117
  audit authority 117
  audit objectives 116
  audit responsibilities 117
  example 123
  key issues 117
  nature of internal auditing 116
  outline of independence 117
  role of 116
  scope of audit work 116
  standards see standards
  structure of 122
cheques, fraudulent encashment of 602–7
Churchill studies 77, 77
CIMA 44
CIPFA 44, 77, 105, 116
  1991 research 79

manual 341, 343
civil service model (risk) 236
claiming losses 557
clearance procedures 319, 338
client
  defining 304
  feedback 407
code C 570
coding systems 451
collusion 164
common body of knowledge 38, 41, 465, 468
communication of results 134
compensating controls 225
competence 65, 386
competitors 461
complaints procedure 460
compliance 12, 29, 33, 40, 252
  auditing 512, 512
  checks 160
  legislation 33
  mechanisms 12
  role 12, 29
  test see testing
compliance officers 152
computer abuse 588
computer audit 53, 503–49, 513, 519
  acquiring facilities 545, 546
  applications 526, 528, 529
  approaches to 511
  computer controls 515
  computer generated evidence 545
  computerised environment 509
  computerised systems, problems with 509
  control cycle 514, 515
  control framework 515
  control objectives 544
  development 520–2
  establishing 516
  exemptions from access 539
  exemptions from disclosure 540
  fraud see computer fraud
  impact of computers 513
  installation 547
  interface issues 523
  interrogation process 542, 543
  managing 518
  objectives 511, 525, 529
  planning 519
  poor developments 521
  real life acquisitions 546
  requirement specification 547
  rights of data subjects 539
  skills 516, 517
  software 548
  staffing and planning 516
  standards 447

systems based approach 530
in systems development 520, *521*
techniques 542
testing 543, *543*, 544
three part SD model *524*
training 517
computer centre 531, *531*, 533, *534*
computer fraud 588–602, *589*
cause of losses **589**
controlling 598, *602*
features of 591
surveys 590–1
types 588
computer hacking 592
Computer Misuse Act 1990 592
confidence levels 270
conflict of interests 61
conflicts, audit 497, *497*
confrontation, degrees of 493
consultancy work 35, 69
consultants, using 483
consumer behaviour 462
contingency allowances 371
contracting out IA 28
control risk *see* risk
control self assessment 32, 96
control systems cycle *95*, 514
control(s) 154–72
of the acquisition process (IT) 546
of applications 526
audit role 167
authority *159*
of benefits frauds 610
breakdown 97, *97*
and change 491, 492
compensating 225
of computer abuse 598
of the computer centre 531
concept of 154
criteria 157
framework 515
IIA briefing note 168
IIA definition 154
of information technology 513
management role 165, 170
MCS (amended) 173
objectives 248
output inspection process *161*
over controls 27
in practice 159
recent developments 169
suitability of 162
system 168, 171–2
traditional *173*
types of 158
converting ideas into action 494

Copyright Design Patents Acts 1988 593
cost benefit analysis 487, **487**
crisis management 85
Cromer, Michael 553
Crown Prosecution Service 578, 579
currency, dynamism of 347
current files 259

Data Protection 152, 449, 538, 587, 588
enforcement *540*
offences under the Act 540
security measures and role of 540, *541*
systems based approach and 542, *542*
dealing with people 82, 88, 384
debate on internal audit (1947) 26
decision support systems 442
defining the system 217
definition of internal audit *8*
1994 changes 5
APB 3
IIA (1991) 4
of internal audit 3–16
system 217
delinquent manager 76, 101
departmental teams 378
development of internal audit 17–37, *21*
as extension of external audit 17
internal check 17, 19
management audit 21
non-financial systems 18
operational audit 20
probity work 18, 19
risk analysis 20
spot checks 20
statement of responsibility 25
statistical sampling 19
systems based approach 20
transaction based approach 19
directed reading 472
directed representations 219
director of finance 22, 23, 24, 67–9, 114, 134, 380
disaster co-ordinator 537
disasters
planning 534, 535, *536*, 537
types of 535
disciplinaries 415
discipline, staff 415, *416*, *417*, *419*, *421*, *422*
diskettes 448
District Auditor 146
Dittenhoffer 124
Dowden 347

education, continuing professional 472
effectiveness audit 34
efficiency and change 489

emotional maturity 388
emotional states (role playing) 81
employee benefits fraud 612
end user computing 441
enforcement process (DP) 540
entropy 202
environmental change 369
establishing IA 8, 51
ethics, code of 38, 124–31, 287, 417, 427
  business, society and *39*
  ethical considerations *131*
  integrity and 385
  moral maze 129
  pre-reporting *130*
  relevant factors 124
  three-part model 130
  underlying models 127
  whistleblowing 128
evaluating systems 53, 217–27, *227*
  advantages 220
  business advice service **223**
  continuous process 224
  defining the system 217
  disadvantages 221
  evaluation by objectives 226
  evaluation cycle *225*
  evaluation techniques 219, *220*
  internal control questionnaires 220, 222, **222**
  managerial systems components 225
  operational questions *226*
  operations *226*
evidence 254–8, 319, 558
  admissibility of 560
  advance disclosure 578
  automation 263
  circumstantial 560
  computer generated 545
  current files 259, *261*
  documentary evidence 559, 573
  filing systems 262, *263*
  information attributes 254
  legal aspects 559
  permanent files 258, *261*
  real 560
  securing 561
  standardisation 261
  types of 255, 561
  weight of 560
examinations 40
executive summaries 298
exemptions
  from access (DP) 539
  from disclosure (DP) 540
expectation gap 96
expectations 8, 30, 42, 57, 96

expertise 10, 49
external audit 17, 22, 27, 42, 71, 119, 138–53, 264, 428
  background 138
  controls versus accounts *142*
  different objectives 138
  inspectorate functions 150
  interfaced planning *147*
  internal versus **145**
  poor cousin of 84
  project teams 151
  report format **139**
  work study 150
external review 428

fear 84
Fearn 62
Federation Against Software Theft 595
feedback and appraisals 401
files **214**
filing systems 262
findings 134
flowcharts
  basic rules *211*, 213
  pros and cons of 215
  symbols *213*
  types of 210
  using 215
follow-ups 134, 298
force field analysis 56
fraud and fraud investigations 11, 21, 36, 55, 143, 184, 225, 277, 550–623, *582*
  allegations 565
  APB guidelines 557
  Audit Commission research 1994 554
  claiming losses 557
  closing 561
  control 620, *621*
  courses of action 580
  computer *see* computer fraud
  defining 550
  defining officer roles 556
  detection 622
  documentation 573, 575
  employee benefits 612
  evidence *see* evidence
  four components of 552
  indicators of 555
  internal audit role 622
  interviews 565, *567*, 568
  local authority benefit 609
  main implications 579
  objectives 564
  PACE 1984 569
  policy on 363
  preventative techniques 614–23

process 583
public sector benefits *see* public sector
  benefits fraud
reason for **553**
risk areas 555
rules 578
strategies 564
surveillance 576
terminology 578
types of 552
see also cheques, fraudulent encashment of
future for IA 32–6

general survey 184, 365
general systems thinking 201
gifts 61
globalisation 29
Government IA manual 6, 45, 341, 343
graphics 325
grievances 413

hearsay 559
Heeschen 340, 342, 344
Herman 490
hostility 84
hourly rates 463
human resource management
  and change 482
  cycle 383

IA liaison 80
ICA 44
I.D.E.A 544
IIA 50, 79, 105, 116, 454
  briefing note 4, 114 5, 128 6, 168 7, 32, 96
  and CIMA survey (computer abuse) 590
  committee 48
  contribution of 50
  definition (1991) 4
  Mints survey 78
  standards *see* IIA standards
  UK 1992 Research 79
  UK professional briefing note 114
IIA standards 43–4, 75, 260
  100 independence 43, 76
  200 professional proficiency 43, 75, 135
  300 scope of work 9, 43, 116, 157, 203
  400 performance of audit work 44, 132
  500 management of IA 44, 140, 182, 293,
    357, 427
image 84, 463
impartiality 58
Impey 340
improvements 426
independence 17, 24, 30, 43, 58–74, *73*, 102,
  113, 117, 380

factors affecting 60
fundamentals 72
impartiality 58
meaning of 58
objectivity 58
receiving gifts *61*
three component model 62
unbiased views 58
valid opinion 59
information analysis 134
information attributes 254
information systems 13, 434–52
  development 436
  effect on audit work 434
  end user computing 441
  hierarchical structure 440
  impact of information *434*
  importance of people involvement 444
  job codes **451**
  need for standards 447
  needs of audit *444*
  storage 446
  time monitoring *449*, *450*
  using *437*
  workstation concept 442
information technology (IT)
  acquisitions 445, 546
  as a strategic resource 437
  strategy 443
information, securing 211
inspector/advisor conflict 84
inspectorate functions 150
instructions 430
intelligence 389
interim audit reports 297
internal audit angle 483
internal check 17, 19
internal control evaluation system 22
internal control questionnaires 215,
  220, 313
internal control teams 12, 149
internal review 428
international standards 48
interrogation
  hundred percent 250
  process, audit 542
interviews 84, 276–95
  barriers to good 289
  behavioural aspects 281
  conduct during 287
  fraud 292, 564, 565, *567*, 568
  non-verbal communication 283
  recording 295
  standardised procedures 293
  structuring 277, *281*
  types of questions 285

intrusion, audit 76
investigations 55, 57
    v systems auditing 55
    see also fraud and fraad investigations
ISO 9000 424

job analysis 391
job codes 451
job descriptions 392
job specification 392
journals 40, 41

King, Jim 98
kitemarks 136
Klem 124

Laboratory of Government Board 575
leavers 412
legislation 30
levels of auditing 56
Lewin, Kurt 490
library 473
local authority benefit fraud 609
Local Government Act 1972 553
London wide fraud initiative 610

management
    of computer audit *see* computer audit
    by fear 20, 87, 93
    of information technology 44
    meeting 85
    needs 13, 54, 76
    participation 92, 365
    role (controls) 165
    style 93
management audit 21
management consultants 148
management control mechanisms 170
management control system 14, 76, 171, 172,
        173, 206, 225, 347
    concept of 170
management information systems 512
manual,audit manual 12, 52, 118, 120, 124,
        127, 338, 340–56, 364, 435, 473
    ability levels **350**
    audit approach and methodology 345
    autonomy and control *352*
    conceptual model 346, 348, *349*
    contents 342
    dynamism of currency 347
    impact on creativity 345, 352
    implementation *355*
    maintaining 356
    management of audit function 348
    management control system 347
    models 347, 350

objectives 341
procedures 160, 408
role of 340
services 350, *351*
sources of information 340
standardised forms 343
structuring *354*
marketing of audit services 85, 100, 453–64
    analysis of competitors 461
    annual report 463
    approaches to 457
    audit image 463
    budget 462,**462**
    business cards 460
    complaints procedure 460
    concept *457*
    consumer behaviour 462
    information brochure 459
    marketing mix 458
    marketing onformation 461
    marketing plans 461, *461*
    marketing profile 453
    service level agreements 463
Mautz 7, 62, 75, 465
Maxwell 31
McGregor 501
meeting management 85
memory, reliance on 164
methodology 429
Metropolitan Police 568
minimum numbers 378
Mints, Frederick 78, **78**
model building 323
monthly progress reports 297
moral maze 39, 129
morality 39
Moulton 501
moving out of accountancy 24

narrative 211
National Audit Office 138, 143
National Health Service 46, 50, 142
    audit manual 341
National Vocational Qualification 478
nationalism 49
NCC, ICL, DT Survey (computer abuse) 591
negotiation skills 98–9
non-executive directors 31, 32
non-financial systems 18
non-verbal communication 283
normal distribution 267
number of auditors 351, 378

objectives and strategies 361–72
    achievable 369
    approved 363

audit 116, 361
business 529
cascading 370, *370*
communicated 352, 369
contingency allowances 371
control 248
environmental change *369*
long-term plans 370, *370*
management participation 365
preliminary surveys 371
resource allocation 368, *368*
risk analysis 365
strategy *364*, 368
successful implementation 371, *372*
types of audit service 363
objectivity 58, 65
obstructive management 86
one minute manager 75, 330
operations 226
oral presentations 298, 331
audit clearance procedures 338
audit manual 338
anxiety 331, *331*, *333*
conducting 335
physical environment *335*
preparation 333
visual aids 334
ordering system 214, *214*
organisational policies 390
output inspection 160, 161

PACE 1984 564, 569, 571
participation
advantages of participation 93
disadvantages of participation 94
with management 88–94
passwords 599
performance indicators 234
performance of audit work 44
performance targets 399, 402
permanent files 258
personal computing
environment 520
policies on 595
personal drive and initiative 387
personality clashes 291
personnel
policies 390, 484
role of 484
see also staffing
persuasion 384
PESTL analysis 190, 365
physical access 160
physical and mental state 385
planning 15, 52, 65, 133, 177–98
action 319

advantages 178
annual audit 190
assigning time budgets to audits 197
assignment 195, 197
audit programme 194
auditing standards 182
basic 92
business 189
for change 92
computer audit work 519
disadvanatges 181
documentation 197
long term 182
preliminary survey 192, 195
process *177*
quarterly audit plan 191
risk profile 187
strategic 86
strategy versus resource 187, *187*
poor cousin of external audit 84
poor products 425
power audit 490
pre-event auditing 525
pre-reporting 130
preliminary surveys 192, 297, 371
presentations 335
Prevention of Corruption Acts 553
pricing strategy 28
probity based work 18, 19, 55
problem solving 54, 327
problem staff 413
procedures 429, 432
productivity 408
professional affiliations 40, 473
professional proficiency 43, 135
professional standards *see* standards, audit
professionalism 38
project teams 151, 376
propping up management 329
public relations 81, 85, *88*
public sector 35
public sector benefits fraud 607–14
controlling 610–11
employee benefits fraud 612
local authority benefit fraud 609
London wide fraud initiative 610
prosecution policies 609
structures 610
types 610

qualifications 39
see also training
quality assurance and procedures 153, 424–33
appropriate approach 426
appropriate structures 427
audit direction 429, *430*

quality assurance and procedures—*cont.*
  audit procedures 429
  barriers and constraints 425
  code of conduct 427
  controlling internal audit 432
  decision making mechanisms 431
  directing internal audit 429
  features 425
  improvements 426
  induction training 431
  instructions 430
  poor products 425
  procedures cycle *432*
  staff discipline 433
  staff meetings 432
  standardised working papers 430
  standards 430
  supervision and review of audit work 431
questionnaires 459

recommendations 312
reconciliation 162
record of control weakness 260, 310
recording systems 210
recruitment 161, 391
regularity 36
relationships, levels of *81*
relevance 76
reports and reporting 296–339
  action plan 319
  activity 298
  annual 86, 296
  annual reporting cycle 299
  audit assignment reports 298
  change management 320
  clearance process 319
  defining the client 304
  drafting 322
  executive summaries 298
  follow-up 298
  fraud investigation 298
  good 327
  interim 297
  lines 379
  logical presentation *321*
  monthly progress 297
  objectives 306
  ongoing drafting 322
  oral 298
  preliminary survey 297
  quarterly 11, 296, 298
  recommendations 312, *313*
  report structure *321*
  review process 316
  staff appraisal 298
  supportive evidence 319

types 296
  residual risk 232
resource allocation 56, 368
resourcing the audit unit 382–423
  human resource management cycle 382, *383*
  management role 382
  management weaknesses 382
  see also staffing
responsibilities, audit 117
Revans, Reg 475
review agencies 148
review process 316
risk 20, 228–38, 365, 535
  analysis 231
  factors 230
  hierarchy *233*
  matrix *234*
  performance indicators 234
  residual *232*
  types 228
risk based audit cover *232*
risk areas (fraud) 555
risk index 189, *231*, 235, **236**, 237
risk parameters 270
risk profile 187
Rittenberg model 64
role of audit 83, 85
role playing 81
role theory 80, 87
Root 340
rotating auditors 61
Rutteman 213

safeguarding assets 11
sampling plans 271
sampling techniques 269
sanctions 38
Sawyer, Lawrence 6, 340, 341, 342, 343, 344, 345, 465
Sayle, Allen 6
SBA versus probity 194
scope of internal audit 9–16, *16*, 43, 116, 361
  assignment planning 14
  audit components *16*
  charter 15
  compliance role 12, *12*
  five elements 9
  implications 10
  information systems 13
  long term plans 15
  medium term plans 15
  safeguarding assets 11
  time frames 15
  value for money 13
Scott and Jaffe 480, 504
security measures (DP) 540

segregation of duties 161
self audit 95, *96*
Selim 345
senior management, audited 59
sensitive areas audited 59
sequential numbering 162
service based auditing 209
service level agreements 463
Sharif 62, 75
shortlisting 393
single audit evaluation 411
skills level 398
skills workshop 470
Skinner 213
small audit units 49
social auditing 21
software acquisitions 548
software piracy 593
Spooner 465
spot checks 20
spying for management 59
staffing
  accounting 92
  appraisal 86, 298, 397
  career developmemt 406, *410*
  counselling 408, *408*, 415
  discipline 433
  grievances 413, *415*
  meetings 432
  motivation 86
  and planning computer audit 516
  problem 413
  training 85
stand-by facilities 536
standardisation 48
standardised forms 343, 430
standards 35, 38–52, *120*, 132–7, *137*, 342, 345
  APB 44, 132, 135
    guidelines (fraud) 557
    statement on IA 145
  analysis of information 134
  applying a suitable model 133
  audit planning 133
  baseline *133*
  communication of results 134
  computer 447
  follow-up 134
  formulation of findings 134
  IA 132, 400
    establishing 51
    implications for 133
    as trustees 42
  international *48*
  local factors 47
  mandatory 47
  nationalism 49

performance 137
professional proficiency 135
role of 41
smaller organisations 49
standardisation 48
translation 48
universality of 47
see also IIA Standards
statement of responsibility 25, 27, 73
see also audit charter
statistical sampling 19, 263–75
  advantages 266
  basic rules 273
  confidence levels *270*
  external audit perspective 264
  normal distribution *267*
  risk parameters 270
  sampling *264*, 269, **271**, 273
  testing *269*
status of internal audit 375
Stearn 340
Stephen's Digest of Law 560
Stewart, Henrietta 343
storage 446
strategic development 485, *486*
strategic planning 86
strategy 364
  versus resources 187
stress 504
structured systems narrative 212
structures for internal audit 373–81, *374*
  departmental teams *378*
  factors influencing 374
  independence 380
  individual work 375
  minimum numbers 378
  project teams 376
  reporting lines 379
  service based 377, *377*
  status of internal audit *375*
  supervisors 380
  trainees 381
success criteria 248
successful strategic development 494
suitability of controls 162
supervision 160
supervisors 380
supplier cycle 532
surveillance 576
SWOT analysis 190, 365, *367*, 411
synergy 200
systems analysts 152
systems approach 20, 34, 55, 69, 171, 200, 199–227, 530, 542
  ascertaining and recording systems 210
  benefits 206

systems approach—*cont.*
  entropy 202
  features of systems 199, *199*
  general 201, *202*
  key systems issues 205, *206*
  management control system 206
  motor cycle system *201*
  service based auditing *209*
  stages 204
  systems auditing 203, *204*
  systems thinking 199
  transactions approach versus 203, *203*, 207, 208
systems design 60
systems developments 60, 520
  involvement in 522
systems managers 151

taped interviews 572
targets, performance 399, 402
technical aspects of audit work 87
test data 544
testing 82, 239–75, *239*, *242*, *249*
  achieving control objectives 248
  analytical review 244
  considerations 242
  dual purpose 241
  in fraud investigations 253
  hundred percent interrogation 250
  meaning of compliance 252
  substantive 253
  techniques 244
  test patterns *241*
  types of 241
  walk through 241
tick and check 83
time frames 15
time monitoring 262, 449
topical issues 28
total quality management 29
traditional control 173
traditional management 382
traditional tick and check 83
trainees 381
training and development 407, 465–79

action learning 475
audit review 473
benefits 466
common body of knowledge 468
of computer auditors 517
directed reading 472
link into development 477
monitoring 476
professional 471, 472
professional affiliations 473
programme 38
role of the IIA 474
skills workshop 470
staff 85
through work 472
training auditors 470
training co-ordinator 472
transaction analysis 81
transaction based approach 19, 203, 208
transactions testing *see* testing
Treadway Committee 105, 169

UK listed companies 105
unbiased views 58
uncaring management (fraud) 620

value for money 9, 13, 21
verification 54, 575
Vinten, Gerald 7, 21, 47, 127, 345, 592
virus, computer 595
visual aids 334
vouching 54

Wade, Keith 64, 206
walk through tests 241
Westwood, Graham 273
whistleblowing 119, 126, 128
Willson 340
Wilson 79
witnesses 563
Wood 79
work study 150
working papers 255, 344
working relations 62
workstation concept 442